Rick Steves'

CROATIA
& SLOVENIA

Rick Steves & Cameron Hewitt

CROATIA & SLOVENIA

=A14= Expressway
Major Road
Major Rail Line
·········· Boat
✈ Airport
■ Ruin, Museum, Other Point of Interest
▮ Castle, Monument, Palace
🌲 Natural Wonder

0 km   50   100 km
0 miles   50 miles

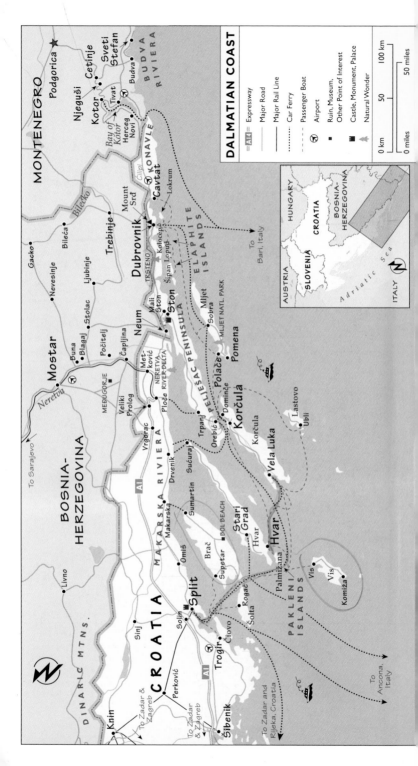

DALMATIAN COAST

Legend:
- **A1** Expressway
- Major Road
- Major Rail Line
- Car Ferry
- Passenger Boat
- ✈ Airport
- ■ Ruin, Museum, Other Point of Interest
- Castle, Monument, Palace
- Natural Wonder

0 km   50   100 km
0 miles   50 miles

CROATIA

DINARIC MTNS.

Knin • Perković • Šibenik • Trogir • Split • Solin • Sinj

To Zadar & Zagreb
To Zadar & Rijeka, Croatia

BOSNIA-HERZEGOVINA

To Sarajevo

Livno • Mostar • Buna • Blagaj • Stolac • Počitelj • Čapljina • Neum
Gacko • Nevesinje • Ljubinje • Bileća • Bilećko • Trebinje

MEDUGORJE • Veliki Prolog • Metković • Ploče • NERETVA RIVER DELTA

Vrgorac • Makarska • Drvenik • Sućuraj

MAKARSKA RIVIERA

Omiš • Supetar • Sumartin • Brač • BOL BEACH • Stari Grad • Hvar

Rogač • Šolta • Čiovo

PAKLENI ISLANDS

Palmižana • Vis • Komiža • Vis

To Ancona, Italy

Hvar • Vela Luka • Korčula • Korčula • Ubli • Lastovo

Trpanj • Orebić • Domince • Polače • Pomena • Sobra • Mljet

PELJEŠAC PENINSULA

MLJET NATL. PARK

Mali Ston • Ston • TRSTENO • Šipan • Lopud • Koločep

ELAPHITE ISLANDS

Dubrovnik • Mount Srd • Lokrum • Cavtat • **KONAVLE** • Cilipi

To Bari, Italy

MONTENEGRO

Podgorica • Cetinje • Sveti Stefan • Njeguši • Kotor • Tivat • Budva
Herceg Novi • Bay of Kotor • **BUDVA RIVIERA**

Inset map:
AUSTRIA • SLOVENIA • HUNGARY • CROATIA • BOSNIA-HERZEGOVINA • ITALY • Adriatic Sea

Palese

Rick Steves'

CROATIA
& SLOVENIA

AVALON
TRAVEL

CONTENTS

Top Destinations in Croatia & Slovenia

INTRODUCTION

Set sail on the shimmering Adriatic, for a remote island whose name you can't pronounce but whose wonders you'll never forget. Corkscrew your way up impossibly twisty mountain roads to panoramic vistas of cut-glass peaks. Lie on a beach in the hot summer sun, listening to the lapping waves as a Venetian-style bell tower clangs out the hour. Ponder the fading scars of a recent war, and admire how skillfully the locals have revitalized their once-troubled region. Dine on a seafood feast and sip a glass of local wine as you watch the sunset dip into the watery horizon... feeling smug for discovering this place before all your friends did. Unfamiliar as they might seem, Croatia and Slovenia have what you've been looking for: some of Europe's most spectacular natural wonders, a fascinating recent history, and a spirit of adventure—much of it still off the beaten path.

Here in the land where the Adriatic meets the Alps, there are countless ways to have fun. Begin your adventure by flipping through this book, which covers Croatia's and Slovenia's best big-city, small-town, and back-to-nature destinations. You'll get all the specifics and opinions necessary to wring the maximum value out of your limited time and money. If you're planning a trip of a month or less, this book is all you need.

Just two decades ago, Croatia and Slovenia—two of Europe's youngest nations—belonged to the union called Yugoslavia. Today they're proudly independent and racing toward the future. Carefree Croatia, with a long and varied coastline, beckons vacationers with its dramatically scenic terrain, romantic old towns, sunshine-bathed pebbly beaches, and irrepressible seafaring spirit. Perky Slovenia surprises travelers with its tidy quaintness, breathtaking mountainscapes, colorful towns, and impossibly friendly natives. And for good measure, I've also included detours into two other

INTRODUCTION

Map Legend

⅄ Viewpoint	✈ Airport		Tunnel	
↑ Entry Arrow	Ⓣ Taxi Stand		Pedestrian Zone	
⊕ Tourist Info	⊞ Tram Stop		Railway	
WC Restroom	Ⓑ Bus Stop		Ferry/Boat Route	
⬛ Castle	Ⓟ Parking		Tram	
⊕ Church	)(Mtn. Pass		Stairs	
▪ Statue/Point of Interest	Park		Walk/Tour Route	
Mosque	◎ Fountain		Trail	

Use this legend to help you navigate the maps in this book.

parts of the former Yugoslavia, each one offering a striking contrast to Croatia or Slovenia: the craggy coast of Montenegro, and a pair of diverse and fascinating Bosnian cities: bite-sized Mostar and bustling Sarajevo.

Experiencing Europe's culture, people, and natural wonders economically and hassle-free has been my goal for three decades of traveling, tour guiding, and writing. With this book, I pass on to you all the lessons I've learned, painstakingly updated for this edition.

Rick Steves' Croatia & Slovenia covers the predictable biggies and adds a healthy dose of "Back Door" intimacy. Along with strolling the walls around Dubrovnik's peerless Old Town, you'll poke your way into a hidden little tavern clinging like a barnacle over the sea. I've been selective, including only the top destinations and sights. For example, Croatia has over a thousand islands. But why not focus on the very best? That's Korčula, Hvar, Rab, and Mljet.

The best is, of course, only my opinion. But after spending half of my adult life researching Europe, I've developed a sixth sense for what travelers enjoy. Just thinking about the places featured in this book makes me want to polka.

About This Book

Rick Steves' Croatia & Slovenia is a personal tour guide in your pocket. Better yet, it's actually two tour guides in your pocket: The co-author of this book is Cameron Hewitt. Cameron writes and edits guidebooks for my travel company, Rick Steves' Europe Through the Back Door. Inspired by his Slavic roots and by the enduring charm of the Slovenian and Croatian people, Cameron has spent the last decade closely tracking the exciting changes in this part of the world. Together, Cameron and I keep this book up-to-date and accurate (though for simplicity we've shed our

Key to This Book

Updates

This book is updated regularly. For the latest, visit www.rick
steves.com/update. For a valuable list of reports and experiences—good and bad—from fellow travelers, check www
.ricksteves.com/feedback.

Abbreviations and Times

I use the following symbols and abbreviations in this book:

Sights are rated:

▲▲▲	**Don't miss**
▲▲	**Try hard to see**
▲	**Worthwhile if you can make it**
No rating	**Worth knowing about**

Tourist information offices are abbreviated as **TI,** and
bathrooms are **WCs.** To categorize accommodations, I use a
Sleep Code (described on page 24).

Like Europe, this book uses the **24-hour clock.** It's the
same through 12:00 noon, then keep going: 13:00, 14:00, and
so on. For anything over 12, subtract 12 and add p.m. (14:00 is
2:00 p.m.).

When giving **opening times,** I include both peak season
and off-season hours if they differ. So, if a museum is listed
as "May-Oct daily 9:00-16:00," it should be open from 9
a.m. until 4 p.m. from the first day of May until the last day of
October (but expect exceptions).

For **transit** or **tour departures,** I first list the frequency,
then the duration. So, a train connection listed as "2/hour, 1.5
hours" departs twice each hour and the journey lasts an hour
and a half.

respective egos to become "I" in this book).

This book is organized by destinations. Each one is a mini-
vacation on its own, filled with exciting sights, strollable neighborhoods, affordable places to stay, and memorable places to eat.

In the following chapters, you'll find these sections:

Planning Your Time suggests a schedule for how to best use
your limited time.

Orientation includes specifics on public transportation,
helpful hints, local tour options, easy-to-read maps, and tourist
information.

Sights describes the top attractions and includes their cost
and hours.

Self-Guided Walks take you through interesting neighborhoods, with a personal tour guide in hand.

Sleeping describes my favorite accommodations, from good-
value private rooms to cushy splurges.

Eating serves up a range of options, from inexpensive eateries to fancy restaurants.

Connections explains your options for traveling to destinations by train, bus, and boat. In car-friendly areas, I've also included route tips for drivers.

Country Introductions for Croatia, Slovenia, and Bosnia give you an overview of each country's culture, customs, money, history, current events, cuisine, language, and other useful practicalities.

The **Understanding Yugoslavia** chapter sorts out the various countries and conflicts, giving you a good picture of how Yugoslavia was formed, and why it broke apart.

The **appendix** is a traveler's tool kit, with telephone tips, useful phone numbers, transportation basics (on trains, buses, boats, car rentals, driving, and flights), recommended books and films, a holiday and festival list, climate chart, handy packing checklist, and Croatian and Slovenian survival phrases.

Browse through this book, choose your favorite destinations, and link them up. Then have a great trip! Traveling like a temporary local, you'll get the absolute most out of every mile, minute, and dollar. As you visit places I know and love, I'm happy that you'll be meeting some of my favorite Croatians, Slovenes, Bosnians, and Montenegrins.

Planning

This section will help you get started planning your trip—with advice on trip costs, when to go, and what you should know before you take off.

Travel Smart

Your trip to this region is like a complex play—easier to follow and fully appreciate on a second viewing. While no one does the same trip twice to gain that advantage, reading this book in its entirety before your trip accomplishes much the same thing.

Design an itinerary that enables you to visit sights at the best possible times. For example, avoid coastal resort towns off-season (when they're deserted) and during the busy months of July and August (when they're miserably crammed). Be sure to mix intense and relaxed periods in your itinerary. To maximize rootedness, minimize one-night stands. It's worth a long drive or bus ride after dinner to be settled into a town for two nights. Accommodations are more likely to give a good price to someone staying more than one night. Every trip (and every traveler) needs at least a few slack days (laundry, picnics, people-watching, and so on). Pace yourself. Assume you will return.

Reread this book as you travel, and visit local TIs. Upon arrival in a new town, lay the groundwork for a smooth departure; write down the schedule for the train, bus, or boat you'll take when you leave. Drivers can study the best route to their next destination. Whether you're traveling by public transportation (trains, buses, and boats) or by rental car, read up on my tips in the appendix.

Get online at Internet cafés or your hotel, and buy a phone card or carry a mobile phone: You can find tourist information, learn the latest on sights (special events, English tour schedules, etc.), book tickets and tours, make reservations, reconfirm accommodations, research transportation connections, and keep in touch with your loved ones.

Connect with the culture. Set up your own quest for the best bell tower, mountain vista, or scenic seafront perch. Enjoy the hospitality of the local people. Slow down and be open to unexpected experiences. Ask questions—most locals are eager to point you toward their idea of the right direction. Keep a notepad in your pocket for confirming prices, noting directions, and organizing your thoughts. Wear your money belt, and learn the local currencies and how to estimate prices in dollars.

A smart trip is a puzzle—a fun, doable, and worthwhile challenge. Those who expect to travel smart, do.

Trip Costs

Croatia and Slovenia—while just two decades removed from communism—are no longer Europe's bargain basement. Although local economies are struggling along with everyone else's due to the global crisis, the cost of living in Croatia and Slovenia has come close to their European neighbors. Things aren't exactly cheap here—but they're still more affordable than similar, better-established tourist countries, such as Italy or Switzerland. If you're careful to avoid inflated tourist-trap prices (by following my tips on where to stay and where to eat), a trip to this region can be a good value. If you detour into Bosnia-Herzegovina, you'll find prices substantially lower (though Montenegro is, if anything, pricier than Croatia and Slovenia).

Five components make up your trip costs: airfare, surface transportation, room and board, sightseeing and entertainment, and shopping and miscellany.

Airfare: A basic round-trip flight from the US to Ljubljana or Dubrovnik can cost $1,300-1,900, depending on where you fly from and when (cheaper in winter). Consider saving time and money in Europe by flying into one city and out of another. For example, flying into Ljubljana and out of Dubrovnik often saves the extra cost (not to mention wasted time) of an overland return trip to Ljubljana.

Surface Transportation: For the two-week whirlwind trip

INTRODUCTION

Croatia & Slovenia at a Glance

Croatia

▲▲Zagreb Croatia's underrated capital city, with interesting museums (the best feature Naive Art and Broken Relationships), lush parks, and a lively urban bustle, plus the nearby town of Samobor.

▲▲▲Plitvice Lakes National Park Arguably Europe's most breathtaking natural wonder: a forested canyon filled with crystal-clear lakes, stunning waterfalls, and easy-to-hike boardwalks and trails.

▲▲Istria Croatia's most Italian-feeling corner, with the super-romantic, Venetian-flavored coastal town of Rovinj; top Roman ruins in the city of Pula; and a rolling interior of vineyards and picturesque hill towns (including Motovun).

The Kvarner Gulf Sparsely populated coastline between Istria and Dalmatia, with the genteel Habsburg resort of Opatija, the port city of Rijeka, and the island of Rab.

▲▲Split Unofficial capital city and transit hub of the Dalmatian Coast, with a bustling urban vibe, people-filled seaside promenade, and lived-in warren of twisting lanes sprouting out of a massive Roman palace, plus the nearby town of Trogir.

▲▲Hvar Ritzy island and old town known for its jet-set appeal, high prices, and seductively relaxing beaches and smaller islands.

▲▲Korčula Low-key island and walled peninsular Old Town with a fjord-like backdrop, a fish-skeleton street plan, and quirky offbeat museums.

▲▲▲Dubrovnik The "Pearl of the Adriatic": a giant walled Old Town with a scenic wall walk, tons of crowds, great beaches, modest but engaging museums, a mountaintop viewpoint, an epic past and difficult but inspiring recent history, and a well-earned reputation as Croatia's single best destination.

Near Dubrovnik Boat excursions from Dubrovnik's Old Port, the art-packed resort village of Cavtat, the nearby Trsteno Arboretum, the walled town of Ston, the vineyard-draped Pelješac Peninsula, and the giant national park at Mljet Island.

Bosnia-Herzegovina

▲▲▲Mostar An easy taste of Bosnia-Herzegovina, with a striking setting, vital Muslim culture, old Turkish architecture, evocative war damage, and an inspiring, rebuilt Old Bridge; plus nearby Muslim sights (scenic gorge at Blagaj, hill town of Počitelj, worka-day burg of Stolac) and the famous Catholic pilgrimage site of Međugorje.

▲▲▲**Sarajevo** Formerly war-torn, now rejuvenated Bosnian capital, with a fascinating layered history and a spectacular mountain-valley setting.

Montenegro ✖

▲▲**The Bay of Kotor** Steep bay with fjord-like inlets, visit-wor-thy towns and sights, and the remarkably fortified Old Town of Kotor.

The Montenegrin Interior Rugged mountain road leading up the cliffs into the Montenegrin heartland, ending at the historic capi-tal of Cetinje.

The Budva Riviera Glitzy emerging beach resort zone.

Slovenia

▲▲**Ljubljana** Slovenia's vibrant yet relaxing capital, with a fun-to-browse riverside market, scintillating architecture, and inviting riverside promenade.

▲▲▲**Lake Bled** Photogenic lake resort huddled in the foothills of the Julian Alps, with a church-topped island, cliff-hanging cas-tle, lakefront walkway, tasty desserts, and appealing side-trips.

▲▲**The Julian Alps** Cut-glass peaks easily conquered by a twisty and scenic mountain road over the Vršič Pass, ending in the tran-quil Soča River Valley, with the fine WWI museum in Kobarid.

▲**Logarska Dolina and the Northern Valleys** Remote mountain valleys with traditional farming lifestyles.

Ptuj and Maribor In Ptuj, a charming-if-sleepy historic town topped by a castle; and Maribor, Slovenia's "second city."

▲**The Karst** Windblown limestone plateau with world-class caves (Škocjan and Postojna), the Lipizzaner Stallion stud farm at Lipica, and the dramatically situated Predjama Castle.

▲**Piran** Slovenia's leading seaside resort town.

INTRODUCTION

described in this chapter, allow $150 per person for public transportation (train, bus, and boat tickets). Train travelers will probably save money by simply buying tickets along the way, rather than purchasing a railpass (see "Transportation," page 704). A basic car rental costs about $450 per week (including tolls, gas, and basic insurance). Renting a car is cheapest if arranged from the US, but exorbitant fees for dropping off in a different country can make it prohibitively expensive if you're going to both Croatia and Slovenia (for strategies to avoid this headache, see "Renting a Car," page 709).

Room and Board: You can thrive in Croatia and Slovenia on an average of $100 a day per person for room and board (much less in Bosnia-Herzegovina). This allows $15 for lunch, $25 for dinner, and $60 for lodging (based on two people splitting the cost of a $120 double room that includes breakfast). Students and tightwads can eat and sleep for as little as $50 a day ($30 per hostel bed, $20 for groceries and snacks).

Sightseeing and Entertainment: Sightseeing is cheap here. Figure about $3-6 per major sight (museums), and $10-25 for splurge experiences (e.g., watching the *Moreška* sword dance in Korčula, or seeing Slovenia's Lipizzaner stallions). You can hire your own private guide for four hours for about $100-150—a good value when divided among two or more people. An overall average of $20 a day works for most people. Don't skimp here. After all, this category is the driving force behind your trip—you came to sightsee, enjoy, and experience Croatia and Slovenia. Fortunately for you, the region's best attractions—the sea, mountains, and sunshine—are free.

Shopping and Miscellany: Figure $2 per postcard, coffee, beer, and ice-cream cone. Shopping can vary in cost from nearly nothing to a small fortune. Good budget travelers find that this category has little to do with assembling a trip full of lifelong and wonderful memories.

When to Go

Tourist traffic in this part of Europe (especially the coastal towns) is extremely seasonal. The peak season hits suddenly and floods the towns like a tidal wave, only to recede a couple months later—leaving empty streets and dazed locals. In general, the tourist season runs roughly from mid-May through early October, reaching a peak in early August. (If you're staying in bigger cities or landlocked towns—including all of Slovenia outside of Piran—the seasonal influence is much less pronounced.)

Peak Season: July and especially August are peak season, when just about everything is likely to be open very long hours daily (with occasional closures for a midday siesta). It's also the busiest time of year—boats, buses, and budget accommodations are packed to the gills. Visiting Croatia in July or August is like spending spring break in Florida—fun, but miserably crowded and hot. Hotels charge top dollar, and you'll miss out on the "undiscovered" quality that pervades most of the region the rest of the year.

Shoulder Season: Early May through June, and September through mid-October are shoulder seasons. Within these time spans, late June and early September are nearly as crowded as peak season, but the rush subsides substantially in May and October; by the second week of October, restaurants are already starting to close down for the winter. Shoulder season is my favorite time to visit—I enjoy the smaller crowds, milder weather, and ability to grab a room almost whenever and wherever I like.

Off-Season: Mid-October through early May are dead as a doornail. Many small coastal towns close down entirely, with only one hotel and one restaurant remaining open during the lean winter months; most residents move to the interior to hibernate. Anything that's open keeps very limited hours (weekday mornings only). The weather can be cool and dreary, and night will draw the shades on your sightseeing before dinnertime. You may find the climate chart in the appendix helpful.

Seasonal Changes: Because of this region's extreme seasonality, specifics such as opening times and prices are especially flexible. It's not unusual for a hotel to charge six different rates for the same room, depending on the time of year. (A hotel receptionist once showed me an entire book with literally hundreds of potential rates they could charge, based on room size, type, views, and season.) With every visit, I dutifully hike around these towns trying to pin down hours for tourist offices, travel agencies, and museums. And every time, they change. If you're here anytime outside of midsummer, don't rely on my hours—call a day or two ahead to double-check that the place you need (like a room-booking agency) will actually be open when you arrive.

Sightseeing Priorities

Depending on the length of your trip, and taking geographic proximity into account, here are my recommended priorities.

3 days:	Dubrovnik
5 days, add:	Mostar, Split
7 days, add:	Korčula or Hvar (for a relaxing island experience); Montenegro's Bay of Kotor (for dramatic scenery); or Sarajevo (for a more in-depth look at Bosnia)
9 days, add:	Lake Bled and the Julian Alps
10 days, add:	Plitvice Lakes

Croatia and Slovenia:
Best Two-Week Trip by Car

Day	Plan	Sleep in
1	Arrive Ljubljana's airport and take a taxi to Lake Bled	Lake Bled
2	Relax at Lake Bled	Lake Bled
3	Pick up car, drive through Julian Alps, end in Ljubljana	Ljubljana
4	Ljubljana	Ljubljana
5	Drive through the Karst and Piran to Rovinj*	Rovinj
6	Tour Istria	Rovinj
7	Drive to Plitvice Lakes via Istria's hill towns	Plitvice
8	Hike the lakes, then drive to Split and drop car	Split
9	Split	Split
10	To Hvar or Korčula	Hvar/Korčula
11	Relax on Hvar or Korčula	Hvar/Korčula
12	To Dubrovnik	Dubrovnik
13	Dubrovnik	Dubrovnik
14	Rent a car or hire a driver to day-trip to Mostar or to Montenegro's Bay of Kotor	Dubrovnik

* To save the substantial extra cost of picking up your car in one country and then dropping it off in another (see page 710), come up with a strategy for turning in your rental car in Slovenia and then taking public transportation to Croatia, where you can pick up a different rental car for your time there. For example, you could take the bus from Ljubljana or Portorož (near Piran) to Rovinj, then pick up a rental car in Pula; or take the train from Ljubljana to Zagreb or Rijeka, then pick up your rental car in one of those cities. It can be a bit of a puzzle to figure out, but it can also save you plenty.

12 days, add:	Ljubljana, more time for Dalmatian islands
14 days, add:	Istria
16 days, add:	Whatever you skipped on day 7 (Korčula/Hvar, Montenegro, or Sarajevo)
18 days, add:	The Karst, Zagreb
21 days, add:	More mountains (Logarska Dolina) or coastal villages (Piran, Rab, Mljet)
More time, add:	Ptuj, Opatija, and even more islands and coastal villages

The map on page 11 and the two-week itinerary on this page include all of the stops in the first 14 days.

By Public Transportation

This itinerary can be done entirely by public transportation, with a few modifications. Skip (or hire a driver for) the Julian Alps, and take the bus from Lake Bled to Ljubljana. Skip Istria; instead, take the train from Ljubljana to Zagreb, see that city, then take a bus to Plitvice. The bus connects Plitvice to Split, and from there, you'll continue down the Dalmatian Coast by boat or bus.

Even if you're using public transportation, seriously consider periodically renting a car for the day to see the Julian Alps, Istria, Mostar, or Montenegro's Bay of Kotor.

As you plan your trip, don't underestimate the long distances. People tell me, "I've got four days, and I want to see Lake Bled and Dubrovnik"—not realizing they'll waste at least a full day driving nonstop to connect those two sights. If you have less than a week, consider focusing either on the Dalmatian Coast (plus Mostar and Montenegro) in the south, or on Slovenia and Istria (and maybe Zagreb) in the north. The worth-a-detour Plitvice Lakes are stranded in no-man's land between these two areas, but reachable (with some effort) from either one. Sarajevo also requires a detour (about 2.5 hours beyond Mostar, and not "on the way" to anything else in this book), but those who make the trek won't regret it.

INTRODUCTION

Top 10 Small Coastal Towns

1. Rovinj (Croatia)
2. Korčula (Croatia)
3. Hvar (Croatia)
4. Piran (Slovenia)
5. Kotor (Montenegro)
6. Rab (Croatia)
7. Cavtat (Croatia)
8. Perast (Montenegro)
9. Trogir (Croatia)
10. Poreč (Croatia)

Where Should I Go?

The perfect Croatian vacation is like a carefully refined recipe—a dash of this, a pinch of that, a slow simmer...and before long, you've got a delicious feast. Overwhelmed with options, people often ask me how to prioritize their time. Here's my tried-and-true recipe:

Begin with the biggies. Dubrovnik is a must, period. If you like big cities, Split is entertaining. Plitvice Lakes National Park, while difficult to reach, rarely disappoints.

Fold in one or two seafront villages. Croatian coastal towns are all variations on the same theme: A warm stone Old Town with a Venetian bell tower, a tidy boat-speckled harbor, ample seafood restaurants, a few hulking communist-era resort hotels on the edge of town, and *sobe* and *apartman* signs by every other doorbell. Of course, each town has its own personality and claims to fame (for a quick run-down of my favorites—including Rovinj, Hvar, Korčula, and Rab—see the "Croatia & Slovenia at a Glance" sidebar). Beach bums, sightseers, yachters, historians, partiers—everyone you'll talk to has their own favorite town. Don't trust this advice blindly. Try out a few and choose your own top town.

Sprinkle liberally with Slovenia. You won't regret splicing Slovenia into your itinerary. Its spectacular mountain scenery, colorful capital (Ljubljana), Germanic efficiency, and extremely friendly natives are a pleasant contrast to Croatia. In hindsight, most travelers wish they'd budgeted more time for Slovenia.

Add some spice. This is my secret ingredient. After you've been to one or two of the coastal resorts, you could head for another one...or you could use that time for something completely different. Some of these options are easy and convenient—the Roman ruins of Pula, the hilltop hamlets of the Istrian interior, the imported-Austrian-resort feel of Opatija. But my favorites involve crossing borders and broadening horizons: the cities of Mostar and Sarajevo, in Bosnia-Herzegovina; and Montenegro's spectacular Bay of Kotor. A year from now, you'll barely remember the difference between all those little seaside towns you toured. But you'll never forget the mosques of Mostar.

Know Before You Go

Your trip is more likely to go smoothly if you plan ahead. Check this list of things to arrange while you're still at home.

You need a **passport**—but no visa or shots—to travel in Croatia, Slovenia, Bosnia-Herzegovina, and Montenegro. You may be denied entry into certain European countries if your passport is due to expire within three to six months of your ticketed date of return. Get it renewed if you'll be cutting it close. It can take up to six weeks to get or renew a passport (for more on passports, see www.travel.state.gov). Pack a photocopy of your passport in your luggage in case the original is lost or stolen.

Book rooms well in advance if you'll be traveling during **peak season** (July and August) or over any major **holidays** or festivals (see page 721).

Call your **debit- and credit-card companies** to let them know the countries you'll be visiting, to ask about fees, and more (see page 18).

Do your homework if you want to buy **travel insurance.** Compare the cost of the insurance to the likelihood of your using it and your potential loss if something goes wrong. It's also worth checking whether your existing insurance (health, homeowners, or renters) covers you and your possessions overseas. For more tips, see www.ricksteves.com/insurance.

If you're bringing a mobile device, you can download free information from **Rick Steves Audio Europe,** featuring hours of travel interviews and other audio content about Croatia and Slovenia (via www.ricksteves.com/audioeurope, iTunes, or the Rick Steves Audio Europe free smartphone app; for details, see page 718).

If you're planning on **renting a car** in Croatia or Slovenia, you'll need your driver's license. An International Driving Permit is required (see page 709). Driving on Slovenia's expressways requires a €15 toll sticker (*vinjeta,* most Slovenian rental cars come with one, otherwise available at shops in Slovenia; see page 715); failure to display one could cost you a €150 fine.

Because **airline carry-on restrictions** are always changing, visit the Transportation Security Administration's website (www.tsa.gov/travelers) for an up-to-date list of what you can bring on the plane with you...and what you must check.

Croatia is known for its glimmering **beaches.** However, most are pebbly or rocky rather than sandy—and spiny sea urchins are not uncommon. In addition to your swimsuit, you may want to pack (or buy in Europe) a pair of water shoes for wading. Bring good sunscreen, and—if you'll be **hiking** on Croatia's many scenic coastal trails, which can be rugged and often lack shade—a sun hat and sturdy shoes.

Practicalities

Emergency and Medical Help: For medical or other emergencies, dial 112 in Croatia, Slovenia, Montenegro, and Bosnia-Herzegovina. For police, dial 92 in Croatia, 113 in Slovenia, or 122 in Bosnia-Herzegovina and Montenegro. If you get sick, do as the locals do and go to a pharmacist for advice. Or ask at your hotel for help; they know of the nearest medical and emergency services.

Theft or Loss: To replace a passport, you'll need to go in person to the appropriate embassy or consulate (see page 702). If your credit and debit cards disappear, cancel and replace them (see "Damage Control for Lost Cards" on page 19). File a police report, either on the spot or within a day or two, and obtain a copy; you'll need it to submit an insurance claim for lost or stolen railpasses or travel gear, and it can help with replacing your passport or credit and debit cards. For more information, see www.ricksteves.com/help. Precautionary measures can minimize the effects of loss: Back up photos and other files frequently, and use passwords to protect any sensitive data on your electronic devices.

Borders: Even though Croatia, Slovenia, Bosnia-Herzegovina, and Montenegro used to be part of the same country, you'll have to stop and show your passport when you cross the border between any of them. But whether by car, train, or bus, you'll find that border crossings are generally a nonevent: Flash your passport, maybe wait a few minutes, and move on. Drivers may be asked to show proof of car insurance ("green card"), so be sure you have it when you pick up your rental car. Now that Slovenia has joined the Schengen open-borders agreement, you don't have to stop or show a passport when crossing between Slovenia and Austria, Italy, or Hungary. (Even after Croatia joins the European Union in 2013, it will likely take until 2015 at the earliest for Croatia to join Schengen—so those borders will remain for a while.) Crossing from Croatia into Bosnia-Herzegovina or Montenegro is fairly straightforward, if occasionally a bit slow. (When entering Montenegro, you'll be required to pay a €10 "eco-tax" and must declare if you're carrying more than €2,000 in cash.) When you change countries, you change phone cards, postage stamps, and, in most cases, money.

Time Zones: Croatia and Slovenia, like most of continental Europe, are generally six/nine hours ahead of the East/West Coasts of the US. The exceptions are the beginning and end of Daylight Saving Time: Europe "springs forward" the last Sunday in March (two weeks after most of North America) and "falls back" the last Sunday in October (one week before North America). For a handy online time converter, try www.timeanddate.com/worldclock.

Business Hours: Particularly in seasonal resort areas along the coast, business hours can be very unpredictable—dictated entirely by demand. (I've tried to list hours throughout this book, but these are just rough guidelines.) A shop may be open daily from 9:00 to 24:00 in August, with its hours becoming progressively shorter in the shoulder season until it closes entirely in mid-October. In larger, less touristy cities and towns—and in most of Slovenia—hours are a bit more predictable (typically Mon-Fri from around 8:00 or 9:00 until 17:00, Sat mornings from 8:00 or 9:00 until 12:00 or 13:00, and closed Sun); however, there's no clear and consistent set of hours from place to place. In both Croatia and Slovenia, you will find a few businesses open on Sundays, but generally only in touristy areas or at bus or train stations. If you have business or shopping chores to take care of, avoid saving them for Sunday.

Watt's Up? Europe's electrical system is 220 volts, instead of North America's 110 volts. Most newer electronics (such as laptops, battery chargers, and hair dryers) convert automatically, so you won't need a converter, but you will need an adapter plug with two round prongs, sold inexpensively at travel stores in the US. Avoid bringing older appliances that don't automatically convert voltage; instead, buy a cheap replacement in Europe.

Discounts: While discounts are not listed in this book, youths (under 18) and students (with International Student Identity Cards, www.isic.org) often get discounts—but only by asking.

Smoking Bans: Both Croatia and Slovenia have recently enacted smoking bans in most public places, though some establishments may have designated smoking and non-smoking areas—and at outdoor tables, all bets are off. Bosnia-Herzegovina and Montenegro have no such bans, so be ready for lots of smoke, indoors and out, in those countries.

News: Americans keep in touch via the *International Herald Tribune* (published almost daily throughout Europe and online at www.iht.com). Another informative site is www.bbc.co.uk/news. Every Tuesday, the European editions of *Time* and *Newsweek* hit the stands with articles of particular interest to travelers in Europe. Sports addicts can get their fix online or from *USA Today*. Many hotels have CNN or BBC News television channels.

Money

This section offers advice on how to pay for purchases on your trip (including getting cash from ATMs and paying with plastic), dealing with lost or stolen cards, VAT (sales tax) refunds, and tipping.

What to Bring

Bring both a credit card and a debit card. You'll use the debit card at cash machines (ATMs) to withdraw local cash for most purchases, and the credit card to pay for larger items. Some travelers carry a third card, in case one gets demagnetized or eaten by a temperamental machine.

For an emergency reserve, bring several hundred dollars in hard cash in easy-to-exchange $20 bills. Avoid using currency exchange booths (lousy rates and/or outrageous fees); if you have foreign currency to exchange, take it to a bank. Don't use traveler's checks—they're not worth the fees or long waits at slow banks.

Cash

Cash is just as desirable in Europe as it is at home. Small businesses (hotels, restaurants, shops, etc.) prefer that you pay your bills with cash. Some vendors will charge you extra for using a credit card, and many won't take credit cards at all. Cash is the best—and usually only—way to pay for bus fare, taxis, and local guides.

Throughout Europe, ATMs are the standard way for travelers to get cash. Most ATMs in Croatia and Slovenia are located outside a bank. Try to use the ATM when the branch is open; if your

card is munched by a machine, you can immediately go inside for help.

To withdraw money from an ATM (known as a *Bankomat* in Croatia and Slovenia), you'll need a debit card (ideally with a Visa or MasterCard logo for maximum usability), plus a PIN code. Know your PIN code in numbers; there are only numbers—no letters—on European keypads. For security, it's best to shield the keypad when entering your PIN at an ATM. Although you can use a credit card for ATM transactions, you will incur expensive interest charges because these are considered cash advances rather than withdrawals.

When using an ATM, try to withdraw large sums of money to reduce the number of per-transaction bank fees you'll pay. If the machine refuses your request, try again and select a smaller amount

Exchange Rates

Croatia and Slovenia use different currencies. For currency information on Bosnia-Herzegovina (which uses the Convertible Mark, KM) and Montenegro (which uses the euro), see those chapters.

Croatia

Croatia still uses its traditional currency, the kuna (abbreviated kn locally, HRK internationally):

5 Croatian kunas (kn) = about $1

A kuna is broken into 100 smaller units, called lipas. There are coins of 1, 2, 5, 10, 20, and 50 lipas; and 1, 2, and 5 kunas. Here's a very easy formula to roughly convert Croatian kunas into dollars: Double the amount and drop the final zero (e.g., 5 kn = about $1; 70 kn = about $14; 200 kn = about $40).

Croatia doesn't officially use the euro, and many vendors there (frustrated by thousands of cruise passengers who don't want to visit an ATM) flat-out refuse to take euros. (Legally, Croatian vendors are not allowed to accept euros, though this law is scarcely enforced.) If you try to spend euros in Croatia, don't be surprised if you're turned away. Confusingly, most hotels quote prices in euros for the convenience of their international guests. Even if rates are quoted in euros, they'll convert the bill to kunas to determine your final payment. While a few hoteliers prefer to list their rates in kunas, for this book, I've converted those rates into euros to make it easier for you to compare options—so you might notice some variation between the actual prices and those listed in this book.

If you need to convert prices between kunas and euros (7.5 kunas = about €1), divide the kuna price by 7.5 to get euros, or multiply the euro price by 7.5 to get kunas.

Slovenia

Slovenia uses the euro currency:

1 euro (€) = about $1.40

Like dollars, one euro (€) is broken down into 100 cents. You'll find coins ranging from one cent to two euros, and bills from five euros to 500 euros. To convert prices in euros to dollars, add 40 percent: €20 is about $28, €45 is about $63, and so on.

So, that 50-kn bottle of Croatian wine is about $10, the €25 Slovenian feast is about $35, and the 300-kn taxi ride through Zagreb is...uh-oh.

(some cash machines limit the amount you can withdraw—don't take it personally). If that doesn't work, try a different machine. It's easier to pay for purchases with smaller bills; if the ATM gives you big bills, try to break them at a major sight or a larger store.

Because Croatia and Slovenia have different currencies, you may wind up with leftover cash when you're leaving a country. Coins can't be exchanged once you leave the country, so spend them before you cross the border. Bills are easy to convert to the "new" country's currency, but remember that regular banks have the best rates for the conversion. Post offices and train stations usually change money if you can't get to a bank.

To keep your cash safe, use a money belt—a pouch with a strap that you buckle around your waist like a belt, and wear under your clothes. Pickpockets target tourists. A money belt provides peace of mind, allowing you to safely carry your passport, credit cards, and lots of cash. Don't waste time every few days tracking down a cash machine—withdraw a week's worth of money, stuff it in your money belt, and travel!

Credit and Debit Cards

For purchases, Visa and MasterCard are more commonly accepted than American Express. Just like at home, credit or debit cards work easily at larger hotels, restaurants, and shops. I typically use my debit card to withdraw cash to pay for most purchases. I use my credit card only in a few specific situations: to book hotel reservations by phone, to cover major expenses (such as car rentals, plane tickets, and long hotel stays), and to pay for things near the end of my trip (to avoid another visit to the ATM). While you could use a debit card to make most large purchases, using a credit card offers a greater degree of fraud protection (because debit cards draw funds directly from your account).

Ask Your Credit- or Debit-Card Company: Before your trip, contact the company that issued your debit or credit cards.

• Confirm your card will work overseas, and alert them that you'll be using it in Europe; otherwise, they may deny transactions if they perceive unusual spending patterns.

• Ask for the specifics on transaction **fees.** When you use your credit or debit card—either for purchases or ATM withdrawals—you'll often be charged additional "international transaction" fees of up to 3 percent (1 percent is normal) plus $5 per transaction. If your card's fees are too high, consider getting a card just for your trip: Capital One (credit cards only, www.capitalone.com) and most credit unions have low-to-no international fees.

• If you plan to withdraw cash from ATMs, confirm your daily **withdrawal limit,** and if necessary, ask your bank to adjust it (withdrawal limits are set by your bank, but foreign banks or ATMs often also set maximum withdrawal amounts—usually about $250-400). Some travelers prefer a high limit that allows them to take out more cash at each ATM stop, while others prefer to set a lower limit in case their card is stolen.

• Ask for your credit card's **PIN** in case you encounter Europe's "chip-and-PIN" system (described next); the bank will not reveal your PIN over the phone, so allow time for it to reach you by mail.

Chip and PIN: If your card is declined for a purchase in Europe, it may be because of chip and PIN, which requires card-holders to punch in a PIN instead of signing a receipt. While chip and PIN is not yet common in Croatia or Slovenia, much of Europe is adopting it (most often at automated payment machines). If, when you're using your card, you're prompted to enter your PIN but don't know it, ask if the cashier can swipe your card and print a receipt for you to sign instead; if they can't, just pay cash.

Dynamic Currency Conversion: If merchants offer to convert your purchase price into dollars (called dynamic currency conversion, or DCC), refuse this "service." You'll pay even more in fees for the expensive convenience of seeing your charge in dollars.

Damage Control for Lost Cards

If you lose your credit, debit, or ATM card, you can stop people from using it by reporting the loss immediately to the respective global customer-assistance centers. Call these 24-hour US numbers collect: Visa (410/581-9994), MasterCard (636/722-7111), and American Express (623/492-8427).

At a minimum, you'll need to know the name of the financial institution that issued you the card, along with the type of card (classic, platinum, or whatever). Providing the following information will allow for a quicker cancellation of your missing card: full card number, whether you are the primary or secondary cardholder, the cardholder's name exactly as printed on the card, billing address, home phone number, circumstances of the loss or theft, and identification verification (your birth date, your mother's maiden name, or your Social Security number—memorize this, don't carry a copy). If you are the secondary cardholder, you'll also need to provide the primary cardholder's identification-verification details. You can generally receive a temporary card within two or three business days in Europe (see www.ricksteves.com/help for more).

If you promptly report your card lost or stolen, you typically won't be responsible for any unauthorized transactions on your account, although many banks charge a liability fee of $50.

Tipping

A decade ago, tipping was unheard of in Croatia and Slovenia. But then came the tourists. Today, some waiters and taxi drivers have learned to expect Yankee-sized tips when they spot an American. Tipping the appropriate amount—not feeling stingy, but also not contributing to the overtipping epidemic—can be nerve-wracking to conscientious visitors. Relax! Many locals still don't tip at all, so any tip is appreciated. As in the US, the proper amount depends on your resources, tipping philosophy, and the circumstances, but some general guidelines apply.

Restaurants: Tip only at restaurants that have table service. If you order your food at a counter, don't tip.

At restaurants that have a waitstaff, round up the bill 5-10 percent after a good meal. My rule of thumb is to estimate about 10 percent, then round down slightly to reach a convenient total. For a 70-kn meal, I pay 75 kn—a tip of 5 kn, or about 7 percent. That's plenty. A 15 percent tip is overly generous, verging on extravagant. At some tourist-oriented restaurants, a 10 or 15 percent "service charge" may be added to your bill, in which case an additional tip is not necessary. If you're not sure whether your bill includes the tip, just ask.

Taxis: To tip the cabbie, round up about 5 percent (for a 71-kn fare, pay 75 kn). If the cabbie hauls your bags and zips you to the airport to help you catch your flight, you might want to toss in a little more. But if you feel like you're being driven in circles or otherwise ripped off, skip the tip.

Special Services: Tour guides at public sites sometimes hold out their hands for tips after they give their spiels. If I've already paid for the tour, I don't tip extra unless they've really impressed me. At hotels, if you let porters carry your luggage, it's polite to give them a euro (or the local equivalent) for each bag they carry—another reason to pack light. If you like to tip maids, leave a euro for each night you were there at the end of your stay.

In general, if someone in the service industry does a super job for you, a small tip of a euro is appropriate...but not required.

When in doubt, ask: If you're not sure whether (or how much) to tip for a service, ask your hotelier or the TI; they'll fill you in on how it's done on their turf.

Getting a VAT Refund

Wrapped into the purchase price of your souvenirs is a Value-Added Tax (VAT) of 23 percent in Croatia, 20 percent in Slovenia, and 17 percent in Bosnia and Montenegro ("VAT" is called "PDV" in this part of the world). You're entitled to get most of that tax back if you make a purchase of more than a certain amount (for example, 500 kn in Croatia, €50 in Slovenia) at a store that participates in the VAT refund scheme. Typically, you must ring up the minimum at a single retailer—you can't add up your purchases from various shops to reach the required amount.

Getting your refund is usually straightforward and, if you buy a substantial amount of souvenirs, well worth the hassle. If you're lucky, the merchant will subtract the tax when you make your purchase. (This is more likely to occur if the store ships the goods to your home.) Otherwise, you'll need to:

Get the paperwork. Have the merchant completely fill out the necessary refund document. You'll have to present your passport at the store. Be sure to retain your original sales receipt.

Get your stamp at the border or airport. Process your VAT document with the customs service at your last stop in the country in which you made your purchase (or, if you bought it in the EU, at your last stop in the EU). If flying, it's best to keep your purchases in your carry-on for viewing. But if your purchases are too large or dangerous (such as knives) to carry on, have them easily accessible in the bag you're about to check, ready to show the customs agent. You're not supposed to use your purchased goods before you leave. If you show up at customs wearing your brand-new Slovenian shoes, officials might look the other way—or deny you a refund.

Collect your refund. You'll need to return your stamped document to the retailer or its representative. Many merchants work with a service, such Global Blue (www.global-blue.com) or Premier Tax Free (www.premiertaxfree.com), that has offices at major airports, ports, or border crossings (after check-in and security, probably strategically located near a duty-free shop). These services, which extract a 4 percent fee, usually can refund your money immediately in cash or credit your card (within two billing cycles). If the retailer handles VAT refunds directly, it's up to you to contact the merchant for your refund. You can mail the documents from home or, more quickly, from your point of departure (using a stamped, self-addressed envelope or one that's been provided by the merchant). You'll then have to wait—it could take months.

Customs for American Shoppers

You are allowed to take home $800 worth of items per person duty-free, once every 30 days. You can also bring in duty-free a liter of alcohol. As for food, you can take home many processed and packaged foods: vacuum-packed cheeses, dried herbs, jams, chocolate, oil, vinegar, and honey. Fresh fruits and vegetables and most meats are not allowed. Any liquid-containing foods must be packed in checked luggage, a potential recipe for disaster. To check customs rules and duty rates, visit www.cbp.gov.

Sightseeing

Sightseeing can be hard work. Use these tips to make your visits to Croatia's and Slovenia's finest sights meaningful, fun, efficient, and painless.

Plan Ahead

Set up an itinerary that allows you to fit in all your must-see sights. For a one-stop look at opening hours, see the "At a Glance" sidebars for each major destination. The hours at sights tend to fluctuate with demand from season to season (especially in coastal towns), but you can easily confirm the latest hours by checking with the TI or the sight's website.

Don't put off visiting a must-see sight—you never know when a place will close unexpectedly for a holiday, strike, or restoration. On holidays (see list on page 721), expect reduced hours or closures. In summer, some sights may stay open late. Off-season, most museums have shorter hours.

When possible, visit major sights in the morning (when your energy is best) and save other activities for the afternoon. Especially in coastal towns, many sights close for a midafternoon siesta.

Study up. To avoid redundancy, many cultural or historical details are explained for one sight in this book and not repeated for another; to get the full picture, read the entire chapter for each destination you'll visit.

At Sights

Here's what you can typically expect:

A few sights require you to check daypacks and coats. They'll be kept safely. If you have something you can't bear to part with, stash it in a pocket or purse. To avoid checking a small backpack, carry it under your arm like a purse as you enter. From a guard's point of view, a backpack is generally a problem, while a purse is not.

Flash photography is often banned, but taking photos without a flash is usually allowed. Look for signs or ask. Flashes damage oil paintings and distract others in the room. Even without a flash, a handheld camera will take a decent picture (or buy postcards or posters at the museum bookstore). If photos are permitted, video cameras generally are OK too.

Museums may have special exhibits in addition to their permanent collection. Some exhibits are included in the entry price, while others come at an extra cost (which you may have to pay even if you don't want to see the exhibit).

Expect changes—items can be on tour, on loan, out sick, or shifted at the whim of the curator. To adapt, pick up any available free floor plans as you enter, and ask museum staff if you can't find a particular item.

Many sights rent **audioguides,** which generally offer recorded descriptions in English (sometimes included in the price, otherwise about $6-8). If you bring along your own pair of headphones and a Y-jack, you can sometimes share one audioguide with your travel partner and save money. As an alternative, several museums now have smartphone audio tours (often free, sometimes for a fee). Use your smartphone (bring earbuds) to access the museum's Wi-Fi network, where you can log on for a room-by-room tour. While this sounds complicated, it generally works great.

Some sights also run short films featuring their highlights and history. These are generally well worth your time—sometimes even better than the rest of the museum. I make it standard operating procedure to ask when I arrive at a sight if there is a film in English.

A few sights may have an on-site café or cafeteria (usually a good place to rest and have a snack or light meal). The WCs at sights are free and generally clean (it's smart to carry tissues in case a WC runs out of TP).

Many places sell postcards that highlight their attractions. Before you leave a sight, scan the postcards and thumb through the biggest guidebook (or skim its index) to be sure you haven't overlooked something that you'd like to see.

Most sights stop admitting people 30-60 minutes before closing time, and some rooms close early (often 45 minutes before the actual closing time). Guards usher people out, so don't save the best for last.

Every sight or museum offers more than what is covered in this book. Use the information in this book as an introduction—not the final word.

Sleeping

The accommodations scene in Croatia and Slovenia is quirky and complicated. You have two basic choices: either a big hotel or what locals call "private accommodations"—a rented apartment (*apartman,* plural *apartmani*) or a room in a private home (*soba,*

pronounced SOH-bah; plural *sobe,* SOH-bay). I've explained the ins and outs of each in this section.

I favor accommodations (and restaurants) that are convenient to your sightseeing activities. I look for places that are friendly, comfortable, clean, professional-feeling, English-speaking, relatively quiet at night, and family-run. I'm more

INTRODUCTION

Sleep Code

To help you sort easily through my listings, I've divided the accommodations into three categories based on the price for a double room with bath during high season:

$$$ **Higher Priced**
$$ **Moderately Priced**
$ **Lower Priced**

I always rate hostels as $, whether or not they have double rooms, because they have the cheapest beds in town. For other updates, see www.ricksteves.com/update.

If I've listed two sets of rates for an accommodation, separated by a slash, I've noted the time period in which the second rate applies (generally off-season, Oct-May); if I've listed three sets of rates, the first is for peak season (July-Aug), the second is for shoulder season (May-June and Sept-Oct), and the third is for off-season (Nov-April). The dates for seasonal rates vary by hotel, and prices can change without notice; verify the hotel's current rates online or by email. When a price range is given for a type of room (such as double rooms listing for €80-100), it generally means the price fluctuates with the size of room.

A modest tourist tax (roughly €1 per person, per night) is added to room rates in Croatia, Slovenia, and Bosnia.

impressed by local character, a handy location, and a fun-loving philosophy than flatscreen TVs and shoeshine machines. Obviously, a place meeting every criterion is unusual, and all of my recommendations fall short of perfection. But I've listed the best values I could find for each price range. My favorites are small, family-run hotels (which are rare) and friendly local people who rent "hotelesque" private rooms without a reception desk (which are, thankfully, abundant).

Book your accommodations well in advance if you'll be traveling during busy times. See page 721 for a list of major holidays and festivals; for tips on making reservations, see page 30.

Travel Review Websites: TripAdvisor.com and similar review websites are popular tools for finding hotels, but have drawbacks. To write a review, people need only an email address—making it easy to hide their true identity. If a hotel is well reviewed in a guidebook or two, and also gets good ratings on TripAdvisor, it's

Abbreviations

To pack maximum information into minimum space, I use the following code to describe accommodations in this book. Prices listed are per room, not per person.

S = Single room (or price for one person in a double).

D = Double or Twin room. Double beds can be two twins sheeted together and are usually big enough for non-romantic couples.

T = Triple (generally a double bed with a single).

Q = Quad (usually two double beds; adding an extra child's bed to a T is usually cheaper).

b = Private bathroom with toilet and shower or tub.

s = Private shower or tub only (the toilet is down the hall).

According to this code, a couple staying at a "Db-€70" place in Dubrovnik would pay a total of €70 (about $100) for a double room with a private bathroom. At hotels, unless otherwise noted, breakfast is included, the staff speaks English, and credit cards are accepted. Note that private accommodations rarely accept cards or include breakfast; most that I list are run by English-speakers, but a few proprietors may rely on relatives or neighbors to help translate.

If I mention "Internet access" in a listing, there's a public terminal in the lobby for guests to use. If I specify "Wi-Fi," you can generally access it in public areas and often (but not always) in your room, but only if you have your own laptop or other wireless device. If you see "cable Internet," it means you can get online in your room with your laptop, provided you have (or borrow) an Ethernet cable to plug in.

probably a safe bet—but I wouldn't stay at a hotel based solely on a TripAdvisor recommendation.

Rates and Deals

In Croatia, most hotels are outrageously expensive, but private accommodations are an excellent value. My recommendations range from $15 bunks to $500-plus splurges, but most cluster somewhere in between: For a well-located standard double room in peak season on the Croatian coast, plan on spending $150-250 in a big resort hotel; $75-120 in a small hotel or a hotelesque private room or apartment (with your own bathroom, TV, and other amenities); or $45-75 for a more basic private room with a shared bathroom.

Slovenia has a wider range of affordable small hotels (about $90-120 in Ljubljana, and $70-90 in small towns and the countryside), which make private accommodations a lesser value there.

I've described my recommended accommodations using a Sleep Code (see the sidebar). Prices listed are for one-night stays in peak season, and assume you're booking directly (not through a TI or online hotel-booking engine). While most Croatian accommodations quote their rates in euros, when you check out, payment is expected in kunas (or, occasionally, by credit card).

Rates vary wildly by season, with August being the most expensive. Short stays (of less than three nights) are discouraged, especially in peak season. Expect to pay 20-50 percent extra if you're staying just one or two nights, and don't be surprised if some places have a multinight minimum in summer. But if you can fill a gap in their reservations schedule, they might waive this surcharge.

Three or four people can save money by requesting one big room. Traveling alone can be expensive: A single room is often only 20 percent cheaper than a double. In general, prices can soften if you do any of the following: offer to pay cash, stay at least three nights, or mention this book. You can also try asking for a cheaper room or a discount, or offer to skip breakfast (if it's offered and included in the rate).

Book direct. Using an online booking service costs the hotel about 15 percent and logically closes the door on special deals. As you look over the listings, you'll notice that some accommodations promise special prices to my readers who book direct (without using a room-finding service or hotel-booking website). To get these rates, you must mention this book when you reserve, and then show the book upon arrival. Some readers with ebooks have reported difficulty getting a Rick Steves discount. If this happens to you, please show this to the hotelier: Rick Steves discounts apply to readers with ebooks as well as printed books.

Helpful Hints

Discos and nightclubs are proliferating in the old town centers of many cities in this book—including Dubrovnik, Split, and Ljubljana. I've noted the specific hotels that suffer the worst noise. If you're a light sleeper, make a point of requesting a quiet room. And bring earplugs.

Perhaps because they tend to be located in musty old stone buildings, many hotels and *sobe* in Croatia use heavily perfumed air fresheners in their rooms. It's usually easy to locate and unplug these, but if you are very sensitive to fragrances, try asking your *sobe* host to remove them before you arrive.

Window screens are rare in this area, so in warm weather be prepared to share your room with mosquitoes and other bugs.

In Slovenia, a recent smoking ban forced many accommodations to become non-smoking, though some larger hotels still have designated smoking rooms. Croatia's smoking ban is still in flux and often not enforced. For this reason, be very specific and assertive if you need a room that's strictly non-smoking.

If there seems to be no hot water, try flipping the switch with a picture of a water tank, usually next to the light switch. (Ideally, discover this switch long before you need to shower, and keep it on—otherwise you'll have to wait for the water to heat up.) In many *sobe,* the hot-water tank is tiny—barely big enough for one American-length shower. So two people traveling together may want to practice the "navy shower" method (douse yourself, turn off water, soap up, then turn water back on for a quick rinse)...or the second person may be in for a chilly surprise. The incredibly high water pressure in most Croatian showers just makes the hot water go that much faster (turn the faucet on only partway to help stretch the precious hot water).

In private accommodations and some hotels, towels aren't replaced, so hang them up to reuse. The cord that dangles over the tub or shower in big resort hotels is not a clothesline—you pull it if you've fallen and can't get up.

To guard against theft in your room, keep valuables out of sight. Some rooms come with a safe, and other hotels have safes at the front desk. Use them if you're concerned.

Your hotelier or *sobe* host can be a great help and source of advice. Most know their city well, and can assist you with everything from public transit and airport connections to finding a good restaurant, the nearest launderette, or an Internet café. But even at the best places, mechanical breakdowns occur: Air-conditioning malfunctions, sinks leak, hot water turns cold, and toilets gurgle and smell. Report your concerns clearly and calmly. For more complicated problems, don't expect instant results. Above all, don't expect things to be the same as back home. Keep a positive attitude. Remember, you're on vacation. If your accommodations are a disappointment, spend more time out enjoying the places you came to see.

Pay your bill the evening before you leave to avoid the time-wasting crowd at the reception desk in the morning, especially if you need to rush off to catch a boat or train. This also gives you time to discuss and address any points of contention. The only tip my recommended accommodations would like is a friendly, easygoing guest. And, as always, I appreciate feedback on your experiences.

Types of Accommodations
Private Accommodations (*Sobe* and Apartments)
Private accommodations offer travelers a characteristic and money-saving alternative for a fraction of the price of a hotel. You have

two options: *sobe* (rooms) or *apartmani* (apartments).

Often run by empty-nesters, private accommodations are similar to British bed-and-breakfasts...minus the breakfast (ask your host about the best nearby breakfast spot). Generally the more you pay, the more privacy and amenities you get: private bathroom, TV, air-conditioning, kitchenette, and so on. The simplest *sobe* allow you to experience Croatia on the cheap, at nearly youth-hostel prices, while giving you a great opportunity to connect with a local family. The fanciest *sobe* are downright swanky and offer near-hotel anonymity. Apartments are bigger and cost more than *sobe*, but they're still far cheaper than hotels.

Registered *sobe* are rated by the government using a system that assigns stars based on amenities. Three or more stars means that you'll have your own bathroom, two stars puts the bathroom down the hall, and one star is rock-bottom basic. If you don't like the idea of sharing a toilet with strangers, look for three stars and you'll do fine. (Apartments always have private bathrooms, plus modest kitchen facilities.) Many, but not all, three-star *sobe* also have TV and air-conditioning (but usually no telephone). The prices for private accommodations generally fluctuate with the seasons, and remember that stays of fewer than three nights usually come with a 20-50 percent surcharge (though this is often waived outside peak season).

Since the best-value *sobe* deservedly book up early, reservations are highly recommended. For the *sobe* listed in this book, **always book direct.** Many of my recommended *sobe* are listed on room-booking websites (Booking.com is especially popular),

but going through a middleman costs your host an extra 15 percent commission and gains you absolutely nothing. (Some *sobe* hosts may give you slightly lower prices if you book direct. Any special prices or discounts I've negotiated for this book are invalidated if you use a middleman.) Do your hosts a favor and email or phone *sobe* directly to request reservations; it's also an opportunity to ask any questions you have about the accommodations, and to start to get to know your host.

After you've reserved, keep in mind that your host loses money if you don't show up. For this reason, some hosts may request your credit-card number to secure the reservation. (They'll generally ask for payment in cash when you're there; your credit card won't be charged.) Other hosts might ask you to wire or mail money as a deposit. Because wiring money can come with substantial fees—

which you (rather than the *sobe* host) will incur—it usually works better to mail them a check or travelers check. Ask your *sobe* host which options they accept. If the request seems too complicated for you, reserve elsewhere.

Sobe hucksters who accost you on the street can be very aggressive about luring travelers away from their reserved rooms. But if you've already booked a room at a particular place, you owe it to them to show up.

If you like to travel spontaneously, during most of the year you'll have no problem finding *sobe* as you go (late July and August are the exceptions). Locals hawking rooms meet each arriving boat, bus, and train. Many of these *sobe* have not been vetted by the government, but they can sometimes turn out to be a good deal. In fact, I've found some of my favorite *sobe* in this book this way. The person generally shows photos of her place, you haggle for a price, then she escorts you to your new home. Be sure you understand exactly where it's located (i.e., within easy walking distance of the attractions) before you accept—ask to see the location on a map, and find out how long it takes to walk into town.

You can also keep an eye out for rooms as you walk or drive through town—you'll see blue *sobe* and *apartmani* signs everywhere. It's actually fun to visit a few homes and make a deal. While it takes nerve to just show up without a room, this is standard operating procedure for backpackers.

As a last resort, you can enlist the help of a travel agency to find you a room—but you'll pay 10-30 percent extra (various agencies are listed in this book; to search from home, try www.dubrovnikapartmentsource.com for Dubrovnik, or www.adriatica.net for all of Croatia).

I'm accustomed to staying in hotels. But a few years ago, I found all the hotels in Dubrovnik booked up. With some trepidation, I stayed in a *soba*...and I'll never go back to a Croatian resort hotel again. I've made it my mission to convince you to sleep in *sobe*, too.

Note that *sobe* aren't as common or as much of a good value in Slovenia as they are in Croatia, but the Slovenes have their own cheap option: tourist farms *(turistične kmetije)*. At these working farms, you can get a hotelesque room, plus breakfast and dinner, for a surprisingly low cost. For more on tourist farms, see page 508.

Making Reservations

It's possible to travel most of the year without reservations, especially if you arrive early in the day (although popular tourist towns can be completely full in late July and August). But given the good value of the accommodations I've found for this book, I'd recommend that you reserve your rooms in advance, particularly if you'll be traveling during peak season. Book several weeks ahead, or as soon as you've pinned down your travel dates. Note that some national holidays jam things up and merit your making reservations far in advance (see "Holidays and Festivals" on page 721).

Because my favorite accommodations tend to be small-time entrepreneurs renting only a few rooms, they book up fast with my readers. I've tried to list several good options, so if your first choice is full, you can simply try others on the list. Sometimes one of my listings might offer to find you somewhere else to stay. This is convenient, and these alternatives can be just as good as the ones I've listed, but don't feel obligated—you'll have more control over your options if you book direct, using my recommendations.

Requesting a Reservation: To make a reservation, contact hotels and *sobe* directly by email, phone, or fax. Email is the clearest and most economical way to make a reservation. Or you can go straight to the hotel website; many have secure online reservation forms and can instantly inform you of availability and any special deals. But be sure you use the hotel's official site and not a booking agency's site—otherwise you'll give up any Rick Steves' discounts and pay higher rates than you should.

The hotelier or *sobe* host wants to know these key pieces of information (also included in the sample request form on page 726):

- number and type of rooms
- number of nights
- date of arrival
- date of departure
- any special needs (e.g., bathroom in the room or down the hall, twin beds vs. double bed, air-conditioning, quiet, view, ground floor, etc.)

When you request a room, use the European style for writing dates: day/month/year. For example, for a two-night stay in July 2012, I would request: "1 double room for 2 nights, arrive

16/07/12, depart 18/07/12." Consider carefully how long you'll stay; don't just assume you can tack on extra days once you arrive. Make sure you mention any discounts—for Rick Steves readers or otherwise—when you make the reservation.

Confirming a Reservation: If the hotel's response tells you its room availability and rates, it's not a confirmation. You must tell them that you want that room at the given rate. Many hoteliers will request your credit-card number to hold the room. While you can email your credit-card information (I do), it's safer to share that confidential info via phone call, fax, split between two successive emails, or via a secure online reservation form (if the hotel has one on its website). Before accepting a room, confirm your understanding of the complete price (including, for example, surcharges for short stays).

Canceling a Reservation: If you must cancel your reservation, it's courteous to do so with as much advance notice as possible. Simply make a quick phone call or send an email. Family-run hotels and *sobe* hosts lose money if they turn away customers while holding a room for someone who doesn't show up. Understandably, many hoteliers bill no-shows for one night.

Cancellation policies can be strict: For example, you might lose a deposit if you cancel within two weeks of your reserved stay, or you might be billed for the entire visit if you leave early. Internet deals may require prepayment, with no refunds for cancellations. Ask about cancellation policies before you book.

If canceling via email, request confirmation that your cancellation was received to avoid being accidentally billed.

Reconfirming a Reservation: Always call to reconfirm your room reservation a day or two in advance. Smaller hotels and *sobe* appreciate knowing your estimated time of arrival. If you'll be arriving late (after 17:00), let them know. On the small chance that a hotel loses track of your reservation, it helps to bring along a hard copy of their emailed or faxed confirmation.

Reserving Rooms as You Travel: You can make reservations as you travel, calling hotels or *sobe* a few days to a week before your arrival. If everything's full, don't despair. Call a day or two in advance and fill in a cancellation. If you'd rather travel without any reservations at all, you'll have greater success snaring rooms if you arrive at your destination early in the day. When you anticipate crowds (weekends are worst), call hotels at about 9:00 or 10:00 on the day you plan to arrive, when the hotel clerk knows who'll be checking out and just which rooms will be available. If you encounter a language barrier, ask the fluent receptionist at your current hotel to call for you.

Hotels

For most travelers, Croatian hotels are a bad value. You basically have two options: over-the-top, fancy, overpriced splurge hotels catering to the international jet-set crowd; or run-down, communist-era, overpriced resort hotels desperate for a renovation. Whether old or new, Croatian hotels all seem to carry on the old Yugoslav aesthetic of mass tourism. That means crowded "beach" access (often on a concrete pad), typically surly staff, a travel-agency desk selling excursions in the lobby, corny live music in the lounge a few nights each week, and a seaview apéritif bar. More money buys you a friendlier, more polished staff and newer decor.

Fortunately, *sobe*, apartments, and a few small guest houses have stepped up to fill the mid-budget accommodations void. Note that the fine line that separates small, family-run guest houses and top-end *sobe* can be blurry.

The hotel situation is more straightforward in Slovenia and Bosnia, which have a wider range of small, reasonably priced hotels. While you will find a few communist-era holdover hotels in resorty parts of these countries, they don't dominate the scene as they do in Croatia.

Hostels

For $25-35 a night, travelers of any age can stay at a youth hostel. While Hostelling International (IYHF) hostels admit nonmembers for an extra fee, it can be easier to join the club's US affiliate before you go (US tel. 301/495-1240 or order online at www.hiusa .org). However, to increase your options, consider the many independent hostels that don't require a membership card.

Hostels are a relatively new concept in Croatia. Usually official IYHF hostels are poorly located, in bad repair, and institutional, while independent hostels are loosely run, tend to attract a youthful party crowd, and are grungier than the European norm. If you need a cheap bed and aren't into the party scene, you'll probably do better for only a little more money by sleeping in basic private accommodations (rooms in private homes with shared bathrooms, described earlier).

Slovenia has a more appealing range of hostels. For example, one of Europe's most innovative hostels is Ljubljana's Celica, a renovated former prison (see page 554).

In each town, I've tried to list the best-established, most reputable hostel options, both independent and official. But this scene is evolving so fast that avid hostelers will do better getting tips from fellow travelers and searching sites such as www.hostels.com, www.hostelworld.com, www.hostelz.com, and www.hostels europe.com.

At any hostel, cheap meals are sometimes available, and

kitchen facilities are usually provided for do-it-yourselfers. Expect crowds in the summer, snoring, and lots of noisy backpacker bonding in the common room while you're trying to sleep. Hosteling is ideal for those traveling single: Prices are per bed, not per room, and you'll have an instant circle of friends. At most hostels, you can reserve online or by phoning ahead (usually with a credit card).

Eating

Croatia and Slovenia offer good food for reasonable prices—especially if you venture off the main tourist trail. Choose a spot filled with locals, not the place with the big neon signs boasting, "We Speak English and Accept Credit Cards." Locals eat better at lower-rent locales. This is affordable sightseeing for your palate.

While not exactly high cuisine, the food of this region is surprisingly diverse. Choosing between strudel and baklava on

the same menu, you're constantly reminded that this is a land where East meets West. I've listed the specific specialties in the introduction to each country in this book, but throughout Croatia and Slovenia you'll sink your teeth into lots of tasty Italian-style food (pizzas and pastas), as well as seafood and fine local wines. You'll also find some pan-Balkan elements, such as grilled meats and phyllo dough, that distinguish the cuisine throughout the former Yugoslavia (see the "Balkan Flavors" sidebar on page 418).

At fish restaurants, seafood is often priced by weight—either by kilogram or by hectogram (100 grams, or one-tenth of a kilogram). A one-kilogram portion feeds two hungry people or three light eaters. When I list price ranges for main dishes at restaurants, I don't include the super-top-end seafood splurges (such as lobster). For more tips on ordering seafood here, see "Croatian Food" on page 50.

While bread, cover, and service charges haven't traditionally been applied in these countries, a few tourist-oriented restaurants have started to pad their bills with these extra fees. If you're concerned about this, ask up front.

When you're in the mood for something halfway between a

INTRODUCTION

How Was Your Trip?

Were your travels fun, smooth, and meaningful? If you'd like to share your tips, concerns, and discoveries, please fill out the survey at www.ricksteves.com/feedback. I value your feedback. Thanks in advance—it helps a lot.

restaurant and a picnic meal, look for bakeries selling *burek* (the savory phyllo-dough pastry) and other goodies, or shops advertising "pizza cut" (pizza by the slice). Many grocery stores sell premade sandwiches, and others might be willing to make one for you from what's in the deli case.

Traveling as a Temporary Local

We travel all the way to Croatia and Slovenia to enjoy differences—to become temporary locals. You'll experience frustrations. Certain truths that we find "God-given" or "self-evident," such as cold beer, ice in drinks, bottomless cups of coffee, hot showers, and bigger being better, are suddenly not so true. One of the benefits of travel is the eye-opening realization that there are logical, civil, and even better alternatives. A willingness to go local ensures that you'll enjoy a full dose of Croatian and Slovenian hospitality.

Europeans generally like Americans. But if there is a negative aspect to the European image of Americans, it's that we are big, loud, aggressive, impolite, rich, and a bit naive.

Meanwhile, most Americans traveling in this region find Slovenes to be extremely gregarious, but tend to be disappointed with the brusqueness of many Croatians they encounter. While tourism is big in Croatia, the finer points of service and hospitality sometimes get lost. Before losing your patience (as I sometimes do), try to remember that these people lived under a communist regime 20 years ago, followed by a devastating war, and today are coping with an unprecedented tourist crush. They're scrambling to keep up.

While Europeans look bemusedly at some of our Yankee excesses—and worriedly at others—they nearly always afford us individual travelers all the warmth we deserve.

Judging from all the happy feedback I receive from travelers who have used this book, it's safe to assume you'll enjoy a great, affordable vacation—with the finesse of an independent, experienced traveler.

Thanks, and *sretan put*—happy travels!

Back Door Travel Philosophy
From *Rick Steves' Europe Through the Back Door*

Travel is intensified living—maximum thrills per minute and one of the last great sources of legal adventure. Travel is freedom. It's recess, and we need it.

Experiencing the real Europe requires catching it by surprise, going casual..."Through the Back Door."

Affording travel is a matter of priorities. (Make do with the old car.) You can eat and sleep—simply, safely, and enjoyably—anywhere in Europe for $120 a day plus transportation costs (allow more for bigger cities). In many ways, spending more money only builds a thicker wall between you and what you traveled so far to see. Europe is a cultural carnival, and time after time, you'll find that its best acts are free and the best seats are the cheap ones.

A tight budget forces you to travel close to the ground, meeting and communicating with the people. Never sacrifice sleep, nutrition, safety, or cleanliness to save money. Simply enjoy the local-style alternatives to expensive hotels and restaurants.

Connecting with people carbonates your experience. Extroverts have more fun. If your trip is low on magic moments, kick yourself and make things happen. If you don't enjoy a place, maybe you don't know enough about it. Seek the truth. Recognize tourist traps. Give a culture the benefit of your open mind. See things as different, but not better or worse. Any culture has plenty to share.

Of course, travel, like the world, is a series of hills and valleys. Be fanatically positive and militantly optimistic. If something's not to your liking, change your liking.

Travel can make you a happier American, as well as a citizen of the world. Our Earth is home to seven billion equally precious people. It's humbling to travel and find that other people don't have the "American Dream"—they have their own dreams. Europeans like us, but with all due respect, they wouldn't trade passports.

Thoughtful travel engages us with the world. In tough economic times, it reminds us what is truly important. By broadening perspectives, travel teaches new ways to measure quality of life.

Globetrotting destroys ethnocentricity, helping us understand and appreciate other cultures. Rather than fear the diversity on this planet, celebrate it. Among your most prized souvenirs will be the strands of different cultures you choose to knit into your own character. The world is a cultural yarn shop, and Back Door travelers are weaving the ultimate tapestry. Join in!

CROATIA
Hrvatska

CROATIA

Sunny beaches, succulent seafood, and a taste of *la dolce vita*...in Eastern Europe?

With thousands of miles of seafront and more than a thousand islands, Croatia's coastline is Eastern Europe's Riviera. Holidaymakers love its pebbly beaches, predictably balmy summer weather, and dramatic mountains. Croatia is also historic. From ruined Roman arenas and Byzantine mosaics to Venetian bell towers, Habsburg villas, and even communist concrete, past rulers have left their mark.

Croatia feels more Mediterranean than "Eastern European." Historically, Croatia has more in common with Venice and Rome

than Vienna or Budapest; especially on the coast, it's sometimes difficult to distinguish this lively place from Italy. If you've become accustomed to the Germanic efficiency of Slovenia, Croatia's relaxed and unpredictable style can come as a shock.

Aside from its fun-in-the-sun status, Croatia is also known as one of the sites, just over a decade and a half ago, of the most violent European war in generations. Locals call it "The Homeland War" or, more casually, "The Last War" (though it's ambiguous whether they mean "final" or "most recent"). Thankfully, the bloodshed is in the past. While a trip to Croatia offers thoughtful travelers the opportunity to understand a complicated chapter of recent history, most visitors focus instead on its substantial natural wonders: mountains, waterfalls, sun, sand, and sea.

Croatia's 3,600 miles of coastline—its main draw for tourists—is loosely divided into three regions. Most people flock to the Dalmatian Coast, in the south—where dramatic limestone cliffs rise from the deep and islands are scattered just offshore (the most appealing are Hvar and Korčula). Here you'll find Croatia's top tourist town, Dubrovnik, and the big city of Split, with its impres-

sive Roman ruins. Way up at the northern corner of the country is the wedge-shaped peninsula called Istria, which has less dramatic scenery but arguably even more romantic towns—including my favorite, the Venetian-flavored Rovinj—along with the city of Pula (more great Roman ruins) and a hilly interior blanketed with vine-yards and topped with hill towns (Motovun is the best). Wedged between Dalmatia and Istria is the Kvarner Gulf, a windy, arid no-man's-land that has few worthwhile attractions, but a few fine islands offshore (including Rab).

Enjoy the coast, but don't ignore the interior. The bustling capital of Zagreb is urban, engaging, and full of great museums. And Croatia's single best natural wonder (in this country that's so full of them) are the stunning waterfalls at Plitvice Lakes National Park.

It's possible to blow a lot of money here. Croatian hotels, espe-cially on the coast, are a terrible value, and there are plenty of tour-isty restaurants happy to overcharge you. But if you know where to look, you can find some wonderful budget alternatives—foremost among them *sobe* (rooms in private homes). *Sobe* are a comfortable compromise: fresh, hotelesque doubles with a private bathroom, air-conditioning, and TV, for a fraction of the cost of an anonymous room in an overpriced resort hotel just down the beach (for details, see page 27).

Europeans are reverent sun-worshippers, and on clear days, virtually every square inch of coastal Croatia is occupied by a sunbather on a beach towel. Nude beaches are a big deal, especially for vacationing Germans and Aus-

trians. If you want to work on an all-around tan, seek out a beach marked *FKK* (from the German *Freikörper Kultur,* or "free body culture"). First-timers get comfortable in a hurry, finding they're not the only pink novices on the rocks. But don't get too excited— these beaches are most beloved by people you'd rather see with their clothes on.

Perhaps because sunshine is so important to the economy, Croatians are particularly affected by weather. They complain that the once-predictable climate has become erratic, with surprise rainy spells or heat waves in the once perfectly consistent, balmy summer months. Historically, the Dubrovnik senate was legally forbidden from making any major decision if the hot, humid Jugo wind was blowing, as that wind tended to make people cranky and ill-tempered. And today, the weather report includes a *biometeorološka prognoza* that indicates how the day's weather will affect your mood. Weather maps come with smiley or frowny faces, and forecasts predict, "People will be tired in the afternoon and not feel like working." Hmm...good excuse.

Every Croatian coastal town has two parts: The time-warp old town, and the obnoxious resort sprawl. Main drags are clogged with gift shops selling shell sculptures and tasteless T-shirts.

While many European visitors enjoy this tacky-trinket tourism, Americans are generally more interested in Old World charm. Fortunately, it's relatively easy to ignore the touristy scene and instead poke your way into twisty old medieval lanes, draped with drying laundry and populated by gossiping neighbors, humble fishermen's taverns, and soccer-playing kids.

Croatian popular music, the mariachi music of Europe, is the ever-present soundtrack of a Dalmatian vacation.

Oliver Dragojević—singing soulful Mediterranean ballads with his gravelly, passionate voice—is the Croatian Tom Jones. Known simply as "Oliver," this beloved crooner gets airplay across Europe and has spawned many imitators (such as the almost-as-popular Gibonni).

More traditional is the hauntingly beautiful *klapa* music—  men's voices harmonizing a cappella, like a barbershop quartet with a soothing Adriatic flavor. Typically the leader begins the song, and the rest of the group (usually 3 to 12 singers) follows behind him with a slight delay. You'll see mariachi-style *klapa* groups performing in touristy areas; a CD of one of these performances (or of a professional group—Cambi is great) is a fun souvenir.

Croatia may be Europe's second most ardently Catholic country (after Poland). Under communism, religion was downplayed and many people gave up the habit of attending Mass regularly. But as the wars raged in the early 1990s, many Croatians rediscovered religion. You may be surprised by how many people you see worshipping in Croatia's churches today.

In the Yugoslav era, Croatia was flooded with tourists—both European and American—who fell in love with its achingly beautiful beaches and coves. In its heyday, Croatia hosted about 10 million visitors a year, who provided the country with about a third of its income. But then, for several years after the war, Croatia floundered. Just a decade ago, the streets of Dubrovnik were empty, lined with souvenir shops tended by desperate-looking vendors. But in the last few years, locals are breathing a sigh of relief as the number of visitors returns to pre-war highs. With astonishing speed, Croatia is becoming one of Europe's top destinations.

Even so, the standards for service (at restaurants, hotels, and so on) can be lower than you might expect. While you'll meet plenty of wonderfully big-hearted Croatians, many of my readers characterize the Croatian waiters or hotel receptionists they've encountered as "gruff" or even "rude." Be prepared for two universal gestures: the classic eye-roll, directed at anyone asking someone to do something that's not precisely in their job description; and the "Croatian Shrug"—a simple gesture meaning, "Don't know, don't care." It helps me to make an attitude adjustment when I cross into Croatia. We're used to thinking, "I should be waited upon." But Croatians think, "This is our world, and you're visiting it...so you can just wait."

Maybe this mindset is understandable, even forgivable. After

Croatia Almanac

Official Name: Republika Hrvatska, or just Hrvatska for short.

Snapshot History: After losing their independence to Hungary in 1102, the Croats watched as most of their coastline became Venetian and their interior was conquered by Ottomans. Croatia was "rescued" by the Habsburgs, but after World War I it became part of Yugoslavia—a decision many Croats regretted until they finally gained independence in 1991 through a bitter war with their Serb neighbors.

Population: Of the country's 4.5 million people, 90 percent are ethnic Croats (Catholic) and 4.5 percent are Serbs (Orthodox). (The Serb population was more than double that before the ethnic cleansing of the 1991-1995 war.) About 1.3 percent of Croatians are Bosniak (Muslim). "Croatians" are citizens of Croatia; "Croats" are a distinct ethnic group made up of Catholic South Slavs. So Orthodox Serbs living in Croatia are Croatians (specifically "Croatian Serbs"), but they aren't Croats.

Latitude and Longitude: 45°N and 15°E (similar latitude to Venice, Italy; Ottawa, Canada; or Portland, Oregon).

Area: 22,000 square miles, similar to West Virginia.

Geography: This boomerang-shaped country has two terrains: Stretching north to south is the long, rugged Mediterranean coastline (3,600 miles of beach, including more than 1,100 off-shore islands), which is warm and dry. Rising up from the sea are the Dinaric Mountains. To the northeast, beginning at about Zagreb, Croatia's flat, inland "panhandle" (called Slavonia) is an extension of the Great Hungarian Plain, with hot summers and cold winters.

Biggest Cities: The capital, Zagreb (in the northern interior), has 780,000 people; Split (along the Dalmatian Coast) has 178,000; and Rijeka (on the northern coast) has 129,000.

Economy: Much of the country's wealth ($78 billion GDP, $17,400 GDP per capita) comes from tourism, banking, and trade with Italy. Unemployment is a stiff 17 percent.

Currency: 1 kuna (kn, or HRK) = about 20 cents, and 5 kunas = about $1. One kuna is broken down into 100 lipa. Kuna is Croatian for "marten" (a foxlike animal), recalling a time when fur pelts were used as currency. A lipa is a linden tree.

all, how would you like it if a tidal wave of sweaty, ill-behaved, clueless tourists took over your entire town for the nicest months of each year? (No, I'm not talking about you...but just look around you.) The one-two punch of several decades of communism, followed by a devastating war, wasn't exactly the best preparation for being the perfect host. On the other hand, it can be a bit jarring in a place so dependent upon tourism to find such a stubborn

Government: The single-house assembly (Sabor) of 153 legislators is elected by popular vote. The country's prime minister (the
head of the majority party in parliament, the center-left Social
Democratic party) is currently Zoran Milanović; the directly
elected (but more fig-
urehead) president is Ivo
Josipović (whose first
term expires in 2015).

Flag: The flag has three
horizontal bands (red on
top, white, and blue) with
a traditional red-and-
white checkerboard shield
in the center.

The Average Croatian: The average Croatian will live to age 76
and have 1.4 children. One in four uses the Internet. The average
Croatian absolutely adores the soccer team Dinamo Zagreb and
absolutely despises Hajduk Split...or vice versa.

Notable Croatians: A pair of big-league historical figures were
born in Croatia: Roman Emperor Diocletian (A.D. 245-313) and
explorer Marco Polo (1254?-1324). More recently, many Americans
whose names end in "-ich" have Croatian roots, including actor
John Malkovich and Ohio politicians Dennis Kucinich and John
Kasich, not to mention baseball legend Roger Marich...I mean,
Maris. More Croatian athletes abound: NBA fans might recognize
Toni Kukoč or Gordan Giricek, and at the 2002 and 2006 Winter
Olympic Games, the women's downhill skiing events were dominated by Janica Kostelić; her brother Ivica Kostelić medaled in
2006 and 2010. Actor Goran Višnjić (from TV's *ER*) was born
and raised in Croatia, and served in the army as a paratrooper.
You've likely never heard of the beloved Croatian sculptor Ivan
Meštrović, but you'll see his expressive works all over the country (see page 208). Inventor Nikola Tesla (1856-1943)—who, as a
rival of Thomas Edison's, invented alternating current (AC)—was
a Croatian-born Serb. And a band of well-dressed 17th-century
Croatian soldiers stationed in France gave the Western world a
new fashion accessory—the *cravate*, or necktie (for the full story,
see page 62).

disregard for the fundamentals of hospitality. The good news is
that I've noticed some improvement over the last few years. My
advice: Expect the worst, then be pleasantly surprised by the positive interactions you have, rather than getting hung up on the frustrating ones.

Today's Croatia is crawling with a Babel of international guests
speaking German, French, Italian, every accent of English...and a

smattering of Croatian. And yet, despite the tourists, this place remains distinctly and stubbornly Croatian. You'd have to search pretty hard to find a McDonald's.

Helpful Hints

Telephones: Croatia's pay phones take insertable phone cards (buy at newsstands or kiosks). Mobile phone numbers begin with 091, 098, or 099. Numbers beginning with 060 are pricey toll lines. For more details on how to dial to, from, and within Croatia, see page 696.

Free Tourist Help by Phone: The "Croatian Angels" service gives free information in English over a toll-free line (tel. 062-999-999, daily June-Aug 8:00-24:00, April-May and Sept-mid-Oct 9:00-17:00, closed mid-Oct-March).

Addresses: Addresses listed with a street name and followed by "b.b." have no street number. In most small towns, locals ignore not only street numbers but also street names—navigate with a map or by asking for directions.

Slick Pavement: Old towns, with their well-polished pavement stones and many slick stairs, can be quite treacherous, especially after a rainstorm. (On a recent trip, one of your co-authors almost broke his arm slipping down a flight of stairs.) Tread with care.

Siesta: Croatians eat their big meal at lunch, then take a traditional Mediterranean siesta. This means that many stores, museums, and churches are closed in the mid-afternoon.

Business Closures on Sundays: During the busier tourist months, from June through December, stores are allowed to be open on Sundays. Off-season, from January through May, most shops are legally required to close.

Landmine Warning: Certain parts of the Croatian interior were once full of landmines. Most of these mines have been removed, and fields that may still be dangerous are usually clearly marked. As a precaution, if you're in a former war zone, stay on roads and paths, and don't go wandering through overgrown fields and deserted villages.

Croatian History

For nearly a millennium, bits and pieces of what we today call "Croatia" were batted back and forth between foreign powers: Hungarians, Venetians, Ottomans, Habsburgs, and Yugoslavs. Only in 1991 did Croatia (violently) regain its independence.

Early History

Croatia's first inhabitants were the Illyrians (ancestors of today's Albanians). During antiquity, the Greeks and Romans both sailed ships up and down the strategic Dalmatian Coast, founding many towns that still exist today, and littering the Adriatic seabed with shipwrecks. Romans built larger settlements on the Dalmatian Coast as early as 229 B.C., and in the fourth century A.D., Emperor Diocletian built his retirement palace in the coastal town of Split. As Rome fell in the fifth century, Slavs (the ancestors of today's Croatians) and other barbarians flooded Europe. The northern part of Croatia's coast fell briefly under the Byzantines, who slathered churches with shimmering mosaics (the best are in the Euphrasian Basilica in Poreč, Istria).

Beginning in the seventh century, Slavic Croats began to control most of the land that is today's Croatia. In A.D. 925, the Dalmatian Duke Tomislav united the disparate Croat tribes into a single kingdom. By consolidating and extending Croat-held territory and centralizing power, Tomislav created the first "Croatia."

Loss of Independence

By the early 12th century, the Croatian kings had died out, and neighboring powers (Hungary, Venice, and Byzantium) threatened the Croats. For the sake of self-preservation, Croatia entered an alliance with the Hungarians in 1102, and for the next 900 years, the Croats were ruled by foreign states. The Hungarians gradually took more and more power from the Croats, exerting control over the majority of inland Croatia. Meanwhile, the Venetian Republic conquered most of the coast and peppered the Croatian Adriatic with bell towers and statues of St. Mark. Through it all, the tiny Republic of Dubrovnik flourished—paying off whomever necessary to maintain its independence and becoming one of Europe's most important shipbuilding and maritime powers...a plucky rival to powerful Venice.

The Ottomans conquered most of inland Croatia in the 15th century and challenged the Venetians—unsuccessfully—for control of the coastline. Most of the stout walls, fortresses, and other fortifications you'll see all along the Croatian coast date from this time, built by the Venetians to defend against Ottoman attack. In the 17th century, the Habsburgs forced the Ottomans out of inland Croatia. Then, after Venice and Dubrovnik fell to Napoleon in the early 19th century, the coast also went to the Habsburgs—beginning a long tradition of Austrians basking on Croatian beaches.

The Yugoslav Era, World War II, and the Ustaše

When the Austro-Hungarian Empire broke up at the end of World War I, the Croats banded together with the Serbs, Slovenes, and Bosnians in the union that would become Yugoslavia. But virtually as soon as Yugoslavia was formed, many Croats began to fear that the Serbs would steer Yugoslavia to their own purposes. So when the Nazis invaded and installed a puppet government—run by the homegrown, fascist Ustaše party—many Croats supported them, believing that fascism could provide them with greater independence. Under the watchful eye of the Nazis, the Ustaše operated one of the most brutal Nazi puppet states during World War II, the misnamed "Independent State of Croatia" (which also controlled most of today's Slovenia and Bosnia). Ustaše concentration camps were used to murder not only Jews and Roma (Gypsies), but also Serbs. Hot-tempered debate rages even today about how many Serbs died at the hands of the Ustaše—estimates vary wildly, from 25,000 to over a million, but most legitimate historians put the number in the hundreds of thousands.

Cardinal Alojzije Stepinac was one Croat who made the mistake of backing the Ustaše. By most accounts, Stepinac was a mild-mannered, extremely devout man who didn't agree with the extremism of the Ustaše...but also did little to fight it. Following the war, Stepinac was arrested, tried, and imprisoned, dying under house arrest in 1960. In the years since, Stepinac has become a martyr for Catholics and Croat nationalists. Even though he's the single most revered figure of Croatian Catholicism, Stepinac remains highly unpopular among Serbs.

At the end of World War II, the Ustaše and the Nazis were forced out by Yugoslavia's homegrown Partisan Army, led by a charismatic war hero named Josip Broz, who went by his nickname, "Tito." Tito became "president for life," and Croatia once again became part of a united Yugoslavia. The union would hold together for more than 40 years, until it broke apart under Serbian President Slobodan Milošević and Croatian President Franjo Tuđman.

For more details on Yugoslavia and its breakup, see the Understanding Yugoslavia chapter.

Independence Regained

Croatia's declaration of independence from Yugoslavia in 1991 was met with fear and anger on the part of its more than half-million Serb residents. Even before independence, the first volleys of a bloody war had been fired. The war had two phases: First, in 1991, Croatian Serbs declared independence from the new nation of Croatia, forming their own state and forcing out or murdering any Croats in "their" territory (with the thinly disguised support of Slobodan Milošević). Then a tense cease-fire fell over the region until 1995, when the second phase of the war ignited: Croatia pushed back through the Serb-dominated territory, reclaiming it for Croatia and forcing out or murdering Serbs living there.

Imagine becoming an independent nation after nine centuries

of foreign domination. Croatians seized their hard-earned freedom with a nationalist fervor that bordered on fascism. It was a heady and absurd time, which today's Croatians recall with disbelief, sadness...and maybe a tinge of nostalgia.

In the Croatia of the early 1990s, even the most bizarre notions seemed possible. Croatia's first post-Yugoslav president, the extreme nationalist Franjo Tuđman (see sidebar on page 48), proposed implausible directives for the new nation—such as privatizing all of the nation's resources and handing them over to 200 super-elite families (which, thankfully for everyone else, never happened). The government began calling the language "Croatian" rather than "Serbo-Croatian" and created new words from specifically Croat roots. The Croats even briefly considered replacing the Roman alphabet with the ninth-century Glagolitic script to invoke Croat culture and further differentiate Croatian from Serbia's Cyrillic alphabet. Fortunately for tourists, this plan didn't take off.

After Tuđman's death in 1999, Croatia began the new millennium with a more truly democratic leader, Stipe Mesić. The popular Mesić, who was once aligned with Tuđman, had split off and formed his own political party when Tuđman's politics grew too extreme. Tuđman spent years tampering with the constitution to give himself more and more power, but when Mesić took over, he reversed those changes and handed more authority back to the parliament.

Croatia Today

In 2003, Croatia applied for membership in the European Union. It cleared the final hurdles in the summer of 2011, and—assuming all goes as scheduled—is slated to officially join the EU on July 1, 2013.

Croatia's road to EU membership has been rocky. Initially, the country's biggest barrier was its human-rights record during the recent war. Several Croatian officers were indicted for war crimes by the International Criminal Tribunal for the Former Yugoslavia (ICTY) in The Hague, Netherlands. But many Croatians feel that the soldiers branded as "war criminals" by The Hague are instead heroes of their war of independence. The highest-profile Croatian figure to be arrested was Ante Gotovina, a lieutenant general accused of atrocities against Serb civilians. After four years in hiding, Gotovina was found and arrested in Spain in December 2005 and sent to stand

GENERAL
ANTE GOTOVINA

Franjo Tuđman
(1922-1999)

Independent Croatia's first president was the controversial Franjo Tuđman (FRAHN-yoh TOOJ-mahn). Tuđman began his career fighting for Tito on the left, but later had a dramatic ideological swing to the far right. His anticommunist, highly nationalistic HDZ party was the driving force for Croatian statehood, making him the young nation's first hero. But even as he fought for independence from Yugoslavia, his own ruling style grew more and more authoritarian. Today Tuđman remains a polemical figure.

Before entering politics, Tuđman was a military officer (he fought for the Partisans in World War II, and later became the youngest general in the Yugoslav People's Army) and a historian. Tuđman revered the Ustaše, Croatia's Nazi-affiliated government during World War II, who murdered hundreds of thousands of Serbs and Jews in concentration camps. (Because the Ustaše governed the first "independent" Croatian state since the 12th century, Tuđman figured that these quasi-Nazis were the original Croatian "freedom fighters.") When Croatia voted for independence and Tuđman was elected president in 1990, he immediately reintroduced many Ustaše symbols, including their currency (the kuna, still used today). His actions raised eyebrows worldwide, and raised alarms in Croatia's Serb communities.

Tuđman espoused many of the same single-minded attitudes about ethnic divisions as the ruthless Serbian leader Slobodan Milošević. Croat forces—which may or may not have been acting under Tuđman's orders—carried out wide-scale ethnic cleansing, targeting Serb and Muslim minorities. Tuđman and Milošević had secret, Hitler-and-Stalin-esque negotiations even as they were ripping into each other rhetorically. According to some reports, at one meeting they drew a map of Bosnia-Herzegovina on a cocktail napkin, then drew lines divvying up

trial in The Hague; he was convicted and sentenced to a prison term in April 2011. As a sign of support, photos of Gotovina have appeared in towns throughout Croatia. Gotovina's name means "cash." Many Croatians grouse, "To get into the EU, we have to pay cash *(gotovina)*!"

Later in the process, when it was time for current EU members to approve Croatia's accession, spunky Slovenia (one of the smallest EU members) flexed its mighty little muscles. For years, Croatia and Slovenia have wrangled over some disputed borders (most notably, the border through the middle of the Bay of Piran). In 2009, when Croatia needed Slovenia's support to join the EU, the Slovenes said, "Not so fast..." and vetoed Croatia's EU bid for 10 months. (Eventually US Secretary of State Hilary Clinton intervened, and cooler heads prevailed.) The EU dust-up has con-the country between themselves. Their so-called "Karađorđevo Agreement" completely left out the Bosniaks, who constituted the largest ethnic group within the nation whose fate was being decided. When Tuđman's successor moved into the president's office, he discovered a top-secret hotline to Milošević's desk.

To ensure that he stayed in power, Tuđman played fast and loose with his new nation's laws. He was notorious for changing the constitution as it suited him. By the late 1990s, when his popularity was slipping, Tuđman extended Croatian citizenship to anyone in the world who had Croatian heritage—a ploy aimed at getting votes from Croats living in Bosnia-Herzegovina, who were sure to line up with him on the far right.

Through it all, Tuđman kept a tight grip on the media, making it illegal to report anything that would disturb the public—even if true. When Croatians turned on their TV sets and saw the flag flapping in the breeze to the strains of the national anthem, they knew something was up...and switched to CNN to get the real story. In this oppressive environment, many bright, young Croatians fled the country, causing a "brain drain" that hampered the postwar recovery.

Tuđman died of cancer at the end of 1999. While history will probably judge him harshly, the opinion in today's Croatia is qualified. Most agree that Tuđman was an important and even admirable figure in the struggle for Croatian statehood, but he ultimately went too far and got too greedy. Tuđman's political party is still active, frequently naming streets, squares, and bridges for this "hero" of Croatian nationalism. The most elaborate tomb in Zagreb's national cemetery (Mirogoj) honors this "Croatian founding father." And yet, if he were alive, Tuđman would be standing trial before the International Criminal Tribunal in The Hague.

tributed to a palpable friction between the Croatians and Slovenes. On my last trip, when I'd show people the cover of my *Croatia & Slovenia* book, people in both countries expressed displeasure that they were grouped together. Ironically, even Croatians who are vehemently opposed to EU membership are bugged that Slovenia tried to prevent it.

Some Croatians remain skeptical about joining the EU for other reasons. One Croatian said to me, "We were just badly divorced. We're not ready to be married again." For the other countries that recently joined the EU, a concern with EU membership was that the new members' citizens would flood to the West. Some Croatians are worried about the opposite: Westerners buying up Adriatic beachfront property.

Perhaps not surprisingly for a post-communist country,

Croatia's government can be excessively bureaucratic. Expats who want to work here find it a tough place to do business. Laws tend to be implemented, then quickly overturned. In the last few years, a ban on shops being open on Sundays, a smoking ban, and a zero blood-alcohol limit for drivers have all come and gone. (The last one was contested by priests, who pointed out that if the blood-alcohol limit is zero, parishioners can't take the wine at communion.) The country also has a penchant for corruption—perhaps best embodied by Croatia's previous prime minister, Ivo Sanader, who served from 2003 to 2009. After abruptly resigning, he was eventually arrested in Austria and extradited to Croatia in 2010 to stand trial for corruption charges.

After a successful decade as president, the term-limited Stipe Mesić stepped down in 2010. Ivo Josipović, running on a strong anti-corruption platform, won by a landslide, and within months had exceeded his predecessor's already high popularity rating. With EU membership on the horizon and some of the growing pains of new nationhood behind it, Croatia seems poised for an ever-brighter future.

Croatian Food

Croatian food is good, but tends to be fairly expensive and unimaginative—and all too often comes with less than cheerful service.

The country's tourist board has gone to great lengths to promote its cuisine and wines as major components of any trip—inflating the culinary dreams of some visitors, only to leave them disappointed by the reality of Croatian restaurants. Adjust your expectations and you'll eat well here—it ain't Tuscany, but it ain't bad, either.

Like its people, the food in Croatia's different regions has been shaped by various influences—predominantly Italian, Turkish, and Hungarian. And yet, the cuisine here is surprisingly uniform: 90 percent of coastal restaurants have a similar menu of seafood, pasta, and pizza. Because it's so easy to get into a culinary rut here, I've tried to recommend a few more exotic alternatives.

Two staples of Croatian food, as in most Mediterranean lands, are wine and olive oil. You'll see vineyards and olive groves blanketing the Croatian countryside and islandscapes. Croatians joke that grapes are like a new bride—they demand a lot of attention, while olives are like a mother—low-maintenance. Another major part of the local diet is the air-dried ham called *pršut* (a.k.a. prosciutto—see sidebar on page 512).

While you'll find places called *restaurant*, you'll more often see the name *konoba*—which means an unpretentious traditional restaurant, like an inn. To request a menu, say, *"Meni, molim"* (MEH-nee, MOH-leem; "Menu, please"). To get the attention of your waiter, say *"Konobar"* (KOH-noh-bahr; "Waiter"). When he brings your food, he'll likely say, *"Dobar tek!"* ("Enjoy your meal!"). When you're ready for the bill, ask for the *račun* (RAH-choon).

Main Dishes

On the coast, seafood is a specialty, and the Italian influence is obvious. According to Dalmatians, "Eating meat is food; eating fish is pleasure." They also say that a fish should swim three times: first in the sea, then in olive oil, and finally in wine—when you eat it. If you see something described as "Dalmatian-style," it usually means with lots of olive oil, parsley, and garlic.

You can get all kinds of seafood: fish, scampi, mussels, squid, octopus, you name it. Remember that prices for fish dishes are listed either by the kilogram (1,000 grams) or by the 100-gram unit (figure about a half-kilo, or 500 grams—that's about one pound—for a large portion). While this is a land of fisherfolk, frozen fish is not unheard of—if you want something fresh from the market, ask. When ordering, be prepared for surprises. For example, *škampi* (shrimp) often come still in their shells (sometimes with crayfish-like claws), which can be messy and time-consuming to eat. Before you order shrimp, ask if it's shelled. The menu item called "small fried fish" is generally a plate of deep-fried minnows. If you're not clear on exactly what something is, feel free to ask for clarification (though some waiters are more forthcoming than others).

Sometimes it's a pleasant surprise. Many menu items that don't sound appetizing can be delicious. Jump at the chance to sample a good, fresh anchovy—which, when done right, has a pleasant

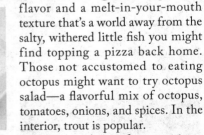

flavor and a melt-in-your-mouth texture that's a world away from the salty, withered little fish you might find topping a pizza back home. Those not accustomed to eating octopus might want to try octopus salad—a flavorful mix of octopus, tomatoes, onions, and spices. In the interior, trout is popular.

If you're not a seafood-eater, there are plenty of meat options. A delicious Dalmatian specialty is *pašticada*—braised beef in a slightly sweet wine-and-herb sauce, usually served with gnocchi. Dalmatia is also known for its mutton. Since the lambs graze on salty seaside herbs, the meat—often served on a spit—has a distinctive flavor. The most widely available meat dish is the

CROATIA

Croatian Wine

The quality of Croatia's wine was devastated by the phylloxera epidemic in the late 19th century, and further declined under the communists, when much of the industry was state-run and focused on mass production. Today vintner families are returning to their roots—literally—and bringing quality back to Croatian wine. Thanks partly to the interest and investment of American vintners, Croatian wines are gaining respect worldwide. Because very few Croatian wines are exported, a visit here is a good chance for wine-lovers to sample some new tastes.

The northern part of the country primarily produces whites *(bijelo vino)*, usually dry *(suho)* but sometimes semi-dry *(polusuho)* or sweet *(slatko)*. The sunny mountains just north of Zagreb are covered with vineyards producing whites. From Slavonia (Croatia's inland panhandle), you'll find *graševina*—crisp, dry, and acidic (like Welsh Riesling); Krauthaker and Enjingi are well-respected brands. The Istrian Peninsula corks up some good whites, including *malvazija*, a very popular, light, mid-range wine (Muscat is also popular).

As you move south, along the Dalmatian Coast, the wines turn red—which Croatians call "black wine" *(crno vino,* TSUR-noh VEE-noh). The most common grape here is *plavac mali* ("little blue")—a distant relative of Californian Zinfandel and Italian *primitivo* grapes. Generally speaking, the best coastal reds are produced on the long Pelješac Peninsula, across from Korčula (the most well-respected regions are Dingač and Postup; see page 359). But each island also produces its own good wines. Korčula makes excellent white wine from *pošip* grapes (espe-

"mixed grill"—a combination of various Balkan grilled meats, best accompanied by the eggplant-and-red-pepper condiment *ajvar* (see the "Balkan Flavors" sidebar on page 418).

The best meat dish in Croatia is veal or lamb prepared under a *peka*—a metal baking lid that's covered with red-hot coals, to allow the meat to gradually cook to tender perfection. (*Ispod peka* means "under the bell.") Available only in traditional

cially near the villages of Čara and Smokvica), as well as *grk* and *korčulanka*. Hvar has *bogdanuša*.

When looking at wine labels, watch for these three official classifications: *stolno* ("table," the lowest grade), *kvalitento* ("quality"—actually mid-range), and *vrhunsko* (top-quality). In general, if only the grape is listed (e.g., *mali plavac*), the quality isn't as good as when the region is prominently noted (e.g., Dingač or Postup)—though there are some exceptions (Miljenko Grgić, described next, produces a top-tier red, with mostly Dingač grapes, that he markets as simply *plavac mali*). You may also see the words *vinogorje* (vineyard) and *položaj* (location).

The big name in Croatian wines is Miljenko Grgić. Born in Croatia in 1923, Grgić emigrated from communist Yugoslavia to the US and—as "Mike Grgich"—worked at the Chateau Montelena in Napa Valley. In the famous so-called "Judgment of Paris" in 1976, Grgić's 1973 Chardonnay beat out several well-respected French wines in a blind taste test. Considered a turning point in the winemaking world, this event brought new respect to American winemakers and put Napa on the mapa.

Having revolutionized American winemaking, Grgić turned his sights on his Croatian homeland. He imported know-how (not to mention equipment) from California to the slopes of the Pelješac Peninsula, where he set about to making some of Croatia's first truly well-respected wines. Grgić grows his red *plavac mali* on the Pelješac Peninsula (at Dingač and nearby, at Trstanik), and his white *pošip* wine on Korčula Island. The prices for Grgić's wines match his reputation; for producers that are comparable but a bit more affordable, look for these red-wine alternatives: Madirazza (they make a great Postup), Frano Miloš (try the full-bodied Stagnum), and Matuško and Škaramuća (good Dingač). Philipp, by a famously meticulous Swiss-Croatian vintner, produces a good Postup, as well as a fine summer white that blends Rukatac and Chardonnay.

restaurants, this dish typically must be ordered in advance and for multiple people. You'll also find a break from seafood in the north (Zagreb) and east (Slavonia), where the food has more of a Hungarian flavor—heavy on meat served with cabbage, noodles, or potatoes.

Budget-conscious tourists reserve meat and fish for splurge dinners and mostly dine on cheaper and faster pastas and pizzas. You'll see familiar dishes, such as spaghetti Bolognese (with meat sauce) and spaghetti carbonara (with a sauce of egg, parmesan, and bacon), gnocchi (*njoki*, potato dumplings), and lasagna. Risotto (*rižoto*, a rice dish) is popular here; most common is "black risotto," mixed with squid ink and various kinds of seafood.

Side Dishes

There are many good local varieties of cheese made with sheep's or goat's milk. Pag, an island in the Kvarner Gulf, produces a famous, very salty, fairly dry sheep's-milk cheese *(paški sir)*, which is said to be flavored by the herbs the sheep eat.

A common side dish is boiled potatoes and mangold *(blitva)*, similar to Swiss chard. When ordering salad, choose between mixed (typically shredded cabbage, tomatoes, and maybe some beets and a little lettuce) or green (mostly lettuce). Throughout Croatia, salad is typically served with the main dish unless you request that it be brought beforehand.

Dessert and Beverages

For dessert, look no further than the mountains of delicious, homemade ice cream *(sladoled)* that line every street in Dalmatia.

I've worked hard to sample and recommend the best ice-cream parlors in each town. (Poor me.) Dalmatia's typical dessert is a flan-like, crème caramel custard, called *rozata*. *Prošek* is a sweet dessert wine.

Water is *voda*, and mineral water is *mineralna voda*. Jamnica is the main Croatian brand of bottled water, but you'll also see Bistra and Studenac. Many restaurants—especially fancier ones—might not want to bring you a glass of tap water, but you can try asking for *voda iz slavine*. For coffee *(kava)*, the easiest choice is *bijela kava* (BEE-yeh-lah KAH-vah)—"white coffee," or espresso with lots of milk (similar to a *caffè latte*). To get it black, ask for *crna kava* (TSUR-nah KAH-vah).

The most popular Croatian beers *(pivo)* are Ožujsko and Karlovačko, but you'll also see the Slovenian brand Laško (which is also brewed here in Croatia). Fans of dark beer *(crno pivo)* enjoy Tomislav. Most places also serve non-alcoholic beers *(bezalkoholno pivo)*; most common are Ožujsko Cool and Stella Artois NA.

Even more beloved in Croatia is wine *(vino;* see "Croatian Wine" sidebar, previous page). Along the coast, locals find it refreshing to drink wine mixed with mineral water (called, as in English, *špricer*). When toasting with some new Croatian friends, raise your glass with a hearty *"Živjeli!"* (ZHEE-vyeh-lee).

Croatian Language

Croatian was once known as "Serbo-Croatian," the official language of Yugoslavia. Most Yugoslav republics—including Croatia, Serbia, and Bosnia-Herzegovina—spoke this same language (though Slovene is quite different). And while each of these countries has tried to distance its language from that of its neighbors since the war, the languages spoken in all of these places are still very similar. The biggest difference is in the writing: Croatians and Bosniaks use our Roman alphabet, while Serbs use Cyrillic letters.

In recent years, Croatia has attempted to artificially make its vocabulary different from Serbian. A decade ago, you'd catch a plane at the *aerodrom*. Today, you'll catch that same flight at the *zračna luka*—a new coinage that combines the old Croatian words for "air" and "port." These new words, once created, are actively injected into the lexicon. Croatians watching their favorite TV show will suddenly hear a character use a word they've never heard before...and think, "Oh, we have another new word." In this way, Croatian really is becoming quite different from Serbian (in much the same way Norwegian evolved apart from Swedish a century ago).

Remember, *c* is pronounced "ts" (as in "bats"). The letter *j* is pronounced as "y." The letters *č* and *ć* are slightly different, but they both sound more or less like "ch"; *š* sounds like "sh," and *ž* sounds like "zh" (as in "leisure"). One Croatian letter that you won't see in other languages is *đ*, which sounds like the "dj" sound in "jeans." In fact, this letter is often replaced with "dj" in English.

When attempting to pronounce an unfamiliar word, remember that the accent is usually on the first syllable (and never on the last). Confusingly, Croatian pronunciation—even of the same word—can vary in different parts of the country. This is because modern Croatian has three distinct dialects, called Kajkavian, Shtokavian, and Chakavian—based on how you say "what?" (*kaj?*, *što?*, and *ča?*, respectively). That's a lot of variety for a language with only five million speakers.

For a smoother trip, take some time to learn a few key Croatian phrases (see the Croatian survival phrases on page 729).

CROATIA

ZAGREB

In this land of time-passed coastal villages, Zagreb (ZAH-grehb) offers a welcome jolt of big-city sophistication. You can't get a complete picture of modern Croatia without a visit here—away from the touristy resorts, in the lively and livable city that is home to one out of every six Croatians (pop. 780,000). In Zagreb, you'll find historic neighborhoods, a thriving café culture, my favorite urban people-watching in Croatia, and virtually no tourists. The city is also Croatia's best destination for museum-going, with wonderful collections highlighting distinctively Croatian artists (the Naive Art movement and sculptor Ivan Meštrović), a quirky exhibit telling the tales of fractured relationships, and a smattering of other fine options (modern art, city history, arts and crafts, and much more). Get your fill here before heading to smaller cities and towns, where worthwhile museums are in short supply.

Zagreb began as two walled medieval towns, Gradec and Kaptol, separated by a river. As Croatia fell under the control of various foreign powers—Budapest, Vienna, Berlin, and Belgrade—the two hill towns that would become Zagreb gradually took on more religious and civic importance. Kaptol became a bishopric in 1094, and it's still home to Croatia's most important church. In the 16th century, the Ban (Croatia's governor) and the Sabor (parliament) called Gradec home. The two towns officially merged in 1850, and soon after, the railroad connecting Budapest with the Adriatic port city of Rijeka was built through the city. Zagreb prospered. After centuries of being the de facto religious, cultural, and political center of Croatia, Zagreb officially became a European capital when the country declared its independence in 1991. Today, while many Croatian destinations are becoming more popular, Zagreb is an underrated, unsung exception that still feels relatively undiscovered. The city rewards those who choose to visit.

Planning Your Time

Most visitors just pass through Zagreb, but the city is worth a look. Throw your bag in a locker at the station and zip into the center for a quick visit—or, better yet, spend the night.

If you're very tight on time, you can get a decent sense of Zagreb in just a few hours. Make a beeline for Jelačić Square to visit the TI and get oriented. Take the funicular up to Gradec, visit the excellent Croatian Museum of Naive Art and/or the Museum of Broken Relationships, and stroll St. Mark's Square. Then wander down through the Stone Gate to the lively Tkalčićeva scene (good for a drink or meal), through the market (closes at 14:00), and on to Kaptol and the cathedral. Depending on how much you linger, this loop can take anywhere from three hours to a full day.

With additional time, visit more of Zagreb's museums (the Meštrović Atelier and City Museum, both in the compact Gradec zone, are both good), wander the series of parks called the "Green Horseshoe" (with even more museums), pay a visit to the beautiful Mirogoj Cemetery (one of Europe's finest final resting places), or head to the enjoyable nearby town of Samobor (see the end of this chapter).

If you're moving on from Zagreb to Plitvice Lakes National Park (described in the next chapter), be warned that the last bus leaves in the mid-afternoon (usually 16:00); confirm your bus departure carefully to ensure that you don't get stranded in Zagreb.

Orientation to Zagreb

(area code: 01)

Zagreb, just 30 minutes from the Slovenian border, stretches from the foothills of Medvednica ("Bear Mountain") to the Sava River. In the middle of the sprawl, you'll find the modern **Lower Town** (Donji Grad, centered on **Jelačić Square**) and the historic **Upper Town** (Gornji Grad, comprising the original hill towns of **Gradec** and **Kaptol**). To the south is a U-shaped belt of parks, squares, and museums that make up the "**Green Horseshoe**." The east side of the

Zagreb Essentials

English	Croatian	Pronounced
Jelačić Square	Trg bana Jelačića	turg BAH-nah YEH-lah-chee-chah
Gradec (original civic hill town)	Gradec	GRAH-dehts
Kaptol (original religious hill town)	Kaptol	KAHP-tohl
Café street between Gradec and Kaptol	Tkalčićeva (or "Tkalči" for short)	tuh-KAHL-chee-chay-vah (tuh-KAHL-chee)
Main train station	Glavni Kolodvor	GLAHV-nee KOH-loh-dvor
Bus station	Autobusni Kolodvor	OW-toh-boos-nee KOH-loh-dvor

U is a series of three parks, with the train station at the bottom (south) and Jelačić Square at the top (north).

Zagrebians have devised a brilliant scheme for confusing tourists: Street names can be given several different ways. For example, the street that is signed as ulica Kralja Držislava ("King Držislav Street") is often called simply Držislavova ("Držislav's") by locals. So if you're looking for a street, don't search for an exact match—be willing to settle for something that just has a lot of the same letters.

Tourist Information

Zagreb has Croatia's best-organized TI, right on Jelačić Square (Mon-Fri 8:30-20:00, until 21:00 in June-Sept; Sat 9:00-18:00, Sun 10:00-17:00; Trg bana Jelačića 11, tel. 01/481-4051, www .zagreb-touristinfo.hr). They also have an office in the train station (Mon-Fri 8:30-20:00, Sat-Sun 12:30-18:30). Both TIs offer piles of free, well-produced tourist brochures; highlights include the one-page city map (with handy transit map and regional map on back), the monthly events guide, and the great *Step By Step* brochure (with a couple of good self-guided walking tours). I'd skip the TI's Zagreb Card (free transportation and discounts at most Zagreb museums, 60 kn/24 hours, 90 kn/72 hours).

Arrival in Zagreb

By Train: Zagreb's main train station (Glavni Kolodvor) is a few long blocks south of Jelačić Square, at the base of the Green Horseshoe. The straightforward arrivals hall has a train information desk, ticket windows, luggage lockers (lining the hallway to the left as you exit the platform, 15 kn/day), ATMs, WCs, Konzum grocery store, and newsstands. To reach the city center, go straight out the front door. You'll run into a taxi stand, and then the tracks for **tram** #6 (direction: Črnomerec zips you to Jelačić Square; direction: Sopot takes you to the bus station—the third stop, just after you turn right and go under the big overpass). You can also take tram #13 to Jelačić Square (direction: Žitnjak). For either tram, buy an 8-kn ticket from the kiosk, and validate it when you board the tram. If you **walk** straight ahead through the long, lush park, you'll wind up at the bottom of Jelačić Square in 10 minutes.

By Bus: The user-friendly but inconveniently located bus station (Autobusni Kolodvor) is a few long blocks southeast of the main train station. The station has all the essentials—ATMs, post office, mini-grocery store, left-luggage counter...everything from a smut store to a chapel. Upstairs, you'll find ticket windows and access to the buses (follow signs to *perone;* wave ticket in front of turnstile to open gate). Tram #6 (direction: Črnomerec) takes you to the main train station, then on to Jelačić Square. Walking from the bus station to Jelačić Square takes about 25 minutes.

By Plane: Zagreb's small airport is 10 miles south of the center (tel. 01/626-5222, www.zagreb-airport.hr). If you have time to kill, head up the stairs (near the main security checkpoint) to the rooftop café view terrace, where you can enjoy a drink while watching planes take off and land, with the Zagreb skyline on the distant horizon. Once you get through security, your only food and drink option is one very expensive bar. While a shuttle bus connects the airport to the bus station (2/hour, 30 minutes, 30 kn), it can be worth the convenience to pay for a taxi right to your hotel (30 minutes; the fair metered rate is around 180-200 kn, but some crooked cabbies might try to charge you more).

Getting Around Zagreb

The main mode of public transportation is the **tram,** operated by ZET (Zagreb Electrical Transport). For longer rides, a single

ticket (good for 1.5 hours in one direction, including transfers) costs 10 kn if you buy it from the driver (8 kn at kiosk, ask for *ZET karta*—zeht KAR-tah). A day ticket *(dnevna karta)* costs 25 kn. The most useful tram for tourists is #6, connecting Jelačić Square with the train and bus stations.

Taxis start at 15-19 kn, then run 5-7 kn per kilometer

ZAGREB

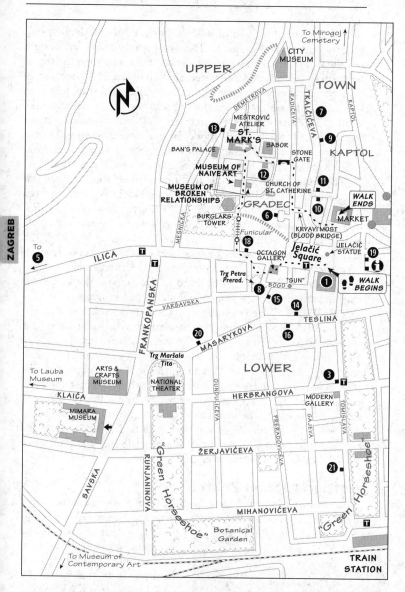

(exact rate depends on company, 20 percent more Sun and 22:00-5:00, 3 kn extra for each piece of baggage). Beware of corrupt cabbies—ask for an estimate up front, or call one of the main companies: Radio Taxi (tel. 01/661-0200 or 060-800-800), Cammeo (tel. 060-700-700), or Oryx (tel. 1888). A typical ride within the city center shouldn't run more than about 30 kn, and the trip to the airport should cost no more than 200 kn (agree on a price first).

Zagreb

1. Hotel Dubrovnik
2. Hotel Astoria
3. Palace Hotel
4. Hotel Central
5. To Hotel Ilica
6. Apartments Lessi & Fulir Backpackers Inn
7. Tkalčićeva St. Eateries
8. Trg Petra Preradovića Eateries
9. Pivnica Medvedgrad Pub
10. Nokturno Restaurant
11. The Cookie Factory
12. Trilogija Wine Bar & Old Pharmacy
13. Konoba Didov San
14. Vinodol Restaurant
15. Ribice i Tri Točkice
16. Sandwich Bar Pingvin
17. Mimice Restaurant
18. Slastičarnica Vincek Ice Cream
19. Gradska Kavana Café
20. Marko Polo Travel Agency
21. Plitvice Lakes Office

Helpful Hints

Schedule Quirks: Virtually all of Zagreb's museums are closed on Sunday afternoon and all day Monday. Some museums stay open late one night a week in summer (usually Thu). On Sunday morning, the city is thriving—but by afternoon, it's extremely quiet.

Changing of the Guard: Zagreb's "Changing of the Guard"

ceremony (a very recent innovation) enlivens the city center on summer weekends. The 17th-century-costumed guards wear jaunty red scarves (an homage to the tale of how Croat soldiers "invented" the necktie) as they proceed through the center of town—passing landmarks such as Tkalčićeva street, St. Mark's Square, Jelačić Square, and the statue of Mary in front of the cathedral (mid-April-mid-Oct only, Sat-Sun 11:40-14:20, ask for complete schedule at TI). While little more than a photo op, this ceremony is one of the many ways Zagreb is working hard to please visitors.

Ferry Tickets: If you're heading for the coast, you can get timetable information and buy Jadrolinija ferry tickets at the **Marko Polo** travel agency (Mon-Fri 9:00-17:00, closed Sat-Sun, Masarykova 24, tel. 01/481-5216).

Plitvice Lakes Office: If you're going to Plitvice Lakes National Park, visit their information office in Zagreb to get your questions answered—I've found this office far better-informed and more helpful than anyplace in Plitvice itself (Mon-Fri 8:00-16:00, closed Sat-Sun, a block in front of main train station at Trg Kralja Tomislava 19, tel. 01/461-3586).

Tours in Zagreb

Local Guide—Dijana Bebek Miletić is an energetic, knowledgeable guide who helps visitors appreciate Zagreb's charms (3-hour walking tour-630 kn, mobile 091-303-3979, dijana.bebek@vip.hr).

Hop-On, Hop-Off Bus Tour—The local transit company runs two hop-on, hop-off routes through the city, a handy way to get to Zagreb's many outlying sights. Unfortunately, the frequency is sparse—only four per day on one route, and three per day on the other (70 kn, May-Sept only, daily 12:00-16:30, details at TI).

Bike Tours—Blue Bike runs three different bike-tour routes through the city, starting in front of the Mimara Museum on the west end of the Green Horseshoe (170 kn, daily at 10:00 and 15:00, for details ask at TI or see www.zagrebbybike.com).

Bus-plus-Walking Tours—This option, which combines a two-hour town walk with a one-hour bus tour, can help you get your bearings (165 kn, April-Oct daily at 10:00, www.ibus.hr).

Self-Guided Walk

▲▲Welcome to Zagreb

The following one-way circular orientation walk begins at Jelačić Square. The entire route takes about an hour at a leisurely pace (not counting museum stops).

▲▲Jelačić Square (Trg bana Jelačića)

The "Times Square" of Zagreb bustles with life. Watching the crowds pile in and out of trams and seeing the city buzz with activ-

ity, you feel the energy of an on-the-rise capital of a vibrant new nation. The city's busy pedestrian scene, sense of style, and utter lack of tourists make it arguably Croatia's best people-watching destination.

It's hard to believe that this frenetic Donji Grad ("lower town") once held the townspeo-

ple's farm fields. Today, it features a prominent equestrian statue of national hero **Josip Jelačić** (YOH-seep YEH-lah-cheech, 1801-1859), a 19th-century governor who extended citizens' rights and did much to unite the Croats within the Habsburg Empire. In Jelačić's time, the Hungarians were exerting extensive control over Croatia, even trying to make Hungarian the official language. Meanwhile, Budapesters revolted against Habsburg rule in 1848. Jelačić, ever mindful of the need to protect Croatian cultural autonomy, knew that he'd have a better shot at getting his way from

Austria than from Hungary. Jelačić chose the lesser of two evils and fought alongside the Habsburgs to put down the Hungarian uprising. A century later, in the Yugoslav era, Jelačić was considered a dangerously nationalistic symbol, and this statue was dismantled and stored away. But when Croatia broke away in 1991, Croatian patriotism was in the air, and Jelačić returned. Though Jelačić originally faced his Hungarian foes to the north, today he's staring down the Serbs to the south.

Get oriented. As you face Jelačić's statue, down a long block to your left is a funicular that takes you up to one of Zagreb's original villages, Gradec. To the right, look for the TI. At the top-right corner of the square is the **Gradska Kavana,** Zagreb's top café (with an elegant white-and-purple Art Deco interior that was recently renovated with gleaming style). If you exit the square ahead and to the right, you'll reach the city's other original village, Kaptol, and the cathedral (you can't miss its huge, pointy, Neo-Gothic spires—visible from virtually everywhere in Zagreb).

Taking the small street behind Jelačić and then going a little to the left would lead you to the market (Dolac) and the lively café street, Tkalčićeva (where this walk ends). On the left side of this small street (still on the square), stop at the modern building with an arcade of blocky pillars to take in a creative bit of public art. Look closely at the first pillar and find the small silver plaque with a little ball labeled *Venus* (about eight feet up, facing the building). This is one piece of the 10-part work called "**Zagreb's Solar System.**" Its center lies a short walk away, two blocks in front of Jelačić (on Bogovićeva street): a large spherical sculpture called *The Grounded Sun*, made in 1971. Decades later, a different artist decided to piggyback on that idea, and created nine new sculptures, together titled *Nine Views*. Scattered around the city are each of the nine planets—completely to scale (both the size of each planet—from the size of a marble to the size of a basketball—and each one's distance from the "sun"). The artist, Davor Preis, did the project in secret, so Zagrebians had to seek out each of the nine planets on their own, in a kind of citywide scavenger hunt. If you've got the time and interest, see if you can track them down (ask locals or search online)—if nothing else, it's a good excuse to see some parts of Zagreb most tourists miss.

But for now, head up to the hill called Gradec. Go a long block down busy Ilica street (to the left as you face Jelačić), then enter the big "**Octagon**" **shopping gallery** on the left (at #5, enter under *Privedna Banka Zagreb* sign). This was the ultimate in iron-and-glass shopping elegance a century ago, and still features a few of the city's top shops (including Croata, the tie store that loves to explain how Croatians invented the necktie; for the whole story, see page 206).

Walk all the way through the gallery, exiting into the inviting café-lined square called **Trg Petra Preradovića.** It hosts a flower market all day, and inviting al fresco cafés throughout the day and into the night. Survey your options for a coffee break, then turn right and head back out to Ilica street, then turn left and continue the way you were headed (noticing, at #18, the popular and recommended ice cream and cake shop Slastičarnica Vincek).

After another block, cross the tram tracks and turn right up Tomičeva, where you'll see a small **funicular** (ZET Uspinjača) crawling up the hill. Dating from the late 19th century, this funicular is looked upon fondly by Zagrebians—both as a bit of nostalgia and as a way to avoid some steps. You can walk up if you want, but the ride is more fun and takes only 55 seconds (4 kn, validate ticket in orange machine before you board, leaves every 10 minutes daily 6:30-22:00).

Gradec

From the top of the funicular, you'll enjoy a fine panorama over

Zagreb. The tall tower you face as you exit is one of Gradec's original watchtowers, the **Burglars' Tower** (Kula Lotršćak). After the Tatars ransacked Central Europe in the early 13th century, King Béla IV decreed that towns be fortified—so Gradec built a wall and guard towers (just like Kraków and Budapest did). Look for the little cannon in the top-floor window. Every day at noon, this cannon fires a shot, supposedly to commemorate a 15th-century victory over the besieging Ottomans. Zagrebians hold on to other traditions, too—the lamps on this hill are still gas-powered, lit by a city employee every evening.

Head up the street next to the tower. Little remains of medieval Gradec. When the Ottomans overran Europe, they never managed to take Zagreb, but the threat was enough to scare the nobility into the countryside. When the Ottomans left, the nobles came back, and they replaced the medieval buildings here with Baroque mansions. At the first square, to the right, you'll see the Jesuit **Church of St. Catherine.** It's not much to look at from the outside, but the interior is intricately decorated. The same applies to several mansions on Gradec. This simple-outside, ornate-inside style is known as "Zagreb Baroque."

As you continue up the street, notice the old-timey **street signs,** holdovers from the Austro-Hungarian era: in both Croatian (Gospodska ulicza) and German (Herren Gasse).

From here, you're a few steps from Zagreb's two most interesting museums: On the right is the **Museum of Broken Relationships,** and a few steps down on the left is the **Croatian Museum of Naive Art** (both listed later, under "Sights in Zagreb").

In the next block, on the left, look for the monument to **Nikola Tesla** (1856-1943), a prominent Croatian-born scientist who moved to America and championed alternating current as a better electrical system than Thomas Edison's direct current. While born in Croatia, Tesla was of Serb ancestry—so both ethnicities claim him.

At the end of the block, you'll come to **St. Mark's Square** (Markov trg), centered on the **Church of St. Mark.** The original church here was from the 13th century, but only a few fragments remain. The present church's colorful tile roof, from 1880, depicts two coats of arms. On the left, the red-and-white checkerboard symbolizes north-central Croatia, the three lions' heads stand for the Dalmatian Coast, and the marten (*kuna*, like the money) running between the two rivers (Sava and Drava) represents Slavonia—Croatia's northern, inland panhandle. On the right is the seal of Zagreb, featuring a walled city. (The seal typically shows wide-open doors—to demonstrate that Zagreb is strong, but still welcoming to visitors—but on this seal, the doors are closed.) The church interior (open sporadically) features frescoes with Bible scenes, and was redecorated in the early 20th century by local artists. Sculptures by the talented artist Ivan Meštrović flank the main altar: a *pietà* on the left, and Madonna and Child on the right (sitting cross-legged, in a typical Meštrović pose). He also sculpted the crucifix over the main altar. If you like these works, consider visiting **Meštrović's former home,** nearby, which is now a museum of his works (it's about a block away: go down the street behind the church on the left-hand side, and you'll see the museum on the right; see the Ivan Meštrović Atelier listing under "Sights in Zagreb").

As you face the church, to the right is the **Sabor,** or parliament. From the 12th century, Croatian noblemen would gather here to make important decisions regarding their territories. This gradually evolved into today's modern parliament. (If you walk along the front of the Sabor and continue straight ahead two blocks, you'll run into the excellent **Zagreb City Museum,** described later, under "Sights in Zagreb.")

Across the square from the Sabor (to your left as you face the church) is **Ban's Palace** (Banski Dvori), today the offices for the prime minister. This was one of the few buildings in central Zagreb damaged in the war following Croatia's independence. In October of 1991, Yugoslav forces shelled it from afar, knowing that Croatian President Franjo Tuđman was inside...but Tuđman survived. (Notice the different-colored tiles where the roof had to be patched.)

Walk from Gradec to Kaptol

For an interesting stroll from St. Mark's Square to the cathedral, head down the street (Kamenita ulica) to the right of the parliament building. Near the end of the street, on the right, you'll see the oldest **pharmacy** in town—recently restored and gleaming (c. 1355, marked *gradska ljekarna*).

Just beyond, you'll reach Gradec's only surviving town gate, the **Stone Gate** (Kamenita Vrata). Inside is an evocative chapel. The focal point is a painting of Mary that miraculously survived a major fire in the adjoining house in 1731. When this medieval gate was reconstructed in the Baroque style, they decided to turn it into

a makeshift chapel. The candles (purchased in the little shop and lit in the big metal bin) represent Zagrebians' prayers. Notice the soot-blackened ceiling over the forest fire of blazing candles in the bin. The stone plaques on the wall give thanks *(hvala)* for prayers that were answered. You may notice people making the sign of the cross as they walk through here, and often a crowd of worshippers gathers, gazing intently at the painting. Mary was made the official patron saint of Zagreb in 1990.

As you leave the Stone Gate and come to Radićeva, turn right and walk downhill. Take the next left, onto the street called **Krvavi Most**—"Blood Bridge." At the end of Krvavi Most, you'll come to Tkalčićeva. This lively café-and-restaurant street used to be a river—the natural boundary between Gradec and Kaptol. The two towns did not always get along, and sometimes fought against each other. Blood was spilled, and the bridge that once stood here between them became known as Blood Bridge. By the late 19th century, the towns had united, and the polluted river began to stink—so they covered it over with this street.

As you cross the pedestrian drag called **Tkalčićeva,** you enter the old town of Kaptol. Consider taking a detour up delightful, in-love-with-life Tkalčićeva to scout your options for a coffee, beer, or meal (I've listed a few recommendations under "Eating in Zagreb," later).

Just beyond Tkalčićeva is the **market** *(dolac),* packed with colorful stalls selling produce of all kinds (Mon-Sat 7:00-14:00, Sun 7:00-13:00). At the back-left corner is the fragrant fish market *(ribarnica),* and under your feet is an indoor part of the market *(tržnica),* where farmers sell farm-fresh eggs and dairy products (same hours as outdoor market, entrance below in the direction of Jelačić Square).

Your walk is over. On the other side of the market, you can visit the **cathedral** (described later, under "Sights in Zagreb").

Sights in Zagreb

Zagreb has more than its share of museums, and many of them are excellent—making up for the lack of great Croatian museums outside of the capital. It would take you days to see all of the city's museums; I've selected the most worthwhile (still enough to fill a couple of days—choose the ones that interest you the most).

▲▲▲Croatian Museum of Naive Art (Hrvatski Muzej Naivne Umjetnosti)

This remarkable spot, founded in 1952 as the "Peasant Art Gallery," is one of the most enjoyable little museums in Croatia. It features expressionistic paintings by untrained peasant artists. On one easy floor, the museum displays 80 paintings made mostly by Croatians from the 1930s to the 1980s.

Cost and Hours: 20 kn, pick up the English explanations as you enter, Tue-Fri 10:00-18:00, Sat-Sun 10:00-13:00, closed Mon, ulica Sv. Ćirila i Metoda 3, tel. 01/485-1911, www.hmnu.org.

Background: Starting in the late 19th century, the art world began to broaden its definition of great art, seeking out worthy art originating outside the esteemed academies and salons of the day. Their goal: to demonstrate that art was not simply a trained skill, but an inborn talent. Intellectuals began to embrace an "anti-intellectual" approach to art. Interest grew in

the indigenous art of Africa, Mesoamerica, and Polynesia (Picasso went through an African mask phase, and Gauguin went to live in Tahiti); composer Béla Bartok collected traditional folk melodies from the Hungarian countryside; the "art brut" movement preserved artwork by people deemed "insane" by mainstream society; the autodidactic (self-taught) painter Grandma Moses became well-known in the US and Europe; and art by children gained acclaim.

Here in Croatia in the 1930s, the focus was on art by untrained peasants. At that time, as in much of rural Europe, 85 percent of Croatians lived virtually medieval lifestyles—with no electricity or other modern conveniences—and about 60 percent were illiterate and uneducated. These artists captured this humble reality, creating figurative works in an increasingly abstract age. By the 1950s and 1960s, Croatian "naive art" had emerged at the forefront of a Europe-wide phenomenon.

This museum presents an easily digestible sampling of the top names from this movement. Viewing these evocative works, it's important to remember that this isn't considered "folk art" or "amateur art"—but top-quality works by great artists who were, by fluke or fate, never formally trained.

❸ Self-Guided Tour: Buy your ticket and follow the one-way route through the six numbered rooms, which you'll circle counter-clockwise.

Room 1: Immediately to the right as you enter is the first of many paintings by **Ivan Generalić** (1914-1992), the founder and star of Croatian naive art (his self-portrait, with a blue background, dominates the room). Generalić was discovered in the 1930s by a Paris-trained Croatian artist. The first few paintings show his evolution as an artist (and the evolution of Croatian naive art in general): While his early works come with a social or political agenda (such as

The Requisition, where two policemen repo a cow from an impoverished couple), he eventually mellows his focus to show simple, typical village scenes. These start out as purely representational of peasant life *(Village Dance),* gradually become more and more fantastical *(Harvesters),* and eventually strip away people entirely to focus on the land (1939's *Landscape).* In 1953, Generalić—still relatively unknown outside his homeland—did a show in Paris, sold everything, and came home rich. This put Croatian naive art on the international map and kick-started a new vigor in the movement.

Woodcutters, from 1959, shows the next phase, as Generalić's works became even more rich with fantasy—the peacock, the men clinging to tree tops, and the trademark "coral trees." Instead of showing, Generalić is evoking; naive art strove to capture the spirit and emotion of peasant life. Paintings such as this one inspired Generalić's followers (called the "Hlebine School," for the village where Generalić lived).

Flanking the door to the next room are works by the next generation of naive art—two big-name followers who were inspired (if not trained) by Generalić: on the left, the gruesome *Evangelists at Cavalry* crucifix, by **Ivan Večenaj,** who focused on religious scenes; and on the right, *Winter Landscape with Woman,* by **Mijo Kovačić,** who specialized in peasant landscapes.

Room 2: The next room features more works by Večenaj and Kovačić. Studying Kovačić's many landscapes, notice how he took a style of painting pioneered by Generalić and brought it to the next level. Winter scenes were most common, because the peasant

artists were busy working the fields the rest of the year. (Early on, such artists were sometimes called "Sunday painters," because they had to work their "real" jobs from Monday to Saturday.) Kovačić also enjoyed winter scenes for the evocative black-and-white contrast they allowed. Like Dalí, Magritte, and other surrealists, Kovačić juxtaposed super-realism (look at each individual hair on the swine in his painting *Swineherd,* pictured below) with fantastical, almost otherworldly settings. Also in this room are some landscapes and portraits by **Dragan Gaži,** a friend and neighbor of Generalić's.

You may notice that these supposedly "untrained" artists seem to borrow from other painters—most notably, the countryside peasant scenes often feel ripped from a Pieter Bruegel canvas. While not formally schooled, there's no doubt that these artists were aware of, and often inspired by, their artistic forebears.

Also notice that naive artists frequently painted on glass. It was cheaper and more readily available in rural areas than art canvases, and—because it required no special technique—was an easier medium for the untrained naive artists to work on.

Room 3: On the right, find the portraits of Roma (Gypsy) people by **Martin Mehkek.** For the one depicting his cross-eyed neighbor Steve, Mehkek mostly painted with his fingers, using brushes only for fine details (such as the Hitler-style moustache). On the other side of the door is *Guiana '78*—by **Josip Generalić,** the founder's less-talented son—showing the gruesome aftermath of the Jim Jones mass suicide, with a pair of monkeys surveying the smiling corpses. (While vivid, this painting doesn't reflect the Croatian peasant experience, and the curator admits it's not the best representative of naive art.) Filling out the room are more of those distinctive coral-style trees that pervade naive works, these

by **Ivan Lacković Croata.**

Room 4: This room shows off two big names from the latter part of the movement. On the left are lyrical landscapes by **Ivan Rabuzin,** arguably the movement's second most important artist, after Ivan Generalić. Like a visual haiku, Rabuzin's dreamlike world of hills, trees, and clouds is reminiscent of Marc Chagall. Rabuzin's works

are especially popular among the museum's many Japanese visitors. On the right are **Emerik Feješ**'s colorful scenes of famous monuments from around Europe—Paris, Venice, Vienna, and Milan. Feješ never traveled to any of these places—his paintings are based on romantic black-and-white postcards of the era, which Feješ "colorized" in his unique style.

Rooms 5 and 6: Room 5 displays works mostly by naive artists from other countries. And Room 6 features pencil sketches used by naive artists to create their works. After the sketch was complete, the artist would put it against a pane of glass to paint the scene—small details first, gradually filling in more and more of the background. Then the glass painting would literally be flipped over to be viewed. All of the works on glass you've seen in this collection were actually painted backward.

ZAGREB

Other Museums in Gradec

▲▲**Museum of Broken Relationships**—Newly opened in 2010, this extremely clever museum lives up to all the attention it's received in the international press. The

museum's mission is simple: collect true stories of failed couples from around the world, tell their story in their own words, and display the tale alongside an actual item that embodies the relationship. The items and stories provide insights into a shared human experience—we can all relate to the anger, sadness, and relief expressed in these poignant, at times hilarious, displays. In addition to the predictable "he cheated on me so I broke his favorite fill-in-the-blank" items, the ever-changing collection delves into other types of fractured connections: an unrequited childhood crush, the slow fade of lovers who gradually grew apart, disappointment in a politician who failed to live up to lofty expectations, the premature end of a love cut short by death, and so on. You'll see discarded wedding albums, sex toys with stories about unreasonable requests for kinky acts, films that attempt to capture the essence of a relationship, children's playthings representing the innocence of young love, and plenty of items broken with vengeful wrath. The museum is small—just a few rooms—but rewards those who take the time to read each story. The collection has been such a hit, they've taken it on the road, garnering fans in cities worldwide.

Cost and Hours: 20 kn, daily June-Sept 9:00-22:30, Oct-May 9:00-21:00, café, 230-kn catalog tells all the stories with photos, Sv. Ćirila i Metoda 2, tel. 01/485-1021, www.brokenships.com.

▲**Ivan Meštrović Atelier**—Ivan Meštrović—Croatia's most famous artist—lived here from 1922 until 1942 (before he fled to the US after World War II). The house, carefully decorated by Meštrović himself, has been converted into a delightful gallery of the artist's works, displayed in two parts: residence and studio. Split's Meštrović Gallery (described on page 209) is the definitive museum of this 20th-century Croatian sculptor, but if you're not going there, Zagreb's gallery is a convenient place to gain an appreciation for this prolific, thoughtful artist. For more on Meštrović, see page 208.

Cost and Hours: 30 kn, 20-kn English catalog, Tue-Fri 10:00-18:00, Sat-Sun 10:00-14:00, closed Mon, behind St. Mark's Square at Mletačka 8, tel. 01/485-1123, www.mestrovic.hr.

Touring the Museum: When you buy your ticket, be sure to pick up the large floor plan—it's the only way to identify the pieces on display here (they're marked only by number). Then enter the high-ceilinged dining room of Meštrović's **home.** He designed the wood-carved chandeliers and the furniture, right down to the carvings on the backs of the chairs. Overlooking the table is a portrait of his mother, legs crossed, hands clasped in intent prayer—a favorite pose of Meštrović's. Head upstairs to see sketches and plaster casts Meštrović did in preparation for some of his larger works. The rooms on this floor are filled with busts and small, characteristically elongated statues, all of them expressive. In the far  room, appreciate his fine ceiling frescoes. Continue up to the top floor, where you'll find several evocative pieces: Meštrović's wife breastfeeding their son; a portrait of Michelangelo, Meštrović's artistic ancestor, holding a chisel and hammer, and portrayed with his trademark high forehead and smashed nose; and a copy of the powerful *pietà* from St. Mark's Church. The next room holds a cowering Job, the head of an archangel, a tender portrait of a mother teaching her child to pray, and a small model of one of Meštrović's biggest and best-known works, *Bishop Gregory of Nin* (in Split, described on page 204).

Head back downstairs and through the courtyard (with the large *Woman in Agony* in the center, and less-agonized women all around) and into Meštrović's **studio.** Immediately to the left as you enter is a skinny, Modigliani-esque sculpture of Meštrović's first wife, Ruža. Farther in the room are two sculptures modeled after his second wife, Olga: The unfinished, walnut-carved *Mother and Child,* and the exquisite, white-marble *Woman Beside the Sea* (one of the collection's highlights). Nearby is a sculpture of the Evangelist Luke. Upstairs around the gallery are smaller pieces, including a study for the spiny-fingered hand of Split's *Bishop Gregory of Nin.*

Now head (or look) out into the **garden,** with several more fine pieces, including another one of the museum's top works: *The History of the Croats,* with a woman sitting cross-legged (remember this pose?) with a book resting on her lap. The top of the book has a unique Croatian spiral design, and along the front of it are the letters of Croatia's Glagolitic alphabet.

▲**Zagreb City Museum (Muzej Grada Zagreba)**—This collection, with a modern, well-presented exhibit that sprawls over two floors of an old convent, traces the history of the city through town models, paintings, furniture, clothing, and lots of fascinating artifacts. After buying your ticket, head through the door and turn left, then work your way up through the ages. Each display has a fine English description. The colorfully painted shooting targets in the 19th-century wing help give it a folk-museum feel. Find the giant map on the floor, punctuated with models of key buildings. The coverage of the tumultuous 20th century is perhaps most engaging, evincing an understandably bad attitude about the Serb-dominated first Yugoslav period. It features stirring videos, a hall of propaganda posters, and artifacts from World War II and the Tito period (when Croatia was a player in Belgrade). The historical heaviness is balanced by a lighthearted exhibit about Zagreb's popular cartoon industry. The finale is a room dedicated to the creation of independent Croatia, including an exhibit on damage sustained during the war, and a film showing the return of the statue of Jelačić to his namesake square.

Cost and Hours: 30 kn, 20-kn audioguide nicely supplements the posted descriptions, Tue-Fri 10:00-18:00, Sat 11:00-19:00, Sun 10:00-14:00, closed Mon, at north end of Gradec at Opatička 20, tel. 01/485-1361, www.mgz.hr.

▲▲Cathedral (Katedrala)

By definition, Croats are Catholics. Before the recent war, relatively few people practiced their faith. But as the Croats fought

against their Orthodox and Muslim neighbors, Catholicism took on a greater importance. Today, more and more Croats are attending Mass. This is Croatia's single most important church.

In 1094, when a diocese was established at Kaptol, this church quickly became a major center of high-ranking church officials. In the mid-13th century, the original cathedral was destroyed by invading Tatars, who actually used it as a stable. It was rebuilt, only to be destroyed again by an earthquake in 1880. The current version—undergoing yet another renovation for the last several years—is Neo-Gothic (about a hundred years old inside and out). Surrounding the church are walls with pointy-topped towers (part of a larger archbishop's palace) that were built for protection against the Ottomans. The full name is the Cathedral of the Assumption of the Blessed Virgin Mary and the Saintly Kings Stephen and Ladislav (whew!)—but most locals just call it "the cathedral."

Cost and Hours: Free, Mon-Sat 10:00-17:00, Sun 13:00-17:00.

Touring the Cathedral: As you stand out front, appreciate the stately facade and modern tympanum (carved semicircular section over the door). Then step inside and wander down the nave.

First, look closely at the silver relief on the main **altar**: a whimsical scene of the Holy Family doing chores around the house (Mary sewing, Joseph and Jesus building a fence...and angels helping out).

In the front-left corner (on the wall, between the confession-

als), find the modern tombstone of **Alojzije Stepinac.** He was the Archbishop of Zagreb during World War II, when he shortsightedly supported the Ustaše (Nazi puppet government in Croatia)—thinking, like many Croatians, that this was the ticket to greater independence from Serbia. When Tito came to power, he put Stepinac on trial and sent him to jail for five years. But Stepinac never lost his faith, and he remains to many the most inspirational figure of Croatian Catholicism. (He's also respected in the US, where some Catholic schools bear his name. But many

Serbs today consider Stepinac a villain who cooperated with the brutal Ustaše.)

Facing the nearby altar, on the right look for the grave of **Josip Jelačić,** the statesman whose statue adorns Zagreb's main square.

As you leave the church, look high on the wall to the left of the door. This strange script is the **Glagolitic alphabet** *(glagoljca),* invented by Byzantine missionaries Cyril and Methodius in the ninth century to translate the Bible into Slavic languages. Though these missionaries worked mostly in Moravia (today's eastern Czech Republic), their alphabet caught on only here, in Croatia. (Glagolitic was later adapted in Bulgaria to become the Cyrillic alphabet—still used in Serbia, Russia, and other parts east.) In 1991, when Croatia became its own country and nationalism surged, the country flirted with the idea of making this the official alphabet.

The Green Horseshoe

With extra time, stroll around the Green Horseshoe (the U-shaped belt of parks and museums in the city center). The museums here aren't nearly as interesting as those on Gradec, but may be worth a peek on a rainy day.

Mimara Museum (Muzej Mimara)—This grand, empty-feeling building displays the eclectic art collection of a wealthy Dalmatian, ranging from ancient artifacts to paintings by European masters. After buying your ticket, head up to the top floor (2) and tour the fine painting gallery. While the names are major—Rubens, Rembrandt, Velázquez, Renoir, Manet—the paintings themselves are minor (I wouldn't prioritize these over the works of Croatian artists on display elsewhere in Zagreb, especially those at the Naive Art Museum or the Meštrović Atelier). The first floor displays sculpture and applied arts, while the ground floor has vases, carpets, and objects from the Far East.

Cost and Hours: 40 kn, 90-kn English guidebook, free and excellent smartphone audio tour available for download on their Wi-Fi network, Tue-Sat 10:00-17:00, Thu until 19:00, Sun 10:00-14:00, closed Mon, Rooseveltov trg 5, tel. 01/482-8100.

Arts and Crafts Museum (Muzej za Umjetnost i Obrt)—This decorative arts collection of furniture, ceramics, and clothes is well-displayed. From the entry, go upstairs, then work your way clockwise and up to the top floor—passing through each artistic style, from Gothic to the present. It's mostly furniture, with a few paintings and other items thrown in. The ground floor features temporary exhibits.

Cost and Hours: 30 kn, some rooms have laminated English descriptions to borrow, otherwise very limited English, Tue-Sat 10:00-19:00, Thu until 22:00, Sun 10:00-14:00—sometimes later depending on special exhibits, closed Mon, Trg Maršala Tita 10, tel. 01/488-2125, www.muo.hr.

Botanical Garden (Botanički Vrt)—For a back-to-nature change of pace from the urban cityscape, wander through this relaxing garden, run by the University of Zagreb.

Cost and Hours: Free, Mon-Tue 9:00-14:30, Wed-Sun 9:00-18:00—until 19:00 in summer, at southwest corner of the Green 'Shoe.

Elsewhere in Zagreb

▲**Mirogoj Cemetery (Groblje Mirogoj)**—Of Europe's many evocative cemeteries, Mirogoj (MEE-roh-goy) is one of the finest, studded with great architecture and beauti-

fully designed tombs. This peaceful spot, a short bus ride from the city center, memorializes many of the greats who built the Croatian nation. Anyone can enjoy a quiet walk here, but to provide context to your stroll, stop by the TI first for their free, thorough booklet of maps and descriptions identifying the most significant graves.

The cemetery was designed by Herman Bollé, an Austrian architect who lived and worked for most of his career in Zagreb, leaving his mark all over the city before becoming a permanent resident in this cemetery. From the stately domed main mausoleum, a long arcade (with VIP tombs) stretches along the road in both directions, punctuated by smaller domes. Entering through the main gate, circle behind the mausoleum to find the biggest tomb here: of Franjo Tuđman, the (now-controversial) leader who spearheaded the creation of independent Croatia. Continuing straight past Tuđman's grave, you'll reach the Central Cross, which usually has a field of flowers around it, and beyond that, a monument to the dead of World War I. In every direction, as far as the eye can see, are the final resting places of great Croatians.

Cost and Hours: Free, daily April-Sept 6:00-20:00, Oct-March 7:30-18:00.

Getting There: Catch bus #106 from in front of the Cathedral (3/hour) and ride six stops, or about 10 minutes, to the stop called simply "Mirogoj" (the one *after* the stop called "Mirogoj Arkada"). The return bus leaves from across the street.

Art Museums—In addition to the art gallery at the Mimara Museum (described earlier), art-lovers may want to visit a trio of other Zagreb art museums. Three different collections cover works from the 20th century through today: The **Modern Gallery** features art from the early 20th century (a few blocks south of Jelačić Square at Andrije Hebranga 1, www.moderna -galerija.hr); the new **Museum of Contemporary Art** focuses on mid-century art (south of the river and not as convenient to visit, avenija Dubrovnik 17, www.msu.hr); and the innovative **Lauba,** with more cutting-edge works from the last few years (Baruna Filipovića 23A, www.lauba.hr). For details on any of these, check their websites or ask at the TI.

Sleeping in Zagreb

Hotels in central Zagreb are expensive. As this is a convention and business town, rates at business-oriented hotels are highest on weekdays mid-February through mid-July, then again from September through November. At other times of year, and week-ends year-round, you'll generally enjoy lower rates. I've listed the average rates—they may be slightly higher or lower with demand. If I've listed two sets of rates separated by slashes, the first is for high season and the second is for low season.

$$$ Hotel Dubrovnik is a professional-feeling, business-class hotel with 245 rooms, ideally located at the bottom of Jelačić Square (small Sb-€95, bigger Sb-€110, Db-€135, bigger and nicer "deluxe" Db-€175, suite-€200-220, extra bed-€35, rooms over-looking the square don't cost extra but come with some tram noise, often cheaper on weekends, prices can flex up or down with demand, air-con, non-smoking floors, elevator, free Internet access and Wi-Fi, Gajeva 1, tel. 01/486-3555, fax 01/486-3506, www .hotel-dubrovnik.hr, reservations@hotel-dubrovnik.hr).

$$$ Hotel Astoria, a Best Western, offers 100 smallish but plush, recently renovated rooms and a high-class lobby. It's con-veniently located between the train station and Jelačić Square, albeit on a somewhat grimy street. If you can get a good price, it's worth considering (Sb-€89/€79, Db-€103/€93, rates flex up and down with demand, various discounts offered—including mili-tary, fancier suites also available, air-con, elevator, non-smoking rooms, free Internet access and Wi-Fi, Petrinjska 71, tel. 01/480-8900, fax 01/480-8908, www.hotelastoria.hr, recepcija@hotel astoria.hr).

Sleep Code

(5 kn = about $1, €1 = about $1.40, country code: 385, area code: 01)

S = Single, **D** = Double/Twin, **T** = Triple, **Q** = Quad, **b** = bathroom. Unless otherwise noted, credit cards are accepted and breakfast is included, but the modest tourist tax (about 7 kn per person, per night) is not. While rates are listed in euros, you'll pay in kunas. Everyone listed here speaks English.

To help you sort easily through these listings, I've divided the accommodations into three categories based on the price for a double room with bath:

$$$ Higher Priced—Most rooms €100 or more.

$$ Moderately Priced—Most rooms between €60-100.

$ Lower Priced—Most rooms €60 or less.

Prices can change without notice; verify the hotel's current rates online or by email. For other updates, see www.ricksteves.com/update.

$$$ Palace Hotel, conveniently located on the big park halfway between the train station and Jelačić Square, comforts business travelers and low-level visiting dignitaries with its Old World elegance. Its 120 rooms are divided between smaller, older, perfectly fine standard rooms (Db-€105/€94), and larger, recently renovated "comfort" rooms (Db-€120/€100; rates can flex with demand, aircon, elevator, non-smoking rooms, free Wi-Fi, Strossmayerov Trg 10, tel. 01/4899600, www.palace.hr, palace@palace.hr).

$$ InZagreb, run by Ivana and Ksandro Kovačić, rents nine mostly one-bedroom apartments in various buildings around the city. While locations vary, most are in untouristy urban zones within a 15- to 20-minute walk of the main square. The units are nicely equipped and come with several welcoming, creative touches. Visit their website, find the apartment that appeals to you, and make a reservation. Clearly communicate your arrival time, and they'll pick you up at the train or bus station (no extra charge) or at the airport (150 kn extra) and take you to your home-away-from-home in Zagreb (Db-€65-89 depending on apartment and location, no 1-night stays, no breakfast, kitchenettes, air-con, free Wi-Fi, laundry machine, mobile 091-652-3201, fax 01/652-3201, www.inzagreb.com, info@inzagreb.com).

$$ Hotel Central's 76 overly perfumed rooms are comfortable and modern, and the price is right. Despite the disinterested staff, the location—right across from the main train station—makes it a good option for rail travelers (Sb-€70, larger Sb-€75, Db with one big bed-€90, twin Db-€95, Tb-€150, rates can flex with demand, air-con, elevator, free Internet access and Wi-Fi, Branimirova 3, tel. 01/484-1122, fax 01/484-1304, www.hotel-central.hr, info @hotel-central.hr).

$ **Hotel Ilica** is a 15-minute walk or short tram ride from Jelačić Square. The hotel's idiosyncratic sense of style—with faux chandeliers and Roman busts that Liberace would find gaudy—helps compensate for its dull urban neighborhood. It's set back on its own courtyard with a garden behind it, making it an oasis of quiet in the heart of the city. With 24 rooms, four apartments, and a staff that prides itself on its personal service, this quirky place is an excellent value if you don't mind commuting to your sightseeing by tram (Sb-€40, Db-€56, twin Db-€60—or €56 for a bunk-bed, Tb-€76, big apartment-€96, air-con, free Internet access and Wi-Fi, off-street courtyard parking-29 kn/€4, Ilica 102, two tram stops from Jelačić Square at Britanski trg stop, tel. 1/377-7522, www.hotel-ilica.hr, info@hotel-ilica.hr).

$ **Apartments Lessi,** run by youthful and English-speaking Tin, are three rooms that share a centrally located courtyard with a bar and the Fulir Backpackers Inn (see next listing). The rooms (one of which is up a tight spiral staircase) have pleasantly rustic decor with modern comforts (smaller room: Sb-€27, Db-€50; apartments: Sb-€47, Db-€60, Tb-€80, Qb-€95; cheaper Jan-April, cash only, no breakfast, air-con, free Wi-Fi, tucked down the courtyard at Radićeva 3a, mobile 091-288-8858, www.lessi.com.hr, info@lessi.com.hr).

$ **Fulir Backpackers Inn,** a funky slumbermill named for a legendary Zagrebian bon vivant, is loosely run by Davor and Leo, a pair of can-do Croats who once lived in Ohio. It's colorful, friendly, and youthful, with a big 10-bunk dorm, one seven-bed dorm, three six-bed rooms, and a quad. Just a few steps from Jelačić Square, this hostel puts you in the heart of Zagreb (€18-20/bunk depending on season—cheaper Oct-April, includes sheets, no breakfast, free lockers, free Internet access and Wi-Fi, self-service laundry, upstairs at the end of the courtyard at Radićeva 3a, tel. 01/483-0882, mobile 098-193-0552, www.fulir-hostel.com, fulir@fulir-hostel.com).

Eating in Zagreb

As a cosmopolitan European capital, Zagreb enjoys a refreshingly varied restaurant scene. If you're heading for (or have just returned from) the coast, consider skipping traditional Croatian food here in Zagreb—your non-Croatian options are limited almost everywhere else in the country. Look beyond restaurants, too: Several enticing boutique sandwich shops and gourmet coffee bars are

ZAGREB

scattered around the center, catering to businesspeople on their lunch breaks.

People-Watching and Coffee-Sipping

One of my favorite Zagreb pastimes is nursing a drink along its thriving people zones, watching an endless parade of fashionable locals saunter past, and wondering why they don't create such an inviting space in my hometown. The best place is on **Tkalčićeva street,** Zagreb's main café street and urban promenade rolled into one. It's a parade of fashionable locals and *the* place to see and be seen (starts a block behind Jelačić Square, next to the market). I've listed my favorite Tkalčićeva eateries next. Honorable mention goes to **Trg Petra Preradovića,** an inviting square just a short walk from Jelačić Square (up Ilica street) that bustles with appealing outdoor cafés and bars.

Eating on or near Tkalčićeva Street

Most places along Tkalčićeva serve only drinks. For a meal, consider these options.

Pivnica Medvedgrad is a rollicking brewpub serving five different in-house beers and heavy, stick-to-your-ribs pub grub that feels closer to Prague than to Dubrovnik. The food offers a welcome break from the pizzas-pastas-and-seafood rut you'll encoun-

ter on the coast, and the outdoor seating right on Tkalčićeva's most colorful stretch will seduce you into staying for another beer—if you can score a table. The pubby interior is convivial, but less enticing (20-60-kn meals, daily 10:00-24:00, food served until 22:00, Tkalčićeva 36, tel. 01/492-9613).

Nokturno, just off of Tkalčićeva, serves up good pizza and pasta in a lively interior and has ample outdoor seating on a terrace that cascades down the street (cheap 20-35-kn pizzas, pastas, and salads; 35-100-kn meat and fish dishes; daily 9:00-1:00 in the morning, Skalinska 4, tel. 01/481-3394).

At the Market **(Dolac):** Zagreb's busy market offers plenty of options (Mon-Sat 7:00-14:00, Sun 7:00-13:00). Assemble a fresh picnic direct from the producers. Or, for something already prepared, duck into one of the many cheap restaurants and cafés on the streets around the market. The middle level of the market, facing Jelačić Square, is home to a line of places with cheap food and indoor or outdoor seating.

Dessert: **The Cookie Factory** has a wide array of American-style cookies, brownies, smoothies, and other goodies. Pull up a table for a brownie à la mode, or get an ice-cream cookie sandwich to go (10-20-kn treats, Mon-Sat 9:00-23:00, Sun 14:00-21:00, next to Nokturno at Skalinska 3, tel. 01/481-3901).

In the Upper Town (Gradec)

Trilogija, just above the Stone Gate, is a casual wine bar serving up delicious, well-presented, and affordable international dishes made with local ingredients. There's no printed menu because they cook what they find at the market—your server will translate and explain the chalkboard menu. Reservations are smart (30-70-kn small dishes, 65-90-kn large dishes, Mon-Sat 11:00-24:00, closed Sun, Kamenita 5, tel. 01/485-1394).

Konoba Didov San ("Grandfather's Dream") serves up traditional food from the Dalmatian hinterland (specifically the Neretva River Delta, near Metković). You'll find the normal Dalmatian specialties, plus eel, frogs, and snails. Choose between the homey, traditional interior and the outdoor tables (25-60-kn starters, 60-120-kn main courses, daily 10:00-24:00, a few steps up from the Ivan Meštrović Atelier at Mletačka 11, tel. 01/485-1154).

In the Lower Town, near Jelačić Square

These places are all within a level five-minute walk of Jelačić Square.

Vinodol is your white-tablecloth-classy dinner spot, with a peaceful covered terrace and a smartly appointed dining room under an impressive vaulted ceiling. The good, reasonably priced cuisine includes veal prepared *peka*-style, in a pot covered with hot coals (*peka* portion costs 90 kn, served only at certain times—generally at 12:30 and 18:30; 50-120-kn main courses, open daily 10:00-24:00, Teslina 10, tel. 01/481-1427).

Ribice i Tri Točkice ("Fish and...") serves up fish, seafood, and...whatever else they feel like. Enjoy the casual, colorful upstairs dining room and the affordably priced fish, bought daily at the market. Restaurants on the coast offer ample opportunity to sample Croatian fish, but this is a good opportunity to have some in the big city (30-80-kn dishes, order sides separately, daily 9:00-24:00, Petra Preradovića 7/1, tel. 01/563-5479).

Fast and Cheap: **Sandwich Bar Pingvin,** busy with locals dropping by for take-away, is a favorite for quick, cheap, tasty sandwiches with chicken, turkey, steak, or fish (plus some pasta dishes). They'll wrap it all in a piece of grilled bread and top it with your choice of veggies and sauces to go—or, to eat here, sit at one of the few tiny tables or stools (17-30 kn, Mon-Sat 8:00-late, Sun 18:00-late, about a block below Jelačić Square at Teslina 7).

Fried and Fishy: **Mimice** is a local institution and an old-habits-die-hard favorite of the older generation. While a bit tired and dreary, I like it as a cheap and memorable time-warp serving up simple fish dishes (15-35 kn, order starches and sauces separately). Choose what you want from the limited menu (if confused, survey the room for a plate that looks good and ask what it is), pay, and take your receipt to the next counter to claim your food. Order the smelt to get a plate of tiny deep-fried fish (Mon-Sat 7:00-21:00, closed Sun, Jurišićeva 21). As Zagreb is a Catholic town, you'll have to wait in line if you're here on a Friday.

Dessert: As the long line out front suggests, Zagreb's favorite *sladoled* (Italian gelato-style ice cream) is at **Slastičarnica Vincek,** two blocks west of Jelačić Square. Choose from a wide variety of flavors (6 kn/scoop), giving special consideration to the Vincek flavor—chocolate and walnuts. They also have other desserts, including *Zagrebačka kremšnita*—a variation on the famous cream-and-custard cake from Lake Bled (see page 585), but with chocolate (Mon-Sat 8:30-23:00, closed Sun, on the busy tram-lined Ilica street at #18).

Zagreb Connections

From Zagreb by Train to: Rijeka (2/day, 4 hours), **Pula** (3/day, 6 hours, transfer in Rijeka), **Split** (3/day, 2/day off-season, 6 hours, plus 1 direct night train, 9 hours), **Sarajevo** (2/day, 9 hours, including a night train), **Mostar** (1/day, 13.5 hours, bus is faster), **Ljubljana** (7/day, 2.5 hours), **Vienna** (2 direct/day, 6-6.5 hours, others with 1-2 changes take 7.5-8.5 hours), **Budapest** (3 direct/day, 6 hours, others with 1-2 changes), **Lake Bled** (via Lesce-Bled, 6/day, 3.5 hours), **Venice** (1 night train/day, 7.5 hours), **Munich** (3/day, 9 hours). Train info: tel. 060-333-444.

By Bus to: Samobor (about 2-3/hour, 30-50 minutes), **Plitvice Lakes National Park** (about hourly until around 16:00, 2-2.5 hours), **Rijeka** (hourly, 2.5 hours), **Rovinj** (6-9/day, 3-6 hours), **Pula** (almost hourly, 3.75-6 hours), **Split** (at least hourly, 5-8 hours), **Mostar** (5/day, 8-9.5 hours, includes a night bus), **Dubrovnik** (7/day including some overnight options, 10 hours), **Korčula** (1/day, 9-13.5 hours depending on route), **Kotor** (1/night, 14.5 hours).

Bus schedules can be sporadic (e.g., several departures clustered around the same time, then nothing for hours)—confirm your plans carefully (inquire locally, or use the good online schedules at www.akz.hr). The TI is very helpful with providing bus information. Popular buses, such as the afternoon express to Split, can fill up quickly in peak season. Unfortunately, it's impossible to buy bus tickets anywhere in the center, so to guarantee a seat, you'll have to get to the station early (locals suggest even two hours in advance). Better yet, call the central number for the bus station to check schedules and reserve the bus you want, ideally at least 24 hours ahead: tel. 060-313-333 (from abroad, dial +385-1-611-2789). If you can't get an English-speaker on the line, and the TI isn't too busy, they might be willing to call for you.

Near Zagreb: Samobor

This charming little town, tucked in the hills between Zagreb and the Slovenian border, is where city dwellers head to unwind, get

away from the clattering trams, and gorge themselves on sausages and cream cakes. While popular with Croatian and German tourists, Samobor is virtually undiscovered by Americans—a true Back Door with small-town warmth. Cuddled by hiker-friendly hills, bisected by a gurgling and promenade-lined stream, favored by artists and poets, and proud of its tidy square, Samobor is made to order for a break from the big city. With a pair of charming, affordable hotels, Samobor works as a small-town home base near Zagreb, but it's perhaps best suited for a low-impact lunch or dinner stop en route between Zagreb and points west or north.

Orientation to Samobor

Samobor (with 15,000 people, plus 20,000 more in the surrounding area) has a pleasantly compact tourist zone. Virtually anything you'd want to see or do is within sight of its centerpiece, King Tomislav Square (Trg Kralja Tomislava). A stream called Gradna cuts through the middle of town.

Tourist Information
The TI, dead center on the main square, hands out free town maps and is eager to offer hiking advice (Mon-Fri 8:00-19:00—until 17:00 in Nov-March, Sat 9:00-17:00, Sun 10:00-17:00, Trg Kralja Tomislava 5, tel. 01/336-0044, www.tz-samobor.hr).

Getting There
Without a car, you can reach Samobor with a **bus** from Zagreb's main bus station (2-3/hour, 25 kn). The trip takes 30-50 minutes,

depending on traffic and the route (if possible, avoid slower buses that stop in smaller villages, such as Novaki and Rakitije). Once at Samobor's bus station, go to the end of the station with all the kiosks. From there, walk five minutes (past the covered produce market) toward the big, yellow steeple that marks the main square.

By **car,** Samobor is just off the main Zagreb-Ljubljana expressway. Exit following signs for Samobor, then follow the bull's-eyes to the *Centar*. Head for the yellow steeple. When you reach the T-intersection with the little fountain next to the church, take the right fork to drive past the main square; soon after, turn left over the little covered bridge to reach the parking lot (10 kn/hour, put ticket on dashboard).

Sights in Samobor

Samobor is more about ambience than about sightseeing. Stroll the main square, sit at a café, gaze at the surrounding hills, and contemplate a hike.

For extra credit, drop into the town's sleepy **Samobor Museum,** an old mansion with miscellaneous bric-a-brac from the town's history—but it's only worthwhile if you're desperate for some sightseeing (8 kn, Tue-Fri 8:00-15:00, Sat 9:00-13:00, Sun 9:00-17:00, closed Mon, across the covered bridge from the main square at Livadićeva 7, tel. 01/336-1014).

Samobor does boast the exquisite **Marton Museum,** with a particularly notable porcelain collection—but most of its items are usually out on loan, and its Samobor home is open only by prior arrangement (call Davor Palinić at least 3 days in advance between 10:00 and 14:00 at mobile 091-111-4489, Jurjevska 7, tel. 01/332-6426, www.muzej-marton.hr).

Those interested in **hiking** find Samobor a pleasant base for venturing into the hills that begin just west of town. One popular option is to drive up to the Šoićeva Kuća mountain lodge, then hike to a nearby peak (either Oštrc or Japetić). Another popular option is to walk from Samobor to Okić and back. You can get specifics and buy hiking maps at the TI.

Sleeping in Samobor

(5 kn = about $1, country code: 385, area code: 01)
Both of central Samobor's hotels are more welcoming and a much better deal than anything in downtown Zagreb. Travelers relying on public transit might find sleeping in Samobor to be too much of a hassle, but drivers may prefer to avoid urban traffic by sleeping here, then day-tripping by bus (30-50 minutes) into Zagreb.

$ **Hotel Livadić,** named for a Croatian patriot and Samobor native, has 21 rooms with elegant, old-fashioned decor. It sits over a classy café right on the main square, with a garden courtyard at its center (Sb-€48-55, Db-€62, bigger "comfort" Db with views on the square-€70, Tb-€70, 6 percent cheaper if you pay cash, non-smoking, air-con in some rooms, free Wi-Fi, Trg Kralja Tomislava 1, tel. 01/336-5850, fax 01/332-5588, www.hotel-livadic.hr, info @hotel-livadic.hr, bubbly Maja offers the warmest welcome in Croatia).

$ **Hotel Lavica,** more businesslike, rents 33 modern rooms next to a pleasant park just across the covered bridge from the main square (Sb-€30, Db-€40, Tb-€50, air-con, free Wi-Fi, Livadi-ćeva 5, tel. & fax 01/336-8000, www.lavica-hotel.hr, info@lavica -hotel.hr).

Eating in Samobor

Samobor is highly regarded among Zagrebians for its filling, rustic cuisine. First, an apéritif: Samobor's own Bermet is a sweet red

wine made with fruits and grasses from the Samobor hills. As it's an acquired taste, start with just a sip. The local sausage, *češnjovke* (sometimes translated on menus as "garlic sausage"), is tradition-ally eaten with the town's own mustard, *Samoborska Muštarda*

(Dijon-esque but without much kick, also sold around town in little ceramic pots). Round out your meal with a piece of *kremšnita* cream cake (curiously similar to Lake Bled's specialty).

Gabreku is every local's top recommendation for good Samobor cooking. It's at the far end of town, a quick drive or 15-minute walk from the main square. The menu includes the Samobor classics described above, a delicious mushroom soup, veal brains and liver, and plenty of other (mostly meat-centric) options (30-55-kn starters, 45-85-kn main dishes, daily 12:00-24:00, free parking across the street, to walk from the main square head upriver on the path after the covered bridge then cross the second bridge, Starogradska 46, tel. 01/336-0722).

Pri Staroj Vuri ("By the Old Clock") has a similar menu of regional dishes, as well as homemade *štrukli* (cheese ravioli). It has a traditional interior with a wall of namesake old clocks and a fine outdoor terrace in a tranquil garden (30-45-kn pastas, 65-100-kn main dishes, Giznik 2, tel. 01/336-0548). From the small foun-tain at the intersection near the end of the church, head uphill for a couple of blocks, veering right at the fork (about a five-minute walk from the square).

Samoborska Klet ("Samobor Cellar") is the most convenient option, tucked in a courtyard on the main square, with a meaty menu, a modern dining room, and a more rustic tavern in the back, but no seating on the square itself (55-110-kn meals, daily 8:00-23:00, Trg Kralja Tomislava 7, tel. 01/332-6536).

PLITVICE LAKES NATIONAL PARK

Nacionalni Park Plitvička Jezera

Plitvice (PLEET-veet-seh) is one of Europe's most spectacular natural wonders. Imagine Niagara Falls diced and sprinkled over a heavily forested Grand Canyon. There's nothing like this lush valley of 16 terraced lakes, laced together by waterfalls and miles of pleasant plank walks. Countless cascades and water that's both strangely clear and full of vibrant colors make this park a misty natural wonderland. Years ago, after eight or nine visits, I thought I really knew Europe. Then I discovered Plitvice and realized you can never exhaust Europe's surprises.

Planning Your Time

Plitvice deserves at least a few good hours. Since it takes some time to get here (two hours by car or bus from Zagreb), the most sensible plan is to spend the night in one of the park's hotels (no character, but comfortable and convenient) or a nearby private home (cheaper, but practical only if you're driving). If you're coming from the north (e.g., Ljubljana), you can take the train to Zagreb in the morning, spend a few hours seeing the Croatian capital, then take the bus (generally no buses after about 16:00) or drive to Plitvice in the late afternoon to spend the night at the park. Get up early and hit the trails (ideally by 8:30); by early afternoon, you'll be ready to move on (by bus to the coast, or back to Zagreb). The most interesting and accessible part of the park can be seen very efficiently, in a three- to four-hour hike; while there are other hiking opportunities, they pale in comparison to this "greatest hits" section. Therefore, two nights and a full day at Plitvice is probably overkill for all but the most avid hikers.

Crowd-Beating Tips: Plitvice is swamped with international tour groups, many of whom aren't shy about elbowing into position for the best photos. The park's trails are most crowded between 10:00 and 15:00. I try to hit the trails by 8:30; that way, the crowds are moving in just as I'm finishing up. If arriving in the afternoon, starting your hike after 15:00 also works well.

Getting to Plitvice

Plitvice Lakes National Park, a few miles from the Bosnian border, is two hours by car south of Zagreb on the old highway #1 (a.k.a. D1).

By car from Zagreb, take the A1 expressway south for about an hour, exiting at Karlovac (marked for *1* and *Plitvice*). From here, D1 takes you directly south about another hour to the park. If you're staying at the park hotels, you can park for free at the hotel lot; to park at the lots at Entrance 1 or Entrance 2, you'll have to pay (7 kn/hour). For information about driving onward from Plitvice, see "Route Tips for Drivers" at the end of this chapter.

Buses leave from Zagreb's main bus station in the direction of Plitvice. Various bus companies handle the route; just go to the ticket window and ask for the next departure (81-95 kn depending on company, trip takes 2-2.5 hours). Buses run from Zagreb about hourly until about 16:00; avoid the sporadic late-night buses, which don't get you to the park until after midnight. Confirm that your bus will actually stop at Plitvice. (The official Plitvice bus stop is along the main road, about a 5- to 10-minute walk beyond the hotels.) Confirm the schedule online (www.akz.hr) or at the Plitvice office in Zagreb (Mon-Fri 8:00-16:00, closed Sat-Sun, Trg Kralja Tomislava 19, tel. 01/461-3586).

By car or bus, you'll see some thought-provoking terrain between Zagreb and Plitvice. As you leave Karlovac, you'll pass through the village of **Turanj,** part of the war zone from two decades ago. The destroyed, derelict houses belonged to Serbs who have not come back to reclaim and repair them. Farther along, about 25 miles before Plitvice, you'll pass through the striking village of **Slunj,** perched picturesquely on travertine formations (like Plitvice's) and surrounded by sparkling streams and waterfalls. If you're in a car, this is worth a photo stop. This town, too, looks very different from how it did before the war—when it was 30 percent Serb. As in countless other villages in the Croatian interior, the Orthodox church has been destroyed...and locals still seethe when they describe how the Serbs "defiled" the town's delicate beauty.

Orientation to Plitvice

(area code: 053)

Plitvice's 16 lakes are divided into the Upper Lakes (Gornja Jezera) and the Lower Lakes (Donja Jezera). The park officially has two entrances *(ulaz)*, each with ticket windows and snack and gift shops. Entrance 1 is at the bottom of the Lower Lakes, across the busy D1 road from the park's best restaurant, Lička Kuća (described later, under "Eating in Plitvice"). Entrance 2 is about 1.5 miles south, below the cluster of Plitvice's three hotels (Jezero, Plitvice, and Bellevue; see "Sleeping in Plitvice," later). There is no town at Plitvice. The nearest village, Mukinje, is a residential community mostly for park workers (boring for tourists, but has some good private room options).

Cost: The price to enter the park during peak season (April-Oct) is 110 kn (80 kn Nov-March; covers park entry, boat, and shuttle bus). Park hotel guests pay the entry fee only once for their entire stay; if you're staying off-site and want to visit the park on several days, you'll have to buy separate tickets each day.

Hours: The park is open every day, but the hours vary by season. In summer, it's generally open 7:00-20:00; in spring and fall, 8:00-18:00; and in winter, 8:00-15:00. The last boats and shuttle buses depart one hour before the park closes. Night owls should note that the park never really "closes"; these hours are for the ticket booths and the boat and shuttle bus system. You can just stroll right into the park at any time, provided that you aren't using the boat or bus. Again, for fewer tour-group crowds, visit early or late in the day.

Tourist Information

A handy map of the trails is on the back of your ticket, and big maps are posted all over the park. The big map is a good investment; the various English-language guidebooks are generally poorly translated and not very helpful (both sold at entrances, hotels, and shops throughout the park). The park has a good website: www.np-plitvicka-jezera.hr.

Getting Around Plitvice

Plitvice is designed for hikers. But the park has a few ways (included in entry cost) to help you connect the best parts.

By Shuttle Bus: Buses connect the hotels at Entrance 2 (stop ST-2, below Hotel Jezero) with the top of the Upper Lakes (stop ST-4) and roughly the bottom of the Lower Lakes (stop ST-1, a 10-minute walk from Entrance 1). Buses start running early and continue until late afternoon (frequency depends on demand—generally 3-4/hour; buses run from March until the first snow—

PLITVICE LAKES

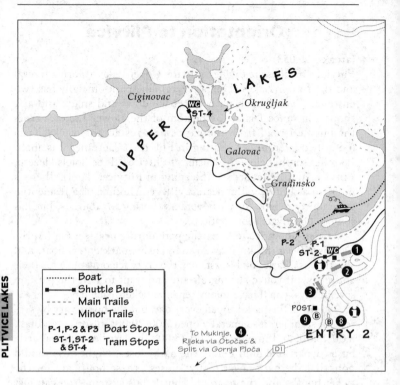

PLITVICE LAKES

often Dec). Note that the park refers to its buses as "trains," which confuses some visitors. Also note that no local buses take you along the major road (D1) that connects the entrances. The only way to get between them without a car is by shuttle bus (inside the park) or by foot (about a 40-minute walk).

By Boat: Low-impact electric boats ply the waters of the biggest lake, Kozjak, with three stops: below Hotel Jezero (stop P-1), at the bottom of the Upper Lakes (P-2), and at the far end of Kozjak, at the top of the Lower Lakes (P-3). From Hotel Jezero to the Upper Lakes, it's a quick five-minute ride; the boat goes back and forth continuously. The trip from the Upper Lakes to the Lower Lakes takes closer to 20 minutes, and the boat goes about twice per hour—often at the top and bottom of every

hour. (With up to 10,000 people a day visiting the park, you might have to wait for a seat on this boat.) Unless the lake freezes (happens about every five years), the boat also runs in the off-season—though frequency drops to hourly, and it stops running earlier.

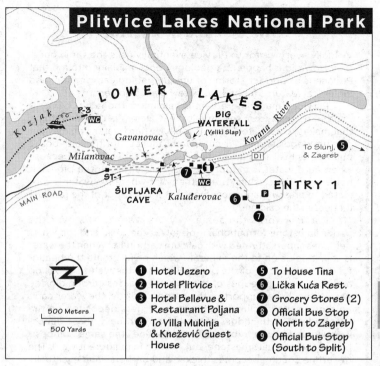

Plitvice Lakes National Park

LOWER LAKES

Kozjak

P-3

WC

Gavanovac

BIG
WATERFALL
(Veliki Slap)

Korana River

Milanovac

To Slunj,
& Zagreb

ST-1

ŠUPLJARA
CAVE

Kaluđerovac

WC

DI

ENTRY 1

P

MAIN ROAD

❶ Hotel Jezero
❷ Hotel Plitvice
❸ Hotel Bellevue &
   Restaurant Poljana
❹ To Villa Mukinja
   & Knežević Guest
   House

❺ To House Tina
❻ Lička Kuća Rest.
❼ Grocery Stores (2)
❽ Official Bus Stop
   (North to Zagreb)
❾ Official Bus Stop
   (South to Split)

500 Meters
500 Yards

PLITVICE LAKES

Sights in Plitvice

Plitvice is a refreshing playground of 16 terraced lakes, separated by natural travertine dams and connected by countless waterfalls. Over time, the water has simultaneously carved out, and, with the help of mineral deposits, built up this fluid landscape.

Plitvice became Croatia's first national park in 1949, and was a popular destination during the Yugoslav period. On Easter Sunday in 1991, the first shots of Croatia's war with Yugoslavia were fired right here—in fact, the war's first casualty was a park policeman, Josip Jović. The Serbs held Plitvice until 1995, and

most of the Croatians you'll meet here were evacuated and lived near the coast as refugees. During those five years, the park saw virtually no tourists, and was allowed to grow wild—allowing the ecosystem to recover from the impact of so many visitors. Today, the war is a fading memory, and the park is again a popular tourist

The Science of Plitvice

Virtually every visitor to Plitvice eventually asks the same question: How did it happen? A geologist once explained to me that Plitvice is a "perfect storm" of unique geological, climatic, and biological features found in very few places on earth.

Plitvice's magic ingredient is calcium carbonate ($CaCO_3$), a mineral deposit from the limestone. Calcium is the same thing that makes "hard water" hard. If you have hard water, you may get calcium deposits on your cold-water faucet. But these deposits build up only at the faucet, not inside the pipes. That's because when hard water is motionless (as it usually is in the pipes), it holds on to the calcium. But at the point where the water is subjected to pressure and movement—as it pours out of the faucet—it releases the calcium.

Plitvice works the same way. As water flows over the park's limestone formations, it dissolves the rock, and the water becomes supersaturated with calcium carbonate. When the water is still, it holds on to the mineral—which helps create the beautiful deep-blue color of the pools. But when the water speeds up and spills over the edges of the lakes, it releases carbon dioxide gas. Without the support of the carbon dioxide, the water can't hold on to the calcium carbonate, so it gets deposited on the lake bed and at the edges of the lakes. Eventually, these deposits build up to form a rock called travertine (the same composition as the original limestone, but formed in a different way). The travertine coating becomes thicker, and barriers—and eventually

destination, with nearly a million visitors each year (though relatively few are from the US).

▲▲▲Hiking the Lakes

Plitvice's system of trails and boardwalks makes it possible for visitors to get immersed in the park's beauty. (In some places, the path

leads literally right up the middle of a waterfall.) The official park map and signage recommend a variety of hikes, but there's no need to adhere strictly to these suggestions; invest in the big map and create your own route.

Most visitors stick to the main paths and choose between two basic plans: uphill or downhill. Each one has pros and cons. Park officials generally recommend hiking uphill, from the Lower Lakes to the Upper Lakes, which offers slightly better head-on views of

dams and new waterfalls—are formed. The moss and grass serve as a natural foundation for the calcification. In other words, the stone hangs down like the foliage because the foliage guides the growth of the stone. Because of this ongoing process, Plitvice's landscape is always changing.

And why is the water so clear? For one thing, it comes directly from high-mountain runoff, giving it little opportunity to become polluted or muddy. And because the water calcifies everything it touches, it prevents the creation of mud—so the bottoms of the lakes are entirely stone. Also, a different mineral in the water, magnesium carbonate, both gives the water its special color (which, park rangers brag, changes with the direction of the sunshine) and makes it highly basic, preventing the growth of plant life (such as certain algae) that could cloud the water.

The park contains nearly 1,300 different species of plants. Wildlife found in the park include deer, wolves, wildcats, lynx, wild boar, voles, otters, 350 species of butterflies, 42 types of dragonflies, 21 species of bats, and more than 160 species of birds (including eagles, herons, owls, grouse, and storks). The lakes (and local menus) are full of trout, and you'll also see smaller, red-finned fish called *klen* ("chub" in English). Perhaps most importantly, Plitvice is home to about 40 or 50 brown bears—a species now extremely endangered in Europe. You'll see bears, the park's mascot, plastered all over the tourist literature (and one scary representative in the lobby of Hotel Jezero).

the best scenery (this is the route described next). It also saves the most scenic stretch of lakes and falls—the Upper Lakes—for last. Hiking downhill, from Upper to Lower, is easier (though you'll have to hike steeply up out of the canyon at the end), and since most groups go the opposite way, you'll be passing—but not stuck behind—the crowds. Either way you go, walking briskly and with a few photo stops, figure on an hour for the Lower Lakes, an hour for the Upper Lakes, and a half-hour to connect them by boat.

Lower Lakes (Donja Jezera)—The lower half of Plitvice's lakes are accessible from Entrance 1. If you start here, the route marked *B* leads you along the boardwalks to Kozjak, the big lake that connects the Lower and the Upper Lakes (described later).

From the entrance, you'll descend a steep path with lots of **switchbacks,** as well as thrilling views over the canyon of the Lower Lakes. As you reach the lakes and begin to follow the boardwalks, you'll have great up-close views of the travertine formations that make up Plitvice's many waterfalls. Count the trout. If you're tempted to throw in a line, don't. Fishing is strictly forbidden. (Besides, they're happy.)

After you cross the path over the first lake, an optional 10-minute detour (to the right) takes you down to the **Big Waterfall** (Veliki Slap). It's the biggest of Plitvice's waterfalls, where the Plitvica River plunges 250 feet over a cliff into the valley below. Depending on recent rainfall, the force of the Big Waterfall varies from a light mist to a thundering deluge.

If you're a hardy hiker, consider climbing the steep steps from the Big Waterfall up to a **viewpoint** at the top of the canyon (marked *Sightseeing Point/Vidikovac*; it's a strenuous 10-minute hike to the top). Take the stairs up, bearing to the right at the top (near the shelter) to find a nice viewpoint overlooking the Big Waterfall. From here, you can carry on along the road that actually goes up over the top of the Big Waterfall, offering more views over the park. (Go as far as you like, then return the way you came.) The giant mill perched at the top of the Big Waterfall was used to grind grains; this very poor part of Croatia was traditionally inhabited by farmers.

After seeing the Big Waterfall, backtrack up to the main trail and continue on the boardwalks. After you pass another bank of waterfalls, a smaller trail branches off (on the left) toward **Šupljara** ("Bottomless") **Cave.** You can actually climb through this slippery cave all the way up to the trail overlooking the Lower Lakes (though it's not recommended). This unassuming cavern is a surprisingly big draw. In the 1960s, several German and Italian "Spaghetti Westerns" were filmed at Plitvice and in other parts of Croatia (which, to European eyes, has terrain similar to the American West). The most famous, *Der Schatz im Silbersee (The Treasure in Silver Lake)*, was filmed here at Plitvice, and the treasure was hidden in this cave. The movie—complete with *Deutsch*-speaking "Native Americans"—is still a favorite in Germany, and popular theme tours bring German tourists to movie locations here in Croatia. (If you drive the roads near Plitvice, keep an eye out for strange, Native American-sounding names such as Winnetou—fictional characters from these beloved stories of the Old West, by the German writer Karl May.)

After Šupljara Cave, you'll stick to the east side of the lakes, then cross over one more time to the west, where you'll cut through a comparatively dull forest. You'll emerge at a pit-stop-perfect clearing with WCs, picnic tables, a souvenir shop, and a self-service restaurant. Here you can catch the shuttle boat across Lake Kozjak to the bottom of the Upper Lakes (usually every 30 minutes).

Lake Kozjak (Jezero Kozjak)—The park's biggest lake, Kozjak, connects the Lower and Upper Lakes. The 20-minute boat ride between Plitvice's two halves offers a great chance for a breather. You can hike between the lakes along the west side of Kozjak, but the scenery's not nearly as good as in the rest of the park.

Upper Lakes (Gornja Jezera)—Focus on the lower half of the Upper Lakes, where nearly all the exotic beauty is. From the boat dock, signs for *B* direct you up to Gradinsko Lake through the most striking scenery in the whole park. Enjoy the stroll, taking your time...and lots of photos.

After Gradinsko Lake, you'll have two options:

1. Make your hike a loop by continuing around the far side of Gradinsko Lake and back to the P2 boat dock, where you can take the boat back over to the hotels (P1 stop).

2. Continue hiking up to the top of the Upper Lakes (following the icon for the shuttle bus); you'll get away from the crowds and feel like you've covered the park thoroughly. From here on up, the scenery is less stunning, and the waterfalls are fewer and farther between. At the top, you'll finish at shuttle bus stop ST4 (with food stalls and a WC), where the bus zips you back to the entrances and hotels.

Nice work!

Sleeping in Plitvice

At the Park

The most convenient way to sleep at Plitvice is to stay at the park's lodges, which are run by the same office (reservation tel. 053/751-015, fax 053/751-013, www.np-plitvicka-jezera.hr, info@np-plitvicka-jezera.hr; reception numbers for each hotel listed below). Warning: Because of high volume in peak season, the booking office often doesn't respond to emails. Instead, to make a reservation, use the park's website to book your room (look for the "Online booking" box). In a pinch, try calling the booking office or the hotel directly (they speak English), or emailing the park information office in Zagreb (np.zg.info@np-plitvicka-jezera.hr), which is more likely to respond in the busy summer months.

$$$ Hotel Jezero is big and modern, with all the comfort—and charm—of a Holiday Inn. It's well-located right at the park entrance and offers 200 rooms that feel newish, but generally have at least one thing that's broken. Rooms facing the park have big glass doors and balconies (July-Aug: Sb-€83/€76/€61, Db-€118/€108/€86; elevator, reception tel. 053/751-400).

$$ Hotel Plitvice, a better value than Jezero, offers 50 rooms and mod, wide-open public spaces on two floors with no elevators. For rooms, choose from economy (fine, older-feeling;

Sleep Code

(5 kn = about $1, €1 = about $1.40, country code: 385, area code: 053)

Unless otherwise noted, credit cards are accepted and breakfast is included, but the tourist tax (about 7 kn per person, per day) is not. While rates are listed in euros, you'll pay in kunas. Everyone listed here speaks English (or has a relative or neighbor who can help translate).

Rates: If I've listed three sets of rates, separated by slashes, the first is for peak season (July-Aug), the second is for shoulder season (May-June and Sept-Oct), and the third is for off-season (Nov-April). The dates for seasonal rates vary by hotel, and prices can change without notice; verify the hotel's current rates online or by email. For other updates, see www.ricksteves.com/update.

Price Ranges: To help you sort easily through these listings, I've divided the accommodations into three categories based on the price for a double room with bath during peak season:

$$$ Higher Priced—Most rooms €100 or more.
  $$ Moderately Priced—Most rooms between €50-100.
    $ Lower Priced—Most rooms €50 or less.

Sb-€72/€65/€50, Db-€96/€82/€70), standard (just a teeny bit bigger; Sb-€77/€70/€55, Db-€106/€96/€74), or superior (bigger still, with a sitting area; Sb-€82/€75/€60, Db-€116/€106/€84, reception tel. 053/751-100).

$$ Hotel Bellevue is simple and bare-bones (no TVs or elevator). It has an older feel to it, but the price is right and the 80 rooms are perfectly acceptable (Sb-€55/€50/€40, Db-€74/€68/€54, reception tel. 053/751-700).

Sobe near the Park

While the park's lodges are the easiest choice for non-drivers, those with a car should consider sleeping at one of the **$-$$** *sobe* (rooms in private homes) near the park. You'll see *sobe* signs for miles on either side of the park. A few that have good reputations include **Villa Mukinja** (in the village of Mukinje just south of the park, tel. 01/652-1857, www.plitvice-lakes.com, info@plitvice -lakes.com), **House Tina** (just north of the park in the village of Grabovac, tel. 04/778-4197), and **Knežević Guest House** (also in the village of Mukinje, tel. 053/774-081, mobile 098-168-7576, www.knezevic.hr, guest_house@vodatel.net, daughter Kristina speaks English).

Eating in Plitvice

The park runs all of the restaurants at Plitvice. These places are handy, and the food is affordable and decent. If you're staying at the hotels, you have the option of paying for half-board with your room (lunch or dinner, €12/90 kn each). This option is designed for the restaurants inside hotels Jezero and Plitvice, but you can also use the voucher at other park eateries (you'll pay the difference if the bill is more). The half-board option is worth doing if you're here for dinner, but don't lock yourself in for lunch—you'll want more flexibility as you explore Plitvice (excellent picnic spots and decent food stands abound inside the park).

Hotel Jezero and **Hotel Plitvice** both have big restaurants with adequate food and friendly, professional service (half-board for dinner, described above, is a good deal; or order à la carte; both open daily until 23:00).

Lička Kuća, across the pedestrian overpass from Entrance 1, has a wonderfully dark and smoky atmosphere around a huge open-air wood-fired grill. They may still be closed following a 2012 fire (pricey, daily 11:00-24:00, tel. 053/751-024).

Restaurant Poljana, behind Hotel Bellevue, has the same boring, park-lodge atmosphere in both of its sections: cheap, self-service cafeteria and sit-down restaurant with open wood-fired grill (same choices and prices as the better-atmosphere Lička Kuća, above; both parts open daily but closed in winter, tel. 053/751-092).

For **picnic** fixings, there's a small grocery store at Entrance 1 and another one with a larger selection across road D1 (use the pedestrian overpass). At the P3 boat dock, you can buy grilled meat and drinks. Friendly old ladies sell homemade goodies (such as strudel and hunks of cheese) throughout the park, including at Entrance 1.

Plitvice Connections

To reach the park, see "Getting to Plitvice," earlier in this chapter. Moving on from Plitvice is trickier. **Buses** pass by the park in each direction—northbound (to **Zagreb**, 2-2.5 hours) and southbound (to coastal destinations such as **Split**, 4-6 hours). The reception desk should have a printout of the schedule, or you can check at www.akz.hr.

There is no bus station at the park—just a low-profile *Plitvice Centar* bus stop shelter. To reach it from the park, go out to the main road from either Hotel Jezero or Hotel Plitvice, then turn right; the bus stops are just after the pedestrian overpass. The one on the hotel side of the road is for buses headed for the coast (southbound); the stop on the opposite side is for Zagreb (north-bound). Try to carefully confirm the bus schedule with the park or hotel staff, then head out to the bus stop and wave down the bus. (It's easy to confuse public buses with private tour buses, so don't panic if a bus doesn't stop for you—look for a bus with your final destination marked in the windshield.)

But here's the catch: If the bus is full, they won't stop at Plitvice to pick you up. This is most common on days when the buses are jammed with people headed to or from the coast. For example, on Fridays—when everyone is going from Zagreb to Split—you're unlikely to have any luck catching a southbound bus at Plitvice after 12:00, as they tend to be full. Similarly, on Sunday afternoons, northbound buses are often full. In general, don't plan on taking the last bus of the day.

While there's a chance you'll miss a bus and have to wait for the next one, in practice bus travel from Plitvice usually works fine...if you're patient.

Route Tips for Drivers

Plitvice's biggest disadvantage is that it's an hour away from the handy A1 expressway that connects northern Croatia to the Dalmatian Coast. You have three ways to access this expressway from Plitvice, depending on which direction you're heading.

Going North: If you're heading north (to Zagreb or Slovenia), get on the expressway at **Karlovac:** From Plitvice, drive about one hour north on D1 to the town of Karlovac, where you can access A1 northbound. Alternatively, you can take A1 southbound to A6, which leads west to Rijeka, Opatija, and Istria (though this route is more boring and only slightly faster than the route via Otočac, next).

Going to Central Croatia: If you're going to central destinations on the coast, such as Istria, Rijeka, Opatija, or Rab, get on the expressway at **Otočac.** From Plitvice, go south on D1, then go west on road #52 to the town of Otočac (about an hour through the mountains from Plitvice to Otočac). After Otočac, you can get on A1 (north to Zagreb, south to the Dalmatian Coast); or continue west and twist down the mountain road to the seaside town of Senj, on the main coastal road of the Kvarner Gulf. From Senj, it's about an hour north along the coast to Rijeka, then on to Opatija or Istria; or an hour south to Jablanac, where you can catch the ferry to Rab Island.

During the recent war, the front line between the Croats and Serbs ran just east of **Otočac** (OH-toh-chawts), and bullet

holes still mar the town's facades. (Watch for minefield warning signs just east of Otočac, but don't let them make you too nervous: It's safe to drive here, but not necessarily safe to get out of your car and wander through the fields.) Today Otočac is putting itself back together, and it's a fine place to drop into a café for a coffee, or pick up some produce at the outdoor market. The Catholic church in the center of town, destroyed in the war but now rebuilt, displays its damaged church bells in a memorial out back. The crucifix nearby is made of old artillery shells. Just up the main street, beyond the big, grassy park, is the Orthodox church. Otočac used to be about one-third Serbian, but the Serbs were forced out during the war, and this church fell into disrepair. But, as Otočac and Croatia show signs of healing, about two dozen Serbs have returned to town and reopened their church (for more on the Serbian Orthodox Church, see page 318).

Going South: If you're heading south (to Split and the rest of Dalmatia) from Plitvice, catch the expressway at **Gornja Ploča.** Drive south from Plitvice on D1, through Korenica, Pećane, and Udbina, then follow signs for the A1 expressway (and *Lovinac*) via Kurjak to the Gornja Ploča on-ramp. Once on A1, you'll twist south through the giant Sveti Rok tunnel to Dalmatia.

ISTRIA

Rovinj • Pula • The Brijuni Islands • Poreč • Hill Towns

Idyllic Istria (EE-stree-ah; "Istra" in Croatian), at Croatia's northwest corner, reveals itself to you gradually and seductively. Pungent truffles, Roman ruins, striking hill towns, quaint coastal villages, carefully cultivated food and wine, and breezy Italian culture all compete for your attention. The wedge-shaped Istrian Peninsula, while not as famous as its southern rival (the much-hyped Dalmatian Coast), is giving Dalmatia a run for its money.

The Istrian coast, with gentle green slopes instead of the sheer limestone cliffs found along the rest of the Croatian shoreline, is more serene than sensational. It's lined with pretty, interchangeably tacky resort towns, such as the tourist mecca Poreč (worthwhile only for its Byzantine mosaic-packed basilica). But one seafront village reaches the ranks of greatness: romantically creaky Rovinj, my favorite little town on the Adriatic. Down at the tip of Istria is big, industrial Pula, offering a bustling urban contrast to the rest of the time-passed coastline, plus some impressive Roman ruins (including an amphitheater so remarkably intact, you'll marvel that you haven't heard of it before). Just offshore are the Brijuni Islands—once the stomping grounds of Marshal Tito, whose ghost still haunts a national park peppered with unexpected attractions.

But Croatia is more than the sea, and diverse Istria offers some of the country's most appealing reasons to head inland. In the Istrian interior, between humble concrete towns crying out for a paint job, you'll find vintners painstakingly reviving a delicate winemaking tradition, farmers pressing that last drop of oil out of their olives, trained dogs sniffing out truffles in primeval forests, and a smattering of fortified medieval hill towns with sweeping

views over the surrounding terrain—including the justifiably popular village of Motovun.

Planning Your Time

Istria offers an exciting variety of attractions compared to the relatively uniform, if beautiful, string of island towns farther south. While some travelers wouldn't trade a sunny island day for anything, I prefer to sacrifice a little time on the Dalmatian Coast for the diversity that comes with a day or two exploring Istria's hill towns and other unique sights.

Istria's main logistical advantage is that it's easy to reach and

Istria at a Glance

▲▲▲**Rovinj** Extremely romantic, Venetian-style coastal town with an atmospheric Old Town and salty harbor. See page 105.

▲▲**Pula** Big, industrial port town with one of the world's best-preserved Roman amphitheaters. See page 131.

▲▲**Motovun** Touristy but enjoyable hill town with a fun rampart walk offering sweeping views over inland Istria. See page 150.

▲**Završje** Picturesque, mostly deserted hill town overlooking Motovun and its valley. See page 161.

▲**Brijuni Islands** Tito's former summer residence, now a national park with a Tito museum, mini-safari, and other offbeat sights. See page 143.

▲**Grožnjan** Sleepy artists' colony hill town in the interior. See page 159.

Buje Big hill town mingling charm with urban flair. See page 158.

Hum Miniscule, touristy town deep in the interior. See page 163.

Poreč Big coastal resort squeezed full of European holidaymakers, plus a church with remarkably intact Byzantine mosaics. See page 146.

Oprtalj Hill town that's striking from afar but all business up close. See page 161.

Livade Modest valley village with some top-notch truffle eateries. See page 162.

Brtonigla Hill town worth visiting only for its great restaurants. See page 157.

to explore by car. Just a quick hop from Venice or Slovenia, compact little Istria is made-to-order for a quick, efficient road trip.

With a car and two weeks to spend in Croatia and Slovenia, Istria deserves two days, divided between its two big attractions: the coastal town of Rovinj and the hill towns of the interior. Ideally, make your home base for two nights in Rovinj or in Motovun, and day-trip to the region's other attractions. To wring the most out of limited Istrian time, the city of Pula and its Roman amphitheater are well worth a few hours. If you have a car, it's easy to go for a joyride through the Istrian countryside, visiting a few hill towns en route. The town of Poreč and the fun but time-consuming Brijuni Islands merit a detour only if you've got at least three days.

Getting Around Istria

Istria is a cinch for **drivers,** who find distances short and roads and attractions well-marked (though summer traffic can be miserable, especially on weekends). Istria is neatly connected by a speedy highway nicknamed the *ipsilon* (the Croatian word for the letter Y, which is what the highway is shaped like). One branch of the "Y" (A9) runs roughly parallel to the coast from Slovenia to Pula, about six miles inland; the other branch (A8) cuts diagonally northeast to the Učka Tunnel (leading to Rijeka). You'll periodically come to toll booths, where you'll pay a modest fee for using the *ipsilon*. Following road signs here is easy (navigate by town names), but if you'll be driving a lot, pick up a good map to more easily navigate the back roads. My favorite is the Kod & Kam 1:100,000 *Istra* map (available in local bookstores and some TIs).

If you're relying on **public transportation,** Istria can be frustrating: The towns that are easiest to reach (Poreč and Pula) are less appealing than Istria's highlights (Rovinj and Motovun). Linking up the coastal towns by bus is doable if you're patient and check schedules carefully, but the hill towns probably aren't worth the hassle. Even if you're doing the rest of your trip by public transportation, consider renting a car for a day or two in Istria.

Driving from Istria to Rijeka (and the Rest of Croatia): Istria meets the rest of Croatia at the big port city of Rijeka (described in the Kvarner Gulf chapter). There are two ways to get to Rijeka: The faster alternative is to take the *ipsilon* road via Pazin to the Učka Tunnel (28-kn toll), which emerges just above Rijeka and Opatija (for Rijeka, you'll follow the road more or less straight on; for Opatija, you'll twist down to the right, backtracking slightly to the seashore below you). Or you can take the slower but more scenic **coastal road** from Pula via Labin. After going inland for about 25 miles, this road jogs to the east coast of Istria, which it hugs all the way into Opatija, then Rijeka. From Rijeka, you can easily hook into Croatia's expressway network (for example, take A6 east

Istrian Food and Wine

Foodies consider Istria the best part of Croatia. Though much of the country is arid and barren, Istria is noticeably greener—its fertile soil bursts with a cor-nucopia of delicious ingredients. Like the Istrian people, Istrian cuisine is a mix of various cultural influences, including Italian-style elements, farmer fare, and sea-food. Truffles are used liberally, if only to please the many tourists who come here for their pungent flavor (see sidebar on page 156). Dishes such as gnocchi, risotto, and fusilli are popular, as is *pršut*,

the air-cured ham that's Istria's answer to prosciutto (see side-bar on page 512). Food here is distinctly Mediterranean, with lots of olives and wine. You'll often find game on the menu.

Istria is also a major wine-growing region, producing about 80 percent whites. Istrian vintners are particularly proud of their *malvazija* (mahl-VAH-zee-yah; better known to English-speakers as Malvasia)—a light white wine that can be either sweet *(slatko)* or dry *(suho)*. *Malvazija* wines are pro-duced throughout Europe, but Istria's *malvazija* is indigenous. The red *teran* is also popular, as is Merlot. *Teran,* a heavy wine from *refošk* grapes, is sometimes blended with Merlot to soften its flavor. *Teran* pairs well with *pršut*. Because many Istrian vintners are relatively new to the job—having gotten into the craft when the industry was privatized at the end of communism—the focus is on quality, not quantity...so few local wines are exported.

ISTRIA

to A1, which zips you north to Zagreb or south to the Dalmatian Coast).

By Boat to Venice, Piran, or Trieste: Venezia Lines (www .venezialines.com) and **Commodore Cruises** (www.commodore -cruises.hr) connect Venice daily in summer with Rovinj, Poreč, and Pula. **Trieste Lines** (www.triestelines.it) connects Rovinj and Poreč to Piran (Slovenia), then Trieste (Italy). While designed for day-trippers from Istria to Venice or Trieste, these services can also be used one-way. Since schedules tend to change from year to year, check their websites for details.

Rovinj

Rising dramatically from the Adriatic as though being pulled up to heaven by its grand bell tower, Rovinj (roh-VEEN; in Italian: Rovigno/roh-VEEN-yoh) is a welcoming Old World oasis in a sea of tourist kitsch. Among the villages of Croatia's coast, there's something particularly romantic about Rovinj—the most Italian town in Croatia's most Italian region. Rovinj's streets are delightfully twisty, its ancient houses are characteristically crumbling, and its harbor—lively with real-life fishermen—is as salty as they come. Like a little Venice on a hill, Rovinj is the stage set for your Croatian seaside dreams.

Rovinj was prosperous and well-fortified in the Middle Ages. It boomed in the 16th and 17th centuries, when it was flooded

with refugees fleeing both the Ottoman invasions and the plague. Because the town was part of the Republic of Venice for five centuries (13th to 18th centuries), its architecture, culture, and even language are strongly Venetian. The local folk groups sing in a dialect actually considered more Venetian than what the Venetians themselves speak these days. (You can even see Venice from Rovinj's church bell tower on a very clear day.)

After Napoleon seized the region, then was defeated, Rovinj became part of Austria. The Venetians had neglected Istria, but the Austrians invested in it, bringing the railroad, gas lights, and a huge Ronhill tobacco factory. (This factory—recently replaced by an enormous, state-of-the-art facility you'll pass on the highway farther inland—is one of the town's most elegant structures, and is slated for extensive renovation in the coming years.) The Habsburgs tapped Pula and Trieste to be the empire's major ports—cursing those cities with pollution and sprawl, while allowing Rovinj to linger in its trapped-in-the-past quaintness.

Before long, Austrians discovered Istria as a handy escape for a beach holiday. Tourism came to Rovinj in the late 1890s, when a powerful Austrian baron bought one of the remote, barren islands offshore and brought it back to life with gardens and a grand villa. Before long, another baron bought another island...and a tourist boom was underway. In more recent times, Rovinj has become a top destination for nudists. The resort of Valalta, just to the north, is a popular spot for those seeking "southern exposure"... as a very revealing brochure at the TI illustrates (www.valalta.hr).

ISTRIA

Whether you want to find PNBs (pudgy nude bodies), or avoid them, remember that the German phrase *FKK* (*Freikörper Kultur*, or "free body culture") is international shorthand for nudism.

Rovinj is the most atmospheric of all of Croatia's small coastal towns. Maybe that's because it's always been a real town, where poor people lived. You'll find no fancy old palaces here—just narrow streets lined with skinny houses that have given shelter to humble families for generations. While it's becoming known on the tourist circuit, Rovinj retains the soul of a fishermen's village; notice that the harbor is still filled not with glitzy yachts, but with a busy fishing fleet.

Planning Your Time

Rovinj is hardly packed with diversions. You can get the gist of the town in a one-hour wander. The rest of your time is for enjoying the ambience or pedaling a rental bike to a nearby beach. When you're ready to overcome your inertia, there's no shortage of day trips (the best are outlined in this chapter). Be aware that much of Rovinj closes down from mid-October through Easter.

Orientation to Rovinj

(area code: 052)

Rovinj, once an island, is now a peninsula. The Old Town is divided in two parts: a particularly charismatic chunk on the oval-shaped peninsula, and the rest on the mainland (with similarly time-worn buildings, but without the commercial cuteness that comes with lots of tourist money). Where the mainland meets the peninsula is a broad, bustling public space called Tito Square (Trg Maršala Tita). The Old Town peninsula—traffic-free except for the occasional moped—is topped by the massive bell tower of the Church of St. Euphemia. At the very tip of the peninsula is a small park.

Tourist Information

Rovinj's TI, facing the harbor, has several handy, free materials, including a town map and an info booklet (June-Sept daily 7:00-22:00; Oct and May daily 8:00-21:00; Nov-April Mon-Fri 8:00-15:00, Sat 8:00-13:00, closed Sun; along the embankment at Obala Pina Budičina 12, tel. 052/811-566, www.tzgrovinj.hr). In summer, the TI may offer a free Old Town walking tour (possibly Tue at

10:00) and a free bike tour (possibly Tue at 16:00); ask for details and reserve a spot at the TI.

Arrival in Rovinj

By Car: Only local cars are allowed to enter the Old Town area. To get as close as possible—whether you're staying in the Old Town, or just visiting for the day—use the big waterfront parking lots just north of the Old Town Peninsula: Approaching Rovinj, follow *Centar* signs, eventually taking you through the little roundabout and directly into the parking lot (July-Aug: 6.5 kn/hour, April-June and Sept: 5 kn/hour, Oct-March: 1-2 kn/hour). There are two big parking lots, side-by-side, called "Valdibora 1" (a.k.a. "Big Valdibora," farther from the Old Town), and "Valdibora 2" (a.k.a. "Little Valdibora," closer to the Old Town). The slightly closer Valdibora 2 is sometimes reserved for residents, in which case you won't be able to take a ticket to enter.

While these Valdibora lots are the most convenient—and come with the classic Rovinj view—the cost adds up fast if you're parking overnight. If it's full, you'll be pushed to another pay lot farther out, along the bay northwest of the Old Town (a scenic 15-minute walk from town; summer: 5-6 kn/hour, free 23:00-6:00; winter: 2 kn/hour, free 20:00-6:00 and on Sun). If you're sleeping at a hotel away from the Old Town, carefully track individual blue hotel signs as you approach town.

By Bus: The bus station is on the south side of the Old Town, close to the harbor. Leave the station to the left, then walk on busy Carera street directly into the center of town. Note that there are plans to move the bus station to the other side of the Old Town, just above the long waterfront parking lots. If your bus stops here instead, simply head down to the main road and walk along the parking lots into town.

By Boat: The few boats connecting Rovinj to Venice, Piran, Trieste, and other Istrian towns dock at the long pier protruding from the Old Town peninsula. Just walk up the pier, and you're in the heart of town.

Helpful Hints

Internet Access: A-Mar Internet Club has several terminals and long hours (40 kn/hour, Mon-Fri 8:00-22:00, Sat-Sun 9:00-23:00, less off-season, on the main drag in the mainland part of the Old Town, Carera 26, tel. 052/841-211).

Laundry: The full-service **Galax** launderette hides up the street beyond the bus station. You can usually pick up your laundry after 24 hours, though same-day service might be possible if you drop it off early enough in the morning (70 kn/load wash and dry; Easter-Sept daily 6:00-20:00, until later in summer;

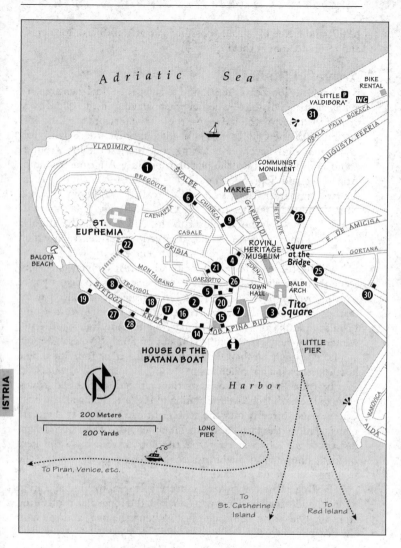

Oct-Easter Mon-Fri 7:00-19:00, Sat 9:00-15:00, closed Sun; up Benussia street past the bus station, on the left after the post office, tel. 052/816-130).

Local Guides: Vukica Palčić is a very capable guide who knows her town intimately and loves to share it with visitors (€50 for a 2-hour tour, mobile 098-794-003, vukica.palcic@pu .t-com.hr). **Renato Orbanić** is a laid-back musician (saxophone player) who also enjoys wandering through town with visitors. While light on heavy-hitting facts, his casual tour somehow suits this easygoing little town (€60 for a 2-hour

Rovinj

1. Hotel Villa Angelo d'Oro
2. Villa Markiz
3. Hotel Adriatic
4. Villa Cissa
5. Casa Garzotto (Reception & Apts.)
6. Casa Garzotto (Rooms)
7. Porta Antica Apartments
8. Trevisol Apartments
9. Miranda Fabris Rooms
10. To Hotels Vila Kristina, Vila Lili, Villa Baron Gautsch, Monte Mulini, Lone & Eden
11. To Hotel Park, Elda Markulin Apts., Apartmani Tomo & Restaurant Maestral
12. Futura Travel Agency
13. Natale Travel Agency
14. Planet Travel Agency
15. Scuba Restaurant
16. Veli Jože Restaurant
17. Santa Croce Restaurant
18. Lampo Restaurant
19. La Puntuleina Restaurant
20. Barba Zuane Restaurant
21. Krčma Ulika Restaurant
22. Monte Restaurant
23. Gostionica/Trattoria Toni
24. Sidro Restaurant
25. Bacchus Wine Bar
26. Piassa Granda Wine Bar
27. Valentino Champagne & Cocktail Bar
28. Monte Carlo Bar
29. Launderette
30. Internet Café
31. Start of Self-Guided Walk

tour, mobile 091-521-6206, rorbanic@inet.hr).

Best Views: The town is full of breathtaking views. Photography buffs will be busy in the "magic hours" of early morning and evening, and even by moonlight. The postcard view of Rovinj is from the parking lot embankment at the north end of the Old Town (at the start of the "Self-Guided Walk," next). For a different perspective on the Old Town, head for the far side of the harbor on the opposite (south) end of town. The church bell tower provides a virtual aerial view of the town and a grand vista of the outlying islands.

Self-Guided Walk

▲▲▲Rovinj Ramble

This orientation walk introduces you to Rovinj in about an hour. Begin at the parking lot just north of the Old Town.

Old Town View

Many places offer fine views of Rovinj's Old Town, but this is the most striking. Boats bob in the harbor, and behind them Venetian-looking homes seem to rise from the deep. (For an aerial perspective, notice the big billboard overhead and to the left.)

The Old Town is topped by the church, whose bell tower is capped by a weathervane in the shape of Rovinj's patron saint, Euphemia. Local fishermen look to this saintly weathervane for direction: When Euphemia is looking out to sea, it means the stiff, fresh Bora wind is blowing, bringing dry air from the interior...a sailor's delight. But if she's facing the land, the humid Jugo wind will soon bring bad weather from the sea. After a day or so, even a tourist learns to look to St. Euphemia for the weather report. (For more on Croatian winds and weather, see the sidebar on page 172.)

As you soak in this scene, ponder how the town's history created its current shape. In the Middle Ages, Rovinj was an island, rather than a peninsula, and it was surrounded by a double wall—a protective inner wall and an outer seawall. Because it was so well-defended against pirates and other marauders (and carefully quarantined from the plague), it was extremely desirable real estate. And yet, it was easy to reach from the mainland, allowing it to thrive as a trading town. With more than 10,000 residents at its peak, Rovinj became immensely crowded, which explains today's pleasantly claustrophobic Old Town.

Over the centuries—as demand for living space trumped security concerns—the town walls were converted into houses, with windows grafted on to their imposing frame. Gaps in the wall, with steps that seem to end at the water, are where fishermen would pull in to unload their catch directly into the warehouses on the bottom level of the houses. (Later you can explore some of these lanes from inside the town.) Today, if you live in one of these houses, the Adriatic is your backyard.

• Now head into town. In the little park near the sea, just beyond the end of the parking lot, look for the big, blocky...

ISTRIA

Communist-Era Monument

Dating from the time of Tito, this celebrates the Partisan Army's victory over the Nazis in World War II and commemorates the

victims of fascism. The minimalist reliefs on the ceremonial tomb show a slow prisoners' parade, the victims prodded by a gun in the back from a figure with a Nazi-style helmet. Notice that one side of the monument is in Croatian, and the other is in Italian. With typical Yugoslav grace and subtlety, this jarring block shatters the otherwise harmonious time-warp vibe of Rovinj. Fortunately, it's the only modern structure anywhere near the Old Town.

• *Now walk a few more steps toward town, stopping to explore the covered...*

Market

The front part of the market, near the water, is for souvenirs. But natives delve deeper in, to the local produce stands. Separating the gifty stuff from the nitty-gritty produce is a line of merchants aggressively pushing free samples. Everything is local and mostly homemade. Consider this snack-time tactic: Loiter around, joking with the farmers while sampling their various tasty walnuts, figs, cherries, grapes, olive oils, honey, *rakija* (the powerful schnapps popular throughout the Balkans), and more. If the sample is good, buy some more for a picnic. In the center of the market, a delightful and practical fountain from 1908 reminds locals of the infrastructure brought in by their Habsburg rulers a century ago. The hall labeled *Ribarnica/Pescheria* at the back of the market is where you'll find fresh, practically wriggling fish. This is where locals gather ingredients for their favorite dish, *brodet*—a stew of various kinds of seafood mixed with olive oil and wine...all of Istria's best bits rolled into one dish. It's slowly simmered and generally served with polenta (unfortunately, it's rare in restaurants).

• *Continue up the broad street, named for **Giuseppe Garibaldi**—one of the major players in late 19th-century Italian unification. Imagine: Even though you're in Croatia, Italian patriots are celebrated in this very Italian-feeling town (see the "Italo-Croatia" sidebar). After one long block, on your left, you'll come to the wide cross-street called...*

Square at the Bridge (Trg na Mostu)

This marks the site of the medieval bridge that once connected the fortified island of Rovinj to the mainland (as illustrated in the small painting above the door of the Kavana al Ponto—"Bridge

Italo-Croatia

Apart from its tangible attractions, one of Istria's hallmarks is its biculturalism: It's an engaging hybrid of Croatia and Italy. Like most of the Croatian Coast, Istria has variously been controlled by Illyrians, Romans, Byzantines, Slavs, Venetians, and Austrians. After the Habsburgs lost World War I, most of today's Croatia joined Yugoslavia—but Istria became part of Italy. During this time, the Croatian vernacular was suppressed, while the Italian language and culture flourished. But this extra chapter of Italian rule was short-lived. After World War II, Istria joined Yugoslavia, and Croatian culture and language returned. What followed was a so-called "Italian exodus," during which many Istrian Italians chose to relocate to Italy—leaving behind hill towns, valley villages, and farm estates that are abandoned even to this day.

The Istrians who stayed behind were saddled with an identity crisis. Many people here found it difficult to abandon their ties to Italy, and continued to speak the language and embrace the culture. Today, depending on who you ask, Istria is the most Italian part of Croatia...or the most Croatian part of Italy. Istria pops up on Italian weather reports. A few years ago, Italy's then-Prime Minister Silvio Berlusconi declared that he still considered Istria part of Italy—and he wanted it back. When I wrote an article about Istria for a newspaper, some Italian readers complained that I made it sound "too Croatian," while some Croatians claimed my depiction was "too Italian."

People who actually live here typically don't worry about the distinction. Locals insist that they're not Croatians and not Italians—they're Istrians. They don't mind straddling two cultures. Both languages are official (and often taught side-by-side in schools), street signs are bilingual, and most Istrians dabble in each tongue—often seeming to foreign ears as though they're mixing the two at once.

As a result of their tangled history, Istrians have learned how to be mellow and take things as they come. They're gregarious, open-minded, and sometimes seem to thrive on chaos. A twentysomething local told me, "My ancestors lived in Venice. My great-grandfather lived in Austria. My grandfather lived in Italy. My father lived in Yugoslavia. I live in Croatia. My son will live in the European Union. And we've all lived in the same town."

Café"). Back then, the island was populated mostly by Italians, while the mainland was the territory of Slavic farmers. But as Rovinj's strategic importance waned, and its trading status rose, the need for easy access became more important than the canal's protective purpose—so in 1763, it was filled in. The two populations integrated, creating the bicultural mix that survives today.

Notice the breeze? Via Garibaldi is nicknamed Val di Bora ("Valley of the Bora Wind") for the constant cooling wind that blows here. On the island side of Trg na Mostu is the Rovinj Heritage Museum (described later, under "Sights in Rovinj"). Next door, the town's cultural center posts lovingly hand-lettered signs in Croatian and Italian announcing upcoming musical events (generally free, designed for locals, and worth noting and enjoying).

Nearby (just past Kavana al Ponto, on the left), the Viecia Batana Café—named for Rovinj's unique, flat-bottomed little fishing boats—has a retro interior with a circa-1960 fishermen's mural that evokes an earlier age. The café is popular for its chocolate cake and "Batana" ice cream.

• *Now proceed to the little fountain in the middle of the square (near Hotel Adriatic).*

Tito Square (Trg Maršala Tita)

This wide-open square at the entrance to the Old Town is the crossroads of Rovinj. The **fountain,** with a little boy holding a water-spouting fish, celebrates the government-funded water system that finally brought running water to the Old Town in 1959. Walk around the fountain, with your eyes on the relief, to see a successful socialist society at the inauguration of this new water system. Despite the happy occasion, the figures are pretty stiff—conformity trumped most other virtues in Tito's world.

Now walk out to the end of the concrete pier, called the **Mali Molo ("Little Pier").** From here, you're surrounded by Rovinj's crowded harbor, with fishing vessels and excursion boats that shuttle tourists out to the offshore islands. If the weather's good, a **boat trip** can be a memorable way to get out on the water for a different angle on Rovinj (see "Activities in Rovinj," later, for details).

Scan the **harbor.** On the left is the MMC, the local meeting and concert hall (described later, under "Nightlife in Rovinj"). Above and behind the MMC, the highest bell tower inland marks the Franciscan monastery, which was the only building on the mainland before the island town was connected to shore. Along

ISTRIA

the waterfront to the right of the MMC is Hotel Park, a typical monstrosity from the communist era, now tastefully renovated inside. A recommended bike path starts just past this hotel, leading into a nature preserve and the best nearby beaches (which you can see in the distance; for more on bike rental, see "Activities in Rovinj," later).

Now head back to the base of the pier. If you were to walk down the **embankment** between the harbor and the Old Town (past Hotel Adriatic), you'd find the TI, the recommended House of the Batana Boat museum, and a delightful "restaurant row" with

several tempting places for a drink or a meal. Many fishermen pull their boats into this harbor, then simply carry their catch across the street to a waiting restaurateur. (This self-guided walk finishes with a stroll down this lane.)

Backtrack 10 paces past the fountain and face the Old Town entrance gate, called the **Balbi Arch.** The winged lion on top is a reminder that this was Venetian territory for centuries.

• *Head through the gate into the Old Town. Inside and on the left is the red...*

Town Hall

On the old Town Hall, notice another Venetian lion, as well as other historic crests embedded in the wall. The Town Hall actually sports an Italian flag (along with ones for Croatia and Rovinj) and faces a square named for Giacomo Matteotti, a much-revered Italian patriot.

Continue a few more steps into town. Gostionica/Trattoria Cisterna faces another little square, which once functioned as a cistern (collecting rainwater, which was pulled from a subterranean reservoir through the well you see today). The building on your left (which often has a *batana* boat out front) is the Italian Union—yet another reminder of how Istria has an important bond with Italy.

• *Now begin walking up the street to the left of Gostionica/Trattoria Cisterna.*

Grisia Street

The main "street" (actually a tight lane) leading through the middle of the island is choked with tourists during the midday rush and lined with art galleries. This inspiring town has attracted many

artists, some of whom display their
works along this colorful stretch.
Notice the rusty little nails speckling
the walls—each year in August, an
art festival invites locals to hang their
best art on this street. With paintings
lining the lane, the entire community comes out to enjoy each other's
creations.

As you walk, keep your camera
cocked and ready, as you can find
delightful scenes down every side
lane. Remember that, as crowded
as it is today, little Rovinj was even more packed in the Middle
Ages. Keep an eye out for arches that span narrow lanes (such as
on the right, at Arsenale street)—the only way a walled city could
grow was up. Many of these additions created hidden little courtyards, nooks, and crannies that make it easy to get away from the
crowds and claim a corner of the town for yourself. Another sign
of Rovinj's overcrowding are the distinctive chimneys poking up
above the rooftops. These chimneys, added long after the buildings were first constructed, made it possible to heat previously
underutilized rooms...and squeeze in even more people.

• *Continue up to the top of Grisia. Capping the town is the can't-
miss-it...*

▲Church of St. Euphemia (Sv. Eufemija)

Rovinj's landmark Baroque church dates from 1754. It's watched
over by an enormous 190-foot-tall campanile, a replica of the

famous bell tower on St. Mark's
Square in Venice. The tower is
topped by a copper weathervane with the weather-predict-
ing St. Euphemia, the church's
namesake.

Cost and Hours: Free,
generally open May-Sept daily
10:00-18:00, Easter-April and
Oct-Nov open only for Mass and with demand, generally closed
Dec-Easter.

Touring the Church: The vast, somewhat gloomy interior
boasts some fine altars of Carrara marble (a favorite medium of
Michelangelo's). Services here are celebrated using a combination
of Croatian and Italian, suiting the town's mixed population.

To the right of the main altar is the church's highlight: the
chapel containing the relics of St. Euphemia. Before stepping into

the chapel, notice the altar featuring Euphemia—depicted, as she usually is, with her wheel (a reminder of her torture) and a palm frond (symbolic of her martyrdom), and holding the fortified town of Rovinj, of which she is the protector.

St. Euphemia was the virtuous daughter of a prosperous early fourth-century family in Chalcedon (near today's Istanbul). Euphemia used her family's considerable wealth to help the poor. Unfortunately, her pious philanthropy happened to coincide with anti-Christian purges by the Roman Emperor Diocletian. When she was 15 years old, Euphemia was arrested for refusing to worship the local pagan idol. She was brutally tortured, her bones broken on a wheel. Finally she was thrown to the lions as a public spectacle. But, the story goes, the lions miraculously refused to attack her—only nipping her gently on one arm. The Romans murdered Euphemia anyway, and her remains were later rescued by Christians. In the year 800, a gigantic marble sarcophagus containing St. Euphemia's relics somehow found its way into the Adriatic and floated all the way up to Istria, where Rovinj fishermen discovered it bobbing in the sea. They towed it back to town, where a crowd gathered. The townspeople realized what it was and wanted to take it up to the hilltop church (an earlier version of the one we're in now). But nobody could move it...until a young boy with two young calves showed up. He said he'd had a dream of St. Euphemia—and, sure enough, he succeeded in dragging her relics to where they still lie.

The small chapel behind the altar is dominated by Euphemia's famous sarcophagus. The front panel (with the painting of Euphemia) is opened with much fanfare every September 16, St. Euphemia's feast day, to display the small, withered, waxen face of Rovinj's favorite saint. The sarcophagus is flanked by frescoes depicting her most memorable moment (protected by angels, as a bored-looking lion tenderly nibbles at her right bicep) and her arrival here in Rovinj (with burly fishermen looking astonished as the young boy succeeds in moving the giant sarcophagus). Note the depiction of Rovinj fortified by a double crenellated wall—looking more like a castle than like the creaky fishing village of today. At the top of the hill is an earlier version of today's church.

• *If you have time and energy, consider climbing the...*

Bell Tower

Scaling the church bell tower's creaky wooden stairway requires an enduring faith in the reliability of wood. It rewards those who brave the climb with a commanding view of the town and surrounding islands. The climb doubles your altitude, and from this perch you can also look down—taking advantage of the quirky little round hole in the floor to photograph the memorable staircase you just climbed.

Cost and Hours: 10 kn, same hours as church, enter from inside church—to the left of the main altar.

• *Leave the church through the main door. A peaceful café on a park terrace (once a cemetery) is a bit to your right. Farther to the right, a winding lane leads down toward the water, then forks. A left turn zig-zags you past a WWII pillbox and leads along the "restaurant row," where you can survey your options for a drink or a meal (see "Eating in Rovinj," later). A right turn curls you down along the quieter northern side of the Old Town peninsula. Either way, Rovinj is yours to enjoy.*

Sights in Rovinj

▲**House of the Batana Boat (Kuća o Batani)**—Rovinj has a long, noble shipbuilding tradition, and this tiny but interesting museum gives you the story of the town's distinctive *batana* boats. Locals say this museum puts you in touch with the soul of this town.

The flat-bottomed vessels are favored by local fishermen for their ability to reach rocky areas close to shore that are rich with certain shellfish. The museum explains how the boats are built, with the help of an entertaining elapsed-time video showing a boat built from scratch in five minutes. You'll also meet some of the salty old sailors who use these vessels (find the placemat with wine stains, and put the glass in different red circles to hear various seamen talk in the Rovinj dialect). Another movie shows the boats at work. Upstairs is a wall of photos of *batana* boats still in active use, a tiny library (peruse photos of the town from a century ago), and a video screen displaying *bitinada* music—local music with harmonizing voices that imitate instruments. Sit down and listen to several (there's a button for skipping ahead). The museum has no posted English information, so pick up the comprehensive English flyer as you enter.

Cost and Hours: 10 kn; June-Sept daily 10:00-14:00 & 19:00-23:00; Oct-Dec and March-May Tue-Sun 10:00-13:00 & generally also 16:00-18:00, closed Mon; closed Jan-Feb; Obala Pina Budicina 2, tel. 052/812-593, mobile 091-154-6598, www.batana.org.

Activities: The museum, which serves as a sort of cultural heritage center for the town, also presents a variety of engaging *batana*-related activities. On some summer evenings, you can take a boat trip on a *batana* from the pier near the museum. The trip, which is accompanied by traditional music, circles around the end of the Old Town peninsula and docks on the far side, where

ISTRIA

a traditional wine cellar has a fresh fish dinner ready, with local wine and more live music (June–mid-Sept, generally 2 days per week—likely Tue and Thu at 20:30, boat trip-50 kn, dinner-120 kn extra, visit or call the museum the day before to reserve). Also on some summer evenings, you can enjoy an out-

door food market with traditional Rovinj foods and live *bitinada* music. The centerpiece is a *batana* boat being refurbished before your eyes (in front of museum, 20-30-kn light food, mid-June–early Sept generally Tue and Sat 20:00–23:00—but confirm details at museum). Even if you're here off-season, ask at the museum if anything special is planned.

Rovinj Heritage Museum (Zavičajni Muzej Grada Rovinja)—This ho-hum museum combines art old (obscure classic painters) and new (obscure contemporary painters from Rovinj) in an old mansion. Rounding out the collection are some model ships, a small archaeological exhibit, and temporary exhibits.

Cost and Hours: 15 kn; mid-June–mid-Sept Tue-Sun 10:00–14:00 & 18:00–22:00, closed Mon; off-season Tue-Sat 10:00–13:00, closed Sun-Mon; Trg Maršala Tita 11, tel. 052/816-720, www.muzej-rovinj.com.

Aquarium (Akvarij)—This century-old collection of local sea life is one of Europe's oldest aquariums. Unfortunately, it's also tiny (with three sparse rooms holding a few tanks of what you'd see if you snorkeled here), disappointing, and overpriced.

Cost and Hours: 20 kn, daily June-Aug 9:00–21:00, Sept 9:00–20:00, Oct-May 10:00–16:00 or longer depending on demand, across the street from the end of the waterfront parking lot at Obala G. Paliage 5, tel. 052/804-712.

Activities in Rovinj

Boat Trips—Excursion boats leave from the end of the concrete pier in the Old Town known as the Mali Molo ("Little Pier"). In Rovinj's own little archipelago, the two most popular islands to visit by boat are **St. Catherine** (Sv. Katarina—the lush, green island just across the harbor, about a 5-minute trip, boats run about hourly in summer, 30 kn) and **Red Island** (Crveni Otok—farther out, about a 15-minute trip, boats run hourly in summer, 40 kn). Each island has a hotel and its own share of beaches.

If you're more interested in the boat trip than the destination, it's also fun to simply go for a **cruise** to the various coves and islands around Rovinj. Your two basic options are a straightforward 1.5-hour loop trip around the offshore islands for around 100 kn (often available—and especially atmospheric—at sunset); or a four-hour, 150-kn sail north along the coast and into the disappointing **"Limski Canal"** (a.k.a. "Limski Fjord"), where you'll have one to two hours of free time. Dolphin sightings are not unusual, and some outfits throw in a "fish picnic" en route for extra. To sort through your options, chat with the captains hawking excursions at the pier.

▲**Swimming and Sunbathing**—Rovinj doesn't have any sandy beaches—just rocky ones. (The nearest thing to a sandy beach is

the small, finely pebbled beach on Red Island/Crveni Otok.) The most central spot to swim or sunbathe is at **Balota Beach,** on the rocks along the embankment on the south side of the Old Town peninsula (no showers, but scenic and central). For bigger beaches, go to the wooded **Golden Cape** (Zlatni Rt) south of the harbor (past the big, waterfront Hotel Park). This cape is lined with walking paths and beaches, and shaded by a wide variety of trees and plants. For a scenic and memorable sunbathing spot, choose a perch facing Rovinj on the north side of the Golden Cape. Another beach, called **Kuvi,** is beyond the Golden Cape. To get away from it all, take a boat to an island on Rovinj's little archipelago (see previous listing).

▲**Bike Ride**—The TI's free, handy biking map suggests a variety of short and long bike rides. The easiest and most scenic is a quick loop around the Golden Cape (Zlatni Rt, described above). You can do this circuit and return to the Old Town in about an hour (without stops). Start by biking south around the harbor

and past the waterfront Hotel Park, where you leave the cars and enter the wooded Golden Cape. Peaceful miniature beaches abound. The lane climbs to a quarry (much of Venice was paved with Istrian stone), where you're likely to see beginning rock climbers inching their way up and down. Cycling downhill from the quarry and circling the peninsula, you hit the Lovor Grill (open daily in summer 10:00-16:00 for drinks and light meals)—a cute little

restaurant housed in the former stables of the Austrian countess who planted what today is called "Wood Park." From there, you can continue farther along the coast or return to town (backtrack two minutes and take the right fork through the woods back to the waterfront path).

Bike Rental: Bikes are rented at subsidized prices from the city parking lot kiosk (5 kn/hour, open 24 hours daily except no rentals in winter, fast and easy process; choose a bike with enough air in its tires or have them pumped up, as the path is rocky and gravelly). Various travel agencies around town rent bikes for much more (10-20 kn/hour); look for signs or ask around.

Nightlife in Rovinj

Rovinj After Dark

Rovinj is a delight after dark. Views that are great by day become magical in the moonlight and floodlight. The streets of the Old Town are particularly inviting when empty and starlit.

Concerts—Lots of low-key, small-time music events take place right in town (ask at the TI, check the events calendar at www .tzgrovinj.hr, and look for hand-written signs on Garibaldi street near the Square at the Bridge). Groups perform at various venues around town: right along the harborfront (you'll see the bandstand set up); in the town's churches (especially St. Euphemia and the Franciscan church); in the old cinema/theater by the market; at the pier in front of the House of the Batana Boat (described earlier, under "Sights in Rovinj"); and at the Multi-Media Center (a.k.a. the "MMC," which locals call "Cinema Belgrade"—its former name), in a cute little hall above a bank across the harbor from the Old Town.

Wine Bars—Rovinj has two good places to sample Istrian and Croatian wines, along with light, basic food—such as prosciutto-like *pršut*, truffles, and olive oil. Remember, two popular local wines worth trying are *malvazija* (a light white) and *teran* (a heavy red). At **Bacchus Wine Bar,** owner Paolo is happy to explain how the local wine has improved since communist times, when wine production stagnated. About 80 percent of his wines are Istrian, with the rest from elsewhere in Croatia and international vint-ners (15-60 kn/deciliter, most around 20-30 kn, 65-250-kn bottles, daily 7:00-1:00 in the morning, shorter hours off-season, Carera 5, tel. 052/812-154). **Piassa Granda,** on a charming little square right in the heart of the Old Town, has a classy, cozy interior and

ISTRIA

140 types of wine (18-25-kn glasses, 30-70-kn Istrian small plates, more food than Bacchus, daily 10:00-24:00, Veli trg 1, mobile 098-824-322, Helena).

Lounging—Valentino Champagne and Cocktail Bar is a memorable, romantic, justifiably pretentious place for an expensive late-night waterfront drink with jazz. Fish, attracted by its underwater lights, swim by from all over the bay...to the enjoyment of those

nursing a cocktail on the rocks (literally—you'll be given a small seat cushion and welcomed to find your own seaside niche). Or you can choose to sit on one of the terraces. Classy candelabras twinkle in the twilight, as couples cozy up to each other and the view. Patricia opens her bar nightly from 19:00 until as late as there's any action. While the drinks are extremely pricey, this place is unforgettably cool (50-65-kn cocktails, 50-kn non-alcoholic drinks, Via Santa Croce 28, tel. 052/830-683). Valentino sometimes plays thumping techno music; if you're in the mood to chill out instead, check out the **Monte Carlo** bar, along the same drag but a bit closer to the harbor, with generally mellower Rat Pack-type music and cheaper cocktails; it has fine waterfront seating, but lacks the atmospheric "on the rocks" setting of Valentino. Or consider **La Puntuleina,** beyond Valentino, with a similarly rocky ambience but lower prices (30-40-kn drinks) and a bit less panache (listed later, under "Eating in Rovinj").

Batana **Boat Activities**—In summer, the House of the Batana Boat often hosts special events such as a boat trip and traditional dinner, and an outdoor food court. For details, see the listing earlier, under "Sights in Rovinj."

Sleeping in Rovinj

Most Rovinj accommodations (both hotels and *sobe*) prefer longer stays of at least four or five nights, so in peak season (mid-July-mid-Sept), you may run into strict minimum-stay requirements or high surcharges for shorter stays (though I've noted the ones that waive this fee). Hoteliers and *sobe* hosts are somewhat more flexible in the shoulder season. Don't show up here without a room in August: Popular Rovinj is packed during that peak month.

In the Old Town
All of these accommodations are on the Old Town peninsula, rather than the mainland section of the Old Town. Rovinj has no real hostel, but *sobe* are a good budget option.

ISTRIA

Sleep Code

(5 kn = about $1, €1 = about $1.40, country code: 385, area code: 052)

S = Single, **D** = Double/Twin, **T** = Triple, **Q** = Quad, **b** = bathroom. The modest tourist tax (about 7 kn per person, per night) is not included in these rates. Hotels generally accept credit cards and include breakfast in their rates, while most *sobe* accept only cash and don't offer breakfast. While rates are listed in euros, you'll pay in kunas. Unless I note otherwise, everyone listed here speaks English (or has a relative or neighbor who can help translate).

Rates: If I've listed three sets of rates, separated by slashes, the first is for peak season (typically mid-July through late Aug), the second is for shoulder season (roughly June-mid-July and late Aug-Sept), and the third is for off-season (Oct-May). If I've listed only two rates, the first is for peak season and the second for shoulder/off-season. The dates for seasonal rates vary by hotel, and prices can change without notice; verify the hotel's current rates online or by email. For other updates, see www.ricksteves.com/update.

Price Ranges: To help you sort easily through these listings, I've divided the accommodations into three categories based on the price for a double room with bath during peak season:

$$$ Higher Priced—Most rooms €110 or more.
$$ Moderately Priced—Most rooms between €70-110.
$ Lower Priced—Most rooms €70 or less.

$$$ Hotel Villa Angelo d'Oro is your Old Town splurge. The location—on a peaceful street just a few steps off the water—is ideal, and the public spaces (including a serene garden bar and sauna/whirlpool area) are rich and inviting. The 23 rooms don't quite live up to the fuss, but if you want your money to talk your way into the Old Town, this is the place (Sb-€137/€121/€103, Db-€222/€204/€170, sea view-€20 more, family room for up to 4 people-€332/€298/€238, no extra charge for 1-night stays, closed Jan-Feb, no elevator, air-con, free Wi-Fi in lobby, free loaner bikes for guests, Vladimira Švalbe 38-42, tel. 052/840-502, fax 052/840-111, www.rovinj.at, hotelangelo@rovinj.at).

$$$ Villa Markiz, run by Danijela, has four extremely mod, stylish apartments in an old shell in the heart of the Old Town. You'll climb a steep and narrow staircase to reach the apartments, each of which has a small terrace (Db-€120/€80-100/€60; gorgeous top-floor apartment with seaview terrace-€250/€150-180/€140; no breakfast, air-con, free Wi-Fi, Pod Lukovima 1, tel. 052/841-380, mobile 095-804-0375, dani7cro@msn.com).

$$$ Hotel Adriatic, a lightly renovated holdover from the communist days, features 27 rooms overlooking the main square, where the Old Town peninsula meets the mainland. The quality of the drab, worn rooms doesn't justify the outrageously high prices... but the location might. Of the big chain of Maistra hotels, this is the only one in the Old Town (rates flex with demand, in top season figure Sb-€150, Db-€225; these prices are per night for 1- or 2-night stays—cheaper for 3 nights or more, all Sb are non-view, most Db have views—otherwise €20 less, closed mid-Oct-March, no elevator, air-con, pay Wi-Fi, some nighttime noise—especially on weekends, Trg Maršala Tita, tel. 052/803-520, fax 052/813-573, www.maistra.hr, adriatic@maistra.hr).

$$ Villa Cissa, run by Zagreb transplant Veljko Despot, has three apartments with tastefully modern, artistic decor above an art gallery in the Old Town. Kind, welcoming Veljko—who looks a bit like Robin Williams—is a fascinating guy who had an illustrious career as a rock-and-roll journalist (he was the only Eastern Bloc reporter to interview the Beatles) and record-company executive. Now his sophisticated, artistic style is reflected in these comfortable apartments. Because the place is designed for longer stays, you'll pay a premium for a short visit (50 percent extra for 2-night stays, prices double for 1-night stays), and it comes with some one-time fees, such as for cleaning. Veljko lives off-site, so be sure to clearly communicate your arrival time (smaller apartment-€98/€88/€78 plus €30 one-time cleaning fee, bigger apartment-€100 more plus €50 one-time cleaning fee, extra person-20 percent more, cash only, air-con, free Wi-Fi, lively café across the street, Zdenac 14, tel. 052/813-080, www.villacissa.com, info @villacissa.com).

$$ Casa Garzotto is an appealing mid-range option, with four apartments, four rooms, and one large family apartment in three different Old Town buildings. These classy and classic lodgings have modern facilities but old-fashioned charm, with antique furniture and historic family portraits on the walls. Thoughtfully run by a friendly staff, it's a winner (rooms—Sb-€80/€80/€70, Db-€110/€105/€90; apartments—Sb-€105/€95/€90, Db-€140/€125/€115; 2-bedroom family apartment—Sb-€105/€95/€90, Db-€145/€125/€115, Tb-€180/€160/€150; includes breakfast, off-site parking, loaner bikes, and other thoughtful extras; 25 percent extra for 1-night stays, air-con, lots of stairs, free Wi-Fi in main building, reception and most apartments are at Garzotto 8, others are a short walk away, tel. 052/811-884, mobile 099-247-9887, www.casa-garzotto.com, casagarzotto @gmail.com).

$$ Porta Antica rents 16 comfortable, nicely decorated apartments in five different buildings around the Old Town (all except La Carera are on the peninsula). Review your options on their website and be specific in your request—though in busy times (July-Aug), you may be asked to pay a surcharge to guarantee a particular apartment (Db-€100/€90/€80, cheaper for longer stays, sea views-€10-20 extra, extra person-€25, no breakfast, air-con, tries to be non-smoking, free Wi-Fi, open year-round, reception and main building next door to TI on Obala Pina Budičina, mobile 099-680-1101, www.portaantica.com, portaantica@yahoo .it, Marino).

$$ Trevisol Apartments has four new, modern units on a sleepy Old Town street, plus a few others around town. Check your options on their website, reserve your apartment, and arrange a time to meet (Db-€90/€75/€50; bigger seaview Db-€110/€80/€60; extra charge for 1-night stays: 50 percent in peak season, 30 percent off-season; no breakfast, air-con, free Wi-Fi, Trevisol 40, main office at Sv. Križa 33, mobile 098-177-7404, www.lvi.hr, Adriano).

$ Miranda Fabris is an outgoing local teacher who rents four basic, tight apartments with kitchenettes. While rough around the edges, the rooms are the cheapest I could find in the Old Town (Db-€50/€40, no extra charge for 1- or 2-night stays, cash only, no breakfast, lots of steep stairs, across from Villa Valdibora at Chiurca 5, mobile 091-881-8881, miranda_fabris@yahoo.com).

$ *Other* Sobe: Try looking for your own room online (www .inforovinj.com is helpful). Several agencies have a line on private rooms in the Old Town—but in peak season, you'll pay about 70 percent extra for a one-night stay, and 30 percent extra for a two- or three-night stay. These agencies are English-friendly and handy to the bus station (open sporadic hours, based on demand): **Futura Travel** (across from bus station at Benussi 2, tel. 052/817-281, fax 052/817-282, www.futura-travel.hr) and **Natale** (Carducci 4, tel. & fax 052/813-365, www.rovinj.com). In the Old Town, try **Planet,** near the TI (Sv. Križa 1, tel. 052/840-494, www.planetrovinj.com).

On the Mainland, Southeast of the Old Town

To escape the high prices of Rovinj's Old Town, consider the resort neighborhood just south of the harbor. These are a 10- to 20-minute walk from the Old Town (in most cases, at least partly uphill), but most of that walk is along the very scenic harborfront—hardly an unpleasant commute. While the big Maistra hotels are an option, I prefer cheaper alternatives in the same area. The big hotels are signposted as you approach town (follow signs for *hoteli*, then your specific hotel). Once you're on the road to Hotels Eden and Park, the smaller ones are easy to reach: Villa Baron Gautsch is right on the road to Hotel Park; Hotel Vila Lili and Vila Kristina are a little farther on the main road toward Eden (to the left just after turnoff for Hotel Park, look for signs).

Guest Houses and Small Hotels

These are a bit closer to the Old Town than the Maistra hotels, and offer much lower rates and more personality. The first three are hotelesque and sit up on the hill behind the big resort hotels, while the last two choices lack personality but are a great budget option relatively close to the Old Town (an easy and scenic 10-minute walk).

$$ Vila Kristina, run by friendly Kristina Kiš and her family, has 10 rooms and five apartments along a busy road. All but one of the units has a balcony (Db-€75/€70, extra bed-€40/€35, includes breakfast, air-con, no elevator, free Wi-Fi, Luje Adamovića 16, tel. 052/815-537, www.kis-rovinj.com, kristinakis@mail.inet.hr).

$$ Hotel Vila Lili is a family-run hotel with 20 rooms above a restaurant on a quiet, leafy lane. While the rooms are a bit overpriced, the extra cost buys you more hotel amenities than the cheaper guest houses listed here (Sb-€60/€50, Db-€105/€75, pricier suites also available, no extra charge for 1-night stays, elevator, air-con, free Wi-Fi, parking-30 kn/day, Mohorovičića 16, tel. 052/840-940, fax 052/840-944, www.hotel-vilalili.hr, info@hotel -vilalili.hr, Petričević family).

$$ Villa Baron Gautsch, named for a shipwreck, is a German-owned pension with 17 comfortable rooms and an inviting, shared view terrace (Db-€72/€62/€52, €10 more for balcony, they also have two Sb for half the Db price, 20 percent more for 1- or 2-night stays, only non-balcony rooms have air-con, closed late Oct-Easter, cash only, no elevator, free Wi-Fi, Ronjgova 7, tel. 052/840-538, fax 052/840-537, www.baron-gautsch.com, baron .gautsch@gmx.net).

$ Elda Markulin, whose son runs the Baccus Wine Bar, rents three rooms and four apartments in a new, modern house a short walk up from the main harborfront road (Db-€50/€45/€40, apart-ment-€75/€60/€50, small surcharge possible for short stays, cash only, air-con, free Wi-Fi, Mate Balote 12, tel. 052/811-018, mobile 091-170-7453, markulin@hi.t-com.hr). To reach it from the Old Town, walk along the waterfront; after you pass the recommended Maestral restaurant and the ragtag boatyard on your right, turn left onto the uphill Mate Balote.

$ Apartmani Tomo, next door to Elda (see directions above), is run with Albanian pride by Tomo Lleshdedaj, who rents seven rooms and nine studio apartments. While the lodgings are basic and communication can be a bit challenging, it's a handy location and the price is right (Db-€40/€35, Db with kitchen-€45/€40, smaller studio Db-€70/€60, bigger studio Db-€60/€50, extra person-€10, cash only, air-con, free Wi-Fi, Mate Balote 10, tel. 052/813-457, mobile 091-578-1518, no email—reserve by phone).

Maistra Hotels

The local hotel conglomerate, Maistra, has several hotels in the lush parklands just south of the Old Town. As all of the hotels were recently either completely renovated or built from scratch, these are a very expensive option; most of my readers—looking for proximity to the Old Town rather than hanging out at a fancy hotel—will prefer to save money and stay at one of my other listings. These hotels have extremely slippery pricing, based on the type of room, the season, and how far ahead you book. (I've listed the starting rate for a 1- or 2-night stay in July-Aug; you'll pay less if you stay longer or visit off-season. Complete rates are explained on the website, www.maistra.hr.) I've listed the hotels in the order you'll reach them as you approach from the Old Town. All hotels have air-conditioning, elevators, free parking, Internet access, and Wi-Fi, and include breakfast in their rates. The Maistra chain also has several other properties (including the Old Town's Hotel Adriatic, described earlier, and other more distant, cheaper options). Most Maistra hotels close during the winter.

$$$ Hotel Park is the humblest of the pack, with just three stars. It has 202 renovated but dull rooms in a colorized communist-era hull, and a seaside swimming pool with sweeping views to the Old Town. This is the handiest for walking into the Old Town—it's a 10-minute stroll, entirely along the stunning harborfront promenade (non-view Sb-€125, non-view Db-€225, view Db-€250, tel. 052/808-000, park@maistra.hr).

$$$ Hotel Monte Mulini is the fanciest of the bunch, with five stars, 99 rooms and 14 suites (all with seaview balconies), a beautiful atrium with a huge glass wall overlooking the cove, an infinity pool, and over-the-top prices (Db-€540, tel. 052/636-000, www.montemulinihotel.com, montemulini@maistra.hr).

$$$ Hotel Lone (LOH-neh), named for the cove it overlooks, is the newest and by far the most striking in the collection—the soaring atrium of this "design hotel" feels like a modern art museum. Also extremely expensive, its 248 rooms come wrapped in a memorable package (Db-€540, tel. 052/632-000, www.lone hotel.com, lone@maistra.hr).

$$$ Hotel Eden offers four stars and 325 upscale, imaginatively updated rooms with oodles of contemporary style behind a brooding communist facade (rates about €30 more than Hotel Park, tel. 052/800-400, eden@maistra.hr).

Eating in Rovinj

It's expensive to dine in Rovinj, but the food is generally very good-quality. Interchangeable restaurants cluster where Rovinj's Old Town peninsula meets the mainland, and all around the harbor. Be warned that most eateries—like much of Rovinj—close for the winter (roughly mid-Oct to Easter). If you're day-tripping into the Istrian interior, consider dining at one of the excellent restaurants in or near Motovun (see page 155), then returning to Rovinj after dark.

Along Rovinj's "Restaurant Row"

The easiest dining option is to stroll the Old Town embankment overlooking the harbor (Obala Pina Budičina), which changes its name to Svetoga Križa and cuts behind the buildings after a few blocks. Window-shop the pricey but scenic eateries along here, each of which has its own personality (all open long hours daily). Some have sea views, others are set back on charming squares, and still others have atmospheric interiors. I've listed these in the order you'll reach them. You'll pay top dollar, but the ambience is memorable.

Scuba, at the start of the row, is closest to the harbor—so, they claim, they get first pick of the daily catch from arriving fishing boats. They serve both seafood and tasty Italian dishes, in a contemporary interior or at a few outdoor tables with harbor views (50-80-kn pastas, 60-150-kn main dishes, daily 11:00-24:00, Obala Pina Budičina 6, mobile 098-219-446).

Veli Jože, with a smattering of outdoor tables (no real views) and a rollicking, folksy interior decorated to the hilt, is in all the guidebooks but still delivers on its tasty, traditional Istrian cuisine (35-80-kn pastas, 45-160-kn main courses, daily 12:00-24:00, Sv. Križa 1, tel. 052/816-337).

Santa Croce, with tables scenically scattered along a terraced incline that looks like a stage set, is well-respected for its pricey seafood and pastas (50-70-kn pastas, 70-160-kn main courses, no sea views, daily 18:00-24:00, Sv. Križa 11, tel. 052/842-240).

Lampo is simpler, with a basic menu of salads, pizzas, and pastas. The only reason to come here is for the fine waterfront seating at a reasonable price (30-45-kn pastas, 60-100-kn main courses, Sv. Križa 22, tel. 052/811-186).

La Puntuleina, at the end of the row, is the most scenic (and most expensive) option. This upscale restaurant/cocktail bar/wine bar features Italo-Mediterranean cuisine served in the contemporary dining room, or outside—either on one of the many terraces, or at tables scattered along the rocks overlooking a swimming hole. The menu is short, and the selection each day is even less, since Miriam and Giovanni insist on serving only what's fresh in the market. I wouldn't pay these prices unless I got a nice table out on a terrace. Reservations are recommended (80-100-kn pastas, 120-160-kn main courses, Thu-Tue 12:00-15:00 & 18:00-22:00, closed Wed except in peak season, closed Nov-Easter, on the Old Town embankment past the harbor at Sv. Križa 38, tel. 052/813-186). You can also order just a drink to sip while sitting down on the rocks.

Just before La Puntuleina, don't miss the inviting **Valentino Champagne and Cocktail Bar**—with no food but similar "drinks on the rocks" ambience (described earlier, under "Nightlife in Rovinj"). If you're on a tight budget, dine cheaply elsewhere, then come here for an after-dinner finale.

Barba Zuane, while not on "Restaurant Row," is just a couple of blocks behind it, buried deep in the Old Town. As it has some of the best indoor atmosphere in Rovinj—with rustic old Venetian coziness, and a well that looks down into a cistern now filled with the kitchen's stock room—it's a good rainy-day option. Chef Boris spent 20 years cooking in Italy before returning to his native Croatia (60-80-kn pastas, 90-130-kn main dishes, daily 12:00-23:00, Via Montalbano 1, tel. 052/811-884).

International Fare on the Old Town Peninsula

Offering upscale, international (rather than strictly Croatian) food and presentation, these options are expensive but memorable.

Krčma Ulika, a classy hole-in-the-wall run by Inja Tucman, has a mellow, cozy, art-strewn interior. Inja enjoys surprising diners with unexpected flavor combinations. The food is a bit overpriced and can be hit-or-miss, but the experience feels like an innovative break from traditional Croatian fare. Explore your options with Inja's help before ordering (12-kn cover, 100-130-kn main courses, daily 19:00-1:00 in the morning, Sun-Thu also 13:00-15:00, until 23:00 in shoulder season, closed Nov-Easter, cash only, Porečka 6, tel. 052/818-089, mobile 098-929-7541).

Monte Restaurant is your upscale, white-tablecloth splurge—made to order for a memorable dinner out. With tables strewn around a covered terrace just under the town bell tower, this atmospheric place features inventive cuisine that melds Istrian products with international techniques. Come here only if you value a fine dining experience, polished service, and the chance to learn about local food and wines more than you value the price tag (plan to spend 350-600 kn per person for dinner, daily 12:00-14:30 & 18:30-23:00, reserve ahead in peak season, Montalbano 75, tel. 052/830-203, Đekić family).

Affordable Alternatives on the Mainland

These options are a bit less expensive than most of those described above. I've listed them in the order you'll reach them as you walk around Rovinj's harbor.

Gostionica/Trattoria Toni is a hole-in-the-wall serving up small portions of good Istrian and Venetian fare. Choose between the cozy interior (tucked down a tight lane), or the terrace on a bustling, mostly pedestrian street (40-95-kn pastas, 40-130-kn main courses, Thu-Tue 12:00-15:00 & 18:00-22:30, closed Wed, just up ulica/via Driovier on the right, tel. 052/815-303).

Sidro offers a break from pasta, pizza, and fish; it's well-respected for its Balkan meat dishes such as *ćevapčići* (see the "Balkan Flavors" sidebar on page 418) and a spicy pork-and-onion stew called *mućkalica*. With unusually polite service and a long tradition (run by three generations of the Paoletti family since 1966), it's a popular local hangout (45-70-kn pastas, 55-90-kn grilled meat dishes, 75-135-kn steaks and fish, daily 11:00-23:00, closed Nov-Feb, harborfront at Rismondo 14, tel. 052/813-471).

Maestral combines affordable, straightforward pizzas and seafood with Rovinj's best view. If you want an outdoor table overlooking bobbing boats and the Old Town's skyline—without breaking the bank—this is the place. It fills a big building surrounded by workaday shipyards about a 10-minute walk from the Old Town, around the harbor toward Hotel Park (30-kn sandwiches, 45-60-kn pizzas and pastas, 45-100-kn fish and meat dishes, May-Sept open long hours daily, closed Oct-April, obala N. Nazora b.b., look for *Bavaria* beer sign).

Breakfast

Most rental apartments come with a kitchenette handy for breakfasts (stock up at a neighborhood grocery shop). Cafés and bars along the waterfront serve little more than an expensive croissant with coffee. The best budget breakfast (and a fun experience) is a picnic. Within a block of the market, you have all the necessary stops: the Brionka bakery (fresh-baked cheese or apple strudel); mini-grocery stores (juice, milk, drinkable yogurt, and so on); market stalls (cherries, strawberries, walnuts, and more, as well as an elegant fountain for washing); an Albanian-run bread kiosk/café between the market and the water...plus benches with birds chirping, children playing, and fine Old Town views along the water. For a no-fuss alternative, you can shell out 50 kn for the buffet breakfast at Hotel Adriatic (daily 7:00-10:00, until 11:00 July-Aug; described earlier, under "Sleeping in Rovinj").

Rovinj Connections

By Bus

Rovinj's bus station is open limited hours (Mon-Fri 6:30-9:15 & 9:45-16:30 & 17:00-20:00, Sat 7:30-13:30, Sun 8:30-13:30). As always, confirm the following times before planning your trip. Fares listed here are approximate and vary based on the company and route. Bus schedules are dramatically reduced on Saturdays and especially on Sundays, as well as (in some cases) off-season. Bus information: tel. 060-333-111.

From Rovinj by Bus to: Pula (about hourly, 45 minutes, 30-40 kn), Poreč (6-9/day, 1 hour, 30-45 kn), Rijeka (4-7/day, 2-3.25 hours, 90-125 kn), Zagreb (6-9/day, 3-6 hours, 150-200 kn), Venice (1/day Mon-Sat departing very early in the morning—likely at 5:40, arriving Venice at 10:00, none Sun, 185 kn). In the summer, you can reach Slovenia—including Piran (2.5 hours) and Ljubljana (5.5 hours)—by hopping on the 8:00 bus from Rovinj (June-late Sept only; off-season, a similar bus may run 2/week at 6:00, stopping at Portorož near Piran en route to Ljubljana). A second bus to Ljubljana may run sporadically on summer afternoons (around 17:00). You can also reach Piran (and other Slovenian destinations) with a transfer in Umag and Portorož. A bus departs Rovinj every evening at 19:00 for the Dalmatian Coast, arriving in Split at 6:00 (445 kn) and Dubrovnik at 11:00 (630 kn). (If this direct bus isn't running, you can take an earlier bus to Pula, from where this night bus leaves at 20:00; also note that Pula has two daytime connections to Split.)

Route Tips for Drivers

Just north of Rovinj, on the coastal road to Poreč, you'll drive briefly along a seven-mile-long inlet dubbed the Limski "Fjord" (Limski Zaljev). Supposedly the famed pirate Captain Morgan was so enchanted by this canal that he retired here, founding the nearby namesake town of Mrgani. Local tour companies sell boat excursions into the fjord, which is used to raise much of the shellfish that's slurped down at local restaurants. Calling this little canal a "fjord" outrages Norwegians—it's not worth going out of your way to see. Along the road above the canal, you'll pass kiosks selling grappa (firewater, a.k.a. *rakija*), honey, and other homemade concoctions.

Pula

Pula (POO-lah, Pola in Italian) isn't quaint. Istria's biggest city is an industrial port town with traffic, smog, and sprawl...but it has the soul of a Roman poet. Between the shipyards, you'll discover some of the top Roman ruins in Croatia, including a stately amphitheater—a fully intact mini-Colosseum that marks the entry to a seedy Old Town with ancient temples, arches, and columns.

Strategically situated at the southern tip of the Istrian Peninsula, Pula has long been a center of industry, trade, and military might. In 177 B.C., the city became an important outpost

of the Roman Empire. It was destroyed during the wars following Julius Caesar's death and rebuilt by Emperor Augustus. Many of Pula's most important Roman features—including its amphitheater—date from this time (early first century A.D.). But as Rome fell, so did Pula's fortunes. The town changed hands repeatedly, caught in the cross-fire of wars between greater powers—Byzantines, Venetians, and Habsburgs. After being devastated by Venice's enemy Genoa in the 14th century, Pula gathered dust as a ghost town...still of strategic military importance, but otherwise abandoned.

In the mid-19th century, Italian unification forced the Austrian Habsburgs—whose navy had been based in Venice—to look for a new home for their fleet. In 1856, they chose Pula, and over the next 60 years, the population grew thirtyfold. (Despite the many Roman and Venetian artifacts littering the Old Town, most of modern Pula is essentially Austrian.) By the dawn of the 20th century, Pula's harbor bristled with Austro-Hungarian warships, and it had become the crucial link in a formidable line of imperial defense that stretched from here to Montenegro. As one of the most important port cities of the Austro-Hungarian Empire, Pula attracted naval officers, royalty...and a young Irishman named James Joyce who was on the verge of revolutionizing the literary world.

Today's Pula, while no longer quite so important, remains a vibrant port town and the de facto capital of Istria. It offers an enjoyably urban antidote to the rest of this stuck-in-the-past peninsula.

ISTRIA

Planning Your Time

Pula's sights, while top-notch, are quickly exhausted. Two or three hours should do it: Visit the amphitheater, stroll the circular Old Town, and maybe see a museum or two. As it's less than an hour from Rovinj, there's no reason to spend the night.

Orientation to Pula

(area code: 052)

Although it's a big city, the tourist's Pula is compact: the amphitheater and, beside it, the ring-shaped Old Town circling the base of an old hilltop fortress. The Old Town's main square, the Forum, dates back to Roman times.

Tourist Information

Pula's TI overlooks the Old Town's main square, the Forum. It offers a free map and information on the town and all of Istria (daily May-Oct 8:00-22:00, Nov-April 9:00-16:00, Forum 3, tel. 052/219-197, www.pulainfo.hr).

Arrival in Pula

By Car: Pula is about a 45-minute drive south of Rovinj. Approaching town, follow *Centar* signs, then look for the amphitheater. You'll find a large pay lot just below the amphitheater, toward the waterfront (4 kn/hour, 20 kn/all day).

By Bus: As you exit the bus station, walk toward the yellow mansion, then turn left onto the major street (ulica 43 Istarske Divizije); at the roundabout, bear left again, and you'll be headed for the amphitheater (about a 10-minute walk total).

By Train: The train station is a 15-minute walk from the amphitheater, near the waterfront (in the opposite direction from the Old Town). Walk with the coast on your right until you see the amphitheater.

By Plane: Pula's small airport, which is served by various low-cost airlines, is about 3.5 miles northeast of the center. Since there's no convenient public bus option, count on paying 100 kn for the taxi ride into town. Airport info: tel. 052/530-105, www.airport-pula.com.

Helpful Hints

Car Rental: To rent a car in Pula, **Avis** is the most central (Riva 14, tel. 052/224-350). Several other companies have offices at the airport, which is a 100-kn taxi ride outside of town (see "Arrival in Pula," above).

Local Guide: If you'd like a local guide to help you uncover the story of Pula, **Mariam Abdelghani** leads great tours of the

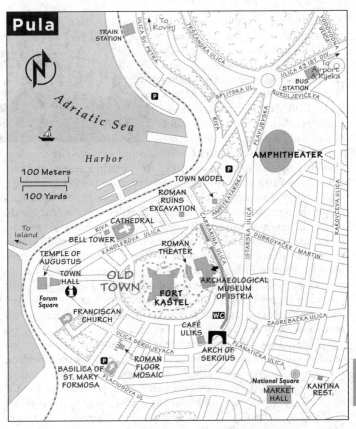

major sites (€80 for a 2-hour city tour, €160 for an all-day tour of Istria, mobile 098-419-560, mariam.abdelghani@gmail .com).

Self-Guided Walk

Welcome to Pula

This walk is divided between Pula's two most interesting attractions: the Roman amphitheater and the circular Old Town. About an hour for each is plenty. More time can be spent sipping coffee al fresco or dipping into museums.

• *Begin at Pula's main landmark, its...*

Amphitheater (Amfiteatar)

Of the dozens of amphitheaters left around Europe and North Africa by Roman engineers, Pula's is the sixth-largest (435 feet long and 345 feet wide) and one of the best-preserved anywhere.

This is the top place in Croatia to resurrect the age of the gladiators.

Cost and Hours: 40 kn, daily May-Sept 8:00-21:00—sometimes later for special events, April 8:00-20:00, Oct 9:00-19:00, Nov-March 9:00-17:00. The 30-kn audioguide narrates 20 stops with 30 minutes of flat, basic data on the structure.

◒ Self-Guided Tour: Go inside and explore the interior, climbing up the seats as you like. An "amphi-theater" is literally a "double theater"—imagine two theaters, without the back wall behind the stage, stuck together to maximize seating. Pula's amphitheater was built over several decades (first century A.D.) under the reign of three of Rome's top-tier emperors: Augustus, Claudius, and Vespasian. It was completed around A.D. 80, about the same time as the Colosseum in Rome. It remained in active use until the beginning of the fifth century, when gladiator battles were outlawed. The location is unusual but sensible: It was built just outside town (too big for tiny Pula, with just 5,000 people) and near the sea (so its giant limestone blocks could be transported here more easily from the quarry six miles away).

Notice that the amphitheater is built into the gentle incline of a hill. This economical plan, unusual for Roman amphitheaters,

saved on the amount of stone needed, and provided a natural foundation for some of the seats (notice how the upper seats incorporate the slope). It may seem like the architects were cutting corners, but they actually had to raise the ground level at the lower end of the amphitheater to give it a level foundation. The four rectangular towers anchoring the amphitheater's facade are also unique (two of them are mostly gone). These once held wooden staircases for loading and unloading the amphitheater more quickly. At the top of each tower was a water reservoir, used for powering fountains that sprayed refreshing scents over the crowd to mask the stench of blood.

And there was plenty of blood. Imagine this scene in the days of the gladiators. More than 25,000 cheering fans from all social classes filled the seats. The Romans made these spectacles cheap or even free—distracting commoners with a steady diet of mindless entertainment prevented discontent and rebellion. (Hmm... *American Idol,* anyone?) Canvas awnings rigged around the top

---

Amphorae

In museums, hotels, and restaurants all along the Croatian coast, you'll see amphorae. An amphora is a jug that was used

to transport goods when the ancient Greeks ruled the seas, through about the second century B.C. Later, the Romans also used their own amphorae. These tall and skinny ceramic jugs—many of them lost in ancient shipwrecks—litter the Adriatic coastline.

Amphorae were used to carry oil, wine, and fish on long sea journeys. They're tapered at the bottom because they were stuck into sand (or placed on a stand) to keep them upright in transit. They also have a narrow neck at the top, often with two large handles. In fact, the name comes from the Greek *amphi pherein*, "to carry from both sides." The taller, skinnier amphorae were generally used for wine, while the fat,

short ones were for olive oil. Because amphorae differ according to their purpose and nationality, archaeologists find them to be a particularly useful clue for dating shipwrecks and determining the country of origin of lost ships. This is made easier by later Roman amphorae, which are actually stamped with the place they came from and what they held.

ISTRIA

of the amphitheater shaded many seats. The fans surrounded the "slaying field," which was covered with sand to absorb blood spilled by man and beast, making it easier to clean up after the fight. This sand *(harena)* gave the amphitheater its nickname...arena.

The amphitheater's "entertainers" were gladiators (named for the *gladius,* a short sword that was tucked into a fighter's boot). Some gladiators were criminals, but most were prisoners of war from lands conquered by Rome, who dressed and used weapons according to their country of origin. A colorful parade kicked off the spectacle, followed by simulated fights with fake weapons. Then the real battles began. Often the fights represented stories from mythology or Greek or Roman history. Most ended in death for the loser. Sometimes gladiators fought exotic animals—gathered at great expense from far corners of the empire—which would enter the arena from the two far ends (through the biggest arches). There were female gladiators, as well, but they always fought other women.

While the life of a gladiator seems difficult, consider that it wasn't such a bad gig—compared to, say, being a soldier. Gladiators were often better paid than soldiers, enjoyed terrific celebrity (both in life and in death), and only had to fight a few times each year.

Ignore the modern seating, and imagine when the arena (sandy oval area in the center) was ringed with two levels of stone seating and a top level of wooden bleachers. Notice that the outline of the arena is marked by a small moat—just wide enough to keep the animals off the laps of those with the best seats, but close enough so that blood still sprayed their togas.

After the fall of Rome, builders looking for ready-cut stone picked apart structures like this one—scraping it as clean as a neat slice of cantaloupe. Sometimes the scavengers were seeking the iron hooks that were used to connect the stone; in those oh-so "Dark Ages," the method for smelting iron from ore was lost. Most of this amphitheater's interior structures—such as steps and seats—are now in the foundations  and walls of Pula's buildings...not to mention palaces in Venice, across the Adriatic. In fact, in the late 16th century, the Venetians planned to take this entire amphitheater apart, stone by stone, and reassemble it on the island of Lido on the Venetian lagoon. A heroic Venetian senator—still revered in Pula—convinced them to leave it where it is.

Despite these and other threats, the amphitheater's exterior has been left gloriously intact. The 1999 film *Titus* (with Anthony Hopkins and Jessica Lange) was filmed here, and today the amphitheater is still used to stage spectacles—from Placido Domingo to Elton John—with seating for about 5,000 fans. Recently, the loudest concerts were banned, because the vibrations were damaging the old structure.

Before leaving, don't miss the museum exhibit (in the "subterranean hall," down the chute marked #17). This takes you to the lower level of the amphitheater, where gladiators and animals were kept between fights. When the fight began, gladiators would charge up a chute and burst into the arena, like football players being introduced at the Super Bowl. As you go down the passage, you'll walk on a grate over an even lower tunnel. Pula is honeycombed with tunnels like these, originally used for sewers and as a last-ditch place of refuge in case of attack. Inside, the exhibit—strangely dedicated to "viniculture and olive-oil production in Istria in the period of antiquity" instead of, you know, gladiators—is surprisingly interesting. Browse the impressive collection of amphorae (see sidebar), find your location on the replica of a fourth-century A.D. Roman map (oriented with east on top), and ogle the gigantic grape press and two olive-oil mills.

• *From the amphitheater, it's a few minutes' walk to Pula's Old Town, where more Roman sights await. Exit the amphitheater to the left and walk one long block up the busy road (Amfiteatarska ulica) along the small wall, bearing right at the fork. When you reach the big park on your right, look for the little, car-sized...*

Town Model

Use this handy model of Pula to get oriented. Next to the amphitheater, the little water cannon spouting into the air marks the blue house nearby, the site of a freshwater spring (which makes this location even more strategic). The big star-shaped fortress on the hill is Fort Kaštel, designed by a French architect but dating from the Venetian era (1630). Read the street plan of the Roman town into this model: At the center (on the hill) was the *castrum*, or military base. At the base of the hill (the far side from the amphitheater) was the forum, or town square. During Pula's Roman glory days, the hillsides around the *castrum* were blanketed with the villas of rich merchants. The Old Town, which clusters around the base of the fortress-topped hill, still features many fragments of the Roman period, as well as Pula's later occupiers. We'll take a counterclockwise stroll around the fortified old hill through this ancient zone.

The huge anchor across the street from the model celebrates Pula's number-one employer—its shipyards.

• *Continue along the street. At the fork, again bear right (on Kandlerova ulica—level, not uphill). Notice the **Roman ruins** on your right. Just about any time someone wants to put up a new building, they find ruins like these. Work screeches to a halt while the valuable remains are excavated. In this case, they've discovered three Roman houses, two churches, and 2,117 amphorae—the largest stash found anywhere in the world. (Notice the harbor just behind, which suggests this might have been a storehouse for off-loaded amphorae.) I guess the new parking garage has to wait.*

After about three more blocks strolling through gritty, slice-of-life Pula, on your right-hand side, you'll see Pula's...

Cathedral (Katedrala)

This church combines elements of the two big Italian influences on Pula: Roman and Venetian. Dating from the fifth century A.D., the Romanesque core of the church (notice the skinny, slitlike windows) marks the site of an early-Christian seafront settlement in Pula. The Venetian Baroque facade and bell tower are much more recent (early 18th century). Typical of the Venetian style, notice how far away the austere bell tower is from the body of the church. The bell tower's foundation is made of stones that were scavenged from the amphitheater. On the square is an instructive poster illustrating the physical development of the town through the ages. The church's interior features a classic Roman-style basilica floor plan, with a single grand hall—the side naves were added in the 15th century, after a fire.

Cost and Hours: Free, generally open daily 7:00-12:00 & 16:00-18:00, but often closed.

• *Keep walking through the main pedestrian zone, past all the tacky souvenir shops and Albanian-run fast-food and ice-cream joints. After a few more blocks, you emerge into the...*

Forum

Every Roman town had a forum, or main square. Twenty centuries later, Pula's Forum not only serves the same function but has kept the old Roman name.

Two important buildings front the north end of the square, where you enter. The smaller building (on the left, with the columns) is the first-century A.D. Roman **Temple of Augustus** (Augustov Hram). Built during the reign of, and dedicated to, Augustus Caesar, this temple took a direct hit from an Allied bomb in World War II. After the war, the Allied occupiers rebuilt it as a sort of mea culpa—notice the patchwork repair job. It's the only one remaining of three such temples that once lined this side of the square. Inside the temple is a single room with fragments of ancient sculptures (10 kn, May-Sept Mon-Sat 9:00-20:00, Sun

10:00-15:00, often closed Oct-April—but you can try asking at the Archaeological Museum if you want to go in, sparse English labels). The statue of Augustus, which likely stood on or near this spot, dates from the time of Christ. Other evocative chips and bits of Roman Pula include the feet of a powerful commander with a pathetic little vanquished barbarian obediently at his knee (perhaps one of the Histri—the indigenous Istrians that the Romans conquered in 177 B.C.).

Head back out on to the square. As Rome fell, its long-subjugated subjects in Pula had little respect for the former empire's symbols, and many temples didn't survive. Others were put to new use: Part of an adjacent temple (likely dedicated to Diana) was incorporated into the bigger building on the right, Pula's medieval **Town Hall** (Gradska Palača). If you circle around behind this building, you can still see Roman fragments embedded in the back. The Town Hall encapsulates many centuries of Pula architecture: Romanesque core, Gothic reliefs, Renaissance porch, Baroque windows...and a few Roman bits and pieces. Notice the interesting combination of flags above the door: Pula, Croatia, Istria (with its mascot goat), Italy (for the large ethnic minority here), and the European Union (since Croatia is a candidate country).

• *Consider dropping by the TI on this square before continuing our circular stroll down the main drag, Sergijevaca. You'll pass by a small park on your right, then a block of modern shops. Immediately after the Kenvelo shop on the right (with a red-and-black K sign), turn right into the white, unmarked doorway. Emerging on the other side, turn left, walk to the metal grill, and look down to see the...*

Roman Floor Mosaic (Rimski Mozaik)

This hidden mosaic is a great example of the Roman treasures that lie below the old center of Pula. Uncovered by locals who were cleaning up from World War II bombs, this third-century floor was carefully excavated and cleaned up for display right where it was laid nearly two millennia ago. (Notice that the Roman floor level was about six feet below today's.) The centerpiece of the mosaic depicts the punishment of Dirce. According to the ancient Greek legend, King Lykos of Thebes was bewitched by Dirce and abandoned his pregnant queen. The queen gave birth to twin boys (depicted in this mosaic), who grew up to kill their deadbeat dad and tie Dirce to the horns of a bull to be bashed against a mountain. This same story is famously depicted in the twisty *Toro Farnese* sculpture partly carved by Michelangelo (on display in Naples' Archaeological Museum).

• *For an optional detour to Byzantine times, walk into the parking lot just beyond the mosaic. Near the end of the lot, on the left-hand side, is a fenced-off grassy field. At the far end of the field is the small...*

Basilica of St. Mary Formosa (Kapela Marije Formoze)

We've seen plenty of Roman and Venetian bric-a-brac, but this chapel survives from the time of another Istrian occupier: Byzantium. For about 170 years after Rome fell (the sixth and seventh centuries A.D.), this region came under the control of the Byzantine Empire and was ruled from Ravenna (now in Italy, across the Adriatic, south of Venice). Much of this field was once occupied by a vast, richly decorated basilica. This lonely chapel is all that's left,

ISTRIA

but it still gives a feel for the architecture of that era—including the Greek cross floor plan (with four equal arms) and heavy brick vaulting. An informational sign posted nearby outlines the original basilica and floor plan.

• *Back on the main drag (Sergijevaca), continue a few more blocks through Pula's most colorful and most touristy neighborhood, until you arrive at the...*

Arch of Sergius (Slavoluk Sergijevaca)

This triumphal arch, from the first century B.C., was Michelangelo's favorite Roman artifact in Pula. Marking the edge of the original

Roman town, it was built to honor Lucius Sergius Lepidus. He fought on the side of Augustus in the civil wars that swept the empire after Julius Caesar's assassination. The proto-feminist inscription proudly explains, "Silvia of the Sergius family paid for this with her own money." Statues of Silvia's husband, Lucius, plus her son and her brother-in-law, once stood on the three blocks at the top of the arch. (Squint to see the *Sergivs* name on each block.) On the underside of the arch is a relief of an eagle (the symbol of Rome) clutching an evil snake in its talons.

• *Before going under the arch, look to your left to see a famous Irishman appreciating the view from the terrace of...*

Café Uliks

In October 1904, a young writer named James Joyce moved from Dublin to Pula with his girlfriend, Nora Barnacle. By day, he taught English to Austro-Hungarian naval officers at the Berlitz language school (in the yellow building just behind). By night, he imagined strolling through his hometown as he penned short stories that would eventually become the collection *Dubliners*. But James and Nora quickly grew bored with little Pula and moved to Trieste in March 1905. Even so, Pula remains proud of its literary connections.

• *Now pass through the arch, into a square next to remains of the town wall. Continue straight ahead (up two bustling blocks, along the in-love-with-life Flanatička street) to...*

National Square (Nardoni Trg) and Market Hall

Pula's market hall was an iron-and-glass marvel when inaugurated in the 19th century. This structure is yet another reminder

of the way the Austro-Hungarian Empire modernized Pula with grace and gentility. You'll find smelly fish on the ground floor (Mon-Sat 7:00-13:30, Sun 7:00-12:00) and an inviting food circus upstairs (Mon-Fri 7:00-15:00, Sat 7:00-14:00, Sun 7:00-12:00). All around is a busy and colorful farmers' market that bustles until about 13:00, when things quiet down.

• *Our tour is finished. If you're ready for lunch, consider one of the cheap options inside the market hall, or walk one block to Kantina (see "Eating in Pula," later).*

*When you're done here, backtrack to the town wall. As you face the Arch of Sergius, take a right and walk under the leafy canopy next to the wall. Keep an eye out (mostly on your left, along the wall) for more Roman remains. Among these are the **Twin Gates** (Porta Gemina), marking the entrance to a garden that's home to the **Archaeological Museum of Istria** (described next, under "Sights in Pula"). With more time, you can also consider a trip to the hilltop fortress, **Fort Kaštel**. Otherwise, we've completed our circular tour—the amphitheater is just around the corner.*

Sights in Pula

Archaeological Museum of Istria (Arheološki Muzej Istre)—If Pula's many ruins intrigue you, here's the place to scratch your Roman itch. This museum, over a century old, shows off some of what you've seen in the streets, plus lots more—stone monuments, classical statues, ancient pottery...you name it.

Cost and Hours: 20 kn; May-Sept Mon-Fri 9:00-20:00, Sat-Sun 10:00-15:00; Oct-April Mon-Fri 9:00-14:00, closed Sat-Sun; Carrarina 3, tel. 052/351-301, www.ami-pula.hr.

Nearby: On the hill behind the museum (and free to visit even if you don't buy a museum ticket) is its highlight, the remains of a **Roman Theater** (Rimsko Kazalište). Part of the stage is still intact, along with the semicircle of stone seats (some of which are still engraved with the names of the wealthy theatergoers who once sat in them). To find it, go up the hill around the right side of the museum. This was the smaller of the two theaters in Roman Pula; the second was south of the center (and is no longer intact).

Fort Kaštel—For a bird's-eye view over the town, head up to its centerpiece fortress. This deserted-feeling place, hosting the Historical Museum of Istria, is worth visiting only for the chance to wander the ramparts. While neither the museum nor the fortress is worth the hike up here, it's a good way to kill some extra time in Pula and sample the views over the town and amphitheater (various trails lead up from the streets below).

Eating in Pula

The best lunch options are in and near the town's **market hall** (which is also where my self-guided walk ends). The top floor of the market is a food circus with a number of cheap and tempting eateries with both indoor and terrace seating. Upstairs in the back, look for **Laterna,** with unusually classy decor and fish specialties. Back outside, **Pekarna Corona**—a bakery across from the right side of the market (as you face the main entrance)—serves up good, fresh, cheap *burek,* the phyllo-dough pastry (Mon-Fri 6:30-18:00, Sat 6:30-15:00, closed Sun).

Kantina Restaurant, a block away, serves good lunches (including veggie options) and hearty, creative 35-kn salads both in an elegant vaulted cellar and on a lazy shady terrace. The service can be slow—if you're in a rush, eat at the market hall instead (50-75-kn pastas, 90-130-kn meat dishes, daily 12:00-23:00, at the end of the pedestrian zone at Flanatička 16, tel. 052/214-054). They also have a smaller café (drinks only, no food) directly across from the market hall.

Pula Connections

By Bus from Pula to: Rovinj (about hourly, 45 minutes, 30-40 kn), **Poreč** (12/day, 1.5 hours, 75 kn), **Opatija** (12-14 day, 2 hours), **Rijeka** (nearly hourly, 2-2.5 hours, 100 kn), **Zagreb** (almost hourly, 3.75-6 hours, 190 kn), **Split** (2/day, 10 hours, plus 1 night bus—described next, 400 kn), **Venice** (1/day departing at 5:30, arrives Venice 10:45). A night bus departs Pula at 20:00, going to **Split** (arrives 6:00), where you can connect to **Dubrovnik** (arrives 11:00). To reach destinations in **Slovenia** (including Piran and Ljubljana), you'll first transfer in Umag; or, in the summer, you can take the 8:00 bus from Rovinj (described on page 130); these buses, which tend to be in flux, may originate in Pula—ask at the bus station. Be aware that bus connections are more frequent on weekdays (fewer departures Sat-Sun). Bus info: toll tel. 060-304-090.

By Train to: Zagreb (3/day, 6 hours, transfer in Rijeka), **Ljubljana** (1/day Thu-Sun mid-July-Aug only, 4.75 hours, transfer in Hrpelje-Kozina).

ISTRIA

The Brijuni Islands

The Brijuni Islands (bree-YOO-nee, Brioni in Italian)—an archipelago of 14 islands just offshore from the southern tip of the Istrian Peninsula—were a favorite haunt of Marshal Tito, the leader of communist Yugoslavia. The main island, called Great Brijuni (Veli Brijun), was where Tito liked to show off the natural wonders of his beloved Yugoslavia to visiting dignitaries and world leaders. Today the island is a national park that combines serene natural beauty with quirky Yugoslav sights—offering a strange but enjoyable time capsule of the Tito years.

As you'll see from the remains of previous occupants (Romans, Byzantines, Venetians, Austrians—even dinosaurs), Tito wasn't the first to fall in love with Brijuni. Its first tourist boom came at the turn of the 20th century, when Austrian entrepreneur Paul Kupelwieser developed Brijuni into a world-class health resort. Between the World Wars, it hosted many notables, from Douglas Fairbanks and John D. Rockefeller to Richard Strauss and Hirohito. But when Tito took power, he claimed the islands for himself, making Brijuni his summer residence from 1949 until 1979. During this time, the island hosted a steady stream of VIP visitors from the East, the West, and the non-aligned world (see sidebar). Just three years after Tito's death, in October 1983, Brijuni opened to the public as a national park.

Getting There: You can get to Great Brijuni Island only on one of the national park's boats. These depart from the town of Fažana, five miles north of Pula and 20 miles south of Rovinj. From Rovinj, drive southeast to Bale, where you'll get on the *ipsilon* highway and continue south. In Vodnjan, watch for the easy-to-miss turnoff (on the right) marked for Fažana and Brijuni. Once in Fažana, follow brown *Brijuni* signs and park along the water (confirm with park ticket office that your parking spot is OK).

Cost and Information: The price varies depending on the time of year: July-Aug-210 kn, June and Sept-200 kn, April-May and Oct-170 kn, Nov-March-125 kn; includes park entry, round-trip by boat to the island, and a guide (see "English Tour," below). Tel. 052/525-882, www.brijuni.hr, izleti@brijuni.hr.

Hours: From April through October, the first boat departure from Fažana is at 6:45 and the last trip is at 21:45 (last return from Brijuni at 23:00). The number of departures varies with the time of year: May-Sept about hourly, 12/day; March-April and Oct 8/day; Nov-Feb 4/day.

English Tour: You're required to go to the island with a four-hour guided tour, much of which is spent on a little tourist train. The only English-language tour usually departs Fažana daily

Brijuni: Center of the Non-Aligned World

Many visitors to the former Yugoslavia mistakenly assume this country was part of the Soviet Bloc. It most decidedly wasn't. While the rest of "Eastern Europe" was liberated by the Soviets at the end of World War II, Yugoslavia's own, homegrown Partisan Army forced the Nazis out themselves. This allowed the country—and its new leader, the war hero Marshal Tito—a certain degree of self-determination following the war. Though the new Yugoslavia was socialist, it was not Soviet-style socialism. After formally breaking ties with Moscow in 1948, Tito steered his country toward a "third way" between the strict and stifling communism of the East and the capitalist free-for-all of the West. (For more on Tito's system, see the Understanding Yugoslavia chapter.)

Many other countries also didn't quite fit into the easy East-versus-West dichotomy embraced by the US, USSR, and Europe. On July 19, 1956, the Brijuni Declaration—signed by Tito, Jawaharlal Nehru of India, and Abdel Nasser of Egypt—created the Non-Aligned Movement (NAM). Members recognized each other's sovereignty and respected each leader's right to handle domestic issues however he or she saw fit.

As Tito's international prominence grew, the list of visitors to his Brijuni Islands hideaway began to read like a Who's Who of post-WWII world leaders. In addition to Nehru and Nasser, Tito hosted Haile Selassie (Ethiopia), Yasser Arafat (Palestine Liberation Organization), Fidel Castro (Cuba), Indira Gandhi (India), Muammar al-Gaddafi (Libya), Queen Elizabeth II (Great Britain), Willy Brandt (West Germany), Leonid Brezhnev (USSR)...not to mention Elizabeth Taylor (US) and Sophia Loren (Italy).

In principle, the NAM was envisioned as a competitor of NATO and the Warsaw Pact. But as the world's politics have changed, many NAM members are now closely allied with other, more powerful nations. And when Yugoslavia broke up, most of the countries that emerged preferred to join NATO and the EU.

So whatever happened to the rest of the NAM? It's still going strong, with 120 member states encompassing virtually all of Africa, the Middle East, Southeast Asia, and Latin America. While the EU and the US wrestle for bragging rights as the world's superpower, the NAM represents a majority (55 percent) of the world's population.

ISTRIA

at 11:30. It's essential to call ahead to confirm the schedule and reserve a space on the tour (call at least a day before, or three days ahead in peak season, tel. 052/525-882).

If you can't make it on the English tour, you're welcome to join any tour you like (Croatian, German, Italian, etc.). While it's possible to slip away from your group and explore the island on your own, park officials discourage it. (But, since hotel guests on the island can move about freely, it's generally no problem.) Staying with the tour for most of the trip is wise in any event, as there's lots of ground to cover in a limited amount of time. It's possible to rent bikes at the hotel where the boat puts in. You're technically required to take the same boat back with the rest of your tour, but this isn't closely monitored.

Visiting the Island: Great Brijuni Island can be visited only with a tour (described above). After a 15-minute crossing from the mainland town of Fažana, visitors arrive at the island's main harbor, a hub of activity and the site of its two hotels (Neptun-Istra Hotel and Karmen Hotel, Sb-€97-110, Db-€160-186 in peak season, www.brijuni.hr). Outside this area, the island is largely undeveloped, with just a few tourist facilities and houses of people who live here. There are virtually no cars—most people get around by bike, golf cart, or the little tourist train you'll board to begin your tour. As you spin around the island, you'll enjoy views over its endlessly twisty coast, with cove after tranquil cove. Your guide will impart both dry facts and eye-rolling legends while you putter past several intriguing sights, periodically giving you a chance to get off the train and explore a few of them up close.

The tour's highlight is the **"Tito on Brijuni"** exhibit. Dating from 1984—four years after his death, but before the end of Yugoslavia—this exhibit celebrates the cult of personality surrounding the head of this now-deceased nation. The museum (with English descriptions) features countless photos of Tito in every Brijuni context imaginable—strolling, sunbathing, skeet shooting, schmoozing with world leaders and movie stars, inspecting military officers, playing with camels given to him by Muammar al-Gaddafi, and so on. (For more on Tito, and why this former dictator remains so beloved in his former lands, see the sidebar on page 680.) Smaller side-exhibits include a taxidermy collection of exotic animals given to Tito by foreign leaders from around the world and photos of Paul Kupelwieser, the Austrian magnate who put Brijuni on the tourist map.

Another high point of the island tour is the **safari,** featuring a diverse menagerie of animals (or their descendants) brought here for Tito as gifts by visiting heads of state. Because many of the non-aligned nations are in Africa, Asia, or other non-European regions, some of these beasts are particularly exotic. Aside from the Istrian ox and Istria's trademark goat, you'll see llamas, Somali sheep, Shetland ponies, chamois, and more. Your train may stop for a visit with Sony and Lanka, a pair of Indian elephants given to Tito by Indira Gandhi, the former prime minister of India. There once were camels, cheetahs, ostriches, monkeys, bears, and bobcats as well, but most of these have gone to the great non-aligned safari in the sky, and their bodies are now preserved at the "Tito on Brijuni" exhibit.

Other attractions you may see on Brijuni: an ancient, gnarled olive tree supposedly dating from the fourth century A.D.; the remains of a mostly first-century A.D. Roman *villa rustica* (country estate); the ruined street plan of a Byzantine fort; a 15th-century Gothic church with an exhibit on frescoes and Glagolitic (early Croatian) script; a Venetian summer house that hosts an archaeology museum; an Austro-Hungarian naval fort (Brijuni was strategically important back when Pula was Austria's main naval base); and footprints left by a dinosaur who vacationed here 120 million years before Tito.

Birders can look for some of the 250 avian species that live on the island in the summer. Gardeners may spot some exotic, non-native plant species (more gifts, to go along with all those animals), such as Australian eucalyptus. And Republicans can drool over the golf course, a reminder that Brijuni is attempting to cultivate a ritzy image. Your tour's lengthy stop at the bar/gift shop is yet another indication that, while some remember Tito fondly, good ol' capitalism is here to stay.

Poreč

When you tell Europeans you're going to Istria, they say, "Ah, you must go to Poreč!" Poreč (poh-RETCH, Parenzo in Italian), the tourist capital of the Istrian coast, is the kind of resort that brags about how many hotel beds it has, rather than how many museums, churches, or gelato stands are packed into its Old Town. They're also proud to have more than their share of "blue-flag beaches" (which they call *laguna*s)—meaning that the water is crystal-clear for swimming. Finally, Poreč has won several "Croatia's cleanest city" contests. None of this makes for very compelling sightseeing, but...there you go.

Despite the town's appeal to Europeans, most American visitors find Poreč too big to be charming, but too small to be exciting. Its only real sight is the basilica, with its exquisite mosaics. Beyond that, it's mostly interesting as a case study on how Germans like to vacation: Set up camp for a week at a distant resort hotel, bake in the sun, and occasionally trek into the Old Town for dinner. Think of it as the Croatian Acapulco.

Planning Your Time

For the typical speedy American visitor, spending time in Rovinj, Piran, Pula, or the Istrian interior is more satisfying. If you're still curious, see Poreč en route or as a day trip: Zip in, stroll the Old Town, ogle the mosaics in the basilica, then move on. Despite its many hotels, Poreč lacks soul—I prefer sleeping elsewhere.

Orientation to Poreč

(area code: 052)

Like so many Croatian coastal towns, the Old Town of Poreč is on a peninsula. Surrounding it are miles of hotels-and-concrete sprawl. Traffic into the city funnels into Zagrebačka street, which passes the TI and ends at the spacious square named Trg Slobode. From there, Decumanus street marches straight through the middle of the Old Town.

Tourist Information

Visit the TI to pick up the information booklet, sightseeing guide, and city map (July-Aug daily 8:00-21:00; progressively shorter hours off-season until winter Mon-Fri 8:00-17:00, Sat 9:00-15:00, closed Sun; a few steps from Trg Slobode at Zagrebačka 9, tel. 052/451-293, www.to-porec.com).

Arrival in Poreč

The bus station and big parking lot straddle the base of the Old Town.

Drivers follow *Centar* and blue *P* signs to reach the big lot nearest the Old Town (8 kn/hour, 50 kn/day, take ticket as you enter and bring it with you; when leaving Poreč, pay at the kiosk before returning to your car, then wave paid ticket at exit to open gate). From the lot, walk uphill past the parking kiosk and the market until you reach big Zagrebačka boulevard, with the grass median. Turn right and continue up Zagrebačka, passing the TI (on your right) en route to Trg Slobode and the Old Town.

The **bus** station is at the other end of the Old Town. Exit the station to the right and go through the little park to the seafront and Old Town. Just up the hill is Trg Slobode and the nearby TI.

Sights in Poreč

▲**Euphrasian Basilica (Eufrazijeva Bazilika)**—This sixth-century church is a gold mine for fans of Byzantine mosaics. The otherwise dull interior is dominated by gorgeous, glittering mosaics in the apse surrounding the main altar. The top row depicts Jesus surrounded by the 12 apostles, the medallions around the

ISTRIA

arch celebrate 12 female martyrs, and front and center are Mary and Jesus surrounded by angels and martyrs—including Bishop Euphrasius, holding his namesake basilica in his arms (second from left). These date from the 170-year period after the fall of Rome (roughly 530-700 A.D.), when Istria was part of the Byzantine Empire

and was ruled from Ravenna (near Venice, across the Adriatic). The more recent (13th-century) canopy over the altar was inspired by the one in St. Mark's Basilica in Venice. Don't miss another set of mosaics in the floor just inside the door.

For more mosaics, drop into the attached **museum,** with several mosaic fragments scattered around two floors. Or climb the **bell tower** to get a bird's-eye view of Poreč.

Cost and Hours: Basilica—free, open long hours daily, no shorts; museum—15 kn, April-Sept daily 10:00-17:00, closed Oct-March; bell tower—15 kn, same hours as museum; a block off the Old Town's main drag on—where else?—Eufrazijeva street; as you walk down the main street, Decumanus, look for the archway with gold mosaics down Sv. Eleuterija street.

Poreč Connections

From Poreč by Bus to: Rovinj (6-9/day, 1 hour), **Pula** (12/day, 1.5 hours), **Piran** (2/day Mon-Fri, 1/day Sun; additional departures to **Portorož,** near Piran).

Hill Towns of the Istrian Interior

Most tourists in Croatia focus on the coast. For a dash of variety, head inland. Some of the best bits of the Croatian interior lie just a short drive from Rovinj. Dotted with picturesque hill towns, speckled with wineries and olive-oil farms, embedded with precious truffles, and grooved by meandering rural roads, the Istrian interior is worth a visit. Tucked below, between, and on top of the many hills are characteristic stone-walled villages, designed to stay cool in summer and warm in winter. The local tourist board is carefully manicuring this region's image as *the* hot new spot to find hill towns, backcountry drives, and a relaxed and relaxing lifestyle. The often-repeated comparisons to Tuscany and Provence are a stretch (if not a little ridiculous). The Istrian landscape is not as idyllic or as stunningly beautiful as those places, and because of the area's complex history, the culture is less deeply rooted. But many visitors still find themselves seduced by the *malvazija* wine, truffles, and laid-back ambience of the Istrian hill towns.

Poking around and exploring on your own is a good option here. For a quick visit, focus on the best hill town: Motovun, a

popular little burg with sweeping views. With more time, consider venturing deeper into the smaller villages that sit above the Mirna River Valley—the scenic, deserted, lost-in-a-time-warp village of Završje; the rugged, relatively untrampled artists' colony of Grožnjan; or the bigger towns of Buje and Oprtalj. Farther east—on the way to Rijeka—is the extremely remote and miniscule, yet touristy, hamlet of Hum.

One of the interior's main draws is its cuisine—especially the truffles that are discovered right here, as fresh as you can get. While Rovinj has some fine restaurants, it's worth planning your day around having lunch or dinner in the interior. Motovun has several great options, or you can head for the countryside: For the ultimate rustic rest stop (but with few truffles), dine at Konoba Astarea in Brtonigla; for truffle dishes surrounded by the forests in which they're foraged, you can go upscale at Zigante in Livade, a notch down at Livade's Konoba Dorjana, or venture into the countryside near Livade to enjoy the more rustic truffle dishes at Konoba Dolina in Gradinje. All of these are described later in more detail. The price ranges I've given for restaurants in this area are

ISTRIA

extremely wide—you can assume that the top-end dishes are truffle splurges, such as steak with white truffles (white truffles are most expensive, followed by black truffles...followed by everything else on the menu).

During the glory days of the Austro-Hungarian Empire, a twisty railway called La Parenzana (Porečanka in Croatian) connected Trieste to Poreč by way of many of northwest Istria's hill towns. While the train itself is long gone, part of its route has been converted

to a "rails-to-trails" path (you'll see signs for this around the area, and a small museum in Livade), and the many bridges and tunnels engineered to make the train line possible have become nostalgic icons of an earlier time.

You may notice that the Istrian hill towns are, in places, pretty rough and rugged. Many are abandoned, only recently having been rediscovered by artists. Remember that after Istria shifted from Italy to Yugoslavia following World War II, the "Italian exodus" saw many local peasants leave their homes behind and move into Italy proper—one reason many of these towns are still in such disrepair.

As you explore, you'll see frequent signs for wineries, olive-oil producers, and truffle shops. There's an itinerary for every interest, and the Istrian tourist board publishes a stack of well-produced brochures on every topic you can imagine (available at local TIs). One recent trend in Istria is the emergence of *agroturizams*. Like Italian *agriturismos* or Slovenian tourist farms, these are working farms that try to involve tourists in a meaningful way—sometimes just for a meal or overnight stay, but occasionally actually participating in the daily workings of the farm. For more information, pick up the free brochure (available locally), or visit www.istra.hr.

Getting Around the Istrian Interior

By Public Transportation: While it's possible to see some parts of inland Istria by public transportation, the rewards are not worth the headaches. The large hill town of Pazin is the region's transit hub, with buses to Rovinj, Pula, Poreč, and Motovun—but not the smaller villages.

By Car: The region is ideal by car. For a quick visit to only the best hill town (Motovun), just zip on the *ipsilon* highway (A9) to the Nova Vas exit, and take the mercifully flat road 44 along the Mirna River Valley straight to Motovun. But for a full day of hill town-hopping in the Istrian interior, follow my suggested route in the "More Hill Towns" section, later.

Motovun

Dramatically situated high above vineyards and a truffle-filled forest, Motovun (moh-toh-VOON, Montona in Italian, pop. 531) is the best-known and most-touristed of the Istrian hill towns. And for good reason: Its hilltop Old Town is particularly evocative, with a colorful old church and a rampart walk with the best spine-tingling vistas in the Istrian interior. It's hard to believe that race-car driver Mario Andretti was born in such a tranquil little traffic-free hamlet. Today Motovun's quiet lanes are shared by locals, tourists, and artists—who began settling here a generation ago, when it was nearly deserted.

Orientation to Motovun

(area code: 052)
Motovun is steep. Most everything of interest to tourists is huddled around its tippy-top. The main, upper entrance gate into town

deposits you at the main square, with the church on your left and Hotel Kaštel on the right. From there, you're just about two blocks in every direction from a sheer drop-off. This hilltop zone is circled by an old rampart that today offers Motovun's most scenic stroll.

Tourist Information

Motovun's main square has a small TI (Mon and Wed-Sat 11:00-15:00, closed Tue and Sun, Trg Andrea Antico 1, tel. 052/681-726); if it's closed, the gang at Hotel Kaštel dispenses tourist information.

Arrival in Motovun

Motovun's striking hilltop setting comes with a catch: Visitors usually have to hike up part of the way. A steep, twisty road connects the base of the hill with the Old Town up top. If it's not too crowded, drive as far up this road as possible until you're directed to park in the lot partway up (near the lower church, a steep 10-minute uphill walk to the main square, 20 kn/day). On extremely busy days, this lot might be full, so you may have to wait a few minutes for a car to leave; or you can park in the big lot at the foot of the hill and walk all the way up (during special events, such as the film festival, a shuttle bus may take visitors up the hill). If you're staying at Hotel Kaštel, follow the procedure explained under "Sleeping in Motovun," later. If staying elsewhere, ask your *sobe* host for advice.

Self-Guided Walk

Welcome to Motovun

The following commentary will bring some meaning to your Motovun hilltop stroll. The walk begins at the traffic barrier halfway up the hill (the highest you can drive unless you're sleeping at Hotel Kaštel).

The main drag leading up into town is lined with wine-and-truffle shops. My favorite is the Lanča family's **Etnobutiga ČA** (just above the parking lot on the right, at Gradiziol 33). This restored 17th-century house has a beautiful view terrace and a wide selection of local wines, brandies, and truffle products (most of them from the Zigante company, just across the valley). Like many people around here, Livio Lanča makes his own mistletoe brandy laced with honey (daily in season 10:00-22:00, closed Mon in Nov and entirely in Feb-mid-March, tel. 052/681-767). On the enclosed terrace downstairs, they also have a small restaurant, **Pod Napun** (45-150-kn pastas, 55-250-kn main dishes, same hours as shop).

Hike several more steep minutes up the hill. Soon you'll pass yet another traffic barrier and reach the base of the town's wall (and the recommended Mondo Konoba restaurant). Continuing up, you'll go through the first of two **defensive gateways.** Inside this passage (under the fortified gate), notice the various insignias from Motovun's history lining the walls—look for the Venetian lion, the Latin family tombstone, and the seal of Motovun (with five towers being watched over by an angel). The area above the gate was a storehouse for weapons in the 15th century, when Motovun first flourished.

Emerging from the gateway, you're greeted by sweeping views of the valley below on your right-hand side. (A coffee or light meal with this view is unforgettable; the town's lone ATM is to your left.) Just up and to the left, you'll find another defensive gateway, which is the main entrance into the heart of the **Old Town.** (Inside this gateway, notice the recommended Konoba pod Voltom restaurant.)

To your left as you come through the main gate is the yellow town church, **St. Stephen's.** The crenellated tower is a reminder of a time when this hilltop town needed to be defended. While unassuming from the outside, this austere house of worship has an impressive pedigree: It's based on designs by the famous Venetian architect Andrea Palladio (1508-1580), who greatly influenced the Neoclassical architecture of Washington, DC. The interior is a little gloomy but refreshingly lived-in—used more by locals than by tourists. On the left, notice a painting of the heart of Jesus, its eyes following you around the church (free, generally open daily 10:00-18:00 and during frequent services).

As you stand on the square in front

of the church, imagine Motovun during its annual **film festival,** when it's filled with 20,000 movie-lovers from throughout the region and around the world—often including a minor celebrity or two. This square fills to capacity, and films are projected on a giant screen at the far end (generally late July or early Aug, www .motovunfilmfestival.com).

Facing the church is the **Italian Cultural Center,** which plays an important role in this very Italian corner of Croatia. While the building is not open to the public, if your timing is right you'll enjoy beautiful music spilling out from its windows and filling the square. The local *klapa* music troupe—with men's voices harmonizing a cappella—practices here twice weekly (usually Mon and Fri evenings, at 21:00 in summer and 20:00 in winter, www.klapa motovun.com). If you hear them, find a bench and enjoy the show.

At the other end of the square is a leafy little piazza dominated by the big **Hotel Kaštel**—the main industry in town. This is also where bigwigs in town for the local film festival call home— ask the staff about recent sightings of B-, C-, and D-list celebrities. (For example, if you're staying here, you may be showering in the same bathroom once graced by Jason Biggs, star of *American Pie*. Lucky you.) In the fall, they can also arrange truffle-finding excursions for tourists (about 400 kn/person).

Between the church and Hotel Kaštel, follow the lane to the **ramparts.** Take the five-minute stroll around the Old Town on

these fortifications. While most of Croatia is overrun by stray cats, Motovun seems populated by dog lovers. If you see or hear dogs in people's backyards, it's a safe bet that they are trained to hunt for truffles in the surrounding forest.

As you breathe in the stunning panorama, notice that well-defended Motovun has been fortified three times—two layers of wall up top, and a third down below.

Sleeping in Motovun

(5kn = about $1, €1 = about $1.40, country code: 385, area code: 052)

Because it's not on the coast, Motovun's accommodations don't charge extra for one- or two-night stays. In fact, if you're staying for three or more nights, try to score a discount. Except for the big hotel, all of the places here keep the same rates all year long. Most Motovun accommodations lack air-conditioning; thick old walls

ISTRIA

and a nice breeze generally keep things cool without it.

$$ Hotel Kaštel, dominating Motovun's hilltop (and its tourist industry), is can-do, ideally located, and the only real hotel in this little burg. Most of the 33 colorful rooms have views. True to its name, the building used to be a castle, so the floor plan can be confusing (Sb-€60/€56/€53, standard Db-€102/€94/€87, Db suite or "superior" Db with air-con-€123/€116/€108, "exclusive" Db with air-con and balcony-€154/€146/€135; 10 percent discount with this book if you book direct, elevator, air-con only in some rooms, laundry service, pay Internet access and Wi-Fi, Trg Andrea Antico 7, tel. 052/681-607, fax 052/681-652, www.hotel-kastel-motovun.hr, info@hotel-kastel-motovun.hr). Guests have free access to part of the spa facilities, with a beautiful indoor pool and a spa offering a wide range of massages (starting at 150 kn/30 min, 10 percent discount with this book). Guests with cars should tell the attendant at the traffic barrier that you're staying here (he'll likely charge you a one-time 20-kn parking fee). If there's room on top, he'll let you drive up. Otherwise he'll tell you where to park and call the hotel, which will send down a free car to shuttle you up (runs until about 18:00); either way, call ahead to the hotel to figure out your options.

$ House of Gold is an injection of creativity in creaky old Motovun, filling a historic house on the road up into town with modern, minimalist, artsy decor. Youthful but still respectable—and just the right kind of funky—the three rooms share a common room with a big-screen TV, wood stove, and kitchen (non-view Db-€50, bigger view Db-€64, huge attic Db-€74, includes breakfast, cash only, free Wi-Fi, Gradziol 46—across from Etno-butiga ČA gift shop at the bottom of town, mobile 098-353-968, www.motovunaccommodation.com, brankarusnov@gmail.com, Branka). It's on the main road just above the parking lot halfway up into town—a steep 10- to 15-minute walk to the main square.

$ At Bella Vista, just below the lower defensive gateway (a five-minute uphill walk to the main square), the Kotiga family rents five apartments with cute decor and balconies that offer sweeping views across the countryside (Db-€50, no breakfast, cash only, air-con, Gradiziol 1, check in at gift shop, clearly communicate arrival time if coming after 21:00 in summer or 20:00 off-season, tel. & fax 052/681-724, mobile 091-523-0321, www.apartmani-motovun.com, info@apartmani-motovun.com, Mirjana).

$ Sobe Nena, run by sweet Nevija and Ricardo, is a good budget option at the very bottom of Motovun's hill. The two rooms are old-fashioned and basic, sharing a bathroom, but there's a fine garden to relax in. Ricardo speaks only a little English (Nevija speaks none), but they can call their daughter Doris to translate if necessary. It's a steep hike up into town, but you can try catching the shuttle bus from the lower parking lot, or—if you have a car—drive up to the parking lot partway up the hill (S-€20, D-€40, cash only, across from the gas station at Kanal 32, tel. 052/681-719, mobile 099-609-0883, sobe.nena@gmail.com).

$ Villa Maria has two fine rooms with view terraces in the Sviličić family home (Db-€50, no breakfast, cash only, air-con, free Wi-Fi, facing the defensive gate turn right and go down and around to Borgo 32, tel. 052/681-559, lorenasvilicic@gmail.com).

$ Antico Rooms is five simple rooms above the lively Café/Bar Antico, a few steps around the corner from the main square. As the rooms are not affiliated with the bar, arrange a meeting time when you reserve (Db-€30, apartment with air-con-€40, no breakfast, cash only, closed Oct-March, some rooms get late-night noise from the café—try requesting a quieter one, Pietra Kandlera 2, mobile 098-173-0019, antico_motovun@hi.t-com.hr, Tomislav and Sandra).

Eating in Motovun

Considering this is a small hill town with just a few real restaurants, all of them are impressively good; the first two listings are particularly notable. Every menu is topped by pricey (but tasty) truffle dishes—but keep in mind that these are a better investment when truffles are in season and the flavors are pungent (see sidebar, next page); otherwise you'll get older, blander truffles. Remember, there are also several excellent restaurants in the countryside near Motovun—if you're serious about food, before choosing, be sure to peruse your options in the "More Hill Towns" section, next page.

ISTRIA

Mondo Konoba, run by a typical Croatian-Italian hybrid family and located just below the lower town gate (on the left, at the base of the wall), serves up Sicilian-Istrian fusion cuisine. Most diners skip the forgettable dining room in favor of the inviting little outdoor terrace. The Mondo family's pack of five truffle-hunting dogs occasionally pays a visit (55-95-kn pastas, 60-170-kn main courses, June-Sept daily 12:00-15:30 & 18:00-22:00, closed Tue Oct-May and all of Jan, Barbakan 1, tel. 052/681-791).

Konoba pod Voltom is actually inside the town's upper, main gate (on the right, with the *Taberna* sign above the door). Motovun's most traditional eatery serves excellent, well-presented Istrian food in a cozy dining room. In good weather (June-Sept only), it's hard to beat their view loggia, just below and outside the gate (40-60-kn pastas, 60-110-kn main courses, 80-260-kn truffle splurges, Thu-Tue 12:00-22:00, closed Wed and Jan, tel. 052/681-923).

Hotel Kaštel's **Palladio Restaurant** has good food and delightful seating right on the leafy main square—but I'd skip the dull interior (40-50-kn pastas, 55-185-kn main dishes, 10

Truffle Mania

A mysterious fungus with a pungent, unmistakable flavor has been all the rage in Istria for the last decade or so. Called *tartufi* in both Croatian and Italian, these precious tubers have been gathered here since Roman times and were favored by the region's Venetian and Austrian rulers. More recently, local peasants ate them as a substitute for meat (often mixed with polenta) during the lean days after World War II.

In 1999, local entrepreneur Giancarlo Zigante discovered a nearly three-pound white truffle. In addition to making Giancarlo Zigante a very wealthy man (see page 162), this giant truffle legitimized Istria on the world truffle scene. Today, Istria is giving France's Provence and Italy's Piedmont a run for their money in truffle production. Most of Istria's truffles are concentrated in the Motovun Forest, the damp, oak-tree-filled terrain surrounding Motovun, Livade, and Buzet.

A truffle is a tuber that grows entirely underground, usually at a depth of eight inches, near the roots of oak trees. Since no part of the plant grows aboveground, they're particularly difficult to find...and, therefore, valuable. Traditionally, Istrian truffle-gatherers use specially trained dogs to find truffles. This is most productive at night, when

percent discount with this book, daily 7:00–22:00; also listed under "Sleeping in Motovun," earlier).

The simple **Montona Gallery** café, with tables along the rampart between the two gates, serves drinks and ice cream with mammoth views (open long hours daily).

More Hill Towns

While Motovun is the top hill town, you can get there by connecting a charm bracelet of appealing villages to flesh out a day exploring. Some are better for visiting (Grožnjan, Završje), others better for a meal (Brtonigla, Livade), and others worth a quick stop if you're passing through (Buje, Oprtalj, Hum). I've listed these roughly in the order you'll reach them, coming from the highway and working your way toward Motovun. While you'll traverse some slow and windy roads, this entire trip is quick—you could do the full circle (including Hum) without stops in less than three hours. This route is just a rough framework. Venture off it.

the darkness forces the dog to rely more on its sense of smell rather than sight.

There are two general types of truffles: white (more valuable and with a milder flavor—*Tuber magnatum,* known as the "Queen of the Truffles") and black. Each type of truffle has a "season"—a specific time of year when its scent is released, making it easier to find (May-Nov for black, Oct-Jan for white). Once dug up, they look pretty unassuming—like a tough, dirty pinecone.

Truffles can be eaten in a variety of ways. Thanks to their powerful and distinctive kick, they're often used sparingly for flavor—grated like parmesan cheese, or as truffle oil sprinkled over a dish. But you'll also find them in cheese, salami, olive oil, pâté, and even ice cream. Some people find that the pungent, musty aftertaste follows them around all day...and all night, when its supposed aphrodisiac qualities kick in. Because they're so rare and difficult to find, truffles are incredibly expensive—but many people are more than happy to pay royally for that inimitable flavor. Long overshadowed by other famous truffle regions, Istria is becoming more well-known for this precious local product. In 2011, American chef and TV personality Anthony Bourdain filmed a show here highlighting Istrian truffle meals (airing in 2012).

If you're a truffle nut, you'll find yourself in heaven here; if not, you may still appreciate the chance to sample a little taste of truffle. While you do that, ponder how one giant tuber changed the economy of an entire region.

ISTRIA

Run down leads from locals. Follow intriguing signs to wine-tastings, restaurants, and *agroturizams.* Sniff out some truffles in the Motovun Forest. You will see some other tourists, but this area isn't overrun...yet. There may just be some overlooked gems in the Istrian interior waiting for you to discover.

• *From Rovinj, take the fast* ipsilon *highway (A9) north. You have two exit options for this area. If you want to enjoy a meal in Brtonigla, take the Nova Vas exit, drive into Nova Vas, then follow signs for five minutes into Brtonigla. But if you want to head straight to the other towns, take the exit for Buje and skip down to that section.*

Brtonigla

Brtonigla (bur-toh-NEEG-lah, Verteneglio in Italian, literally "black soil") is a tiny wine village surrounded by vineyards. It's a bit closer to the sea than the other hill towns in this chapter, and sits above gentle slopes rather than a dramatic hilltop. But this deserted-feeling place is home to a luxurious hotel/restaurant and a well-regarded local eatery. Still, if you're not eating or sleeping here, give it a pass. Once in town, you'll find just a handful of hap-hazard streets.

Sleeping and Eating in Brtonigla: $$$ **San Rocco Hotel and Restaurant** is a family-run hotel suitable for a serious splurge. A few years ago this was the abandoned shell of a traditional Istrian house; now, after an extensive renovation, it's a cushy and elegant hotel with traditional beams-and-stone decor and all the modern amenities. With 12 rooms, an outdoor pool, a big indoor hot tub and sauna, and distant views of the Adriatic, it's a welcoming retreat. "Tradition" rooms come with views or Jacuzzi tubs (Db-€209/€199/€179), but the simpler and smaller "classic" (Db-€189/€179/€139) and mid-sized "comfort" (Db-€199/€189/€159) rooms are plenty comfortable (Sb costs 35 percent less than Db, no extra charge for 1- or 2-night stays, air-con, elevator, Internet access, loaner bikes, other fun extras explained on their website, Srednja ulica 2, tel. 052/725-000, fax 052/725-026, www.san-rocco .hr, info@san-rocco.hr, Rita and the Fernetich family). Its **restaurant**—open to guests and non-guests alike—features traditional Istrian cuisine in a dressy dining room or outside, with poolside elegance (350-600-kn fixed-price meals, à la carte dishes for 80-250 kn, daily 13:00-24:00).

Konoba Astarea, a restaurant down the street and around the corner (on the main road toward Buje), is a local favorite for tradi-

tional, take-your-time Istrian cuisine with a focus on fish and lamb. While this isn't gourmet cooking and truffles are an afterthought, it's rustic food done well. Anton and Alma Kernjus don't print an English menu, but Anton will pull up a chair to explain your options. Choose between the warmly cluttered, borderline-kitschy dining room huddled around the blazing open fire, where Alma does a lot of the cooking, or the cool and welcoming terrace with faraway sea views. It's smart to reserve ahead (figure 210 kn per person for a full-blown multicourse meal, or 70-120 kn for individual dishes, daily 11:00-23:00, closed Nov, tel. 052/774-384).

• *From Brtonigla, simply follow signs into...*

Buje

Close to the Slovenian border, Buje (BOO-yeh, Buie in Italian) is big and striking from afar, but pretty functional up close. Still, it's worth a visit if you're passing through and curious to take a stroll through a hill town that feels more alive and workaday than the norm. Just above the parking lot are the small TI and the

ISTRIA

town museum (facing each other across the street), and higher up is another parking-lot plaza in front of Buje's pastel-yellow Church of Our Mother of Mercy (marked in Latin, *Mater Misericordiae*); from the nearby terrace, you have (distant) views of the sea. From this square, you can hike on cobbles through workaday neighborhoods. Up and to the left you'll find the squat remains of a mid-15th-century octagonal defensive tower, the small Sv. Martin church with its evocative graveyard, and a viewpoint overlooking the countryside (though views from Motovun and other towns are better). Up and to the right from the main square is the main Sv. Servol church, whose big bell tower—visible from miles around—dominates the hilltop. With a rough, unfinished facade, the church shares a fine little piazza with the local elementary school.

Sleeping and Eating near Buje: In Volpia, a nondescript village five minutes outside of Buje (toward Slovenia), you'll find a charming stone country house offering reasonably priced rooms and good food. **$$ La Parenzana,** named for the long-extinct and lamented Istrian rail line, is well-run by Guido Schwengersbauer. He rents 16 woody, simple-but-comfortable, Germanic-feeling rooms (Sb-€38, Db-€76, includes breakfast, no air-con, free Wi-Fi, rental bikes, Volpia 3, tel. 052/777-460, fax 052/777-459, www.parenzana.com.hr, info@parenzana.com.hr) and also runs a restaurant serving up truffle specialties and other dishes cooked over an open fire (60-110-kn pastas, 60-190-kn main dishes, daily 12:00-23:00). The former route of the Parenzana rail line—now a handy hiking and biking trail—runs just behind the property, and Guido runs a sweet little mini-museum about that nostalgic train trip. To get here from Buje, leave town following signs for *Trieste*, then turn off toward *Plovanija*, *Portorož*, and the Slovenian border; after a couple of minutes, watch for *Casa Parenzana* signs to the right.

• *Leaving Buje, look for signs that take you along a twisty, narrow road (via Triban) right to Grožnjan.*

▲Grožnjan

Grožnjan (grohzh-NYAHN, Grisignana in Italian) is your trapped-in-a-time-warp Istrian hill town. Its setting, artfully balanced on the tip of a vine-and-olive-tree-covered promontory, is pleasing, if not thrilling. The time-passed character of its sleepy lanes invites you to get lost and leave your itinerary on your dashboard. Not long ago, Grožnjan was virtually forgotten. But now several artists have taken up residence here, keeping it Old World but with a spiffed-up, bohemian ambience. If gallery-browsing is your idea of fun, you'll like this place.

Grožnjan has virtually no "sights," but it's a delightful place to go for a stroll. All roads lead to the convenient and free parking lot, a few steps from the traffic-free village. A few English panels are posted around town, identifying what passes for "important" buildings in this sleepy burg. The town church's bell tower is its only landmark. Inside the church, the big wall painting over the altar is shows angels intervening in the Pula amphitheater to save Christians who were thrown to the lions and tigers.

To get the lay of the land, take a 10-minute town wander: Facing the church's front door, go left and loop clockwise through town. Walking along the main street, you'll pass the Enoteka Zigante wine-and-truffle shop, then the **TI** (which doesn't have a lot to do; Gorjan 12, tel. 052/776-131, www.tz-groznjan.hr). Then you'll reach the shaded square with Café Pintur and the Bastia restaurant, then the Italian Cultural Center. Don't worry about addresses or finding a particular place; whether you want to or not, you'll find yourself walking in circles, and quickly see what there is to see. Instead, let your pulse slow and enjoy being a castaway on this isolated, tranquil hilltop.

Sleeping and Eating in Grožnjan: **$ Café Pintur,** a nondescript restaurant on a cozy Grožnjan square just downhill from the church, rents four tiny and basic but comfy top-floor rooms. The Černeka family doesn't speak much English, but the rooms are cheap and work well in a pinch (Sb-€25, Db-€40, includes breakfast Sept-May, or €5 extra June-Aug; cash only, lots of stairs with no elevator, air-con, Mate Gorjana 9, mobile 098-586-188, tel. & fax 052/776-397, ivan.cerneka@pu.t-com.hr).

Café Pintur's restaurant, open long hours daily in summer, serves up basic pasta and grilled meats (30-100-kn pastas, 45-100-kn main dishes).

Bastia, across the square and sharing a leafy terrace with Pintur, is a bit bigger, with a menu focusing on truffles (40-110-kn starters, 60-140-kn main dishes, daily 8:00-24:00, 1 Svibnja 1, tel. 052/776-370).

For a scenic **picnic,** shop at the grocery store facing the church; nearby is a fine shady terrace with benches.

Enoteka Zigante, a branch of the Istrian truffle empire described earlier, has a gifty little wine-and-truffle bar offering a more genteel nibbling experience. A glass of the best local wine with a plate of cheese and meat makes a good little lunch for about

80 kn. For dessert, step into the adjacent truffle shop and nibble a few samples (Mon-Thu 10:00-20:00, Fri-Sun 10:00-21:00, until 22:00 in peak season, ulica Gorjan 5, tel. 052/721-998).

• *From Grožnjan, follow signs for* Oprtalj. *Along the way, you'll see* Završje *signs directing you to the right.*

▲Završje

If you've ever wanted to visit a nearly deserted hill town, Završje (ZAH-vur-shyeh) is your place. Called "Piemonte d'Istria" in

Italiano, this hamlet seems to have more truffle-hunting dogs than people. One of the smallest, most compact, and most picturesquely set hill towns in the area, Završje was once just a double-walled fortress clinging to the top of its bulbous hill. Over time it sprawled just a bit outside its

original walls, but it was deserted after the post-WWII Italian exodus and remains almost uninhabited today; only a few locals live here, and virtually all of the buildings are abandoned skeletons. There's very little to actually "see" or "do" here—no museums, no restaurants, and a sporadically open church with a leaning tower and a colorfully painted Baroque altar. But the EU has taken notice in this precious little burg, and has invested in restoring its pretty pink schoolhouse (at the base of the hill, near the parking lot) and posting informative English descriptions along the street through town. Walk up through the village on this cobbled lane, peering into ruined stone houses and pondering their potential. Thanks to its priceless setting, convenient location a short drive from Motovun, and inherent charm, Završje won't be overlooked for long. If I were an entrepreneurial Istrian restaurateur, I'd set up a fancy truffle restaurant here posthaste. A stroll through here today will have a big payoff a decade from now, after little Završje has been rediscovered and repopulated with artists, hotels, and restaurants—as it surely will. You'll be able to say, "Yeah, I was there back when it was a ghost town."

• *If you want to head directly to Motovun, you can simply proceed on the road past Završje and twist down into the valley. Or, for a more scenic approach, backtrack the way you came for a couple of minutes, turning right to follow signs to* Oprtalj.

Oprtalj

Oprtalj (oh-per-TAL; Portole in Italian) has a particularly scenic approach, along a twisting driveway lined with pointy cypress trees. But once in the town itself, you'll find that there's not much to see.

Oprtalj lines up along a plateau with a busy road ripping through its middle. Like Motovun, it has a pink loggia across from its main gate, containing an old stone-carved winged lion of St. Mark and other stony fragments from the town's history. If you poke up through the gate and wander  the town, you'll find a fairly nondescript, largely deserted burg. Near the gate is the town's *konoba*, with seating under a tree out on the view terrace across the street. The fancy yellow building at the Motovun end of town is the elementary school, named for local hero Milan Šorgo, a Partisan who was killed during the fighting to retake his native Istria from the Nazis.

• *The road through Oprtalj leads directly down into Livade, then across the valley highway to Motovun.*

Livade

The flat little crossroads village of Livade, sitting in the valley facing the back of Motovun's hill, is home to the first and last name in Istrian truffles. In 1999, Giancarlo Zigante unearthed the biggest white truffle the world had ever seen—2.9 pounds, as verified by *The Guinness Book of World Records*. (In 2007, the record was broken by a 3.3-pound Tuscan truffle.) Zigante's hunk of fungus—now revered as if a religious relic—kicked off a truffle craze that continues in Istria today (see sidebar on page 156). Today Zigante has a virtual monopoly on Istria's truffle industry, producing a wide range of truffle goodies. If you're a connoisseur, or just curious, make a pilgrimage to this truffle mecca. The valley is enlivened by Livade's Tuberfest, which typically occurs the first three Sundays of October; white tents are filled with local producers showing off their truffles, wines, olive oils, and more. While here, you can also drop into Livade's little museum about La Parenzana, the railway that once linked these hill towns; follow its route on the light-up map (across the street from Konoba Dorjana, sporadic hours).

Eating in Livade: Zigante's large facility here is divided into two parts: The **Zigante Tartufi shop** offers shelves upon shelves of both fresh and packaged truffle products (plus local wines, olive oils, brandies, and more). There's also a little tasting table where you can sample the earthy goods, and a brain-sized replica of that famously massive chunk of white truffle. A small jar of preserved truffles will run you 80-150 kn, depending on the size, type of truffle, and preparation. You can even pick up a recipe sheet telling you what to do with the precious stuff once you get it home (daily 9:00-21:00, off-season 10:00-20:00, Livade 7, tel. 052/664-

030, www.zigantetartufi.com). The adjacent **Restaurant Zigante,** one of Istria's fanciest (and most expensive), dishes up all manner of truffle specialties. The decor—inside or out on the terrace—is white-tablecloth classy, the service is deliberate but friendly, and the truffles, as if on a cooking game show, are prepared in a dizzying variety of ways. If you want the full dose of this local delicacy from a place that knows its truffles, this is a worthwhile splurge (250-350-kn main dishes, 500-kn-plus fixed-price meals—even more during white truffle season, daily 12:00-23:00, until 22:00 in winter, Livade 7, tel. 052/664-302).

Livade's more affordable dining option, **Konoba Dorjana,** is across the roundabout and just down the street from Zigante. This family-run eatery has a cozy old-fashioned dining room around a giant fireplace, an inviting terrace covered by a canopy of ivy, and plenty of truffle options (45-150-kn pastas, 50-200-kn main dishes, Thu-Tue 11:00-22:00, closed Wed, Livade 4a, tel. 052/664-093).

Eating near Livade, in Gradinje: A five-minute drive east of Livade, in the hamlet of Gradinje, is a rustic, unpretentious eatery serving up the most affordable truffle dishes around. **Konoba Dolina** ("Valley Inn") has a nondescript interior and a pleasant terrace out front. Because it's just beyond the tourist trail, the prices are reasonable and the ambience is more authentic (45-95-kn meals, truffle splurges up to 120 kn, Wed-Mon 12:00-22:00, closed Tue, tel. 052/664-091). First make your way to Gradinje (go into Livade and turn right at the main roundabout, then drive through the countryside for a few minutes). Once in Gradinje, go all the way through town, then look for signs on the left.

• *Motovun hovers on the hill just across the valley from Livade (described earlier in this chapter).*

Once you've seen this area, if you have more time and interest, you can carry on another 40 minutes to reach Hum (follow the main valley road east to Buzet, then to Roč, then look for the turn-off on the right to Hum, along the Glagolitic Lane). Most people won't find the Hum detour worth the miles, but it works great if you're headed east anyway (such as to Opatija or Rijeka).

Hum

According to its market-ing plan, Hum (pronounced "hoom," Colmo in Italian) is the "smallest town in the world." While there are, no doubt, hamlets even tinier than its population of 16 peo-ple, as of a few decades ago— when first it laid claim to this

ISTRIA

honor—Hum had a Town Hall, church, school, post office, and all the other trappings of a "town"...so it wins the title on a technicality. Smart gimmick.

Unfortunately, these days Hum is also, per capita, the most touristy town in the world—crammed with visitors who come to stroll through its streets, drop some kunas in its souvenir shops, or dine at its lone restaurant, **Humska Konoba,** with fine outdoor terrace seating (70-kn fixed-price meals, 25-95-kn à la carte dishes, daily mid-May-mid-Oct 11:00-22:00, closed Mon mid-March-mid-May and mid-Oct-mid-Nov, Sat-Sun only mid-Nov-mid-March, tel. 052/660-005).

But despite its quirks and its one-trick commercialism, Hum is engaging. At the far corner of Istria—just up the road from Mount Učka, which forms the natural boundary with the neighboring Kvarner Gulf—Hum feels incredibly remote, rugged, and (if you don't run into any tour buses) forgotten by modern times.

You'll enter Hum through its main gate, formed by part of its 11th-century castle. Once inside the characteristic Old Town, you'll find cobbled lanes connecting the stone houses and 19th-century town church (with five altars). It's more rustic-feeling than many other villages, with rougher paving stones, more overgrowth, and an even more pronounced yesteryear quality. And yet, you'll still spot several *sobe* signs and souvenir shops. Popular mementos—sold at the restaurant and the shops—are little ceramic tiles with your initials using the Glagolitic alphabet (see below).

Getting There: Coming from Motovun on the road following the Mirna River, you'll pass through Buzet, following signs for *Lupoglav* and *Rijeka*. The turn-off for Hum (and the Glagolitic Lane, described next) is on the right, near the village of Roč. (If you're coming from the highway, get off at the Lupoglav exit, turn toward Ročko Polje, then continue through that village—ignoring the turn-off for Hum—until you reach Roč, with a better route to Hum.) When you're finished in Hum, you're not far from the A8 highway back to the south (the coast) or onward to the east (Rijeka or Opatija via the Učka Tunnel).

Nearby: The road between Hum and the Mirna Valley is dubbed the **Glagolitic Lane** (Aleja Glagoljaša), and commemorates a ninth-century alphabet once used for written Croatian. While the alphabet hasn't been widely used for centuries, Croatians recognize it as an integral and unique part of their cultural heritage. And in the area around Hum, they've clung to the dinosaur alphabet even more than in other parts of the country—claiming it was commonly used here into the 20th century. Today, the alphabet is even taught in some schools, and children have poetry contests and spelling bees in Glagolitic. Along the Glagolitic Lane to Hum, you'll see various monuments to this alphabet, including giant Glagolitic characters standing in a field, as well as a sort of "Rosetta Stone" on top of a hill comparing the Glagolitic, Cyrillic, and (our) Roman alphabet.

• *From Hum, you're very close to the northeast branch of the* ipsilon highway (A8). *You can take this either west to Rovinj (via Pazin), or east to the Učka Tunnel, Opatija, and Rijeka.*

THE KVARNER GULF

Opatija • Rijeka • Rab

The long stretch of Croatian coast from Istria to Dalmatia—between the cities of Rijeka and Zadar—offers twisty seaside roads, functional port towns and fishing villages, some of the country's most rugged scenery, and no real knockout sights. Croatia offers more bang for your buck to the north (Istria) and the south (Dalmatia)—but if you're connecting those areas, the Kvarner Gulf offers several suitable stopovers.

Kvarner's best mainland town is its northern gateway: the former Habsburg resort of Opatija. Shot through with faded elegance of an upper-crust history, Opatija is, if nothing else, a welcome change of pace from the salty Venetian-flavored towns along the rest of the Croatian coast. Nearby, the big industrial port city of Rijeka is best avoided, unless you need to change buses or boats there.

South of Opatija and Rijeka, the Kvarner coastline is stark and desolate—any traces of settlement have been long since blown away by the battering Bora wind (see sidebar on page 172). But offshore, sheltered from the elements, are several inviting island getaways. Each of the main islands—Krk, Cres, Lošinj, Rab, and Pag—has its own character and appeal. The best Kvarner village is Rab, on the island of the same name. Rab's pretty, peninsular Old Town, bristling with Venetian-style bell towers, overlooks a shimmering harbor and beaches full of happy swimmers and sunbathers.

Planning Your Time

The Kvarner Gulf is "passing-through" territory. While destinations in this chapter have their fans, first-timers seeing Croatia in a hurry should give the region a miss. But if you have plenty of time

The Kvarner Gulf

To Zagreb
Karlovac
Turanj
To Ljubljana
Učka
Opatija
Rijeka
Bakar
To Rovinj
Brestova
Porozina
Krk
Krk
Valbiska
Cres
Baška
Senj
Prvić
Grgur
Goli Otok
Cres
Rab
Rab Town
Jablanac
Mišnjak
Prizna
Unije
Pag
Mali Lošinj
Lošinj
Karlobag
Pag
Adriatic Sea
Olib
Vir
Zadar
CROATIA
Ogulin
Slunj
BOSNIA-HERZ.
Grabovac
Plitvice Lakes National Park
PARK ENTRANCES
Otočac
Korenica
Velebit Mtns.
Gospić
Udbina
Kurjak
Gornja Ploča
Lovinac
SVETI ROK (tunnel)
To Split & Dalmatian Coast

20 Kilometers
20 Miles

Expressway
Other Road
Boat

and your own wheels, and you're driving through anyway, Opatija and Rab are worthy overnight stops. Even with less time, Opatija still merits a quick stopover if it's on the way between your main destinations.

Driving Between Northern Croatia and Dalmatia

If you're driving between northern Croatia (Zagreb, Plitvice, Istria, or Opatija) and the Dalmatian Coast (Zadar, from where the expressway zips to Split), you have two options: Use the fast inland A1 expressway, or follow the slow Kvarner Gulf coastal road all the way down.

The **A1 expressway** option is boring but faster and far more efficient, especially from Zagreb or Plitvice. If you're coming from Zagreb, just take A1 directly to Split; from Plitvice, drive south through Korenica to access A1 at Gornja Ploča (see page 99). From Istria or Opatija, you have two options for accessing A1 that take about the same amount of time: Head east (inland) from Rijeka on

A6 to join A1; or, more interesting (and better for southern destinations), drive the Kvarner coastal road as far south as Senj, then cut inland and up over the mountains to Otočac, where you can get on A1.

The two-lane **Kvarner coastal road** (national road #8, a.k.a. E65) is twisty and slow, but more scenic. Speedy sightseers won't find it worth the time. Compared to the expressway, you'll lose at least an hour if you're coming from Istria or Opatija, and much more if you're starting in Zagreb or Plitvice. Along this road, you'll enjoy good but not spectacular views—similar to what you'll see in Dalmatia, but less developed. To find this road from Rijeka, just follow signs for *Split* and *Zadar* (being careful not to get on the expressway).

If you want to visit **Rab,** be sure to take the Kvarner coastal road; at Jablanac, catch the car ferry to Rab (see "Route Tips for Drivers" at the end of this chapter).

Opatija

Opatija (oh-PAH-tee-yah) is not your typical Croatian beach town. In the late 19th-century golden age of the Austro-Hungarian Empire, this unassuming village near the port of Rijeka was transformed into the Eastern Riviera, one of the swankiest resorts on the Mediterranean. While the French, British, and German aristocracy sunbathed on France's Côte d'Azur, the wealthy elite from the eastern half of Europe—the Habsburg Empire, Scandinavia, and Russia—partied in Opatija. Baroque, Neoclassical, and Art Nouveau villas popped up along its coastline as it became the sunny playground for barons, dukes, and other aristocrats.

Though the Habsburgs are long gone, Opatija retains the trappings of its genteel past. Most of Croatia evokes the time-passed Mediterranean, but Opatija whispers "belle époque." It may be the classiest resort town in Croatia, with more taste and less fixation on postcards and seashells. Most people don't come to Croatia for this chic scene. But if rustic seaside villages are wearing on you, Opatija—which hosts equal numbers of tourists and convention-going businesspeople—is a pleasant return to high-class civilization.

Thanks to its sheltered location nestled under high mountain peaks, Opatija is protected from the Bora wind, enjoying instead a light, refreshing breeze from Učka Mountain.

This gives Opatija a particularly mild and enjoyable climate—the perfect match for its refined ambience.

Orientation to Opatija

(area code: 051)
Opatija is basically a one-street town: Ulica Maršala Tita, lined on both sides by stately hotels, follows the seafront. The town's focal point is its beach area, called Slatina. You can walk from one end of the tourist zone to the other in about 20 minutes.

Tourist Information

Opatija's helpful TI is just a short walk up ulica Maršala Tita from Slatina. Pick up the map, information booklet, and list of hotels (mid-July-Aug daily 8:00-22:00, progressively shorter hours off-season until Nov-Easter Mon-Sat 8:00-16:00, closed Sun; from Slatina, just head a block toward Rijeka and look on the left/non-sea side of road, Maršala Tita 128; tel. 051/271-310, www.opatija -tourism.hr).

Sights in Opatija

Begin at Opatija's centerpiece, the waterfront beach-and-park area called **Slatina,** with sweeping sea views, a marbled Croatian "Walk of Fame" (with one or two names you might recognize), and a seawater swimming pool. From here, Opatija lines up along its main drag, **ulica Maršala Tita,** still fronted by ornate villas that would seem more at home in Vienna than they do in Croatia. Austrians and other tourists stroll here hand-in-hand, taking in the views, dipping into high-class boutiques, and snapping photos of the fancy facades as they go. Joining them, you, too, may soon find yourself thinking of this place as the "Monte Carlo of Croatia."

A few steps toward the sea, stretching in either direction along the waterfront, is a scenic promenade called the **Lungomare.** This is another wonderful spot for rocky seafront strolling, and it offers striking views across the bay to Rijeka (which looks much better from afar). Near the Slatina end of the Lungomare is one of Opatija's trademarks: a **statue** of a woman surrounded by seagulls, called *Greetings to the Sea.* Much as I'd like to relay some romantic legend behind this evocative monument, the truth is that there's no story behind it—like Opatija itself, it's just pretty to look at.

As for sightseeing...well, Opatija is not that kind of place. If you like, you can drop into the *opatija* (abbey) that gave the town its name, the **Abbey of St. James** (Opatija Sv. Jakov, right along the Lungomare below the TI). On the dome above the altar is a strangely eerie relief showing St. James standing in a boat, cradling this church in his arm, accom-

panied by his trademark gourd-on-a-stick, and flanked by palm trees.

Beyond the abbey, the Lungomare cuts through one of Opatija's many manicured parks and hits the harbor. Here you'll find an outdoor theater that shows movies or concerts nightly in peak season (weather permitting, check with TI for schedule).

Sleeping in Opatija

Opatija is chock-a-block full of swanky resort-slash-business hotels. While prices are high, you get a lot of luxury for your money (unlike hotels in most small coastal villages). The busiest—and most expensive—times are August (tourists) and September through late October (conventions). Sleeping in Opatija is definitely preferable to overnighting in Rijeka.

$$$ Big and Fancy: These two chain hotels are my favorites of the many opulent Opatija hotels. They have the most striking Habsburg facades in town, and both have luxurious rooms (air-con, elevator, non-smoking rooms, free Wi-Fi, and all the amenities). Each can also refer you to other, similar chain properties (price range depends on season—top price is for Aug). **Hotel Bristol,** part of the Vienna International chain, has 78 rooms. It's gone to great pains to maintain its late 19th-century decor inside and out—mixing modern comfort with period moldings, chandeliers, and a cheery yellow facade (Sb-€77-111, bigger deluxe Sb-€85-120, Db-€108-157, bigger deluxe Db-€115-165, last-minute deals possible, pay Internet access, gorgeously restored coffee shop in lobby, parking-€10, Maršala Tita 108, tel. 051/706-300, fax 051/706-301, www.hotel-bristol.hr, info@hotel-bristol.hr). **Hotel Agava,** part of the Milenij chain, also has an impressively restored old shell, but its 76 rooms feel more businesslike and contemporary. The cheaper "economy" rooms are in the attic, with small skylight windows (economy Sb-€76/€58, standard Sb-€96/€84, economy Db-€95/€82, standard Db-€144/€126, higher rates are

THE KVARNER GULF

Sleep Code

(5 kn = about $1, €1 = about $1.40, country code: 385, area code: 051)

S = Single, **D** = Double/Twin, **T** = Triple, **Q** = Quad, **b** = bathroom. The modest tourist tax (about 7 kn per person, per night) is not included in these rates. Hotels generally accept credit cards and include breakfast in their rates, while most *sobe* accept only cash and don't offer breakfast. While rates are listed in euros, you'll pay in kunas. Everyone listed here speaks English.

Rates: If I've listed two sets of rates for an accommodation, I've noted the time period in which the second rate applies (generally off-season, Oct-April); if I've listed three sets of rates, separated by slashes, the first is for peak season (July-Aug), the second is for shoulder season (May-June and Sept), and the third is for off-season (Oct-April). The dates for seasonal rates vary by hotel, and prices can change without notice; verify the hotel's current rates online or by email. For other updates, see www.ricksteves.com/update.

Price Ranges: To help you sort easily through these listings, I've divided the accommodations into three categories based on the price for a standard double room with bath in peak season:

$$$ Higher Priced—Most rooms €100 or more.
  $$ Moderately Priced—Most rooms between €60-100.
    $ Lower Priced—Most rooms €60 or less.

for mid-June–mid-Sept, sea view–€5 extra, hotel dinner–€4 extra/person, free cable Internet, Maršala Tita 89, tel. 051/278-200, fax 051/278-287, www.milenijhoteli.hr, info@milenijhoteli.hr).

$$$ *Smaller and Family-Run:* These two small hotels, run by the Brko family, are well-located a few steps from the lively Slatina scene (to the right as you face the water; both have air-con, elevators, free Wi-Fi, and limited €7 parking—reserve ahead). **Hotel Galeb,** with 25 comfortable rooms and three stars, has more character than most Opatija hotels, but is a tad overpriced. Guests at the Galeb have access to the pool and beach at the Savoy, described next (Sb-€100/€79/€71, Db-€125/€106/€95, €10 more for sea view and balcony, 10 percent less if you pay cash, pricier suites also available, Maršala Tita 160, tel. 051/271-177, fax 051/711-935, www.hotel-galeb.hr, hotel-galeb@ri.t-com.hr). **Hotel Savoy,** across the street, comes with four stars, more class, 32 nicely appointed rooms, an enticing swimming pool with a great view, a private beach, and higher prices. Request the type of room you want when you reserve: Most rooms have balconies and sea views for no extra

The Bora
Or, How to Predict Croatian Coastal Weather

When asked what tomorrow's weather will bring, a salty Croatian fisherman looks to the mountains and feels the stiff wind on his face. "Sun," he says. "The Bora brings good weather."

Like any people whose fate is tied to the sea, coastal Croatians can extrapolate a breeze or a front of clouds into a full-blown weather report. While this is a precise art cultivated over a lifetime, even the casual tourist can learn a few tried-and-tested clues from the natives.

Croatian coastal weather is shaped by a mighty wind called the Bora (named for the Greek Boreas, the North Wind; sometimes called "Bura" in Croatian, or "Burja" in Slovene). Much like France's infamous mistral wind, an unavoidable fact of life in Provence, the Bora has an indelible impact on this region's weather, vegetation, architecture, and tourism.

The Dinaric Mountains, which rise sharply up from the sea for nearly the full length of the Croatian Coast, act as a barrier for cold, cloudy weather. As the air on the coastal side of the mountains heats up, the air behind the snow-capped peaks stays cool. Something's gotta give to equalize this temperature and pressure differential. A white fringe of clouds builds up along the ridge of the mountains, as the cool air moves toward the warm air—a sure sign that the Bora is about to blow. When all that pent-up air finally escapes, the Bora comes screaming down the slopes to the sea.

The Bora occurs anywhere that mountains create two different climates in nearby terrains, including Slovenia's Karst. But the Bora's power is at its peak along the Kvarner Gulf—especially where a gap in the mountains provides a natural funnel toward the sea (such as at Senj and at Karlobag). It's strongest in the winter, when the temperature differential between the interior and the coast is most pronounced. Farther south, such as in Dalmatia, the inland remains warmer and the Bora is milder (but still strong—Bora winds blowing through the "funnel" near Dubrovnik's airport occasionally force incoming flights to divert to Split).

The Bora is not constant—it's strongest at midday and

charge, but many of these face a noisy nightclub; for maximum quiet, you can request a back (non-view) room facing the street (rates about 20 percent more expensive than Galeb, Maršala Tita 129, tel. 051/710-500, fax 051/272-680, www.hotel-savoy.hr, info @hotel-savoy.hr).

$ **Sobe:** There are no cheap hotels or hostels in Opatija, but several people rent private rooms (many on or near the main drag). You can check your options at www.opatijaholiday.com. If you show up without a room, consider stopping by one of the many

made up of intermittent, fierce gusts that can reach 150 miles per hour. Young children have been known to "fly" through the air for short distances because of the Bora. The Kvarner coastal road is closed several times each year to trucks, buses, and other high-profile vehicles, which can be tipped over by the gusts. Occasionally, Kvarner Gulf ferries (such as the Jablanac-Mišnjak connection to Rab Island) must wait patiently for the Bora to die down before they can sail safely. After a day or two of a stiff winter Bora, everything is coated with a thin layer of salt, like ash after a volcano.

The good news: As the Bora rushes toward the coast, it sweeps bad-weather clouds away with it—leaving in its wake clear, cooler air and sunshine.

In summer, the much milder version of this wind—which usually bathes the coast in a refreshing breeze each evening, when the interior cools faster than the sea—is called a Maestral. Sporadic mini-Bora gusts at night are known as Burin.

The Bora's unpopular cousin is the wind called Jugo (YOO-goh, meaning "south," as in "Yugo-slavia"). The Jugo originates as a moist air mass gathering over the Adriatic, which creates a low-pressure vortex. Finally it blows northward toward Croatia, bringing with it hot, humid, and stormy weather. Because humid conditions foster disease, an ancient superstition considers the Jugo wind evil, and the refreshing Bora wind good. The Bora and the Jugo are the yin and yang of Croatian winds, blowing in opposite directions and with opposite effects.

When all else fails, you can always fall back on the reliable old saying, which also exists in Croatian: "Red sky at night, sailor's delight." If light from the sunset is able to leak through the bottom of a bank of clouds on the western horizon, it's a sign that clearer weather lies just beyond...and should arrive by morning.

Of course, these adages are highly generalized. Croatia's coast is made up of a series of microclimates. Each island has its own very specific weather conditions, which is why one island may excel at growing olives, the next one lavender, the next red wine grapes, and the next white wine grapes. If you really want to know what sort of weather is on the way, ask a local.

room-booking agencies in town, including **Kvarner Touristik** (Maršala Tita 162, tel. 051/703-723, www.kvarner-touristik.com, office@kvarner-touristik.com).

Eating in Opatija

Many hotels offer a "half-board" option (dinner at the hotel) that can be a good value for a decent, affordable meal. Otherwise, touristy restaurants abound (especially cheap snack and pizza joints).

To browse for your own picnic, drop by the old-fashioned indoor market hall (*tržnica*, on the left a 10-minute walk up Maršala Tita from Slatina). Several hotel lobbies also have refined Vienna-style coffee houses with late 19th-century appeal. For a good sit-down meal, consider one of the following options.

Ružmarin, tucked in a residential zone just behind a row of big hotels, has an inviting covered terrace, a modern dining room, and good pizzas, pastas, and other dishes (30-50-kn pizzas, 45-70-kn pastas, 40-120-kn main dishes, daily 10:00-1:00 in the morning, up the road behind Grand Hotel Palace at Veprinački put 2, tel. 051/712-673).

Roko, along the busy main drag, has a cozy stone-and-brick interior, a small terrace, and a busy wood-fired oven turning out tasty Italian meals. If you find this place calming, it may be because it was the home of Opatija native Leo Henryk Sternbach, who invented Valium (40-80-kn pizzas and pastas, 60-140-kn main dishes, daily 11:00-24:00, Maršala Tita 114, tel. 051/711-500).

Near Opatija, in Volosko

Just to the west of Opatija—enveloped in that city's resort sprawl— is the real-feeling village of Volosko, with a busy fishing harbor surrounded by restaurants and cafés. The best-regarded is **Le Mandrać,** named for the enclosed, square fishing harbor that it sits on. With a contemporary-styled interior and a partially glassed-in terrace, this splurge restaurant serves up classic Croatian flavors using modern methods (such as *sous-vide*), upscale presentation, and a touch of French and Asian-fusion flair. As it earns raves for its creative approach to local cooking, reservations are smart in the summer (60-190-kn dishes, four-course "mini-*menu*" for 270 kn, nine-course "exploring *menu*" for 490 kn, obala F. Supila 10, tel. 051/701-357). Volosko is adjacent to Opatija, in the direction of Rijeka; you can walk from Opatija to Volosko in about 30 minutes, or drive there in five (you'll dive along the top of town, then take a hard right to head down to the lower street and look for parking, and finally walk down one more level to the waterfront and harbor).

Opatija Connections

Opatija is connected to the nearby transportation hub of **Rijeka** twice each hour by bus (20-30-minute trip). A few long-distance buses depart from Opatija, near Slatina square. Buses to the east depart from in front of Grand Hotel Palace, including **Zagreb** (5-6/day), **Split** (2/day), and **Dubrovnik** (1/night); connections to Istria, to the west, depart from the bus stalls in the middle of the square, including **Pula** (12-14/day, 2 hours) and **Rovinj** (4/day).

Rijeka

The industrial city of Rijeka (ree-YAY-kah; it translates as "River") became Croatia's biggest port under Austro-Hungarian rule. It's dainty little Opatija's bigger, burlier brother. Like Opatija, much of Rijeka's architecture is reminiscent of the glory days of the Habsburgs. But unlike Opatija, most of Rijeka's buildings haven't been renovated in the last century or so, giving it a seedy, gritty, past-its-prime feel. Avoid Rijeka if you can. However, since it's a major transportation hub, there's a good chance you'll pass through. Here are the basics.

The bus station, train station, and ferry terminal are within a few blocks of each other in a bustling waterfront business zone. The sector is crossed by two one-way streets (going in opposite directions): Ivana Zajca (or the "Riva," along the waterfront, runs west to east) and Adamićeva (which changes its name a few times as it cuts east to west through town).

A block above these two streets is the **Korzo,** an almost-charming pedestrianized zone packed with shops, restaurants, and the **TI** (mid-June-mid-Sept Mon-Sat 8:00-20:00, Sun 9:00-14:00; mid-Sept-mid-June Mon-Fri 8:00-19:30, Sat 8:00-13:30, closed Sun; Korzo 14, tel. 051/335-882, www.tz-rijeka.hr).

The **train station** is a few blocks west of the Korzo. On arrival, exit the station to the right and walk 10 minutes to the water. You'll first come to the bus station, then the ferry terminal. The Korzo is just above them.

The **bus station** is basically a big parking lot in the middle of the chaos, near the west end of the Korzo. You'll see the big boats along the waterfront as you exit your bus. To get to the train station, face the water and turn right, following the busy street about 10 minutes.

The **ferry terminal** is at the east end of the waterfront. The Jadrolinija ticket office is in the building with the big *Jadrolinija* sign (at Riva 16, second building east of bus station, ticket office at far right end of building as you face it).

Some of Rijeka's **car-rental** offices are conveniently located right downtown, on the main harborfront street: **Avis** is at Riva 8 (tel. 051/311-135), and **Hertz** is at Zadarska 3B (tel. 051/311-098).

Rijeka Connections

From Rijeka by Boat to: Rab (1/day, 1.75 hours by passenger catamaran—see "Rab Connections," later), the **Dalmatian Coast** (slow
Jadrolinija car ferry, 2/week June-Sept only, departs in the evening
and goes overnight to Split, then onward down the coast; figure 11
hours to **Split**, 18 hours to **Korčula**, 21 hours to **Dubrovnik**).

From Rijeka by Train to: Zagreb (2/day, 4 hours), **Ljubljana**
(2-3/day direct, 2.75 hours).

From Rijeka by Bus to: Opatija (2/hour, 30 minutes, 25 kn),
Senj (hourly, 1.5 hours, 70 kn), **Rab town** (2-3/day, 3 hours, 135
kn), **Pula** (nearly hourly, 2-2.5 hours, 100 kn), **Rovinj** (4-7/day,
2-3.25 hours, 90-125 kn), **Zagreb** (hourly, 2.5 hours, 120-165 kn),
Split (7-10/day including some night buses, 7.75-8.5 hours, 260-350
kn), **Dubrovnik** (1-3/day, 12.5-13 hours, 410-510 kn), **Ljubljana** (2/
day in summer, less off-season, 2.5 hours, 170 kn). For schedules,
see www.autotrans.hr or call 051/213-821.

Rab

Rab (pronounced "Rob," like the man's name) is the most appealing Croatian island north of the Dalmatian Coast. Though it's one
of the greenest islands in the northern Adriatic, its landward half
(including where the ferry from the mainland docks) is an eerily
dry, rocky moonscape—the result of saltwater blown ashore by
harsh Bora winds. But on the seaward side of the island, you'll
find lush vegetation, as well as the island's main town, also called
Rab. Rab's Old Town peninsula is nestled along a sleepy harbor.
Along the spine of the Old Town are four different Venetian-style

campaniles (bell towers)—Rab's
claim to touristic fame. A relaxing seafront promenade runs behind the Old Town.

Rab was independent and strong in
the 14th century, but soon after became
a backwater outpost of Venice. In the
19th century, when Rab was part of the
Habsburg Empire, Austrians found its
beaches a fine place to catch some rays
(their descendants still do). In fact, Rab
Island kicked off the nude-beach boom
that's still going strong in Croatia: In
1936, England's King Edward VIII
came to Rab on holiday with his soon-to-be wife, Wallis Simpson.
Edward wanted to work on an all-over tan, so he went through

THE KVARNER GULF

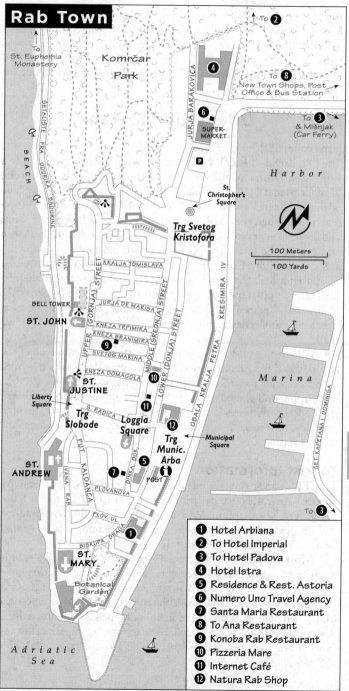

Rab Town

THE KVARNER GULF

1 Hotel Arbiana
2 To Hotel Imperial
3 To Hotel Padova
4 Hotel Istra
5 Residence & Rest. Astoria
6 Numero Uno Travel Agency
7 Santa Maria Restaurant
8 To Ana Restaurant
9 Konoba Rab Restaurant
10 Pizzeria Mare
11 Internet Café
12 Natura Rab Shop

the proper channels to have one of Rab's beaches designated for nudists. Inspired by the English monarch's example, other visitors to Rab followed suit (er, dropped suit)...and a phenomenon was born. Keep your eyes peeled for the letters *FKK* (*Freikörper Kultur*, German for "free body culture"), which is pan-European code for nudism.

Orientation to Rab

(area code: 051)
The Old Town of Rab is on a long, tapering peninsula alongside a tidy harbor. Three parallel streets run the length of the peninsula: **"Lower Street"** (Donja ulica, just off the harbor, a narrow lane with a few cafés and discos); **"Middle Street"** (Srednja ulica, a few steps higher, the bustling main drag lined with souvenir shops and ice-cream stands); and **"Upper Street"** (Gornja ulica, a steep climb up at the top of the peninsula, with most of Rab's churches and campaniles). Along the harbor are Rab's two biggest squares: St. Christopher's Square (Trg Svetog Kristofora), with a makeshift art gallery and steps leading up into the park; and businesslike Municipal Square (Trg Municipium Arba), with a huddle of al fresco café umbrellas surrounded by the TI, post office, and Town Hall.

Where the Old Town peninsula attaches to the rest of the island, you'll find the extensive, lush **Komrčar Park,** which is filled with trees and crisscrossed with walking paths. A few steps off the harbor, beyond the park from the Old Town, is a **"New Town"** (called Palit) with modern amenities such as grocery stores, travel agencies, bakeries, an open-air produce market, a post office, and the bus station.

Tourist Information
The **TI,** with a smattering of local brochures, is on Municipal Square (generally open daily June-Sept 7:00-21:00, Oct-May 8:00-15:00, Trg Municipium Arba 8, tel. 051/724-064, www.tzg-rab.hr). In peak season (June-Sept), there's a second, smaller branch near the bus station in the New Town.

Most of Rab's travel agencies—where you can find a *soba* or apartment, rent bikes and scooters, and sign up for excursions—are in the New Town. More convenient is the only travel agency in the Old Town, **Numero Uno,** at the corner of the harbor where the Old Town peninsula meets the mainland (open long hours daily in season, shorter hours off-season, between the big supermarket and Hotel Istra on Šetalište Markantuna de Dominisa, tel. 051/724-688, www.numero-uno.hr).

Self-Guided Walk

Rab's Old Town

Don't get bogged down figuring out which campanile is which, or trying to make too much of Rab's humdrum history. Simply enjoy the lazy ambience. Instead of sightseeing, use Rab as an excuse to take a vacation from your vacation. This 30-minute walk will give you the lay of the land.

Begin at the big **St. Christopher's Square** (Trg Svetog Kristofora). Peruse the starving artists' work and admire the sculpture

fountain. These star-crossed lovers, from the island's two big feuding families, are the protagonists of Rab's favorite legend. Kalifront (the bronze guy with the goatee) was desperately in love with a peasant girl named Draga (in the fountain). But since Draga had taken a vow of celibacy to the Roman goddess Diana, she couldn't give in to Kalifront's advances. Draga begged Diana for help, and Diana turned her to stone to prevent any hanky-panky. Tears from the petrified Draga became the spring of a fountain of youth. Diana punished the

randy Kalifront by turning him into a half-man-half-tree, fed by the spring of his unrequited lover—and sentenced to watch her eternally from afar.

Look across the harbor to the ridge that runs along the spine of the island. Notice the little **stone walls** climbing up the hill. These walls, called *gromače*—which you'll see throughout the region—traditionally served three purposes: to mark property boundaries, to prevent erosion, and to provide a convenient place for farmers to get rid of big rocks unearthed while tilling.

Continue into town on **Middle Street** (Srednja ulica, near the base of the big staircase). You'll pass restaurants, galleries, tacky souvenir shops (with T-shirts so obscene you can only admire their creativity), and the town's Internet café (look for @ sign on left). Along the way, stop to drool over a few of the ice-cream *(sladoled)* stands—many run by Kosovo Albanians who live on Rab. When you emerge into the little piazza with the pillared loggia, detour through the tunnel on the left.

THE KVARNER GULF

The Dark History of Rab

For some more serious, somber sightseeing—and a severe contrast to otherwise lighthearted Rab—you can pay your respects at the remains of a **concentration camp** operated by Mussolini's occupying forces during World War II. Tens of thousands of Jews and political prisoners (many of them Slovenes) were interned here; thousands of them died. It's odd to think this facility was Italian, rather than German—making this, for many, a surprising footnote in WWII history. The site is now a graveyard memorial (on the road to Lopar, about three miles northwest of Rab town).

Offshore from Rab Island (to the north) are two smaller islands with a troubled history. After Yugoslav president-for-life Tito split from Moscow in 1948 to pursue his own brand of communism, he arrested Yugoslavs who remained loyal to the Soviet Union. Many of them ended up on the "gulag island" of **Goli Otok** ("Barren Island"). In a strange parallel to the US's McCarthyism, the late 1940s and early 1950s were an era of great anti-Soviet paranoia in communist Yugoslavia. This period—called *Informbiro*, after the Soviet secret police—is the subject of the Oscar-nominated Croatian film *When Father Was Away on Business*. Near Goli Otok, **Grgur Island** hosted a women's prison in the early Yugoslav era. Prisoners were forced to carve Tito's name and a giant star of communism into the hillside (still faintly visible). It's difficult to visit these islands, but you may see them as you drive around Rab Island and along the mainland.

Municipal Square (Trg Municipium Arba), the second of Rab's two harborfront squares, is home to several outdoor cafés, the recommended Astoria restaurant, and the TI (at the far corner, near the waterfront). Also on this square is the family-run **Natura Rab** shop, selling all-organic, all-local products from Rab, including various types of olive oil, honey, lavender, and *rakija*—the local firewater, like Italian grappa (July-Aug daily 9:30-13:00 & 19:00-23:00, shorter hours in shoulder season, closed in winter, www.natura-rab.hr). Just to the right of Natura Rab is the old Rector's Palace (marked with a distinctively carved balcony), the former residence of the Venetian governor.

With your back to the harbor, go to the top-left corner of the square, with the post office (notice the wall of old-fashioned wooden mailboxes inside). Walk down the street the P.O. is on (Biskupa Draga) until you emerge into a sweet little **botanical garden.** This peaceful oasis is watched over by a statue of St. Marin—the Rab-born stonecutter who went to Italy and founded the statelet of San Marino, which remains an independent nation today. (If you continue out the far end of the garden, you'll reach the tip of the Old Town peninsula.)

Take the ramp up from the garden, and find your way to the start of **Upper Street** (Gornja ulica), marked by a big church and a piazza with palm trees. As you stroll along this street with the sea on your left, you'll pass several little monasteries and churches, four of which boast Rab's trademark bell towers (named for, in order, Saints Mary, Andrew, Justine, and John the Evangelist). If a church is open, poke inside (or look through the grate to see the interior); some of them have modest museums attached. You can climb the first **bell tower** (St. Mary, 10 kn, closed for a long mid-day siesta), but it's better to climb the fourth tower, by the ruins of the seventh-century Church of St. John (Sveti Ivan), because it's free and always open.

Halfway along Upper Street, you'll reach **Liberty Square** (Trg Slobode), marked by a single, huge Holm oak. Stairs behind the tree lead down to the embankment that runs behind the peninsula—a fine place for swimming or strolling (see "Activities in Rab").

Beyond the fourth bell tower, Upper Street runs into a small staircase. Go up the stairs and into the garden courtyard, where more stairs on the right lead up to the top of a rampart with a fine view over Rab's rooftops. Continuing past the courtyard leads you into the park—a nicely shaded place to relax.

Activities in Rab

Swimming—As with most beaches in Croatia, Rab's are largely pebbly or rocky. The best swimming area is along the back (non-harbor) side of the Old Town peninsula and park (accessed from Liberty Square/Trg Slobode on Upper Street). This concrete sidewalk running along the waterfront has a few low-key cafés and several sets of steps descending into the sea that make things easy for swimmers. (To stretch your legs, continue along this embankment for about 30 minutes to the Franciscan Monastery of St. Euphemia—not worth going out of your way for, but a suitable excuse for a waterfront stroll.)

Reaching the island's sandy beaches (away from the Old Town) takes a little more effort. Sahara Beach, the best beach, is clothing-optional (some people wear swimsuits, but most are nude). It's at the north end of the island, past the town of Lopar (easiest to take the bus

to the town of San Marino, then water taxi or walk to Sahara—get details at Rab TI).

Shopping—Trinkets don't get much tackier than the ones on Rab. But with a little searching, you can find some worthwhile souvenirs (try the Natura Rab shop on the Municipal Square—described earlier, in the "Self-Guided Walk"). Look for local honey, grape brandy, and lavender. The next island over, Pag, produces a tasty cheese called *paški sir*—with an herby/salty flavor that is said to come from the sea-air-blown vegetation the sheep graze on.

Other Activities—To get out and see the island, you can rent a bike or scooter, or join an excursion by bus or boat (all are available at hotel reception desks and at travel agencies—see "Tourist Information," on page 178). Boat captains along the harborfront offer cruises to various secluded coves on Rab and nearby islands. With a bike, you can ride the trails in Kalifront and Frkanj (get a good map when you rent your bike).

Sleeping in Rab

(€1 = about $1.40, country code: 385, area code: 051)
Rab's season is very brief. If I've listed three rates, separated by slashes, they indicate high season (late July-late Aug), shoulder season (early June-late July and late Aug-mid-Sept), and low season (mid-Sept-early June); some rates can be even lower in winter.

$$$ **Hotel Arbiana** is a splurge hotel with 28 plush rooms at the tip of Rab's Old Town peninsula (Sb-€90/€80/€70, standard Db-€165/€130/€100, superior Db-€30 extra, air-con, elevator, free Wi-Fi, Obala Petra Krešimira 12, tel. 051/775-900, www.arbiana hotel.com, sales@arbianahotel.com).

$$$ *Imperial Rab Hotels:* Most of Rab's big hotels are run by this company. These communist-era hotels have been nicely renovated, but—as is usual for big resort hotels in little island towns—the prices are too high. The best-located option is the **Hotel Imperial,** with 134 rooms in the park just beyond the end of the harbor (Sb-€73/€56/€50, non-view Db-€120/€90/€80, seaview Db-€136/€102/€90, "superior" seaview Db-€140/€110/€100, €3 more for a balcony, tel. 051/724-522, www.imperial.hr, imperial @imperial.hr). **Hotel Padova** looms across the harbor from the Old Town (a 20-minute walk away; non-view Sb-€90/€68/€60, seaview Sb-€105/€75/€65, non-view Db-€120/€94/€80, seaview Db-€140/€106/€90, tel. 051/724-544, www.imperial.hr, padova @imperial.hr). Both hotels have elevators, air-conditioning, and Internet access and Wi-Fi in the lobby.

$$$ **Hotel Istra,** at the corner of the harbor where the Old Town peninsula meets the mainland, is an old communist-style hotel now run by the Renić family. Its 100 rooms are dingy and not

air-conditioned, but the location and lack of other options makes it worth considering (Sb-€63/€48/€45, Db-€106/€76/€70, €4 extra/person for a balcony, elevator, Šetalište Markantuna de Dominisa b.b., tel. 051/724-134, fax 051/724-050, www.hotel-istra.hr, hotel -istra@hi.t-com.hr).

$$ Residence Astoria rents five comfortable apartments over the restaurant of the same name, in a restored Venetian palazzo right in the center of town. It overlooks the bustling Municipal Square, but the rooms have air-conditioning that helps keep things quiet (Db-€60-110/€50-100/€40-80, specific price depends on size and amenities, one-week minimum July-Aug, 30 percent extra for 1- or 2-night stays, Trg Municipium Arba 7, tel. 051/774-844, mobile 098-907-2654 or 099-227-9357, www.astoria-rab.com, astoria@astoria-rab.com).

$ Sobe *and Apartments:* As with elsewhere in Croatia, the best budget option is to stay in a room in a private home *(soba)* or rent an apartment. Every travel agency in Rab has a line on rooms; Numero Uno is well-located and well-established (see "Tourist Information" on page 178).

Eating in Rab

Rab has a cuisine scene that's typical for a Croatian resort town—a dozen pizzerias, a half-dozen seafood joints, and some splurges—but a few eateries stand above the rest. All of these recommendations (except Ana) are in the Old Town. As with everything in Rab, opening times flex with the season (long hours daily in summer with a mid-afternoon break, shorter hours or closed entirely off-season).

Astoria is a good choice for a splurge, with lots of delectable seafood options. Sit inside or out on the terrace overlooking the Municipal Square (open daily for lunch and dinner, closed 15:00-18:00 and off-season, on Trg Municipium Arba 7, tel. 051/774-844).

Ana Restaurant serves up pastas, seafood, and Balkan-style grilled meats in a residential-feeling area just beyond the New Town commercial center. My only listing outside the Old Town, it lacks the charm—and crowds—of the Old Town eateries, but the food is delicious (daily 11:00-15:00 & 18:00-24:00; go up the New Town's main drag, then turn right just after the open-air produce stalls and look for signs, Palit 80, tel. 051/724-376).

Konoba Rab, run by the father-and-son Vidas family, has good seafood and an over-the-Croatian-village-rooftops interior (daily 10:00-14:00 & 17:00-23:00; about halfway down Middle Street, look for sign leading up the stairway to Upper Street, Kneza Branimira 3, tel. 051/725-666).

Santa Maria specializes in grilled meat, but you'll also find fish on the menu. Though the food gets mixed reviews, it has the most impressive interior in town, including nautical decor reminiscent of its namesake ship and a giant old-fashioned skylight that pulls in a refreshing breeze (daily 10:00-14:00 & 17:00-23:00; just beyond the end of Middle Street, continue straight up the narrow alley after the piazza with the loggia, on the right at Dinke Dokule 6, tel. 051/724-196).

Pizza: There's no shortage of pizza and pasta eateries in Rab's Old Town. I enjoy **Pizzeria Mare,** serving up pizza with a soft and tasty crust (daily 9:00-22:00, entrances from both Middle and Lower Streets, Srednja ulica 8).

Rab Connections

By Public Transportation

Getting to Rab can be frustrating by public transportation. It's easy to reach by boat from Rijeka, but it's slow and complicated to continue southward. This makes it difficult to visit Rab efficiently between northern destinations (such as Slovenia or Istria) and the Dalmatian Coast.

Without a car, the easiest way to reach Rab is by **fast passenger catamaran** from Rijeka (1/day in each direction; generally leaves from Rab's harborfront early in the morning—Mon-Fri at 6:45, Sun at 9:45, return boat leaves Rijeka at 17:00; 1.75-hour trip, 60 kn in June-Sept, 50 kn off-season). Rab Island is also connected by other ferries and by taxi boats to nearby islands (such as Krk to the north), and a regular car ferry keeps it linked to the mainland (see "Route Tips for Drivers," next).

Buses connect Rab to the mainland using the Mišnjak-Jablanac ferry. Buses to the north are easy and straightforward: **Rijeka** (2-3/day, 3 hours, 135 kn), **Senj** (partway up the coast to Rijeka—see below; 2-4/day, 1-2 hours, 70 kn), and **Zagreb** (3/day direct in summer, 5.5 hours, 210 kn; off-season you'll probably transfer in Senj).

Taking the bus to destinations to the south (such as **Zadar,** at the start of the Dalmatian Coast) is more complex and very slow, since you'll be following the windy coastal road all the way down to Zadar (connections speed up from Zadar to Split). To get on a southbound bus from Rab, you'll have to take one of the northbound buses across to the mainland, then transfer to a southbound bus. After the ferry docks at Jablanac, the bus climbs up to a roadside bus stop called Magistrala, where you can transfer (often requires a long wait for the next bus); or continue another 45 minutes north to **Senj** to transfer. Carefully confirm the transfer schedule at the station before you set out. Rab's bus station is in the New Town (bus info: tel. 051/724-189).

Route Tips for Drivers

Rab is a relatively straightforward stopover if you have a **car.** Driving along the Kvarner coastal road between Rijeka and Zadar, you'll pass above Jablanac (follow signs off the main road down a twisty one-way road to this coastal ferry-port town). In summer, the Rapska Plovidba car ferry makes the 20-minute crossing more or less continuously between Jablanac and Mišnjak, a lonely dock at the very barren end of Rab Island (a 15-minute drive along the length of the island from Rab town). In the busiest times (weekends in July-Aug), you may have to wait up to a few hours to drive your car on. Off-season, the ferry still crosses at least eight times per day.

It's striking how desolate it feels as you drive along the Kvarner coastal road. Between Jablanac (with the Rab ferry) and Rijeka, the most appealing spot for a break is **Senj** (pronounced "sehn"—the j is mostly silent, but has a slight *y* sound). Senj has a little harbor and a modest square with a jumble of outdoor cafés. The town is watched over by the boxy fortress of a band of pirates called the Uskoks. These were Serb and Croat refugees forced out of their homes in the interior when the Ottomans invaded in the 16th century. After resettling here in Senj, they became pirates and began terrorizing the Adriatic coastline. While they claimed to target only Ottoman ships, they also harassed anyone who traded with the Ottomans—including the Venetians. Finally the Austrians—bowed by political pressure from Venice—put down the Uskoks. Today Senj is the best jolt of civilization along this road, with busloads of tour groups constantly dropping off here for a coffee-and-WC break. This means that the natives of Senj—perhaps harkening back to their pirate ancestors—are adept at overcharging and shortchanging visitors. Check your bill carefully against the posted menu prices.

Senj is also the easiest point where the Kvarner coastal road connects to the speedy A1 expressway that runs parallel to the coast inland. From Senj, a well-traveled road cuts away from the coast and soon begins twisting up the coastal mountain range. After about an hour, you'll arrive at the A1 expressway, followed by the war-scarred town of Otočac. (For more on Otočac, see page 99.)

SPLIT

Dubrovnik is the darling of the Dalmatian Coast, but Split (pronounced as it's spelled) is Croatia's "second city" (after Zagreb), bustling with 178,000 people. If you've been hopping along the coast, landing in urban Split feels like a return to civilization. While most Dalmatian coastal towns seem made for tourists, Split is real and vibrant—a shipbuilding city with ugly sprawl surrounding an atmospheric Old Town, which teems with Croatians living life to the fullest.

Though today's Split throbs to a modern, youthful beat, its history goes way back—all the way to the Roman Empire. Along with all the trappings of a modern city, Split has some of the best Roman ruins this side of Italy. In the fourth century A.D., the Roman Emperor Diocletian (245-313) wanted to retire in his native Dalmatia, so he built a huge palace here. Eventually, the palace was abandoned. Then locals, fleeing seventh-century Slavic invaders, moved in and made themselves at home, and a medieval town sprouted from the rubble of the old palace. In the 15th century, the Venetians took over the Dalmatian Coast. They developed and fortified Split, slathering the city with a new layer of Gothic-Renaissance architecture.

But even as Split grew, the nucleus remained the ruins of Diocletian's Palace. To this day, 2,000 people live or work inside the former palace walls. A maze

Split Overview

To Airport & Trogir

HRVATSKE MORNARICE

To Bene Beach

ARCHAEOLOGICAL MUSEUM

SUBURBAN BUS STATION

KAŠTELANSKA

ZRINSKO FRANKOPANSKA

DOMOVINSKOG RATA

LOVREČEK

MAŽURANIĆEVO ŠET.

MATOŠEVA

MANDALINSKA PUT.

VUKOVARSKA

See Detail maps

MARJAN PENINSULA

(TUNNEL)

MATEJUŠKA (FISHERMEN'S PORT)

VAROŠ

OLD TOWN

KRIŽEVA

MARMONTOVA

DIOCLETIAN'S PALACE

LUČAC

Zoo

SENJSKA

RIVA

ZVONIMIRA

MARASOVIĆEVA

MIHANOVIĆEVA

JADROLINIJA CATAMARAN

TRAIN STATION

MEŠTROVIĆ GALLERY

MUSEUM OF CROATIAN ARCH. MONUMENTS

City Harbor

KRILO CATAMARAN

BUS STATION

Bus to/from Airport

ŠET. IVANA MEŠTROVIĆA

OBALA BRANIMIRA

MAIN FERRY TERMINAL

JEŽINAC BEACH

BAČVICE BEACH

To Kaštelet Chapel

500 Meters

500 Yards

Adriatic Sea

To Zadar & Rijeka

To Hvar, Korčula & Dubrovnik

of narrow alleys is home to fashionable boutiques and galleries, wonderfully atmospheric cafés, and Roman artifacts around every corner.

Today's Split has a split personality, as it struggles to decide how it fits into Croatia's tourist-mecca image: Is it a big, drab metropolis; a no-nonsense transit point; an impressive destination in its own right, with sights to rival Dubrovnik's...or all three? While largely lacking Dubrovnik's over-the-top romance, Split settles for being nobody's "second-best." It is its own city—an antidote to all that's quaint and cutesy in Dalmatia.

Planning Your Time

Split is southern Croatia's hub for bus, boat, train, and flight connections to other destinations in the country and abroad. This means that many visitors stop in Split only long enough to change boats. But the city is the perfect real-life contrast to the lazy, prettified Dalmatian beach resorts—it deserves a full day. Begin by strolling the remains of Diocletian's Palace, then take a coffee break along the Riva promenade or have lunch in the Old Town. After lunch, browse the shops or visit a couple of Split's museums (the Meštrović Gallery, which is a long walk or short bus or taxi ride from the Old Town, is tops). Promenading along the Riva with the natives is *the* evening activity, while nursing a drink at an atmospheric open-air café is a close second.

With a second day (or en route to or from northern destinations), you could spend some time in nearby Trogir—an enjoyable Dalmatian seaside village (described at the end of this chapter).

Orientation to Split

(area code: 021)

Split sprawls, but almost everything of interest to travelers is around the City Harbor (Gradska Luka). At the top of this harbor is the Old Town (Stari Grad). Between the Old Town and the sea is the Riva, a waterfront pedestrian promenade lined with cafés and shaded by palm trees. The main ferry terminal (Trajektni Terminal, a.k.a. Trajektna Luka) juts into the harbor from the east side. Along the harborfront embankment between the ferry terminal and the Old Town are the long-distance bus station (Autobusni Kolodvor) and the forlorn little train station (Željeznička Stanica). West of the Old Town, poking into the Adriatic, is the lush and hilly Marjan peninsula.

Split's domino-shaped Old Town is made up of two square sections. The east half was once Diocletian's Palace, and the west half is the medieval town that sprang up next door. The shell of Diocletian's ruined palace provides a checkerboard street plan, with a gate at each end. But the streets built since are anything but straight, making the Old Town a delightfully convoluted maze (double-decker in some places). At the center of the former palace is a square called the Peristyle (Peristil), where you'll find the TI, cathedral, and highest concentration of Roman ruins.

Tourist Information

Split's TI is in the little chapel on the square called the Peristyle, in the very center of Diocletian's Palace (Easter-mid-Oct Mon-Sat 8:00-20:30, Sun 8:00-13:00; mid-Oct-Easter Mon-Fri 8:00-20:00, Sat 8:00-13:00, closed Sun; tel. 021/345-606, www.visitsplit.com). Pick up the free town map, monthly *Visit Split* booklet (with information on museums, events, restaurants, and more), and other brochures.

Sightseeing Pass: The TI sells the **Splitcard,** which includes free admission to several sights (including the City Museum, Ethnographic Museum, and cathedral), a 50 percent discount at

Split Essentials

English	Croatian	Pronounced
Old Town	Stari Grad	STAH-ree grahd
City Harbor	Gradska Luka	GRAHD-skah LOO-kah
Harborfront promenade	Riva	REE-vah
Peristyle (old Roman square)	Peristil	PEH-ree-steel
Soccer team	Hajduk	HIGH-dook
Local sculptor	Ivan Meštrović	EE-vahn MESH-troh-veech
Adriatic Sea	Jadran	YAH-drahn

other sights (including the Meštrović Gallery, Archaeological Museum, and Museum of Fine Arts), and minor discounts at other attractions, shops, and restaurants around town (35 kn/72 hours). This card might save busy sightseers some money—do the arithmetic. The Splitcard is free if you're staying at least three nights in town; to claim yours, bring a note from your hotel to the TI.

Arrival in Split

By Boat, Bus, or Train: Split's ferry terminal (Trajektni Terminal),

main bus station (Autobusni Kolodvor), and train station (Željeznička Stanica) all share a busy and practical strip of land called Obala Kneza Domagoja, on the east side of the City Harbor. From any of them, you can see the Old Town and Riva; just **walk** around the harbor toward the big bell tower (about a 10-minute walk). Along the way, you'll pass travel agencies, baggage-storage offices, people trying to rent rooms, a post office, Internet cafés, shops, and cafés. Arriving or leaving from this central location, you never need to deal with the concrete, exhaust-stained sprawl of outer Split.

Boats arrive at various piers. The **Jadrolinija passenger catamaran** to and from Hvar and Korčula docks at the Obala Lazareta embankment, right in front of the Old Town. The *Krilo* **passenger catamaran** to those destinations uses pier #11, the shorter pier partway along the harbor. Bigger **car ferries** use various docks along the harbor. The main terminal, at the far end, has ATMs,

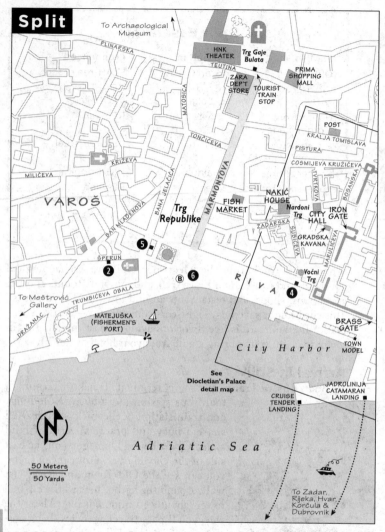

Split

To Archaeological Museum

PLINARSKA

HNK THEATER

Trg Gaje Bulata

ZARA DEP'T STORE

TOURIST TRAIN STOP

PRIMA SHOPPING MALL

TEUTINA

MATOŠIĆA

TONČIĆEVA

POST

KRALJA TOMISLAVA

PISTURA

COSMIJEVA   KRUŽIČEVA

KRIŽEVA

TKVRTKOVA

BOSANSKA

MILIČEVA

NAKIĆ HOUSE

IRON GATE

VAROŠ

BAN MLADENOVA

BANA JELAČIĆA

MARMONTOVA

FISH MARKET

Trg Republike

Nardoni Trg

CITY HALL

ZADARSKA

SUBIĆEVA

GRADSKA KAVANA

MARULIĆEVA

ŠPERUN

5

2

B   **6**

Voćni Trg

4

R I V A

To Meštrović Gallery

TRUMBIĆEVA OBALA

DRAŽANAC

MATEJUŠKA (FISHERMEN'S PORT)

BRASS GATE

TOWN MODEL

C i t y   H a r b o r

See Diocletian's Palace detail map

CRUISE TENDER LANDING

JADROLINIJA CATAMARAN LANDING

N

A d r i a t i c   S e a

50 Meters
50 Yards

To Zadar, Rijeka, Hvar, Korčula & Dubrovnik

WCs, a grocery store, and offices for all of the main ferry companies. The large Jadrolinija ticket and information office, which is open long hours daily, generally has a helpful English-speaking staff.

By Cruise Ship: In recent years—as packed-to-the-gills Dubrovnik has had to turn away cruise ships—Split has become a popular port of call for Mediterranean cruises. Dubrovnik's loss is Split's gain—and passengers' gain, as the city is particularly easy to see in a quick visit. Cruise ships either dock along the main harbor in front of the Old Town, or anchor in the harbor and send

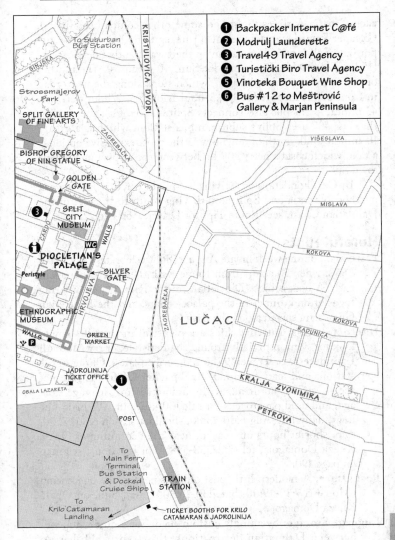

tenders into the harbor (for directions on the short walk to the Old Town, see above).

By Plane: Split's airport (Zračna Luka Split-Kaštela) is across the big bay, 15 miles northwest of the center, near the town of Trogir (tel. 021/203-506, www.split-airport.hr). A handy Croatia Airlines bus connects the airport with downtown Split (30 kn, 40 minutes). This bus meets most arriving flights at the airport—just exit the airport, turn right, and look for the bus stop. To take this *to* the airport, catch it at the stop just beyond the bus station, across the street from the main ferry terminal (departs 1.5 hours before each Croatia Airlines flight and some other companies' flights). Cheaper long-distance buses also run regularly between the airport and Split's main bus station on their way to other destinations (15 kn, 7/day Mon-Fri, none Sat-Sun, 40 minutes). Yet another option is to take public bus #37, which stops along the main road in front of the airport (20 kn, 3/hour Mon-Fri, 2/hour Sat-Sun, 45 minutes; this bus also connects Split and Trogir); the catch is that bus #37 uses Split's suburban bus station, which is a dreary 10-minute walk north of downtown. The most expensive option is a taxi, which costs a hefty 300 kn between the airport and downtown Split.

By Car: For details on arriving in Split by car, driving between northern Croatia and Split, and driving south to the rest of the Dalmatian Coast, see "Route Tips for Drivers," on page 229.

Helpful Hints

Festivals: For one week in late August, Split celebrates Diocletian Days, when 50 actors from Rome walk the streets in ancient garb. A boat brings "Diocletian" to the Riva, people wearing togas attend dinner in the palace cellars, and the Diocletian Games are staged along the Riva.

Internet Access: Internet cafés are plentiful in the Old Town; look for signs, especially around the Peristyle, or try **Modrulj Launderette** or **Travel49** (both described later). Closer to the stations and ferry terminal, **Backpacker C@fé** has Internet access, coffee and drinks with outdoor seating, luggage storage, and used paperbacks for sale (30 kn/hour, Wi-Fi-15 kn/hour, daily July-Aug 6:00-23:00, shoulder season 6:30-22:00, even shorter hours off-season, near the beginning of Obala Kneza Domagoja, tel. 021/338-548). For locations, see map on page 190.

Post Office: A modern little post office is next to the bus station (Mon-Fri 7:30-19:00, Sat 7:30-14:30, closed Sun, on Obala Kneza Domagoja).

Luggage Storage: Seemingly custom-made for a quick stopover between Dalmatian destinations, this transit hub has no shortage of luggage-storage options. The train station has lockers (15 kn), and the adjacent bus station has a left-luggage desk *(garderoba)*. A small luggage-storage kiosk is along the sidewalk between the stations and the Old Town. Other options in and near the Old Town include Backpacker C@fé (listed earlier) and Modrulj Launderette and Travel49 (both listed later).

Laundry: Modrulj Launderette, a rare coin-operated launderette, is well-run by an Australian couple, Shane and Julie. It's conveniently located in the Varoš neighborhood at the west end

SPLIT

of the Old Town, near several recommended restaurants—handy if multitasking is your style (self-service-50 kn/load, full-service-75 kn/load, air-con, Internet access, left-luggage service; April-Oct daily 8:00-20:00; Nov-March Mon-Sat 9:00-17:00, closed Sun; Šperun 1—see map on page 190, tel. 021/315-888).

Bike Rental: The staff at **Travel49** can rent you some wheels and enjoys suggesting biking routes. One good—if strenuous—option is a loop around the nearby Marjan peninsula, with a stop at a beach (15 kn/hour, 60 kn/4 hours, 100 kn/day, 20 percent discount with this book; for contact information, see below). They also offer three-hour **bike tours** (180 kn, 20 percent discount with this book).

Travel Agencies: Travel49, run by gregarious Josip, is a jack-of-all-trades agency buried deep in the Old Town. Josip offers walking tours (see "Tours in Split," later), bike tours, excursions, a room-booking service, car and bike rental, Internet access, luggage storage, and other services (daily May-Nov 8:00-22:00, Dec-April 9:00-17:00, Dioklecijanova 5, mobile 098-858-141, www.travel49.com). **Turistički Biro,** between the two halves of the Old Town on the Riva, books *sobe* and hotels; they also sell guidebooks, maps, and tickets for excursions (May-Sept daily 8:00-20:00; Oct-April Mon-Fri 8:00-20:00, Sat 8:00-13:00, closed Sun; Riva 12, tel. & fax 021/347-100, turist.biro.split@st.t-com.hr). For locations, see map on page 190.

Wine Shop: At **Vinoteka Bouquet,** at the west end of the Riva (near the restaurants and launderette on Šperun street), knowledgeable Denis can help you pick out a bottle of Croatian wine to suit your tastes (Mon-Fri 8:30-12:30 & 17:00-20:30, Sat 9:00-13:30, closed Sun, Obala Hrvatskog Narodnog Preporoda 3, tel. 021/348-031). For a wine primer before you visit, see page 52.

Who's Hajduk?: You'll see the word *Hajduk* (HIGH-dook), and a distinctive red-and-white checkerboard circle design (or red-and-blue stripes), all over town and throughout northern Dalmatia. Hajduk Split is the fervently supported soccer team, named for a band of highwaymen bandits who rebelled against Ottoman rule in the 17th-19th centuries. Most locals adore Hajduk as much as they loathe their bitter rivals, Dinamo Zagreb.

G'day, *Gospod*: You may notice a surprising concentration of Australians in Split. Many of them are actually Australian-born Croats, returning to the cosmopolitan capital city of their parents' Dalmatian homeland.

Getting Around Split

Most of what you'll want to see is within walking distance, but some sights (such as the Meštrović Gallery) are more easily reached by bus or taxi.

By Bus: Local buses, run by Promet, cost 10 kn per ride (or 9 kn if you buy a ticket at a newsstand or Promet kiosk, ask for a *putna karta;* zone I is fine for any ride within Split, but you need the 20-kn zone IV ticket for the ride to Trogir). For a round-trip within the city, buy a 16-kn transfer ticket, which works like two individual tickets (must buy at kiosk). Validate your ticket in the machine or with the driver as you board the bus. Suburban buses to towns near Split (such as Trogir) generally use the suburban bus station (Prigradski Autobusni Kolodvor), a 10-minute walk due north of the Old Town on Domovinskog rata. Bus information: www.promet-split.hr.

By Taxi: Taxis start at 20 kn, then cost around 7 kn per kilometer. Figure 50 kn for most rides within the city (for example, from the ferry terminal to most hotels)—but if going from one end of the Old Town to the other, it can be faster to walk. To call for a taxi, try Radio Taxi (tel. 021/970).

By Tourist Train: An hourly tourist train leaves from the square at the top of Marmontova and does a loop around the Marjan peninsula with a stop at Bene Beach (20 kn one-way, departs on the hour 9:00-20:00, mobile 095-530-6962).

Tours in Split

Walking Tours—Various companies offer walking tours of Split's Old Town. The most established is **Unique Walking Tours,** part of Travel49, whose 1.5-hour tours depart from the Peristyle (80 kn, 20 percent discount if you buy tickets at Travel49 office and show this book; May-Oct daily at 10:30, 12:00, and 19:00; April and Nov daily at 11:00 only; Dec-March no scheduled tours but possible upon request; mobile 098-858-141, www.diocletianpalace tour.com).

Local Guides—Consider hiring an insider to show you around. Maja Benzon is a smart and savvy local guide; she leads good walking tours through the Old Town (500 kn/up to 2 hours, 600 kn/3 hours, mobile 098-852-869, maja.benzon@gmail.com). You can also hire a guide through the **guide association,** which has an office at the Peristyle (525 kn/1.5-2 hours; June-Aug Mon-Fri 9:00-17:00, closed Sat-Sun; Sept-May generally open weekday mornings only; tel. 021/360-058, tel. & fax 021/346-267, mobile 098-361-936, www.guides.hr, info@guides.hr).

From Split

Bus Tours—Various companies run excursions to outlying sights. Options include the town of Trogir; the Roman ruins of Solin (ancient Salona); whitewater rafting on the Cetina River; the islands of Brač, Hvar, and Šolta (either separately or together); the pilgrimage site at Međugorje; Dubrovnik; and the waterfalls at Krka National Park or Plitvice Lakes National Park. This can be an efficient way to get to places that take a while to reach by public transportation. **Travel49** runs youthful, fun-loving excursions, and offers a 20 percent discount to Rick Steves readers if you book at their office (listed earlier, under "Helpful Hints"). **Atlas Travel** is a much larger operation and offers a wider variety of excursions, but their guiding can be hit-or-miss (about 300-700 kn, most are full-day tours). For details on excursions, look for fliers around town. Buy tickets at any travel agency, such as the Turistički Biro on the Riva (listed earlier, under "Helpful Hints").

Self-Guided Walk

▲▲▲Diocletian's Palace (Dioklecijanova Palača)

Split's top activity is visiting the remains of Roman Emperor Diocletian's enormous retirement palace, sitting on the harbor in the heart of the city. This monstrous complex was two impressive structures in one: luxurious villa and fortified Roman town. My walk takes you through Diocletian's back door; down into the labyrinth of cellars that supported the palace; up to the Peristyle (the center of the palace); into Diocletian's mausoleum—now the town's cathedral, with a crypt, treasury/museum, and climbable tower; over to Jupiter's Temple (later converted into a baptistery); down the main artery of the palace; and ends at what was once the front entrance to the palace. The ruins themselves are now integrated with the city's street plan, so exploring them is free—except for the cellars and the cathedral sights/temple, which you'll pay to enter. In peak season, the cellars are open late (on most days until 20:00 or 21:00), and the cathedral sights generally close at 19:00. If visiting off-season, do this walk as early as possible, as the cathedral sights close at noon. For exact hours, see the individual sight listings.

Fragments of the palace are poorly marked, and there are no good guidebooks or audioguides for understanding the remains. For most visitors, this walk provides enough details; for more in-depth information, consider joining a walking tour or hiring a guide (see "Tours in Split," earlier).

Background

Diocletian grew up just inland from Split, in the town of Salona (Solin in Croatian), which was then the capital of the Roman prov-

ince of Dalmatia. He worked his way up the Roman hierarchy and ruled as emperor for the unusually long tenure of 20 years (A.D. 284-305). Despite all of his achievements, Diocletian is best remembered for two questionable legacies: dividing the huge empire among four emperors (which helped administer it more efficiently, but began a splintering effect that arguably led to the empire's decline); and torturing and executing Christians, including thousands right here on the Dalmatian Coast.

As Diocletian grew older, he decided to return to his homeland for retirement. Since he was in poor health, the medicinal sulfur spring here was another plus. His massive palace took only 11 years to build—and this fast pace required a big push (more than 2,000 slaves died during construction). Huge sections of his palace still exist, modified by medieval and modern developers alike.

• *Start in front of the palace, at the east end of the Riva. To get a sense of the original palace, check out the big illustration posted across from the palace entry. Across the street at the end of the Riva, notice the big car-size model of today's Old Town, which is helpful for orientation. (Both the sign and the model are usually crowded with tour groups.) Now study the...*

Palace Facade

The "front" of today's Split—facing the harbor—was actually the back door of Diocletian's Palace. There was no embankment in front of the palace back then, so the water came right up to this door—sort of an emergency exit by boat. Looking out to the water, appreciate the palace's strategic location: It's easy to fortify, and to spot enemies approaching either by land or by sea.

Visually trace the outline of the gigantic palace, which was more than 600 feet long on each side. On the corner to the right stands a big, rectangular guard tower (one of the original 16). To the left, the tower is gone and the corner is harder to pick out (look for the beginning of the newer-looking buildings). Mentally erase the ramshackle two-story buildings added 200 years ago, which obscure the grandeur of the palace wall.

Halfway up the facade, notice the row of 42 arched window frames (mostly filled in today). Diocletian and his family lived in the seaside half of the palace. Imagine him strolling back and forth

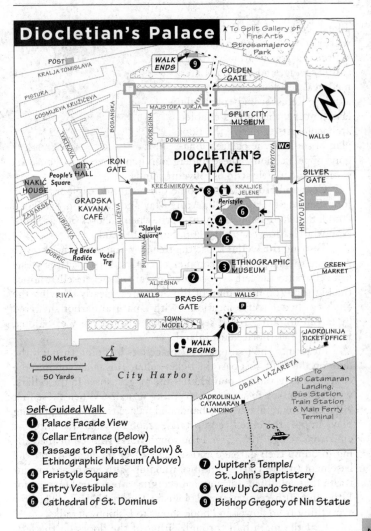

Diocletian's Palace

Self-Guided Walk
1. Palace Facade View
2. Cellar Entrance (Below)
3. Passage to Peristyle (Below) & Ethnographic Museum (Above)
4. Peristyle Square
5. Entry Vestibule
6. Cathedral of St. Dominus
7. Jupiter's Temple/St. John's Baptistery
8. View Up Cardo Street
9. Bishop Gregory of Nin Statue

along this fine arcade, enjoying the views of his Adriatic home-land. The inland, non-view half of the palace was home to 700 servants, bodyguards, and soldiers.

• Go through the door in the middle of the palace (known as the "Brass Gate," located under the Substructure of Diocletian's Palace banner). Just inside the door and to the left is the entrance to...

Diocletian's Cellars (Podromi)

Since the palace was constructed on land that sloped down to the sea, these chambers were built to level out a foundation for the massive structure above (like a modern "daylight basement").

These cellars were filled with water from three different sources: a freshwater spring, a sulfur spring, and the sea. Later, medieval residents used them as a dump. Rediscovered only in the last century, the cellars enabled archaeologists to derive the floor plan of some of the palace's long-gone upper sections. These underground chambers now house art exhibits and a little strip of souvenir stands.

Cost and Hours: 35 kn, some posters inside explain the site; June-Sept daily 9:00-21:00; April-May and Oct Mon-Sat 9:00-20:00, Sun 9:00-18:00 except in April, when it closes Sun at 14:00; Nov-March Mon-Sat 9:00-18:00, Sun 9:00-14:00.

Touring the Cellars: Use the free map you get at the entry to navigate this labyrinthine complex of cellars. First visit the **western cellars** (to the left as you enter). Near the ticket-seller, notice the big **topographical map** of the Split area, clearly showing the city's easily defensible location—with a natural harbor sheltered by tall mountains. You'll see the former Roman city of Salona, Diocletian's birthplace, just inland.

Head into the main part of the cellars by going through the door on the right, just past the ticket-seller. This takes you into the complex's vast, vaulted **main hall**—the biggest space in the cellars, with stout pillars to support everything upstairs. When those first villagers took refuge in the abandoned palace from the rampaging Slavs in 641, the elite lived upstairs, grabbing what was once the emperor's wing. They carved the rough holes you see in the ceiling to dump their garbage and sewage. Over the generations, the basement (where you're standing) filled up with layers of pungent waste that solidified, ultimately becoming a precious bonanza for 19th- and 20th-century archaeologists. Today this hall is used for everything from flower and book shows to fashion catwalks.

Exit the main hall through either of the doors on the left, cross through the narrow corridor, and enter the long room. Look just overhead—the holes you see once held beams to support floorboards, making this a two-story cellar. Face the giant replica of a golden Diocletian coin at the far end, and turn left, then immediately right into a small circular room, which has a headless, pawless black granite sphinx—one of 13 that Diocletian brought home from Egypt (only four survive, including a mostly intact one we'll see soon on the Peristyle). Look up to admire the circular brickwork. Then continue straight. In the small room just beyond is a stone olive-oil press.

Backtrack past the round room and into a room that displays two petrified beams, like the ones that once filled the double-decker holes we saw earlier. At the far end of this room is an unexcavated wing—a compost pile of ancient lifestyles, awaiting the tiny shovels and toothbrushes of future archaeologists.

Facing the mound of ancient garbage, turn left into another round room, featuring a bust of Diocletian (or is it Sean Connery?). From here, loop through a few more rooms back into the long room you were in earlier, then turn right and exit out the bottom of this hall. On your right, look for original Roman sewer pipes—square outside and round inside—designed to fit into each other to create long pipes.

From here, head back out to the exit. If you'd like to see more cellars—mostly with their ceilings missing, so they're open to the air—cross over into the **eastern cellars** (same ticket). This section is less interesting than the western part, but worth a quick visit.

• *When you're finished, head back to the main gallery. Ignore the tacky made-in-Malaysia trinket shops as you head down the passage and up the stairs into the...*

Peristyle (Peristil)

This square was the centerpiece of Diocletian's Palace. As you walk up the stairs, the entry vestibule into the residence is above

your head, Diocletian's mausoleum (today's Cathedral of St. Dominus) is to your right, and the street to Jupiter's Temple is on your left. The TI is in the small chapel. Straight ahead, beyond the TI/chapel, is the narrow street that leads to the palace's former main entrance, the Golden Gate.

Go to the middle of the square and take it all in. The red granite pillars—which you'll see all over Diocletian's Palace—are from Egypt, where Diocletian spent many of his pre-retirement years. Imagine the pillars defining fine arcades—now obscured by medieval houses. The black sphinx is the only one of Diocletian's collection of 13 that's still (mostly) intact.

In summer (mid-June–mid-Sept), costumed pageantry brings the square to life. "Roman soldiers" pose for tips (daily 9:00–17:00), and every day at noon an actor playing Diocletian appears at the top of the stairs to address the crowd in Latin.

• *Climb the stairs (above where you came in) into the domed, open-ceilinged...*

Entry Vestibule

Impressed? That's the idea. This was the grand entry to Diocletian's living quarters, meant to wow visitors. Emperors were believed

to be gods. Diocletian called himself "Jovius"—the son of Jupiter, the most powerful of all gods. Four times a year (at the changing of the seasons), Diocletian would stand here and overlook the Peristyle. His subjects would lie on the ground in worship, praising his name and kissing his scarlet robe. Notice the four big niches at floor level, which once held statues of the four tetrarchs who ruled the unwieldy empire after Diocletian retired. The empty hole in the ceiling was once capped by a dome (long since collapsed), and the ceiling itself was covered with frescoes and mosaics.

In this grand space, you'll likely run into an all-male band of *klapa* singers, performing traditional a cappella harmonies. Just stand and enjoy a few glorious tunes—you'll rarely find a better group or acoustics. A 100-kn *klapa* CD is the perfect souvenir.

Wander out back to the harbor side through medieval buildings (some with seventh-century foundations), which evoke the way local villagers came in and took over the once-spacious and elegant palace. Back in this area, you'll find the beautifully restored home of the **Ethnographic Museum** (described later, under "Sights in Split").

• *Now go back into the Peristyle and turn right, climbing the steps to the...*

Cathedral of St. Dominus (Katedrala Sv. Duje)

The original octagonal structure was Diocletian's elaborate mausoleum, built in the fourth century. But after the fall of Rome, it was converted into the town's cathedral. Construction of the bell tower began in the 13th century and took 300 years to complete. Before you go inside, notice the sarcophagi ringing the cathedral. In the late Middle Ages, this was prime post-mortem real estate, since being buried closer to a cathedral improved your chances of getting to heaven.

Cost and Hours: You'll need a ticket for the cathedral interior, the crypt, the unimpressive treasury/museum, the tower climb, and—a block away—Jupiter's Temple (described later). Various combo-ticket options are available (but note that these are constantly changing and may be different during your visit). A basic 15-kn ticket covers the cathedral, crypt, and Jupiter's Temple (probably your best option on a brief visit). The 35-kn combo-ticket adds the tower and the treasury/museum. You can also buy individual tickets for the tower climb (10 kn, buy ticket at tower door) and the treasury/museum (15 kn). All of the sights are open similar hours, but the cathedral can close unexpectedly for services. In general, hours are summer Mon-Sat 8:00-19:00, Sun 12:30-18:30, cathedral often closed Sat afternoons for weddings; winter daily 7:00-12:00, maybe later on request; Kraj Sv. Duje 5, tel. 021/344-121.

Touring the Cathedral: To get inside in peak season (April-Oct), you must loop around the outside of the cathedral. Facing the main door at the bottom of the stairs, circle around the left side to find the door in the building behind. Buy your ticket here and climb up the stairs to the **treasury/museum.** This single room contains dusty display cases of vestments, giant books, icon-like paintings, reliquaries, chalices, monstrances, and other church art, with very sparse English descriptions. Go up one more floor to get into the cathedral. In winter (Nov-March), you can simply enter the cathedral through the main door.

Step into the church **interior.** This is the oldest—and likely smallest—building used as a cathedral anywhere in Christendom. Imagine the place in pre-Christian times, with Diocletian's tomb in the center. The only surviving pieces of decor from those days are the granite columns and the relief circling the base of the dome (about 50 feet up)—a ring of carvings heralding the greatness of the emperor. The small red-marble pillars around the top of the pulpit (near the entry) were scavenged  from Diocletian's sarcophagus. These pillars are all that remain of Diocletian's remains.

Diocletian brutally persecuted his Christian subjects. Just before he moved to the Dalmatian Coast, he had Bishop Dominus of Salona killed, along with several thousand Christians. When Diocletian died, there were riots of happiness. In the seventh century, his mausoleum became a cathedral dedicated to the martyred bishop. The extension behind the altar was added in the ninth century. The sarcophagus of St. Dominus (to the right of the altar, with early-Christian carvings) was once the cathedral's high altar. To the left of today's main altar is the impressively detailed,

Renaissance-era altar of St. Anastasius, who is lying on a millstone that is tied to his neck. On Diocletian's orders, this Christian martyr was drowned in A.D. 302. To the left of St. Anastasius' altar is the "new" altar of St. Dominus; his relics lie in the 18th-century Baroque silver reliquary, above a stone relief showing him being beheaded. Posthumous poetic justice: Now Christian saints are entombed in Diocletian's mausoleum... and Diocletian is nowhere to be found. As you exit through the 13th-century main doors, notice the 14 panels on each of the two wings—showing 28 scenes from the life of Christ.

Climbing the 183 steep steps to the top of the 200-foot-tall **bell tower** rewards you with sweeping views of Split, but it's not for claustrophobes or those scared of heights.

If you circle down and around the right side of the cathedral as you face the main stairs, you'll find the entrance to the **crypt** *(kripta)*. This musty, domed cellar (with eerie acoustics) was originally used to level the foundation of Diocletian's mausoleum. Later, Christians turned it into another chapel. The legend you'll likely hear about Diocletian torturing and murdering Christians in this very crypt, which began about the same time this became a church, is probably false.

• *Remember that Diocletian believed himself to be Jovius (Jupiter, Jr.). As worshippers exited the mausoleum of Jovius, they would look straight ahead to the temple of Jupiter. (Back then, there were none of these medieval buildings cluttering up the view.) Make your way through the narrow alley (directly across from the cathedral entry), past another headless, pawless sphinx, to explore the small...*

Jupiter's Temple/St. John's Baptistery

About the time the mausoleum became a cathedral, this temple was converted into a baptistery (same ticket and hours as cathedral; off-season, if it's locked, go ask the person at the cathedral to let you in). Inside, the big 12th-century baptismal font—large enough to immerse someone (as was the tradition in those days)—is decorated with the intricate, traditional *pleter* design also used around the border of Croatia's current passport stamp. On the font, notice the engraving: a bishop (on the left) and the king on his throne (on the right).

At their feet (literally under the feet of the bishop) is a submissive commoner—neatly summing up the social structure of the Middle Ages. Standing above the font is a statue of St. John the Baptist counting to four, done by the great Croatian sculptor Ivan Meštrović (see page 208). The half-barrel vaulted ceiling, completed later, is considered the best-preserved of its kind anywhere. Every face and each patterned box is different.

• *Back at the Peristyle, stand in front of the little chapel with your back to the entry vestibule. The small street just beyond the chapel (going left to right) connects the east and west gates. If you've had enough Roman history, head right (east) to go through the Silver Gate and find Split's busy, open-air Green Market. Or, head to the left (west), which takes you to the Iron Gate and People's Square (see "Sights in Split," later) and, beyond that, the fresh-and-smelly fish market. But if you want to see one last bit of Roman history, continue straight ahead up the...*

Cardo

A traditional Roman street plan has two roads: Cardo (the north-south axis) and Decumanus (the east-west axis). Split's Cardo street was the most important in Diocletian's Palace, connecting the main entry with the heart of the complex. As you walk, you'll pass several noteworthy sights: in the first building on the right, a bank with modern computer gear all around its exposed Roman ruins (look through window); at the first gate on the left, the courtyard of a Venetian merchant's palace (a reminder that Split was dominated by Venice from the 15th century on); on the right, an alley to the **City Museum** (described later, under "Sights in Split"); and, on the right, **Nadalina,** an artisan chocolatier selling mostly dark chocolate creations with some innovative Dalmatian flavors (30 kn/100 grams, 13-kn chocolate bars, Mon-Fri 9:00-21:00, Sat 9:00-12:00, closed Sun).

Just before the Golden Gate, detour a few steps to the left along skinny **Majstora Jurja** street—lined with some of the most appealing outdoor cafés in town, lively both day and night (described later, under "Nightlife in Split"). Near the start of this street, just after its initial jog, stairs climb to the miniscule **St. Martin's Chapel,** burrowed into the city wall. Dating from the fifth century, this is one of the earliest Christian chapels anywhere. St. Martin is the patron saint of soldiers, and the chapel was built for the troops who guarded this gate (free, sporadic hours—just climb the stairs to see if it's open).

• *Backtrack to the main drag and go inside the huge...*

Golden Gate (Zlatna Vrata)

This great gate was the main entry of Diocletian's Palace. Its name wasn't literal—rather, the "gold" suggests the importance of this gateway to Salona, the Roman provincial capital at the time. Standing inside the gate itself, you can appreciate the double-door design that kept the palace safe. Also notice how this ancient building is now being used in very different ways from its original purpose. Above, on the outer wall, you can see the bricked-in windows that contain part of a Dominican convent. At the top of the inner wall is somebody's garden terrace.

Go outside the gate and look back at the recently restored fortification—with all its structural elements gleaming. This mostly uncluttered facade gives you the best opportunity in town to visu-

alize how the palace looked before so many other buildings were grafted on. Straight ahead as you exit this gate is Salona (Solin), which was a major city of 60,000 (and Diocletian's hometown) before there was a Split. The big statue by Ivan Meštrović is **Bishop Gregory of Nin,** a 10th-century Croatian priest who tried to convince the Vatican to allow sermons during Mass to be said in Croatian, rather than Latin. People rub his toe for good luck (though only non-material wishes are given serious consideration). The big building beyond the statue houses Split's **Gallery of Fine Arts** (described later, under "Sights in Split").

· *Your tour is finished. Now enjoy the rest of Split.*

Sights in Split

In or near the Old Town

In addition to the palace, cellars, and cathedral described on my self-guided walk, you can also enjoy these attractions.

▲**People's Square (Narodni Trg)**—Locals call this lively square at the center of the Old Town *Pjaca*, pronounced the same as the Italian *piazza* (PYAH-tsah).

Stand in the center and enjoy the bustle. Look around for a quick lesson in Dalmatian history. When Diocletian lived in his palace, a Roman village popped up here, just outside the wall. Face the former wall of Diocletian's Palace (behind and to the right of the 24-hour

clock tower). This was the western entrance, or so-called "Iron Gate." By the 14th century, a medieval town had developed, making this the main square of Split.

On the wall just to the right of the lane leading to the Peristyle, look for the life-size relief of **St. Anthony.** Notice the creepy "mini-me" clutching the saint's left leg—depicting the sculptor's donor, who didn't want his gift to be forgotten. Above this strange statue, notice the smaller, faded relief of a man and a woman arguing.

Turn around and face the square. On your left is the city's grand old café, **Gradska Kavana,** which has been the Old Town's venerable meeting point for generations. Today it's both a café and a restaurant with disappointing food but the best outdoor ambience in town (35-kn breakfasts, 60-80-kn pastas, 85-145-kn main courses, daily 7:00-24:00, Narodni trg 1, tel. 021/317-835).

Across the square, the white building jutting into the square was once the **City Hall,** and now houses temporary exhibitions. The loggia is all that remains of the original Gothic building.

At the far end of the square is the out-of-place **Nakić House,** built in the early 20th-century Viennese Secession style—a reminder that Dalmatia was part of the Habsburg Empire, and ruled by Vienna, from Napoleon's downfall through World War I.

The lane on the right side of the Nakić House leads to Split's **fish market** (Ribarnica), where you can see piles of the still-wriggling catch of the day. No flies? It's thanks to the sulfur spring in the nearby spa building (with the gray statues, on the corner). Just beyond the fish market is the pedestrian boulevard Marmontova (described on page 211).

Ethnographic Museum (Etnografski Muzej)—This museum uses well-presented temporary exhibits to show off the culture, costumes, furniture, tools, jewelry, weapons, and paintings of Dalmatia. It's all displayed in a gorgeously renovated early-medieval palace with a confusing treehouse floor plan. You'll find it in the upper level of the Old Town, behind Diocletian's entry vestibule. Check out the artsy "golden fleece" entry door. The ground floor sports the remains of a seventh-century church, and the exhibits usually include a good look at traditional folk dress. Your ticket also includes access to the roof of the vestibule (find the stairs at the far end of the museum); while it's not high enough to be thrilling, and you can't actually see down into the vestibule, it provides a nice view over the rooftops of Split.

Cost and Hours: 10 kn, some English explanations; July-mid-Sept Mon-Fri 9:00-21:00, Sat 9:00-13:00, closed Sun; June Mon-Fri 9:00-18:00, Sat 9:00-13:00, closed Sun; mid-Sept-May Mon-Fri 9:00-15:00, Sat 9:00-13:00, closed Sun; Severova 7, tel. 021/344-164, www.etnografski-muzej-split.hr.

Split City Museum (Muzej Grada Splita)—This museum traces how the city grew over the centuries. It's a bit dull, but it can help you appreciate a little better the layers of history you're seeing in the streets. The ground floor displays Roman fragments (including coins from the days of Diocletian), temporary exhibits, and the museum's highlight: a semicircular marble table used by the Romans. As depicted in Hollywood movies, the Romans ate lying down (three people would lounge and feast, while servants dished things up from the straight side). This table has been painstakingly reconstructed from shards and splinters discovered in the cellars. The upstairs focuses on the Middle Ages (find the terrace displaying carved stone monuments), and the top floor covers the 16th century to the present.

The 15th-century Papalić Palace, which houses the City Museum, is a sight all its own. At the end of the palace, near Cardo street, look up to see several typical Venetian-style Gothic-Renaissance windows. The stone posts sticking out of the wall next to them were used to hang curtains.

Cost and Hours: 10 kn, some English descriptions, 40-kn guidebook is overkill; May-Oct Tue-Fri 9:00-21:00, Sat-Mon 9:00-16:00; Nov-April generally Tue-Fri 10:00-17:00, Sat-Sun 10:00-13:00, closed Mon, possibly even shorter hours off-season, Papalićeva 1, tel. 021/360-171, www.mgst.net.

Radić Brothers Square (Trg Braće Radića)—Also known as Voćni Trg ("Fruit Square") for the produce that was once sold here, this little piazza is just off the Riva between the two halves of the Old Town. Overhead is a **Venetian citadel.** After Split became part of the Venetian Republic, there was a serious danger of attack by the Ottomans, so octagonal towers like this were built all along the coast. But this imposing tower had a second purpose: to encourage citizens of Split to forget about any plans of rebellion.

In the middle of the square is a studious sculpture by Ivan Meštrović of the 16th-century poet **Marko Marulić,** who is considered the father of the Croatian language. Marulić was the first to write literature in the Croatian vernacular, which before then had generally been considered a backward peasants' tongue.

On the downhill (harbor) side of the square is **Croata,** a necktie boutique that loves to explain how Croatian soldiers who fought with the French in the Thirty Years' War (1618-1648) had a distinctive way of tying their scarves. The French found it stylish, adopted it, and called it *à la Croate*—or eventually, *cravate*—thus creating the modern necktie that many people wear to work every day throughout the world. Croata's selection includes ties with traditional Croatian motifs, such as the checkerboard pattern from the flag or writing in the ninth-century Glagolitic alphabet. Though pricey, these ties make nice souvenirs (250-700 kn, Mon-Fri 8:00-20:30, Sat 8:00-13:00, closed Sun, shorter hours off-season). Croata has a bigger, second location on the Peristyle.

SPLIT

Green Market—This lively open-air market bustles at the east end of Diocletian's Palace. Residents shop for produce and clothes here, and there are plenty of tourist souvenirs as well. Browse the wide selection of T-shirts, and ignore the creepy black-market tobacco salesmen who mutter at you: *"Cigaretta?"*

Split Gallery of Fine Arts (Galerija Umjetnina Split)—This collection, beautifully displayed in a finely restored old hospital just behind Diocletian's Palace, features mostly Croatian artwork from the 14th to the 21st centuries. It's basically a hodgepodge with few highlights—best reserved for art-lovers. Cross through the courtyard, climb up the stairs, and follow the one-way route through the chronologically displayed collection, which is heavy on the 20th century.

Cost and Hours: 20 kn; May-Sept Mon 11:00-16:00, Tue-Fri 11:00-19:00, Sat 11:00-15:00, closed Sun; Oct-April Mon 9:00-14:00, Tue-Fri 9:00-17:00, Sat 9:00-13:00, closed Sun; mod café, go straight out the Golden Gate and a bit to the left—behind the statue of Gregory of Nin—to Kralja Tomislava 15, tel. 021/350-110, www.galum.hr.

Archaeological Museum (Arheološki Muzej)—If you're intrigued by all the "big stuff" from Split's past (buildings and ruins), consider paying a visit to this collection of its "little stuff." A good exhibit of artifacts (mostly everyday domestic items) traces this region's history chronologically, from its Illyrian beginnings through its notable Roman period (items from Split and Salona) to the Middle Ages. About a 10-minute walk north of the Old Town, it's worth the trip for archaeology fans. Don't confuse this with the less-interesting Museum of Croatian Archaeological Monuments, on the way to the Ivan Meštrović Gallery.

Cost and Hours: 20 kn; June-Sept Mon-Sat 9:00-14:00 & 16:00-20:00, closed Sun; Oct-May Mon-Fri 9:00-14:00 & 16:00-20:00, Sat 9:00-14:00, closed Sun; Zrinsko Frankopanska 25, tel. 021/329-340, www.mdc.hr/split-arheoloski.

Ivan Meštrović Sights, West of the Old Town

The excellent Meštrović Gallery and nearby Kaštelet Chapel are just outside the Old Town. Both sights are covered by the same ticket and have the same hours.

Cost and Hours: 30 kn, covers both the gallery and the chapel; May-Sept Tue-Sun 9:00-19:00, closed Mon; Oct-April Tue-Sat 9:00-16:00, Sun 10:00-15:00, closed Mon; gallery tel. 021/340-800, chapel tel. 021/358-185, www.mdc.hr/mestrovic.

Getting There: Both sights are located along Šetalište Ivana Meštrovića. You can take **bus #12** from the little cul-de-sac at the west end of the Riva (departs hourly, get off at the stop in front of the gallery—just after your bus passes a museum prominently

SPLIT

Ivan Meštrović
(1883-1962)

Ivan Meštrović (EE-vahn MESH-troh-veech), who achieved international fame for his talents as a sculptor, was Croatia's answer to Rodin. You'll see Meštrović's works everywhere, in the streets, squares, and museums of Croatia.

Meštrović came from humble beginnings. He grew up in a family of poor, nomadic farm workers just inland from Split. At an early age, his drawings and wooden carvings showed promise, and a rich family took him in and made sure he was properly trained. He eventually went off to school in Vienna, where he fell in with the Secession movement and found fame and fortune. He lived in Prague, Paris, and Switzerland, fully engaged in the flourishing European artistic culture at the turn of the 20th century (he counted Rodin among his friends). After World War I, Meštrović moved back to Croatia and established an atelier, or workshop, in Zagreb (now a museum—see page 72).

Later in life—like Diocletian before him—Meštrović returned to Split and built a huge seaside mansion (today's Meštrović Gallery). The years between the World Wars were Meštrović's happiest and most productive. It was during this time that he sculpted his most internationally famous works, a pair of giant Native American warriors on horseback in Chicago's Grant Park. But when World War II broke out, Meštrović—an outspoken supporter of the ideals of a united Yugoslavia—was briefly imprisoned by the anti-Yugoslav Ustaše (Croatia's Nazi puppet government). After his release, Meštrović fled to Italy, then the US, where he lectured at prominent universities such as Notre Dame and Syracuse. After the war, the Yugoslav dictator Tito invited Meštrović to return, but the very religious artist refused to cooperate with an atheist regime. (Meštrović was friends with the Archbishop Alojzije Stepinac, who was imprisoned by Tito.) Meštrović died in South Bend, Indiana.

Meštrović worked in wood, plaster, marble, and bronze, and dabbled in painting. His sculptures depict biblical, mythological, political, and everyday themes. Meštrović's figures typically have long, angular fingers, arms, and legs. Whether whimsical or emotional, Meštrović's expressive, elongated faces—often with prominent noses—powerfully connect with the viewer.

SPLIT

marked *Muzej Hrvatskih Arheoloških Spomenika*). You can also **walk** (about 25 minutes): Follow the harbor west of town toward the big marina, swing right with the road, and follow the park until you see the gallery on your right (at #46). A **taxi** from the west end of the Old Town to the gallery costs about 50 kn (much more from the east end of the Old Town). To reach the chapel, it's a five-minute walk past the gallery down Šetalište Ivana Meštrovića to #39 (on the left, in an olive grove).

▲▲**Meštrović Gallery (Galerija Meštrović)**—Split's best art museum is dedicated to the sculptor Ivan Meštrović, the most

important of all Croatian artists. Many of Meštrović's finest works are housed in this palace, designed by the sculptor himself to serve as his residence, studio, and exhibition space. If you have time, it's worth the trek. The gallery offers a free guide-booklet and pricey, downloadable smartphone audio tours. The 80-kn guidebook is overkill for most visitors.

❍ **Self-Guided Tour:** After buying your ticket (and asking about the time for your return bus to the Old Town), climb the stairs toward Meštrović's house, pausing in the **garden** to admire a smattering of sculptures (including several female nudes, Cyclops hurling a giant shot put, and an eagle).

Go up another set of stairs to reach the **Entrance Hall,** which displays sculptures mostly of Carrara marble, Michelangelo's favorite medium. Notice the black sculptures by the two staircases: on the left, representing birth, and on the right, representing death—Meštrović strove to capture the full range of human experience in his work.

Go to the left, and enter the **Dining Room** at the end of the main floor. It's decorated with portraits of Meštrović's wife, mother, and children. Meštrović often used his mother as a model for older women and his second wife Olga as a model for younger women. Also look for the self-portrait and two painted portraits of Meštrović (one as a young man, another shortly before his death). A painting of the *Last Supper* hangs in virtually every Dalmatian dining room. Meštrović's is no exception—he painted this version himself. At the end of the room are two giant caryatids carved from Dalmatian stone (embedded with fragments of seashells).

Now climb the stairs and go to the right, into the **Secession Room.** Some of these works—including the girl singing and the intimate portrait of a family—show the influence of Meštrović's contemporary, Rodin.

Pass through the room of drawings into the **Long Hall,** lined with life-size figures and a view terrace. The woman sitting with her knees apart and feet together is demonstrating a favorite pose of Meštrović's.

At the end of the hall is the **Study Room,** filled with miniature sculptures Meštrović created to prepare for larger-scale works. Notice the small study of *Job,* then go into the small side-room to see the much larger final version. One of Meštrović's most powerful works, *Job*—howling with an agony verging on insanity—was carved by the artist in exile, as his country was turned upside-down by World War II. Meštrović sketched his inspiration for this piece (displayed on the wall) while he was imprisoned by the Ustaše.

Head down the stairs and turn left into the **Sacral Room.**

Meštrović was very religious, and here you can see some of his many works depicting biblical figures. The giant, wood-carved *Adam* and *Eve* dominate the room, but don't miss the smaller side-room, with another of the gallery's highlights: the quietly poignant *Roman Pietà.* Meštrović follows the classical pyramid form, with Joseph of Arimathea (top), Mary (left), and Mary Magdalene (right) surrounding the limp body of Christ. But the harmony is broken by the painful angles of the mourning faces. While this sculpture is plaster, Meštrović also completed a marble version for the campus of The University of Notre Dame in the US.

▲**Kaštelet Chapel**—If you enjoy the gallery, don't miss the nearby Kaštelet Chapel ("Chapel of the Holy Cross"). Meštrović bought this 16th-century fortified palace to display his 28 wood reliefs of Jesus' life. You can see how Meštrović's style changed over time, as he carved these over a nearly 30-year span, completing the last 12 when he was in the US. (However, note that he didn't carve the reliefs in chronological order—ask for a booklet identifying the topic and year for each one.) While the earlier pieces are well-composed and powerful, the later ones seem more hastily done, as Meštrović rushed to complete his opus. Work clockwise around the room, tracing the life of Christ. Notice that some of the Passion scenes are out of order (a side-effect of Meštrović's nonlinear schedule). The beautiful *pietà* near the end still shows some of the original surface of the wood, demonstrating the skill required to create depth and emotion in just a few inches of medium. Dominating the chapel is an extremely powerful wooden crucifix, with Christ's arms, legs, fingers, and toes bent at unnatural angles—a typically expressionistic flair Meštrović used to exaggerate suffering.

Activities in Split

▲▲**Strolling the Riva**—The official name for this seaside pedestrian drag is the "Croatian National Revival Embankment" (Obala

Hrvatskog Narodnog Preporoda), but locals just call it "Riva" (Italian for "harbor"). This is the town's promenade, an integral part of Mediterranean culture. After dinner, Split residents collect their families and friends for a stroll on the Riva. It offers some of the best people-watching in Croatia; make it a point to be here for an hour or two after dinner. The stinky smell that sometimes accompanies the stroll (especially at the west end) isn't from a sewer. It's sulfur—a reminder that the town's medicinal sulfur spas have attracted people here since the days of Diocletian.

The Riva recently underwent an extensive, costly, and controversial renovation. The old potholed pavement and scrubby gardens were torn up and replaced with a broad, sleek, carefully landscaped people zone. A clean, synchronized line of modern white lampposts and sun screens sashays down the promenade. But many residents miss the colorful quirks of the old version. For example, when the promenade was first renovated, cafés were forced to buy identical tables and chairs to make everything match. In protest, some cafés offered no outdoor seating at all... until the city relented, and now any chairs are allowed. Some think that the starkly modern strip is at odds with the rest of the higgledy-piggledy Old Town, while others see this as simply the early-21st century's contribution to the architectural hodgepodge that is Split.

At the west end of the Riva, the people-parade of Croatian culture turns right and heads away from the water, up **Marmontova.** Although it lacks the seafront cachet, this drag is equally enjoyable and feels more local. As you walk up Marmontova, on the left is the plain-Jane outer facade of the arcade that defines Trg Republike, a grand and genteel Napoleonic-era square. Duck through the passage across from the fish market to bask in its "poor man's St. Mark's Square" ambience, and maybe to linger over a drink at the recommended Bajamonti café. A bit farther up Marmontova, on the right, look for the whimsical fountain nicknamed "The Teacup," with a hand squirting water across the sidewalk into a funnel. At the top of Marmontova are some department stores, a lively café square, and the Croatian National Theater (Hrvatsko Narodno Kazalište, HNK).

Exploring Matejuška Fishermen's Port—While Split's harborfront Riva is where the beautiful people stroll, the city's fishermen roots still thrive just to the
west. The neighborhood called
Matejuška—at the little harbor
where the Varoš district hits the
water (a five-minute walk beyond
the end of the Riva, with the
water on your left)—has long been
Split's working fishermen's harbor. While the area has received a

facelift to match the one along the Riva, it still retains its striped-collar character. The enclosed harbor area is filled with working fishing boats and colorful dinghies that bob in unison. Along the breakwater, notice the new fishermen's lockers, where people who earn their living from the Adriatic still keep their supplies. You'll see the most fisherman action here in the mornings.

The far side of the breakwater—all glitzy white marble—is another world, with a pebbly beach, inviting plaza, and some of the best views looking back on the Riva. After its recent facelift, this jetty has become a popular open-air, after-hours hangout spot for young people. Like Split itself, these two worlds—the grizzled fishermen mending their nets, and the teenagers laughing and flirting—coexist more smoothly than anyone might have guessed.

Hiking the Marjan Peninsula—This huge, hilly, and relatively undeveloped spit of parkland—improbably located right next to Split's Old Town—feels like a chunk of Dalmatian island wilderness, a stone's throw from the big city. With out-of-the-way beaches and miles of hiking trails, the Marjan (MAR-yahn) Peninsula is where residents go to relax; most people here seem to have their favorite hidden paths and beach coves, so ask around for tips.

From the Šperun neighborhood at the west end of the Old Town, you can hike to various lookout points. The best views are from the lowest point. If you're in shape, figure about an hour to hike to the top viewpoint, then another 45 minutes back down.

Start by climbing the stairs past the recommended Šperun Restaurant, and continue straight up Senjska ulica. Follow the

stairs all the way up for 10-15 steep minutes to reach a spectacular view terrace (with sweeping vistas over Split's Old Town), next to a little café.

If you like, you can keep ascending for more good views (though you can't really see the Old Town beyond here). To continue on, curl around past the restaurant (following signs for *Crkva sv. Nikole* and *Sedlo*) and follow the steep pathway up, passing the fenced-in park on your right. Soon you'll reach the small chapel of St. Nicholas. Just behind it, find the steps up and to the right (look for *Marjanske Skale* signs). At the top of these stairs is Split's very humble zoo (adults-10 kn, kids-5 kn, daily 8:00-18:00). From here, a broad path cuts through the woods, with smaller paths branching off downhill. For the highest viewpoint, follow signs for *Sedlo* and hike up the steps to the terrace. This top-of-the-world perch offers a 360-degree panorama of Split's urban sprawl, receding layers of jagged and majestic mountains, offshore islands, and the bay behind the Marjan peninsula (but little in the way of Old Town views).

It's easiest to go back down the way you came. But for a longer hike, continue down the stairs at the far end of the view terrace, and follow signs for *Crkva sv. Jere*. This path takes you along the length of the peninsula, mostly through trees (read: no views). A series of switchbacks leads back down to the main road running along the perimeter of Marjan; from here, you can turn left to get back to town or right for an even longer walk around the far end of Marjan.

The peninsula also has a pair of good beaches (Ježinac and Bene, described next).

Hitting the Beach—Since it's more of a big city than a resort, Split's beaches aren't as scenic (and the water not as clear) as small towns elsewhere along the coast. The beach that's most popular—and crowded—is **Bačvice,** in a sandy cove just a short walk east of the main ferry terminal. As it's very shallow, it's especially popular with kids. After dark, it becomes a hopping meat-market nightlife zone for older "kids." You'll find less crowded beaches just to the east of Bačvice.

Or head in the other direction to Marjan, the peninsular city park, which is ringed with several sunbathing beaches. Along the southern edge of Marjan, just below the Meštrović Gallery, is a rocky but more local-feeling and less crowded beach called **Ježinac** (Croatian for "sea urchin"...be sure to wear water shoes). **Bene Beach** is along the northern edge of Marjan—reachable by bus #12 (the same one that goes to the Meštrović Gallery), tourist train (described earlier, under "Getting Around Split"), bike, or foot (about a 45-minute walk from the Old Town).

Nightlife in Split

The Riva—Every night, the sea of Croatian humanity laps at the walls of Diocletian's Palace along the town's pedestrian promenade. Choose a bench and watch life go by, or enjoy a drink at one

of the many outdoor cafés. Live
music (funded by the tourist
board) enlivens the Riva nightly
through the summer (June-mid-
Sept).

Old Town Bars—The labyrinthine lanes of the Old Town
are packed with mostly interchangeable bars and cafés featuring inviting tables crammed
between ancient stone buildings under a starry Croatian sky. If
you're staying in the Old Town, you'll hear bar-goers late into the
night. If you can't beat 'em, join 'em. One way is to simply lose
yourself in the twisty lanes by following the music and the sound
of socializing Croatians to the spot you like best. Or, if you prefer a
little direction to your ramblings, explore the following neighborhoods. Note that, while each of the bars listed here has an interior,
there's little reason to sit anywhere but under the open sky. Prices
and menus are similar at most places (beer, wine, cocktails, coffee
drinks); ordering something simply gives you an excuse to sit in a
gorgeous outdoor space, nurse a drink, and focus on your travel
partner. The action at these places really gets rolling around 22:00
and peaks around 23:00 (when bars are supposed to close their
outdoor seating areas—but rarely do).

On the Peristyle: The obvious choice is right on the main
square of the Old Town, Diocletian's former entry hall. All day
long, the Peristyle steps serve as makeshift café tables for the bar
called **Luxor,** with red cushions and small tables scattered along
the steps. If you sit on a cushion, you're expected to order a drink
(but you can sit or stand elsewhere for free). In the evening—as
twilight encroaches and floodlights transform the square into
one of the most atmospheric public spaces in Europe—live music
breaks out (generally starting between 20:00 and 21:00 and continuing until around midnight). The smooth marble tiles of the
Peristyle—worn to a slippery sheen by two millennia of visitors—
becomes a dance floor, as people salsa, foxtrot, or pop-and-lock
their way around the majestic space. Where else can you cut a rug
in the grand entry hall of a Roman palace?

Majstora Jurja: This street, which runs along the north edge
of Diocletian's Palace (just inside the wall), is lined with a mellow gaggle of low-key hangouts. Some mood music plays, but the
soundtrack here is mostly chatting, laughing, and flirting. West
of the Golden Gate, the lineup of café/bars includes **Teak** (with a
namesake woody interior that feels almost distinguished) and the
nondescript **Kala** and **Mosquito.** Up the side street at Dominisova
9, **Galerija** has the classiest atmosphere, with an upscale-feeling

(but not stuffy), gallery-like ambience and a display case of cakes. East of the Golden Gate is the requisite **Irish Pub** (the best place in town to watch a rugby match) and **Red Room,** filling a large square with tables.

"**Slavija Square**": This is my own nickname for the tight, stepped area that's squeezed in front of Hotel Slavija, near Radić Brothers Square (Trg Braće Radića; from the square's statue of Marulić, enter the Old Town and bear right, following the beat). This area is more youthful and rowdy, with throbbing techno music and cocktails that flow freely. Clambering up the steps are several bars, including the hip and roughly interchangeable **Puls** and **Fluid,** with predictable thumpa-thumpa atmosphere. Near the top of the stairs, the engagingly scruffy **Rakijarnica** boasts magic-marker walls, free stick-on moustaches, the motto "User Friendly," and *rakija*, the ubiquitous Balkan firewater, in several different flavors (mostly fruit). A few steps beyond, through the enclosed courtyard on the right, **Ghetto** has a mellower sailors' bordello-theme interior, with heart-shaped tables, red velvet, and randy graffiti. In the opposite direction, around the corner toward Jupiter's Temple, is a pair of bars facing each other (**Jupiter** and **San Giovanni**), with outdoor café tables and corny American music.

Behind the Loggia: For the youngest, trendiest scene in the Old Town, head for the zone locals call *Iza Lođa* ("Behind the Loggia"). From the grand People's Square, follow the beat behind the former City Hall loggia to discover a well-dressed meat market populated by sleazy young men and tipsy American girls determined to make bad decisions. The main magnet here is the standing-room-only **Gaga,** with a pounding dance beat, indoor and outdoor bar areas, and a laser-light show on the ancient stones above. At the far end of the little square, like a mellow grandparent observing the rowdy younger generation, is **La Linea** (which locals call simply "taverna")—an old sailors' pub decorated with nautical flags.

Other Areas: The large square at the top of Marmontova, just before the **Zara** store, is crammed with tables belonging to a half-dozen, identical-feeling cafés. And with the arrival of the recommended Bajamonti café, **Trg Republike** (the grand Napoleonic square just west of the Riva) could also become a happening and inviting nightlife option.

Clubbing at Bačvice Beach—This family-friendly beach by day becomes a throbbing party area for young locals late at night. Since all Old Town bars have to close by 1:00 in the morning, night owls hike on over to the Bačvice crescent of clubs. The three-floor club complex is a cacophony of music, with the beat of one club melting into the next—all with breezy terraces overlooking the harbor.

Sleeping in Split

Split has very expensive sleeps. Since there aren't enough beds in peak season, many hoteliers are shameless about gouging their customers. Lower your expectations. Split also suffers from perhaps the worst nighttime noise of any destination in this book—bring earplugs, and always ask for a quiet room (if possible). If you're on your own for breakfast, see my suggestions on page 224.

Outside of the Old Town

These good values are within a five-minute walk of the Old Town. They're nearly as convenient as the Old Town options, but cheaper. Note that none of these places has a full-time reception desk; call ahead to arrange your arrival time.

In the Lučac Neighborhood, East of the Old Town

The Lučac neighborhood—which lines up along the busy street called Kralja Zvonimira—feels urban and a bit gritty, but it's handy to the Old Town. You'll find more Old World atmosphere on Petrova street, a block below the main road.

$$$ Hotel Luxe, a mod, minimalist hotel with 30 elegant-feeling rooms, is your best bet near the Old Town for sea views. While it fronts a dreary, busy urban street, all of its rooms face the quieter back side, and most have views over the harbor (non-view Sb-€140/€115/€105, sea-view Sb-€160/€130/€115, non-view Db-€155/€130/€120, sea-view Db-€200/€165/€140, bigger "superior" room with balcony for about €50 more, cheaper Nov-Feb, one-time €25 cleaning fee, air-con, elevator, free Wi-Fi, spa with small gym and Jacuzzi, Kralja Zvonimira 6, tel. 021/314-444, www.hotelluxesplit.com, hotelluxe@hotelluxesplit.com).

$$$ Villa Diana has six overpriced, mostly small rooms in a stone house over a restaurant (Sb-€104/€90/€80, Db-€129/€115/€100, Tb-€159/€145/€130, pricier apartment also available, cheaper Nov-March, air-con, free Wi-Fi, free parking, next door to Villa Ana at Kuzmanića 3—see directions in next listing, tel. & fax 021/482-460, www.villadiana.hr, info@villadiana.hr).

$$ Villa Ana, my favorite small hotel in Split, has five modern, comfortable rooms in a smart little freestanding stone house (Sb-€80, Db-€100, Tb-€115, roughly €20 less Nov-March, includes breakfast, air-con, free Wi-Fi, reception open sporadically 7:00-22:00, may be closed mid-Dec-mid-Jan, a few tight free parking spots out front; 2 long blocks east of Old Town up busy Kralja Zvonimira, follow the driveway-like lane opposite the lonely skyscraper to Vrh Lučac 16; tel. 021/482-715, fax 021/482-721, www.villaana-split.hr, info@villaana-split.hr, Danijel Bilobrk and helpful Branka).

Sleep Code

(5 kn = about $1, €1 = about $1.40, country code: 385, area code: 021)

S = Single, **D** = Double/Twin, **T** = Triple, **Q** = Quad, **b** = bathroom. The modest tourist tax (about 7 kn per person, per night) is not included in these rates. Hotels generally accept credit cards and include breakfast in their rates, while most *sobe* accept only cash and don't offer breakfast. While rates are listed in euros, you'll pay in kunas. Everyone listed here speaks English.

Rates: If I've listed two sets of rates for an accommodation, I've noted when the second rate applies (generally off-season, Oct-May); if I've listed three sets of rates, separated by slashes, the first is for peak season (July-Sept), the second is shoulder season (May-June and Oct), and the third is off-season (Nov-April). The dates for seasonal rates vary by hotel, and prices can change without notice; verify the hotel's current rates online or by email. For other updates, see www.ricksteves.com/update.

Price Ranges: To help you sort easily through these listings, I've divided the accommodations into three categories based on the price for a standard double room with bath in peak season:

$$$ Higher Priced—Most rooms €125 or more.
$$ Moderately Priced—Most rooms between €70-125.
$ Lower Priced—Most rooms €70 or less.

$ Villa Art, run by sweet Tatijana, has five color-coded rooms that are unusually thoughtfully appointed. Decorated by a local artist, they have an almost French flair. Although it's on a drab alley, it's handy to the center (Db-€70/€55, apartment-€100/€85, lower prices are for Sept-June, no extra charge for 1- or 2-night stays, air-con, free Wi-Fi, Vickotina 7, tel. 021/482-288, mobile 098-170-4769, www.splitartapartments.com, booking@splitartapartments.com).

$ Dioclecijan Apartments, run by Tomislav Skalić and his wife Ivana, has two small rooms and one apartment in a pleasant local neighborhood. The decor is a tasteful mix of new and traditional (Db-€55/€40, apartment-€80/€65, lower price is for Oct-March, 1-night stays cost €5 more in rooms or €10 more in apartment, prices soft, cash only, no breakfast, air-con, free Wi-Fi, Petrova 19, Tomislav's mobile 091-537-1826, Ivana's mobile 091-536-7486, tskalic@globalnet.hr). From near the Green Market, head up Kralja Zvonimira, and turn right down Petrova. The apartments are on your left as the road bends.

Split Hotels & Restaurants

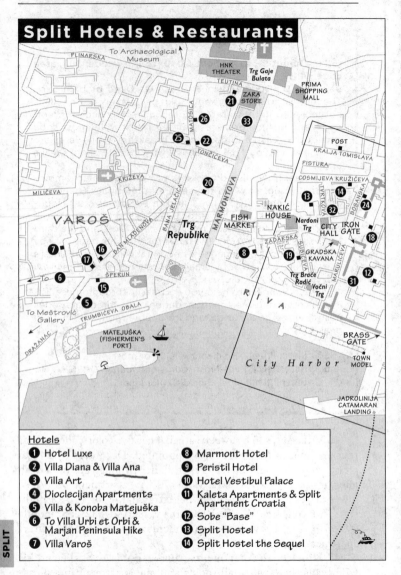

Hotels

1. Hotel Luxe
2. Villa Diana & Villa Ana
3. Villa Art
4. Dioclecijan Apartments
5. Villa & Konoba Matejuška
6. To Villa Urbi et Orbi & Marjan Peninsula Hike
7. Villa Varoš
8. Marmont Hotel
9. Peristil Hotel
10. Hotel Vestibul Palace
11. Kaleta Apartments & Split Apartment Croatia
12. Sobe "Base"
13. Split Hostel
14. Split Hostel the Sequel

In the Varoš Neighborhood, West of the Old Town

In addition to hosting the following accommodations, the atmospheric Varoš neighborhood—with twisty lanes climbing up towards the forested peak of the Marjan peninsula—is also home to several recommended eateries and the self-service Modrulj Launderette.

$$ Villa Matejuška has six apartments with old-fashioned beams and stone walls on a tight lane (small apartment-€109/€79,

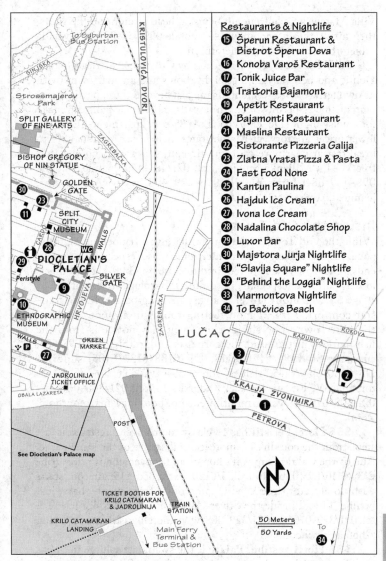

bigger apartment-€117/€79, biggest apartment-€136/€89, lower prices are for Oct-mid-April, cash only, no extra charge for 1-night stays, no breakfast, air-con, free Wi-Fi, Tomića Stine 3, mobile 098-222-822, www.villamatejuska.hr, info@villamatejuska.hr or villamatejuska93@gmail.com). A second branch, **$$ Villa Urbi et Orbi,** has six cheaper units a steep five-minute hike up the street (Sb-€79/€59, Db-€89/€59, small apartment-€119/€89, big apartment-€169/€129, lower prices are for Oct-mid-April; from

Villa Matejuška, continue up Senjska, head straight up the stairs, then turn right on Šenoina to #2; mobile 099-734-2777, www.villa urbietorbi.hr, info@villaurbietorbi.hr).

$$ Villa Varoš, run with class by Croatian-American Joanne Đonlić and her son Jure, has eight rooms and an apartment (with its own terrace) on a residential lane just beyond the appealing, restaurant-lined Šperun street. Thin walls and echoey halls can make for a noisy night (Db-€80/€65, Tb-€85/€70, apartment-€120/€90, lower prices are for Oct-March, rates include tax, optional 30-kn breakfast at nearby restaurant, air-con, stairs with no elevator, free Wi-Fi, Miljenka Smoje 1, tel. 021/483-469, Joanne's mobile 098-469-681, Jure's mobile 098-229-408, www.villavaros.hr, joanne.d.o.o@st.t-com.hr).

Inside the Old Town

While the Old Town is convenient, it's also a happening nightlife zone, so you're likely to encounter some noise (especially on weekends). Old Town bars are required to close by 23:00, though this is loosely enforced (especially in summer). Earplugs are essential.

$$$ Marmont Hotel is a very inviting oasis offering four-star comfort, with 21 mod-feeling rooms in a quiet corner of the Old Town. The slight aroma you may notice is from the fish market, just around the corner (standard Sb-€145/€95/€85, superior Sb-€185/€120/€118, Db-€188/€136/€105, superior Db-€260/€189/€145, "deluxe" rooms also available, air-con, elevator, free Wi-Fi, sun terrace, Zadarska 13, tel. 021/308-060, fax 021/308-070, www.marmonthotel.com, booking@marmonthotel .com).

$$$ Hotel Peristil has 12 classy rooms over a restaurant just steps from the couldn't-be-more-central square of the same name. Run by the Caktaš family, it's homey and convenient, if pricey (Sb-€135/€110/€95, Db-€160/€135/€120, extra bed-€15, air-con, stairs with no elevator, free Wi-Fi, some noise from nearby bars, just behind TI and inside the Silver Gate at Poljana Kraljice Jelene 5, tel. 021/329-070, fax 021/329-088, www.hotelperistil.com, booking @hotelperistil.com).

$$$ Hotel Vestibul Palace is the swankiest splurge in Split's Old Town, with modern decor in an old shell. Tucked in a corner just behind the entry vestibule on the upper level of Diocletian's Palace, this plush place offers seven rooms with maximum comfort and style for maximum prices. Throughout the day, you'll hear the harmonious voices of the *klapa* singers echoing up from the vestibule below (Sb-€190/€158/€126, small Db-€230/€189/€147, standard Db-€315/€275/€217, pricier suites also available, air-con, no elevator, free Internet access and Wi-Fi, valet parking-100 kn, Iza Vestibula 4, tel. 021/329-329, fax 021/329-333, www.vestibul

palace.com, info@vestibulpalace.com). They also have four more rooms in a nearby annex, called Villa Dobrić.

$$ Kaleta Apartments, run by the Raić family, consists of several tastefully decorated apartments spread across two buildings. Two stylish, modern apartments are squeezed between cafés along a tight alley in a lively area at the back of the Old Town (the good windows do a heroic job of keeping noise to a minimum). Their other three units, including a larger one with a couch and eat-in space, share a common lounge in a quieter building a few blocks away, near the People's Square (Db-€75-90, €60-80 in Oct-May, price depends on size of room, cash only, air-con, free Internet access and Wi-Fi, Majstora Jurja 4, mobile 099-509-4299, www.kaletaapartments.hr, kaletaapartments@email.t-com.hr).

$$ Split Apartment Croatia, run by go-getter Nikša, is an agency with a line on apartments around Split. Nikša rents two of his own rooms, near the People's Square (Db-€75/€55/€40, air-con, free Wi-Fi). He can also arrange a room for you elsewhere for similar prices (you pay him 20 percent, then the rest to the owner, cash only; his office at Majstora Jurja 4 serves as a sort of reception desk, offering free coffee and Internet access; mobile 091-390-9411, www.split-apartment.com, info@split-apartment.com).

$ Sobe "Base" has three of the nicest rooms in the Old Town. Tina and her dad, retired ship's captain Ivo, offer many amenities unusual for this price range, including free Wi-Fi and Internet terminals in each room. You can't be more central: All of the colorful rooms—located over a gift shop—overlook the front steps of the cute little Jupiter's Temple. Although it's in the midst of some bustling bar action, the double-paned windows do their darnedest to provide reasonable peace; earplugs help, too (Db-€70, €60 in Sept-June, cash only, no extra charge for 1- or 2-night stays, no breakfast, air-con, Kraj Svetog Ivana 3, tel. 021/317-375, mobile 098-361-387, www.base-rooms.com, mail@base-rooms.com).

$ *Other* Sobe: Several *sobe* are inside Split's Old Town, and many more are within a 10-minute walk. As in any coastal town, you can simply show up at the boat dock or bus station, be met by locals trying to persuade you into their rooms, and check out the best offer (Db-about 250 kn). Or you can try booking through a travel agency, such as **Travel49** or **Turistički Biro** (both listed earlier, under "Helpful Hints"), or **Split Apartment Croatia** (listed above).

$ Split Hostel is centrally located just off the People's Square in the heart of town. This small, youthful hostel has 23 beds in four cramped rooms and a shared outdoor terrace to give everyone some much-needed breathing room. Run by a pair of Croat-Aussie women with the simple slogan "booze & snooze," it's Split's most central hostel option (bunk in 6-bed room-€25/€20/€17/€15, cash only, no breakfast, free Internet access and Wi-Fi, laundry service, excursions, 8 Narodni Trg, tel. 021/342-787, www.splithostel.com, info@splithostel.com). Their second location—**Split Hostel the Sequel**—is also in the Old Town, a short walk away, and has 25 dorm beds in five rooms at similar prices, plus a wider range of rooms, including 8-, 5-, 4-, and 2-bed rooms (D-€70 in summer, downstairs bar, Kružićeva 5).

Eating in Split

Split's Old Town has oodles of atmosphere, but the Varoš district, just a couple of blocks west of the Old Town, has several characteristic *konoba*s (traditional restaurants). I've listed options in both areas. Service in Split's restaurants tends to be a bit grouchy, and you may be unceremoniously turned away if they're very busy (reservations are wise, especially for dinner).

In Varoš, West of the Old Town

Šperun Restaurant has a classy, cozy Old World ambience and a passion for good Dalmatian food. Owner Damir Banović (with the help of his animated dad, Zdravko) serves a mix of Croatian and "eclectic Mediterranean," specializing in seafood. A "buffet" table of *antipasti* (starters) in the lower dining room shows you what you're getting, so you can select your ideal meal (not self-service— order from the waiter). This place distinguishes itself by offering a warm welcome and good food for reasonable prices (35-70-kn pastas, 50-120-kn meat and seafood dishes, daily 9:00-23:00, air-con, a few sidewalk tables, reservations wise in summer, Šperun 3, tel. 021/346-999). Their annex across the street, **Bistrot Šperun Deva,** has a simpler and cheaper menu, lots of outdoor seating, and a handy à la carte breakfast for *sobe*-dwellers (20-50-kn salads, 50-60-kn main courses, daily 8:00-23:00, closed off-season, Šperun 2).

Konoba Matejuška offers charm, good food, and fair prices in a cozy, inviting, mellow, five-table cellar (30-55-kn starters, 50-150-kn main courses, daily 13:00-16:00 & 19:00-23:00, below Villa Matejuška hotel at Tomića Stine 3, tel. 021/355-152).

Konoba Varoš, though bigger and more impersonal than others listed here, is beloved by natives and tourists alike for its great food. Serious waiters serve a wide range of Croatian cooking (including pastas, seafood, and meat dishes) under droopy fishnets in a slightly gloomy throwback interior (50-80-kn pastas, 60-110-

kn main courses, daily 9:00-24:00, lots of groups, reservations smart—busiest 20:00-22:00, Ban Mladenova 7, tel. 021/396-138).

Smoothies and Fruit Juices: For a healthier energy boost, head for **Tonik Juice Bar,** run by Croat-Aussie Stefanie. Select from the diverse menu of smoothies and juice combos (16-40 kn). In summer, they also serve light meals (30-kn wraps, 25-kn muesli for breakfast, June-Sept daily 7:00-22:00, shoulder season daily 8:00-21:00, closed Nov-March, near the launderette and Šperun street restaurants at Ban Mladenova 5, mobile 098-641-376).

In and near the Old Town

Trattoria Bajamont, not to be confused with Bajamonti (listed below), is buried on a narrow lane deep in the Old Town. This is a great choice for unpretentious, affordable Dalmatian home cooking with an emphasis on fish. The handwritten menu pinned to a bulletin board informs you of the day's options—all fresh from the market. In this tight, casual, and cozy eatery, the busy kitchen and seven tables are all crammed into a single room. Because the place can get crowded, you may have to share your table—and be prepared for the service to be chaotic and a bit quirky (60-80-kn pastas, 70-150-kn fish dishes, Mon-Sat 8:00-24:00, closed Sun, Bajamontijeva 3, mobile 091-253-7441).

Apetit serves up traditional Dalmatian cuisine in an appealingly modern, second-floor dining room (the restaurant on the ground floor of the same building, which enjoys hijacking Apetit's customers, is a different operation). As there's no outdoor seating, this is a good bad-weather option (50-70-kn pastas, 60-115-kn main courses; 90-kn daily special in summer includes soup, salad, and main dish; lots of groups, daily 10:00-24:00, Šubićeva 5, tel. 021/332-549).

Bajamonti sits regally at the top of Split's beautiful, arcaded square, Trg Republike, just off the west end of the Riva. This place brings a certain grand-café elegance to Split's otherwise rustic-*konoba*-heavy dining scene. The interior is classy, with checkerboard-tiled, split-level elegance, but the best seating is on the grand square out front (55-80-kn pastas, 80-160-kn main courses, daily 7:30-24:00, Trg Republike 1, tel. 021/341-033).

Maslina ("Olive"), an unpretentious family-run spot filled with locals, hides behind a shopping mall on the busy Marmontova pedestrian street. They serve a wide range of 45-70-kn pizzas and pastas, plus 65-110-kn meat and fish dishes (Tue-Sat 10:00-24:00, Sun-Mon 12:00-24:00, Teutina 1A, tel. 021/314-988, Pezo family). It's virtually impossible to find on your own, so follow these directions carefully: Approaching the top of Marmontova from the harbor, look for the low-profile archway on the left beyond the café tables (just before the big Zara store). Walk along the skinny

SPLIT

path behind the building to reach the restaurant.

Pizzerias: **Ristorante Pizzeria Galija,** at the west end of the Old Town, has a boisterous local following and good wood-fired pizza, pasta, and salads (40-70 kn, Mon-Sat 9:00-24:00, Sun 12:00-24:00, air-con, just a block off of Marmontova at Tončićeva 12, tel. 021/347-932; the recommended Hajduk ice-cream shop is nearby). **Zlatna Vrata** ("Golden Gate"), right in the Old Town, offers wood-fired pizzas and pasta dishes. The food and interior are nothing special, but there's wonderful outdoor seating in a tingle-worthy Gothic courtyard with pointy arches and lots of pillars (40-60 kn, Mon-Sat 7:00-24:00, closed Sun, just inside the Golden Gate and—as you face outside—up the skinny alley to the left, on Majstora Jurja, tel. 021/345-015).

Take-Away: **Fast Food None** ("Grandma's") is a stand-up or take-away pizza joint handy for a quick bite in the Old Town. In addition to pizzas and bruschettas with various toppings, they serve up a pair of traditional pizza-like specialties (with crust on bottom and top, like a filled pizza): *viška pogača,* with tomatoes, onion, and anchovy; and *soparnik,* with a thin layer of spinach, onion, and olive oil. They can also make you a grilled sandwich—just point to what you want (10-30 kn, Mon-Sat 7:00-23:00, closed Sun, just outside Diocletian's Palace on the skinny street that runs along the wall at Bosanska 4, tel. 021/347-252). **Kantun Paulina** ("Paulina's Corner") is a local favorite for take-away *ćevapčići*—Balkan grilled meats (17-20 kn, Mon-Sat 8:00-23:00, Sun 17:00-23:00, Matošića 1). For descriptions of your options, see the "Balkan Flavors" sidebar on page 418.

Breakfast: **Hotel Peristil** serves breakfast to non-guests for 50 kn (all-you-can-eat, including eggs; daily 7:00-12:00); the adjacent **Duje Restaurant,** just behind the cathedral, has a similar deal. The only place serving breakfast along the Riva is **Adriana,** which charges a hefty 80 kn for eggs, rolls, coffee, and juice; alternatively, you could just buy some pastries at a bakery and eat them on a harborfront bench. For a cheap alternative, head over to the Matejuška fishermen's port, where **Leut** restaurant serves a 30-kn breakfast on their terrace (from 10:00). Several of my recommended restaurants also serve breakfast.

Gelato: Split has several spots for delicious ice cream *(sladoled)*. Most ice-cream parlors *(kuća sladoleda)* are open daily 8:00-24:00. Natives recommend two in particular: **Hajduk,** named for Split's soccer team, is a block off the main Marmontova pedestrian drag; ask them to dip your cone in milk chocolate for no extra charge (around the corner from Pizzeria Galija at Matošićeva 4). More central, at the east end of the Riva, look for **Ivona** (near entrance to Diocletian's cellars at Kaštelanska cesta 65).

Split Connections

By Boat

As the transport hub for the Dalmatian Coast, Split has good boat connections to nearly anywhere you want to go. The fast passenger  catamarans dock close to the Old Town: the *Krilo* catamaran uses dock #11, which is along the pier halfway between the main ferry terminal and the Old Town; and the Jadrolinija catamaran arrives and departs at the handy Obala Lazareta embankment just in front of the Old Town. Big car ferries can arrive or depart from all along the harbor (electronic boards display which dock each boat leaves from). Note that these locations sometimes change according to boat traffic.

Note: The following boat information is subject to change—always confirm before you make your plans. To check Jadrolinija schedules, see www.jadrolinija.hr; for *Krilo* catamaran schedules, see www.krilo.hr. Or drop by Split's helpful Jadrolinija boat ticket office, in the main ferry terminal (open 24/7 in summer, daily 5:30-24:00 off-season, tel. 021/338-333).

Buying Tickets

Tickets for the fast passenger **catamarans** (either *Krilo* or Jadrolinija) are not sold until 6:00 in the morning on the day of departure. As these boats can sell out quickly in peak season, buy your tickets in the morning. For the 11:30 Jadrolinija catamaran, try to get your tickets by 9:00 (or, on busy days in July-Aug, even earlier—by about 8:30). For afternoon boats, purchase tickets by noon (or earlier on summer weekends). *Krilo* tickets are only sold at the kiosk at its departure dock (#11). For Jadrolinija catamarans, you can buy tickets at three locations: the kiosk on the parking island right in front of the Old Town; next to the *Krilo* kiosk alongside the harbor; and in the main terminal (if the kiosk near the Old Town has a long line, consider walking five minutes to the next one, where the wait is probably shorter).

If you're a passenger walking onto a Jadrolinija **car ferry,** there's no need to buy tickets in advance. However, if you're driving onto a car ferry, it's smart to buy your tickets from one of the Jadrolinija kiosks mentioned above and line up early—ask locally for advice on your particular boat. For the connections below, I've listed the passenger fare.

Sailing Between Croatia and Italy

Many travelers are tempted to splice a little bit of Croatia into their Italian itinerary, or vice versa. But zipping across the Adriatic isn't as effortless as it seems. Most sea crossings involve an overnight on the boat, and the Italian towns best connected to Croatia—Ancona, Pescara, and Bari—are far from Italy's top sights. Plan thoughtfully. For example, if you're in northern Italy and want to sample Croatia, it's much easier to dip into Istria than it is to get all the way down to Croatia's Dalmatian Coast.

If you decide to set sail, you have several options, run by various companies. Split is the primary hub, but you can also go from other cities (usually Dubrovnik or Zadar; some international ferries also call at the small Dalmatian islands). Almost all boats go to Ancona, Italy, which is about two-thirds of the way up the Italian coast (on the calf of Italy's "boot"). Others go to Pescara, about 100 miles south of Ancona; and to Bari, near the southern tip of Italy (the "heel"). Most trips are overnight and last 8-10 hours, but there are faster daytime catamarans. Note that these connections are highly subject to change from year to year; do an Internet search to be confident you know all of your options.

Slow Night Boats: Figure about €55 per person for one-way deck passage (about 10-20 percent more in peak season, roughly July-Aug; sometimes even more on weekends). Onboard accommodation costs extra (about €20 per person for a couchette in a 4-berth compartment, €60-75 per person in 2-bed compartment with private shower and WC). These companies operate night boats to Italy:

Jadrolinija goes from Split to Ancona, from Zadar to Ancona, and from Dubrovnik to Bari (tel. 051/211-444 or 021/338-333, www.jadrolinija.hr).

Blue Line sails from Split to Ancona; on weekends in Aug, it stops en route at Stari Grad on Hvar Island (can book at Split Tours travel agency in Split, tel. 021/352-533, www.blueline -ferries.com).

SPLIT

If I've listed a price range for a specific journey, it depends on the season.

Weather Disruptions: Catamarans are the quickest way to the islands, but they're also the most susceptible to bad weather. In very rough or windy weather, cancellations are possible (decisions are made a couple of hours before departure—ask at the ticket booth what time you should come back to check). In poor weather, the *Krilo* is more stable (and provides a more comfortable ride) than Jadrolinija's *Adriana* catamaran; if you have an option, go with *Krilo*. If the catamarans aren't running, look into taking the slower car ferries instead (which typically go in any weather).

Azzurra Line/Jadrolinija goes between Bari and Dubrovnik, and between Bari and Kotor, Montenegro (Croatian tel. 020/313-178, Montenegrin tel. 085/313-617, Italian tel. 080-592-8400, www.azzurraline.com).

Other companies serving these routes come and go each year—ask the Split TI or poke around Split's main terminal building to discover the latest.

Fast Daytime Boats: Some speedier crossings are available. But because these boats are faster and smaller, they're also weather-dependent—so they don't run off-season. In recent years, due to decreased demand, these boats have run only in July and August—check online for a current schedule. **SNAV** connects Split and Ancona in just 4.5 hours; they also zip from Split to Stari Grad (on Hvar Island), then on to the Italian town of Pescara (6 hours total; either trip €60-100 one-way, depending on season; Croatian tel. 021/322-252, Italian tel. 081-428-5555, www.snav.it).

Trains Within Italy: From **Ancona,** you can catch a train to Venice (almost hourly, 4.25-5.25 hours, most transfer in Bologna), Florence (almost hourly, 3-4.25 hours, most transfer in Bologna), or Rome (8/day direct, 3-4.5 hours). From **Pescara,** trains head to Rome (6/day direct, 3.75-4.25 hours) and Florence (almost hourly, 4.5-5.25 hours, transfer in Bologna). From **Bari,** you can hop a train to Naples (6/day, 3.75-6 hours, most transfer in Caserta), Rome (3/day direct, 4.75 hours), or Florence (8/day, 6.75-8.5 hours, transfer in Rome or Bologna). For timetables, check www.ferroviedellostato.it or www.bahn.com (Germany's excellent all-Europe website).

Northern Italy/Croatia: Venice is connected by boat to several seaside towns in northern Croatia and Slovenia. For details, see page 104.

Note that in Italian, Split is called "Spalato" (which is also the sound you hear if seasickness gets the best of you).

Getting from Split to Other Destinations in Croatia

Big Jadrolinija Car Ferries: Twice weekly in summer, these hulking boats make the long trip down the Dalmatian Coast, connecting key destinations. They leave Split early in the morning (at 7:30) and head south, stopping at **Stari Grad on Hvar Island** (20-minute bus ride from Hvar town; 1.75 hours, 39-47 kn; the catamarans described next are faster and take you right to Hvar town), **Korčula town** (6 hours, 90-110 kn; again, catamarans to Korčula island are faster), **Sobra on Mljet Island** (1.25-hour bus ride from the national park; 8.75 hours, 110-130 kn), and **Dubrovnik** (11 hours, 110-130 kn). You can also take a boat to **Rijeka,** on the northern Croatian coast, 4 hours by train from Zagreb and 2.75 hours by train from Ljubljana (2/week, June-Sept only, 11 hours overnight, 160- to 190-kn deck passage, more if you want a bed).

Other Boats to Hvar Island: To reach Hvar, ideally catch a boat heading to Hvar town, the most interesting part of the island. Two companies run speedy catamarans (50-60 minutes) from Split to Hvar town: **Jadrolinija** (June-Sept: 2/day, departing Split at 11:30 and 15:00, 45-47 kn; Oct-May: 1/day, departing Split at 14:00, 45 kn; occasionally stops at Milna on Brač Island; a different catamaran, bound for Vis, stops at Hvar only on Tuesdays) and *Krilo* (June-Sept: departs Split daily at 17:00; Oct-May: departs Split daily at 16:00; 35-45 kn). You can also reach Hvar Island on the **local car ferries** from Split; these are frequent but take longer and are less convenient, since they take you to the town of Stari Grad, across the island and a 20-minute bus trip from Hvar town. On the other hand, these are the only way to get to Hvar in the morning—and a good backup plan if the 11:30 catamaran sells out, or if the catamaran stops running due to bad weather (7/day in summer, 3/day in winter, 1.75 hours, 39-47 kn).

Other Boats to Korčula Island: Many of the same boats that go to Hvar town continue on to Korčula Island. The most convenient is the *Krilo* **catamaran,** which takes you right to Korčula town (June-Sept: departs Split daily at 17:00; Oct-May: departs Split daily at 16:00; 2.5-2.75 hours; 60-65 kn; in summer, it also stops en route at Prigradica on Korčula Island). The other boats leave you at Vela Luka, at the far end of the island from Korčula town (buses meet arriving boats to take passengers on the one-hour trip into Korčula town). One **Jadrolinija catamaran** goes from Split to Hvar town, then to Vela Luka (June-Sept: departs Split at 15:00, Oct-May: departs at 14:00, 2 hours, 40-50 kn). You can also take Jadrolinija's slower **local car ferries** from Split to Vela Luka (1-2/day, 3 hours, 50-60 kn).

By Bus

Each of the following routes is served by multiple companies, which charge slightly different rates, so the prices listed here are rough estimates. Always ask about the fastest option—which can save hours of bus time. It's smart to arrive about 30 minutes before your bus departs to buy tickets (better yet, during peak season, come to the station to buy them earlier in the day). The generally English-speaking staff at Split's bus station gives out handy little schedules for popular journeys. Bus info: www.ak-split.hr, toll tel. 060-327-777.

By Bus to: Zagreb (at least hourly, 5-8 hours, depending on route, about 175-200 kn), **Dubrovnik** (almost hourly, less off-season, 3.5-5 hours, 100 kn), **Korčula** (1 night bus leaves at 1:00 in the morning and arrives at 6:00, 125 kn), **Trogir** (1-2/hour,

30 minutes, about 20 kn), **Zadar** (at least hourly, 3 hours, about 80-120 kn), **Mostar** (6/day, 4-4.5 hours, about 115 kn), **Međugorje** (3/day, 3.5 hours, about 100 kn), **Sarajevo** (5/day in summer, 3/day in winter, 5.5-6 hours, 7.5 hours, about 200 kn), **Rijeka** (7-10/day including some night buses, 7.75-8.5 hours, 260-350 kn). Zagreb-bound buses sometimes also stop at **Plitvice** (confirm with driver and ask him to stop at the national park entrance; about 4/day, 4-6 hours, 155 kn).

By Train

From Split, trains go to **Zagreb** (3/day, 6 hours, 190 kn; 1 direct night train, 9 hours, 172 kn); in Zagreb, you can transfer to **Ljubljana** (1/day, 9 hours total). Train info: tel. 021/338-525 or toll tel. 060-333-444, www.hznet.hr.

Route Tips for Drivers

Driving around the city center can be tricky—Split is split by its Old Town, which is welded to the harbor by the pedestrian-only Riva promenade. This means drivers needing to get 300 yards from one side of the Old Town to the other must drive about 15 minutes entirely around the center, which can be miserably clogged with traffic. A semicircular ring road and a tunnel under the Marjan peninsula help relieve the situation a bit.

Arriving in Split: Drivers are treated to the ugly side of Split as they approach town (don't worry—it gets better). From the expressway, you'll pass through an industrial zone, then curl through a few tunnels as you twist your way down into Split's striking, bowl-like setting. While you're still quite a distance from downtown, you'll come to a fork where you'll have to make a decision about which side of town you want to drive to (east or west); ask your hotel in advance for directions, and be ready for your turn. (While many hotels are individually signposted at the fork, it's a long list and hard to read quickly as you zip past.)

At the main fork, turning to the right (marked with *Centar* signs) takes you to the **west end** of the Old Town, including the Varoš neighborhood. Or, if you continue straight (marked *Trajekt*—"ferry"), you'll eventually reach other *Centar* signs and the **east end** of the Old Town, with the ferry terminal, the bus and train stations, and the Lučac neighborhood. You'll pop out right at the southeast corner of Diocletian's Palace (by the Green Market). For handy (but expensive) parking, when the road swings left to the ferry terminal, continue straight, right into a parking lot just outside the palace walls (10 kn/hour).

Connecting Split with Destinations to the North: Thanks to Croatia's A1 super-expressway, the road trip from Zagreb to Split takes less than five hours. You can leave Zagreb after an early dinner and arrive in Split before bedtime. If you're heading north from Split, simply drive up out of the city's bowl-like setting and follow signs to the A1 expressway north (toward Zagreb; if you're going to Plitvice, turn off at Otočac and drive east from there).

Connecting Split with Destinations to the South: If you're heading to Dubrovnik, other Dalmatian Coast destinations, or Mostar—it's a bit more complicated, as the expressway southbound from Split is only partially completed (to check the latest progress, see www.hac.hr or www.hak.hr). You have two options. The main **coastal road** twists slowly but scenically along some fantastic scenery, in an area dubbed the "Makarska Riviera." (Along this road is the town of Drvenik, where you can take a ferry to Sućuraj on Hvar Island; from Sućuraj, a surprisingly long and twisty road traverses the length of the island to Hvar town. If you're going to Hvar Island, taking a car ferry directly from Split to Stari Grad is much faster and less stressful.) Continuing south, you'll wind up in the town of Ploče (described later).

To save some time, most travelers prefer to take the **expressway** part of the way. To do this, as you leave Split, follow blue expressway signs to *Dubrovnik*. You can take A1 south as far as it goes; it cuts inland from the sea, running behind the tall coastal mountain range, near the Bosnian border. As of early 2012, A1 was complete to the remote town of Vrgorac, about 100 km (60 miles) south of Split; a small section around the coastal town of Ploče, about 25 km (15 miles) south of Vrgorac, was also complete. Until A1 is finished (possibly in late 2012 or early 2013), you'll have to transfer to rough and rugged surface roads between Vrgorac and Ploče. (Note that if you're headed to Mostar, the fastest way from here is to pass into Bosnia-Herzegovina just south of Vrgorac, at Veliki Prolog, then follow signs to *Mostar* from there.)

Ploče has a ferry that runs to the town of Trpanj, on the landward side of the Pelješac Peninsula—not far from Orebić, where another boat plods across to Korčula town. If you're headed to Korčula and plan your timing to catch this ferry, it could save you some driving.

Just south of Ploče is the dramatic Neretva River Delta, a scenic and lush zone of farmland (described on page 448). This also marks the end of the A1 expressway. Here you'll hop on the main Dalmatian coastal road. Halfway along the delta, you'll see the turnoff to Metković, the gateway town on the main, heavily touristed road between Croatia and Mostar.

South of the Neretva River Delta—after twisting up to a high perch overlooking the delta—is a border crossing. Here begins an odd little stretch of coastline that's technically in Bosnia, around the town of Neum (for details on Neum—and the bridge Croatia is building to bypass it—see "A Bridge Too Far?" on page 357).

Have your passport ready, but don't panic—the border is generally a quick wave-through. After a few more miles, you'll cross back into Croatia, and shortly come to a crossroads where, if you like, you can turn right and detour a few minutes to the impressively walled little villages of Ston and Mali Ston, at the base of the Pelješac Peninsula (all described on page 356). If you're headed to Korčula, continue beyond Ston to the far end of the Pelješac Peninsula, where the ferry plods from Orebić to Dominče, near Korčula town.

After Ston, you're less than an hour from Dubrovnik. Along the way, you'll have fine views of Mljet and the Elaphite Islands. As you near Dubrovnik, you'll pass through the town of Trsteno, which has a good arboretum (described on page 355). When you cross the giant, modern bridge, you'll know Dubrovnik is just around the bend; for arrival tips, see page 286.

Near Split: Trogir

Just 12 miles northwest of Split, across a giant bay, is Trogir, a tiny, medieval-architecture-packed town surrounded by water. This made-for-tourists village lacks the real-world heart and soul of Split, and it's reminiscent of a dozen other Croatian coastal resort towns (Hvar and Korčula are bigger and better). But Trogir's proximity to Split makes it appealing to yachters; the proud masts of tall ships line the harbor three deep. Although Trogir is nothing to jump ship for, it's an easy day trip for those looking to get away from urban Split.

Getting There

The easiest option in summer is to take the Sestrice **boat,** which avoids traffic and includes a mini-cruise on the Adriatic. The boat departs from the embankment in front of the Riva (24 kn, 4/day June-Sept only, 1 hour, stops at Čiovo Island en route, www.bura line.com).

You also have two bus options for reaching Trogir from Split, both roughly the same price (20-25 kn): The faster, easier option is to take a bus from Split's **main bus station,** next to the City Harbor. Any bus going north (for example, to Šibenik, Zadar, or even Rijeka) will usually stop at Trogir (1-2/hour, 30 minutes, simply go to ticket window and ask for next bus to Trogir). Note

SPLIT

that in the busiest summer months, long-distance bus drivers may not want to take you (preferring to give your seat instead to someone paying for a longer trip). The other, slower option is **local bus #37;** because this bus makes several stops along the way, it can take longer (3/hour Mon-Fri, 2/hour Sat-Sun; 45-60 minutes, depending on traffic; departs from Split's suburban bus station—Prigradski Autobusni Kolodvor, a 10-minute walk north of Old Town on Domovinskog rata; buy 20-kn ticket for zone IV at ticket window or on bus). Note that bus #37 also stops at the **airport** on its way between Split and Trogir; if you're sleeping in Trogir before catching a flight, this bus is handy (about 10 minutes from Trogir; taxis from Trogir to the airport are exorbitantly priced).

Orientation to Trogir

(area code: 021)
Trogir is a small island, wedged between the mainland and the much bigger Čiovo Island. Busy bridges connect it to the rest of the world at its east end, and a big soccer field squeezed between imposing watchtowers anchors the west end. In the middle is a tight medieval maze of twisty marble-stone lanes.

Tourist Information: At the main square, named for Pope John Paul II (Trg Ivana Pavla II), you'll find the TI (mid-June-Aug Mon-Sat 8:00-23:00, Sun 8:00-12:00; Sept-mid-June Mon-Fri 8:00-20:00, Sat 8:00-13:00, closed Sun; tel. 021/881-412).

Arrival in Trogir: Buses drop you off at the mainland market, just across the canal from the island. Cross the bridge into town and wander straight ahead for two blocks (bearing left); you'll run into the main square.

Sights in Trogir

On the main square is the town's centerpiece, the **Cathedral of St. Lawrence** (Katedrala Sv. Lovre). Built from the 13th through the 17th centuries, the cathedral drips with history. The bell tower alone took 200 years to build, leaving it a textbook lesson in Dalmatian architecture styles: straightforward Gothic at the bottom, Venetian Gothic in the middle, and Renaissance at the top. The cathedral's front entryway—the ornately decorated, recently restored Radovan's Portal—is worth a gander. Inside, it's dark, very old-feeling, and packed with altars. The treasury features some beautiful 15th-century carved-wood cabinets filled with ecclesiastical art and gear.

The town's other sights are the **Town Museum** (Muzej Grada), a few blocks north (toward the mainland) from the main square; and the **Monastery of St. Nikola** (Samostan Sv. Nikole), a few blocks south (toward Čiovo Island).

But Trogir isn't for museum-going; it's for aimless strolling. And the best place for that is along the wide, beautifully manicured **harborfront promenade** along the southern edge of town (Obala bana Berislavića). Lined with expensive restaurants, and clogged with giddy, ice-cream-licking tourists, this promenade is the highlight of a visit to Trogir. Often the enormous yachts of the rich and famous stern-tie into the good life here, giving wanderers something to gaze at and yak about. At the far end of the promenade, the **Kamerlengo Fortress** has a lookout tower with fine views over the town and region.

Sleeping in Trogir

(5 kn = about $1, €1 = about $1.40, country code: 385, area code: 021)

Some travelers prefer sleepy Trogir to bustling Split. But, since Trogir is also lively after-hours, and is in the airport's flight path, it's not the quietest place in Dalmatia.

$$$ Hotel Pašike is a family-run place with lots of character. Situated over a restaurant in the Old Town, its 14 rooms come with over-the-top traditional formality (standard Db-€115/€96/€92, fancier "exkluziv" Db-€129/€129/€103, superior Db-€143/€143/€115, less Nov-April, a few euros cheaper if you pay cash or stay longer than 3 nights, air-con, free Internet access and Wi-Fi, ulica Sinjska, tel. 021/885-185, mobile 091-484-8434, www.hotelpasike.com, info@hotelpasike.com, Buble family).

$$ Hotel Concordia, with 11 outmoded, slightly overpriced rooms at the end of the embankment, is run with warmth by the Bulum family (Sb-€60, small Db with view or bigger Db without view-€80/€75, big Db with view-€100/€90, lower prices are for Sept-June, only partially open in winter, air-con, free Wi-Fi, Obala bana Berislavića 22, tel. 021/885-400, fax 021/885-401, www.concordia-hotel.net, concordia-hotel@st.t-com.hr).

$ Palaća Stafileo has three apartments in a 15th-century Venetian palace buried in a quiet part of town. Well-run by gentle Thomas, it's the best *sobe* option I've found in Trogir (Db-€60-70/€55-65/€50-60, price depends on size of apartment, cash only, no breakfast, air-con, lots of stairs, ulica Budislavićeva 6, tel. 021/885-680, mobile 098-131-3171, www.trogironline.com/stafileo, stafileo@vip.hr).

$ Hostel Trogir is a basic, institutional-feeling hostel with four dorm rooms on Čiovo Island, a 10-minute walk across the bridge from downtown Trogir (bunk in 6- to 8-bed dorm-€14, air-con, free Internet access, Marin Rožić, tel. 021/884-916, mobile 091-579-2190, www.hosteltrogir.com, hosteltrogir@yahoo.com).

HVAR

Hvar's hip cachet, upscale-ritzy "Croatian Riviera" buzz, and easy proximity to Split have quickly turned this tidy little Dalmatian fishing village into one of the most popular (and most expensive) destinations in Croatia. The island desperately wants to be thought of as Croatia's answer to Mykonos or St-Tropez... and it's getting there. Although some travelers may find all of the glitz and high prices off-putting, the setting is undeniably gorgeous, and the island provides an interesting contrast to its low-brow rival, Korčula.

Unlike Korčula, with its fortified mini-Dubrovnik feel, Hvar's straightforward main town, also called Hvar, melts into the harbor instead of dominating it. But as you get to know it, Hvar reveals itself to be a fun-loving, easygoing place to be on vacation. Its quirky museums, while far from time-consuming, are enjoyable. The formidable fortress hovering above town provides restless beach bums with a good excuse for a hike and rewards hikers with stunning views. And if you're seeking nightlife, you'll find that happening Hvar can become a party town after hours.

Hvar is aggressively courting the big-money yachting crowd. This means that its hotels and restaurants are pricier than other Croatian destinations (including famous towns like Dubrovnik). And who sails into town on a yacht? Celebrities. Locals claim their laid-back attitude is perfect for high-profile visitors who just want to be left alone. Recent celeb visitors have included Beyoncé and Britain's Prince Harry.

Despite Hvar's newfound fame, it has plenty of history. Its tongue-twisting name comes from the ancient Greek settlement here: Pharos. Greeks from the island of Paros migrated here in the

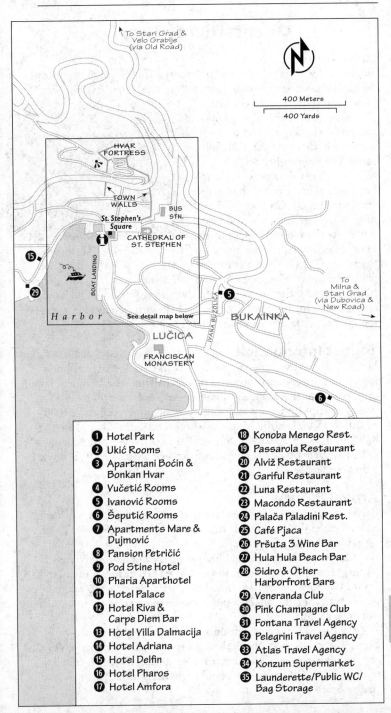

To Stari Grad & Velo Grablje (via Old Road)

N

400 Meters

400 Yards

HVAR FORTRESS

TOWN WALLS

BUS STN.

St. Stephen's Square

CATHEDRAL OF ST. STEPHEN

BOAT LANDING

Harbor

See detail map below

IVANA BUZOLICA

To Milna & Stari Grad (via Dubovica & New Road)

BUKAINKA

LUČICA

FRANCISCAN MONASTERY

HVAR

1. Hotel Park
2. Ukić Rooms
3. Apartmani Boćin & Bonkan Hvar
4. Vučetić Rooms
5. Ivanović Rooms
6. Šeputić Rooms
7. Apartments Mare & Dujmović
8. Pansion Petričić
9. Pod Stine Hotel
10. Pharia Aparthotel
11. Hotel Palace
12. Hotel Riva & Carpe Diem Bar
13. Hotel Villa Dalmacija
14. Hotel Adriana
15. Hotel Delfin
16. Hotel Pharos
17. Hotel Amfora
18. Konoba Menego Rest.
19. Passarola Restaurant
20. Alviž Restaurant
21. Gariful Restaurant
22. Luna Restaurant
23. Macondo Restaurant
24. Palača Paladini Rest.
25. Café Pjaca
26. Pršuta 3 Wine Bar
27. Hula Hula Beach Bar
28. Sidro & Other Harborfront Bars
29. Veneranda Club
30. Pink Champagne Club
31. Fontana Travel Agency
32. Pelegrini Travel Agency
33. Atlas Travel Agency
34. Konzum Supermarket
35. Launderette/Public WC/ Bag Storage

Orientation to Hvar

(area code: 021)

First off, "Hvar" is pronounced like it's spelled, but the H is nearly silent. If you struggle with it, just say "var" (but don't say "huh-var," which just sounds silly to locals).

Hvar town (with about 4,000 residents) clusters around its harbor. The harbor's eastern embankment (to the right, with your back to the water) is where the big boats put in, and is home to the Jadrolinija boat ticket office, most travel agencies, and the post office. At the top of the harbor is Hvar's long, wide main square, St. Stephen's Square (Trg Svetog Stjepana). The Old Town scampers up the hills in either direction from the square. Overlooking the town and harbor is a mighty hilltop fortress. Sprawling in both directions from the Old Town are nondescript residential zones packed with good-value apartment rentals, many with sensational sea views.

Tourist Information

Hvar's informative, no-nonsense TI is in the big Arsenal building right on the main square, a few steps from the harbor. Pick up the helpful free map, ask about events, and confirm details for your day trips and ferry connections (mid-June-Aug daily 8:00-14:00 & 15:00-21:00; May-mid-June and Sept-Oct Mon-Sat 8:00-14:00 & 16:00-20:00, Sun 8:00-12:00; Nov-April Mon-Sat 8:00-14:00, closed Sun; Trg Svetog Stjepana, tel. 021/741-059, www.tzhvar.hr).

Arrival in Hvar

By Boat: Passenger boats to **Hvar town** arrive on the harbor's eastern embankment. Simply exit and walk to the left—you'll run right into St. Stephen's Square.

Car ferries to Hvar Island (including the big Jadrolinija coastal ferries) arrive just outside the town of **Stari Grad,** across the island from Hvar town. Buses are timed to meet arriving boats and take passengers over the island's picturesque spine to Hvar town (20 minutes, 25 kn).

By Bus: Hvar's bus station is just beyond the far end of St. Stephen's Square from the harbor. As you get off your bus, you can see the main tower of the cathedral—marking the town center, a two-minute walk away. The island's few **taxis** usually hang out at the bus station.

HVAR

By Car: Car ferries from Split and most other destinations arrive on Hvar Island at the town of Stari Grad. There are two ways to drive from Stari Grad to Hvar town: the speedy, newer road via Dubovica to the south; or the slower, windy road (through prettier, less-traveled terrain) via Brusje to the north. In Hvar, you can park by the bus station. Be warned that the car ferries can be crowded in summer—waiting two hours or more is not unusual.

A second ferry crossing is at the opposite tip of Hvar Island, connecting the island's settlement of Sućuraj to the mainland town of Drvenik. But the road connecting Sućuraj to Hvar town is long, twisty, and challenging to drive—most visitors prefer arriving and departing at Stari Grad instead.

Helpful Hints

Boat Tickets: Tickets for the fast catamarans to Split and Korčula Island sell out fast in peak season—buy them as early as possible (they generally go on sale 24 hours in advance). You can get tickets for **Jadrolinija** connections at their office in Hvar town (open long hours daily in summer but closed about 12:00-14:30—inconvenient for those arriving on the morning catamaran from Split and needing to buy tickets; office is along the embankment where the big boats put in, tel. 021/741-132). To buy tickets for the *Krilo* catamaran to Split or Korčula, go to the **Pelegrini** travel agency at the opposite end of Hotel Riva (tel. 021/742-743, www.pelegrini-hvar.hr, pelegrini@inet.hr).

Live Music: The Hvar Summer Festival fills the entire peak season (mid-May–early Oct) with frequent concerts. Ask the TI for a Summer Festival *Program* with the latest schedule.

Addresses: Everyone in Hvar ignores house numbers (you'll constantly see *b.b.*, meaning "without number") and even street names. Making things more complicated, the town recently renamed and renumbered many streets and addresses, seemingly in an effort to impose a bit of order. It backfired. Locals (who don't much cotton to addresses) tend to ignore both the old and the new systems, so you now have twice as many ways to get lost. Navigate with maps (a good one is available free at the TI) and by asking for directions.

Post Office: It's along the harbor's main (eastern) embankment, inside a little fenced courtyard (Mon-Fri 7:00-20:00, Sat 7:00-13:00, closed Sun).

Laundry and Baggage Storage: Hvar has a rare and expensive self-service launderette, at the public toilets under the market on the main square (50-kn wash, 40-kn dry, 5-kn soap, they'll stick it in the dryer for you if you ask nicely and thank them with a small tip). The same place has pricey luggage storage (10 kn/1 hour, 15 kn/2 hours, 20 kn/3 hours, 40 kn/4-12 hours) and pay showers (25 kn)—handy if you're day-tripping here and want to swim in the sea (unpredictable hours, but generally daily June-Aug 7:00-23:00, May and Sept 7:00-20:00, Oct 8:00-13:30 & 16:00-19:00, shorter hours and no laundry off-season, to the left as you face the cathedral at Trg Svetog Stjepana 1—look for big, blue *toilet* sign).

Summer Fun: You name it, Hvar has it. Various agencies in town rent cars, scooters, bikes, motorboats, and more—just look for signs or ask at the TI.

Tours in Hvar

Old Town and Island Tours—Secret Hvar's owner Siniša prides himself on introducing you to undiscovered corners of Hvar that most tourists miss. He or one of his guides—guaranteed to be a Hvar native—can take you on a private walking tour around Hvar town (€100/up to 2.5 hours); an "off-road" tour that includes a *peka* lunch and some off-the-beaten-path sights on Hvar (€70/person, 8 hours); a wine-tasting trip with visits to two wineries, including eight tastings and some finger foods (€70/person for up to 4 hours); or a private full-island tour that includes Hvar town, Jelsa, Stari Grad, Vroboska, and more (€200/1-3 people, €300/4-7 people, up to 5 hours; mobile 095-805-9075, tel. 021/717-615, www.secrethvar .com, info@secrethvar.com).

Other Excursions from Hvar—Joining a day-trip excursion is a handy way to reach nearby destinations (generally available June-Oct). The best-selling options for getting off Hvar Island include the nearby Pakleni Islands (described later); Vis Island and its "Blue Cave"; Brač Island and the beach at Bol; Korčula; Mljet National Park; Dubrovnik; river-rafting; and more. The main operation is **Atlas** (at the top of the harbor), but other salespeople along the embankment also hawk various boat excursions.

Sights and Activities in Hvar

In and near the Old Town

▲▲**St. Stephen's Square (Trg Svetog Stjepana)**—Hvar's main square, which is supposedly Dalmatia's biggest, is a relaxed and relaxing people zone surrounded by inviting cafés filled with deliriously sun-baked tourists. For a quick tour, begin by the harbor and face the cathedral.

To your right is the **Arsenal** building (housing the TI)—a reminder of Hvar's nautical importance through history, thanks to its ideal location on the sailing route between Venice and the Mediterranean. During the town's seafaring heyday, ships were repaired and supplied in this huge building that still dominates the

HVAR

town. In 2012, the Arsenal wraps up a very lengthy and costly renovation (in honor of its 400th anniversary). The beautiful barrel-vaulted space inside, often used for special exhibits, may eventually house a permanent museum—ask the TI for details. From near the TI, you can climb the stairs up to the terrace atop the Arsenal for fine views over the square.

Many of Hvar's buildings date from the 16th and 17th centuries, when it was an important outpost of the Venetian Republic. Facing the cathedral, notice that the Old Town spreads out in two directions. During the Venetian period, the population was segregated along this axis. To the left lived the well-to-do patricians, protected within the city wall (from the fortress, crenellated walls reach down to embrace this neighborhood—not quite visible from here). To the right, outside the wall, dwelled the humble

plebeians—who worked hard and paid high taxes, but had no say in government. In the 16th century, these two populations came to blows, scuffling sporadically over the course of a century. The Venetians finally decided enough was enough and sent a moderator to restore peace...and this medieval Dr. Phil pulled it off. As a symbol of the reconciliation, part of the Arsenal building was converted into a **communal theater.** Built in 1612, this was the first municipal theater in Europe. It still serves this purpose.

Across the square from the Arsenal, the building with the arches and tower is the **Loggia,** all that remains of a 15th-century palace for the rector (who ruled the island as a representative of Venice). This was the town's court of justice, and important decisions were announced from the stepped pillar in front (with the flagpole). This pillar also served as the town pillory, for publicly humiliating prisoners. During Habsburg control in the early 20th century, most of the palace was torn down to build the town's first resort hotel; today, that building—appropriately called the Palace Hotel—still stands just behind the Loggia.

Walk toward the cathedral, stopping at the first big gap on the left. You can see the top of a never-finished **Venetian palace,** with its distinctive Venetian-style windows. A descendant of the former owner recently bought back this palace and has restored it. The renovation took longer than expected when workers began to uncover layer after layer of Hvar's history: blocks of stone from the Greek island of Paros, Illyrian coins, and Roman mosaics. If you were to head two blocks up this street, you'd run into the yellow **Benedictine Convent** and its loveable lace museum; if you continued beyond the convent, you'd reach the trailhead for the **fortress** up above (all described later). But before leaving the square, visit the cathedral (see below).

Then poke around Hvar's **back streets.** As you wander, especially on the left (north) side of the square, look up to find more characteristic Venetian windows. You'll also spot stone tabs jutting from house facades. The ones with holes were used to hang color-coded curtains: white for a birth, black for a death. Also notice the gleaming white limestone everywhere, which is quarried locally. An often-repeated (but false) legend that the US White House was built of this same stone is temptingly plausible.

Cathedral of St. Stephen (Sv. Stjepan)—Hvar's centerpiece is its Renaissance-era cathedral, with a distinctive three-humped gable (representing the Holy Trinity) and open-work steeple. The interior comes with a few tales from Hvar's storied past.

Cost and Hours: 10 kn, daily 9:00-13:00 & 17:00-21:00.

Touring the Cathedral: The bronze entrance doors, completed by a popular Croatian sculptor in 1990, combine religious themes with important elements of life on  Hvar. On the left door, top to bottom, you'll see the Creation; Madonna and Baby Jesus surrounded by the circle of stars (representing the European Union—reflecting Croatians' desire to be considered part of Europe); vineyards (both literal and as a symbol of heaven); and a procession of penitence, a fixture of life among religious locals. On the right door, you'll see a dove (representing peace and the Holy Spirit); the crucified Christ; fishermen (an actual part of Hvar life, but also representing the Church's "fishers of men" evangelical philosophy); and a boat, sailing into the future.

Inside, work your way counterclockwise around the church. At the right-front chapel, the tabernacle embedded in the yellow cloth (under the big crucifix) holds an important piece of Hvar history: a crucifix that supposedly shed tears of blood on the eve of a major 1510 uprising of the plebeians against the patricians. (This spooked the rebels enough to postpone the uprising a few months.) Behind the main altar are wooden choir stalls rescued from an earlier Gothic church destroyed during an Ottoman attack in 1571. Notice the two pulpits: The right one, with St. Paul and his sword, is for reading or singing the Epistles; the left one, with the eagle (representing St. John), is used for reading the Gospels. The left-front chapel features the tomb of St. Prosperus, Hvar's "co-patron saint," who shares the credit with the more famous St. Stephen. People pray to Prosperus for good health. On his feast day, May

10, the lid is opened and you can actually see his preserved body. The figures flanking the tomb represent Faith and Strength.

▲▲**Benedictine Convent (Benediktinski Samostan) and Lace Museum**—Hvar's most appealing sight is this nun-run attraction, inside a convent where 13 Benedictine sisters spend their lives (they never go outside). When they're not praying, the sisters make lace using fibers from the *agava* (a cactuslike plant with broad, flat, tapered, spiny leaves—see the sample next to the desk as you enter). First, they tease the delicate threads out of the plant, then wash, bleach, and dry them. Finally, they weave the threads into intricate lace designs. The painstaking procedure is made even more challenging by Hvar's unpredictable weather: The humid southerly Jugo wind causes tangles, while the dry northern Bora wind makes the fibers stiff and difficult to work with.

You'll see astonishingly delicate samples of the nuns' work, both new and old—some yellowed specimens date from the late 19th century (the oldest ones are in the back room). The sisters are particularly happy to make lace for bishops and cardinals. And when the *other* Benedict—the XVI—became pope in 2005, they created a lace papal emblem for him as a gift.

Rounding out the museum are ecclesiastical gear, some bishops' vestments (with the Baby Jesus below them wearing an *agava*-lace shirt), ancient kitchenware discovered in this house, a stone sink and baptismal font, an actual well, and some amphora jugs. Out in front of the building is a statue of St. Benedict, the patron saint of Europe, reading his daily routine in a book: *ora et labora* ("pray and work"). You'll notice the museum is also called the Hanibal Lucić Museum, for a prominent Renaissance poet whose daughter-in-law donated this property to the church.

Cost and Hours: 20 kn, skimpy 20-kn multilingual booklet, extremely expensive samples for sale; June-Aug Mon-Sat 10:00-12:00 & 17:00-19:00, closed Sun; generally closed Sept-May, but you can try ringing the bell to the right of the main door to get in during these same hours—use the door in the yellow building; tel. 021/741-052.

▲**Franciscan Monastery (Franjevački Samostan)**—Starting in the 15th century, this monastery was a hospice for sailors who encountered illness on treacherous sea journeys. These days it's worth the five-minute stroll from the Old Town to visit its offbeat museum, Hvar's most famous painting, an ancient tree, and a pair of monks.

Cost and Hours: 25 kn; May-Oct Mon-Sat 9:00-15:00 & 17:00-19:00, closed Sun; usually closed Nov-April but the TI can call to see if they'll let you in during these hours.

Touring the Monastery: Out front, notice the statue of a kneeling St. Francis—the twin of the prayerful St. Benedict, who stands in front of the Benedictine Convent. As you enter, notice that the cloister's floor is slanted inward to capture rainwater. Pipes took this pure water out to the waterfront, where passing ships could use it to replenish their supplies.

Inside, the focal point of the monastery is its impressive painting of the **Last Supper** (c. 1640). According to legend, a passing ship had a passenger who was severely ill with scurvy, so they left him on a small offshore island, where monks took pity on him. He asked for the biggest canvas they could find and painted this. (This may be more than a myth—historians recently found a letter inviting the presumed artist to Hvar.) The U-shaped table in the painting provides the framework for some bold experimentation with perspective. Facing Jesus, front and center, is Judas, identified by several clues. In his left hand (hard to see) is a bag of coins, and his right hand is dipping bread into wine (after Jesus had predicted that the one who did this would betray him). The yellow of his garment symbolizes betrayal, and the red indicates that the betrayal led to the spilling of blood. Under the table by Judas is a cat, representing lust. On the lower right, we see a beggar (accompanied by a dog, symbolizing fidelity)—likely a self-portrait by the artist, grateful to the monks who nursed him back to health.

The museum has a few more rooms, including an exhibit of currency from the fourth century B.C. (Greek coins with an image of Zeus) until today (see the rapid evolution of Croatia's currency since its independence); a collection of amphora jugs; and paintings by Venetian artists and modern Croatian artists.

The final attraction, out in the relaxing garden (beyond the museum), is an enormous **cypress tree** whose gnarled branches are held up by big supports. Scientists believe this ancient tree—probably around 250 years old—was struck by lighting, which caused the branches to spread out and become flatter than usual.

Nearby: On the way to or back from the monastery, peek inside the recommended Gariful Restaurant to see fish swimming around inside the floor. This is also a good place for a scenic meal.

▲**Hvar Fortress (Fortica Hvar)**—Visiting this mighty castle above the Old Town is a good excuse for a sturdy 20- to 30-minute hike to break up your lazy Hvar day.

Cost and Hours: 25 kn, daily June–mid-Sept 8:00–22:00, Easter–May and mid-Sept–Oct 8:30–20:00, Nov–Easter much shorter hours and sometimes closed.

Getting There: From the Old Town, hike up the steep street called Groda to the road passing above town. Once on that road, look for the nearby gate with the picture of a castle for another steep hike up a switchback trail (stay on the main path—side paths that seem like shortcuts are actually dead-ends).

Touring the Fortress: This huge fortification was built over several generations, beginning in the 13th century. In the 14th century, Spanish engineers did their part to bulk up the fortress (giving it the nickname "Španjola"). In 1571, the townspeople fled here for sanctuary during an attack by the Ottomans (on their way to the famous Battle of Lepanto), but just a few years later, the fortress was devastated when lightning hit a gunpowder store. In the 19th century, the occupying Austrians put their own touches on the castle. Today it's used as a catering facility and tourist attraction.

Inside the fort, there's very little in the way of posted descriptions, but the views over town are terrific. You can also climb down into the prison, sip a drink at the café/bar, and visit the one-room "Marine Archaeological Collection" (hiding inside the blocky central part of the fortress; look for *amphorae* and *muzej* signs). This display features booty found at three different Dalmatian shipwrecks, including a collection of amphora jugs (for more on these jugs, see the sidebar on page 135). According to the exhibit, one out of every 50 voyages in antiquity ended in a shipwreck. (And you thought flying was dangerous.)

The complex on the higher hill nearby was built by Napoleon (which is also its nickname among locals). In the 1970s, it was converted into an astronomic and seismographic observatory.

Strolling and Swimming—With typically Dalmatian crystal-clear water, Hvar is a great place to swim. Also typically

Dalmatian, virtually all of the swimming areas are rocky or pebbly. As you walk along the coastline in either direction from town, you'll spot concrete pads and ladders trying to seduce you into the cool blue (these are generally open to the public; you may have the option of renting a beach chair).

East of the Old Town: Whether or not you plan to swim, take a waterfront walk east of town (past the Franciscan Monastery). This delightful path leads past swimmers, sunbathers, and boats bobbing just offshore. After about a 20-minute walk, you'll reach the town's main beach, **Pokonji Dol**, which faces a small, barren island of the same name topped with a lonely little lighthouse. After Pokonji Dol, the path becomes more challenging and is not as well-marked, offering little shade. Bring water and wear good shoes if planning to venture this far. If you continue eastward along the coast, you'll find more beaches—first the one nicknamed **"Robinson,"** then the even better one at **Milna** (2.5 miles from Hvar town). Beyond Robinson, the waterfront path to Milna is challenging and very poorly marked, so instead, consider taking a taxi, water taxi (about 50 kn one-way between Hvar and Milna), or the bus (any bus taking the new road to Stari Grad stops at Milna).

West of the Old Town: This path leads along a series of bays, one of them dominated by the huge Hotel Amfora (with a row of private cabanas, below the trail). On the next bay over, the super-popular **Hula Hula** beach bar serves light meals and cocktails on platforms and rocks over the beach, with chill-out music all day and a live DJ starting at 17:00 (see "Nightlife in Hvar," later). The farther you get from town, the more remote-feeling the beaches become, ending at the mellow cocktail bar under Pod Stine Hotel.

Many sun worshippers—especially the clothing-optional crowd—prefer to take a water taxi to the beaches of the nearby **Pakleni Islands,** across the bay from Hvar town (described later).

More Sights on Hvar Island

If you have more time, Hvar is an interesting island to explore. A good way to efficiently hit several sights in a single day is to take a trip with Secret Hvar (listed earlier, under "Tours in Hvar"). Otherwise, consider one of these outings.

Hike from Velo Grablje to Milna—For a vigorous but mostly downhill hike in the interior of Hvar Island, you can bus to a partially abandoned town, hike down through a ravine to a nearly empty village, then pop out along the sea at Milna for a bus ride back to Hvar. Allow a half-day for the whole trip, including about two hours for the hike itself. This is best for hardy hikers and those who enjoy getting away from touristy beaches to explore the artifacts of an earlier age of Hvar; most of the route is in a ravine without sea views. As this is a challenging trail with little shade, wear good shoes and load up on water, sunscreen, and anything else you might need before setting out.

To reach the start of the hike, take the one daily bus that uses the scenic old road to Stari Grad (generally departs Hvar town at 12:10 in summer, 12:20 in winter—confirm at TI or bus station), and get off about five miles east of Hvar town at the village of Velo Grablje. From the Velo Grablje stop, hike down the switchback road into the town. For a more scenic arrival, stay on the bus a few

Hvar Wine and Lavender

The hillsides of Hvar Island are striped with the faint outlines of an elaborate network of terraces, once used to cultivate grapes for wine. But in 1910, a phylloxera pest infestation devastated vineyards and nearly decimated the island's winemaking industry. Many vintners moved to the US, Australia, and Argentina, where they became pioneers in wine production. Today winemaking on Hvar is only about five percent of its historic peak, and the focus is on quality, not quantity.

In the 1930s, in an effort to boost the economy, the island began producing lavender, which was mostly exported for industrial use to Germany and the UK (peaking in the 1960s and 1970s). This dramatically improved the quality of life on Hvar, though devastating forest fires in 1984, 1997, 2003, and 2007 burned up much of this cash crop. As the island's tourism industry expands, it's become less critical to the economy to replant after each fire, so many lavender farmers have left their fields fallow. These days most lavender is produced for the sake of tradition—and for tourists.

hundred yards longer and ask the driver to let you off at Vidikovac (vee-dee-koh-vats), a viewpoint restaurant with panoramic vistas across the far side of the island; from here, cross the road and walk down the gravel path into town.

Velo Grablje, once famous for its lavender oil production, is

now a near-ghost town on a rugged plateau with far-off views of the sea. Most people migrated to Hvar town in the 1970s and 1980s, though seven natives still reside here.

From Velo Grablje, follow the medieval footpath through the ravine downhill about two miles to the abandoned village of **Malo Grablje.** After the phylloxera epidemic, most people from this village moved down to Milna, on the sea (where tourism provided them with better prospects for earning income). The last holdout left in 1968. But recently the grandson of the first villager who left returned to Malo Grablje and opened a rustic restaurant called Konoba Stari Komin (open 16:00-23:00 only, run by Berti Tudor—the surname of virtually everyone who originated in this village, possible to call ahead to arrange a *peka* dinner, mobile 091-527-6408). Even if the *konoba* is closed, you can explore the streets of Malo Grablje. Poke into the ruined buildings to find a giant, still-functioning olive press.

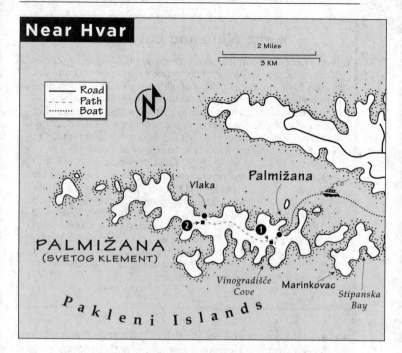

The humble church hosts a Mass twice per year, when people from Milna return to their ancestral village. Next to the church is a huge reservoir and cistern for catching rainwater.

Leaving Malo Grablje, follow the gravel road down into the beach town of **Milna.** The seafront path from Milna back to Hvar (about 2.5 miles) is extremely rugged and can be nearly impossible to follow; unless you're very adventurous, it's best to walk along the main road (not very scenic) or take a public bus back to Hvar (any bus that goes between Stari Grad and Hvar along the new road stops in Milna—likely in summer at 16:05 and 18:40, in winter at 16:00, but confirm times at Hvar TI before heading out). You can also take a water taxi between Milna and Hvar for about 50 kn one-way.

Note: It's possible to drive from Milna up to Malo Grablje and Velo Grablje, but the road consists of very rough gravel—not advisable with a rental car.

Vrboska and Nearby—While many visitors to Hvar see only the main town and the road to Stari Grad (where the island's main car-ferry port is), if you have a car it can be fun to head east of Stari Grad to some nearby settlements. Driving eastbound on the main road from Stari Grad takes you into a plain with fertile **farm fields.** This unassuming patch of land is one of the only agricultural areas in Europe that's still divided according to its original plots—which

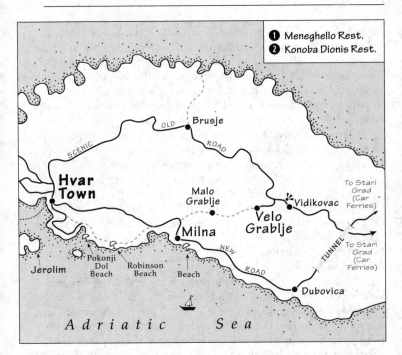

Meneghello Rest.
Konoba Dionis Rest.

date all the way back to the first ancient Greek settlers. Soon you'll reach the seafront village of **Vrboska**, nicknamed "Little Venice" (this endearing hyperbole is typical of local pride). While the name is a stretch, this pleasant town does have a canal with picturesque bridges, the fortress/church of St. Mary's (built during a time of Turkish naval threat), and an island with a lone palm tree.

Near Hvar: Pakleni Islands (Pakleni Otoci)

These islands, just offshore from Hvar town, are a popular and easy back-to-nature day-trip destination. The name means the

"Devil's Islands" in Croatian, but in the local dialect, *pakleni* refers to the resin used to seal the hulls of ships. These days, the islands harbor some popular nude beaches: The island of Jerolim and the bay of Stipanska (or is it *Strip*anska?) on the island of Marinkovac are particularly good places to spot—or sport—some bare skin. For a bit more civilization, set your sights on the biggest island, known as **"Palmižana"** (pahl-mee-ZHAH-nah; sounds like "parmesan-a") for its main settlement (the island's official name is Svetog Klement, but nobody calls it that). The beach at Palmižana is a popular swim destination because it's partly "sandy" (translation: smaller pebbles). The only real town on this island is Palmižana, which is basically a modest marina and a handful of cafés huddled around a beach. From there, you can hike through the woods and scramble your way to some postcard-perfect hidden coves.

Getting There: Excursion boats ferry tourists out to the islands every summer morning from the harbor in front of the Hvar TI—just look for signs to the specific island, beach, or cove that you want. It costs about 60 kn round-trip per person to Palmižana; most boats take people over between 9:00 and 11:00, then go back to fetch them around 16:00 or 17:00 (they run more or less constantly in peak season; figure about 20 minutes each way to Palmižana). This works well, provided you want to spend the entire day stranded on a tropical island. Visiting Jerolim or Marinkovac costs 35 kn round-trip.

An efficient sightseer might prefer just a few hours of island time—enough for a quick dip, a hike, and maybe a meal. For this purpose, you can pay double for a faster, private **water taxi** to zip you there in just 15 minutes, and then pick you up whenever you like. I had a good experience with one of these speedy taxis, helmed by English-speaking Luka. I called him 15 minutes before I wanted to head over, and again 15 minutes before I came back—door-to-door service to any island you like (300 kn round-trip for up to 3 people, mobile 098-959-5094). Luka's small, inflatable boat is built for speed but not comfort, so the ride can be rough.

Planning Your Time: If you're relatively fit and have a few hours to spare, try this plan: Ride with Luka to Palmižana, hit the Vinogradišće beach, hike across the island to the settlement of Vlaka, have lunch or dinner at Konoba Dionis, call Luka, and ride with him from Vlaka back to Hvar.

Beach at Vinogradišće Cove: The most popular spot for swimming on the island is the beach at Vinogradišće. To get here from the Palmižana marina, hike up the trail (to the left, past the little cantina). When the road forks, take the middle fork and follow the restaurant signs (they're all at the beach). While it's not as "undiscovered" as you might hope, Vinogradišće is a picturesque spot, with a small patch of semi-sand surrounded by rocks and concrete pads for catching some rays. A smattering of sailboats on the horizon rounds out the idyllic Croatian scene.

Hike to Vlaka: For a hardy 45-minute (2-mile) hike on a rough trail with some pleasant views—and a restaurant reward at the end (Konoba Dionis, described later)—trek across the top of the island to the little settlement of Vlaka (wear good shoes and bring water). From Palmižana, first follow signs to Meneghello.

After you pass Meneghello Restaurant and some of its bungalows (described next), go right at the fork in the path (following the faint red marking on the wall to *Vlaka*). You'll climb up to the crest of the island, on a very narrow and rocky trail. A few side paths fork down to various bays, but stay on the main trail along the top of the island (generally marked with red-painted rocks). You'll periodically break through the trees for views over secluded coves and nearby islands. Finally, the path leads down along yet another pretty cove before sending you back over the top of the island to Vlaka and Konoba Dionis.

Eating at Palmižana: Several lazy cafés surround the Vino-gradišće beach at Palmižana. A bit higher on the hill is **Meneghello,** run by a family of the same name that's been in Palmižana for over a century. They serve mostly seafood on a colorful, funky terrace (open long hours daily April-Oct, reservations smart for dinner, follow signs from the Palmižana marina, tel. 021/717-270). Meneghello Restaurant is the centerpiece of a complex of rentable, color-coded bungalows that bunny-hop through an overgrown botanical garden down to the beach (www.palmizana.hr).

Eating at Vlaka: The culinary highlight of the island is at the other end, in Vlaka. **Konoba Dionis** is a charming stone hut with just six tables on a covered terrace, overlooking vineyards, an olive grove, and the distant sea. The electricity comes from a generator, and the water comes from the sky (except during droughts, when it's brought over from the mainland)—so the cuisine is straightforward, traditional Dalmatian dishes, and the focus is on relaxation. Their "aubergine pie" is a tasty eggplant lasagna (figure about 250 kn per person for a meal, mid-May-mid-Oct daily 12:00-23:00, closed off-season, mobile 098-167-1016 or 091-765-6044). Tourists often make the long journey over to Dionis, only to find it's already full—reservations (especially for lunch) are a must. Note that there are boats from Hvar to Vlaka in peak season (but the schedule is sparse; ask at TI).

Shopping in Hvar

Little souvenir kiosks are everywhere on Hvar. The big item here is lavender, produced on the island for the last century or so (see "Hvar Wine and Lavender" sidebar, earlier). In addition to making things smell good, lavender is acclaimed by some locals for its medicinal properties: Massage some lavender oil on your temples to cure a headache, or rub it on your chest for asthma. You'll see it sold in bottles or sachets—a fragrant souvenir that helps keep your luggage smelling fresh, too. Hvar town also has plenty of jewelry shops selling coral and other pieces made from semi-precious stones.

Nightlife in Hvar

This island town is known for its nightlife, but it tends to gravitate to the loud and young.

Mellow Nightlife—Strolling the harbor, then continuing out of town along the waterfront promenade, is a fine way to pass a warm, starry evening. **Pršuta 3** wine bar, right in the heart of town, is a cozy and chill place to hang out, socialize, and sip some of the island's wines with light food (25-75-kn wines by the glass, cash only, nightly 18:00-late, mobile 098-969-6193).

Lively Nightlife—Hvar probably has Dalmatia's most happening "après-beach" scene. Expect very high prices for drinks, and prepare to share the nightspots with a very flush, international jet-set crowd. On balmy summer evenings, partying is best enjoyed in three stages. (Note that virtually all of the places below are closed from about early October through early May.)

Stage 1: Watch the sunset from the groovy **Hula Hula** beach bar, with drinks—and tables—"on the rocks" (literally). Don't expect a relaxed vibe here—in summer, it's absolutely jam-packed (drinks with light food and snacks, open daily from 9:00, "chill-out music" until 17:00, then a live DJ with dance-club ambience, hopping until about 23:00; for directions, see page 236). When I asked if older guests would be comfortable here, they smirked and said, "When they come here, everybody feels young!"

Stage 2: Head for the bars in the center of town, along the harbor (including **Sidro**—known for its cheap drinks and friendly service—as well as **Nautica, Lion's Pub,** and so on). Just above this strip of bars, on the ground floor of Hotel Park, is **Club Park,** with elegant Tuscan living-room ambience.

Stage 3: If you're still going strong, continue to one of the late-night options. While these places brag about their rich and famous guests, many travelers find them overpriced and overrated. But, when in Hvar... **Veneranda,** with giant tentlike canopies filling the courtyard of an old stone monastery-turned-fortress-turned-nightspot, is in the parkland just west of the harbor. This trendy dance bar has gained an international reputation (pricey cover, daily 22:00-5:00, July-Aug only, www.veneranda.hr). **Carpe Diem** is an exclusive-feeling cocktail bar along the harbor, right next to Hotel Riva (Carpe Diem also has their own beach bar on Stipanska Island, www.carpe-diem-hvar.com). **Pink Champagne,** the most exclusive of the bunch, is up the lane beyond the bus station and parking lot, near the police station.

HVAR

Sleeping in Hvar

In keeping with its posh reputation, Hvar has some of the most expensive accommodations in Croatia. As usual, *sobe* and apartments are a more affordable option (see page 254), but there are relatively few in the center of town; you'll have to walk 10 to 20 minutes to reach many of them (fortunately, the ones I've listed are cozy, well-equipped, well-run, and worth the walk). Very few Hvar accommodations involve a level stroll from the harbor or bus station (and those that do are very expensive); plan on climbing several steps to reach most of these places. The farther and steeper you're willing to walk, the better the price and views (most of those requiring an uphill climb come with glorious seaview balconies on a pauper's budget). As some of my listings are tucked away in residential areas, they can be tricky to find; get clear directions from your host, or arrange to meet them at the boat. In general, it can be challenging to find a room in July and especially August (when all accommodations boost their rates); book as far ahead as possible

Sleep Code

(5 kn = about $1, €1 = about $1.40, country code: 385, area code: 021)

S = Single, **D** = Double/Twin, **T** = Triple, **Q** = Quad, **b** = bathroom. The modest tourist tax (about 7 kn per person, per night) is not included in these rates. Hotels generally accept credit cards and include breakfast, while most *sobe* accept only cash and don't offer breakfast. While rates are listed in euros, you'll pay in kunas. Unless I note otherwise, everyone listed here speaks English (or has a relative or neighbor who can help translate).

Rates: If I've listed two sets of rates for an accommodation, separated by slashes, the first price is for peak season (mid-July–late Aug), and the second is for shoulder season (May–mid-July and late Aug–Oct); those that remain open in winter are often even cheaper then. If I've listed three sets of rates, the third is for off-season (Nov–April). The dates for seasonal rates vary by hotel, and prices can change without notice; verify the hotel's current rates online or by email. For other updates, see www.ricksteves.com/update.

Price Ranges: To help you sort easily through these listings, I've divided the accommodations into three categories based on the price for a double room with bath during peak season:

  $$$ Higher Priced—Most rooms €100 or more.
  $$ Moderately Priced—Most rooms between €55-100.
  $ Lower Priced—Most rooms €55 or less.

HVAR

for these times.

Sobe Tips: I've organized my listings by neighborhood, with a few *sobe*/apartments scattered in each area. It's standard for *sobe* and apartments to charge 30 percent more for stays shorter than three nights. This is rarely waived in high season, but you can try to negotiate your way out of this at other times.

The options I've listed are just a few of Hvar's many *sobe*. Stepping off the boat or bus, you'll be approached by hordes of people hoping to recruit you into their rooms; throughout the streets, *sobe* and *apartman* signs are everywhere. To find one from home, look on the TI's website (www.tzhvar.hr; click "Accommodation," then "Private Accommodation"). Or, once you've arrived, consider going through a Hvar room-booking agency (all are open sporadic hours, based on season): **Fontana** (tel. 021/742-133, www.happy hvar.com, info@happyhvar.com) and **Pelegrini** (tel. 021/742-743, www.pelegrini-hvar.hr, pelegrini@inet.hr) are along the embankment where the big boats dock. **Atlas** is across the harbor (tel. 021/741-911, atlas-hvar@st.t-com.hr).

In the Old Town

$$$ Hotel Park, a rare independent hotel, sits right in the heart of town, above the harbor and next to Hotel Palace. While not cheap, its 15 rooms (most of them very spacious suites) offer a small-hotel alternative to the big boys. Its restaurant/breakfast terrace, overlooking the harbor, is a momentum-killer. Despite its bottom-floor nightclub and locale near the harborfront disco zone, good windows minimize the noise (standard seaview Db-€230-250/€190-210/€100-150; a few cheaper non-view and more expensive large "superior" rooms also available—see website, air-con, free Wi-Fi, Bankete, tel. 021/718-337, www.hotelparkhvar.com, park.hvar@st.t-com.hr).

$$ Ivana and Paško Ukić offer the only real *sobe* I've found in the center of Hvar, with three cozy apartments (with kitchens) and one double room. The house has one of Hvar's most convenient locations, buried deep in the Old Town and sharing a quiet square with a little church a few steep blocks above the main square (apartment-€70/€60/€50, cheaper Oct-May, Db about €5 less, no breakfast, 30 percent extra for 1-night stays, no extra charge for 2-night stays, air-con, Matija Ivanića 10, tel. 021/741-810, Ivana speaks just enough English to make a reservation, or call fluent daughter Lidija at mobile 098-917-0652, www.hvar-apartments -center.com, ivanaukic@net.hr). From the cathedral, walk three blocks up toward the fortress, then look for the little church (Sv. Duh) to your left.

Higher Up, on the Main Road

Two places sit side-by-side on the main road above the Old Town (halfway up to the castle), with a third around the corner. While these are a bit older and a lesser value than some of the options listed later, their relative proximity to town (10-minute-or-less uphill walk) makes them worth considering.

$$ Apartmani Boćin, run by Eta Rosso Domančić, has two spacious one-bedroom apartments and one rustic studio apartment, all with seaview terraces (Db-€80/€50, €10 less for studio, air-con, free Wi-Fi, Gojava bb, mobile 091-536-1744, www.hvar-rosso.com, josip.rosso@st.t-com.hr).

$$ Bonkan Hvar, next door, has four air-conditioned apartments (Db-€70/€50) and two simple rooms with no air-conditioning, tree-trunk accents, and affordable prices (Db-€50/€40; free Wi-Fi, D. Novaka 17, mobile 091-734-5313, www.myhvar.com).

$ Jozo and Danica Vučetić, around the corner and a few steps down toward town, rent one room (€40/€30) and one apartment (€50/€40, €10 extra if you use kitchen). While they don't speak much English, their English-speaking daughter-in-law Katija is helpful (no air-con, free Wi-Fi, Skaline od Gojave 6, tel. 021/741-051, katija.vucetic@yahoo.com).

East of the Old Town, in Bukainka

The residential neighborhood called Bukainka sits on a high plateau just east of the harbor, hemmed in by the main road to Stari Grad. To reach this area, figure on a steep 10- to 15-minute uphill walk from the Old Town and waterfront.

$$ Ivanka Ivanović rents five apartments and two rooms in a big, modern house with view balconies (Db-€50-60/€40, price depends on size, air-con, free Wi-Fi, Ivana Buzolića 9, tel. 021/741-332, mobile 091-517-7038, www.ivanovic-hvar.com, ivanka.ivanovic@st.t-com.hr).

$$ Dino Šeputić is a hardworking young Hvarin renting seven apartments, all with kitchens and harbor-view balconies (Db-€40-70, huge three-room apartment-€100-200, rates depend on season, air-con, free Wi-Fi, walk straight uphill from the Franciscan Monastery, Vrisak bb, tel. 021/742-534, mobile 098-526-099, www.seputic.hr, info@seputic.hr).

West of the Old Town

In Zastup

These places are along the street called Biskupa Dubokovića, the main drag leading west of town, about a 10- to 15-minute walk from the Old Town (directly above and behind Hotel Amfora), though Pansion Petričić is a bit farther out and higher up.

$$ Apartments Mare, run by Marica Dujmović, has three small freestanding houses that bunny-hop up through a delightful garden behind the main house, which has three more apartments. All come with seaview terraces and the aroma of a well-tended garden (Db-€60/€40-50, air-con, free Wi-Fi, Biskupa Dubokovića 34, tel. 021/741-454, mobile 091-552-2014, www.apartments-mare -hvar.com, maricadujmovic@gmail.com).

$$ Ana Dujmović, next door, has nine apartments with seaview balconies (bigger Db-€75/€55, smaller and older but still nice Db-€60/€45, air-con, free Wi-Fi, Biskupa Dubokovića 36, tel. 021/742-010, mobile 098-838-434, www.hvar-croatia.com /dujmovic, ana.dujmovic@st.t-com.hr).

$ Pansion Petričić, high up in a residential zone, has four rooms (sharing a kitchen) and two apartments that are a bit older. The kindly owners, Živko and Marija, enjoy getting to know their guests—and so does their big but friendly dog Arix (Db-€54/€48/€28/€24, 2-person apartment-€64/€56/€36/€30, 4-person apartment-€120/€100/€68/€60, rates are for Aug/July/June and Sept-off-season, discount if it rains a lot, air-con, free Wi-Fi, Biskupa Dubokovića 25, tel. 021/742-481, www.hvar-petricic.com, z.petricic@inet.hr).

Hotels in Podstine, Beyond Zastup

These two hotels are in a quiet, nondescript residential neighborhood just beyond the big Hotel Amfora west of the Old Town (about a 15- to 20-minute walk).

$$$ Pod Stine Hotel ("Under Stones") feels like the sunny hideout of a reclusive writer. At the edge of town overlooking a mini-arboretum and a beautiful cove, this place features smart contemporary decor, 52 upscale-feeling rooms, a cocktail terrace, and pool. If you don't mind the 20-minute walk into town, it's a more intimate and enjoyable splurge than the big hotels (standard non-view Sb-€147/€131/€114, superior Sb with seaview-€185/€164/€143, bigger superior exclusive Sb with seaview-€239/€213/€186, standard non-view Db-€198/€174/€153, superior Db with seaview-€247/€218/€187, bigger superior exclusive Db with seaview-€320/€283/€250, cheaper Oct and May, closed Nov-late April, no extra charge for 1- or 2-night stays, air-con, elevator, free Internet access and Wi-Fi in lobby, free parking, free use of spa facilities—including gym and swimming pool, put Podstina 11, tel. 021/740-400, fax 021/740-499, www.podstine .com, hotel@podstine.com).

$$$ Pharia Aparthotel has 10 straightforward rooms and 11 apartments in two buildings. Though more expensive than a comparable *sobe* or apartment, this place comes with the services of a modern hotel, and the location is fairly handy to the Old

Town (Sb-€68/€50/€38, non-view Db-€108/€78/€58, seaview Db-€124/€92/€68, non-view apartment-€134/€107/€77, seaview apartment-€155/€116/€83, closed mid-Oct-April, air-con, free Wi-Fi, put Podstina 1, tel. 021/778-080, fax 021/778-081, www .orvas-hotels.com, pharia@orvas.hr).

Sunčani Hvar Hotels

Most of the big hotels in town are operated by the same company, Sunčani Hvar. These hotels are currently undergoing a long-term, multiphase renovation to bring them all up to four- and five-star (read: expensive) status, so some of them might be closed for your visit. Those that are fully renovated boast super-modern rooms with strikingly contemporary decor; the unrenovated hotels give you a taste of the drab old communist days. Prices vary dramatically depending on season, view, size, how recently the rooms were renovated, and the direction the wind is blowing. I've listed the price per night for a two-night stay in a standard double room with no view in peak season (July-Aug). You'll pay more for a sea view, a "superior" room, or other special features, but prices can be much lower off-season—check specific rates on their website (www.suncani hvar.com). I'd save some kunas and enjoy more local color by sleeping in one of the *sobe* or apartments listed earlier instead, but if you prefer a well-located home base with big-hotel amenities, here are your options: **$$$ Hotel Palace,** a few steps off the main square, at the end of the harbor (not yet fully renovated but extremely central, some rooms get noise from nearby bars—request a quieter room, 73 rooms, Db-€127); **$$$ Hotel Riva,** along the embankment where the big boats dock (renovated to top-class quality, with artsy mod decor and nude sketches in the halls, suffers from disco noise at the adjacent Carpe Diem nightclub—try requesting a quieter room, 54 rooms, Db-€265); **$$$ Hotel Villa Dalmacija,** around the corner from Hotel Riva, just east of the Old Town (21 unrenovated rooms in main hotel, Db-€163; 37 lightly renovated rooms in adjacent, youth-oriented "beach lodge," Db-€128); **$$$ Hotel Adriana,** across the harbor from Hotel Riva (recently renovated and even more plush than the Riva, full-service spa and 59 rooms, noise from rooftop disco, Db-€312); **$$ Hotel Delfin,** just beyond the Adriana (55 unrenovated rooms, Db-€87); and two others farther along past the Adriana and Delfin, a 5- to 10-minute walk from the Old Town: **$$$ Hotel Pharos** (200 unrenovated rooms, Db-€106) and **$$$ Hotel Amfora** (nicely renovated but not quite as fancy as the Riva or Adriana, great resort vibe with wonderful swimming-pool complex that reaches down to the beach, 324 rooms, Db-€242). You can book any of the Sunčani Hvar hotels through the same office: tel. 021/750-750, fax 021/750-751, www .suncanihvar.com, reservations@suncanihvar.com.

Eating in Hvar

Hvar is packed with similar places serving up plates of grilled fish and meat, with pasta and pizza rounding out the predictable options. Fortunately—unlike some other small resort towns (such as Korčula)—Hvar also has some more inventive alternatives that provide a nice break from the same old seaside fare. Prices on Hvar are high, but (for the most part) so is quality. No matter where you dine, reservations are smart July through September.

Konoba Menego, run by Dinko and the Kovačević family, offers the chance to try typical cuisine from Dalmatia and throughout Croatia. (Dinko stubbornly refuses to serve anything that's not authentically Dalmatian—including Coca-Cola, spaghetti, or beer.) The user-friendly menu lists the town or region of origin for each specialty. Portions are small, so think of it as Croatian tapas: Two people can order three or four dishes to share, and sample a variety of regional flavors. Dine in the cozy enclosed terrace or in the atmospheric dining room, with air-dried ham *(pršut)* hanging from the rafters (45-70-kn portions, bigger 130-140-kn two-person combination plates, Mon-Sat 11:30-14:30 & 17:00-24:00, Sun 17:00-24:00 only, closed mid-Oct-March, on the steep lane called Groda leading up to the fortress, reservations smart, tel. 021/742-036 or 021/717-411).

Passarola is Hvar's classy splurge, with a trendy, minimalist interior (white arches, black tables), outdoor seating on the roof surrounding an open ceiling, and an impressive guest list of celebrity diners. Chef Hrvoje Zirojević combines Dalmatian food with graceful nouvelle cuisine presentation; considering the quality, he keeps his prices reasonable. Reservations are recommended (70-140-kn starters, 95-160-kn main dishes, daily 10:00-14:00 & 17:00-24:00, Mate Miličića 10, tel. 021/717-374, mobile 099-733-2438).

Alviž, just outside the Old Town near the bus station, is where locals mingle with tourists. Dine on affordable pizzas, pastas, and other dishes in a woody interior or on a welcoming terrace out back with a busy open grill. The food is unpretentious but delicious, including one of the best *pašticadas* I've had (40-60-kn pizzas, 50-70-kn pastas, 60-110-kn meat and fish dishes, daily 18:00-24:00, across parking lot from bus station, Hanibala Lucića 1, tel. 021/742-797).

Gariful Restaurant ("Carnation") owns Hvar's best waterfront location, at the end of the yacht-lined embankment. They have a fine outdoor terrace and a small dining room, and the service is crisp and helpful. You know the fish is fresh, because it's swimming around beneath the floor inside (55-95-kn pastas, 85-150-kn meat dishes, 95-190-kn seafood dishes, daily 10:00-23:00; at the end of the embankment, by the green lighthouse; tel. 021/742-999, mobile 098-916-0173).

Hvar's "Restaurant Row": The streets just above the main square (to the left, as you face the cathedral) are full of restaurants slinging similar Dalmatian and Mediterranean fare in an upscale atmosphere. Outdoor tables make it easy to window-shop and find your favorite. In this zone, three places are particularly well-regarded: **Luna** has colorful, lively decor and a delightful rooftop terrace (70-90-kn pastas, 80-150-kn main courses, 9-kn cover charge, daily 12:00-24:00, closed Nov-March, tel. 021/741-400). **Macondo,** one street up, offers fun, tight sidewalk seating and a nondescript dining room serving mostly fish dishes (95-100-kn pastas, 90-150-kn main courses; April-Oct Mon-Sat 12:00-14:00 & 18:30-24:00, Sun 18:30-24:00; closed Nov-March, tel. 021/742-850). **Palača Paladini,** in a 500-year-old-palace, has a large enclosed garden courtyard and a small dining room (60-85-kn pastas, 85-120-kn meat dishes, 200-300-kn fish splurges, daily 12:00-24:00, across the street from Luna, tel. 021/742-104).

Breakfast: If you're sleeping in a *soba,* you're on your own for breakfast. Small **bakeries** are scattered around town. For something more substantial, drop into **Café Pjaca,** with ideal outdoor seating on the main square across from the TI (30-60-kn options, daily 7:00-23:00, cool modern decor). **Hotel Park**'s enticing terrace overlooking the square and harbor is a scenic place for a pricey breakfast (69 kn, daily 7:00-11:00).

Picnics: A big, handy **Konzum** supermarket is near the bus station (Mon-Sat 7:00-21:00, Sun 7:00-13:00).

Hvar Connections

By Boat

Big car ferries use the port at Stari Grad, across the island from Hvar town (a 20-minute bus ride; local buses are scheduled to connect Hvar town with these boats). Smaller passenger-only catamarans leave from the harbor in the heart of Hvar town. For nondrivers going to either Split or Korčula, the catamarans are much better, since their departure point is more convenient and they make the trip faster. As always, it's essential to confirm your plans in advance—boat schedules are subject to change. If I've listed a range of prices for a journey, the specific fare varies by season.

Boats from Hvar Town to Split and Korčula Island: The handy *Krilo* **catamaran,** which runs daily year-round, heads for Split in the morning (departs Hvar at 7:45 in June-Sept, 7:30 in Oct-May, 50-60 minutes, 35-45 kn) and for Korčula town in the afternoon (departs Hvar at 17:10 year-round, 1.5 hours, 40-50 kn; in summer also stops at Prigradica on Korčula Island en route to Korčula town). In Hvar, buy *Krilo* tickets at Pelegrini travel agency (confirm schedule at www.krilo.hr). In summer (June-Sept), a **Jadrolinija catamaran** connects Hvar town twice daily to Split (departs Hvar at 6:30 Mon-Sat or 10:00 Sun, also daily at 13:45, 50-60 minutes, 45-47 kn) and once daily to Vela Luka (at the far end of Korčula Island, a 1-hour bus ride to Korčula town; departs Hvar at 16:00, 45 minutes, 27-32 kn). Off-season (Oct-May), Jadrolinija's catamaran runs once daily in each direction (departs for Split at 6:30 Mon-Sat or 10:00 Sun, departs for Vela Luka daily at 15:00).

Note: Remember, it's smart to buy tickets for these popular catamarans as early as possible. This is especially important for the morning departures to Split, which always sell out (afternoon departures to Korčula Island are a bit less crowded). Tickets go on sale about 24 hours in advance—as soon as one day's catamaran departs, you can buy tickets for the next day's boat (try to do this when you arrive).

Big Jadrolinija Car Ferries from Stari Grad: Twice weekly in summer (June-Sept only), these big boats run up and down the Dalmatian coast, heading north to **Split** (1.75 hours, 39-47 kn); and south to **Korčula town** (3.75 hours, 90-110 kn) and **Dubrovnik** (8.75 hours, 110-130 kn). Jadrolinija also runs frequent local car ferries from Stari Grad to **Split** (7/day in summer, 3/day in winter, 1.75 hours, 39-47 kn).

Overland Connections

Hvar's **buses** only connect you to other parts of the island. For farther-flung destinations (such as Dubrovnik or Zagreb), you'll take a boat to Split, then connect by bus from there. About six buses a day cross the island between Hvar town and Stari Grad, and there's always a bus coordinated to meet the big ferries at Stari Grad (in which case you want Stari Grad's "Trajekt" stop rather than its Old Town stop). Most of the Stari Grad buses use the new road and stop at Milna, while one per day uses the old road.

Drivers heading north can drive 20 minutes to Stari Grad and catch the car ferry right to Split. If you're heading south (or to Mostar), you can also drive the very twisty roads (about 1.5 hours) down the length of Hvar Island to the town of Sućuraj, where you can catch the car ferry to Drvenik; from Drvenik, you can drive along the mainland, or catch a different ferry to Korčula town (confirm all ferry schedules at Hvar TI before making the trip).

HVAR

KORČULA

The island town of Korčula (KOHR-choo-lah) boasts an atmospheric Old Town, a smattering of surprisingly engaging museums, and a dramatic, fjord-like mountain backdrop. Simpler and humbler than its glitzy big sister Hvar, Korčula—while certainly on the tourist trail—is sleepier and has an appealing (and occasionally frustrating) backwater charm. All things considered, Korčula is the most enjoyable Back Door stopover between Split and Dubrovnik.

Like so many other small Croatian coastal towns, Korčula was founded by the ancient Greeks. It became part of the Roman Empire and was eventually a key southern outpost of the Venetian Republic. Four centuries of Venetian rule left Korčula with a quirky Gothic-Renaissance mix and a strong siesta tradition. Korčulans take great pride in the fact that Marco Polo was born here in 1254—the explorer remains the town's poster boy. Korčula is also known for its traditional *Moreška* sword dance.

You'll discover that there are two Korčulas: the tacky seaside resort and the historic Old Town. Savvy visitors ignore the tourist sprawl and focus on Korčula's medieval quarter, a mini-Dubrovnik poking into the sea on a picture-perfect peninsula. Tiny lanes branch off the humble main drag like ribs on a fish's backbone. This street plan is designed to catch both the breeze and the shade. All in all, this laid-back island village is an ideal place to take a vacation from your busy vacation.

Planning Your Time

For general Dalmatian Island tips, see "Planning Your Time" for Hvar (page 235).

...orčula deserves the better part of a day, but you'll quickly
e..aust the town's sightseeing options. With a single day, spend
the morning wandering the medieval Old Town and exploring
the handful of tiny museums (many close for siesta in the early
afternoon, especially outside of peak season). In the afternoon,
kick back at a café or restaurant and bask on the beach. If you're
here on a Thursday, be sure to catch the performance of the
Moreška dance (also Mon July-Aug). With a second day, unwind
more, or consider a one-day package excursion to Mljet Island
and its national park (not quite doable in one day by public transportation; see page 278).

If you're trying to choose between Hvar and Korčula, why not
do both? For example, if heading south, you can take an early boat
from Split to Hvar, have a few hours there, then take the evening
boat on to Korčula to set up for a day or two of vacation. If you're
in a rush, you can spend one night on Korčula, see the town in the
morning, then zip out on the evening *Nona Ana* boat to Dubrovnik
(July-Aug 4/week)—but it's much more sane and relaxing to hang
out here for two nights.

Off-Season Challenges: While Korčula is reasonably well-
connected to the rest of Dalmatia in the summertime, things
change off-season. The handy *Nona Ana* express boat to Dubrovnik
runs only in July and August. From October to May, things get
even more sparse: The Dubrovnik car-ferry is discontinued entirely,
bus connections to Dubrovnik are cut in half (leaving only one
early-morning option), and express boat service from Split and
Hvar is also halved. You may find that you'll have to spend two
nights in Korčula just to have any daylight time here.

Orientation to Korčula

(area code: 020)

The long, skinny island of Korčula runs alongside the even longer, skinnier Pelješac Peninsula. The main
town and best destination on the island—
just across a narrow strait from Pelješac—is
also called Korčula.

Korčula town is centered on its compact **Old Town** (Stari Grad) peninsula,
which is connected to the mainland at a big
staircase leading to the Great Land Gate.
In the area in front of this staircase, you'll
find ATMs, travel agencies, the Jadrolinija
ferry office, Internet cafés, the Konzum
supermarket, a colorful outdoor produce
market, and other handy tourist services.

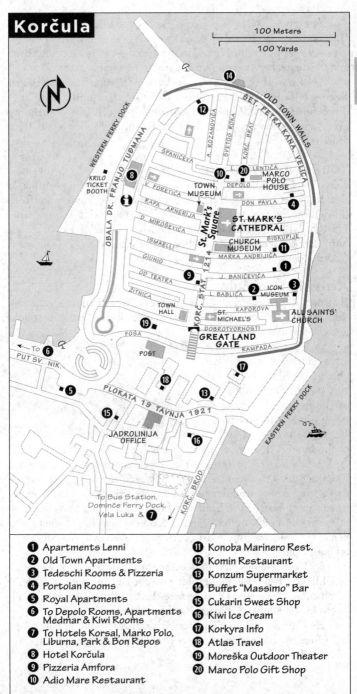

Korčula

100 Meters
100 Yards

OLD TOWN WALLS
ŠET. PETRA KANAVELIĆA

WESTERN FERRY DOCK

OBALA DR. FRANJO TUĐMANA

KRILO
TICKET
BOOTH

ŠPANIĆEVA
A. ROZANOVIĆA
SVETOG ROKA
KORČ. BRAĆ
LENTIĆA

V. FORETIĆA
TOWN
MUSEUM
DEPOLO
MARCO
POLO
HOUSE

RAFA ARNERIJA
St. Mark's Square
DON PAVLA

D. MIROŠEVIĆA
ST. MARK'S
CATHEDRAL

ISMAELLI
CHURCH
MUSEUM
BISKUPIJE

GIUNIO
MARKA ANDRIJIĆA

OD TEATRA
KORČ. STAT. 1214
J. BANIČEVIĆA

ŽITNICA
L. BABLIĆA
ICON
MUSEUM

TOWN
HALL
ST.
MICHAEL'S
KAPOROVA
ALL SAINTS'
CHURCH

DOBROTVORNOSTI
GREAT LAND
GATE

FOSA
RAMPADA

To
PUT SV. NIK.
POST

PLOKATA 19 TRAVNJA 1921

JADROLINIJA
OFFICE

EASTERN FERRY DOCK

KORČ. BROD.

To Bus Station,
Dominče Ferry Dock,
Vela Luka &

❶ Apartments Lenni
❷ Old Town Apartments
❸ Tedeschi Rooms & Pizzeria
❹ Portolan Rooms
❺ Royal Apartments
❻ To Depolo Rooms, Apartments
  Medmar & Kiwi Rooms
❼ To Hotels Korsal, Marko Polo,
  Liburna, Park & Bon Repos
❽ Hotel Korčula
❾ Pizzeria Amfora
❿ Adio Mare Restaurant

⓫ Konoba Marinero Rest.
⓬ Komin Restaurant
⓭ Konzum Supermarket
⓮ Buffet "Massimo" Bar
⓯ Cukarin Sweet Shop
⓰ Kiwi Ice Cream
⓱ Korkyra Info
⓲ Atlas Travel
⓳ Moreška Outdoor Theater
⓴ Marco Polo Gift Shop

Stretching to the south and east of the Old Town is **"Shell Bay,"** surrounded by a strip of tacky tourist shops and resort hotels. This seamier side of Korčula—best avoided—caters mostly to Brits and Germans here to worship the sun for a week or two.

To the west of Old Town is the serene waterfront street **Put Svetog Nikole,** where you'll find a few *sobe* (including some recommended under "Sleeping in Korčula," later), inviting swimming areas, great views back on the Old Town, and more locals than tourists.

Tourist Information

Korčula's TI, run by Stanka Kraljević and slyly smiling Smilija, is next to Hotel Korčula on the west side of the Old Town waterfront (mid-June-Sept Mon-Sat 8:00-15:00 & 16:00-22:00, Sun 9:00-13:00 & 17:00-20:00; Oct-mid-June Mon-Sat 8:00-14:00, closed Sun, may be open Sun in shoulder season; tel. 020/715-701, www .korcula.net).

Arrival in Korčula

By Boat: In general, the big Jadrolinija car ferries arrive on the east side of the Old Town peninsula, while the Orebić passenger boat and the fast catamarans dock at the west side of town. (But inclement weather can change the arrival or departure point.) From either side of the peninsula, it's just a two-minute walk to where it meets the mainland and all of the services described under "Orientation to Korčula," earlier.

A few boats (car ferries from Orebić and Drvenik) use the Dominče dock two peninsulas east of Korčula, about a five-minute drive from town. Regular buses connect this dock with Korčula town. Some boats from Split and Hvar town arrive at Vela Luka, at the far end of Korčula Island. Each boat arriving at Vela Luka is met by a bus waiting to bring arriving travelers to Korčula town (about 1 hour).

By Bus: The bus station is at the southeast corner of Korčula's Shell Bay. If you leave the station with the bay on your right, you'll reach the Old Town. If you leave with the bay on your left, you'll get to hotels Korsal, Liburna, Park, and Marko Polo.

By Car: See "Route Tips for Drivers" at the end of this chapter. Once in Korčula town, there's free parking at the bus station along the marina.

Helpful Hints

Boat Tickets: On arrival, plan for your departure (for your options, see "Korčula Connections," later). Don't dawdle buying your tickets to leave Korčula—they can sell out. The **Jadrolinija** office, selling tickets for the big car ferries, short hops across to the Pelješac Peninsula, and the catamaran that departs from Vela Luka at the far end of the island, is located where the Old Town meets the mainland (June-Sept Mon-Fri 8:00-20:00, Sat 8:00-13:30 & 18:00-22:00, Sun 6:00-13:30; Oct-May generally open Mon-Fri 8:00-14:00, Sat 8:00-13:00, closed Sun; tel. 020/715-410, www.jadrolinija.hr). But they don't sell tickets for two of the handy, fast catamarans: the *Krilo* catamaran to Hvar town and Split (buy *Krilo* tickets at the small kiosk on the embankment near Hotel Korčula the night before the boat departs—tickets sold June-Sept 19:00-20:00 only, Oct-May 18:00-19:00 only), and the *Nona Ana* catamaran to Mljet and Dubrovnik (buy *Nona Ana* tickets at the Korkyra Info travel agency, listed next).

Travel Agencies: Korčula has several travel agencies where you can book an excursion, browse shelves of books and souvenirs, and get information about car rental and other activities. **Korkyra Info,** well-run by Vlado, provides all the usual services (car rental, room booking, excursions) and runs a handy shuttle bus to Dubrovnik (May-Sept daily 9:00-22:00, until 20:00 and sometimes closed for mid-afternoon break in shoulder season, just outside the Great Land Gate, mobile 091-571-4355, www.korkyra.info, info@korkyra.info). **Atlas Travel** is well-established but more institutional (long hours daily in summer, closed for mid-afternoon break and sometimes closed Sun in shoulder season, open Mon-Sat mornings and closed Sun in winter; a few steps down from the Great Land Gate at Trg 19 Travnja, tel. 020/711-231).

Sights in Korčula

Korčula's few sights cluster within a few yards of each other in the Old Town. I've listed them roughly in order from the Great Land Gate (the Old Town's main entry) to the tip of the Old Town peninsula. All museums are officially "closed" November through April, but most will usually open by request (ask the TI to call for you...or just try knocking on the door).

▲▲*Moreška* **Dance**—Lazy Korčula snaps to life when locals perform a medieval folk dance called the *Moreška* (moh-REHSH-kah). The plot helps Korčulans remember their hard-fought past: A bad king takes the good king's bride, the dancing forces of good and evil battle, and there's always a happy ending.

Cost and Hours: 100 kn, June-mid-Oct every Thu at 21:00, July-Aug also Mon at 21:00, in outdoor theater next to the Great Land Gate—to the left as you face the gate, or in a nearby congress center if bad weather; buy tickets from travel agency, at your hotel, or at the door.

▲**Great Land Gate (Veliki Revelin)**—A noble staircase leads up to the main entrance to the Old Town. Like all of the town's towers, it's adorned with the Venetian winged lion and the coats of arms of the doge of Venice (left) and the rector of Korčula (right; the offset coat of arms below was the rector who later renovated the gate). Climb the tower to visit a small exhibit with costumes and photos from the *Moreška* dance, then head up to the top level to enjoy panoramic town views.

Cost and Hours: 15 kn, daily 10:00-16:00, until 19:00 or 21:00 in summer, generally closed Nov-May, English descriptions.

Nearby: On the left inside the gate is the 16th-century **Town Hall and Rector's Palace.** The seal of Korčula (over the center arch) symbolizes the town's importance as the southernmost bastion of the Venetian Republic: St. Mark standing below three defensive towers. The little church on the other side of the square is dedicated to **St. Michael** (Crkva Sv. Mihovila). Throughout Croatia, many towns have churches dedicated to St. Michael just inside the town gates, as he is believed to offer saintly protection from enemies. Notice that a passageway connects the church to the building across the street—home to the Brotherhood of St. Michael, one of Korčula's many religious fraternal organizations (see "Icon Museum," later).

• *Now begin walking up the...*

Street of the Korčulan Statute of 1214 (Ulica Korčulanskog Statuta 1214)—This street is Korčula's backbone, in more ways than one: While most medieval towns slowly evolved with twisty, mazelike lanes, Korčula was carefully planned to resemble a fish skeleton. The streets to the west (left) of this one are straight, to allow the refreshing northwesterly Maestral winds into town. To the east (right), they're curved (notice you can't see the sea) to keep out the bad-vibe southeasterly Jugo winds.

The street's complicated name honors a 1214 statute—the oldest known written law in Central Europe—with regulations about everyday life and instructions on maintaining the city walls, protecting nature, keeping animals, building a house, and so on. As you head up the street, look up to notice some interesting decorations on the houses' upper floors.

• *If you continue up the street, you'll reach St. Mark's Square (Trg Sv. Marka). From here, you're a few steps from the next four sights.*

▲**St. Mark's Cathedral (Katedrala Sv. Marka)**—Korčula became a bishopric in the 14th century. In the 19th century—36

bishops later—the Habsburgs decided to centralize ecclesiastical power in their empire, and they removed Korčula's bishop. The town still has this beautiful "cathedral"—but no bishop. On the ornately decorated tympanum above the main door, you'll see another Venetian statue of St. Mark (flanked by Adam and Eve). Inside, above the main altar, is an original Tintoretto painting. At the altar to the left, find the statue of St. Rok (better known by his Italian name, San Rocco) pointing to a wound on his leg. This French saint is very popular in Croatia; it's believed he helps cure disease. As you leave, notice the weapons on the back wall, used in some of the pivotal battles that have taken place near strategically situated Korčula.

Cost and Hours: Free except in Aug, when you'll pay 4 kn; open May-Oct daily 9:00-14:00 & 17:00-19:00, may be open all day long in peak season, closed during church services, generally closed Nov-April but may be open Mon-Fri 9:00-12:00 after Easter.

▲**Church Museum (Opatska Riznica)**—This small museum has an eclectic and fascinating collection. Go on a scavenger hunt for the following items: a ceremonial necklace from Mother Teresa (who came from Macedonia, not far from here—she gave this necklace to a friend from Korčula), some 12th-century hymnals, copies of two tiny drawings by Leonardo da Vinci, a coin collection (including a 2,400-year-old Greek coin minted here in Korčula), some Croatian modern paintings, three amphora jugs, and two framed reliquaries with dozens of miniscule relics.

Cost and Hours: 20 kn, 25-kn guidebook covers both museum and cathedral; May-Oct Mon-Sat 9:00-14:00 & 17:00-19:00, closed Sun except sometimes open in the morning; generally closed Nov-April but may be open Mon-Fri 9:00-12:00 after Easter.

▲**Town Museum (Gradski Muzej)**—Housed in an old mansion, this museum does a fine job of bringing together Korčula's various claims to fame. It's arranged like a traditional Dalmatian home: shop on the ground floor, living quarters in the middle floors, kitchen on top. Notice that some of the walls near the entry have holes in them. Archaeologists are continually doing "digs" into these walls to learn how medieval houses here were built.

On the ground floor is a lapidarium, featuring fragments of Korčula's stone past (see the first-century Roman amphora jugs). Upstairs is a display on Korčula's long-standing shipbuilding industry, including models of two modern steel ships built here (the town still builds ship parts today). There's also a furnished living room and, in the attic, a kitchen. This was a smart place for the kitchen—if it caught fire, it was less likely to destroy the whole building. Notice the little WC in the corner. A network of pipes took kitchen and other waste through town and out to sea.

Cost and Hours: 20 kn, limited posted English information but free smartphone audiotour available for download on their Wi-Fi network; June-Sept Mon-Sat 10:00-21:00, closed Sun; Oct and April-May Mon-Sat 8:00-14:00, closed Sun; Nov-March Mon-Fri 8:00-14:00, closed Sat-Sun; tel. 020/711-420. If it's locked, try knocking.

Marco Polo's House (Kuća Marka Pola)—Korčula's favorite son is the great 13th-century explorer Marco Polo. Though Polo sailed under the auspices of the Venetian Republic, and technically was a Venetian (since the Republic controlled this region), Korčulans proudly claim him as their own. Marco Polo was the first Westerner to sail to China, bringing back amazing stories and exotic goods (like silk) that Europeans had never seen before. After his trip, Marco Polo fought in an important naval battle against the Genoese near Korčula. He was captured, taken to Genoa, and imprisoned. He told his story to a cellmate, who wrote it down, published it, and made the explorer a world-class and much-in-demand celebrity. To this day, kids in swimming pools around the world try to find him with their eyes closed.

Today, Korčula is the proud home to "Marco Polo's House"—actually a more recent building on the site of what may or may not have been his family's property, with a stubby tower you can climb for an uninspiring view...and nothing else. In the future, the town hopes to turn the complex into a world-class museum about the explorer, with exhibits about Polo himself, Korčula in the 13th century, the big 1298 naval battle during which Polo was taken prisoner, and the Silk Road trading route.

Cost and Hours: 15 kn, daily July-Aug 9:00-21:00, Easter-June and Sept-Oct 10:00-13:00 & 15:00-18:00, closed Nov-Easter, just north of cathedral on—where else?—ulica Depolo.

Nearby: Across the street from the house's entrance, you'll find a clever **Marco Polo gift shop** selling various items relating to the explorer—herbs, brandies, honey, ice cream, and so on. Each one comes with a little tag telling a legend about M.P.—for example, how the word "million" was based on his middle name, Emilio (because no existing word was superlative enough for his discoveries). There are even life-size figures of Marco Polo and Kublai Khan keeping an eye on the cash register (daily in summer 9:00-24:00, progressively shorter hours and closed for mid-afternoon break off-season, closed in winter, ulica Depolo 1A, mobile 091-189-8048).

▲**Icon Museum (Zbirka Ikona)**—Korčula is known for its many brotherhoods—centuries-old fraternal organizations that have sprung up around churches. The Brotherhood of All Saints has been meeting every Sunday after Mass since the 14th century, and they run a small but interesting museum of icons. Maja, who lives upstairs, speaks no English but will point out what's worth seeing. These golden religious images were brought back from Greece in the 17th century by Korčulans who fought the Ottomans on a Venetian warship.

Brotherhoods' meeting halls are often connected to their church by a second-story walkway. Use this one to step in to the Venetian-style **All Saints' Church** (Crkva Svih Svetih). Under the loft in the back of the church, notice the models of boats and tools—donated by Korčula's shipbuilders. Look closely at the painting to the right of the altar. See the guys in the white robes kneeling under Jesus? That's the Brotherhood, who commissioned this painting.

Cost and Hours: 15 kn, hours depend on demand—generally May-Oct daily 10:00-14:00 & 17:00-20:00, may be open all day in peak season, closed Nov-April—but try ringing the bell, on Kaprova ulica at the Old Town's southeast tip.

▲**Old Town Walls**—For several centuries, Korčula held a crucial strategic position as one of the most important southern outposts of the Venetian Republic (the Republic of Dubrovnik started at the Pelješac Peninsula, just across the channel). The original town walls around Korčula date from at least the 13th century, but the fortifications were extended (and new towers built) over several centuries to defend against various foes of Venice—mostly Ottomans and pirates.

The most recent tower dates from the 16th century, when the Ottomans attacked Korčula. The rector and other VIPs fled to the mainland, but a brave priest remained on the island and came up with a plan. All of the women of Korčula dressed up as men, and then everybody in town peeked over the wall—making the Ottomans think they were up against a huge army. The priest prayed for help, and the strong northerly Bora wind blew. Not wanting to take their chances with the many defenders and the weather, the Ottomans sailed away, and Korčula was saved.

By the late 19th century, Korčula was an unimportant Habsburg beach town, and the walls had no strategic value. The town decided to quarry the top half of its old walls to build new

KORČULA

homes (and to improve air circulation inside the city). Though today's walls are half as high as they used to be, the town has restored many of the towers, giving Korčula its fortified feel. Each one has a winged lion—a symbol of Venice—and the seal of the rector of Korčula when the tower was built.

Activities in Korčula

Swimming—The water around Korčula is clean and suitable for swimming. You'll find pebbly beaches strewn with holiday-goers all along Put Svetog Nikole, the street that runs west from the Old Town. While this shoreline doesn't have much flat land for sunning yourself, you can generally find a relatively comfy rock to recline on. Another good swimming spot is at the very end of the Old Town peninsula. Or trek to the beaches near Lumbarda (described next).

Lumbarda—For a break from Korčula town, venture about three miles southeast to Lumbarda, a tranquil end-of-the-road village. Lumbarda is known for its wine (the sweet *grk* dessert wine) and for its beaches: the pebbly Bilin Žal, just east of town; and the sandy Vela Pržina, about a 20-minute walk through vineyards to the south. While not worth going out of your way for, Lumbarda and its beaches are fun to explore on a lazy vacation day. From Korčula town, you can get to Lumbarda by water taxi (50 kn) or by bus (hourly Mon-Sat, fewer buses Sun, 15 minutes, 15 kn).

Excursions—Various companies offer day-long excursions to nearby destinations (generally available June-Oct, each itinerary offered 2-4 times per week). The most popular options are Dubrovnik and the national park on Mljet Island. Korkyra Info runs their own tours, with smaller groups, or you can go with the bigger, most established, and more impersonal Atlas (see "Helpful Hints," earlier). Several new, more active tour companies have popped up recently, offering canoe trips, snorkeling, kayaking, and other "adventures"—look for flyers around town.

Other Activities—You'll see travel agencies all over where you can rent a car, bike, scooter, boat, sea kayak, or anything else you want for some vacation fun. Local captains take tourists on cruises to nearby bays and islands to get out on the water, swim, and enjoy a local-style "fish picnic." Inquire at any travel agency, or simply talk to a captain at the harbor (near the eastern ferry dock, at Shell Bay; figure about 200 kn per hour regardless of number of people). If you're a wine-lover,

consider hiring a driver to take you on a tour of Korčula Island, including stops at some wineries (ask at TI or travel agency).

Nightlife in Korčula

This town is much sleepier than Hvar, but you'll still find a fair share of late-night discos in the summertime, including one near the eastern base of the Old Town peninsula, and others along the waterfront between the Old Town and the resort hotels (east of town). Just below the Great Land Gate, Caffe Bar Step often has live music outside.

The best setting for drinks is at **Buffet "Massimo,"** a youthful-feeling cocktail bar in a city-wall tower at the very tip of the Old Town peninsula. You can have a drink on one of three levels: the downstairs bar, the main-floor lounge, or climb the ladder (at your own risk) to the tower-top terrace (terrace is only for cocktail-sippers—no beer or wine). If you're up top, notice the simple dumbwaiter for hauling up drinks (50-55-kn cocktails, 20-kn beer, daily in summer 18:00-2:00 in the morning, shoulder season 17:00-1:00 in the morning, closed Nov-April, tel. 020/715-073).

Sleeping in Korčula

Korčula has six hotels—five of which are owned by the same company (which is, in turn, government-run). The lack of competition keeps quality low and prices ridiculously high—which makes *sobe* a particularly good alternative.

Sobe

My favorite *sobe* in Korčula offer similar comfort to the hotels at far lower prices—most of them with TVs and air-conditioning, to boot. If you arrive without a room and all of my recommendations are full, you still have several options: Entertain the offers that greet you as you step off your boat or bus; walk through an area with lots of *sobe* and *apartman* signs (such as the Put Svetog Nikole waterfront and the streets just above it) and ring some doorbells; or enlist the help of a local travel agency, such as Korkyra Info or Atlas (see "Helpful Hints," earlier). If you book a place sight-unseen, be very clear on the location, and expect locals to underestimate walking times (a place they swear is a "10-minute walk" from town may take you more like 15 or 20 minutes). The options I've listed here are safe bets and worth reserving ahead.

Apartments come equipped with kitchens, and *sobe* often have refrigerators and kettles. For something more substantial, several cafés in town offer breakfast for 30-40 kn; ask your *sobe* host for suggestions.

Sleep Code

(5 kn = about $1, €1 = about $1.40, country code: 385, area code: 020)

S = Single, **D** = Double/Twin, **T** = Triple, **Q** = Quad, **b** = bathroom. The modest tourist tax (about 7 kn per person, per night) is not included in these rates. Hotels generally accept credit cards and include breakfast in their rates, while most *sobe* accept only cash and don't offer breakfast. While rates are listed in euros, you'll pay in kunas. Unless I note otherwise, everyone listed here speaks English (or has a relative or neighbor who can help translate).

Rates: If I've listed two sets of rates for an accommodation, prices for peak season (generally July and August) precede those for shoulder season (May-June and Sept-Oct). The few places that remain open through the winter charge even less during those months. The dates for seasonal rates vary by hotel, and prices can change without notice; verify the hotel's current rates online or by email. For other updates, see www.ricksteves.com/update.

Price Ranges: To help you sort easily through these listings, I've divided the accommodations into three categories based on the price for a double room with bath during peak season:

$$$ Higher Priced—Most rooms €100 or more.
  $$ Moderately Priced—Most rooms between €55-100.
    $ Lower Priced—Most rooms €55 or less.

In the Old Town

Sleeping in the Old Town nestles you squarely in the historic heart of Korčula, in immediate proximity to all of the sights. The likely trade-offs: steep and tight staircases, small rooms in centuries-old houses, and no sea views.

$$ Apartments Lenni is run by Lenni and Periša (Peter) Modrinić, both of whom are outgoing and speak good English. They rent three tight, modern, comfortable rooms (one with a private bathroom across the hall) and three apartments in a nicely renovated house right in the heart of the Old Town. Since they live off-site, confirm your reservation the day before and let them know your arrival time (Db-€65/€55, apartment-€90/€70, book direct for these rates, air-con, free Wi-Fi, near Konoba Marko Polo restaurant at Jakova Baničevića

13, tel. 020/721-444, fax 020/711-400, mobile 091-551-6592, www
.ikorcula.net/lenni, perisa.modrinic@du.t-com.hr). Peter offers
minibus transfers to Dubrovnik with a few fun stops en route
(1,100 kn for groups of 1-8 people—team up with other guests to
cut costs), and can drive you on a day trip to Mostar (1,500 kn) or
on a four-hour tour around the island (750 kn).

$$ Old Town Apartments, well-run by Branko and Ulrike
Ristić (who lived in Germany for many years), has three modern
apartments wedged into an old shell right in the heart of town
(studio-€75/€65, bigger "comfort" studio-€85/€75, one-bedroom
apartment-€95/€85, air-con, free Wi-Fi, Don Iva Matijace 14,
tel. 020/711-320, mobile 098-180-2553, www.juristic.de/korcula,
branko.r@onlinehome.de).

$ Ivo and Katja Tedeschi, who also run a recommended piz-
zeria, rent four small, simple rooms and a big, low-ceilinged, top-
floor apartment up lots of steep stairs just inside the seawall. The
apartment and two of the rooms have sea views and air-condition-
ing, while two other rooms have neither (Db-€50/€40-45, apart-
ment-€90/€60, Don Iva Matijace, tel. 020/711-354, Ivo's mobile
091-762-7803, tedeschi@hi.t-com.hr).

$ Anka Portolan, with her helpful English-speaking grand-
daughter Vesna, rents two fine, older-feeling rooms perfectly
located near the wall in the Old Town (Db-€35/€30, bigger
apartment-€50/€40, 30 percent more for 1- or 2-night stays, cash
only, air-con, Don Pavla Poše 7, tel. 020/711-711, ankaportolan
.apartmani@gmail.com).

West of the Old Town

The pleasant residential neighborhood west of the Old Town,
along the waterfront drag called Put Svetog Nikole, comes with
an easy, level walk into town and gorgeous views of the Old Town
peninsula. The main advantages to sleeping here are a bit more
space and (in many cases) sea views. I've listed these in the order
you'll reach them as you walk along the water—from one minute
(the first listing) to 10 minutes (last listing) away from the Old
Town.

$$ Royal Apartments are run by Zvonko and Marija Jelavić,
who have lived in Toronto and have built some of the most hote-
lesque (and most expensive) rooms in town—using comfortingly
familiar North American fixtures imported from Home Depot.
Their five classy apartments feel more like a small hotel with no
real reception desk (small apartment-€80, big apartment-€95,
same prices all season, closed mid-Oct-mid-April, no extra charge
for 1- or 2-night stays, air-con, free Wi-Fi, well-marked with green
awning just west of Old Town at Trg Petra Šegedina 4, mobile
098-184-0444, royalapt@ica.net, Jelavić family).

$ Rezi and Andro Depolo, probably distant relatives of Marco, rent four comfy, good-value rooms on the bay west of the Old Town. Three of the rooms offer beautiful views to the Old Town, and the five-minute stroll into town is pleasant and scenic. Friendly, English-speaking Rezi works to make her guests feel welcome (Db-€40/€35, room with kitchen-€5 more, about €3 cheaper without sea view, 30 percent more for 1-night stays, continental breakfast-25 kn, big breakfast-35 kn, air-con, free Wi-Fi; walk along waterfront from Old Town with bay on your right to the yellow house at Put Svetog Nikole 28—it's set back from the street, just before the two monasteries; tel. 020/711-621, mobile 098-964-3687, rezi.depolo@gmail.com).

$ Apartments Medmar, run by colorful Mađa Marović, has three well-appointed, well-stocked apartments and two rooms in a modern yellow house with great sea views at the tip of land just beyond the monastery. Ursa-Međa (as in "Ursa Major") speaks limited English, but her son Pero translates reservation emails (Db-€45 year-round but discounted for longer stays off-season, apartment-€80/€50, air-con, Put Svetog Nikole 38—just as the road bends left, above the family's natural-products shop, tel. 020/711-640, mobile 098-244-974, marovicp@yahoo.com).

$ Kiwi Rooms, run by gregarious English-speaking Nado Andrijić and his artist wife Marica, has two bright, modern, nicely decorated rooms with gorgeous seaview balconies. While there's no air-conditioning, they often get a good breeze and there's only a bit of road noise (Db-€50/€40, 25 percent more for 1-night stays, Put Svetog Nikole 42, tel. 020/711-608, mobile 091-543-8265).

Hotels

$$$ Hotel Korsal is Korčula's best hotel option—and the only one in town not owned by the sinking ship called HTP Korčula (see next listing). The Korsal's 10 rooms fill two buildings just above the promenade connecting the Old Town to the resort area, less than a 10-minute walk from downtown. While the standard rooms are smallish, all rooms come with sea views and stylish, colorful decor (standard Db-€156/€136, bigger "comfort" Db-€196/€176, family room for up to four-€296/€260, 20 percent more for 1-night stays, includes breakfast, free Wi-Fi, air-con, closed Nov-April, Šetalište Frana Kršinića 80, tel. 020/715-722, mobile 091-533-8302, www.hotel-korsal.com, info@hotel-korsal.com). Their restaurant has a good menu that mixes traditional Dalmatian cooking with international dishes; you can sit inside, or out on the seaview terrace—ask about the proposal-perfect tables (60-95-kn pastas and starters, 80-170-kn main dishes, daily 12:00-24:00).

HTP Korčula

This company owns Korčula's five big hotels, all in need of renovation. But if you don't want to stay in a *soba*, and the Korsal is full, these are the only game in town. You can reserve rooms at any of them through the main office (tel. 020/726-336, fax 020/711-746, www.korcula-hotels.com, marketing@htp-korcula.hr). I've listed peak-season prices with breakfast only; rates are progressively lower the further you get into off-season. You can pay €10 more per person for half-board (dinner at the hotel). It's much cheaper to stay a week or longer. There's a long-term plan to renovate all of these hotels, but so far the Marko Polo is the only one that's seen any progress (and the only one that has air-conditioning).

$$$ Hotel Korčula has by far the best location, right on the waterfront alongside the Old Town. It has a fine seaside terrace restaurant and friendly staff, even if the 20 rooms are outmoded and waaay overpriced. The rooms are on two floors: The more expensive "first-floor" rooms (actually on the third floor) have big windows and sea views; the cheaper "second-floor" rooms (actually on the fourth floor) have tiny windows and no views (Sb-€105-120/€85, Db-€140-160/€120, less off-season, reception tel. 020/711-078).

$$$ Hotel Marko Polo, the only one of the chain that has been renovated, has 94 rooms, air-conditioning, an elevator, and a big pool. All of this makes it the town's only real "splurge"...and it's priced accordingly (Db-€120-165/€85-132 depending on size and amenities, cheaper off-season, pay Wi-Fi, reception tel. 020/726-100).

$$$ *Other Hotels:* Three more HTP hotels cluster a 15-minute walk away, around the far side of Shell Bay. All are rough around the edges, overpriced, and relatively inconvenient to the Old Town, but they share a nice beach. **Hotel Liburna,** with a clever split-level design that reflects the skyline of the Old Town, has 109 rooms, most of them accessible by elevator; half the rooms face the sea and cost an additional 10 percent (Db-€130/€100-110, pay Wi-Fi, reception tel. 020/726-006). Dreary **Hotel Park** has 153 cheaper rooms (some the same price as Liburna, others cheaper, reception tel. 020/726-100). The fifth hotel, **Hotel Bon Repos**—another 15 minutes by foot from the Old Town—is, in every sense, the last resort.

Eating in Korčula

Korčula lacks the burgeoning culinary scene of Hvar; things are pretty static here, and the place is awash in interchangeable *konobas*—simple restaurants serving pastas and seafood dishes. These are all decent options, but everything in town is pretty similar—make your decision based on atmosphere and what looks best to you. Note that almost all of these eateries close from mid-October to Easter.

Pizzeria Amfora, on a side lane off the people-parade up Korčula's main drag in the Old Town, features delicious and well-priced pastas and pizzas—nothing fancy, just good ol' comfort food. Squeeze into the small dining room or enjoy the sidewalk tables (50-70-kn pizzas and pastas, 60-100-kn main courses, daily 11:00-24:00, closed 15:00-18:00 and Sun dinner for a few weeks at start and end of season, closed mid-Oct-mid-April, ulica od Teatra 4, tel. 020/711-739).

Adio Mare, with fine seafood, may have the best decor in town: a cavernous stone dining room with long shared tables and a thick vine scaling one wall. Or climb the stairs and cross the little bridge to the delightful rooftop garden terrace. Either way, carefully review your bill (60-70-kn pastas, 50-120-kn main courses, descriptive menu, Mon-Sat 12:00-24:00, Sun 17:30-24:00, on the main drag just past Marco Polo's House, tel. 020/711-253).

Konoba Marinero has pleasantly nautical decor, outdoor tables on an atmospherically tight lane, and a simple menu of Dalmatian specialties (70-120-kn main courses, Easter-mid-Oct daily 17:00-24:00, Marka Andrijića 13, tel. 020/711-170).

Along the Seawall: Various restaurants line up scenically along the Old Town's seawall, providing al fresco dining with salty views. Their tables, spilling out along the seafront, are ideal for romantic harborside meals. On the eastern side of the peninsula, several interchangeable places serve uninspired, overpriced crank-'em-out food with jaded service; for something more affordable, try **Pizzeria Tedeschi,** which serves up good pizzas closer to the base of the peninsula (40-50-kn pizzas and pastas, daily 9:00-24:00, closed mid-Oct-April, tel. 020/711-586). On the western side, near the tip and perfectly situated for viewing the sunset, **Komin** offers traditional Dalmatian meals cooked on a grill inside (45-70-kn pastas, 65-150-kn main dishes, daily 9:00-24:00, Šetalište Petra Kanavelica 26, mobile 098-847-057).

Around Shell Bay: Prices inside the Old Town are generally the highest in Korčula. But several cheaper eateries lie just outside the Old Town. Window-shop the menus along the harbor, then hang a left at the bus station and continue up the road toward the big resort hotels. You'll find plenty of cafés, pizzerias, and *konoba*s (traditional restaurants), most with outdoor seating. For something a bit more upscale, consider the restaurant at **Hotel Korsal,** which strives to bring a bit more class to Korčula's cuisine scene (see "Sleeping in Korčula," earlier).

Picnics: Just outside the main gate, you'll find a lively produce market and a big, modern, air-conditioned **Konzum** supermarket

(Mon-Sat 7:00-20:00, Sun 8:00-13:00). A short stroll from there down Put Svetog Nikole takes you to rocky seafront perches with the best Korčula views. Otherwise, there are many inviting picnic spots along the Old Town embankment.

Sweet Shop: For good (if pricey) local sweets, stop by **Cukarin,** which sells tasty traditional cookies such as the delicious flourless (and gluten-free) *amareta* almond cake; the Marko Polo cake (flourless chocolate cake with buttercream); and the walnut-cream-filled *klašun.* They also sell homemade wine, liqueur, honey, and jam (Mon-Sat 8:30-12:00 & 17:30-20:00, closed Sun and Jan-Feb, a block behind the Jadrolinija office on Hrvatske Bratske Zajednice, tel. 020/711-055).

Ice Cream: My favorite *sladoled* in Korčula is at **Kiwi** (just up the lane across from Konzum supermarket, open long hours daily).

Korčula Connections

Korčula is reasonably well-connected to the rest of the Dalmatian Coast by boat, but service becomes sparse in the off-season. If you're here during a lull in the sailing schedule, buses are your ticket out of town (making the short crossing to the Pelješac Peninsula on the Dominče-Orebić ferry). No matter when you travel, it's smart to carefully study current boat schedules, as they are always subject to change.

By Boat

Boats big and small depart from the embankment surrounding Korčula's Old Town peninsula. Which side of the peninsula a boat uses can depend on the weather—be flexible and inquire locally about where to meet your boat. Some boats leave from other parts of the island, most notably the town of Vela Luka (at the opposite tip of the island, a 1-hour bus ride from Korčula town—described later). Other boats, including the car ferries to Orebić and Drvenik (described later, under "Route Tips for Drivers"), leave from the Dominče dock, about a five-minute drive east of Korčula town. If I've listed two prices for a journey, the specific fare depends on the season.

Big Jadrolinija Car Ferries: Running twice weekly in summer (June-Sept only), these huge, handy vessels go north from Korčula town to **Stari Grad** on Hvar Island (20-minute bus ride from Hvar town; 3.75 hours, 90-110 kn; the catamaran described next is faster and takes you right to Hvar town) and **Split** (6 hours, 90-110 kn—catamaran described next is faster and cheaper); or south, to **Sobra** on Mljet Island (1.25-hour bus ride from the national park, 2.25 hours, 75-90 kn; see details below) and **Dubrovnik** (4.5 hours,

90-110 kn). These ferries do not run off-season (Oct-May).

Speedy *Krilo* Catamaran from Korčula Town to Hvar Town and Split: The speedy *Krilo* catamaran leaves Korčula town at 6:00 in the morning every day year-round (except Sun in Oct-May, when it departs at 13:00 instead), and zips to Hvar town and Split (to Hvar: 1.5 hours, 40-50 kn; to Split: 2.5-2.75 hours, 60-65 kn; in summer, it also stops en route at Prigradica on Korčula Island). In Korčula, tickets for the *Krilo* are sold at a small waterfront kiosk near Hotel Korčula—not at the Jadrolinija office. While you can, in theory, buy *Krilo* tickets starting a half-hour before the boat departs (at 5:30), they often sell out—so it's essential to buy them the night before (they're sold at the kiosk only during a one-hour time period, which is posted at the kiosk—generally June-Sept 19:00-20:00, Oct-May 18:00-19:00, mobile 099-194-6903). Since it returns from Split and Hvar the same afternoon, this extremely handy catamaran allows you to effortlessly day-trip to either place (see "Connections" for each town). For the latest schedule, see www.krilo.hr.

Speedy *Nona Ana* Catamaran to Mljet and Dubrovnik: In July and August, this convenient boat zips travelers from Korčula to Polače (on Mljet Island, handy to the national park there), then to Sobra (a less-appealing spot on Mljet) and on to Dubrovnik (4/week, generally departs Korčula at 16:00; to Polače: 1 hour, 39 kn; to Sobra: 1.25 hours, 45 kn; to Dubrovnik: 2.75 hours, 58 kn). Unfortunately, the boat doesn't serve Korčula at other times (Sept-June). Confirm schedules at www.gv-line.hr, and buy tickets at the Korkyra Info travel agency (see "Helpful Hints," earlier).

From Vela Luka to Hvar Town and Split: Additional boats connect to points north, but they depart from the port at Vela Luka, an hour away from Korčula town, at the other end of the island. A Jadrolinija **fast catamaran** goes daily from Vela Luka to both Hvar town and Split; unfortunately, on most days it leaves extremely early, with no bus connection from Korčula to get you there in time—if you're desperate, you could pay about 400 kn for an early-morning taxi, or sleep overnight in Vela Luka (Mon-Sat departs at 5:30, Sun at 8:00; to Hvar: 45 minutes, 27-32 kn; to Split: 2 hours, 40-50 kn). A **car ferry** also travels daily from Vela Luka to Split—it's slower, but generally departs at a more convenient time and is coordinated with a bus from Korčula (1-2/day, 3 hours, 50-60 kn, no stop at Hvar town). Since reaching Vela Luka from Korčula town is a hassle, carefully confirm these boat schedules at the Korčula TI or Jadrolinija office, and understand all your options before you get up early to make the trip.

To the National Park on Mljet Island: Unfortunately, day-tripping from Korčula to Mljet National Park by public transportation is not possible (see the Near Dubrovnik chapter). The

Nona Ana catamaran (described above) gets you there in the evening with no return boat that day to Korčula. However, you can day-trip to Mljet from Korčula by taking an excursion (described on page 368). To do Mljet en route from Korčula to Dubrovnik, you'll have to sleep on Mljet, then take the afternoon catamaran to Dubrovnik the next day (only possible July-Aug).

Bus Connections

All buses from Korčula town (except those to Vela Luka) first drive to Dominče, where they meet the car ferry to cross over to Orebić, on the Pelješac Peninsula. Don't be surprised if you have to get off the bus, walk onto the ferry, and meet a different bus across the channel. It takes just over an hour to drive the length of the Pelješac Peninsula and meet the main coastal road.

From Korčula Town by Bus to: Dubrovnik (peak season: 2/day, 3.5 hours, likely departs at 6:45 and 15:45; off-season: 1/day, Mon-Sat generally at 6:45, Sun at 14:45; trip costs 90 kn), **Zagreb** (1/day, 9-13.5 hours depending on route), **Split** (1/day, 5 hours, inconveniently timed—departs Korčula at 19:45 and arrives in Split after midnight, same bus goes to Zagreb), **Vela Luka** (at far end of island, Mon-Fri 7/day, Sat 6/day, Sun 4/day, 1 hour).

Shuttle Bus to Dubrovnik: Korkyra Info travel agency runs a handy minibus that costs only slightly more than the bus and takes you right to your accommodations in Dubrovnik (150 kn one-way, runs daily March-Oct generally at 9:00, Nov-Feb by request only, 2 hours, includes croissant, juice, and room-finding help through their Dubrovnik agency if needed, reserve ahead, mobile 091-571-4355, www.korkyra.info, info@korkyra.info).

Route Tips for Drivers: Between Korčula and the Mainland

The island of Korčula is connected to the mainland by a small car ferry that runs between Dominče—about a mile east of Korčula town—and Orebić, across the channel on the Pelješac Peninsula (76 kn/car, 16 kn/passenger, 15-minute crossing, departs Dominče at the top of most but not all hours—check carefully in Korčula, departs Orebić at :30 past most hours).

If you're driving via the mainland, you'll first cross on this car ferry to Orebić on the vineyard-strewn Pelješac Peninsula. The Pelješac Peninsula is extremely long and narrow, and the roads are very rough, so it can take longer than you'd expect to reach the main coastal road (figure 1-1.5 hours from Orebić). Where the peninsula meets the mainland, you'll see the cute little "Great Wall of Croatia" town of Ston. For more on the Pelješac Peninsula and Ston—including a self-guided driving tour of the vineyards between here and Dubrovnik—see page 356.

If you're heading south to **Dubrovnik,** the coastal road zips you right there (about an hour from Ston). If you're heading north to **Split,** soon after joining the coastal road you'll actually pass through Bosnia-Herzegovina for a few miles (around the town of Neum; for details, see page 230).

Because of the ferry crossing and the long drive along the Pelješac Peninsula, driving **between Split and Korčula** is time-consuming and tiring. Instead, I prefer to take the longer car ferry the whole way between Split and Vela Luka, at the far end of Korčula Island (described earlier; allow 1 hour for the drive from Korčula town to Vela Luka, costs about 300 kn per car for ferry ride). The scenic and relaxing 2.75-hour boat ride from Vela Luka to Split saves you more than that much driving time.

If you're headed north, note that there's also a car ferry from Dominče north, to **Drvenik** on the mainland (about halfway to Split).

DUBROVNIK

Dubrovnik is a living fairy tale that shouldn't be missed. It feels like a small town today, but 500 years ago, Dubrovnik was a major maritime power, with the third-biggest navy in the Mediterranean. Still jutting confidently into the sea and ringed by thick medieval walls, Dubrovnik deserves its nickname: the Pearl of the Adriatic. Within the ramparts, the traffic-free Old Town is a fun jumble of quiet, cobbled back lanes; low-impact museums; narrow, steep alleys; and kid-friendly squares. After all these centuries, the buildings still hint at old-time wealth, and the central promenade (Stradun) remains the place to see and be seen. If I had to pick just one place to visit in Croatia, this would be it.

The city's charm is the sleepy result of its no-nonsense past. Busy merchants, the salt trade, and shipbuilding made Dubrovnik rich. But the city's most valued commodity was always its freedom—even today, you'll see the proud motto *Libertas* displayed all over town (see *"Libertas"* sidebar).

Dubrovnik flourished in the 15th and 16th centuries, but an earthquake destroyed nearly everything in 1667. Most of today's buildings in the Old Town are post-quake Baroque, although a few palaces, monasteries, and convents displaying a rich Gothic-Renaissance mix survive from Dubrovnik's earlier Golden Age. Dubrovnik remained a big tourist draw through the Tito years, bringing in much-needed hard currency from Western visitors. Consequently, the city never acquired the hard socialist patina of other Yugoslav cities (such as the nearby Montenegrin capital Podgorica, then known as "Titograd").

As Croatia violently separated from Yugoslavia in 1991, Dubrovnik became the only coastal city to be pulled into the

Libertas

Libertas—liberty—has always been close to the heart of every Dubrovnik citizen. Dubrovnik was a proudly independent republic for centuries, even as most of Croatia became Venetian and then Hungarian. Dubrovnik believed so strongly in *libertas* that it was the first foreign state in 1776 to officially recognize an upstart, experimental republic called the United States of America.

In the Middle Ages, the city-state of Dubrovnik (then called Ragusa) bought its independence from whichever power was strongest—Byzantium, Venice, Hungary, the Ottomans—sometimes paying off more than one at a time. Dubrovnik's ships flew whichever flags were necessary to stay free, earning the nickname "Town of Seven Flags." It was sort of a Hong Kong of the Middle Ages—a spunky, trading-oriented statelet that maintained its sovereignty while being completely surrounded by an often-hostile mega-state (in Dubrovnik's case, the Ottoman Empire). As time went on, Europe's big-league nations were glad to have a second major seafaring power in the Adriatic to balance the Venetian threat; Dubrovnik emerged as an attractive alternative at times when Venetian ports were blockaded by the Ottomans. A free Dubrovnik was more valuable than a pillaged, plundered Dubrovnik.

In 1808, Napoleon conquered the Adriatic and abolished the Republic of Dubrovnik. After Napoleon was defeated, the fate of the continent was decided at the Congress of Vienna. But Dubrovnik's delegate was denied a seat at the table. The more powerful nations, no longer concerned about Venice and fed up after years of being sweet-talked by Dubrovnik, were afraid that the delegate would play old alliances off each other to re-establish an independent Republic of Dubrovnik. Instead, the city became a part of the Habsburg Empire and entered a long period of decline.

Libertas still hasn't died in Dubrovnik. In the surreal days of the early 1990s, when Yugoslavia was reshuffling itself, a movement for the creation of a new Republic of Dubrovnik gained some momentum (led by a judge who, in earlier times, had convicted others for the same ideas). Another movement pushed for Dalmatia to secede as its own nation. But now that the dust has settled, today's locals are content and proud to be part of an independent Republic of Croatia.

fighting (see "The Siege of Dubrovnik" sidebar). Imagine having your youthful memories of good times spent romping in the surrounding hills replaced by visions of tanks and warships shelling your hometown. The city was devastated, but Dubrovnik has been repaired with amazing speed. The only physical reminders of the war are lots of new, bright-orange roof tiles. Locals, relieved the fighting is over but forever hardened, are often willing to talk openly about the experience with visitors—offering a rare opportunity to grasp the harsh realities of war from an eyewitness perspective.

Though the war killed tourism in the 1990s, today the crowds are most decidedly back—even exceeding prewar levels. In fact, Dubrovnik's biggest downside is the overwhelming midday crush of multinational tourists who converge on the Old Town when their cruise ships dock. These days the city's economy is based almost entirely on tourism, and most locals have moved to the suburbs so they can rent their Old Town apartments to travelers. All of this can make the Old Town feel, at times, like a very pretty but soulless theme park. Dubrovnik lacks the gritty real-world vibe of Split or the charming local vitality of Ljubljana. But, like Venice, Dubrovnik rewards those who get off the beaten path and stick around beyond the normal midday cruise-ship window. Europeans set up here for a full week or two to explore the entire region, and even busy Americans might want to build some slack into their Dubrovnik time for a wide array of worthwhile side-trips (outlined in the Near Dubrovnik, Montenegro, and Mostar chapters).

Planning Your Time

While Dubrovnik's museums are nothing special, the town is one of those places that you never want to leave. The real attraction here is the Old Town and its relaxing, breezy ambience. While Dubrovnik could easily be "seen" in a day, a second or third day to unwind (or even more time, for side-trips) makes the long trip here more worthwhile.

To hit all the key sights in a single day, start at the Pile Gate, just outside the Old Town. Walk around the city's walls to get your bearings (before it gets too hot and crowded), then work your way down the main drag (following my "Strolling the Stradun" self-guided walk). As you explore, drop in at any museums or churches that appeal to you. To squeeze the most into a single day (or with a second day), hit the beach or consider a boat excursion from the Old Port (Lokrum Island, just offshore, requires the least brainpower).

Dubrovnik also makes an excellent home base for day trips into the surrounding area, including a dizzying array of island

DUBROVNIK

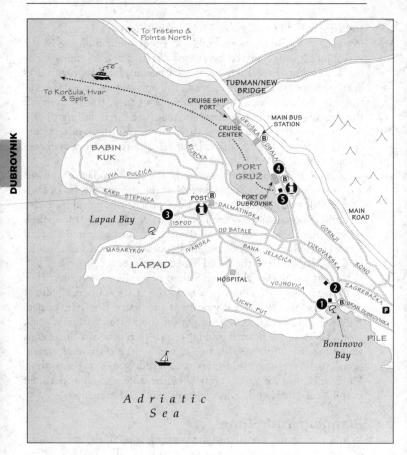

getaways, plus a pair of particularly striking international destinations: Bosnia-Herzegovina's Mostar and Montenegro's Bay of Kotor. I enjoy staying three or four nights, for maximum side-tripping flexibility.

Orientation to Dubrovnik

(area code: 020)

Nearly all of the sights worth seeing are in Dubrovnik's traffic-free, walled **Old Town** (Stari Grad) peninsula. The main pedestrian promenade through the middle of town is called the **Stradun;** from this artery, the Old Town climbs steeply uphill in both directions to the walls. The Old Town connects to the mainland through three gates: the **Pile Gate,** to the west; the **Ploče Gate,** to the east; and the smaller **Buža Gate,** at the top of the stepped lane called Boškovićeva. The **Old Port** (Gradska Luka), with lei-

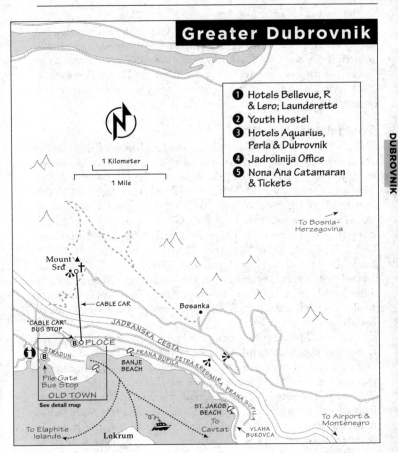

Greater Dubrovnik

1 Hotels Bellevue, R & Lero; Launderette
2 Youth Hostel
3 Hotels Aquarius, Perla & Dubrovnik
4 Jadrolinija Office
5 Nona Ana Catamaran & Tickets

DUBROVNIK

To Bosnia-Herzegovina

Mount Srđ

CABLE CAR

Bosanka

"CABLE CAR" BUS STOP

JADRANSKA CESTA

PLOČE

STRADUN

FRANA SUPILA

PETRA KREŠIMIRA FRANA SUPILA

BANJE BEACH

Pile Gate Bus Stop

OLD TOWN

See detail map

ST. JAKOB BEACH
To Cavtat

VLAHA BUKOVCA

To Airport & Montenegro

To Elaphite Islands

Lokrum

1 Kilometer

1 Mile

sure boats to nearby destinations, is at the east end of town. While greater Dubrovnik has about 50,000 people, the local population within the Old Town is just a few thousand in the winter—and even smaller in summer, when many residents move out to rent their apartments to tourists.

The **Pile** (PEE-leh) neighborhood, a pincushion of tourist services, is just outside the western end of the Old Town (through the Pile Gate). In front of the gate, you'll find the main TI, ATMs, a post office, taxis, buses (fanning out to all the outlying neighborhoods), a cheap Konzum grocery store, and the Atlas Travel Agency (described later, under "Helpful Hints"). Just off this strip are some good *sobe* (rooms in private homes—described under "Sleeping in Dubrovnik"). This is also the starting point for my "Strolling the Stradun" self-guided walk.

A mile or two away from the Old Town are beaches peppered with expensive resort hotels. The closest area is **Boninovo Bay** (a

20-minute walk or 5-minute bus trip from the Old Town), but most cluster on the lush **Lapad Peninsula** to the west (a 15-minute bus trip from the Old Town); I've recommended accommodations in each of these areas. Across the bay from the Lapad Peninsula is **Port Gruž,** with the main bus station, ferry terminal, and cruise-ship port.

Tourist Information

Dubrovnik's main TI is just outside the Old Town's **Pile Gate,** at the far end of the big terrace with the modern video-screens sculpture (July-Aug daily 8:00-22:00; June and Sept daily 8:00-21:00; May and Oct daily 8:00-20:00; Nov-April Mon-Sat 8:00-19:00, Sun 8:00-16:00; Brsalje 5, tel. 020/312-011, www.tzdubrovnik .hr). There are also locations at **Port Gruž,** across the street from the Jadrolinija ferry dock (June-Sept daily 8:00-21:00; May and Oct daily 8:00-20:00; Nov-April Mon-Fri generally 9:00-15:00, Sat 9:00-14:00, closed Sun; Gruška obala, tel. 020/417-983); in the **Lapad** resort area, at the head of the main drag (May-Oct daily 8:00-20:00, until 21:00 in July-Aug; closed Nov-April; Šetalište Kralja Zvonimira 25, tel. 020/437-460); and at the arrivals area of the **airport.**

All the TIs are government-run and legally can't sell you anything except a Dubrovnik Card—but they can answer questions and give you a copy of the free town map and two similar information booklets: the annual *Dubrovnik Riviera* and the monthly *The Best in Dubrovnik* (with a current schedule of events and performances); both contain helpful maps, bus and ferry schedules, museum hours, specifics on side-trip destinations, and more. If you need a room and the TI isn't busy, they might be willing to unofficially call around to find a place for you.

Sightseeing Pass: The heavily promoted **Dubrovnik Card** covers local public transportation; admission to the City Walls (one time only), Rector's Palace, Rupe Museum, and a few other minor sights; and various discounts around town. If you're here for three days and plan to do a lot of sightseeing and take the bus a few times, this may add up—do the math (130 kn/24 hours includes unlimited transit, 180 kn/3 days includes 10 transit rides, 220 kn/7 days includes 20 transit rides, sold at TIs and many sights and hotels).

Arrival in Dubrovnik

As is the case throughout Croatia, you'll be met at the boat dock or bus station by locals trying to get you to rent a room *(soba)* at their house. If you've already reserved elsewhere, honor your reservation; if not, consider the offer (but be very clear on the location before you accept—many are nowhere near the Old Town).

Dubrovnik Essentials

English	Croatian	Pronounced
Old Town	Stari Grad	STAH-ree grahd
Old Port	Stara Luka	STAH-rah LOO-kah
Pile Gate	Gradska Vrata Pile	GRAHD-skah VRAH-tah PEE-leh
Ploče Gate	Gradska Vrata Ploče	GRAHD-skah VRAH-tah PLOH-cheh
Main Promenade	Stradun	STRAH-doon
Adriatic Sea	Jadran	YAH-drahn

By Bus: Dubrovnik's **main bus station** (Autobusni Kolodvor) is just beyond the ferry terminal along the Port Gruž embankment (about 2.5 miles northwest of the Old Town). It's straightforward and user-friendly, with pay toilets, baggage storage, and a helpful bus information window. To reach the Old Town's Pile Gate, walk straight ahead through the bus stalls, then bear right at the main road to the city bus stop, where you can hop on a bus (#1, #1a, #1b, or #1c) to the Pile stop. A taxi from the main bus station to the Old Town and most accommodations runs about 75 kn.

Some buses (especially southbound regional buses, such as those to Cavtat) originate at the main bus station, but also use another stop, much handier to the Old Town. The **"cable car" bus stop** (a.k.a. "fire station" bus stop) is just uphill from the Buža Gate, overlooking the old wall, right next to the bottom station of the cable car up to Mount Srđ. From this bus stop, simply walk downhill (and through the pedestrian underpass)—you'll be inside the Old Town walls within a few minutes.

By Car Ferry or Catamaran: The big car ferries currently arrive at Port Gruž, two miles northwest of the Old Town. On the road in front of the ferry terminal, you'll find a bus stop (#1, #1a, #1b, and #1c go to the Old Town's Pile Gate; wait on the embankment side of the street) and a taxi stand (figure 70 kn to the Old Town and most accommodations). Across the street is the Jadrolinija office (with an ATM out front) and a TI. You can book a private room *(soba)* at Atlas Travel Agency (room-booking desk in boat terminal building, May-Sept only) or at Gulliver Travel Agency (behind TI). The fast *Nona Ana* catamaran from Mljet and Korčula also arrives near this big ferry dock.

By Cruise Ship: Some ships anchor just offshore from the Old Port, then send their passengers into the Old Town on tenders. Others put in at Port Gruž, just beyond the bus station. To reach the Old Town, take a public bus or pay 80 kn for a taxi (described

Dubrovnik at a Glance

▲▲▲**Stradun Stroll** Charming walk through Dubrovnik's vibrant Old Town, ideal for coffee, ice cream, and people-watching. **Hours:** Always open. See page 295.

▲▲▲**Town Walls** Scenic mile-long walk along top of 15th-century fortifications encircling the city. **Hours:** July-Aug daily 8:00-19:30, progressively shorter hours off-season until 10:00-15:00 in mid-Nov-mid-March. See page 304.

▲▲▲**Mount Srđ** Napoleonic fortress above Dubrovnik with spectacular views and a modest museum to the recent war. **Hours:** Mountaintop—always open; cable car—daily June-Aug 9:00-24:00, April-May and Sept-Oct 9:00-20:00, Feb-March and Nov 9:00-17:00, Dec-Jan 9:00-16:00; museum—same hours as cable car except closes at 22:00 in summer. See page 319.

▲**Franciscan Monastery Museum** Tranquil cloister, medieval pharmacy-turned-museum, and a century-old pharmacy still serving residents today. **Hours:** Daily April-Oct 9:00-18:00, Nov-March 9:00-17:00. See page 309.

▲**Rector's Palace** Sparse antiques collection in the former home of rectors who ruled Dubrovnik in the Middle Ages. **Hours:** Daily May-Oct 9:00-18:00, Nov-April 9:00-16:00. See page 310.

▲**Cathedral** Eighteenth-century Roman Baroque cathedral and treasury filled with unusual relics, such as a swatch of Jesus' swaddling clothes. **Hours:** Church—daily 8:00-20:00, treasury—generally open same hours as church, both have shorter hours off-season. See page 312.

▲**Dominican Monastery Museum** Another relaxing cloister with precious paintings, altarpieces, and manuscripts. **Hours:** Daily May-Sept 9:00-18:00, Oct-April 9:00-17:00. See page 313.

▲**Synagogue Museum** Europe's second-oldest synagogue and Croatia's only Jewish museum, with 13th-century Torahs and

earlier, under "By Bus").

By Plane: Dubrovnik's small airport (Zračna Luka) is near a village called Čilipi, 13 miles south of the city. A Croatia Airlines bus meets arriving flights for most major airlines at the airport, and brings you to the main bus station (35 kn, 40 minutes; may also stop near the Old Town—ask driver or airport TI). Legitimate cabbies charge around 220 kn for the ride between the airport and the center (though some cabbies charge as much as 300 kn; con-

Holocaust-era artifacts. **Hours:** May-mid-Nov daily 10:00-20:00; mid-Nov-April Mon-Fri 10:00-13:00, closed Sat-Sun. See page 316.

▲**War Photo Limited** Thought-provoking photographic look at contemporary warfare. **Hours:** June-Sept daily 10:00-22:00; May and Oct Tue-Sun 10:00-16:00, closed Mon; closed Nov-April. See page 316.

▲**Serbian Orthodox Church and Icon Museum** Active church serving Dubrovnik's Serbian Orthodox community and museum with traditional religious icons. **Hours:** Church—daily May-Sept 8:00-14:00 & 16:00-21:00, until 19:00 in shoulder season, until 17:00 in winter; museum—May-Oct Mon-Sat 9:00-13:00, closed Sun; Nov-April Mon-Fri 9:00-13:00, closed Sat-Sun. See page 317.

▲**Rupe Granary and Ethnographic Museum** Good folk museum with tools, jewelry, clothing, and painted eggs above immense underground grain stores. **Hours:** Wed-Mon 9:00-16:00, closed Tue. See page 318.

Maritime Museum Contracts, maps, paintings, and models from Dubrovnik's days as a maritime power and shipbuilding center. **Hours:** Flex with demand, usually March-Oct Tue-Sun 9:00-18:00, until 16:00 in Nov-Feb, closed Mon year-round. See page 315.

Aquarium Tanks of local sea life housed in huge, shady old fort. **Hours:** Daily July-Aug 9:00-21:00, progressively shorter hours off-season until 9:00-13:00 Nov-March. See page 315.

Institute for the Restoration of Dubrovnik Photos and videos of the recent war and an exhibit on restoration work. **Hours:** Completely unpredictable—just drop by and see if it's open. See page 316.

sider arranging your transfer in advance with one of the drivers listed on page 294, or through your *sobe* host). Airport info: tel. 020/773-333, www.airport-dubrovnik.hr.

To get *to* the airport, you can take the same Croatia Airlines bus, which typically leaves from Dubrovnik's main bus station 1.5 hours before each Croatia Airlines or Austrian Airlines flight, or two hours before other airlines' international flights (the schedule is posted the day before—ask at the TI). It's possible that the bus may also stop at a point closer to the Old Town (maybe at the Pile Gate, or possibly at the Buža Gate above the Old Town). As of this writing, this has not been decided—ask at the TI to see if it can save you some time.

Bad-Weather Warning: If you're considering flying into or out of Dubrovnik, be aware that the airport is located right in the blast zone of the fierce Bora winds that periodically howl along the Dalmatian Coast (especially in the late fall). It's not uncommon for flights coming into Dubrovnik to be diverted to Split instead, with passengers forced to take a dull five-hour bus journey to their intended destination. Departing flights are usually less affected (though disruptions to incoming planes could, obviously, cause delays for departures as well). Personally, I've flown out of Dubrovnik a dozen times without incident, but it's not unheard-of for travelers to be inconvenienced by this.

Nearby: If you have time to kill at the airport, you can go spelunking in the karstic **Đurović Cave,** which was recently discovered beneath the runway and opened to the public. It's filled with a "skycellar," allowing you to sample local wines in an underground cavern while waiting for your flight...no joking (40 kn to enter, 75 kn to taste up to 10 wines, sporadic hours; as you face the terminal, go to the right end and buzz the bell, or enter through the cafeteria).

By Car: Coming from the north, you'll drive over the supermodern Tuđman Bridge (which most locals, mindful of their former president's tarnished legacy, call simply "the New Bridge"). Immediately after crossing the bridge, you have two options: To get to the main bus station, ferry terminal (with some car-rental drop-off offices nearby), and Lapad Peninsula, take the left turn just after the bridge, wind down to the waterfront, then turn left and follow this road along the Port Gruž embankment. Or, to head for the Old Town, continue straight after the bridge. You'll pass above the Port Gruž area, then take the right turn-off marked *Dubrovnik* (with the little bull's-eye). You'll go through a tunnel, then turn left for *Centar,* and begin following the brown signs for *Grad* (Old Town); individual big hotels are also signed from here. Turn right to get to the Buža Gate at the top of the Old Town; first you'll pass the Old Town parking garage (described next), then wind up just above the walls (with more parking options—also described next). From this point, the direction you choose determines which one-way loop you'll be stuck on. Turning right takes you to the Pile Gate, then back up out of town toward Boninovo Bay and Lapad; turning left takes you the pretty Viktorija area, then (after looping down again) to the Ploče Gate.

If you're sleeping in or near the Old Town, **parking** is tricky. The handiest place to park long-term is the Old Town garage,

which you'll pass on the right as you
(15 kn/hour, 180 kn/day, half-pri
about a 10-minute downhill walk to
a shuttle bus (2/hour, free if you'r
like to be closer to the Old Tow
finding a spot—either on the stre
town walls (pay at meter), or in the conve
pay lot nicknamed "the tennis court," just behinu
hour). Another option is to drive to this area near the Ol
unload your bags, then leave your car at the Old Town garage (o.
cheaper, more distant one) for the duration of your visit. When in
doubt, ask your *sobe* host or hotel for parking tips.

If you're sleeping at Lapad or Boninovo Bay, you'll have an
easier time finding parking at or near your hotel—ask.

Helpful Hints

Festivals: Dubrovnik is most crowded during its Summer Festival,
a month and a half of theater and musical performances held
annually from July 10 to August 25 (www.dubrovnik-festival
.hr). This is quickly followed by the "Rachlin & Friends" classical music festival in September (www.julianrachlin.com).
For other options, see "Entertainment in Dubrovnik," later.

Crowd-Beating Tips: Dubrovnik has been discovered—especially
by cruise ships (nearly 800 of which visit each year, bringing
a total of around 900,000 passengers). Cruise-ship crowds
descend on the Old Town on most summer days, roughly
between 8:30 and 14:00 (the streets are most crowded 9:00-
13:00). In summer, try to avoid the big sights—especially
walking around the wall—during these peak times, and hit
the beach or take a siesta midday, when the town is hottest
and most crowded. On very busy days, as many as 9,000
cruise-ship day-trippers deluge Dubrovnik (three big ships'
worth). If you're caught off-guard, it can be miserable. For
others, it's entertaining to count the dozens of tour guides toting numbered paddles through the Old Town, and to watch
the blocky orange tenders going back and forth to the ships
moored offshore.

No Euros: Dubrovnik's merchants can be stubborn about accepting only kunas—no euros. (While it's technically illegal for
vendors to accept any payment other than kunas, this is rarely
enforced.) Even some of the top sights—including the City
Walls and the cable car to Mount Srđ—accept only kunas (or,
sometimes, credit cards). Even if you're in town for just a few
hours, visit an ATM to avoid hassles when it comes time to pay.

Wine Shop: For the best wine-tasting selection in a cool bar atmosphere, don't miss **D'Vino Wine Bar** (described on page 325).

t to shop rather than taste, **Vinoteka Miličić** offers
ariety of local wines; wry Dolores can explain your
s, though she does tend to push Miličić wines (daily
-Aug 9:00-23:00, April-May and Sept-Oct 9:00-20:00,
ov-March 9:00-16:00, near the Pile end of the Stradun, tel.
020/321-777).

ternet Access: Most accommodations in Dubrovnik offer
free Wi-Fi, and several cafés and bars around town provide
Wi-Fi for customers. In the Old Town, the modern **Netcafé**
has several speedy terminals and pay Wi-Fi right on Prijeko
street, the "restaurant row" (daily 9:00-24:00, Prijeko 21, tel.
020/321-025).

English Bookstore: The **Algoritam** shop, right on the Stradun, has
a wide variety of guidebooks, nonfiction books about Croatia
and the former Yugoslavia, novels, and magazines—all in
English (July-Aug Mon-Sat 9:00-23:00, Sun 10:00-13:00 &
18:00-22:00; June and Sept Mon-Sat 9:00-21:00, Sun 10:00-
14:00; shorter hours off-season; Placa 8, tel. 020/322-044).

Laundry: Hotels charge a mint to wash your clothes; *sobe* hosts
are cheaper, but often don't have the time (ask). The handy,
fun, retro, self-service **Sanja and Rosie's Launderette** is just
outside the Ploče Gate (cross the bridge and look left; 50-kn
wash, 30-40-kn dry, clear English instructions, machines
take bills, daily 8:00-22:00, 100-kn drop-off service available
Mon-Sat before 14:00, put od Bosanke 2, mobile 099-254-
6959, www.dubrovniklaundry.com). Two full-service laun-
derettes are near the hotels at **Boninovo Bay**, a 20-minute
uphill walk or five-minute bus trip from the Pile Gate: one
at Pera Čingrije 8 (145-kn wash and dry in about 3 hours, no
self-service, Mon-Fri 9:00-13:00 & 15:00-18:00, Sat 9:00-
15:00, closed Sun, shorter hours off-season, across from the
big seafront Hotel Bellevue, tel. 020/333-347), and another a
few steps toward the main road at bana Jelačića 1 (120 kn to
wash and dry up to an 11-pound load, same-day service possible if you bring it in by 10:00, open Mon-Fri 8:00-20:00, Sat
9:00-14:00, closed Sun, mobile 091-190-0888).

Car Rental: The big international chains, such as **Avis** (tel.
020/313-633), have offices both at the airport and near the
Port Gruž embankment where the big boats come in. In addition, the many travel agencies closer to the Old Town also
have a line on rental cars. Figure €50-60 per day, including
taxes, insurance, and unlimited mileage (at the bigger chains,
there's usually no extra charge for drop-off elsewhere in
Croatia). Be sure the agency knows if you're crossing a border
(such as Bosnia-Herzegovina or Montenegro) to ensure you
have the proper paperwork.

Travel Agency: You'll see travel agencies all over town. At any of them, you can buy seats on an excursion, rent a car, book a room, buy Jadrolinija ferry tickets, and pick up a pile of brochures. The most established company is **Atlas,** with an office just outside the Pile Gate from the Old Town—though the location might change (June-Sept Mon-Sat 8:00-21:00, Sun 8:00-13:00; Oct-May Mon-Sat 8:00-20:00, closed Sun; down the little alley at Sv. Đurđa 4, otherwise look for signs to new location around the bus-stop area, tel. 020/442-574, fax 020/323-609, www.atlas-croatia.com, atlas.pile@atlas.hr).

Best Views: Walking the **Old Town walls** late in the day, when the city is bathed in rich light, is a treat. The cable car up to **Mount Srđ** provides bird's-eye panoramas over the entire region, from the highest vantage point without wings. The **Fort of St. Lawrence,** perched above the Pile neighborhood cove, has great views over the Old Town. A stroll up the road east of the city walls offers nice views back on the Old Town (best light early in the day). Better yet, if you have a car, head south of the city in the morning for gorgeously lit Old Town views over your right shoulder; various turn-offs along this road are ideal photo stops. The best one, known locally as the **"panorama point,"** is where the road leading up and out of Dubrovnik meets the main road that passes above the town (look for the pull-out on the right, with tour buses). Even if you're heading north, in good weather it's worth a quick detour south for this view.

Getting Around Dubrovnik

If you're staying in or near the Old Town, everything is easily walkable. But those sleeping on Boninovo Bay or the Lapad Peninsula will want to get comfortable using the buses. Once you understand the system, commuting to the Old Town is a breeze.

By Bus: Libertas runs Dubrovnik's public buses. Tickets, which are good for an hour, are cheaper if you buy them in advance from a newsstand or your hotel (10 kn, ask for *autobusna karta,* ow-toh-BOOS-nah KAR-tah) than if you buy them from the bus driver (12 kn). A 24-hour ticket costs 30 kn (only sold at special bus-ticket kiosks, such as the one near the Pile Gate bus stop).

When you enter the bus, validate your ticket in the machine next to the driver (insert it with the orange arrow facing out). Because most tourists can't figure out how to validate their tickets, it can take a long time to load the bus (which means drivers are understandably grumpy, and locals aren't shy about cutting in line).

All buses stop near the Old Town, just in front of the Pile Gate (buy tickets at the newsstand or bus-ticket kiosk right by the stop). From here, they fan out to just about anywhere you'd want to go (hotels on Boninovo Bay, Lapad Peninsula, and the ferry terminal and main bus station). You'll find bus schedules and a map in the TI booklet (for more information, visit www.libertas dubrovnik.hr).

By Taxi: Taxis start at 25 kn, then charge 8 kn per kilometer. The handiest taxi stand for the Old Town is just outside the Pile Gate. The biggest operation is Radio Taxi (tel. 0800-0970).

Tours in Dubrovnik

Walking Tours—Two companies—**Dubrovnik Walking Tours** and **Dubrovnik Walks**—offer similar one-hour walking tours of the Old Town daily at 10:00 and usually also at 18:00 (90 kn, also other departures and topics—look for fliers at TI). I'd skip these tours—they're pricey and brief, touching lightly on the same information explained in this chapter.

Local Guide—For an in-depth look at the city, consider hiring your own local guide. **Štefica Curić** is a sharp professional guide who offers a great by-the-book tour and an insider's look at the city (500 kn/2 hours, mobile 091-345-0133, www.dubrovnikprivate guide.com, dugacarapa@yahoo.com). If Štefica is busy, she can refer you to another good guide for the same price. **Roberto de Lorenzo** and his mother **Marija Tiberi** are both warm people enthusiastic about telling evocative stories from medieval Dubrovnik, including some off-the-beaten-path stops tailored to your interests (480 kn/2 hours, mobile 091-541-6637, bobdel70@yahoo.com). The TI can also suggest guides.

Bus-plus-Walking Tours—Two big companies (**Atlas** and **Elite**) offer expensive tours of Dubrovnik (about 250 kn, 2 hours).

From Dubrovnik

Package Excursions—For information on tour boats and guided big-bus excursions from Dubrovnik to nearby destinations, see the next chapter.

Hire Your Own Driver—I enjoy renting my own car to see the sights around Dubrovnik (see "Helpful Hints," earlier). But if you're more comfortable having someone else do the driving, consider hiring a driver. While the drivers listed here are not official tour guides, they speak great English and offer ample commentary as you roll, and can help you craft a good day-long itinerary to Mostar, Montenegro, or anywhere else near Dubrovnik (typically departing around 8:00 and returning in the early evening). They're flexible about tailoring the tour to your interests: Because there are lots of options en route to either Mostar or Montenegro, do your homework so you can tell them what you'd like to see (and not see).

Or you can just leave it up to them and go along for the ride.

Friendly **Pepo Klaić,** a veteran of the recent war, is enjoyable to get to know and has a knack for making the experience both informative and meaningful (€250/day, €125 for half-day trip to nearer destinations, airport transfer for about €30—cheaper than a taxi, these prices for up to 4 people—more expensive for bigger group, mobile 098-427-301, www.dubrovnikshoretrip.com, pepo klaic@yahoo.com). For €70, Pepo can drive you to the fortress at Mount Srđ up above the Old Town, with sweeping views of the entire area (about 1-1.5 hours round-trip). **Petar Vlašić** does similar tours for similar prices, and specializes in wine tours to the Pelješac Peninsula, with stops at various wineries along the way (€30 airport transfers, €190-200 for 2-person trip to Pelješac wineries, €230 to Mostar including guide, €250 to Montenegro including local guide and boat to Our Lady of the Rock, these prices for 1-3 people—more for larger groups, mobile 091-580-8721, www.dubrovnikrivieratours.com, meritum@du.t-com.hr). **Pero Carević,** who runs the recommended Villa Ragusa guest house, also drives travelers on excursions (similar prices, mobile 098-765-634, villa.ragusa@du.t-com.hr). If your destination is Mostar, like-able Bosnian driver **Ermin Elezović** will happily come pick you up for less than the Dubrovnik-based drivers (for up to 3 people: €100 for one-way transfer from Dubrovnik to Mostar, €150 for an all-day excursion with stops en route, €200 for round-trip to Mostar with same-day return to Dubrovnik; for contact information and details, see page 425).

Self-Guided Walk

▲▲▲Strolling the Stradun

Running through the heart of Dubrovnik's Old Town is the 300-yard-long Stradun promenade—packed with people and lined with sights. This walk offers an ideal introduction to Dubrovnik's charms. It takes about a half-hour, not counting sightseeing stops.

• *Begin at the busy square in front of the west entrance to the Old Town, the Pile (PEE-leh) Gate.*

Pile Neighborhood

This bustling area is the nerve center of Dubrovnik's tourist indus-try—it's where the real world meets the fantasy of Dubrovnik (for details on services offered here, see "Orientation to Dubrovnik," earlier). Near the modern, mirrors-and-TV-screens monument (which honors the "Dubrovnik Defenders" who protected the city during the 1991-1992 siege) is a leafy café terrace. Wander over to the edge of the terrace and take in the imposing walls of the Pearl of the Adriatic. The huge, fortified peninsula just outside the city

DUBROVNIK

walls is the **Fort of St. Lawrence** (Tvrđava Lovrijenac), Dubrovnik's oldest fortress and one of the top venues for the Dubrovnik Summer Festival. Shakespearean plays are often performed here, occasionally starring Goran Višnjić, the Croatian actor who became an American star on the TV show *ER*. You can climb this fortress for great views over the Old Town (30 kn, or covered by same ticket as Old Town walls on the same day).

• *Cross over the moat (now a shady park) to the round entrance tower in the Old Town Wall. This is the...*

Pile Gate (Gradska Vrata Pile)

Just before you enter the gate, notice the image above the entrance of **St. Blaise** (Sveti Vlaho in Croatian) cradling Dubrovnik in his arm. You'll see a lot more of Blaise during your time here—we'll find out why later on this walk.

Inside the outer wall of the Pile Gate and to the left, a white **map** shows where each bomb dropped on the Old Town during the siege. Once inside town, you'll see virtually no signs of the war—demonstrating the townspeople's impressive resilience in rebuilding so well and so quickly.

Passing the rest of the way through the gate, you'll find a lively little square surrounded by landmarks. To the left, a steep stairway leads up to the imposing **Minčeta Tower.** It's possible to enter here to begin Dubrovnik's best activity, walking around the top of the wall (described later, under "Sights in Dubrovnik")—but this walk ends near a better entry point.

Next to the stairway is the small **Church of St. Savior** (Crkva Svetog Spasa). Appreciative locals built this votive church to thank God after Dubrovnik made it through a 1520 earthquake. When the massive 1667 quake destroyed the city, this church was one of the only buildings left intact. And during the recent war, the church survived another close call when a shell exploded on the ground right in front of it (you can still see faint pockmarks from the shrapnel).

The big building on the left just beyond the small Church of St. Savior is the **Franciscan Monastery Museum.** This building, with a delightful cloister and one of Europe's oldest pharmacies, is worth touring (described later).

The giant, round structure in the middle of the square is **Onofrio's Big Fountain** (Velika Onofrijea Fontana). In the Middle Ages, Dubrovnik had a complicated aqueduct system that brought water from the mountains seven miles away. The water ended up here, at the town's biggest fountain, before continuing through the city. This plentiful supply of water, large reserves of salt (a key source of Dubrovnik's wealth, from the town of Ston—see page 356), and a massive granary (now the Rupe Granary and Ethnographic Museum, described later) made little, independent Dubrovnik very siege-resistant.

Tucked across the square from the church is the **Visia Dubrovnik Multimedia Museum,** showing a badly produced 3-D film about the city's history that isn't worth your 35 minutes or 75 kn (schedule posted at entry). In the evening, the theater shows first-run 3-D movies.

• *When you're finished taking in the sights on this square, continue along...*

The Stradun

Dubrovnik's main promenade—officially called the Placa, but better known as the Stradun—is alive with locals and tourists alike. This is the heartbeat of the city: an Old World shopping mall by day

and sprawling cocktail party after dark, when everybody seems to be doing the traditional evening stroll—flirting, ice-cream-licking, flaunting, and gawking. A coffee and some of Europe's best people-watching in a prime Stradun café is one of travel's great $3 bargains.

When Dubrovnik was just getting its start in the seventh century, this street was a canal. Romans fleeing from the invading Slavs lived on the island of Ragusa (on your right), and the Slavs settled on the shore. In the 11th century, the canal separating Ragusa from the mainland was filled in, the towns merged, and a unique Slavic-Roman culture and language blossomed. While originally much more higgledy-piggledy, this street was rebuilt in the current, more straightforward style after the 1667 earthquake.

DUBROVNIK

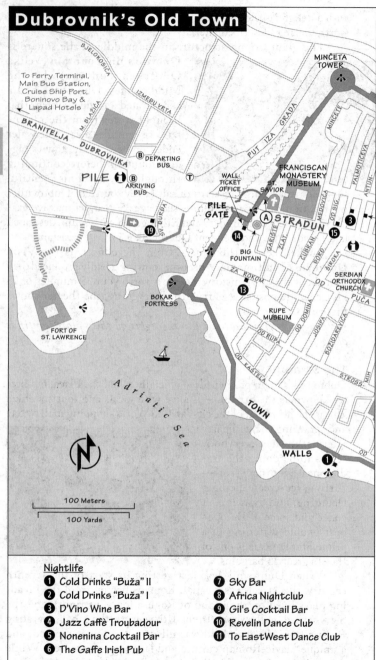

Dubrovnik's Old Town

To Ferry Terminal,
Main Bus Station,
Cruise Ship Port,
Boninovo Bay &
Lapad Hotels

BJELOKOSICA

IZMEĐU VRTA

BRANITELJA DUBROVNIKA

M. BLAŽICA

PILE

DEPARTING
BUS

ARRIVING
BUS

SV. ĐURĐA

PILE
GATE

PUT IZA GRADA

MINČETA
TOWER

MINČETE

FRANCISCAN
MONASTERY
MUSEUM

WALL
TICKET
OFFICE

ST.
SAVIOR

STRADUN

BIG
FOUNTAIN

ZA ROKOM

ZLAT.

GARIŠTE

ĐURĐEVIĆ

PORD

OD SIG.

MEDOVIĆA

PALMOTIĆEVA

ANTUN-

ŠIROKA

SERBIAN
ORTHODOX
CHURCH

PUČA

BOKAR
FORTRESS

FORT OF
ST. LAWRENCE

RUPE
MUSEUM

OD DOMINA

OD RUPA

OD KAŠTELA

JOSIPA

BOŽIDAREVIĆA

STROSS.

MIH.

Adriatic Sea

N

TOWN

WALLS

100 Meters

100 Yards

Nightlife

1. Cold Drinks "Buža" II
2. Cold Drinks "Buža" I
3. D'Vino Wine Bar
4. Jazz Caffè Troubadour
5. Nonenina Cocktail Bar
6. The Gaffe Irish Pub
7. Sky Bar
8. Africa Nightclub
9. Gil's Cocktail Bar
10. Revelin Dance Club
11. To EastWest Dance Club

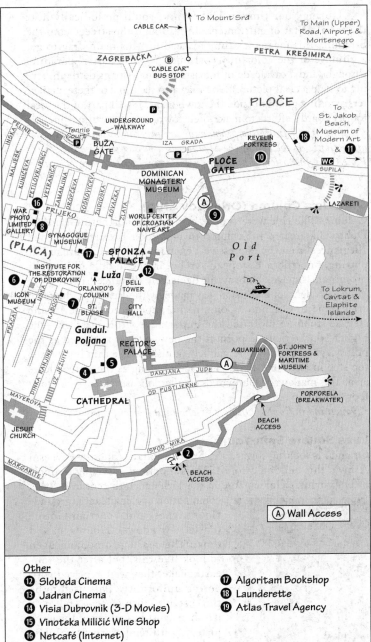

DUBROVNIK

Other

① Sloboda Cinema
① Jadran Cinema
① Visia Dubrovnik (3-D Movies)
① Vinoteka Miličić Wine Shop
① Netcafé (Internet)

① Algoritam Bookshop
① Launderette
① Atlas Travel Agency

During your time in Dubrovnik, you'll periodically hear the rat-a-tat-tat of a drum echoing through the streets from the Stradun. This means it's time to head for this main drag to get a glimpse of the colorfully costumed **"town guards"** parading through (and a cavalcade of tourists running alongside them, trying to snap a clear picture). You may also see some of these characters standing guard outside the town gates. It's all part of the local tourist board's efforts to make their town even more atmospheric.

• *Branching off from this promenade are several museums and other attractions. At the end of the Stradun is a passageway leading to the Ploče Gate. Just before this passage is the lively Luža Square. Its centerpiece is...*

Orlando's Column (Orlandov Stup)

Columns like this were typical of towns in northern Germany. Dubrovnik erected the column in 1417, soon after it had shifted allegiances from the oppressive Venetians to the Hungarians. By putting a northern European symbol in the middle of its most prominent square, Dubrovnik decisively distanced itself from Venice. Whenever a decision was made by the Republic, the town crier came to Orlando's Column and announced the news. The step he stood on indicated the importance of his message—the higher up, the more important the news. It was also used as the pillory, where people were publicly punished. The thin line on the top step in front of Orlando is exactly as long as the statue's forearm. This mark was Dubrovnik's standard measurement—not for a foot, but for an "elbow."

• *Now stand in front of Orlando's Column and orient yourself with a...*

Luža Square Spin-Tour

Orlando is looking toward the **Sponza Palace** (Sponza-Povijesni Arhiv). This building, from 1522, is the finest surviving example of Dubrovnik's Golden Age in the 15th and 16th centuries. It's a

combination of Renaissance (ground-floor arches) and Venetian Gothic (upstairs windows). Houses up and down the main promenade used to look like this, but after the 1667 earthquake, they were replaced with boring uniformity. This used to be the customs office *(dogana),* but now it's an exhaustive archive of the city's history, with temporary art exhibits and a war memorial. The poignant **Memorial Room of Dubrovnik Defenders** (on the left as you enter) has photos of dozens of people from Dubrovnik who were killed fighting Yugoslav forces in 1991. A TV screen and images near the ceiling show the devastation of the city. Though the English descriptions are pointedly—if unavoidably—slanted to the Croat perspective, it's compelling to look in the eyes of the brave young men who didn't start this war...but were willing to finish it (free, long hours daily in peak season, shorter hours off-season). Beyond the memorial room, the impressive **courtyard,** which generally displays temporary exhibits, is worth a peek (25 kn, generally free after-hours).

To the right of Sponza Palace is the town's **Bell Tower** (Gradski Zvonik). The original dated from 1444, but it was rebuilt when it started to lean in the 1920s. The big clock may be an octopus, but only one of its hands tells time. Below that, the golden circle shows the phase of the moon. At the bottom, the old-fashioned digital readout tells the hour (in Roman numerals) and the minutes (in five-minute increments). At the top of each hour (and again three minutes later), the time is clanged out on the bell up top by two bronze bell-ringers, Maro and Baro. (If this all seems like a copy of the very similar clock on St. Mark's Square in Venice, locals are quick to point out that this clock predates that one by several decades.) The clock still has to be wound every two days. Notice the little window between the moon phase and the "digital" readout: The clock-winder opens this window to get some light. The Krasovac family was in charge of winding the clock for generations (1877-2005). During the 1991-1992 siege, their house was destroyed—with the winding keys inside. For days, the clock bell didn't run. But then, miraculously, the keys were discovered lying in the street. The excited Dubrovnik citizens came together in this square and cheered as the clock was wound and the bell chimed, signaling to the soldiers surrounding the city that they hadn't won yet.

It's possible to climb up to the **gallery** next to the tower for a fine view of the Stradun, but only in the evening (July-Aug nightly 20:00-23:00, spring and fall nightly 19:00-21:00 or 22:00, closed in winter) and—as of this writing—only if you have a Dubrovnik Card. Even if you don't have the card, you can try asking nicely (the entrance is in the passageway just to the left of the tower).

The big building to the right of the Bell Tower is the **City Hall** (Vijećnica). Next to that is **Onofrio's Little Fountain** (Mala Onofrijea Fontana), the little brother of the one at the other end of the Stradun. Beyond that is the **Gradska Kavana,** or "Town Café." This hangout—historically Dubrovnik's favorite spot for gossiping and people-watching—has pricey drinks and seating all the way through the wall to the Old Port. Just down the street from the Town Café is the Rector's Palace, and then the cathedral (for more

The Siege of Dubrovnik

In June 1991, Croatia declared independence from Yugoslavia. Within weeks, the nations were at war (for more on the war, see the Understanding Yugoslavia chapter). Though warfare raged in the Croatian interior, nobody expected that the bloodshed would reach Dubrovnik.

As refugees from Vukovar (in northeastern Croatia) arrived in Dubrovnik that fall, telling horrific stories of the warfare there, local residents began fearing the worst. Warplanes from the Serb-dominated Yugoslav People's Army buzzed threateningly low over the town, as if to signal an impending attack.

Then, at 6:00 in the morning on October 1, 1991, Dubrovnik residents awoke to explosions on nearby hillsides. The first attacks were focused on Mount Srđ, high above the Old Town. First the giant cross was destroyed, then a communications tower (both have been rebuilt and are visible today). This first wave of attacks cleared the way for Yugoslav land troops—mostly Serbs and Montenegrins—who surrounded the city. The ragtag, newly formed Croatian army quickly dug in at the old Napoleonic-era fortress at the top of Mount Srđ, where just 25 or 30 soldiers fended off a Yugoslav takeover of this highly strategic position.

At first, shelling targeted military positions on the outskirts of town. But soon, Yugoslav forces began bombing residential neighborhoods, then the Pearl of the Adriatic itself: Dubrovnik's Old Town. Defenseless townspeople took shelter in their cellars, and sometimes even huddled together in the city wall's 15th-century forts. It was the first time in Dubrovnik's long history that the walls were actually used to defend against an attack.

Dubrovnik resisted the siege better than anyone expected. The Yugoslav forces were hoping that residents would flee the town, but the people of Dubrovnik stayed.  Though severely outgunned and outnumbered, Dubrovnik's defenders managed to hold the fort atop Mount Srđ, while Yugoslav forces controlled the nearby mountaintops. All supplies had to be carried up to the fort by foot or by donkey. Dubrovnik wasn't prepared for war, so its citizens had to improvise their defense. Many brave young locals lost their lives when they slung old hunting rifles over their shoulders and, under cover of darkness, climbed the hills above Dubrovnik to meet Yugoslav soldiers face-to-face.

After eight months of bombing, Dubrovnik was liberated by the Croatian army, which attacked Yugoslav positions from the north. By the end of the siege, 100 civilians were dead, as well as more than 200 Dubrovnik citizens who lost their lives actively fighting for their hometown (much revered today as "Dubrovnik Defenders"); in the greater Dubrovnik area, 420 "Defenders" were killed, and another 900 wounded. More than two-thirds of Dubrovnik's buildings had been damaged, and more than 30,000 people had to flee their homes—but the failed siege was finally over.

Why was Dubrovnik—so far from the rest of the fighting—dragged into the conflict? Yugoslavia wanted to catch the city and surrounding region off-guard, gaining a toehold on the southern Dalmatian Coast so they could push north to Split. They also hoped to ignite pro-Serb passions in the nearby Serb-dominated areas of Bosnia-Herzegovina and Montenegro. But perhaps most of all, Yugoslavia wanted to hit Croatia where it hurt—its proudest, most historic, and most beautiful city, the tourist capital of a nation dependent on tourism. (It seems their plan backfired. Locals now say, "When Yugoslavia attacked Dubrovnik, they lost the war"—because images of the historic city under siege swayed international public opinion *against* Yugoslavia.)

The war initially devastated the tourist industry. Now, to the casual observer, Dubrovnik seems virtually back to normal. Aside from a few pockmarks and bright, new roof tiles, there are scant reminders of what happened here two decades ago. But even though the city itself has been repaired, the people of Dubrovnik are forever changed. Imagine living in an idyllic paradise, a place that attracted and awed visitors from around the world...and then watching it gradually blown to bits. It's understandable if Dubrovnik's citizens are a little less in love with life than they once were.

It's clear that in the case of this siege, the Croats of Dubrovnik were the largely innocent victims of a brutal surprise attack. But keep in mind the larger context of the war: The cousins of these Croats, who were defending the glorious monument that is Dubrovnik, bombarded another glorious monument—the Old Bridge of Mostar (see page 429). It's just another reminder that the "good guys" and "bad guys" in these wars are far from clear-cut.

Dubrovnik has several low-key attractions related to its recent war, including the museum in the ruined fortress atop Mount Srđ, the Memorial Room of Dubrovnik Defenders in the Sponza Palace on Luža Square, and the Institute for the Restoration of Dubrovnik. Another sight, War Photo Limited, expands the scope to war photography from around the world.

on each, see "Sights in Dubrovnik").

Behind Orlando is **St. Blaise's Church** (Crkva Sv. Vlaha), dedicated to the patron saint of Dubrovnik. You'll see statues and paintings of St. Blaise all over town, always holding a model of the city in his left hand. According to legend, a millennium ago St. Blaise came to a local priest in a dream and warned him that the up-and-coming Venetians would soon attack the city. The priest alerted the authorities, who prepared for  war. Of course, the prediction came true. St. Blaise has been a Dubrovnik symbol—and locals have resented Venice—ever since.

• *Your tour is finished. From here, you've got plenty of sightseeing options (all described next, under "Sights in Dubrovnik"). As you face the Bell Tower, you can go up the street to the right to reach the Rector's Palace and cathedral; you can walk through the gate straight ahead to reach the Old Port; or you can head through the gate and jog left to find the Dominican Monastery Museum. Even more sights—including an old synagogue, an Orthodox church, two different exhibits of war photography, and the medieval granary—are in the steep streets between the Stradun and the walls.*

Sights in Dubrovnik

Nearly all of Dubrovnik's sights are inside the Old Town's walls.

Combo-Tickets: The Rector's Palace, Maritime Museum, and Rupe Granary and Ethnographic Museum—which normally cost 40 kn apiece—are covered by a combo-ticket (55 kn to visit any two, 70 kn to visit all three, tickets sold at all three sights, valid for three days). The TI's Dubrovnik Card—which covers the same three sights, plus the City Walls and a few lesser attractions—can also be a good deal for busy sightseers (see "Tourist Information," earlier).

▲▲▲Town Walls (Gradske Zidine)

Dubrovnik's single best attraction is strolling the scenic mile-and-a-quarter around the city walls. As you meander along this lofty perch—with a sea of orange roofs on one side, and the actual sea on the other—you'll get your bearings and snap pictures like mad of the ever-changing views. Bring your map, which you can use to pick out landmarks and get the lay of the land.

Cost: 70 kn to enter walls, also includes the St. Lawrence Fort outside the Pile Gate (kunas or credit cards only—no euros).

Hours: July-Aug daily 8:00-19:30, progressively shorter hours off-season until mid-Nov-mid-March 10:00-15:00. Since the hours change with the season, confirm them by checking signs posted at the entrance (essential if you want to time your wall walk to avoid the worst crowds—explained below). The posted closing time indicates when the walls shut down, *not* the last entry—ascend well before this time if you want to make it all the way around. (If you want to linger, begin at least an hour ahead; if you're speedy, you can ascend 30

minutes before closing time.) Attendants begin circling the walls about 30 minutes after the posted closing time to lock the gates. There's talk of someday illuminating the walls at night, in which case the hours would be extended until after dark.

Entrances and Strategies: There are three entry points for the wall (see map on page 298), and wall-walkers are required to proceed counterclockwise. The best plan is to begin at the far side of the Old Town, using the entrance **near the Ploče Gate** and Dominican Monastery. This entrance is the least crowded, and you'll tackle the steepest part (and enjoy the best views) first, as you climb up to the landward side of the wall with magnificent views across the entire Old Town and the Adriatic. If you're wiped out, overheated, or fed up with crowds after that, you can bail out halfway (at the Pile Gate), having seen the best—or you can continue around the seaward side. The other two entrances are **just inside the Pile Gate** (by far the most crowded; for this location only, you must buy your tickets at the desk across the square; if you begin here, you'll reach the Minčeta Tower—with the steepest ascent and best views—last) and **near St. John's Fort** overlooking the Old Port (next to the Maritime Museum).

Crowd Control: Because this is Dubrovnik's top attraction, it's extremely crowded. Your best strategy is to avoid the walls during the times when the cruise ships are in town. On days when the walls open at 8:00, try to get started around that time. The walls are the most crowded from about 8:30 until 11:00, when the cruise ships are docked. There's generally an afternoon lull in the crowds (11:00-15:00), but that's also the hottest time to be atop the walls. Crowds pick up again in the late afternoon (starting around 15:00), peaking about an hour before closing time (18:30 in high season). So your peak-season options are either early, crowded, or hot; the ticket-takers told me that, all things considered, they'd ascend either at 8:00 or 30-60 minutes before closing.

Tips: Speed demons with no cameras can walk the walls in about an hour; strollers and shutterbugs should plan on longer. Because your ticket is electronically scanned as you enter, you can't leave and re-enter the wall later; you have to do it all in one go. If you have a Dubrovnik Card—even a multiple-day one—you can only use it to ascend the walls once.

Warning: The walls can get deliriously hot—all that white stone and seawater reflect blazing sunshine something fierce, and there's virtually no shade. It's essential to bring sunscreen, a hat, and water. Take your time: There are several steep stretches, and you'll be climbing up and down the whole way around. A few scant shops and cafés along the top of the wall (mostly on the sea side) sell water and other drinks, but it's safest to bring what you'll need with you.

Audioguide: You can rent a 40-kn audioguide, separate from the admission fee, for a dryly narrated circular tour of the walls (look for vendors near the Pile Gate entrance—not available at other entrances). But I'd rather just enjoy the views and lazily pick out the landmarks with my map.

Background: There have been walls here almost as long as there's been a Dubrovnik. As with virtually all fortifications on the Croatian Coast, these walls were beefed up in the 15th century, when the Ottoman navy became a threat. Around the perimeter are several substantial forts, with walls rounded so that cannon-balls would glance off harmlessly. These stout forts intimidated would-be invaders during the Republic of Dubrovnik's Golden Age, and protected residents during the 1991-1992 siege.

◉ Self-Guided Tour: It's possible to just wander the walls and snap photos like crazy as you go. And trying to hew too closely to guided commentary kind of misses the point of being high above the Dubrovnik rooftops. But this brief tour will help give you bearings to what you're seeing, as you read Dubrovnik's unique and illustrious history into its street plan.

Part 1—Ploče Gate to Pile Gate: Begin by ascending near the **Ploče Gate** (go through the gate under the Bell Tower, walk along the stoutly walled passageway between the port and the Dominican Monastery, and look for the wall entrance on your right). Buy your ticket, head up, turn left, and start walk-ing counterclockwise, with Mount Srđ and the cable car on your right. Passing the Dominican Monastery's fine courtyard on the left, you're walking above what was the poorest part of medieval Dubrovnik, the domain of the craftsmen—with narrow, stepped lanes that had shops on the ground floor and humble dwellings up above.

As you walk, keep an eye on the different-colored **rooftops** for an illustration of the damage Dubrovnik sustained during the 1991-1992 siege. It's easy to see that nearly two-thirds of Dubrovnik's roofs were replaced after the bombings (notice the new, bright-orange tiles—and how some buildings salvaged the old tiles, but have 20th-century ones underneath). The pristine-seeming Old Town was rebuilt using exactly the same materials and methods with which it was originally constructed.

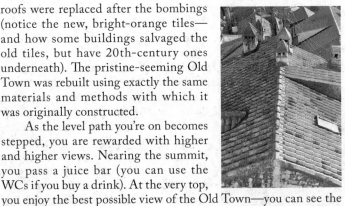

As the level path you're on becomes stepped, you are rewarded with higher and higher views. Nearing the summit, you pass a juice bar (you can use the WCs if you buy a drink). At the very top, you enjoy the best possible view of the Old Town—you can see the

rooftops, churches, and the sea. For an even better view, if you have the energy, huff up the steep stairs to the (empty) **Minčeta Tower.** From either viewpoint, observe the valley-like shape of Dubrovnik. It's easy to imagine how it began as two towns—one where you are now, and the other on the hilly island with the church spires across the way—originally separated by a seawater canal. Notice the relatively regular, grid-like pattern of houses on this side, but the more higgledy-piggledy arrangement on the far side (a visual clue that the far side is older).

The sports court at your feet is a reminder that Dubrovnik is a living city—though it's not as vibrant as it once was. While officially 2,000 people live within these walls, most locals estimate the real number at about half that; the rest rent out their homes to tourists. And with good reason: Imagine the challenges that come with living in such a steep medieval townscape well into the 21st century. Delivery trucks rumble up and down the Stradun early each morning, and you'll see hardworking young men delivering goods on hand carts throughout the day. Looking up at the fortress atop Mount Srđ—seemingly custom-made for keeping an eye on a large swathe of coast-

line—the strategic position of Dubrovnik is clear. Independent Dubrovnik was not just this walled city, but an entire region.

Now continue downhill (you've earned it) until you get to the flat stretch. If you're bushed and ready to head back to town, you can turn left and head downstairs to the exit—but be aware that once you leave, you can't re-enter on the same ticket. Better yet, carry on straight for part 2.

Part 2—Pile Gate to Old Port: Pause to enjoy the full frontal view of the **Stradun,** barreling right at you. In the Middle

Ages, lining this drag were the merchants, and before that, this was a canal. At your feet is Onfrio's Big Fountain, which supplied water to a thirsty town. From here, you can see a wide range of church steeples representing the cosmopolitan makeup of a thriving medieval trade town (from left to right): Dominican, Franciscan (near you), the town Bell Tower, St. Blaise's (the round dome—hard to see from here), Serbian Orthodox, Cathedral, and (high on the hill) Jesuit. Sit and watch the river of humanity, flowing constantly up and down one of Europe's finest main streets.

Carry on through the guard tower and along the wall, climbing uphill again. On the right across the little cove is the **Fort of St. Lawrence,** which worked in concert with these stout walls to make Dubrovnik virtually impenetrable. Climbing higher and looking to your left, into town, you'll see that this area is still damaged—not from the 1991-1992 siege, but from the 1667 earthquake. Notice that, unlike the extremely dense construction on the poorer far side of town, this area has more breathing space—and even some gardens. Originally this was also densely populated, but after the quake, rather than rebuild, the wealthy folks who lived here decided to turn some former homes into green space. Grates cover the openings to old wells and grain stores that once supplied homes here—essential for surviving a siege.

As the walkway levels out, you pass a bar with drinks; more (with WCs) are coming up. Farther along, at the picturesque little turret, are gift shops and WCs. Looking down to your right (outside the wall), you'll begin to see tables and umbrellas clinging to the rocks at the base of the wall. This is the recommended Cold Drinks "Buža" II, the best spot in town for a scenic drink. On the horizon is the isle of Lokrum and—often—cruise ships at anchor, sending their passengers to and fro on ten-

ders. After passing Buža, look down on the left to see the local kids' makeshift soccer pitch, wedged between the walls—the best they can do in this vertical town. Soon you'll see the "other" Buža (technically Buža I) ahead; nearby, notice the little statue of St. Blaise, Dubrovnik's patron, enjoy some shade under the turret.

Rounding the bend, you see the facade of the Jesuit church. Notice that the homes in this area are much larger. These are aristocratic palaces—VIPs wanted to live as close as possible to the Cathedral and Rector's Palace, which are just below—and this also happens to be the oldest part of town, where "Ragusa" was born on a steep offshore island.

Continue around the wall, passing another snack bar (with WCs) and more ruined houses. From the high plateau, you have another opportunity to head down into town. (In the little plant-filled square at the bottom of these stairs is a cute little cat hospice, with a donation box for feeding some homeless feline residents.) But the final stretch of our wall walk is shorter than the other two, and mostly level.

Part 3—Old Port to Ploče Gate: Continuing along the wall, you'll pass near the entrance to the skippable Maritime Museum, then walk along the top of the wall overlooking the Old Port. Imagine how this heavily fortified little harbor (facing away from Dubrovnik's historic foes, the Venetians) was busy with trade in the Middle Ages. Today it's still the economic lifeline for town—watch the steady stream of cruise-ship tenders injecting dose after dose of tourist cash into town. As you curl around the far side of the port, you'll see the inviting outdoor tables of Gil's, a cocktail bar/restaurant catering to high-rolling yachters. While it looks appealing, it's a very exclusive place that frowns on would-be visitors who dress like normal people. Gussied-up jet-set diners enjoy coming here for good but extremely expensive designer fare. (One local told me, "The food is great—just eat a hamburger before you go.")

Just past Gil's, you come to the stairs back down to where you started this wall walk. Nice work. Now head on down and reward yourself with an ice-cream cone...and some shade.

The "Other" Wall Climb: Your ticket for the Old Town Walls also includes the Fort of St. Lawrence just outside the Old Town (valid same day only; fort described on page 308). If you've already bought a 30-kn ticket there, show it when buying your main wall ticket and you'll pay only the difference.

Near the Pile Gate
This museum is just inside the Pile Gate.

▲**Franciscan Monastery Museum (Franjevački Samostan-Muzej)**—In the Middle Ages, Dubrovnik's monasteries flourished. While all you'll see here are a fine cloister and a one-room museum in the old pharmacy, it's a delightful space. Enter through the gap between the small church and the big monastery. Just inside the door (before the ticket-seller), a century-old pharmacy still serves residents.

Explore the peaceful, sun-dappled **cloister.** Examine the capitals at the tops of the 60 Romanesque-Gothic double pillars. Each one is different. Notice that some parts of the portals inside the courtyard are made with a lighter-colored stone—these had to be repaired after being hit during the 1991-1992 siege. The damaged 19th-century frescoes along the tops of the walls depict the life of St. Francis, who supposedly visited Dubrovnik in the early 13th century.

In the far corner stands the monastery's original medieval **pharmacy.** Part of the Franciscans' mission was to contribute to

the good health of the citizens, so they opened this pharmacy in 1317. The monastery has had a pharmacy in continual operation ever since. On display are jars, pots, and other medieval pharmacists' tools. The sick would come to get their medicine at the little window (on left side), which limited contact with the pharmacist and reduced the risk of passing on disease. Around the room, you'll also find some relics, old manuscripts, and a detailed painting of early 17th-century Dubrovnik.

The adjoining **church** (enter next door) has a fine Baroque interior.

Cost and Hours: 30 kn, daily April-Oct 9:00-18:00, Nov-March 9:00-17:00, Placa 2, tel. 020/321-410, www.malabraca.hr.

Near Luža Square

These sights are at the far end of the Stradun (nearest the Old Port). As you stand on Luža Square facing the Bell Tower, the Rector's Palace and cathedral are up the wide street called Pred Dvorom to the right, and the Dominican Monastery Museum is through the gate by the Bell Tower and to the left.

▲**Rector's Palace (Knežev Dvor)**—In the Middle Ages, the Republic of Dubrovnik was ruled by a rector (similar to a Venetian doge), who was elected by the nobility. To prevent any one person from becoming too powerful, the rector's term was limited to one month. Most rectors were in their 50s—near the end of the average life span and when they were less likely to shake things up. During his term, a rector lived upstairs in this palace. Because it's been plundered twice (most recently by Napoleon's forces, who stole all the furniture), this empty-feeling museum isn't as interesting as most other European palaces. What little you'll see was donated by local aristocrats to flesh out the pathetically empty complex.

The palace collection, which requires a ticket and has good English explanations, is skippable, but it does offer a glimpse of Dubrovnik in its glory days. Even if you pass on the interior, the palace's exterior and courtyard are viewable at no charge.

Cost and Hours: 40 kn, covered by 55-kn or 70-kn combo-ticket, daily May-Oct 9:00-18:00, Nov-April 9:00-16:00, some posted English information, 6-kn English booklet is helpful, Pred Dvorom 3, tel. 020/322-096.

Visiting the Palace: The **exterior** is decorated in the Gothic-Renaissance mix (with particularly finely carved capitals) that was so common in Dubrovnik before the 1667 earthquake. Above the entrance is the message *Obliti privatorum publica curate*—loosely translated, "Forget your personal affairs and concern yourself with the affairs of state." This was a bold statement in a feudal era before democracy, when aristocrats were preoccupied exclusively with their self-interests.

Standing at the main door, you can generally get a free look at the palace's impressive **courtyard**—a venue for the Summer Festival, hosting music groups ranging from the local symphony to the Vienna Boys' Choir. In the courtyard (and also visible from the door) is the only secular statue created during the centuries-long Republic. Dubrovnik republicans, mindful of the dangers of hero-worship, didn't believe that any one citizen should be singled out. They made only one exception—for Miho Pracat (a.k.a. Michaeli Prazatto), a rich citizen who donated vast sums to charity and willed a fleet of ships to the city. But notice that Pracat's statue is displayed in here, behind closed doors, not out in public.

If you pay to go **inside,** you'll start on the ground-floor, where you'll see dull paintings, the green-stucco courtroom (with explanations of the Republic's unique governmental system), and one of the palace's highlights, the original bronze bell-ringers from the town Bell Tower (named Maro and Baro). Like antique robots (from the Renaissance, c. 1470), these eerily lifelike sculptures

could pivot at the waist to ring the bell. Then you'll see some iron chests (including a few with elaborate locking mechanisms) before entering some old prison cells, which supposedly were placed within earshot of the rector's quarters, so he would hear the moans of the prisoners...and stay honest. Leaving the prison, you'll enter the courtyard described earlier, where you can get a better look at the Pracat statue.

On the mezzanine level (stairs near the main entrance, above the prison), you'll find a decent display of furniture, a wimpy gun exhibit, votive offerings (mostly silver), a ho-hum coin collection, and an interesting painting of "Ragusa" in the early 17th century—back when it was still bisected by a canal.

Head back down to the courtyard and go to the upper floor (using the staircase across from mezzanine stairs, near the Pracat statue—notice the "hand" rails). Upstairs, you'll explore old apartments that serve as a painting gallery. The only vaguely authentic room is the red room in the corner, decorated more or less as it was in 1500, when it was the rector's office. Mihajlo Hamzić's exquisite *Baptism of Christ* painting, inspired by Italian painter Andrea Mantegna, is an early Renaissance work from the "Dubrovnik School" (see "Dominican Monastery Museum" listing, later).

▲**Cathedral (Katedrala)**—Dubrovnik's original 12th-century cathedral was funded largely by the English King Richard the Lionhearted. On his way back

from the Third Crusade, Richard was shipwrecked nearby. He promised God that if he survived, he'd build a church on the spot where he landed—which happened to be on Lokrum Island, just offshore. At Dubrovnik's request, Richard agreed to build his token of thanks inside the city instead. It was the finest Romanesque church on the Adriatic...before it was destroyed by the 1667 earthquake. This version is 18th-century Roman Baroque.

Cost and Hours: Church—free, daily 8:00-20:00; treasury—15 kn, generally open same hours as church; both have shorter hours off-season.

Touring the Cathedral: Inside, you'll find a painting from the school of Titian *(Assumption of the Virgin)* over the stark contemporary altar, and a quirky treasury *(riznica)* packed with 187 relics. Examining the treasury collection, notice that there are three locks on the treasury door—the stuff in here was so valuable, three different VIPs (the rector, the bishop, and a local aristocrat) had to agree before it could be opened. On the table near the door are several of St. Blaise's body parts (pieces of his arm, skull, and leg—all encased in gold and silver). In the middle of the wall directly opposite the door, look for the crucifix with a piece of the True Cross. On a dig in Jerusalem, St. Helen (Emperor Constantine's mother) discovered what she believed to be the cross that Jesus was crucified on. It was brought to Constantinople, and the Byzantine czars doled out pieces of it to Balkan kings. Note the folding three-paneled altar painting (underneath the cross). Dubrovnik ambassadors packed this on road trips (such as their annual trip to pay off the Ottomans) so they could worship wherever they traveled.

On the right side of the room, the silver casket supposedly holds the actual swaddling clothes of the Baby Jesus (or, as some locals call it somewhat less reverently, "Jesus' nappy"). Dubrovnik bishops secretly passed these clothes down from generation to generation...until a nun got wind of it and told the whole town. Pieces of the cloth were cut off to miraculously heal the sick, especially new mothers recovering from a difficult birth. No matter how often it was cut, the cloth always went back to its original form. Then someone tried to use it on the wife of a Bosnian king. Since she was Muslim, it couldn't help her, and it never worked again. True or not, this legend hints at the prickly relationships between faiths (not to mention the male chauvinism) here in the Balkans.

▲Dominican Monastery Museum (Dominikanski Samostan-Muzej)—You'll find many of Dubrovnik's art treasures—paintings, altarpieces, and manuscripts—gath-

ered around the peaceful Dominican Monastery cloister inside the Ploče Gate. Historically, this was the church for wealthy people, while the Franciscan Church (down at the far end of the Stradun) was for poor people. Services were staggered by 15 minutes to allow servants to drop off their masters here, then rush down the Stradun for their own service.

Cost and Hours: 20 kn, art buffs enjoy the 50-kn English book, daily May-Sept 9:00-18:00, Oct-April 9:00-17:00.

Touring the Museum: Turn left from the entry and work your way clockwise around the cloister. The room in the far corner contains paintings from the **"Dubrovnik School,"** the Republic's circa-1500 answer to the art boom in Florence and Venice. Though the 1667 earthquake destroyed most of these paintings, about a dozen survive, and five of those are in this room. Don't miss the triptych by Nikola Božidarović with St. Blaise holding a detailed model of 16th-century Dubrovnik (left panel)—the most famous depiction of Dubrovnik's favorite saint. You'll also see reliquaries shaped like the hands and feet that they hold.

Continuing around the courtyard, duck into the next room. Here you'll see a painting by **Titian** depicting St. Blaise, Mary Magdalene, and the donor who financed this work.

At the next corner of the courtyard is the entrance to the striking **church** at the heart of this still-active monastery. Step inside.

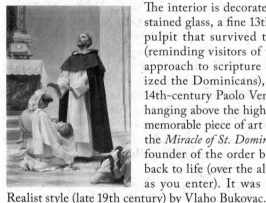

The interior is decorated with modern stained glass, a fine 13th-century stone pulpit that survived the earthquake (reminding visitors of the intellectual approach to scripture that characterized the Dominicans), and a precious 14th-century Paolo Veneziano crucifix hanging above the high altar. The most memorable piece of art in the church is the *Miracle of St. Dominic,* showing the founder of the order bringing a child back to life (over the altar to the right, as you enter). It was painted in the Realist style (late 19th century) by Vlaho Bukovac.

World Center of Croatian Naive Art—Just inside the entrance to the Dominican Monastery complex, look left to find this Croatian naive art center. The gallery displays and sells works of this little-known art movement (described in detail on page 68). In addition to some less-impressive starving artists, the gallery has some pieces by movement founder Ivan Generalić (priced at €15,000), Ivan Večenaj, and Mijo Kovačić. If you're not going to the excellent Croatian Museum of Naive Art in Zagreb, this is a good chance to get a peek at this unique art form.

Cost and Hours: Free, Mon-Sat 10:00-18:00, closed Sun, 4 Sv. Dominika, tel. 020/321-565.

Museum of Modern Art (Umjetnička Galerija)—While salty old Dubrovnik and modern art don't quite seem to go together, the city has a fine modern art gallery a 10-minute walk outside the Ploče Gate. You'll see a permanent collection with 20th-century Croatian art (including some paintings by local artist Vlaho Bukovac—whose home in Cavtat offers a more intimate look at his life and works), as well as changing exhibits.

Cost and Hours: 30 kn, Tue-Sun 10:00-20:00, closed Mon, put Frana Supila 23, tel. 020/426-590, www.ugdubrovnik.hr.

Near the Old Port (Stara Luka)

The picturesque Old Port, carefully nestled behind St. John's Fort, faces away from what was Dubrovnik's biggest threat, the  Venetians. At the port, you can haggle with captains selling excursions to nearby towns and islands (described in the next chapter) and watch cruise-ship passengers coming and going on their tenders. The long seaside building across the bay on the left is the Lazareti, once the medieval quarantine house. In those days, all visitors were locked in here for 40 days before entering town. (Today it hosts folk-dancing shows—described later, under "Entertainment in Dubrovnik.") A bench-lined harborside walk leads around the fort to a breakwater, providing a peaceful perch. From the breakwater, rocky beaches curl around the outside of the wall.

Maritime Museum (Pomorski Muzej)—By the 15th century, when Venice's nautical dominance was on the wane, Dubrovnik emerged as a maritime power and the Mediterranean's leading shipbuilding center. The Dubrovnik-built "argosy" boat (from "Ragusa," an early name for the city) was the Cadillac of ships, even mentioned by Shakespeare. This small museum traces the history of Dubrovnik's most important industry with contracts, maps, paintings, and models—all well-described in English. The main floor takes you through the 18th century, and the easy-to-miss upstairs covers the 19th and 20th centuries. Boaters will find the museum particularly interesting.

Cost and Hours: 40 kn, covered by 55-kn or 70-kn combo-ticket, 5-kn English booklet, hours flex on demand—usually March-Oct Tue-Sun 9:00-18:00, until 16:00 in Nov-Feb, closed Mon year-round, upstairs in St. John's Fort, at far/south end of Old Port, tel. 020/323-904.

Aquarium (Akvarij)—Dubrovnik's aquarium, housed in the cavernous St. John's Fort, is an old-school place, with 31 tanks on one floor. A visit here allows you a close look at the local marine life and provides a cool refuge from the midday heat.

Cost and Hours: 40 kn, kids-15 kn, English descriptions, daily July-Aug 9:00-21:00, progressively shorter hours off-season until 9:00-13:00 Nov-March, ground floor of St. John's Fort, enter from Old Port, tel. 020/323-484.

Between the Stradun and the Mainland

These two museums are a few steps off the main promenade toward the mainland.

▲**Synagogue Museum (Sinagoga-Muzej)**—When the Jews were forced out of Spain in 1492, a steady stream of them passed through here en route to today's Turkey. Finding Dubrovnik to be a flourishing and relatively tolerant city, many stayed. Žudioska ulica ("Jewish Street"), just inside Ploče Gate, became the ghetto in 1546. It was walled at one end and had a gate (which would be locked at night) at the other end. Today, the same street is home to the second-oldest continuously functioning synagogue in Europe (after Prague's), which contains Croatia's only Jewish museum. The top floor houses the synagogue itself. Notice the lattice windows that separated the women from the men (in accordance with Orthodox Jewish tradition). Below that, a small museum with good English descriptions gives meaning to the various Torahs (including a 14th-century one from Spain) and other items—such as the written orders *(naredba)* from Nazi-era Yugoslavia, stating that Jews were to identify their shops as Jewish-owned and wear armbands. (The Ustaše—the Nazi puppet government in Croatia—interned and executed not only Jews and Roma/Gypsies, but also Serbs and other people they considered undesirable; see page 45.) Of Croatia's 24,000 Jews, only 4,000 survived the Holocaust. Today Croatia has about 2,000 Jews, including a dozen Jewish families who call Dubrovnik home.

Cost and Hours: 20 kn, 10-kn English booklet; May-mid-Nov daily 10:00-20:00; mid-Nov-April Mon-Fri 10:00-13:00, closed Sat-Sun; Žudioska ulica 5, tel. 020/321-028.

▲**War Photo Limited**—If the tragic story of wartime Dubrovnik has you in a pensive mood, drop by this gallery with images of warfare from around the world. The brainchild of Kiwi-turned-Croatian photojournalist Wade Goddard, this thought-provoking museum attempts to show the ugly reality of war through raw, often disturbing photographs taken in the field. You'll find well-displayed exhibits on two floors; a small permanent exhibit depicts the wars in the former Yugoslavia through photography and video footage. Each summer, the gallery also houses various temporary exhibits. Note that the focus is not solely on Dubrovnik, but on war anywhere and everywhere.

Cost and Hours: 30 kn; June-Sept daily 10:00-22:00; May and Oct Tue-Sun 10:00-16:00, closed Mon; closed Nov-April; Antuninska 6, tel. 020/322-166, www.warphotoltd.com.

Between the Stradun and the Sea

Institute for the Restoration of Dubrovnik (Zavod za Obnovu Dubrovnika)—This small photo gallery considers the eight-month siege of Dubrovnik from late 1991 to mid-1992 (see "The Siege of Dubrovnik" sidebar, earlier). You'll see images of bombed-out Dubrovnik, each one juxtaposed with an image of the same building after it was rebuilt, as well as rotating exhibits about efforts to restore Dubrovnik to its pre-siege glory. The photos are too few, but still illuminating. The highlight of the exhibit is a video showing a series of breathless news reports from a British journalist stationed here during the siege. As you watch shells devastating this glorious city, and look in the eyes of its desperate citizens at their darkest hour, you might just begin to grasp what went on here not so long ago.

Cost and Hours: Free, completely unpredictable hours—just drop by and see if it's open, a half-block off the Stradun at Miha Pracata, tel. 020/324-060.

▲**Serbian Orthodox Church and Icon Museum (Srpska Pravoslavna Crkva i Muzej Ikona)**—Round out your look

at Dubrovnik's major faiths (Catholic, Jewish, and Orthodox) with a visit to this house of worship—one of the most convenient places in Croatia to learn about Orthodox Christianity. Remember that people from the former Yugoslavia who follow the Orthodox faith are, by definition, ethnic Serbs. With all the (perhaps understandably) hard feelings about the recent war, this church serves as an important reminder that all Serbs aren't bloodthirsty killers.

Dubrovnik never had a very large Serb population (an Orthodox church wasn't even allowed inside the town walls until the mid-19th century). During the recent war, most Serbs fled, created new lives for themselves elsewhere, and saw little reason to return. But some old-timers remain, and Dubrovnik's dwindling, aging Orthodox population is still served by this **church.** The candles stuck in the sand (to prevent fire outbreaks) represent prayers: The ones at knee level are for the deceased, while the ones higher up are for the living. The gentleman selling candles encourages you to buy and light one, regardless of your faith, so long as you do so with the proper intentions and reverence.

A few doors down, you'll find the **Icon Museum.** This small collection features 78 different icons (stylized paintings of saints, generally on a golden background—a common feature of Orthodox churches) from the 15th through the 19th centuries, all identified in English. In the library—crammed with old shelves holding some 12,000 books—look for the astonishingly detailed calendar, with portraits of hundreds of saints. The gallery on the ground floor, run by Michael, sells original icons and reproductions (open longer hours than museum).

Cost and Hours: Church—free but donations accepted, good

The Serbian Orthodox Church

The emphasis of this book is on the Catholic areas of the former Yugoslavia, but don't overlook the rich diversity of faiths in this region. Dubrovnik's Serbian Orthodox church, as well as Orthodox churches in Kotor, Montenegro (see page 395); Sarajevo, Bosnia-Herzegovina (pages 473 and 482); and Ljubljana, Slovenia (page 540); offer invaluable opportunities to learn about a faith that's often unfamiliar to American visitors.

As you explore an Orthodox church, keep in mind that these churches carry on the earliest traditions of the Christian faith. Orthodox and Catholic Christianity came from the same roots, so the oldest surviving early-Christian churches (such as the stave churches of Norway) have many of the same features as today's Orthodox churches.

Notice that there are no pews. Worshippers stand through the service, as a sign of respect (though some older parishioners sit on the seats along the walls). Women stand on the left side, men on the right (equal distance from the altar—to represent that all are equal before God). The Orthodox Church uses essentially the same Bible as Catholics, but it's written in the Cyrillic alphabet, which you'll see displayed around any Orthodox church. Following Old Testament Judeo-Christian tradition, the Bible is kept on the altar behind the iconostasis, the big screen in the middle of the room covered with curtains and icons (golden

20-kn English book explains church and museum; daily May-Sept 8:00-14:00 & 16:00-21:00, until 19:00 in shoulder season, until 17:00 in winter; short services daily at 8:30 and 19:00, longer liturgy Sun 9:30-11:00; museum—10 kn; May-Oct Mon-Sat 9:00-13:00, closed Sun; Nov-April Mon-Fri 9:00-13:00, closed Sat-Sun, Od Puča 8, tel. 020/323-283.

▲**Rupe Granary and Ethnographic Museum (Etnografski Muzej Rupe)**—This huge, 16th-century building was Dubrovnik's biggest granary, and today houses the best folk museum I've seen in Croatia. *Rupe* means "holes"—and it's worth the price of entry just to peer down into these 15 cavernous underground grain stores, designed to maintain the perfect temperature to preserve the seeds (63 degrees Fahrenheit). When the grain had to be dried, it was moved upstairs—where today you'll find a surprisingly well-presented Ethnographic Museum, with tools, jewelry, clothing, instruments, painted eggs, and other folk artifacts from Dubrovnik's colorful history. Borrow the free English information guide at the entry. The museum hides several blocks uphill from the main promenade, toward the sea (climb up Široka—the widest side street from the Stradun—which becomes Od Domina on the way to the museum).

paintings of saints), which separates the material world from the spiritual one. At certain times during the service, the curtains or doors are opened so the congregation can see the Holy Book.

Unlike the decorations in many Catholic churches, Orthodox icons are not intended to be lifelike. Packed with intricate symbolism, and cast against a shimmering golden background, they're meant to remind viewers of the metaphysical nature of Jesus and the saints rather than of their physical form, which is considered irrelevant. You'll almost never see a statue, which is thought to overemphasize the physical world...and, to Orthodox people, feels a little too close to violating the commandment, "Thou shalt not worship graven images." Orthodox services generally involve chanting (a dialogue that goes back and forth between the priest and the congregation), and the church is filled with the evocative aroma of incense.

The incense, chanting, icons, and standing up are all intended to heighten the experience of worship. While many Catholic and Protestant services tend to be more of a theoretical and rote consideration of religious issues (come on—don't tell me you've never dozed through the sermon), Orthodox services are about creating a religious experience. Each of these elements does its part to help the worshipper transcend the physical world and join in communion with the spiritual one.

Cost and Hours: 40 kn, covered by 55-kn or 70-kn combo-ticket, Wed-Mon 9:00-16:00, closed Tue, od Rupa 3, tel. 020/323-013.

Above Dubrovnik

▲▲▲**Mount Srđ**—After adding Dubrovnik to his holdings, Napoleon built a fortress atop the hill behind the Old Town to

keep an eye on his new subjects (in 1810). During the city's 20th-century tourism heyday, a cable car was built to effortlessly whisk visitors to the top so they could enjoy the fine views from the fortress and the giant cross nearby. Then, when war broke out in the 1990s, Mount Srđ (pronounced like "surge") became a crucial link in the defense of Dubrovnik—the only high land that locals were able to hold. The fortress was shelled and damaged, and the cross and cable car were destroyed. Minefields and unexploded ordnance left the hilltop a dangerous no-man's land. But more recently, the mountain's fortunes have reversed. The landmines have been removed, and in 2010, the cable car was rebuilt to once again connect Dubrovnik's Old Town to its mountaintop. Visitors head to the top both for the spectacular sweeping views and for the ragtag museum about the war.

Warning: While this area has officially been cleared of landmines, nervous locals remind visitors that this was once a war zone. Be sure to stay on clearly defined paths and roads.

Getting There: The <u>cable car</u> is easily the best option for reaching the summit of Mount Srđ (80 kn round-trip, 50 kn one-way, kunas or credit cards only—no euros; 2/hour—generally departing at :00 and :30 past each hour, maybe more frequent with demand, 3-minute ride; daily June-Aug 9:00-24:00, April-May and Sept-Oct 9:00-20:00, Feb-March and Nov 9:00-17:00, Dec-Jan 9:00-16:00; doesn't run in Bora wind or heavy rain, last ascent 30 minutes before closing, tel. 020/325-393, www.dubrovnikcablecar.com). The lower station is just above the Buža Gate at the top of the Old Town (from the main drag, huff all the way to the top of Boškovićeva, exit through gate, and climb uphill one block, then look right). You may see travel agencies selling tickets elsewhere in town, but there's no advantage to buying them anywhere but here.

If you have a **car,** you can drive up. From the high road above the Old Town, watch for the turnoff to Bosanka, which leads you to that village, then up to the fortress and cross—follow signs for Srđ (it's twisty but not far—figure a 20-minute drive from the Old Town area). If you're coming south from the Old Town, once you reach the main road above, you'll have to turn left and backtrack a bit to reach the Bosanka turnoff. A **taxi** to the top is needlessly expensive (figure €50-70 round-trip, including some waiting time at the top); this is worthwhile only if you hire recommended driver Pepo Klaić to take you to the summit while sharing his firsthand experiences defending the fortress (€70, listed on next page). For **hikers,** a switchback trail (used to supply the fortress during the siege) connects the Old Town to the mountaintop—but it's very steep and provides minimal shade. (If you're in great shape and it's not too hot, you could ride the cable car up, then hike down.)

Mountaintop: From the top cable-car station, head up the stairs to the panoramic terrace. The bird's-eye **view** is truly spectacular, looking straight down to the street plan of Dubrovnik's Old Town. From this lofty perch, you can see north to the Dalmatian islands (the Elaphite archipelago, Mljet, Korčula, and beyond); south

to Montenegro; and east into Bosnia-Herzegovina. Gazing upon those looming mountains that define the border with Bosnia-Herzegovina—which, centuries ago, was also the frontier of the huge and powerful Ottoman Empire—you can appreciate how impressive it was that stubborn little Dubrovnik managed to remain independent for so much of its history.

The **cross** was always an important symbol in this very Catholic town. After it was destroyed, a temporary wooden one was erected to encourage the townspeople who were waiting out the siege below. During a visit in 2003, Pope John Paul II blessed the rubble from the old cross; those fragments are now being used in the foundations of the city's newest churches.

To reach the museum in the old fortress, walk behind the cable-car station along the rocky red soil.

Fort and Museum: The Napoleonic-era Fort Imperial (Tvrđava Imperijal) houses the **Dubrovnik During the Homeland War (1991-1995) Museum** (20 kn, 40-kn booklet, same hours as cable car except closes at 22:00 in summer). Photos, video clips, documents, and artifacts tell the story (with English descriptions) of the overarching war with Yugoslavia and how the people defended this fortress. The descriptions are too dense and detailed for casual visitors, but you'll see lots of photos and some actual items used in the fighting: primitive, rusty rifles (some dating from World War II) that the Croatians used for their improvised defense, and mortar shells and other projectiles that Yugoslav forces hurled at the fortress and the city. Look for the wire-guided Russian rockets. After being launched at their target, the rockets would burrow into a wall, waiting to be detonated once their operators saw the opportunity for maximum destruction. You'll also learn how a squadron of armed supply ships became besieged Dubrovnik's only tether to the outside world.

While the devastation of Dubrovnik was disturbing, this museum could do a far better job of fostering at least an illusion of impartiality. Instead, descriptions rant one-sidedly against "Serbian and Montenegrin aggression" and the "Serbian imperialist war," and the exhibits self-righteously depict Croats exclusively as victims (which was basically true here in Dubrovnik, but ignores Croat atrocities elsewhere). All of this serves only to trivialize and distract from the human tragedy of this war.

After seeing the exhibit, climb up a few flights of stairs to the **rooftop** for the view. The giant communications tower overhead flew the Croatian flag during the war, to inspire the besieged residents below. You might see some charred trees around here—these were claimed not by the war, but more recently, by forest fires. (Fear of landmines and other explosives prevented locals from fighting the wildfires as aggressively as they might otherwise, making these fires more dangerous than ever.)

Eating: Boasting undoubtedly the best view in Dubrovnik, **Restaurant/Snack Bar Panorama** has reasonable prices and drop-dead, astonishing views over the rooftops of the Old Town and to the most beautiful parts of three different countries (25-35-kn drinks, 55-70-kn cocktails, 10-kn ice cream, 27-kn cakes, 65-90-kn pastas, 85-145-kn main dishes, open same hours as cable car).

Activities in Dubrovnik

Swimming and Sunbathing—If the weather's good and you've had enough of museums, spend a sunny afternoon at the beach.

There are no sandy beaches on the mainland near Dubrovnik, but there are lots of suitable pebbly options, plus several concrete perches. The easiest and most atmospheric place to take a dip is right off the Old Town. From the Old Port and its breakwater, uneven steps clinging to the outside of the wall lead to a series of great sunbathing and swimming coves (and even a showerhead sticking out of the town wall). Another delightful rocky beach hangs onto the outside of the Old Town's wall (at the bar called Cold Drinks "Buža" I; for more on this bar, and how to find it, see page 324). Locals prefer to swim on Lokrum Island, because there are (relatively) fewer tourists there; for details on taking a boat to Lokrum, see page 349. Other convenient public beaches are Banje (just outside Ploče Gate, east of Old Town) and the beach in the middle of Lapad Bay (near Hotel Kompas).

My favorite hidden beach—**St. Jakob**—takes a lot longer to reach, but if you're up for the hike, it's worth it to escape the crowds. Figure about a 25-minute walk (each way) from the Old Town. Go through the Ploče Gate at the east end of the Old Town, and walk along the street called Frana Supila as it climbs uphill above the waterfront. At Hotel Argentina,

take the right (downhill) fork and keep going on Vlaha Bukovca. Eventually you'll reach the small church of St. Jakob. You'll see the beach—in a cozy protected cove—far below. Curl around behind the church and keep an eye out for stairs going down on the right. Unfortunately, these stairs are effectively unmarked, so it might take some trial and error to find the right ones. (If you reach the rusted-white gateway of the old communist-era open-air theater, you've gone too far.) Hike down the very steep stairs to the gentle cove, which has rentable chairs and a small restaurant for drinks (and a WC). Enjoy the pebbly beach and faraway views of Dubrovnik's Old Town.

Sea Kayaking—Paddling a sleek kayak around the outside of Dubrovnik's imposing walls is a memorable experience. Several outfits in town offer half-day tours (most options 250-350 kn); popular itineraries include loops along the City Walls, to secluded beaches, and around Lokrum island. As this scene is continually evolving, look for fliers locally.

Shopping in Dubrovnik

Most souvenirs sold in Dubrovnik—from lavender sachets to plaster models of the Old Town—are pretty tacky. Whatever you buy, prices are much higher along the Stradun than on the side streets.

A classy alternative to the knickknacks is a type of local jewelry called *Konavoske puce* ("Konavle buttons"). Sold as earrings,

pendants, and rings, these distinctive and fashionable filigree-style pieces consist of a sphere with several small posts. Though they're sold around town, it's least expensive to buy them on Od Puča street, which runs parallel to the Stradun two blocks toward the sea (near the Serbian Orthodox Church). The high concentration of jewelers along this lane keeps prices reasonable. You'll find the "buttons" in various sizes, in both silver (affordable) and gold (pricey).

You'll also see lots of jewelry made from red coral, which can only be legally gathered in small amounts from two small islands in northern Dalmatia. If you see a particularly large chunk of coral, it's likely imported. To know what you're getting, shop at an actual jeweler instead of a souvenir shop.

Gift-Shop Chains: Several pleasant gift shops in Dubrovnik (with additional branches throughout Dalmatia) hawk fun, if sometimes made-in-China, items. Look for these chains, which are a bit classier than the many no-name shops around town: **Aqua**

DUBROVNIK

sells pleasant nautical-themed gifts, blue-and-white-striped sailor shirts, and other gear. **Bonbonnière Kraš** is Croatia's leading chocolatier, selling a wide array of tasty candies.

Entertainment in Dubrovnik

Musical Events

Dubrovnik annually hosts a full schedule of events for its Summer Festival (July 10-Aug 25, www.dubrovnik-festival.hr). Lovers of classical music enjoy the "Rachlin & Friends" festival in September (www.julianrachlin.com). But the town also works hard to offer traditional music outside of festival time. Spirited folk-music concerts are performed for tourists twice weekly in the Lazareti (old quarantine building) just outside the Old Town's Ploče Gate (100 kn, usually at 21:30). About one night per week through the winter, you can watch the Dubrovnik Symphony Orchestra (usually at the Rector's Palace in good weather, or Dominican Monastery in bad weather). And since Dubrovnik is trying to become a year-round destination, the city also offers tourist-oriented musical events most nights throughout the winter (often at a hotel). For the latest on any of these festivals and concerts, check the events listings in the *Best in Dubrovnik* brochure, or ask the TI.

Also consider the folk dancing and market each Sunday morning at Čilipi, a small town near the airport (see page 354). Dubrovnik-based companies offer excursions that include transportation there and back (230 kn).

Nightlife

Dubrovnik's Old Town is one big, romantic parade of relaxed and happy people out strolling. The main drag is brightly lit and packed with shops, cafés, and bars, all open late. This is a fun scene. And if you walk away from the crowds or out on the port, you'll be alone with the magic of the Pearl of the Adriatic. Everything feels—and is—very safe after dark.

If you're looking for a memorable bar after dark, consider these:

▲▲▲**Drinks with a View—Cold Drinks "Buža"** offers, without a doubt, the most scenic spot for a drink. Perched on a cliff above the sea, clinging like a barnacle to the outside of the city walls, this is a peaceful, shaded getaway from the bustle of the Old Town... the perfect place to watch cruise ships disappear into the horizon.

Buža means "hole in the wall"—and
that's exactly what you'll have to go
through to get to this place. There
are actually two different Bužas, with
separate owners. My favorite is Buža
II (which is actually the older and
bigger of the pair). Filled with mellow
tourists and bartenders pouring wine
from tiny screw-top bottles into plastic cups, Buža II comes with castaway
views and Frank Sinatra ambience.
This is supposedly where Bill Gates
hangs out when he visits Dubrovnik

(25-40-kn drinks, summer daily 9:00-into the wee hours, closed
mid-Nov-Jan). Buža I, with a different owner, is more casual, plays
hip rather than romantic music, and has concrete stairs leading
down to a beach on the rocks below (18-45-kn drinks). If one Buža
is full, check the other one.

Getting There: Both Bužas are high above the bustle of the
main drag, along the seaward wall. To reach them from the cathedral area, hike up the grand staircase to St. Ignatius' Church, then
go left to find the lane that runs along the inside of the wall. To
find the classic Buža II, head right along the lane and look for the
Cold Drinks sign pointing to a literal hole in the wall. For the hip-
per Buža I, go left along the same lane, and locate the hole in the
wall with the *No Toples No Nudist* graffiti.

Wine-Tasting—D'Vino Wine Bar, just a few steps off the main
drag, has a relaxed atmosphere and a knowledgeable but unpretentious approach—making it the handiest place in Dalmatia to taste
and learn about Croatian wines. Run by gregarious Aussie-Croat
Sasha, this cozy bar (with a few outdoor tables) sells more than 60
wines by the glass and lots more by the bottle. The emphasis is on
Croatian wines by small-production wineries, but they also have
a few international vintages. Each wine is well-described on the
menu, and the staff is happy to guide you through your options—
just tell them what you like (18-80-kn glasses—most around 25-35
kn, 50-kn wine flights; light food—70-kn 2-person cheese plate,
90-kn antipasti plate; daily 10:30-2:00 in the morning, possibly less
in winter, Palmotićeva 4a, tel. 020/321-130, www.dvino.net). Sasha
takes wine-lovers on all-day wine tours to the Pelješac Peninsula
(see page 359); also ask about his wine dinners.

Cocktails and People-Watching—Jazz Caffè Troubadour is a
cool place, originally owned by a former member of the Dubrovnik
Troubadours—Croatia's answer to the Beatles (or, perhaps more
accurately, the Turtles). On balmy evenings, 50 chairs with tiny
tables are set up theater-style in the dreamy alley facing the

musicians. Step inside to see old 1970s photos of the band (50-60-kn cocktails, daily 9:00-24:00, happy hour 14:00-19:00 with 20-kn drinks, live jazz nightly from about 20:30, often live piano at other times, next to cathedral at Bunićeva Poljana 2).

The square just around the corner from Troubadour, alongside the cathedral, is another happening nightspot. Several cafés that ring the square have outdoor seating, filling the entire space with a convivial hubbub of people out enjoying the al fresco ambience.

Nonenina, a few steps from the cathedral on Pred Dvorom, is an outdoor lounge with big, overstuffed chairs at a fine vantage point for people-watching. They brag that they serve 180 different types of cocktails (55-80 kn, also 35-45-kn beers, daily 9:00-2:00 in the morning, shorter hours off-season, across from Rector's Palace).

The Gaffe Irish Pub, with a nice pubby interior and a small courtyard, is a rollicking spot to drain a pint and watch some rugby (Miha Pracata 4, mobile 098-196-2149, see full listing under "Eating in Dubrovnik," later).

Nightclubs—Dubrovnik has a variety of nightclubs. The streets branching off from the Stradun are lined with several options with drinks and pumping music, including **Sky Bar** (toward the water on Marojice Kaboge) and **Africa** (toward the mountain at Vetranićeva 3). Just follow the beat.

More places are near or just beyond the Ploče Gate at the east end of town. Head under the Bell Tower, then up the street past the Dominican Monastery. You'll pass the hole-in-the-wall entrance (right) for the snobby, upscale **Gil's** cocktail bar and "pop lounge" (www.gilsdubrovnik.com). Then, after crossing the bridge, look (on the left) for the entrance to **Revelin**—a dance club that fills one of the city wall's fortress towers (nightly 22:00-6:00, www.revelinclub-dubrovnik.com). Then head out and up the street until you reach Banje Beach, half of which is occupied by the **EastWest** dance club (www.ew-dubrovnik.com). Note that some of these are more exclusive and may charge admission on weekends.

Movies

The Old Town has a trio of movie theaters showing American blockbusters (usually in English with Croatian subtitles, unless the film's animated or for kids). The **Sloboda** cinema, right under the Bell Tower on Luža Square, is nothing special. But in good weather, head for the fun outdoor **Jadran** cinema, where you can lick ice cream (B.Y.O.) while you watch a movie with a Dubrovnik-mountaintop backdrop. This is a cheap, casual, and very Croatian scene, where people smoke and chat, and the neighbors sit in their windowsills to watch the movie (most nights in summer only, shows begin shortly after sundown; in the Old Town near the Pile

Gate). For first-run 3-D movies, head to the **Visia Dubrovnik Multimedia Museum** just inside the Pile Gate (tel. 020/324-714, www.visiadubrovnik.com).

Sleeping in Dubrovnik

You basically have two options in Dubrovnik: a centrally located room in a private home *(soba)*; or a resort hotel on a distant beach, a bus ride away from the Old Town. Since Dubrovnik hotels are generally a poor value, I highly recommend giving the *sobe* a careful look. For locations, see the map on page 328.

Be warned that the Old Town is home to many popular discos. My listings are quieter than the norm, but if you're finding a place on your own, you may discover you have a late-night soundtrack—particularly if you're staying near the Stradun.

No matter where you stay, prices are much higher mid-June through mid-September, and highest in July and August. Reserve ahead for these peak times, especially during the Summer Festival

---

Sleep Code

(5 kn = about $1, €1 = about $1.40, country code: 385, area code: 020)

S = Single, **D** = Double/Twin, **T** = Triple, **Q** = Quad, **b** = bathroom. The modest tourist tax (about 7 kn per person, per night) is not included in these rates. Hotels generally accept credit cards and include breakfast in their rates, while most *sobe* accept only cash and don't offer breakfast. While rates are listed in euros, you'll pay in kunas. Unless otherwise noted, everyone listed here speaks English.

Rates: If I've listed two sets of rates for an accommodation, I've noted when the second rate applies (generally off-season, Oct-May); if I've listed three sets of rates, separated by slashes, the first is for peak season (July-Aug), the second is for shoulder season (May-June and Sept-Oct), and the third is for off-season (Nov-April). The dates for seasonal rates vary by hotel, and prices can change without notice; verify the hotel's current rates online or by email. For other updates, see www.ricksteves.com/update.

Price Ranges: To help you sort easily through these listings, I've divided the accommodations into three categories based on the price for a double room with bath in peak season:

$$$ Higher Priced—Most rooms €95 or more.
$$ Moderately Priced—Most rooms between €55-95.
$ Lower Priced—Most rooms €55 or less.

DUBROVNIK

Old Town Hotels & Restaurants

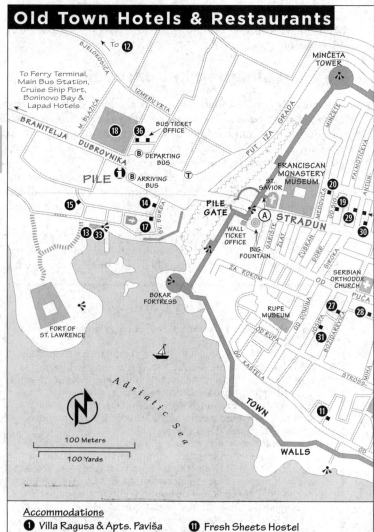

To ⑫

BJELOKOSIĆA

To Ferry Terminal,
Main Bus Station,
Cruise Ship Port,
Boninovo Bay &
Lapad Hotels

IZMEĐU VRTA

M. BLAŽICA

BRANITELJA DUBROVNIKA

PILE

⑱   ㊱

BUS TICKET
OFFICE

Ⓑ DEPARTING
BUS

❶ Ⓑ ARRIVING
BUS

Ⓣ

MINČETA
TOWER

PUT IZA GRADA

MINČETE

PALMOTIĆEVA

FRANCISCAN
MONASTERY
MUSEUM
ST.
SAVIOR

⑳

OD SIG

MEDOVIĆA

ANTUN

⑲

⑮   ⑭

SV. ĐURĐA

⑰

PILE
GATE

Ⓐ STRADUN

㉙

⑬ ㉝

WALL
TICKET
OFFICE

GARIŠTE

BIG
FOUNTAIN

ZLAT

ČUBRAN.

BORO

ŠIROKA

㉚

ZA ROKOM

OD

SERBIAN
ORTHODOX
CHURCH

BOKAR
FORTRESS

RUPE
MUSEUM

OD DOMINA

OD RUPA

㉗

PUCA

㉘

FORT OF
ST. LAWRENCE

Adriatic Sea

OD KAŠTELA

BOŽIDAREVIĆA

JOPA

㉛

MIHA

BTROSS.

N

100 Meters

100 Yards

TOWN

⑪

WALLS

Accommodations

❶ Villa Ragusa & Apts. Paviša
❷ Apartments Martecchini
❸ Raič Apartments
❹ Plaza Apartments
❺ Minerva Apartments
❻ Karmen Apartments
❼ Apartments Amoret (3)
❽ Apartments Placa
❾ Garden Cottage
❿ Renata Zijadić Rooms

⑪ Fresh Sheets Hostel
⑫ To Jadranka Benussi Rooms
⑬ Rest. Orhan Guest House
⑭ Nedjeljka Benussi Rooms
⑮ Paulina Čumbelić Rooms
⑯ Villa Adriatica
⑰ Atlas Travel Agency
⑱ Hilton Imperial Dubrovnik
⑲ Hotel Stari Grad

DUBROVNIK

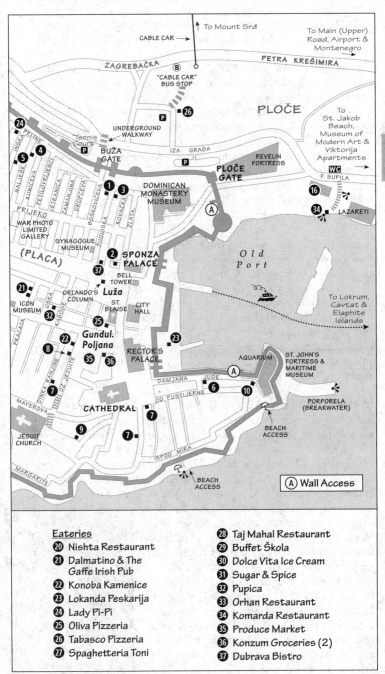

DUBROVNIK

(July 10-Aug 25 every year). Most accommodations prefer to list their rates in euros (and I've followed suit), but you'll pay in kunas.

Sobe (Private Rooms): A Dubrovnik Specialty

In Dubrovnik, you'll almost always do better with a *soba* than with a hotel. Before you choose, carefully read the information on page 27. All of my favorite *sobe* are run by friendly English-speaking Croatians and are inside or within easy walking distance of the Old Town. There's a range of places, from simple and cheap rooms where you'll share a bathroom, to downright fancy places with private facilities, air-conditioning, kitchenettes, and satellite TV, where you can be as anonymous as you like. Most *sobe* don't include breakfast, so I've listed some suggestions later, under "Eating in Dubrovnik."

Book direct, using the email addresses I've listed for each place—middleman agencies (including booking websites) tack on fees, making it more expensive for both you and your host. Note that many Dubrovnik *sobe* hosts might ask you to send them a deposit to secure your reservation. Sometimes they'll accept your credit-card number; others might want you to mail them a check or traveler's check (the better option) or wire them the money (which can be expensive). While it's a bit of a hassle, this request is reasonable and part of the experience of sleeping at a *soba*. Remember that you'll usually need to pay your bill in cash (kunas), not with a credit card.

In the Old Town, Above the Stradun Promenade

These are some of my favorite accommodations in Dubrovnik. All are located at the top of town, high above the Stradun, and all are excellent values. The first three are within a few steps of each other, along a little block dubbed by some "Rickova ulica." If you don't mind the very steep hike up, you'll find this to be a wonderful enclave of hospitality. When one of these places is full, they work together to find space for you. The last two listings are a few blocks over, and nearly as nice (and equally steep). Because all of these hosts live off-site, be sure to let them know when you'll arrive so they can let you in.

$$ Villa Ragusa, offers my favorite rooms for the price in the Old Town. Pero and Valerija Carević have renovated a 600-year-old house at the top of town that was damaged during the war. The five comfortable, modern rooms come with atmospheric old wooden beams, antique furniture, and thoughtful touches. There are three doubles with bathrooms (including a top-floor room with breathtaking Old Town views for no extra charge—request when you reserve) and two singles that share a bathroom (S-€40/€35/€25, Db-€80/€70/€50, €8 breakfast can be eaten here or at nearby Stradun café, cash only, air-con, lots of stairs with no elevator, free Wi-Fi, Žudioska ulica 15, tel. 020/453-834, mobile 098-765-634, www.villaragusa-dubrovnik.com, villa.ragusa@du.t-com.hr). Pero offers his guests airport transfers for a reasonable €30, and can drive you on an all-day excursion (such as to Montenegro or Mostar) for €250—if you can split this cost with other guests, it's a good value (same price for up to 6 people).

$$ Apartments Paviša, next door to Villa Ragusa and run by Pero and Davorka Paviša, has three good, older-feeling rooms at the top of the Old Town (Db-€100/€70/€50, 10 percent discount if you book direct with this book, no breakfast, cash only, air-con, lots of stairs, free Wi-Fi, Žudioska ulica 19, mobile 098-427-399 or 098-175-2342, www.apartmentspavisa.com, davorka.pavisa @du.t-com.hr). They have two more rooms in the **Viktorija** neighborhood, about a 20-minute mostly uphill walk east of the Old Town. While it's a long-but-scenic walk into town, the views from these apartments are spectacular (same prices as in-town rooms, Frana Supila 59, bus stop nearby). Pero and Davorka also manage **Apartments Martecchini,** three units a bit closer to the main drag in the Old Town (small apartment-€100/€70/€50, bigger apartment-€110/€80/€50, biggest apartment-€120/€90/€60; 10 percent discount if you book direct with this book, prices depend on size and views, no breakfast, cash only, air-con, free Wi-Fi, www .apartmentsmartecchini.com).

$$ Ivana and Anita Raič are sisters renting three new-feeling apartments with kitchenettes and air-conditioning (Db-€90/€70/€50-60, no extra charge for 1- or 2-night stays, no breakfast, cash only, air-con, free Wi-Fi, Žudioska ulica 16, Ivana's mobile 098-996-0858, Anita's mobile 091-537-6035, www .apartments-raic.com, ivanaraic@gmail.com).

$$ Plaza Apartments, run by Lidija and Maro Matić, rents three clean, well-appointed apartments on a plant-filled lane— the steepest and most appealing stretch of stairs leading up from the Stradun. Lidija's sweet personality is reflected in the cheerful rooms, which are a great value if you don't mind the hike (Db-€75/€60/€55, cheaper Nov-April, these special prices for Rick Steves readers, no breakfast, cash only, air-con, free Wi-Fi, climb the stairs past Dolce Vita gelato shop to Nalješkovićeva 22, tel. 020/321-493, mobile 091-517-7048, www.dubrovnik-online.com /apartment_plaza, lidydu@yahoo.com).

$$ Minerva Apartments has two cozy ground-floor units near the top of a similar lane, in the home of Dubravka Vidosavljević-

Vučić (Db-€80/€75/€65, cheaper Nov-April, cash only, no breakfast, air-con, free Wi-Fi, washing machine, Antuninska 14, mobile 091-252-9677, duvivu@gmail.com).

In the Old Town, near the Cathedral and St. John's Fort

The following places are south of the Stradun, mostly clustering around the cathedral and St. John's Fort, at the end of the Old Port. To find the Karmen and Zijadić apartments from the cathedral, walk toward the big fort tower along the inside of the wall (follow signs for *akvarji*).

$$$ Apartments Amoret, run by Branka Dabrović and her husband Ivica, are in all the guidebooks. The pricey but comfortable apartments, with furnishings that are a step up from the norm, are in three different buildings: two over Amoret Restaurant in front of the cathedral (at Restićeva 2); eight more sharing an inviting terrace on a quiet, untouristy lane a few blocks east (at Dinka Ranjine 5); and three more nearby (at Ilije Sarake 4). All three classes of apartments are comparably good; in every case, the furnishings are a tasteful mix of traditional and modern. Since Branka and Ivica don't live on-site, arrange a meeting time and place when you reserve ("regular" apartments-€100/€90/€80; "standard" apartments-€120/€110/€100; "superb" apartments-€140/€130/€110; cheaper Nov-April, 30 percent more for 1-night stays, 20 percent more for 2-night stays, 10 percent more for 3-night stays, no breakfast, cash only, air-con, free Wi-Fi, mobile 091-530-4910, tel. & fax 020/324-005, www.dubrovnik-amoret.com, dubrovnik@post.t-com.hr).

$$ Karmen Apartments are well-run by a Brit named Marc and his Croatian wife Silva, who offer four apartments just inside the big fort. The prices are very high, and they're in all the guidebooks, but the apartments are big, well-equipped, and homey-feeling, each with a bathroom and kitchen. The decor is eclectic but tasteful, and Marc and Silva are good hosts, with a virtual minimuseum of historic Dubrovnik maps and documents in the stairwell (smaller apartment-€90/€70, mid-sized apartment-€135/€108, bigger apartment-€155/€110; higher price is for May-Sept, less Dec-March, usually 3-night minimum, no breakfast, cash only, air-con, free Wi-Fi, near the aquarium at Bandureva 1, tel. 020/323-433, mobile 098-619-282, www.karmendu.com, marc.van-bloemen@du.t-com.hr).

$$ Apartments Placa (PLAH-tsah; not to be confused with Plaza Apartments, described earlier) is run by Tonči (TOHN-chee). He rents three apartments with some antique furnishings and some modern, overlooking the market square in the heart of the Old Town. You might get some early-morning noise from the market set-up, but the double-paned windows help, and the location is wonderfully central. Since Tonči lives elsewhere, clearly communicate your arrival time (Db-€90/€80/€70, cheaper Nov-April, no breakfast, cash only, no extra charge for 1- or 2-night stays, several flights of stairs, air-con, free Wi-Fi, Gundulićeva poljana 5, mobile 091-721-9202, www.dubrovnik-online.com /apartments_placa, tonci.korculanin@du.t-com.hr).

$$ Garden Cottage is exactly that: a small freestanding house nestled in a very rare patch of green. It's a peaceful oasis smack-dab in the heart of the bustling city (just off the plaza in front of the Jesuit church). Roberto and his mother Marija (also recommended tour guides—see page 294) live in an old Dubrovnik mansion with a fine little garden, and they've converted the old laundry building into a simple rental apartment that sleeps up to four people. When you book this place, you're also renting the entire garden for your own use...very cool, particularly in a city with virtually no green space (€80/€70/€60 per night for 4 or more nights, €90/€80/€70 per night for 2-3 nights, €100/€90/€80 for 1 night, extra bed-€15, cash only, air-con, washing machine, kitchenette, mobile 091-541-6637, bobdel70@yahoo.com).

$$ Renata Zijadić, a friendly mom who speaks good English, offers four well-located rooms with slanting floors, funky colors, and over-the-top antique furniture. A single and a double (both with great views) share one bathroom; another double features an ornate old cabinet and its own bathroom; and the top-floor apartment comes with low ceilings and fine vistas (S-€30/€28, D-€50/€45, Db-€60/€50, apartment-€85/€75, second price is for June and Sept, cheaper Oct-May, no extra charge for 1- or 2-night stays, no breakfast, cash only, all rooms have air-con except the single, free Wi-Fi; follow signs for wall access and walk up the steps marked *ulica Stajeva* going over the street to find Stajeva 1; tel. 020/323-623, www.dubrovnik-online.com/house_renata, renatadubrovnik@yahoo.com).

$ Fresh Sheets, a bright, stylish, and appealingly funky hostel run by a fun-loving Canadian-Croatian couple, is your best youth hostel option in the Old Town. The 22 bunks (two 8-bed dorms, one 4-bed dorm, and a double room) sit above a tight but enjoyable common area. Located at the very top of Dubrovnik just inside the town walls, it's a steep hike up from the main drag, but worth it if you enjoy youthful backpacker bonding (€22-33/bunk in a dorm, €25-38/person in a private room, likely closed Nov-March, free breakfast, free Internet access and Wi-Fi, lockers, kitchen, Svetog Šimuna/Smokvina 15, mobile 091-799-2086, www.freshsheets hostel.com, beds@igotfresh.com).

In the Pile Neighborhood, Just Outside the Old Town

There's a concentration of good *sobe* just outside the Old Town's Pile Gate. The Pile (PEE-leh) neighborhood offers all the conveniences of the modern world (grocery store, bus stop, post office, travel agency, etc.), just steps from Dubrovnik's magical Old Town. The first place is up the hill (away from the water) from the Pile Gate's bus stop; the rest cluster around a quiet, no-name cove near Restaurant Orhan. From the bus stop area in front of Pile Gate, various lanes lead down toward this cove.

$$ Jadranka and Milan Benussi, a middle-aged professional couple, rent four rooms in a quiet, traffic-free neighborhood. Their delightful stony-chic home, complete with a leafy terrace, is a steep 10-minute hike above the Old Town—close enough to be convenient, but far enough to take you away from the bustle and into a calm residential zone. Jadranka speaks good English, enjoys visiting with her guests, and gives her place a modern Croatian class unusual for a *soba*. This is one of your best values and most comfortable home bases in Dubrovnik, if you don't mind the walk (small Db-€60/€55, big Db-€70/€65, small apartment-€90/€85, big apartment with balcony-€100/€95, cheaper Oct-May, 20 percent more for stays less than 4 nights, no breakfast, cash only, aircon, kitchenettes, free Wi-Fi, Miha Klaića 10, tel. 020/429-339, mobile 098-928-1300, www.dubrovnik-benussi.com, jadranka @dubrovnik-benussi.com). To find the Benussis, go to the big Hilton Hotel just outside the Pile Gate (across from the TI). Walk up the little stepped lane called Marijana Blažića at the upper-left corner of the Hilton cul-de-sac. When that lane dead-ends, go left up ulica Don Iva Bjelokosića (more steps) until you see a little church on the left. The Benussis' house is just before this church.

$$ Restaurant Orhan Guest House allows hotel anonymity at *sobe* prices. Its 11 basic, old-fashioned, ramshackle rooms—in a couple of different buildings around the corner from the restaurant—are well-located and quiet, with modern bathrooms. As the rooms are an afterthought to the restaurant, don't expect a warm welcome (Sb or Db-€60-75/€40, includes breakfast, cash only, aircon, free Wi-Fi, Od Tabakarije 1, tel. & fax 020/414-183, www .restaurant-orhan.com, restoran.orhan@yahoo.com). Their restaurant is also a good spot for a scenic meal (described later, under "Eating in Dubrovnik").

$$ Nedjeljka Benussi, the sister-in-law of Jadranka Benussi (listed earlier), rents three modern, spacious, straightforward rooms sharing two bathrooms and a pretty view (D-€70/€55, T-€80/€75, cheaper Dec-March, same price for 1-night stays, no breakfast, cash only, fans but no air-con, Sv. Đurđa 4, tel. 020/423-062, mobile 098-170-5699).

$ Paulina Čumbelić is a kind, gentle woman renting four old-fashioned rooms in her homey, clean, and peaceful house (S-€30/€27, D-€50/€40, T-€60/€55, 20 percent more for 1- or 2-night stays, no breakfast, cash only, closed in winter, can be noisy outside, Od Tabakarije 2, tel. 020/421-327, mobile 091-530-7985).

Beyond the Ploče Gate, East of the Old Town

To reach these options, you'll go through the Ploče Gate and walk along the road stretching east from the Old Town (with fine views back on the Old Port). This area is shared by giant waterfront luxury hotels and residential areas, so it has a bit less character than the Pile and Old Town listings (which I prefer).

$$ Apartments Paviša, described on page 331, has two fine apartments in the Viktorija neighborhood about a 20-minute walk or short bus ride from town.

$$ Villa Adriatica has four old-fashioned rooms above a travel agency and a family home just outside the Ploče Gate, a few steps from the Old Town. The rooms are antique-furnished, but have modern bathrooms, TVs, and air-conditioning. While impersonal and a lesser value than my other listings, it's worth considering just for the huge, shared terrace with priceless Old Port views, plus a common living room and kitchen furnished with museum-piece antiques. Teo manages the rooms; ask for him at the Perla Adriatic travel agency, just outside the Ploče Gate (Db-€85-95/€80-90/€75-85, cheaper Nov-April, price depends on size and view, 20 percent more for 1- or 2-night stays, no breakfast, cash only, air-con, free Wi-Fi in some areas, Frana Supila 4, mobile 098-334-500, tel. 020/411-962, fax 020/422-766, www.villa-adriatica.net, booking @villa-adriatica.net, Tomšić family).

Sobe-Booking Websites and Agencies

Several websites put you in touch with Dubrovnik's *sobe* and apartments. Of course, you'll save yourself and your host money if you book direct, but these sites are convenient. For example, www .dubrovnikapartmentsource.com, run by an American couple, offers a range of carefully selected, well-described accommodations. You can browse a variety of options, then reserve your choice and pay a nonrefundable deposit by credit card. Another, bigger operation—with a wider selection but less personal attention—is www.adriatica.net; international sites such as www.booking.com are another good option.

If you arrive without a reservation and the TI isn't too busy, they might be able to call around and find you a *soba* for no charge. Otherwise, just about any travel agency in town can help you, on the spot or in advance...for a fee. **Atlas** is the biggest company (figure Db-€55-60 and apartment-€75-100 in June-Sept, €15-20 less in shoulder season; for more on Atlas, see page 293).

Hotels
If you must stay in a hotel, you have only a few good options. There are just two hotels inside the Old Town walls—and one of them charges $500 a night (Pucić Palace, www.thepucicpalace.com). Any big, resort-style hotel within walking distance of the Old Town will run you at least €200. These inflated prices drive most visitors to Boninovo Bay or the Lapad Peninsula, a bus ride west of the Old Town. In the mass-tourism tradition, many European visitors choose to take the half-board option at their hotel (i.e., dinner in the hotel restaurant). This can be convenient and a good value—especially considering the relatively low quality of Dubrovnik's restaurants (explained later, under "Eating in Dubrovnik")—but the Old Town is a much more atmospheric place to dine.

In and near the Old Town
$$$ Hilton Imperial Dubrovnik, sitting regally just outside the Pile Gate, is the closest big hotel to the Old Town. This grand 19th-century building was recently overhauled to create 147 plush rooms. If you want predictable Hilton comfort at outlandish prices a short walk from the Old Town, this is the place (Db-€300, less off-season, €55 extra for sea view, €65 extra for balcony but no view, €120 extra for balcony and view, most rates include breakfast but not the 10 percent tax, elevator, air-con, pay Wi-Fi in lobby and pay cable Internet in rooms, parking-€27/night, $7 bottles of water at the reception desk, Marijana Blažića 2, tel. 020/320-320, fax 020/320-220, www.hilton.com, sales.dubrovnik@hilton.com).

$$$ Hotel Stari Grad knows it's the only real hotel option inside the Old Town—and charges accordingly. It has eight modern yet nicely old-fashioned rooms a half-block off the Old Town's main drag. The rooftop terrace enjoys an amazing view over orange tiles. This place books up fast, so reserve early (Sb-€180/€134/€99, Db-€240/€192/€140, no extra charge for 1- or 2-night stays, includes breakfast, air-con, lots of stairs with no elevator, free Wi-Fi, Od Sigurate 4, tel. 020/322-244, fax 020/321-256, www .hotelstarigrad.com, info@hotelstarigrad.com).

Near Boninovo Bay
Boninovo Bay (boh-NEE-noh-voh) is your best bet for an affordable and well-located hotel. Above this bay are Dubrovnik's only three-star hotels within walking distance of the Old Town (not

to mention the city's only official youth hostel). These places offer slightly better prices and closer proximity to the Old Town than the farther-out Lapad Bay resorts. They're on or near the water, but don't have views of the Old Town (which is around the bend). Boninovo Bay is an uphill 20-minute walk or five-minute bus ride from the Old Town (straight up Branitelja Dubrovnika). Once you're comfortable with the buses, the location is great: Any bus that leaves the Pile Gate stops first at Boninovo Bay. You'll see the bay on your left as you climb the hill, then get off at the stop after the traffic light (or stay on bus #4, which stops even closer to the hotels). To reach the hotels from the Boninovo bus stop, go up Pera Čingrije (the busy road running along the top of the cliff overlooking the sea). There's a super little bakery, Pekarnica Klas, on the right (across the street from Hotel Bellevue).

$$$ Hotel Bellevue has a striking location, with its back against the cliff rising up from Boninovo Bay and an elevator plunging directly to its own pebbly beach. Completely gutted and rebuilt just a few years ago, its 91 top-notch rooms—all but two with sea views, many with balconies—offer upscale wood-grain elegance (standard Db-generally €250/€220, less Nov-April, very flexible rates, €50 more for balcony, air-con, elevator, free Internet access and Wi-Fi, Pera Čingrije 7, tel. 020/330-000, fax 020/330-100, www.hotel-bellevue.hr, welcome@hotel-bellevue.hr).

$$$ Hotel R, a homey enclave with just 10 rooms, feels friendlier and less greedy than all the big resort hotels. Well-run by the Rešetar family, it's a good small-hotel value (Sb-€72/€56/€50, Db-€110/€86/€77, closed Nov-Easter, 10 percent more for balcony, half-board-€13, air-con, free Wi-Fi, just beyond the big Hotel Lero at Iva Vojnovića 16, tel. 020/333-200, fax 020/333-208, www.hotel-r.hr, helpdesk@hotel-r.hr).

$$$ Hotel Lero, 250 yards up the street from the bus stop, has 140 recently renovated rooms and a fine outdoor pool. Choose between so-so sea views with some road noise, or quieter back rooms (soft rates, but generally Sb-€110/€85, Db-€140/€106, cheaper mid-Oct-April; in busy times, you may be quoted more than these rates—try asking for a better deal; "superior" rooms with balcony not worth the extra €30/person, air-con, elevator, pay Internet access, free Wi-Fi, half-board-€6, Iva Vojnovića 14, tel. 020/341-333, fax 020/332-123, www.hotel-lero.hr, sales@hotel-lero.hr).

$ Dubrovnik's official **Youth Hostel** is quiet, modern, and well-run by proud manager Laura. It's institutional, with 82 beds in 19 fresh, woody dorms and few extra hostel amenities (bunk in 4- to 6-bed dorm-€18/€17/€16, cheaper Nov-March, €1.50 more for nonmembers, includes sheets, includes breakfast, no air-con in rooms, free Internet access, no Wi-Fi; reception open daily June-Oct 7:00-3:00 in the morning, Nov-May 8:00-14:00 &

18:00-20:00; 2:00 a.m. curfew in summer, none in winter; up the steps at ulica bana Jelačića 15-17 to ulica Vinka Sagrestana 3, tel. 020/423-241, fax 020/412-592, www.hfhs.hr, dubrovnik@hfhs.hr). From the Boninovo bus stop, go down Pera Čingrije toward Hotel Bellevue, but take the first right uphill onto ulica bana Jelačića and look for signs up to the hostel on your left, on ulica Vinka Sagrestana. Several houses nearby rent rooms to those who prefer a double...and pick off would-be hostelers as they approach.

In Lapad

For a real resort-style vacation (at premium prices), many travelers call the touristy area around Lapad (LAH-pahd) Bay home. The main drag running through the middle of this scene, called Šetalište Kralja Zvonimira, is a nicely pedestrianized people zone buzzing with tourists, restaurants, cafés, and mild diversions. From the bus stop, the main drag leads to a pleasant pebble beach good for swimming and a romantic bayside path. While I much prefer sleeping near the Old Town, this is an appealing place to be on vacation (even if the Old Town weren't just a short bus ride away). To get here from the Old Town's Pile Gate, pile onto bus #6 with all the other tourists and get off at the Pošta Lapad stop (poorly marked—after bus turns left away from the big harbor, watch for low-profile yellow *pošta* sign on left; 4-6 buses/hour until 24:30, 15 minutes). A taxi costs about 60 kn.

$$$ *Small Hotels in Lapad:* In this area, I like three new-ish, interchangeable small hotels. While not affiliated with each other, each one has similar amenities—air-con, elevator (except Hotel Dubrovnik), Internet access either in lobby or in room—and similar prices (roughly Db-€160/€140/€110, but prices are very soft and can flex with demand, season, and length of stay; check online for the latest, and ask for a deal when you reserve). **Hotel Aquarius,** hiding a block off the main drag, has 24 comfortable, plush-feeling rooms and an inviting terrace out front (Mata Vodopića 8, tel. 020/456-111, fax 020/456-100, www.hotel-aquarius.net, stjepanka@hotel-aquarius.net). **Hotel Perla,** right on the main drag, has 25 modern rooms (tel. 020/438-244, fax 020/438-245, www.perla-dubrovnik.com, info@perla-dubrovnik.com). **Hotel Dubrovnik,** two doors up from the Perla, has 25 simpler rooms (tel. 020/435-030, fax 020/435-999, www.hoteldubrovnik.hr, info@hoteldubrovnik.com).

Eating in Dubrovnik

Dubrovnik disappoints diners with high prices, surly service, and mediocre quality. With the constant influx of deep-pocketed tourists corrupting greedy restaurateurs, places here tend to go down-

hill faster than a game of marbles on the *Titanic*. Promising new restaurants open all the time, but most quickly fade, and what's great one year can be miserable the next. Therefore, lower your expectations, take my suggestions with a grain of salt, and ask around locally for what's good this month. Don't bother looking for a "local" favorite anywhere near the Old Town—people who live here eat out at restaurants in the 'burbs. The good news is that it's atmospheric. Anywhere you dine, breezy outdoor seating is a no-brainer, and scrawny, adorable kittens beg for table scraps. In general, seafood restaurants are good only at seafood; if you want pasta, go to a pasta place.

In the Old Town

Nishta ("Nothing"), featuring a short menu of delicious vegetarian fusion cuisine with Asian flair, offers a welcome change of pace from the Dalmatian seafood-pasta-pizza rut. Busy Swiss owner/chef Gildas cooks, while his wife Ruža cheerfully serves a steady stream of return diners. This tiny place—which, in my experience, is just about the only reliably good eatery in town—has just a few indoor and outdoor tables. Even if you're not a vegetarian, it's worth a visit; reserve the day ahead in peak season (60-85-kn main courses, May-Oct Mon-Sat 11:30-22:00, Nov-April generally open Mon-Sat for lunch only, closed Sun year-round, on the restaurant-clogged Prijeko street—near the Pile Gate end of the street, tel. 020/322-088).

Dalmatino offers some of the best traditional Dalmatian cooking in the city—and doesn't charge a premium. South African-Croatian owner Robert prides himself on cooking each dish to order; while this may take a few minutes longer, you can taste the results. While there's no seating on a street or square, you'll find cozy tables tucked along the alley leading to the spacious, classy-but-not-stuffy dining room (45-110-kn pastas, 65-125-kn main dishes, daily 11:00-23:00, Miha Pracata 6, tel. 020/323-070).

Konoba Kamenice, a no-frills fish restaurant, is a local institution offering inexpensive, fresh, and good meals on a charming market square, as central as can be in the Old Town. On the limited menu, the seafood dishes are excellent (try their octopus salad, even if you don't think you like octopus), while the few non-seafood dishes are uninspired. Some of the waitstaff are notorious for their playfully brusque service, but loyal patrons happily put up with it. Arrive early, or you'll have to wait (35-70-kn main courses, daily 8:00-23:00, until 22:00 off-season, Gundulićeva poljana 8, tel. 020/323-682).

Lokanda Peskarija enjoys an enticing setting, with a sea of tables facing the Old Port. Servings are hearty and come in a pot, "home-style." The 70-kn seafood risotto easily feeds two, and sharing is no problem. The menu's tiny—with only seafood options, and not much in the way of vegetables. Locals complain that the quality has taken a nosedive (crank-'em-out food and disinterested service) ever since the restaurant's following has grown and its idyllic dining area has been expanded to the hilt. But for reasonably priced seafood dishes on the water, this remains an acceptable option (60-85-kn main courses, daily 12:00-24:00, very limited indoor seating fills up fast, plenty of outdoor tables—which can also fill up, tel. 020/324-750, no reservations taken in summer).

Lady Pi-Pi, named for a comical, anatomically correct, and slightly off-putting statue out front, sits high above town just inside the wall. The food, prepared on an open grill, is just an excuse to sit out on their terrace, with several tables overlooking the rooftops of Dubrovnik (65-70-kn pastas, 65-110-kn main dishes, daily May-Sept 9:00-24:00, closed Oct-April, Peline b.b., tel. 020/321-288).

Pizza: Dubrovnik seems to have a pizzeria on every corner. Little separates the various options—just look for a menu and outdoor seating option that appeals to you. I've eaten well at **Oliva Pizzeria,** just behind St. Blaise's Church (40-65-kn pizzas, Lučarica 5, daily 10:00-24:00, tel. 020/324-594). Around the side is a handy take-out window for a bite on the go (though **Tutto Bene,** a few blocks down on od Puča, has better take-away slices). Close to the Old Town, but just far away to be frequented mostly by locals, **Tabasco Pizzeria** is tucked at the corner of the parking lot beneath the cable-car station. Unpretentious and affordable, this is the place to come if the pizza is more important than the setting—though the outdoor terrace does have views of the Old Town walls...over a sea of parked cars (40-50-kn pizzas, 70-80-kn "jumbo" pizzas, daily 9:00-23:00, Hvarska 48A, tel. 020/429-595).

Pasta: **Spaghetteria Toni** is popular with natives and tourists. While nothing fancy, it offers good pastas at reasonable prices. Choose between the cozy 10-table interior or the long alley filled with outdoor tables (45-80-kn pastas, 45-65-kn salads, daily in summer 11:00-23:00, closed Sun in winter, closed Jan, Nikole Božidarevića 14, tel. 020/323-134).

Bosnian Cuisine: For a break from Croatian fare, consider the grilled meats and other tasty Bosnian dishes at the misnamed **Taj Mahal.** Though the service can be lacking, the menu offers an enticing taste of the Turkish-flavored land to the east. Choose between the tight interior, which feels like a Bosnian tea house, or tables out on the alley (40-55-kn salads, 50-120-kn main courses, daily 10:00-24:00, Nikole Gučetića 2, tel. 020/323-221). For a primer on

Bosnian food, see the "Balkan Flavors" sidebar on page 418.

Sandwiches: **Buffet Škola** is a rare bit of pre-glitz Dubrovnik just a few steps off the Stradun, serving take-away or sit-down sandwiches on homemade bread. Squeeze into the hole-in-the-wall interior, or sit at one of the outdoor tables (25-30 kn, 60-80-kn plates, daily 8:00-22:00 or 23:00, Antuninska 1, tel. 020/321-096).

Pub Grub: **The Gaffe Irish Pub** offers a break from traditional Dalmatian food, with a simple menu of British Isles-style pub food, including burgers and some international flavors (Thai curry, tandoori, and so on). It isn't exactly high cuisine...but at least it's a break from seafood risotto (40-52-kn light meals, 50-90-kn big meals, open long hours daily, Miha Pracata 4, mobile 098-196-2149).

Ice Cream: Dubrovnik has lots of great *sladoled*, but locals swear by the stuff at **Dolce Vita** (daily 9:00-24:00, a half-block off the Stradun at Nalješkovićeva 1A, tel. 020/321-666).

Other Desserts: Two good dessert shops in Dubrovnik have been getting raves from locals and visitors. If you have a sweet tooth, drop by one or both to survey their display cases (12-20-kn cakes). They're within a few short blocks of each other: **Sugar and Spice** (pink-and-stone hole-in-the-wall, "global desserts with a Dalmatian twist," Mon-Sat 9:00-22:00, Sun 11:00-19:00, Sv. Josipa 5, mobile 091-361-9550) and **Pupica** (also has good coffee drinks, long hours daily, Cvijete Zuzorić b.b., mobile 099-216-545).

The Old Town's "Restaurant Row," Prijeko Street: The street called Prijeko, a block toward the mainland from the Stradun promenade, is lined with outdoor, tourist-oriented eateries—each one with a huckster out front trying to lure in diners. (Many of them aggressively try to snare passersby down on the Stradun, as well.) Don't be sucked into this vortex of bad food at outlandish prices. The only place worth seeking out here is Nishta (described earlier); the rest are virtually guaranteed to disappoint. Still, it can be fun to take a stroll along here—the atmosphere is lively, and the sales pitches are entertainingly desperate.

Just Outside the Old Town, with a View

Orhan Restaurant, overlooking the tranquil cove at the Pile neighborhood outside the Old Town, feels just beyond the tourist crush. It features disinterested service and unremarkable food, but great views on a large terrace (reserve a seat here in advance). Watch the people walk the Old Town walls across the cove. This is a handy spot for a scenic breakfast (75-100-kn pastas, 80-180-kn main courses, daily 8:00-23:00, cash only, Od Tabakarije 1, tel. 020/414-183).

Komarda serves up forgettable food on a memorably romantic terrace, with views of Dubrovnik's walls and Old Port. Tables are scattered around a tranquil garden just above the sea and a concrete beach. As there's no point eating here unless you have a good view, consider dropping by early in the day to pick out and reserve the table of your choice for dinner (50-80-kn pastas, 75-135-kn main courses, 60-kn lunch special, daily 7:00-2:00 in the morning, reservations essential in summer, mobile 098-428-239). To find it, exit the Old Town through the Ploče Gate (east). After walking through the final fortification, you'll reach a block of travel agencies. Once you pass these, look for the stairs down to Komarda, on the right.

Picnic Tips

Dubrovnik's lack of great restaurant options makes it a perfect place to picnic. You can shop for fresh fruits and veggies at the open-air produce market (each morning near the cathedral, on the square called Gundulićeva Poljana). Supplement your picnic with grub from the cheap **Konzum grocery store** (one location on the market square near the produce-vendors: Mon-Sat 7:00-21:00, Sun 7:00-13:00; another near the bus stop just outside Pile Gate: Mon-Sat 7:00-21:00, Sun 8:00-13:00). Good picnic spots include the shaded benches overlooking the Old Port; the Porporela breakwater (beyond the Old Port and fort—comes with a swimming area, sunny no-shade benches, and views of Lokrum Island); and the green, welcoming park in what was the moat just under the Pile Gate entry to the Old Town.

Breakfast

If you're sleeping in a *soba*, you'll likely be on your own for breakfast. Fortunately, you have plenty of cafés and pastry shops to choose from, and your host probably has a favorite she can recommend. In the Old Town, **Dubrava Bistro**—which locals call "Snack Bar"—has great views and fine outdoor seating at the most colorful end of the Stradun. While the ham resembles Spam and the continental breakfast is paltry, you can't beat the real estate. Locals who hang out here—catching up with their friends as they stroll by—call this their low-tech version of "Facebook" (basic 38-46-kn egg dishes, 24-kn caffè lattes; you'll pay 25 percent less if you sit inside—but then there's no point eating here; daily 8:00-24:00, Placa 6, tel. 020/321-229). For better food in a less atmospheric setting, **The Gaffe Irish Pub** has a good menu of breakfast options (30-42 kn, served daily 9:00-11:30, Miha Pracata 4, mobile 098-196-2149). In the Pile neighborhood, I like **Restaurant Orhan,** right on the cove (described earlier; 50 kn for omelet or continental breakfast, served daily 8:00-11:00). Some of the other restaurants listed in this section (including **Konoba Kamenice**) also serve breakfast. Not many places serve before 9:00 or 10:00; if you'll be departing early, stock up on groceries the night before.

DUBROVNIK

On Lapad Bay

If you want a break from the Old Town, consider venturing
to Lapad Bay. The ambience is pleasant and Lapad is worth an
evening stroll (for details on getting here, see page 338 under
"Sleeping in Dubrovnik"). This area's main drag, **Šetalište Kralja
Zvonimira,** is an amazingly laid-back pedestrian lane where bars
have hammocks, Internet terminals are scattered through a forested park, and a folksy Croatian family ambience holds its own
against the better-funded force of international tourism. Stroll
from near Hotel Zagreb to the bay, marked by Hotel Kompas.
From Hotel Kompas, a romantic walk—softly lit at night—leads
past some splurge restaurants along the bay through the woods,
with plenty of private little stone coves for lingering.

Dubrovnik Connections

Note that the boats listed here leave from Dubrovnik's Port Gruž, a
bus ride away from the Old Town (described earlier, under "Arrival
in Dubrovnik—By Car Ferry or Catamaran"). Be aware that eventual redevelopment of the port area will likely move the Jadrolinija
ferries and *Nona Ana* catamaran departure point out to the far end
of the port, under the big bridge. If I've listed a range of prices, the
specific fare depends on the season.

From Dubrovnik by Big Jadrolinija Car Ferry: From June
to September only, the big boats leave Dubrovnik twice weekly
in the morning and go to **Sobra** on Mljet Island (1.25 hours, plus
a 1.25-hour bus ride to the national park, 75-90 kn), **Korčula** (4.5
hours, 90-110 kn), **Stari Grad** on Hvar Island (8.75 hours, 110-130
kn), **Split** (11 hours, 110-130 kn), and **Rijeka** (21 hours including
overnight from Split to Rijeka, 215-255 kn). These ferries do not
run October through May, and the price range depends on the
season. However, boat schedules are subject to change—confirm
your plans at a local TI, or see www.jadrolinija.hr.

From Dubrovnik by Speedy *Nona Ana* Catamaran: This
handy service connects Dubrovnik to popular islands to the north
(Mljet, Korčula, and Lastovo). This schedule is subject to change
from year to year, so carefully confirm the details before planning
your trip. In the summer (June-Sept), the boat departs Dubrovnik
each morning and heads for **Sobra** (1.5 hours, 40 kn) and **Polače**
(1.75 hours, 54 kn) on Mljet Island. In the peak months of July
and August, it sometimes continues on to **Korčula** (4/week, 2.75
hours, 58 kn) and **Lastovo Island** (2/week, 4 hours, 68 kn). In the
winter (Oct-May), the boat goes each afternoon at 14:30 to Sobra
and Polače on Mljet, but does not go all the way to Korčula or
Lastovo. The catamaran leaves from Dubrovnik's Port Gruž (buy
tickets at the kiosk next to the boat, ticket window opens 1 hour

before departure; in peak season, it's smart to show up about an hour ahead to be sure you get on the boat). Confirm schedules at the Dubrovnik TI, or check www.gv-line.hr.

By Bus to: Split (almost hourly, generally at the top of each hour, less off-season, 3.5-5 hours, 100 kn), **Korčula** (summer: 2/day at 9:00 and 15:00; off-season: Mon-Sat 1/day at 15:00, Sun 2/day at 15:00 and 18:00; 3.5 hours, 90 kn; also consider the shuttle-bus service described next), **Rijeka** (5/day, 12.5-13 hours, 410-510 kn), **Zagreb** (7/day including some overnight options, 10 hours, 200-220 kn), **Kotor** in Montenegro (2/day, 2.5 hours, 90-110 kn), **Mostar** (5/day in summer, 3/day in winter, 4-5 hours, 80-115 kn), **Sarajevo** (2/day at 8:00 and 15:15, 5-6.5 hours, 245-255 kn; also a night bus at 21:00; only 1/day in winter), **Pula** and **Rovinj** (nightly, 15 hours to Pula, 16 hours to Rovinj). As usual, schedules are subject to change—confirm locally before making the trip to the bus station. For bus information, call 060-305-070 (a pricey toll line, but worth it).

By Shuttle Bus to Korčula: Korčula-based Korkyra Info Travel Agency runs a handy door-to-door shuttle service from your Dubrovnik accommodations to Korčula (departs at various times—call to ask and to reserve, may stop briefly in Ston if you want, by request only Nov-Feb, 2 hours, 150 kn one-way, mobile 091-571-4355, www.korkyra.info, info@korkyra.info).

By Plane: To quickly connect remote Dubrovnik with the rest of your trip, consider a cheap flight. For information on Dubrovnik's airport, see "Arrival in Dubrovnik—By Plane," earlier.

By Car: For tips on driving along the Dalmatian Coast between Dubrovnik and Split, see page 230 in the Split chapter.

Can I Get to Greece from Dubrovnik? Not easily. Your best bet is to fly (though there are no direct flights, aside from the occasional charter flight from Dubrovnik to Athens—you'll generally have to transfer elsewhere in Europe). Even though Croatia and Greece are nearly neighbors, no direct boats connect them, and the overland connection is extremely long and rugged.

What About Italy? Flying is the easiest option, though there are only a few direct flights (on Croatia Airlines to Rome, Venice, or Milan; or on easyJet to Rome or Milan). You can take a direct night boat from Dubrovnik to Bari, or head to Split for more boat connections (for more on all of these boats, see page 225). The overland connection is overly long (figure 5 hours to Split, then 5 hours to Zagreb, then 7 hours to Venice).

NEAR DUBROVNIK

Excursions from Dubrovnik's Old Port • Cavtat • Trsteno Arboretum • Pelješac Peninsula • Mljet National Park

The more time you spend here, the clearer it becomes: Dubrovnik isn't just a town, it's an entire region. Stretching up and down the glimmering Dalmatian Coast from Dubrovnik are a variety of worthwhile getaways. Just off-shore from the city's Old Town—and accessible via scenic boat trip from its historic port—are enticing islands and villages, where time stands still for lazy vacationers: the playground islet of Lokrum and the sight-studded archipelago of the Elaphite Islands. The serene resort town of Cavtat, just south of Dubrovnik, has some of the best art treasures of this part of Dalmatia (including a gorgeous mausoleum designed by Ivan Meštrović). To the north is a lush arboretum called Trsteno, with a playful fountain, a 600-year-old aqueduct, a villa, a chapel...and, of course, plants galore. Poking into the Adriatic is the vineyard-covered Pelješac Peninsula, anchored by the mighty little town of Ston. And out at sea is the sparsely populated island called Mljet, a third of which is carefully protected as one of Croatia's most appealing national parks, where you can hike, bike, boat, and swim to your heart's content. Best of all, there's no better place to "come home to" than Dubrovnik—after a busy day exploring the coastline, strolling the Stradun to unwind is particularly sweet.

Planning Your Time

Give yourself at least a full day and two nights to experience Dubrovnik itself. But if you can spare the time, set up in Dubrovnik for several nights and use your extra days for some of these excursions. (This also gives you the luxury of keeping an eye on the weather reports and saving the most weather-dependent

NEAR DUBROVNIK

Dubrovnik Day Trips at a Glance

The international excursions to Bosnia-Herzegovina and Montenegro—which are worth considering for overnight stops—are covered in their own chapters.

In Bosnia-Herzegovina

▲▲▲**Mostar** The side-trip with the highest degree of cultural hairiness—but, for many, also the most rewarding—lies to the east, in Bosnia-Herzegovina. With its iconic Old Bridge, intriguing glimpse of European Muslim lifestyles, and still-vivid examples of war damage, Mostar is unforgettable. Though not for everyone, this trip is a

must for adventurous travelers interested in Islam or in recent history. Allow a full day or more (best reached by bus or car).

Međugorje Devout Catholics may want to consider a trip to this pilgrimage site in Bosnia-Herzegovina, with a holy hill that some believe is visited regularly by an apparition of the Virgin Mary. Allow a full day or more (best reached by car or bus).

In Montenegro

▲▲**The Bay of Kotor** For rugged coastal scenery that arguably rivals anything in Croatia, head south of the border to Montenegro. The Bay of Kotor is a dramatic, fjord-like inlet crowned by the historic town of Kotor, with twisty Old World lanes, one of Europe's best town walls, and oodles of atmosphere. Allow a full day or more (best reached by car or bus).

The Montenegrin Interior A visit to Montenegro's scruffy but historic former capital, Cetinje, comes with a twisty drive up a mountain road and across a desolate, forgotten-feeling plateau. Allow a full day or more (best reached by car).

Budva Riviera Montenegro's best stretch of sandy beaches isn't worth a special trip, but it's a fun excuse for a drive if you've got extra time to kill. The highlight is the famous resort peninsula of Sveti Stefan. Allow a full day or more (best reached by car).

On the Mainland near Dubrovnik

▲**Cavtat** A charming resort/beach town, unassuming Cavtat holds a pair of wonderful and very local art experiences: an elaborate mausoleum designed by the sculptor Ivan Meštrović, and the house and museum of Cavtat-born modern painter Vlaho

Bukovac. Allow a few hours (best reached by boat or bus).

▲**Pelješac Peninsula** This long, narrow spit of land—between the main coastal road and Korčula Island—is a favorite of wine-lovers, who can joyride through its vineyards and sample its product. Allow a half-day to a full day (best reached by car).

Trsteno Arboretum Plant-lovers will enjoy this surprisingly engaging botanical garden just outside Dubrovnik, punctuated by a classical-style fountain and aqueduct. Allow a half-day (best reached by bus or car).

Ston A small town with giant fortifications, Ston (on the Pelješac Peninsula) is worth a short stop to scramble up its extensive walls. Allow an hour (best reached by car or bus).

Off the Coast of Dubrovnik

▲**Mljet National Park** While this largely undeveloped island is time-consuming to reach from Dubrovnik, Mljet offers an opportunity to romp on an island without all those tacky tourist towns. This is for serious nature-lovers eager to get away from civilization. Allow a full day (best reached by boat).

Lokrum Island The most convenient excursion from Dubrovnik, this little island—just a short hop offshore from the Old Port—is a good chance to get away from (some of) the tourists. Allow a few hours (best reached by boat).

Elaphite Islands This inviting archipelago offers a variety of island experiences without straying too far from Dubrovnik. With more time, Korčula (for a small town) or Mljet (for a back-to-nature experience) is better, but the "Elafiti" (as they're known) are more convenient. Allow a half-day to a full day (best reached by boat).

NEAR DUBROVNIK

Near Dubrovnik

[Map showing region near Dubrovnik with locations including:]
To Sarajevo • Foča • BOSNIA-HERZEGOVINA • Mostar • Neretva • To Split • Makarska • MEĐUGORJE • Buna • Nevesinje • Drvenik • Vrgorac • Ploče • Čapljina • Počitelj • Gacko • NERETVA DELTA • Metković • Stolac • To Split • CROATIA • Ljubinje • Bileća • MONTENEGRO • Orebić • Neum • Mali Ston • Trebinje • Korčula • Pelješac Peninsula • Ston • Korčula • Polače • Trsteno • Trsteno Arboretum • Pomena • Sobra • Elaphite Islands • Dubrovnik • Lastovo • Mljet National Park • Lokrum • Ćilipi • KONAVLE • Kotor • Podgorica • Herceg Novi • Cetinje • Cavtat • Bay of Kotor • Budva • Budva Riviera • Sveti Stefan • To Bari, Italy

50 Kilometers
25 Miles

activities for the sunniest days.) For suggestions on how much time to allow per destination, see the sidebar on page 346. Use a map to strategically line up these attractions—for example, you can easily do Trsteno, Ston, and the Pelješac Peninsula on a drive between Dubrovnik and Korčula, while Cavtat pairs nicely with a trip to the airport or Montenegro.

I've listed these day trips in order of ease from Dubrovnik—the farther down the list, the more difficult to reach (Montenegro and Mostar, the most time-consuming, are covered in their own chapters). Choose the trips that sound best to you, and ask locals and other travelers for their impressions...or for new leads.

Getting There

Lokrum, Cavtat, and the Elaphite Islands are easy to reach by **excursion boat** from Dubrovnik's Old Port; Cavtat also works by bus. The other destinations are farther afield, best reached by **boat** (Mljet) or by **car** or **bus** (Montenegro, Mostar, Trsteno, Pelješac Peninsula). I've listed public transportation options for each, but consider renting a car for the day—or even splurging for your own private driver (see page 294).

Alternatively, the big Atlas Travel Agency in Dubrovnik offers **guided excursions** (by bus and/or boat) to nearby destinations. Popular itineraries include everything mentioned in this chapter, plus Korčula and others (figure €30-100/person, depending on the itinerary; book tickets at Atlas in Dubrovnik—see page 293—or at other travel agencies; Atlas tel. 020/442-574, www.atlas-croatia .com). While these excursions can be a convenient way to see otherwise difficult-to-reach destinations, the experience is generally disappointing. I've been on two of these trips, and have gotten reports about several others. The consensus is that the buses are packed, the guides are uninspired (reading from a dull script— often in multiple languages), and quality time at the destinations is short. If you have no other way to reach a place you're dying to visit, guided excursions can be worth considering. But explore your other options first—consider renting a car for the day or hiring your own driver (expensive, but less so if you can split the cost with other travelers).

Excursions run by **other companies** can be smaller, more personalized, and more satisfying than Atlas' big-bus tours. Unfortunately, since this scene is constantly evolving, it's difficult to recommend one company in particular. Look around for flyers and ask locals for their best tips—but be aware that many smaller agencies simply sell seats on the big Atlas trips.

Excursions from Dubrovnik's Old Port

At Dubrovnik's salty Old Port, local captains set up tiny booths to hawk touristy boat trips. It's fun to chat with them, page through their sun-faded photo albums, and see if they can sell you on a short cruise. The basic option is a 50-minute "panorama cruise" out into the water and back again (75 kn, departures every hour). Among your vessel choices is the **Sv. Ivan,** a cargo boat dating from 1878. Or consider visiting one of the following destinations.

In addition to the islands noted below, you can also take a boat from the Old Port to **Cavtat** (described later).

Lokrum Island
This island, just offshore from the Old Town, provides a handy escape from the city. Lokrum features a monastery-turned-Habsburg-palace, a small botanical garden, an old military fort, hiking trails, a café, some rocky beaches, and a little lake called

the "Dead Sea" (Mrtvo More) that's suitable for swimming. Since the 1970s, when Lokrum became the "Island of Love," it's been known for its nude sunbathing. If you'd like to (carefully) subject skin that's never seen the sun to those burning rays, follow the *FKK* signs from the boat dock for about five minutes to the slabs

of waterfront rock, where naturists feel right at home. Boats run regularly from Dubrovnik's Old Port (50 kn round-trip, 10 kn for a map, runs April-Sept, 2/hour, 9:00-17:00, mid-June-Aug until 19:00, none Oct-March).

Elaphite Islands (Elafiti)

This archipelago, just north of Dubrovnik, is popular among day-trippers because you can hit three different islands in a single day. The main island, **Lopud,** has most of the attractions: a lively little town, boat and bike rental, and some rare sandy beaches. The other two islands—**Koločep** and **Šipan**—are less developed and (for some) a bit boring. Along the way, you'll discover fishing ports, shady forests, and forgotten escape mansions of old Dubrovnik aristocracy. The easiest way to cruise the Elafiti is to buy an excursion at Dubrovnik's Old Port, which includes a "fish picnic" cooked up by the captain as you cruise (about 250 kn with lunch, 180 kn without, several boats depart daily around 10:30-11:00, return around 15:45-19:30; so they can buy enough food, companies prefer you to reserve and pay a 50-kn deposit the day before). You generally spend about three hours on Lopud and about an hour each on Koločep and Šipan, with about 2.5 hours on the boat. To get to the Elaphite Islands without a tour (on a cheap ferry), you'll sail from Dubrovnik's less convenient Port Gruž. Note that if you're going to Korčula or Hvar, this trip is redundant—skip it unless you've got time to kill, need a break from Dubrovnik's crowds, and want a lazy day cruising Dalmatia.

Cavtat

This sleepy little resort town—just 12 miles to the south, near the Montenegrin border—offers a milder alternative to bustling Dubrovnik. With its strategic location sheltered inside a nearly 360-degree bay, this settlement was thriving long before there was a Dubrovnik. The Greeks called it Epidaurus, while the Romans called it Epidaurum—but these days, it's Cavtat (TSAV-taht). The town is best known as a handy spot to find a room when Dubrovnik's booked up, and a fun excuse to take a cruise from Dubrovnik's Old Port. Even those suffering from beach-resort fatigue will enjoy a side-trip to Cavtat, if they appreciate local art. The restaurant- and people-lined promenade is inviting, but the town's best features are its two gems of Croatian art: a breathtaking hilltop mausoleum by the great Croatian sculptor Ivan Meštrović, and the former home-turned-museum of the Cavtat-born, early 20th-century painter Vlaho Bukovac.

Getting to Cavtat

Boats to Cavtat leave about hourly from Dubrovnik's Old Port (80 kn round-trip, 50 kn one-way, about 45 minutes each way, hourly return boats from Cavtat). The boat deposits you right along Cavtat's main seafront promenade. Note that a round-trip ticket is cheaper, but you'll have to return with the same company (rather than on whichever boat is leaving next).

You can also reach Cavtat by public **bus #10**, which leaves from Dubrovnik's main bus station and also stops at the "cable car" bus stop above the Old Town (1-2/hour, 30-40 minutes, 17 kn). The bus brings you to Cavtat's parking lot (described next). For variety, consider going to Cavtat by boat (buy a one-way ticket), then returning by bus.

Drivers find Cavtat an easy detour when heading to points south, including Montenegro or the airport; the town is well-signed off the main road. The big parking lot is at the back of Cavtat's peninsula, just around the corner from the main part of town and seafront promenade: Just walk past the TI, hook right at the busy street, and head for the waterfront.

Orientation to Cavtat

Cavtat is set within an idyllic, horseshoe-shaped harbor hemmed in by a pair of peninsulas. Tucked around the back side of the peninsula is the parking lot, left-luggage office *(garderoba)*, and **TI** (July-Aug daily 8:00-21:00; Sept and June daily 8:00-20:00; May and Oct Mon-Sat 8:00-19:00, Sun 8:00-14:00; Nov-April

Mon-Fri 8:00-15:00, closed Sat-Sun; Zidine 6, tel. 020/479-025, www.tzcavtat-konavle.hr). Cavtat is basically a one-street town, but that street is a fine pedestrian promenade running along the harbor, with a few narrow lanes winding steeply up into the hill. Capping the hill above town is a cemetery with the Meštrović mausoleum.

Sights in Cavtat

NEAR DUBROVNIK

Waterfront Wander—Strolling along Cavtat's waterfront, you'll be immersed in a wrap-around bay and surrounded by Europeans vacationing well. At the near end of the promenade, notice the big water polo court roped off in the bay; Cavtat and Dubrovnik provide the core for the Croatian national water-polo team. Across the street is **St. Nicholas Church,** with a humble, dull interior (though hanging high in the altar area are Bukovac paint-

ings of the four evangelists). Next door is the skippable **Baltazar Bogišić Collection,** a museum with a library and other items once belonging to a wealthy lawyer. About halfway along the drag, one of the narrow lanes leading up the hill (appropriately named Bukovčeva) takes you to the fine **Vlaho Bukovac House** (described next). At the end of the main waterfront area is the **Church of Our Lady of the Snows,** commemorating a freak (and seemingly miraculous) mid-summer snowstorm in ancient Rome, believed to have been a sign sent by the Virgin Mary. Inside, above the altar, is a Vlaho Bukovac painting (from 1909) of Mary and the Baby Jesus watching over Cavtat. Climbing the steep steps up to the right of the church leads you up to Ivan Meštrović's **Račić Mausoleum** (described later). With more time, consider continuing your walk around the peninsula to its pointy tip for distant views of Dubrovnik's Old Town. This is one of the favorite spots in this area for watching the sunset. (If you continue all the way around the point, in about 20 minutes you'll wind up back at the parking lot at the start of town.)

▲**Vlaho Bukovac House (Kuća Bukovac)**—One of the joys of traveling is getting the opportunity to learn about locally beloved artists who are little known outside their homelands. Cavtat proudly introduces you to native son Vlaho Bukovac (1855-1922), who grew up in this very house and went on to become the most important Croatian painter of the modern period. Bukovac moved to New York City with his uncle at age 11, beginning a life of great adventure. After a brief career as a sailor (traveling to Peru and San Francisco), he trained as an artist in Paris, then in Zagreb. For his last 20 years, Bukovac spent his summers in Prague and his winters here in Cavtat. Touring the collection (with good English explanations), you'll get to know Bukovac's life and his works. Bukovac's paintings are mostly realistic (in accordance with his formal Salon training in Paris), but shimmer with a hint of

Post-Impressionism; his later works echo the slinky Art Nouveau Slavic pride of the Czech painter Alfons Mucha, who was Bukovac's contemporary. The ground floor displays photos of his

early life; upstairs you'll find old furniture, early sketches, and portraits of Bukovac and his family (the painting of his children's disembodied heads hanging on the wall is macabre but strangely tender). The top floor houses one big atelier room filled with canvases from various periods, allowing you to survey his impressive artistic development with a sweep of the head. Throughout the house are murals painted by Bukovac in his early days, offering a glimpse of a burgeoning artist who would go on to make Cavtat very proud.

Cost and Hours: 20 kn, good 40-kn guidebook; May-Oct Tue-Sat 9:00-13:00 & 16:00-20:00, Sun 16:00-20:00, closed Mon; Nov-April Tue-Sat 9:00-13:00 & 14:00-17:00, Sun 14:00-17:00, closed Mon; Bukovčeva 5, tel. 020/478-646, www.kuca-bukovac.hr.

▲▲Račić Family Mausoleum (Mauzolej Obitelji Račić)— This harmonious masterwork of Croatia's greatest artist is the gem of Cavtat, and worth ▲▲▲ to fans of Ivan Meštrović's powerful

sculptures. To learn more about Meštrović before you visit, read the sidebar on page 208.

Cost and Hours: 10 kn, Mon-Sat 10:00-17:00, closed Sun and mid-Oct-mid-April. If she's not too busy, helpful Nena will

show you around.

Getting There: Capping the hill above town, it's a steep 10-minute walk from the Cavtat waterfront. From the Church of Our Lady of Snows at the far end of the waterfront, climb up the stairs (following *mauzolej* signs).

Touring the Mausoleum: Over the course of one tragic year, all four members of the wealthy Račić family—father, mother, son, daughter—died of the Spanish flu. From 1920-1922, in accordance with their will, Ivan Meštrović was commissioned to craft their final resting place. He used the opportunity to create a cohesive meditation on Christian faith and death, made entirely of brilliant white stone from the island of Brač. As you enter, take a moment to appreciate how the interior ponders birth, life, and death. The four inner walls of the octagonal hall hold the tombs of the departed; above each tomb, an angel lovingly carries their soul up to heaven—spiriting them into a cupola studded with angel heads. The floor has symbols for the four

evangelists: Matthew (angel), Mark (lion), Luke (bull), and John (eagle). The chapel to the left holds a crucifix; to the right, an altar to St. Rok (the patron saint of illness, to whom the chapel is dedicated—the dog licking the wound in his leg is his symbol). Straight ahead is an altar with Mary holding the Baby Jesus above a relief of the Lamb of God, and below that, Jesus' body being taken down from the cross. Flanking this altar, notice the bases of the twisting candelabras: alternating angels look down to honor the dead. The chapel rewards those who linger over the details, such as the bronze doors, with four saints, Glagolitic inscriptions, and the 12 Apostles. The saints chosen for this door preach both ecumenism and Yugoslav unity: Cyril and Method (the Byzantine missionaries who first brought Christianity to this region), along with a Catholic bishop (Bishop Gregory of Nin) and an Orthodox saint (St. Sava). Taken together, the mausoleum is an astonishing display of talent, especially considering it was Meštrović's first architectural work.

Nearby: The mausoleum sits in the middle of a tranquil cemetery that's still used for the funerals of Cavtat residents (a plot costs €20,000). As you exit the mausoleum, head straight out and a bit to the right to find two communal graves for the poor—with smaller markers lined up along a large plinth. Also in this cemetery is the grave of the artist Vlaho Bukovac.

Near Cavtat

A village near Cavtat, **Čilipi,** hosts a Sunday-morning folk festival through the summer (Easter-Oct, starting at 9:00). There's a special Mass at the church, an open-air market, and—starting at 11:15—a costumed folk-dancing show (tel. 020/771-007, www .cilipifolklor.hr).

Trsteno Arboretum

Take a stroll through the shaded, relaxing botanical garden in Trsteno (worth ▲), just up the coast from Dubrovnik. Non-gardeners may find it a bit dull, but Trsteno is a horticultural-

ist's heaven. Spread over 63 acres on a bluff overlooking the sea, this arboretum features hundreds of different Mediterranean, Asian, and American plants (each one labeled in six languages, including English). The whole complex is laced with easy footpaths and sprinkled with fun attractions—a column-studded Renaissance Garden, a desolate villa, a little chapel, an old mill and olive-oil press, and a seaview pavilion.

As you wander, the world melts away and you're alone with the sounds of nature: wind, water, birds, and frogs. The garden's centerpiece is the whimsical 18th-century Neptune Fountain, featuring the god of the sea flanked by water-spouting nymphs and fishes, and holding court over a goldfish-stocked, lily-padded pond. Circling around behind the fountain, you'll discover that it's fed by an impressive 230-foot-long aqueduct that was built in the 15th-century.

Cost and Hours: 35 kn, daily May-Oct 8:00-19:00, Nov-April 8:00-16:00, tel. 020/751-019.

Nearby: On the waterfront below the arboretum, next to the little village harbor, you'll see the shell of a once-grand 18th-century palace, which was damaged during the siege of Dubrovnik and is now abandoned. It's still owned by the government, but investors are lin-ing up for a chance to buy this prime real estate—possibly the most desirable ruin in Croatia.

Getting There: Trsteno works best with a car, particularly if you're taking your time driving to Dubrovnik from the north (the main coastal road goes through the town of Trsteno, right past the well-marked arboretum). You also have two bus options from Dubrovnik (around 20 kn, 20-30 minutes). Any long-distance northbound bus can drop you in Trsteno—ask about the next bus at the main station. Alternatively, the slower local buses #12 and #15 also reach Trsteno. Coming back from Trsteno to Dubrovnik is trickier: Wait at the bus stop with the glass canopy by the park entrance and wave down any Dubrovnik-bound bus that passes (at least hourly).

Pelješac Peninsula

North of Trsteno, the skinny, 55-mile-long Pelješac (PEHL-yeh-shahts) Peninsula—practically an honorary island—splits off from the Croatian coastline as if about to drift away to Italy. (The far tip of Pelješac comes within a stone's throw of Korčula island.) This sparsely populated peninsula, famous for its rugged terrain—and the grapes that thrive here—is worth a detour for wine-lovers. But its heavily fortified town of Ston, just a short side-trip from the main coastal road, merits a stretch-your-legs visit for anyone. Notice that if you're connecting from Korčula to anywhere else in Croatia by car, you'll probably be taking the ferry to the Pelješac Peninsula anyway; consider slowing down to sample a few wines, to scramble up the walls at Ston, or to have a meal at Mali Ston.

Getting There: Buses between Dubrovnik and Korčula traverse the Pelješac Peninsula, but drivers have the option of stopping where they like (such as at Ston or a winery). Some public buses also stop at Ston.

Ston

The town of Ston, at the base of the peninsula, is the gateway to Pelješac. This "Great Wall of Croatia" town is famous for the impressive wall that climbs up the mountain behind it (about a half-mile encloses the town itself, while another three miles clamber up the hillsides). The unassuming town was heavily fortified (starting in 1333) for two reasons: to defend its strategic location, where mountains and bays create  a bottleneck along the road from Dubrovnik to Pelješac, near the Republic of Dubrovnik's northern boundary; and to protect its impressive salt pans, which still produce salt. Filling a low-lying plain that sprawls in front of Ston's doorstep, these pans provided

A Bridge Too Far?

If you're driving along the coast between Split and Dubrovnik, you may be surprised when you have to stop and show your passport to enter another country—Bosnia-Herzegovina, around the resort town of Neum. How is it that Bosnia wound up with its very own five-and-a-half-mile stretch of the Dalmatian Coast? During the heyday of the Republic of Dubrovnik, the city's leaders granted this land to the Ottoman Empire to provide a buffer between Dubrovnik's holdings and the Republic of Venice, to the north. (They knew the Venetians would never enter the territory of the Ottomans—their feared enemy—in order to invade Dubrovnik.) Later, as the borders of Europe were being redrawn in modern times, Bosnia retained possession of this strip of land as a sort of inheritance from their former rulers.

For years, coastal Bosnians and their Croatian neighbors have coexisted, albeit tensely at times. Prices for hotel rooms, groceries, and other staples are slightly cheaper in Neum, whose rest stops lure tourist buses with low prices and generous kickbacks for bus drivers. Visitors are inconvenienced by having to go through a passport checkpoint as they enter Bosnia and again, just a few minutes later, as they exit Bosnia. From a practical standpoint, this is rarely an issue. But on busy days, there can be lines, and it's always smart to have your passport and rental car's "green card" (proof of insurance) ready.

Croatians are irritated with the red tape, and—even more—by the way Neum merchants undersell the Croatian alternatives nearby. As Croatia extends its expressway southward, the most logical approach would be a route through Bosnia to Dubrovnik. But some Croatian politicians have been looking for a way to avoid Neum altogether. One solution is to build a 1.5-mile-long bridge from just north of Neum to the Pelješac Peninsula, then re-join the coastal road back in Croatia, just south of Neum—effectively bypassing Bosnian territory. Environmentalists worry about the impact the bridge will have on the ecosystem around Mali Ston. But, because of the proposed bridge's popularity with a certain segment of the voting population, work actually began on this project prior to a recent election (notice that one mountaintop on Pelješac has already been cleared). After the election—and with the global economic crisis—plans were put on hold. It remains to be seen whether this very expensive project will ever come to fruition...and if so, whether the bridge will be completed before Croatia and Bosnia both join the EU and open their borders anyway.

Dubrovnik with much of its wealth, back in the days when salt was worth more than its weight in gold. The pans would be flooded with saltwater, then sealed and left to evaporate—leaving the salt easy to harvest.

Today, the sleepy town—with more than its share of outdoor cafés and restaurants—is notable only for the chance to scramble up its massive **fortifications** (park your car in the big lot, then cross the street into town and look right; the entrance to the walls is in the big tower). These walls have been undergoing an extensive restoration, and the long, skinny strip running over the ridge to the town of Mali Ston (described

next) is already complete. For a short wall experience, you can just do a circle around the stout lower walls (about 20-30 minutes); for a more serious hike, you can climb all the way up and over to Mali Ston (figure 45-60 minutes). Be warned that the walls—with all that glistening limestone reflecting heat—are much hotter than ground level, and there's virtually no shade (30 kn to enter walls regardless of how far you walk, daily May-Sept 8:00-19:00, April and Oct 8:00-18:00, Nov-March generally 9:00-16:00).

Other than the walls, there's not much to do in Ston. The town's deserted feel is a result of a devastating 1996 earthquake, from which Ston is still rebuilding. But there are several inviting cafés for a lazy drink. If you want a meal, skip Ston's mediocre offerings and head over to Mali Ston instead.

Eating near Ston, in Mali Ston: From Ston, the walls scamper over a ridge to its little sister, the bayside village of Mali Ston ("Small Ston"). Surrounded by a similar, but smaller, fortified wall, Mali Ston is known for its many mussel and oyster farms, and for its good restaurants. A local favorite is **Kapetanova Kuća,** a memorable restaurant with a fine location on Mali Ston's waterfront. Celebrity chef Lidija Kralj prides herself on her unpretentious but delicious food, made with fresh produce from the restaurant's own garden. For dessert, her bizarre macaroni cake is tastier than it sounds (10-kn cover charge, 75-100-kn pastas, 100-130-kn seafood and meat dishes, daily 9:00-23:00, tel. 020/754-264).

Pelješac Wine Country

Farther along, the sparsely developed Pelješac Peninsula is blanketed with vineyards. Wine is a big draw here, and several vintners open their doors for passing visitors to sample their products. While it's a bit distant from Dubrovnik (about a two-hour drive to the heart of the wine-producing area), it's a worthwhile pilgrimage for wine-lovers and an easy stop-off for those driving from Korčula.

Tours of Pelješac: To really do the peninsula justice, consider hiring a guide to take you for a spin around Pelješac. **Sasha Lušić,** who runs the D'Vino Wine Bar in Dubrovnik, is a gregarious Aussie-Croat guide. He prides himself on taking you to a wide variety of vintners, who represent the best of what's happening here. Sasha's tours can go late into the evening (also offers cheaper half-day tours to the Molinat area closer to Dubrovnik, www .dvino.net, sasha@dvino.net). Other Dubrovnik-based drivers also do good wine tours (which also include several other worthwhile, scenic stops), including **Petar Vlašić** (see page 295).

● **Self-Guided Driving Tour:** I've arranged this tour in the order you'll come from the tip of Pelješac (Orebić, just across the channel from Korčula). If you're doing it from Dubrovnik, begin by driving all the way to the village of Potomje (you can skip the section between there and Orebić) and visit the wineries on your way back (since it's a long, skinny peninsula, you'll have to backtrack anyway). I've included a detour to some of Croatia's finest (and largely undiscovered) vineyards, and saved the best wines for last. For a primer before you start, see "Croatian Wine" on page 52.

If you're crossing from Korčula Island, you'll begin the tour in **Orebić.** It's basically one main road from here back to Ston (where you'll meet up with the main coastal road to Dubrovnik or Split), so you can't really get lost—though we will make an off-the-beaten-path vineyard detour.

Follow the main road (toward *Ston*) up, up, up to a dramatic **viewpoint** (there's a pullout on the right with benches) looking back toward Korčula. The jagged cliffs to your left are the Pelješac Peninsula (where we're about to drive), and the island straight ahead (left of Korčula) is Mljet National Park. On a clear day, you can almost see to Italy. This also gives you a good view of the two best wine-growing regions of Pelješac: Below you and to the right, you can see some vineyards in the **Postup** region; to the left (not quite visible from here) are the vineyards of **Dingač.** Both areas are steeply angled, so they catch a maximum amount of sun, which creates very sweet grapes that produce high-alcohol, very dark (actually called "black" in Croatian) wine with strong legs (or, as Croatians call them, "tears"). The rugged, rocky limestone provides natural irrigation (since water can flow freely through it), and the high winds here keep off bugs and other pests. It all adds up to extremely healthy vines; because disease is rare, pesticides are not needed.

Continuing along the road, you'll crest the hill and drop down into a **plateau** surrounded by cliffs. The vines you'll see in this so-called "continental" area are the same kind of grapes as in Postup and Dingač, but they receive less sun and are less sweet. These *plavac mali* ("little blue") grapes are a distant relative of California Zinfandel and Italian *primitivo*. Notice that many of the vines appear to be almost wild; these are older vineyards, which aren't irrigated, so they must let the vines grow this way to help them survive the hot summer months. This method maximizes yield but reduces quality. Newer vineyards are irrigated and use guide wires, and generally look more manicured.

Soon you'll arrive in the village of **Potomje,** which is at the center of this important wine-growing area. Several wineries cluster here, including some that are open for tastings and tours. Two are particularly accessible to visitors and—while a bit touristy (with big bus tours passing through occasionally)—offer a helpful introduction to Pelješac wines: Madirazza and Matuško. Both are staffed by friendly  English-speakers who are eager to introduce you to their wines; while the tastings are free, they're hoping you'll buy a bottle or two. Both are open long hours daily (around 8:00-20:00, close earlier in shoulder season, generally closed Nov-March—but call ahead and they may be able to open for you, cash only).

The reds are the real draw here; I'd skip the whites. The wines, which are quite fruity, come in various types. In general, bottles marked with the type of grape *(plavac mali)* are lower-quality, from the vines here in the valley. The ones marked with the specific region (Dingač and Postup) come from the sunny slopes and are of better quality, more full bodied, and more expensive; they go well with red meat and dark chocolate. Both Madirazza and Matuško also have various brandies to try (including *travarica*, an herb-infused brandy).

First, near the far end of town, look for the big, pink building of the **Madirazza** winery. Notice the roses that line the vineyards—like a canary in a coal mine, these are more quickly affected by disease than the vines, offering an early-warning system in the event of an unwanted infestation. Madirazza's fairly acidic wines cost 30-90 kn per bottle (mobile 099-700-5146, www.dingac.hr).

Across the main road from Madirazza's parking lot is a smaller road (marked with a *Matuško* sign) leading to the **Matuško** winery. With smoother wines than Madirazza's, this place also has a sprawling network of atmospheric cellars where tour groups sip wines between aging barrels (20-110-kn bottles, most 20-60 kn, reserve bottles for 150-700 kn, free tastings upstairs, good place for a WC stop, tel. 020/742-399, www.matusko-vina.hr). **Miličić,** also in Potomje, is a well-regarded winery, but its hours are less predictable than Madirazza and Matuško.

Very near the Matuško parking lot, look for the **tunnel** through the mountain marked *Dingač Winery*, with the picture of a donkey. Before this tunnel was dug, beasts of burden trod surefootedly up and over this mountain to carry the grapes from Dingač, on the far side, to this village. The donkey remains a symbol of this wine-growing region. In the 1970s, this tunnel was built to make everyone's lives easier. Take advantage of it by driving through the mountain and into another world.

Popping out at the sea, you're in the heart of the **Dingač** vineyards. Turn left (toward *Borak*) and drive on the one-lane road

above all those vines, with a green and jagged waterline that looks almost Celtic. Croatia's best reds are lovingly raised right here, bathed in ample sunshine and struggling against a very rocky soil. At the fork, continue down to the right, toward *Borak;* at the next fork, when the Borak road

turns sharply to the right, keep going straight onto the smaller road.

As you enter an area of trees, look across the harbor to see a building perched on a cliff over the water—that's our next stop. Turn right to pass through the village of Trstanik and drive along its little waterfront. At the far end of town, on the way up the hill, turn into the parking lot for the **Grgić** winery. Perhaps the best-known and best-regarded Croatian vintner, Mike Grgić's facility here is less appealing than the others

we've visited, and you have to pay for the tasting (20 kn)...but the quality of the wine compensates. Keeping things simple, Grgić does a white wine (*pošip*, with grapes grown on Korčula but produced here, 135 kn per bottle) and a red wine (210 kn per bottle); breaking with convention, he names his red simply *plavac mali* partly to help promote this largely unknown and underappreciated grape (grown here in Trstanik and in Dingač). He also sells wines from his California winery, Grgich Hills, at or below their California prices (230-440 kn). While Grgić's staff doesn't speak

NEAR DUBROVNIK

much English, they enjoy sharing the wines (Mon-Fri 10:00-17:00, sometimes also Sat-Sun—call ahead, tel. 020/748-090).

Exiting the winery, turn right (uphill) and twist up to the main road, where you'll turn right, toward Ston. (Another good winery, **Roso,** is to the left, back toward Potomje in the village of Kuna, but its opening times are unpredictable.) From here, you'll continue straight along all the way to Ston. You may be tempted by the *vino* signs in **Janjina,** but these are geared mainly for Croatians buying table wine in bulk—100 liters at a time. After Drače, the road takes you along the **Bay of Ston,** which is famous for its shell-fish production. Here where the Neretva River (which runs under Mostar's Old Bridge) empties into the sea, conditions are perfect for cultivating mussels, oysters, and clams. You can already see the mainland on the far side of the bay. The road climbs up once more, passing a viewpoint café overlooking the dock for the ferry to the national park on Mljet Island, before continuing into the walled town of Ston. For more on that town—and a good restaurant in nearby Mali Ston—see page 358.

Leaving Ston, turn right (toward Dubrovnik) once you hit the main road; from here, it's about an hour back into town. En route, watch out for the speed traps at the towns of Doli and Orešac.

Mljet National Park

Carefully protected against modern development, the island hideaway of Mljet National Park offers a unique back-to-nature escape. With ample opportunities for hiking, swimming, biking, and boating—and without a nightclub, tacky T-shirt, or concrete "beach" pad in sight—Mljet (muhl-YAYT) is a potential highlight for active, outdoorsy travelers.

Though Mljet Island is one of Dalmatia's largest, it has fewer than 1,500 residents. Nearly three-quarters of the island is covered in forest, leaving it remarkably untamed. Aside from its beautiful national park, Mljet has inspired some of the most memorable tales of the Croatian coast—the poet Homer, his protagonist Ulysses, and the Apostle Paul all spent time here...or so the locals love to boast.

Many Croatians swoon over Mljet. Take it with a grain of salt. They appreciate it primarily for its relative lack of people. One local told me, "Mljet is basically Hvar or Korčula with no towns." For foreign visitors, the park, while enjoyable, is a bit overrated. Still, if a peaceful, uncrowded island sounds like your kind of scene, make the trip.

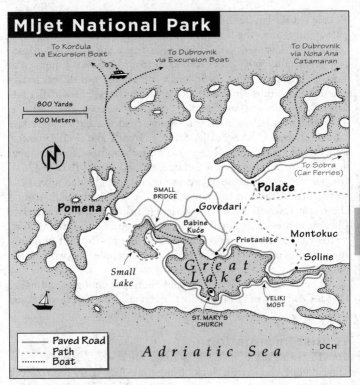

Mljet National Park

To Korčula via Excursion Boat

To Dubrovnik via Excursion Boat

To Dubrovnik via *Nona Ana* Catamaran

800 Yards
800 Meters

To Sobra (Car Ferries)

SMALL BRIDGE

Polače

Pomena

Govedari

Babine Kuće

Pristanište

Montokuc

*G r e a t
L a k e*

*Small
Lake*

Soline

VELIKI MOST

ST. MARY'S CHURCH

A d r i a t i c   S e a

DCH

Paved Road
Path
Boat

NEAR DUBROVNIK

Planning Your Time

Thanks to a handy catamaran connection, Mljet works perfectly as a full-day side-trip from Dubrovnik (only possible in summer). But because of inconvenient boat schedules to other destinations, it's challenging to splice it into a one-way itinerary (say, between Korčula and Dubrovnik). So if you want to visit Mljet, either do it as a day trip on your own from Dubrovnik, or buy a package day-trip excursion from Korčula, Hvar, or Split. For details, see "Mljet Connections," at the end of this chapter.

No matter how you arrive, one day is plenty for Mljet. I've suggested a day-trip plan under "Sights on Mljet."

Be warned that everything's very seasonal and weather-dependent, so visiting outside of peak season (June-Sept) may come with some frustration.

Orientation to Mljet

The island of Mljet is long (23 miles) and skinny (less than two miles wide). The national park occupies the western third of the island. You're likely to reach Mljet via one of three port towns.

Polače (POH-lah-cheh) and **Pomena** (POH-meh-nah) are handy entry points into the national park, while **Sobra** (SOH-brah) is much less convenient (a 1.25-hour bus trip across the island from the park). The *Nona Ana* catamaran from Dubrovnik puts in at Polače and Sobra; most excursions use Pomena; and the car ferries (the big Jadrolinija Korčula-Dubrovnik car ferry, plus smaller ferries to the mainland) use Sobra.

Polače and Pomena flank the heart of the national park, a pair of saltwater "lakes" called simply **Great Lake** (Veliko Jezero) and **Small Lake** (Malo Jezero). The two bodies of water meet at a cute little bridge, appropriately named **Small Bridge** (Mali Most), where you can rent kayaks and bikes and catch a boat out to the little **island** in the Great Lake. A 15-minute walk around the Great Lake from the Small Bridge brings you to **Pristanište** (meaning, roughly, "transit hub"), where you can also catch a boat to the island or a shuttle bus to Polače. The nearby cliff-climbing town of **Goveđari** is home to many of the people who work at the park, but is not interesting to tourists.

Everything's well-signed, and there are enough landmarks that it's difficult to get really lost. Even so, I bought the detailed park map (at the entry kiosk) and was glad I had it.

Tourist Information

The **TI** is in Polače, just across from where the *Nona Ana* catamaran from Dubrovnik docks (mid-June-Aug daily 8:00-20:00; early June and Sept daily 8:00-13:00 & 17:00-20:00; Oct-May Mon-Fri 8:00-13:00, closed Sat-Sun; tel. 020/744-186). The island's lone hotel, the **Hotel Odisej** in Pomena, acts as a second tourist information point. The hotel is a hub of services for visitors (whether you stay there or not): bike, scooter, car, and boat rentals; scuba diving lessons; walking tours around the island; cruises to some of the island's caves; and even help finding private accommodations. For more on the hotel, see "Sleeping and Eating on Mljet," later.

The general-information website for the island (which covers the towns, Hotel Odisej, *sobe* and apartments, and more) is www.mljet.hr; for information on the national park, visit www.np-mljet.hr.

Arrival in Mljet

At Polače: Arriving on the *Nona Ana* catamaran from Dubrovnik, exit the boat to the right, walk a few steps, and look for the TI on your left. A few minutes' walk up the coast (near the Roman ruins) is a kiosk where you can buy your park entry ticket and catch a minibus to the Pristanište transit hub at the Great Lake (runs hourly, scheduled to coincide with boat arrival). From Pristanište, you can take a boat out to the island in the Great Lake (about hourly), or walk around the lake toward the Small Bridge, Small Lake, and on to Pomena.

At Pomena: If you arrive at Pomena, you're most likely on a package excursion, in which case your park entry ticket is included and you'll probably stick with your guide for a while. But in case you're on your own, exit the boat to the left (passing Hotel Odisej) and buy your park entry ticket at the kiosk. A few steps up the road beyond the kiosk, you'll see a shortcut to the right that takes you up and down some steps on your way to the Small Lake; once at the lake, bear left and continue to the Small Bridge, where you can catch the boat to the island in the Great Lake or rent a bike or kayak.

Note that there's no official bus between Polače and Pomena, but Hotel Odisej operates a shuttle to coincide with the Dubrovnik catamaran. Several informal minibus-taxis can also take you for a fee.

At Sobra: If you come on a car ferry, you're in for a long haul over to Polače and Pomena—about a 1.25-hour bus trip on twisty roads. Avoid arriving via Sobra unless you're desperate.

Sights on Mljet

▲Mljet National Park
All of the following attractions are inside the park.

Cost and Hours: The steep 90-kn entry fee includes the shuttle bus from Polače to the Great Lake and a boat ride to the lake's island. The park is open daily May-mid-Oct 7:00-19:00, shorter hours in shoulder season, closed Nov-Feb; park information tel. 020/744-041.

Day-Trip Plan: If you're doing the trip on your own from Dubrovnik, try this itinerary: From Polače, take the minibus to Pristanište, where you can catch the boat to the island in the Great Lake. Take the boat back to Mali Most (Small Bridge), where you can rent a bike for a ride along the shore of the Great Lake. If you're heating up, take a dip in the Small Lake at the beach near the Small Bridge. When you're ready for a bit of civilization, walk into Pomena and relax by the seaside, then take the hotel's shuttle bus or a minibus-taxi back to Polače to catch the catamaran back home to Dubrovnik. With more energy, skip Pomena and hike up to Montokuc (you can hike down to Polače on the other side).

The Lakes—The "Great Lake" and "Small Lake" are technically saltwater bays—fed by the sea and affected by ocean currents (as you'll clearly see if you're at the little channel by the Small Bridge at the right time of day). Scientists love these lakes, which contain various shellfish species unique to Mljet.

The Tales of Mljet

For a mostly undeveloped island, Mljet has had a surprisingly busy history. Home to Illyrians, Greeks, Romans, Slavs, Venetians, Habsburgs, Yugoslavs, and now Croatians, the island has hosted some interesting visitors (or supposed visitors) that it loves to brag about.

Around the eighth century B.C., the Greek epic poet Homer possibly spent time here. He was so inspired by Mljet that he used it as the setting for one of the adventures of his hero Ulysses (a.k.a. Odysseus). This is the island where Ulysses fell in love with a beautiful nymph named Calypso and shacked up with her in a cave for seven years. Today there's a much-vaunted "Ulysses' Cave" (Odisejeva Spilja), a 40-minute hike below the island's main town, Babino Polje (at the far end of the island—skip it unless you're a Ulysses groupie).

Flash forward nearly a millennium, when a real-life traveler found his way to Mljet. According to the Bible (Acts 28), the Apostle Paul was shipwrecked on an island called "Melita"—likely this one—for three months. While on the island, Paul was bitten by a deadly snake, which he threw into a fire. The natives were amazed that he wasn't affected by the poison, and he proceeded to cure their ailments. This event was long believed to have happened on the similarly named isle of Malta, in the Mediterranean Sea. But more recently, many historians began to believe that Paul was on Mljet. The most convincing argument: Malta never had poisonous snakes. Incidentally, Mljet no longer does, either—the Habsburgs imported an army of Indian mongooses to rid the island of problematic serpents. Because of this historical footnote, people from Mljet are nicknamed "mongooses" by other Croatians.

The heroics continue with today's "mongooses." There have been more than 100 fires on the island in the last 20 years (most caused by lightning, some by careless visitors), but only three have spread and caused significant destruction. That's because the people of Mljet—well aware of the fragility of the island that provides their income—are also a crack volunteer firefighting force, ready to spring into action and save their island at the first wisp of smoke.

The Island—The main activity in the park is taking a boat out to the Great Lake's little island-in-an-island (boats depart about hourly from the Small Bridge and from Pristanište). The tiny island's main landmark is St. Mary's Church (Sv. Marija) and the attached monastery, left behind by Benedictine monks who lived on Mljet starting in the 12th century. Though the monastery complex has been modified over the ages, fragments of the original Romanesque structure still survive. You can hike the easy trail up to the top of the island, passing remains of fortifications and old chapels, and look for the island's only permanent residents: a handful of goats, donkeys, and chickens. You'll have about an hour on the island, but it only takes half that to see everything—then relax with an overpriced drink at the restaurant by the boat dock.

Biking—The Great Lake is surrounded by a paved, mostly level road that's good for an hour or two of pedaling (unfortunately, you can't go all the way around because the path is broken by the channel connecting the lakes to the sea). The unpaved path around the Small Lake is rough and rocky, making biking there more difficult. The handiest place to rent a bike for a quick ride around the Great Lake is right at the lake itself, by the Small Bridge. Other bike rental points are scattered around the island, including in both Polače and Pomena. But those towns are separated from the lakes—and from each other—by steep hills, making cycling from either town to the lakes a headache for casual bikers.

Swimming—Options are everywhere, most temptingly at the Great Lake and Small Lake. In fact, even though it's fed by seawater, the Small Lake is always about seven degrees Fahrenheit warmer than the sea. The beach by the Small Bridge is particularly handy (but there are no showers or WCs).

Boating—You can rent kayaks at the Small Bridge. Motorized boats—except for the occasional local resident's dinghy—aren't allowed on the island's lakes.

Hiking to Montokuc—The most rewarding hike takes you up to the national park's highest point, Montokuc. At 830 feet above sea level, this is a serious hike up a steep hill—skip it unless you're in good shape, and be sure to bring water (allow at least one hour round-trip at a steady pace). The trail runs between Polače, at the north end of the island, and the village of Soline, beyond the far end of the Great Lake (past the old, broken bridge called Veliki Most). If you're doing this or any other hike, the park map is essential (sold at park entry kiosks and other merchants).

Sleeping and Eating on Mljet

(€1 = about $1.40, country code: 385, area code: 020)

$$$ Hotel Odisej, the only hotel on the island, has more charm than most renovated communist hotels. Sitting right on the waterfront, with 157 rooms, it's a predictably comfortable home base (July-Aug: non-view Sb-€80-90, Sb with sea view and balcony-€95-110, non-view Db-€100-120, Db with sea view or balcony-€120-145, Db with sea view and balcony-€140-160; cheaper in shoulder season, no extra charge for 1- or 2-night stays, closed mid-Oct-mid-April, air-con, elevator, tel. 020/362-111, fax 020/744-042, www.hotelodisej.hr, info@hotelodisej.hr).

$-$$ Sobe *and Apartments:* Mljet has a wide range of private accommodations, with a few in each town or village. *Sobe* run about €15-20 per person in peak season, or €10-15 off-season; for apartments, figure €40-60 for two people in peak season, €25-40 off-season (20 percent more for 1- or 2-night stays). If you arrive without a room, the TI in Polače or Hotel Odisej in Pomena can help you find something. If you're looking in advance, check out the island website, www.mljet.hr. I'd choose a place in the population centers of Polače or Pomena (for their easy access to the park) or in the cute Great Lake-front village of Babine Kuće (near the Small Bridge). To really get away from it all, little end-of-the-road Soline (near the channel connecting the Great Lake to the sea) is rustic and remote, and has several options.

For **eating,** many good restaurants are scattered around the island. There isn't one that's particularly worth seeking out—just eat when it fits your itinerary (or bring a picnic).

Mljet Connections

To Dubrovnik and Korčula by Catamaran: The speedy, made-for-day-trippers catamaran called *Nona Ana* runs daily in each direction between Dubrovnik and Mljet. In the summer (June-Sept), it goes every morning from **Dubrovnik** to **Sobra,** then on to **Polače** (the best stop for the national park, 1.75 hours, 54 kn). In the peak months of July and August, it sometimes continues to **Korčula** town (1 hour beyond Polače, 4/week) and **Lastovo Island** (2.25 hours beyond Polače, 2/week). In the afternoon, it returns to Dubrovnik via the same route, bringing tired but happy side-trippers back to the city. It's less handy in the winter (Oct-May), when it departs Dubrovnik in the afternoon and goes only as far as Sobra and Polače. Confirm the schedule at www.gv-line.hr, and double-check your plans with the Dubrovnik TI. To be sure you get a ticket in peak season, show up early (at least an hour before the boat leaves).

Even though this boat works perfectly in summer for day-tripping from Dubrovnik to Mljet National Park, it doesn't work as well for connecting to Korčula, because it just goes there on some mornings and is handy only if you're heading north after spending the night on Mljet.

Between Mljet and Other Destinations: All other destinations (including Hvar, Split, and day-tripping from Korčula) are more conveniently connected to Mljet by **excursion** than by public transit. The approximately €50 price tag for an all-day excursion seems high, but remember that it includes the 90-kn (€12) park admission fee and saves you the hassle of getting to the island on your own. Otherwise, you can reach Mljet only by the **car ferry** that stops at Sobra (2-3/week in peak season going between Dubrovnik and Korčula, plus other connections from the mainland).

There's no good, straightforward way to visit Mljet in a single day en route between destinations (say, on the way from Dubrovnik to Korčula). But it might work if you're lucky, flexible, and adventurous. If the excursion boats aren't full—and they rarely are—you can buy a last-minute, one-way ticket for a fraction of the full price. So, for example, you can take the morning catamaran from Dubrovnik to Mljet, enjoy the park, then continue on to Korčula in the evening on one of the day-trip boats. (It works vice versa, too: Pay for a morning excursion from Korčula to Mljet, then continue to Dubrovnik on the public catamaran.) Call the staff at Hotel Odisej—who know which excursions are coming to town—the night before to see if they have any ideas. The downside: You can't arrange this in advance, and there's always a chance the boat will be full—and you'll be stranded on Mljet for the night.

MONTENEGRO
Crna Gora

MONTENEGRO

*The Bay of Kotor • Kotor • The Montenegrin Interior •
The Budva Riviera*

If Dubrovnik is the grand finale of a Croatian vacation, then Montenegro is the encore. One of Europe's youngest nations awaits you just south of the border, with dramatic scenery, a refreshing rough-around-the-edges appeal, and the excitement of a new independence. If you're looking for the "next Croatia," this is it.

And yet, crossing the border, you know you've left sleek, prettified-for-tourists Croatia for a place that's gritty, raw, and a bit exotic. While Croatia's showpiece Dalmatian Coast avoided the drab, boxy dullness of the Yugoslav era, less affluent Montenegro wasn't so lucky. Between the dramatic cliffs and time-passed villages, you'll drive past grimy, broken-down apartment blocks and some truly unfortunate concrete architecture. Montenegro is also a noticeably poorer country than its northern neighbor...with all that entails.

Historically, Montenegro has been even more of a crossroads of cultures than the rest of the Balkans. In some ways, there are two Montenegros: the remote, rugged, rustic mountaintop kingdom that feels culturally close to Serbia; and this chapter's focus, the staggeringly strategic, sun-drenched coastline that has attracted a steady stream of rulers over the millennia. At one point or another, just about every group you can imagine—from the usual suspects (Venetians, Austrians) to oddball one-offs (Bulgarian kingdoms, Napoleon's Ljubljana-based Illyrian Provinces, Russian czars)—has planted its flag here. In spite of their schizophrenic lineage, or maybe because of it, Montenegrins have forged a unique cultural identity that defies many of the preconceived notions of the Balkans. Are they like Serbs or Croats? Do they use the Cyrillic or the Roman alphabet? Do they worship the Roman Catholic God or the Eastern Orthodox one? Yes, all of the above.

Since gaining independence in 2006, the Montenegrin coast has become a powerful magnet for a very specific breed of traveler: millionaires from Russia (and, to a lesser extent, Saudi Arabia), who have chosen to turn this impressionable, fledgling country—with its gorgeous coastline—into their very own Riviera. The Tivat airport is jammed with charter flights from Moscow, signs along the coast advertise Russian-language radio stations, and an extravagant luxury yacht marina is being built near Tivat (Porto Montenegro, www.portomontenegro.com). And so Montenegro finds itself in an awkward position: trying to cultivate an image as a high-roller luxury paradise, while struggling to upgrade what is—in places—a nearly Third World infrastructure. Glittering new €500-a-night boutique hotels are built, then suffer power and water outages. It sometimes feels as if Montenegro is skipping right past an important middle step in its tourist development (that of an on-the-rise, moderately priced destination). I guess what I'm saying is…lower your expectations, and don't expect a fancy facade and high prices to come with predictable quality.

Still, nothing can mar the natural beauty of Montenegro's mountains, bays, and forests. For a look at the untamed Adriatic, a

spin on the winding road around Montenegro's steep and secluded Bay of Kotor is a must. The area's main town, also called Kotor, has been protected from centuries of would-be invaders by its position at the deepest point of the fjord—and by its imposing town wall, which scrambles in a zig-zag line up the mountain behind

it. Wander the enjoyably seedy streets of Kotor, drop into some Orthodox churches, and sip a coffee at an al fresco café.

With more time, romantic historians can corkscrew up into the mountains to visit the remote original capital of the country at Cetinje, beach bums will head for the Budva Riviera, and celebrity-seekers can daydream about past glories at the striking hotel-peninsula of Sveti Stefan.

Getting to Montenegro

This chapter is designed for day-tripping to Montenegro from Dubrovnik; all of the sights are within about a three-hour drive of Dubrovnik, and within about an hour of each other.

By Car: Driving is easily the best option, giving you maximum flexibility for sightseeing—but be aware of possible border delays (see "Helpful Hints," later). I've narrated a handy self-guided

Montenegro Almanac

Official Name: After being part of "Yugoslavia," then "Serbia and Montenegro," it's now the Republic of Montenegro (Republika Crna Gora)—which means "Black Mountain" in the native language. It might have gotten its name from sailors who saw darkly forested cliffs as they approached, or it may have been named for a mythical mountain in the country's interior.

Snapshot History: Long overshadowed by its Croatian and Serbian neighbors, Montenegro finally achieved independence on June 3, 2006, in a landmark vote to secede from Serbia—its influential and sometimes overbearing "big brother."

Population: Montenegro is home to 662,000 people. Of these, the vast majority are Eastern Orthodox Christians (45 percent Montenegrins, 29 percent Serbs), with minority groups of Muslims (including Bosniaks and Albanians, about 13 percent total) and Catholics (1 percent).

Area: 5,415 square miles (slightly smaller than Connecticut).

Red Tape: Americans and Canadians need only a passport (no visa required) to enter Montenegro. Drivers must pay a €10 "eco-tax" at the border.

Geography: Montenegro is characterized by a rugged, rocky terrain that rises straight up from the Adriatic and almost immediately becomes a steep mountain range. The country has 182 miles of coastline, about a third of which constitutes the Bay of Kotor. The only real city is the dreary capital in the interior, Podgorica (144,000 people). Each of Yugoslavia's six republics had a town called Titograd, and Podgorica was Montenegro's.

Economy: Upon declaring independence in 2006, Montenegro's economy was weak. But the privatization of its economy

driving tour of the Bay of Kotor, and another for the most accessible slice of the Montenegrin interior. Even if you don't have a rental car during your Dubrovnik visit, consider renting one just for the day to visit Montenegro. Perhaps most satisfying—but expensive—is to hire your own Dubrovnik-based driver to bring you here (my favorites are recommended on page 294). While this is pricey (€250 for the day), you can try to team up with other travelers to split the cost.

By Bus: Bus service between Dubrovnik and Montenegro is workable but infrequent (2/day each way between Dubrovnik and Kotor town, 2.5 hours). Unfortunately, the bus schedules don't line up conveniently for a day trip—you can take a morning bus from Dubrovnik to Kotor (departing Dubrovnik around 10:30), then take an early-afternoon bus back to Dubrovnik (departing Kotor at 14:45)—leaving you very little time in the town itself. And, of

(including its dominant industry, aluminum) and the aggressive development of its tourist trade (such as soliciting foreign investment—mostly Russian—to build new luxury hotels) have turned things around. In fact, in 2008, Montenegro had the most foreign investment, per capita, of any country in Europe. Its unemployment rate has dropped from the high-20s to a somewhat more respectable 15 percent. But it's still a poor place: Montenegro's per capita GDP is just $10,100—a fraction of Croatia's or Slovenia's.

Currency: Though it's not a member of the European Union, Montenegro uses the euro as its currency: €1 = about $1.40.

Language and Alphabet: The official language is Montenegrin, which is nearly identical to Serbian but predominantly uses "our" Roman alphabet (rather than Cyrillic). Still, you'll see plenty of Cyrillic here—targeting the country's large Serb minority as well as Russian tourists and investors.

Telephones: Montenegro's country code is 382. When calling from another country, first dial the international access code (00 from Europe, 011 from the US), then 382, then the area code (minus the initial zero), then the number. Note that Montenegro recently changed its area codes. If you see the former code for the Bay of Kotor area, 082, you'll have to replace it with the new one: 032.

Flag: It's a red field surrounded by a gold fringe. In the middle is the national seal: a golden, two-headed Byzantine eagle topped with a single crown, holding a scepter in one hand and a ball in the other (symbolizing the balance between church and state). The eagle's body is covered by a shield depicting a lion with one paw raised (representing the resurrected Christ).

course, if you ride the bus, you can't stop to explore the sights along the way. As the schedule is always in flux, it's important to confirm times carefully at the Dubrovnik TI or bus station.

It's also possible to take a bus directly from Montenegro to **Mostar** in Bosnia-Herzegovina. The daily bus (run by Globtour in Mostar) departs Budva at 14:15 and Kotor at 15:00, arriving in Mostar at 20:00. The return bus from Mostar departs at 7:00, and arrives at Kotor at 12:30 and Budva at 13:30.

By Excursion: As a last resort, consider taking a package excursion that follows basically the same route covered in this chapter (sold by various travel agencies in Dubrovnik; see page 349).

Planning Your Time

Assuming you have your own car, for a straightforward one-day plan, drive to Kotor and back (figure about eight hours, including driving time and sightseeing stops). To extend your time, you can add as much Montenegro as you like. Get an early start (to avoid lines at the border, I'd leave Dubrovnik at 7:30 in the morning). It takes about two hours to drive from Dubrovnik to Kotor (add about 1.5 hours if you stop in Perast for the boat trip out to the island). Kotor is worth two or three hours. From Kotor, you can return directly to Dubrovnik (about 1.5 hours if you use the ferry shortcut—see page 388); or drive another hour up to Cetinje in the Montenegrin interior, or a half-hour to the Budva Riviera (from either place, figure about 2.5-3 hours back to Dubrovnik). To cram everything into one extremely long day, you can do Dubrovnik-Kotor-Cetinje-Budva Riviera-Dubrovnik. If you're taking the bay-side road home (not the ferry shortcut) and don't mind getting to Dubrovnik late, consider stopping for dinner at the recommended Konoba Ćatovića Mlini or Stari Mlini restaurants.

Helpful Hints

Border Delays: Crossing the Croatian-Montenegrin border at **Debeli Brijeg** is relatively straightforward—though you will need to stop, show your passport (and potentially your rental car's proof of insurance, called a "green card"), and pay a one-time "eco-tax" of €10. While I've gotten across this border within about 15 or 20 minutes on each visit, on busy days it's possible you'll be delayed. You'll most likely encounter long waits (of an hour or more) on Saturdays and Sundays in August, and to a lesser degree in July and early September. Locals suggest trying to reach the border by 8:00 (leaving Dubrovnik around 7:30 or 7:45) to beat the tour buses. Getting an early start also gives you even more time to enjoy Montenegro once across the border.

In a pinch, there's a second crossing, called **Konfin,** that rarely has a line, although the road leading there may be torn up from an aborted construction project. If you don't mind driving along a stretch of unfinished gravel, it could save you some time: To reach this road coming from Dubrovnik, branch off to the right soon after Gruda and before the main border (following signs for *Pločice*). At the fork, continue straight following signs toward *Vitaljina* and *Molunat,* then go through the villages of Đurinići, Višnjići, and Vitaljina. At the next fork, head left toward *Park Prevlaka* (an old Austro-Hungarian and Yugoslav army fortress that has recently been converted into a park). Along this stretch, you may be driving along some very rough, unfinished roads, so proceed carefully. At the turnoff for the fort (look for it out on a peninsula to the right), take the left turn, following signs for *granični prijelaz Konfin* to reach the border. After entering Montenegro, you'll curve along the small bay into Igalo, where you can pick up the self-guided driving tour described later.

Local Guide: While many Dubrovnik-based drivers/guides can bring you to Montenegro, if you really want the Montenegrin perspective, consider hiring a local guide here. I spent a great day learning about this area from **Stefan Đukanović,** a young, energetic, knowledgeable guide who speaks good English and has an infectious enthusiasm for his homeland. Hiring Stefan is a great value. The catch is that he can't come and get you in Dubrovnik, so it works best if you drive yourself to Montenegro and pick him up when you get there. Stefan is also an excellent choice if you're arriving in Kotor by cruise ship (€60/half-day, €80/day, mobile 069-297-221 or 069-369-994, djukan@t-com.me).

Cruise Passengers: Kotor is becoming an increasingly popular destination for cruises. If you arrive on a cruise ship, you'll likely dock along the pier directly in front of Kotor's Old Town—so your sightseeing options couldn't be easier: Simply walk across the street and you're in the heart of town. To see farther-flung sights in Montenegro, you may want to hire a local guide or driver (consider Stefan Đukanović, recommended above).

The Bay of Kotor

With dramatic cliffs rising out of the glimmering Adriatic, ancient towns packed with history and thrilling vistas, an undeveloped ruggedness unlike anything in Croatia, and a twisty road to tie it all together, the Bay of Kotor represents the best of Montenegro. To top it off, it's easy to reach by car from Dubrovnik.

Self-Guided Driving Tour

▲▲Bay of Kotor Day Trip (from Dubrovnik)

The Bay of Kotor (Boka Kotorska—literally the "Mouth of Kotor"; sometimes translated as "Boka Bay" in English) is Montenegro's most enjoyable and convenient attraction for those based in Dubrovnik. This self-guided driving tour narrates the drive from the Croatian border to the town of Kotor, in the Bay of Kotor's deepest corner.

The Montenegrin border is about 30 to 45 minutes south of Dubrovnik (don't forget your passport). Simply follow the main coastal road south, past Cavtat and the airport. You'll be passing through the Croatian region called **Konavle** (literally "canal,"

MONTENEGRO

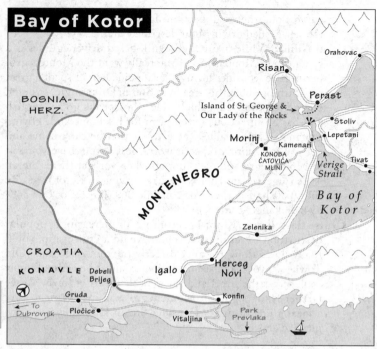

Bay of Kotor

MONTENEGRO

recalling how the Romans built aqueducts through this area to supply their settlement at today's Cavtat). Historically part of the Republic of Dubrovnik, this farming region was badly damaged during the recent war, when the Yugoslav People's Army invaded from the south, forcing villagers to flee to safety in Dubrovnik.

Approaching the **border,** if there's a long back-up, consider turning off to take the much less-traveled road to the secondary border at Konfin (see "Helpful Hints," earlier). Regardless of where you enter Montenegro, you'll pay a one-time "eco-tax" of €10 at the border. (Your rental car might already have a toll sticker for this tax—ask when you pick up your car.) If you don't have your rental car's proof of insurance (called a "green card"), you may be asked to pay another fee as well.

From the border, you can make it to Kotor in about an hour without stopping, but with all the diversions en route you should plan for much more time. Coming back, you can trim a good half-hour off the drive by crossing the fjord at its narrowest point, using the Lepetani-Kamenari ferry (described on page 388). Navigating on this tour is really simple: It's basically the same road, with no turn-offs, from Dubrovnik to Kotor.

• *From the Croatian border, you'll approach the coast at the town called...*

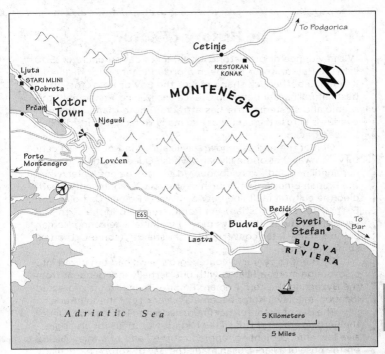

Igalo

Driving through Igalo, keep an eye out (on the right) for a big concrete hotel called **Institut Dr. Simo Milošević** (no relation to war-
criminal Slobodan). This internationally regarded spa, especially
popular among Scandinavians, offers treatment for arthritis and
nerve disorders. Capable of hosting more than 1,000 patients at
once, this complex boasts that it's one of the world's premier treatment facilities for these conditions. Yugoslav President-for-Life
Tito had a villa nearby and took treatments here.

• *A couple of miles beyond Igalo, you enter the biggest city you'll see
today...*

Herceg Novi

The drab economic and industrial capital of the Bay of Kotor,
Herceg Novi (with 25,000 people) is hardly the prettiest introduction to this otherwise striking landscape. Herceg Novi flourished
during the Habsburg boom of the late 19th century, when a railroad line connected it to Dubrovnik, Sarajevo, and Vienna. Back
then, Austrians vacationed here—but more recent development
has been decidedly less elegant than the Habsburgs'. While there
is a walled Old Town core to Herceg Novi, it's not worth stopping
to see.

The History of Kotor

With evidence of prehistoric settlements dating back to 2500 B.C., the Bay of Kotor has been a prized location for millennia. Its unique bottleneck shape makes the Bay of Kotor the single best natural harbor between Greece and Venice. Predictably, this scenic and strategic strip has attracted more than its share of overlords across the centuries—so many, in fact, that it's difficult to keep track.

One of the earliest known civilizations in Kotor (third century B.C.) was that of the Illyrians, whose Queen Teuta held court here until her lands were conquered by the Romans. Later, when the Roman Empire split (fourth century A.D.), Montenegro straddled the cultural fault line between West (Roman Catholic) and East (Orthodox Christian). As Rome crumbled in the sixth and seventh centuries, the Slavs moved in. Initially rejecting Roman culture, many later converted to Christianity (some Orthodox, some Catholic).

By the 10th century, Montenegro's Slavs had organized into a sovereign state, affiliated with but partially independent from the Byzantine (Eastern Roman) Empire. Thanks to its protected location, medieval Kotor became a major city of the salt trade.

The Bay of Kotor further flourished in the 14th century, under the Serbian emperor Dušan the Mighty. Notorious for his aggressive law enforcement—chopping off the hand of a thief, slicing off the nose of a liar—Dušan made the Bay of Kotor a particularly safe place to do business. One of his strategies was making the nobility responsible for safe passage. If a visiting merchant was robbed, the nobleman who controlled that land would be ruthlessly punished. Soon 2,000-horse caravans could pass without a worry along this fjord. During storms, ships would routinely

Passing through the Old Town, keep an eye out on the right for Herceg Novi's stout 15th-century **fortress,** which was built by the Ottomans—who controlled this area, but never made it deeper into the bay.

Also in Herceg Novi, keep an eye out for **banana trees.** Locals pride themselves on their particularly mild climate, kept warm year-round thanks to the mitigating effects of the water from the adjacent fjord. Supposedly, "it never drops below 50 degrees Fahrenheit." While these banana trees are just decorative (the fruit they produce is too small to eat), they're a local symbol. So is the mimosa flower, which blooms all winter long, and is the inspiration for the town's annual Mimosa Festival—held each February, when much of Europe (including most of Montenegro) is under a blanket of snow.

Other than its banana trees and mimosas, Herceg Novi is basically a mess. (Don't worry—the drive gets better.) Why so much

seek protection in this secluded bay.

But the Serbian Empire went into steep decline after Dušan. As the Ottomans threatened to invade in the 15th century, Kotor's traders turned to Venice for help. The Venetian Republic would control this bay for the next 450 years, and it was never taken by enemies. In fact, Montenegro managed to evade Ottoman rule entirely...unlike its neighbors Albania, Kosovo, Serbia, and Bosnia-Herzegovina. (Meanwhile, neighboring Croats enjoy pointing out that, while the Bay of Kotor was nominally part of Venice, much of the territory was privately owned by a Croat family.)

In the late 19th century, when Venice fell to Napoleon, the Bay of Kotor came briefly under the control of France, then Russia, then Austria. Feudal traditions fell by the wayside, industry arrived, and the area's old-fashioned economy went into a sharp decline. As trading wealth dried up, the Bay of Kotor entered a period of architectural stagnation. But thanks to this dark spell in Montenegrin history, today's visitors can enjoy some wonderfully preserved time-warp towns.

When Montenegro became part of Yugoslavia following World War I, the Serbs (who felt a cultural affinity with the Montenegrins that wasn't always reciprocated) laid claim to the Montenegrin coast as their own little patch of seafront. Serbs flooded into Montenegro, altering the demographics and making it, in effect, an outpost of the Republic of Serbia. This helped Montenegro avoid the initial violence of the breakup of Yugoslavia, but put them in an awkward position when it came time for them to request secession a few years later. For the rest of the story, see the "Montenegro: Birth of a Nation" sidebar, later.

MONTENEGRO

ugliness compared to Croatia? For one thing, Tito viewed Croatia's Dalmatian Coast as a gold mine of hard Western currency—so he was inclined to keep it Old World-charming. And Croatia remained in the cultural and political orbit of Zagreb, which was motivated to take good care of its historic towns. But Belgrade, which exerted more influence on Montenegro, didn't offer it the same degree of TLC. And because Montenegro has traditionally been poorer than Croatia, its officials are more susceptible to bribery and corruption. ("Would a few thousand dinar convince you to ignore my new hotel's code violations?") From an architectural point of view, it's a sad irony that gorgeous Dubrovnik was devastated by bombs and the gritty cities of Montenegro survived the war essentially unscathed. To this day, locals aren't crazy about the Serbs who flock here in summer for as-cheap-as-possible beach holidays. Instead, Montenegrins are encouraging the construction of top-end resort hotels to lure high rollers from around the world (such as James Bond, who played poker in the 2006 movie version of *Casino Royale* in "Montenegro"—though it was actually filmed in the Czech Republic). But even this new development is poorly regulated, threatening to turn Montenegro into a charmless, concrete Costa del Sol-style vacation zone. Enjoy the Bay of Kotor's pristine areas (which we'll enter soon) while you still can.

• *As you go through Herceg Novi, follow signs for* Kotor. *Leaving town, you'll pass through* **Zelenika,** *once the end of the line for the Habsburg rail line from Vienna, which first brought tourism to this area.*

After a few more dreary towns, you'll emerge into a more rustic setting. This fjordside road is lined with fishing villages, some now developed as resorts (including a few with severe communist-era touches). You'll pass through the town of **Kamenari,** *which has a handy ferry that you could use to shave time off your return trip to Dubrovnik (described at the end of this drive). Two minutes after leaving Kamenari (just after the* Kostanjica *sign), watch for a convenient gravel pull-out on the right (likely packed with tour buses, by the small white lighthouse). Pull over to check out the narrowest point of the fjord, the...*

Verige Strait

This tight bottleneck at the mouth of the bay is the secret to the Bay of Kotor's success: Any would-be invaders had to pass through here to reach the port towns inside the bay. It's narrow enough to carefully monitor (not even a quarter-mile wide), but deep enough to allow even today's large megaships through (more than 130 feet deep). Because this extremely narrow strait is relatively easy to defend, whoever controlled the inside of the fjord was allowed to thrive virtually unchecked.

Centuries before Christ, even before the flourishing of Roman culture, the Bay of Kotor was home to the Illyrians—the mysterious ancestors of today's Albanians. In the third century B.C., Illyrian Queen Teuta spanned this strait with an ingenious ship-wrecking mechanism to more effectively collect taxes. To this day, many sunken ships litter the bottom of this bay. (Teuta was a little too clever for her own good—her shrewdness and success attracted the attention of the on-the-rise Romans, who seized most of her holdings.)

In later times, chains were stretched across the bay here to control the entrance (the name "Verige" comes from a Slavic word for "chain"). Later still, the Venetians came up with an even more elaborate plan: Place cannons on either side of the strait, with a clear shot at any entering ships. Looking across the wide part of the bay, notice the town of Perast (by the two islands). Perast—where we'll be stopping soon—was also equipped with cannons that could easily reach across the bay. Thanks to this extensive defense network, Ottomans or any other potential invaders were unlikely to penetrate the bay, either by sea or by land.

Montenegro is currently drafting plans to build a bridge across the strait (effectively replacing the ferry connection we just passed)—though concerns about both securing funding and preserving the unique ecosystem of the bay have delayed progress. Stay tuned.

• *Continue driving around the fjord. You'll pass through the village of...*

Morinj

This town is known for two starkly different reasons: First, it's the home of a recommended restaurant with fine food in a gorgeous setting (Konoba Ćatovića Mlini, see page 400). And second, it was the site of a concentration camp for Croat prisoners captured during the 1991-1992 siege of Dubrovnik. Some 300 civilians from in and near Dubrovnik were forcibly brought here, where they lived in horrifying conditions. After the war, six of the guards from this camp were convicted of war crimes.

• *After going through Morinj and some other small villages, you'll pass through the larger resort town of...*

Risan

Back in Greek times, when the Bay of Kotor was known as *"Sinus Rhizonicus,"* Risan was the leading town of the bay. Later, during the Illyrian Queen Teuta's brief three-year reign, Risan was her capital. Today the town is still home to the scant remains of Teuta's castle (on the hilltop just before town), but it's mostly notable for its giant communist eyesore hotel—named, appropriately enough, Hotel Teuta.

• *Continue on to Perast. As you approach the town, take the right fork (marked with brown sign) directly down into Perast; or you can first take the left fork to pass above town for sweeping views over the bay, then backtrack down into the town center.*

Perast

This second-most appealing town on the fjord (after Kotor) is considered the "Pearl of Venetian Baroque." It's worth taking some time to wander and explore its buildings and enjoy its relaxed small-town feel (minus the bustle

of bigger Kotor). During the summer, you're required to park near the entrance of town (€0.50), and then walk or ride the free shuttle bus into the town center; at other times, you'll be allowed to drive along the waterfront road and park for free in front of the church.

Montenegro: Birth of a Nation

Montenegro, like Croatia and Slovenia, was one of the six republics that constituted the former Yugoslavia. When these republics began splitting away in the early 1990s, Montenegro—always allied closely with Serbia, and small enough to slip under the radar—decided to remain in the union. When the dust had settled, four of the six Yugoslav republics had seceded (Croatia, Slovenia, Bosnia-Herzegovina, and Macedonia), while only two remained united as "Yugoslavia": Serbia and Montenegro.

At first, Montenegrin Prime Minister Milo Đukanović was on friendly terms with Serbia's Slobodan Milošević. But in the late 1990s, as Milošević's political stock plummeted, Montenegro began to inch away from Serbia. Eager to keep its access to the coast (and the many Serbs who lived there), Serbia made concessions that allowed Montenegro to gradually assert its independence. In 1996, Montenegro boldly adopted the German mark as its official currency to avoid the inflating Yugoslav dinar.

By 2003, the country of Yugoslavia was no more, and the loose union was renamed "Serbia and Montenegro." Thus began a three-year transition period that allowed Montenegro to test the waters of real independence. During this time, Serbia and Montenegro were united only in defense—legislation, taxation, currency, and most governmental functions were separate. And it was agreed that after three years, Montenegro would be allowed to hold a referendum for full independence.

That fateful vote took place on May 21, 2006. In general, ethnic Montenegrins tended to favor independence, while ethnic Serbs wanted to stay united with Serbia. To secede, Montenegro needed 55 percent of the vote. By the slimmest of margins—half a percent, or just 2,300 votes—the pro-independence faction won. On June 3, 2006, Montenegro officially declared independence. (To save face, two days later, Serbia also "declared independence" from Montenegro.)

Today's Montenegrins are excited to have their own little country and enthusiastic about eventually joining the European Union. Serbia's greatest concern was that in losing Montenegro, it would also lose its lone outlet to the sea—both for shipping and for holiday-making. The Serbs also feared that Montenegrin independence might inspire similar actions in the Serbian province of Kosovo (which did, in fact, declare independence from Serbia less than two years later).

But for many people in both countries, independence is an epilogue rather than a climax. Shortly after the referendum, I asked a Montenegrin when the countries officially separate. He chuckled and said, "Three years ago."

Remember that Perast, with its cannons aimed at the Verige Strait across the bay, was an essential link in the Bay of Kotor's fortifications. In exchange for this important duty, Venice rewarded Perast with privileged tax-free status, and the town became extremely wealthy. Ornate mansions proliferated here during its 17th- and 18th-century heyday. But after Venice fell to Napoleon, and the Bay of Kotor's economy changed, Perast's singular defensive role disappeared. With no industry, no hinterland, and no natural resources, Perast stagnated—leaving it a virtual open-air museum of Venetian architecture.

Go to the tallest steeple in town, overlooking a long and narrow harborfront square. Perast is centered on its too-big (and incomplete) church, **St. Nicholas**—dedicated to the patron saint of fishermen. It was originally designed to extend out into the sea (the old church, still standing, was to be torn down). But Napoleon's troops came marching in before the builders got that far, so the plans were scuttled—and this massive partial-church was instead simply grafted on to the existing, modest church.

Go inside (free, €1 to enter treasury, sporadic hours, generally open April-Nov daily 9:00-18:00, July-Aug until 19:00, closed dur-

ing Mass, closed Dec-March except by request—ask locals around the church if someone can let you in). Beyond the small sanctuary, you'll find a treasury with relics and icons. Look for the priceless crucifix from the school of the 18th-century Venetian artist Giovanni Battista Tiepolo (#1, in the display case in the center of the room), with Jesus on one side, and Mary and the saints on the other. Beyond the treasury is what was to be the main apse (altar area) of the unfinished massive church (notice it's at a right angle to the actual, in-use altar of the existing smaller church). The rough, unadorned brick walls make it clear that they didn't get very far. Check out the model of the ambitious but never-built church. The Baroque main altar is by Bernini's student Francesco Cabianca, who lived in this area and was always trying to earn money to pay off his gambling debts. The small room at the end displays old vestments.

If you have the time and energy, pay €1 to climb the **church tower** for the view.

Perast's only other "sight" is its **Town Museum,** which fills a grand old hall with paintings, furniture, navy uniforms, pistols, portraits of VIPs (very important Perastians), medals, traditional musical instruments, and other historic bric-a-brac. It's pretty dull

MONTENEGRO

but has nice sea views (€2.50; May-Oct Mon-Sat 9:00-18:00, Sun 9:00-14:00; Nov-April Mon-Sat 9:00-13:00 or 14:00, closed Sun; along the water near the start of town, in the ornate building with the arcade and balcony).

Eating in Perast: For an enjoyable drink or meal, consider the **Conte** restaurant, filling a pier on the bay in the middle of town (€8-12 pastas, €11-20 main dishes). On the far side of the square is another, well-shaded pier restaurant, **Admiral** (€8-10 pastas, €11-20 main dishes). Both are open daily and attached to recommended hotels.

• *Before leaving Perast, take a close look at the two islands just offshore (and consider paying a visit).*

St. George (Sv. Đorđe) and Our Lady of the Rocks (Gospa od Škrpjela)

These twin islands—one natural, the other man-made—come with a fascinating story.

The **Island of St. George** (the smaller, rocky island with trees and a monastery—closed to tourists), named for the protector of Christianity, was part of the fortification of the Bay of Kotor. This natural island had a small underwater reef nearby. According to legend, two fishermen noticed a strange light emanating from this reef in

the early-morning fog. Rowing out to the island, they discovered an icon of Our Lady. They attempted to bring it ashore, but it kept washing back out again to the same spot. Taking this celestial hint, local seamen returning home from a journey began dropping rocks into the bay in this same place. The tradition caught on, more and more villagers dropped in rocks of their own, and eventually more than a hundred old ships and other vessels were filled with stones and intentionally sunk in this spot. And so, over two centuries, an entire island was formed in the middle of the bay.

Flash forward to today's **Our Lady of the Rocks** (the flat island with the dome-topped Catholic church). In the 17th century, locals built this Baroque church on this holy site and filled it with symbols of thanks for answered prayers. Step inside (free entry) to explore the collection: silver votive plaques—many of them with images of ships in storms or battles—given by appreciative sailors who survived; 1,700 silver and gold votive plaques from other grateful worshippers; 68 canvases by local Baroque painter Tripo Kokolja; and a huge collection of dried wedding bouquets given by those who had nothing else to offer (the church is a popular place for weddings).

The adjacent **museum** is an entertaining mishmash of items, and the entry price includes a fun little tour by Davorka, Nešo, or Nataša (€1, June-Oct daily 9:00-19:00, April-May and Nov opens sporadically with boat arrival, closed Dec-March). You'll see a wide range of ancient arti-facts, 65 paintings of ships com-missioned by local sailors (notice that most have a saintly image of Mary and the Baby Jesus hover-ing nearby), and other gifts given through the ages. Upstairs, near the gift shop counter, look for the amazing embroidery made by a local woman who toiled over it

for more than 25 years. She used her own hair for the hair of the angels—which you can see fade from brown to gray as she aged (beginning at around 3 o'clock and going clockwise, you'll see the subtle change in color).

Getting There: Boats to Our Lady of the Rocks leave from in front of St. Nicholas' Church in Perast—look for the guys milling around the harborfront with boats ready to go (€5/person round-trip, but show them this book to pay €4/person, or €3/person for a group of 4 or more).

• *When you're ready to move on, continue driving around the fjord. After the large town of Orahovac, you'll see part of the bay roped off for a mussel farm; these farms do best when located where mountain rivers spill into the bay. And a hundred or so yards later, you cross a bridge spanning the don't-blink-or-you'll-miss-it...*

Ljuta River

According to locals, this is the "shortest river in the world"—notice that the source (bubbling up from under the cliff) is just to the left of the bridge, and it meets the sea just to the right. Short as it is, it's hardly a trickle—in fact, its name means "Angry River" for its fierce flow during heavy rains. The river actually courses under-ground for several miles before emerging here. Like the Karst area south of Ljubljana, this is a karstic landscape—limestone that's honeycombed with underground rivers, caves, and canyons. Many other waterfalls and streams feed the Bay of Kotor with snowmelt from the surrounding mountains. Because of this steady natural flushing, locals brag that the bay's water is particularly clear and clean.

• *Immediately after the bridge, look for the turnoff (on the right) to the recommended Restoran Stari Mlini—a tranquil spot for a meal or drink. Continuing along the fjord, as you pass through the town of Dobrota, look across the bay to the village of...*

Prčanj

This town is famous as the former home of many centuries' worth of wealthy sea captains. When the Bay of Kotor was part of the Austrian Empire, Emperor Franz Josef came to Prčanj. Upon being greeted by some 50 uniformed ship captains, he marveled that such a collection of seafarers had been imported for his visit... not realizing that every one of them lived nearby.

• *Keep on driving. When you see the giant moat with the town wall, and the smaller wall twisting up the hill above, you'll know you've arrived in* **Kotor** *(see facing page).*

Before leaving Kotor, make a decision about where you want to go next. You have three basic options: Budva Riviera; Montenegrin interior; or back to Croatia (see instructions for the third option in the next section).

Continuing past Kotor's Old Town, you'll follow the edge of the fjord. At the far end of town (and the fjord), you'll come to a roundabout. Bearing left at the roundabout takes you toward the handy tunnel to the **Budva Riviera**—*or, along this same road, if you turn right after the cemetery and just before the tunnel, you'll take the extremely twisty road up, up, up into the* **Montenegrin interior** *(Njeguši and Cetinje).*

Once you're finished in Montenegro, it'll be time to head...

MONTENEGRO

Back to Croatia: Lepetani-Kamenari Ferry Shortcut

When you're ready to return to Dubrovnik, you can go back the way you came. Or, for a quicker route, consider the ferry that cuts across the narrow part of the fjord (between the towns of Lepetani and Kamenari). On the Kotor side of the bay, the boat departs from the town of Lepetani.

From Kotor, you have two options to reach the ferry: The easiest option is to leave Kotor, bear left at the roundabout at the far end of town, and take the tunnel toward Budva. Once through the tunnel, follow signs into Tivat, and continue straight through Tivat on the main road to reach Lepetani, which is a few miles beyond the end of town. Or, for a more challenging but more scenic route, you can simply turn right at the roundabout and continue driving on the waterfront road clockwise around the bay (through Prčanj and Stoliv) until you land in Lepetani. But be warned that this road is extremely narrow (one lane with an Adriatic shoulder) and can be exhausting if oncoming traffic is heavy.

No matter how you approach, remember that "ferry" is *trajekt* (it's also signed for *Herceg Novi*—the big city across the bay). The boat goes continuously (in slow times, you may have to wait briefly for enough cars to show up), and the crossing takes just four minutes (it takes longer to load and unload all the cars than it does to cross). A small car and its passengers pay €4 each way.

Kotor

Butted up against a steep cliff, cradled by a calm sea, naturally sheltered by its deep-in-the-fjord position, and watched over by an imposing network of fortifications, the town of Kotor is as impressive as it is well-protected. Though it's enjoyed a long and illustrious history, today's Kotor is a time-capsule retreat for travelers seeking a truly unspoiled Adriatic town.

There's been a settlement in this location at least since the time of Christ. The ancient town of Catarum—named for the Roman word for "contracted" or "strangled," as the sea is at this point in the gnarled fjord—was first mentioned in the first century A.D. Like the rest of the region, Kotor's next two millennia were layered with history as it came under control of a series of foreign powers: Illyrians, Romans, Serbs, Venetians, Russians, Napoleonic soldiers, Austrians, Tito's Yugoslavia...and now, finally, Montenegrins. Each group left its mark, and Kotor has its share of both Catholic and Orthodox churches (sometimes both at once), plus monuments and reminders of plenty of past colonizers and conquerors.

Through all those centuries, Kotor avoided destruction by warfare. But it was damaged by earthquakes—including the same 1667 quake that leveled Dubrovnik (known here as the "Great Shaking"), as well as a devastating 1979 earthquake from which the city is still cleaning up. While only 3,000 people live within the Old Town walls, greater Kotor has a population of about 12,000.

With an extremely inviting Old Town that seems custom-built for aimless strolling, Kotor is an idyllic place to while away a few hours. Though it's sometimes called a "little Dubrovnik," Kotor is more low-key, less ambitious, less historic, flatter, and much smaller than its more famous neighbor. And yet, with its own special spice that's exciting to sample, Kotor is a hard place to tear yourself away from.

Orientation to Kotor

Kotor (or Cattaro in Italian) has a compact Old Town shaped like a triangle. The two sides facing the bay are heavily fortified by a thick wall, and the third side huddles under the cliff face. A meandering defensive wall climbs the mountainside directly behind and above town.

The Old Town's mazelike street plan is confusing, but it's so small and atmospheric that getting lost is more fun than frustrating. The natives virtually ignore addresses, including the names of streets and squares. Most Old Town addresses are represented simply as "Stari Grad," then a number (useless if you're trying to navigate by streets). To make matters worse, a single square can have several names—so one map labels it Trg od Katedrale (Cathedral Square), while another calls it Pjaca Sv. Tripuna (Piazza of St. Tryphon). My advice: Don't fret about street or square names. Simply navigate with a map and by asking locals for directions. Thanks to the very manageable size of the Old Town, this is easier than it sounds.

Tourist Information

The TI is in a kiosk just outside the Old Town's main entrance gate (daily May-Oct 8:00-20:00, Nov-April 8:00-17:00, tel. 032/325-950, www.tokotor.com). Pick up the free map and browse the collection of guidebooks and brochures. They can help you find a room for no fee.

Arrival in Kotor

By Car: Approaching town, you'll first see Kotor's substantial wall, which overlooks a canal. You can park in one of two pay lots: "Parking Riva," immediately across from the main gate (more expensive but convenient, to the right just after crossing the bridge by the wall); or "Parking Benovo," in the lot across the canal (on the left just before the bridge by the wall—you'll be sent back here if the first lot is full). Either is a quick walk from the Old Town entrance. Be sure you've parked legally; some of my readers report having been towed and fined for parking in what they thought were legal spaces. When in doubt about a parking spot, either don't park there or ask the TI if it's OK.

By Bus: The bus station is about a half-mile south of the Old Town. Arriving here, simply exit to the right and walk straight up the road—you'll run into the embankment and town wall in 10 minutes.

Sights in Kotor

Because of its tangled alleys and irregular street plan, Kotor feels bigger than it is. But after 10 minutes of wandering, you'll discover you're going in circles and realize it's actually very compact. (In fact, aimless wandering is Kotor's single best activity.) How such a cute town manages to be so delightfully lazy and traffic-free without being overrun by tourists, I'll never know (though the recent arrival of cruise ships is threatening Kotor's until-now-untrampled appeal).

As you ramble, keep an eye out for these key attractions. I've listed them roughly in the order of a counterclockwise route through town, beginning outside the main entrance gate.

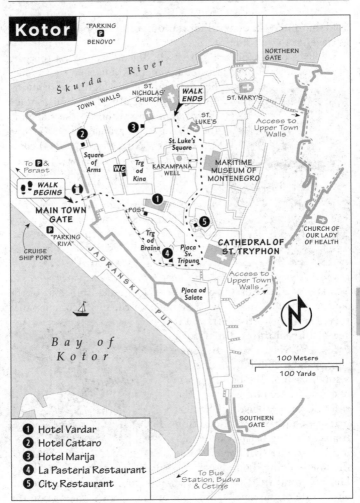

Kotor

"PARKING BENOVO"

Škurda River

TOWN WALLS

NORTHERN GATE

ST. NICHOLAS' CHURCH

WALK ENDS

ST. MARY'S

Access to Upper Town Walls

❸

ST. LUKE'S

St. Luke's Square

❷

Square of Arms

WC

Trg od Kina

KARAMPANA WELL

MARITIME MUSEUM OF MONTENEGRO

To P & Perast

WALK BEGINS

MAIN TOWN GATE

POST

❶

❺

CHURCH OF OUR LADY OF HEALTH

P "PARKING RIVA"

CRUISE SHIP PORT

Trg od Brašna

❹

Pjaca Sv. Tripuna

CATHEDRAL OF ST. TRYPHON

JADRANSKI PUT

Pjaca od Salate

Access to Upper Town Walls

N

Bay of Kotor

100 Meters
100 Yards

MONTENEGRO

❶ Hotel Vardar
❷ Hotel Cattaro
❸ Hotel Marija
❹ La Pasteria Restaurant
❺ City Restaurant

SOUTHERN GATE

To Bus Station, Budva & Cetinje

▲**Main Town Gate (Glavna Gradska Vrata)**—The wide-open **square** fronting the bay and waterfront marina now welcomes visitors. But for centuries, its purpose was exactly the opposite. As the primary point of entry into this heavily fortified town, it was the last line of defense. Before the embankment was built, the water came directly to this door, and there was only room for one ship to tie up at a time. If a ship got this far (through the gauntlet we saw back at the Verige Strait), it was carefully examined here again (and taxes were levied) before its passengers could disembark. This double-checkpoint was designed to foil pirates who might fly the flag of a friend to get through the strait, only to launch a surprise attack once here. By the way, pirates' primary booty wasn't silver or gold, but men—kidnapped for ransom, or, if ransom wasn't paid, as slaves to row on ships.

Check out the pinkish **gate** itself. The oldest parts of this gate date from 1555. It once featured a Venetian lion, then the double-

headed eagle of the Habsburg Empire. But today, most of the symbolism touts Tito's communism (notice the stars and the old Yugoslav national seal at the top). The big date (November 21, 1944) commemorates when this area was liberated from the Nazis by Tito's homegrown Partisan Army. The Tito quote *(tuđe nećemo svoje nedamo)* means, roughly, "Don't take what's ours, and we won't take what's yours"—a typically provocative statement in these troubled Balkans.

• *Notice the **TI** in the kiosk just to the left of the gate. Then go through the gate into town. You'll emerge into the...*

Square of Arms (Trg od Oržja)—Do a quick spin-tour of the square, which is ringed with artifacts of the city's complex his-

tory. Looking to the left, you'll see a long building lined with cafés, ATMs (which dispense euros), and (behind the umbrellas) a small casino. The building was once the palace of the rector, who ruled Kotor on behalf of Venice; princes could watch the action from their long balcony overlooking the square, which served as

the town's living room. Later, the palace became the Kotor Town Hall. Beyond that, two buildings poke out into the square (on either side of the lane leading out of the square). The one on the right is the Venetian arsenal, the square's namesake. The one on the left is the "French Theater," named for its purpose during the time this area was under Napoleon's control. Directly across from the gate you just came through, you'll see the town's Bell Tower, one of Kotor's symbols. The odd triangular structure at its base was once the town pillory. Wrongdoers would be chained to this with their transgression printed on a placard hanging from their neck, open to public ridicule of the rudest kind imaginable. In the little recessed square just right of that, you'll spot the recommended, copper-roofed Hotel Vardar.

• *Walk down the long part of the square directly ahead of where you entered (toward Hotel Vardar). About 20 yards in front of the hotel, take the broad lane angling off to the right (paved with red-and-white-*

striped tiles), which leads past mansions of Kotor's medieval big shots. Turn left down the little lane next to the Montenegro Airlines office. Soon you'll hit Pjaca Sv. Tripuna (a.k.a. Trg od Katedrale), home to the...

▲Cathedral of St. Tryphon (Katedrala Sv. Tripuna)—Even though most Kotorians are Orthodox, Kotor's most significant church is Catholic. According to legend, in A.D. 809, Venetian merchants were sailing up the coast from Nicea (in today's Turkey) with the relics of St. Tryphon—a third-century martyr and today's patron saint of gardeners. A storm hit as they approached the Bay of Kotor, so they took shelter here. Every time they tried to leave, the weather worsened...so they finally got the message that St. Tryphon's remains should remain in Kotor.

Take in the cathedral's **exterior.** The earliest, Romanesque parts of this church, dating from the mid-12th century, are made of limestone from the Croatian island of Korčula. But the church has been rebuilt after four different earthquakes—most extensively after the 1667 quake, when it achieved its current Renaissance-Baroque blend. That earthquake, which also contributed to Dubrovnik's current appea rance, destroyed three-quarters of Kotor's buildings. A fire swept the city, and all of the dead bodies attracted rats (and with them, the plague)—a particularly dark chapter in Kotor's history.

Why are the two **towers** different? There are plenty of legends, but the most likely is that restorers working after 1667 simply ran out of money before they finished the second one. Notice the Church of Our Lady of Health way up on the hill above this church—built in thanks to God by survivors of the plague (it also serves as part of the town fortifications—described later).

Cost and Hours: €2.50, daily June-Sept 9:00-19:00, April-May and Oct 9:00-18:00, Nov-March 9:00-15:00, Mass on Sun at 10:00.

Touring the Cathedral: Within the cathedral, the **nave** of the church is marginally interesting: stout columns; surviving Byzantine-style frescoes under the arches—all that's left of paintings that once covered the church; and a fine 15th-century silver-and-gold altar covered by a delicate canopy.

But the best part is the **reliquary** upstairs. Find the stairs at the rear and walk up to the chapel. Behind the Baroque altar (by Bernini's student Francesco Cabianca, whose work we saw in

Perast) and the screen are 48 different relics. In the center is St. Tryphon—his bones in a silver casket and his head in the golden chalice to the right. In the small room up the stairs, examine the fascinating icon of the Madonna and Child from the 15th century. The painting (like the icons in the adjacent room) exemplifies this town's position as a bridge between Western and Eastern Christianity: The faces, more lifelike, are Western-style (Catholic) Gothic; the stiff, elongated bodies are more Eastern (Orthodox) and Byzantine-style. From here, take a slow walk around the upper gallery of the church to see its displays of paintings, vestments, and other ecclesiastical items.

• *Exit the church. Notice the recommended La Pasteria restaurant immediately across from the cathedral, with Italian- and Serb-style fare and scenic al fresco tables. On the right, the trees mark another recommended eatery, City Restaurant.*

When you're ready to continue, face the cathedral facade and exit the square to your left (at the back-left corner of the square, down the street near City Restaurant). In a block, you'll wind up on a little square that's home to the...

MONTENEGRO

Maritime Museum of Montenegro (Pomorski Muzej Crne Gore)

—Like so many Adriatic towns, Kotor's livelihood is tied to the sea. This humble museum explores that important heritage. As you climb the stairway, notice the evocative maps and etchings of old Kotor. Portraits of salty swashbucklers, traditional costumes, and 98 coats of arms representing aristocratic families who have lived here (ringing the main room upstairs) are all reminders of the richness of Kotor's history. You'll see a display of rifles and swords (some with fun ornamental decorations illustrating the art of killing) and lots of model ships. The museum is housed in the Gregorina Palace, one of dozens of aristocratic mansions that dot the Old Town—yet another reminder of the historically high concentration of wealth and power in this little settlement.

Cost and Hours: €4, includes English audioguide; July-Aug Mon-Fri 8:00-23:00, Sat-Sun 10:00-16:00; mid-April-June and Sept-mid-Oct Mon-Fri 8:00-18:00, Sat-Sun 9:00-13:00; mid-Oct-mid-April Mon-Fri 9:00-17:00, Sat-Sun 9:00-12:00; on Trg Grgurina, tel. 032/304-720, www.museummaritimum.com.

• *Facing the museum, go around the left side. After 10 yards, you'll pass a well on your left called the...*

Karampana

—This well served as Kotor's only public faucet until the early 20th century (swing the pendulum to get things flowing). As such, it was also the top place in town for gossip, like the office water cooler. It's said that if your name is mentioned here, you know you've arrived. Today, though the chatter is no longer raging on this square, the town's gossip magazine is called *Karampana*.

• *Continue straight past the well into the next square...*

▲▲**St. Luke's Square (Trg Svetog Luke)**—There are two Serbian Orthodox churches on this pretty square, each with the typical Orthodox church features: a squat design, narrow windows, and portly domes. Little **St. Luke's Church** (Crkva Sv. Luka), in the middle of the square, dates from the 12th century. Locals debate long and hard as to whether St. Luke's was originally built as a Catholic church or an Orthodox one. (Although it "looks" Orthodox, it was constructed during the rule of Serbian King Vukan Nemanjić, when even Catholic churches were built in the Orthodox style.) Regardless of its origin, during the Venetian era, the church did double duty as a house of worship for both. These days, it's decidedly Orthodox (free, daily May-Oct 10:00-20:00, Nov-April 8:00-13:00 & 17:00-19:00).

The bigger and much newer **St. Nicholas' Church** (Crkva Sv. Nikola), at the far corner of the square, was built in 1909—because of its Neo-Byzantine design, it has similarly spherical domes and slitlike windows (free, same hours as St. Luke's).

Notice how the Orthodox crosses on the steeples of St. Nicholas' Church differ from the cross seen in Roman Catholic churches (known as a Latin cross). In addition to the standard crossbar, Orthodox crosses often also have a second, smaller crossbar near the top (representing the *I.N.R.I.* plaque that was displayed above Jesus' head). Sometimes Orthodox crosses also feature a third, angled crossbar at the bottom. Many believe that rather than being nailed directly to the cross, Jesus' feet were nailed to a crossbar like this one to prolong his suffering. The slanted angle repre-

sents Jesus' forgiveness of the thief crucified to his right (the side that's pointing up)...and suggests where the unrepentant thief on his left ended up.

Stepping into these (or any other Orthodox) churches, you'll immediately notice some key differences from Catholic churches: no pews (worshippers stand through the service as a sign of respect), tall and skinny candles (representing prayers), and a screen of icons, called an iconostasis, in the middle of the sanctuary to separate the material world from the holy world (where the Bible is kept). For more about Orthodox worship, see the sidebar on page 318.

Before continuing on, enjoy this square's lazy ambience. The big building fronting the square is a music school, and the students practicing here fill this already pleasant public space with an appealing soundtrack.

• *If you go down the street to your left as you face St. Nicholas, you'll wind up back at the Square of Arms. But first try getting lost, then found again, in Kotor's delightful maze of streets. The town's final attraction is above your head (to head there directly, face St. Nicholas' Church, turn right, and walk straight for two blocks).*

▲▲**Town Walls (Gradske Zidine)**—Kotor's fortifications begin as stout ramparts along the waterfront, then climb up the sheer cliff face behind town in a dizzying zigzag line. If there's a more elaborate city wall in Europe, I haven't seen it. A proud Kotorian bragged to me, "These fortifications cost more to build than any palace in Europe."

Imagine what it took to create this "Great Wall of Kotor": nearly three miles long, along extremely inaccessible terrain. It

was built in fits and starts over a millennium (9th-19th centuries, though most of it was during the Venetian occupation in the 17th and 18th centuries). Its thickness varies from 6 to 50 feet, and the tallest parts are 65 feet high. Sections higher on the hill—with thinner walls, before the age of gunpowder—are the oldest, while the thick walls along the water are most recent. It was all worth it: The fortified town survived many attacks, including a two-month Ottoman siege in 1657.

If you're in great shape, consider scrambling along the walls and turrets above the Old Town.

Cost and Hours: You'll pay €3 to enter the walls if you visit May-Oct daily 8:00-20:00; otherwise they're free.

Hiking the Walls: If you go all the way up to the top fortress and back again, it'll take around an hour and a half round-trip (depending on how fast you go). This involves climbing 1,355

steps (an elevation gain of more than 700 feet)—don't overestimate your endurance or underestimate the heat. ("Am-I-*that*-out-of-shape?" tourists routinely find themselves winded and stranded high above town.) Bring plenty of water, along with a hat and sunscreen, and wear sturdy shoes. Most of the way, there's both a ramp and uneven stairs, but the route is in poor repair, with a lot of rough, rocky patches.

It's best to tackle the walls clockwise. (Even if you're not doing the hike, you can visually trace this route.) Find the entrance at the back-left corner of town (near St. Mary's Church, through the alley with the two arches over it, including one with a Venetian lion). Pay the entry fee and begin hiking up. On the way up, notice the sign explaining that the fortress reconstruction was funded by the United States (Nov 2004)—if you're a US taxpayer, consider this hike your tax dollars at work.

First climb as high as the **Church of Our Lady of Health** (Crkva Gospe od Zdravlj). This is the halfway mark—about 20 minutes from the base at a good pace. While some believe this church has miraculous healing powers, most everyone agrees it offers some of the best views down over Kotor.

From this church, you can either cut back down toward the Old Town, or—if you're not exhausted yet—keep hiking up to the tippy-top **Fortress of St. John** (figure another 25-30 minutes from the church, if you're in decent shape). Built on the remains of fortifications from the Illyrians (you can scan the third-century B.C. remains just beyond the fort), this was the headquarters for the entire wall network below it. There's not much to see here, but it is fun to play "king of the castle" exploring the ruined shell—and the views, with 360 degrees of Montenegrin cliffs, are spectacular.

Then head back down, enjoying your reward: a downhill walk with head-on views of the Bay of Kotor. On the way down, watch

your step on the slippery-even-when-dry marble stairs, highly polished by the feet of centuries of visitors. At the round terrace below the church, you can head to the right (back the way you came); or, for a different path, head left following *powder magazine* signs, then down (right) at the fork. The ticket-seller warned me that he's often seen people wipe out on the very last step on their way down—so exhausted after the demanding hike that they let their guard down.

Sleeping in Kotor

Kotor's hotels are a poor value, and they feel very "Balkan" (a mix of colorful, tacky, and chaotic). You'll sleep cheaper in Dubrovnik, but Kotor might seduce you into spending the night. My recommendations are all inside the Old Town. Be warned that

Sleep Code

(€1 = about $1.40, country code: 382, area code: 032)
S = Single, **D** = Double/Twin, **T** = Triple, **Q** = Quad, **b** = bathroom.
Unless otherwise noted, credit cards are accepted and break-
fast is included, but the modest tourist tax (about €1 per person, per night) is not. Everyone listed here speaks English.

Rates: If I list two rates for an accommodation, the
second rate applies off-season (generally Oct-May); if I list
three rates, separated by slashes, the first is for peak season
(July-Aug), the second is for shoulder season (May-June and
Sept), and the third is for off-season (Oct-April). The dates for
seasonal rates vary by hotel, and prices can change without
notice; verify the hotel's current rates online or by email. For
other updates, see www.ricksteves.com/update.

To help you sort easily through these listings, I've divided
the accommodations into two categories based on the price
for a double room with bath during high season:

$$ Higher Priced—Most rooms €100 or more.
$ Lower Priced—Most rooms less than €100.

loud nightclubs can bother light sleepers, especially in summer.
Most of the town's cheaper *sobe* are outside the city walls (ask for
details at TI).

$$ Hotel Vardar has 24 rooms with mod bathrooms smack
dab in the middle of the Old Town. This classic old copper-roofed
hotel was recently renovated from top to bottom, leaving it stylish
but not gaudy. While convenient, the dead-central location can
come with some noise, especially on weekends—request a quieter room (Sb-€125/€115/€95, Db-€185/€155/€125; 20 percent less
Fri-Sat nights for two people, pricier and larger apartments have
views on the square, air-con, elevator, free Wi-Fi in lobby, free
cable Internet, Stari Grad 476, tel. 032/325-084, www.hotelvardar
.com, info@hotelvardar.com).

$$ Hotel Cattaro offers 20 newish, Balkan-plush rooms—
with dark wood and bold old-meets-new decor—above a casino
right on the Square of Arms (Sb-€89/€69, Db-€119/€99, cheaper
rates are for Nov-April, pricier suites, some noise from square, air-
con, elevator, free Wi-Fi, tel. 032/311-000, fax 032/311-080, www
.cattarohotel.com, cattarohotel@t-com.me).

$ Hotel Marija, a somewhat ramshackle throwback on an
Old Town square, offers 17 rooms and wood-paneled halls. Rooms
overlooking the square come with noise and the windows are thin,
so request a quieter room in the back. Communicating with the
staff can be challenging but is workable (Sb-€65/€50, Db-€90/€70,

Tb-€103/€90, Qb-€130/€110, air-con, free Wi-Fi, on Trg od Kina, Stari Grad 449, tel. 032/325-062, hotel.marija.kotor@t -com.me).

Near Kotor, in Perast

If you're overnighting in Montenegro, tiny Perast is sleepier than Kotor—which is both good (quiet after dark) and bad (quiet after dark). These two hotels flank the main square along the waterfront road, right in the heart of town. Both have restaurant piers with fine seating right on the water (see page 386).

$$ Conte Hotel has 10 apartments, each one with a sea view (small studio-€100/€80/€70, big studio-€120/€90/€80, more for larger apartments, air-con, free Wi-Fi, Obala Kapetana Marka Martinovića bb, tel. 032/373-687, www.hotel-conte.com, hotel conte@yahoo.com).

$$ Admiral Hotel has eight rooms in an old officer's mansion (Db-€60-120/€50-100, lower rates are for Sept-Oct and May-June, closed Nov-April, price depends on size—highest are for rooms with seaview balcony, air-con, free Wi-Fi, Obala Kapetana Marka Martinovića 82, tel. 032/373-556, mobile 069-209-052, www.admiralperast.com, hoteladmiral@t-com.me).

Eating in Kotor

There's no shortage of dining options in Kotor's Old Town; even locals suggest simply wandering the streets and squares, following your nose, and choosing the ambience you like best. Truly great cuisine is rare here—I'd just settle for something scenic and functional. I've eaten well at **La Pasteria,** which has good pizzas and pastas, and breezy outdoor tables facing St. Tryphon's Cathedral (€6-9 pizzas and pastas, €11-15 main courses, daily 8:00-1:00 in the morning, Pjaca Sv. Tripuna/Trg od Katedrale, tel. 032/322-269). Nearby, **City Restaurant** lacks cathedral views but offers a fine, shady perch—its well-varnished picnic tables are set within the little forest in the Old Town, and more tables fill a small square out front (€6-10 pizzas, pastas, and salads; €7-17 main courses; daily 8:00-1:00 in the morning; mobile 069-049-653).

Near Kotor

For eateries in Perast, see page 386. Or consider these two very scenic options, also situated along the bayside road.

In Ljuta

Restoran Stari Mlini has a cozy interior and wonderful outdoor seating scattered around a spring-fed stream near an old, name-sake water mill. Surrounded by trickling water, you'll dine on local cuisine—you can even choose your own trout from the pond (€12-18 pastas, €13-22 main dishes, long hours daily, tel. 032/333-555).

Near the Verige Strait, in Morinj

Konoba Ćatovića Mlini is a memorable restaurant worth going out of your way to reach. Hiding in a sparse forest off the main fjordside road, this oasis is situated amidst a series of ponds, streams, waterfalls, and bubbling springs. The traditionally clad waiters are stiffly formal, and the cuisine is good and surprisingly affordable. Choose between several different stony seating options, indoors and out. Family-run for 200 years,

this place is a local institution, yet it feels like a well-kept secret (despite the crowds in summer). Reservations are essential (€8-14 pastas, €10-24 fish dishes, extensive wine list—Vranac is a popular local dry red, daily 11:00-23:00, tel. 032/373-030). The best plan might be to dine here on your way back to Dubrovnik from Kotor.

Getting There: At the town of Morinj, watch for burgundy *Konoba Ćatovića Mlini* signs and fish-shaped signs leading away from the water. You'll make several turns, but the signs will lead you right to the restaurant.

Kotor Connections

From Kotor by Bus to: Herceg Novi (2/hour, 1 hour), **Budva** (1-4/hour, 40 minutes), **Cetinje** (2-3/hour, 1 hour), **Dubrovnik** (daily at 8:30 and 14:45, also sporadic connections on other days, 2.5 hours), **Mostar** via Trebinje (1/day in the afternoon, 5.5 hours), **Zagreb** (daily at 14:45). Bus info: tel. 032/325-809, www.autobuskastanica kotor.me.

The Montenegrin Interior

Although Montenegro is trying to cultivate a glitzy beach-break cachet, for most of its history it has been thought of as a rugged mountain kingdom. While the coast—the focus of most of this chapter—was traditionally Venetian or Austrian, the real heart of Montenegro beat behind the sheer wall of mountains rising up from that seafront. Romantics, caught up in outdated Balkan fantasies, still think of this inland area as the "real" Montenegro.

While the Bay of Kotor is the most accessible and appealing

part of the country, if you have more time, consider a joyride up into the mountains. For a quick look at this area, the easiest loop takes you to the historic capital of Cetinje—a dull little town in its own right, but a fine excuse for a mountain drive. You could do this whole loop in about two and half hours without stopping (about an hour from Kotor to Cetinje, then another hour to Budva, then a half-hour back to Kotor), but if you want to stretch your legs in Njeguši or Cetinje, allow more time.

Self-Guided Driving Tour

The Road into the Mountains

The road to Cetinje twists you up the mountain face that stretches high above Kotor—it's an incredibly scenic, white-knuckle drive.

From Kotor, leave town toward Budva (bearing left at the roundabout). At the edge of Kotor, after the cemetery but before the big tunnel, take a right (marked for *Cetinje*) and begin your ascent. Cresting the first hill, go left to get to Cetinje (also marked for *Njeguši*). You'll wind up and up (past a small Roma encampment) on 25 numbered switchbacks. The road is a souvenir from the Habsburg era (1884). While Venetian rule brought sea trade, Austrian rule brought fortresses and infrastructure. After switchback #13, you'll pass an old customs house marking the former border between the Austro-Hungarian Empire and the Kingdom of Montenegro—a reminder that the coastline was not historically an integral part of Montenegrin cultural identity. As you near the top, look across the canyon to the left to spot the impossibly rough little donkey path that once was Cetinje's connection with the coast...like a tenuous umbilical cord tethering the mountainous interior to the outside world.

As you crest the hill, the vegetation changes—you're high above the Adriatic, with commanding views of Kotor and its bay (and great photo-op pull-outs; the best is just after switchback #25). Continuing inland, you find yourself in another world: poor, insular, and more Eastern (you'll see more Cyrillic lettering). Country farmhouses sell smoked ham, mountain cheese, and *medovina* (honey brandy). Before long, you reach a broad plain and the hamlet of...

Njeguši

The humble-seeming village of Njeguši (NYEH-goo-shee) is actually well-known among Montenegrins, with two very important claims to fame. This was the hometown of the House of Petrović-Njegoš, the dynasty that ruled Montenegro for much of its history (1696-1918). The family's favorite son was Petar II Petrović-Njegoš (1813-1851). Aside from ruling the country,

Petar II is remembered most fondly as a great poet and playwright—sort of the Montenegrin Shakespeare.

Njeguši is also famous for producing its own special type of air-dried ham, called *Njeguški pršut*. Locals explain that, because this meadow overlooks the sea on one side, and the mountains on the other, the wind changes direction 10 times each day, alternating between dry mountain breeze and salty sea air—perfect for seasoning and drying ham hocks. For good measure, the *pršut* is also smoked with beech wood. The blocky, white buildings lining the road that look like giant Monopoly houses are actually smokehouses, jammed with five layers of hanging ham hocks—thousands of euros' worth—silently aging. (More industry than you realize hides out in sleepy villages.) A couple of traditional restaurants at the heart of the village are happy to serve passing tourists a lunch of this local specialty. For more on *pršut*, see the sidebar on page 512.

From Njeguši to Cetinje

Continuing through Njeguši toward Cetinje, you'll twist up into more mountains—soon arriving in an even more rugged and inhospitable landscape than you passed on the road that brought you here from the coast. Eyeing this desolate scenery, you can understand why the visiting Lord Byron said of this place, "Am I in paradise or on the moon?" Along the mountain road that drops you down into Cetinje, each rock has the phone number of a vulture-esque road repair service *(auto slep)* spray-painted onto it. Low-profile plaques mark the site of Tito-era ambush assassinations.

Keep an eye out (on the horizon to the right) for the pointy peak of the mountain called **Lovćen,** which is capped by an elaborate mausoleum, designed by the great Croatian sculptor Ivan Meštrović, and devoted to King Petar II Petrović-Njegoš. With more time, you could actually drive up to the top of this mountain for sweeping views across Montenegro.

When you get into Cetinje, take a right when you hit a fork and find a place to park. To find your way into the old center, ask "guh-DEH yeh TSEHN-tar?"

Cetinje

Cetinje (TSEH-teen-yeh)—the historic capital of Montenegro—is a fine but fallen-on-hard-times little burg that sits cradled in a desolate valley surrounded by mighty peaks. Run-down as Cetinje is, it's still more pleasant than the current, drab capital, Podgorica.

Observing Cetinje from afar, it seems made to order as the historic capital of a remote and rustic people. It was the home of the Montenegrin king since the 15th century, but has always been pretty humble. In fact, it's said that when the Ottomans conquered it and moved in ready to rampage, they realized there wasn't much to pillage and plunder—so they just destroyed the town and moved on. The town was destroyed several other times, as well—and each time, the local people rebuilt it.

This "Old Royal Capital," once the leading city in the realm, is today a victim of Tito's quirky economic program for Yugoslavia. It used to provide shoes and refrigerators for the country, but when Yugoslavia disintegrated, so did the viability of Cetinje's economy. As you explore the two-story town today, it seems there's little more than a scruffy dollop of tourism to keep its 17,000 people housed and fed. Many of its younger generation have left for employment along the coast in the tourism industry.

Stroll the main street (Njegoševa) past kids on bikes, old-timers with hard memories, and young adults with metabolisms as low as the town's. At the end of this drag is the main square (Balšića Pazar), surrounded by low-key sights with sporadic opening hours: the **Ethnographic Museum** (traditional costumes and folk life), **Historical Museum** (tracing the story of Montenegro), **Njegoš Museum** (dedicated to the beloved poet-king Petar II Petrović-Njegoš), and **National Museum,** which honors King Nikola I, who ruled from 1860 until 1918. While his residence is as poor and humble a royal palace as you'll see in Europe, Nikola I thought big. He married off five of his daughters into the various royal families of Europe.

A short walk from the palace is the birthplace of the town, **Cetinje Monastery.** It's dedicated to St. Peter of Cetinje, a leg-

endary local priest who carried a cross in one hand and a sword in the other, established the first set of laws among Montenegrins, and inspired his people to defend Christianity against the Muslims. The monastery also holds the supposed right hand of St. John the Baptist. You are free to wander respectfully through the courtyard and church of this spiritual capital of Serbian Orthodox Montenegro.

From Cetinje Back to the Coast

To avoid backtracking down the same twisty road you came up, consider heading more directly back toward the coast from Cetinje. Just follow signs for *Budva.* A few miles outside of Cetinje along this road, look for the good **Restoran Konak,** which serves up tasty traditional dishes with indoor and outdoor seating (open long hours daily, tel. 041/761-011).

Continuing along this road, you'll pop out high above the

Budva Riviera. Looking out to sea, you'll spot the distinctive peninsula of Sveti Stefan off to the left, and the town of Budva to the right. If you have even more time, linger along the coast to visit these sights (described next). Otherwise, head right to return to Kotor or Dubrovnik.

The Budva Riviera

Montenegrins boast, "Croatia's got islands, but we've got beaches!" Long swaths of coarse-sand and fine-pebble beaches surround the resort town of Budva, just south of Kotor. This 15-mile stretch of coast, called the "Budva Riviera," is unappealingly built up, with endless strings of cheap resort hotels (and quite a few new five-star ones)—making it pale in comparison to the jagged saltiness of the Bay of Kotor or the romantic tidiness of Dalmatia. This region has recently become a mecca for super-wealthy Russians, staking their claim to this patch of Adriatic seafront. But the area isn't without its charm. Aside from the pleasant Old Town of the region's unofficial capital, Budva, you'll discover a near-mythical haunt of the rich and famous: the highly exclusive resort peninsula of Sveti Stefan (not possible to visit, but alluring from afar). For me, more time in Kotor or an earlier return to Dubrovnik would be more satisfying than the trek to the Budva Riviera. But beach-lovers who have plenty of time and a spirit of adventure will find this area merits a look.

Getting to the Budva Riviera

Budva is about a 30-minute drive south of **Kotor.** The easiest approach is to continue past Kotor along the fjord, left at the roundabout, then through the tunnel (following *Budva* signs; exiting the tunnel, notice the sign in Cyrillic letters for Russki Radio 107.3—catering to the Russian jet-setters). For a more scenic route, take a right before the tunnel for the upper road to Budva that twists over the mountain (described earlier, under "The Montenegrin Interior"). After winding up several switchbacks (with giddy views back over the Bay of Kotor) and cresting the hill, go right (again following *Budva* signs). You'll coast down into a valley, through the town of Lastva, then back over another mild hill that deposits you above the beaches of Budva.

First you'll reach the town of **Budva** (turn right at traffic light, following brown *Stari Grad* signs to the Old Town; parking is well-marked in modern complex next to Old Town). Continuing around the bay, you'll pass the busy, modern resort cluster of Bečići before reaching **Sveti Stefan.**

Sights on the Budva Riviera

Between the strings of resort hotels are two towns that deserve a quick visit.

Budva

The Budva Riviera's best Old Town has charming Old World lanes crammed with souvenir shops and holiday-making Serbs and

Russians. While far less appealing than Kotor (and Dalmatian towns such as Korčula, Hvar, and Trogir), Budva at least offers a taste of romance between the resort sprawl.

Budva's ancient history (dating back at least to the fifth century B.C.) is arguably more illustrious than Kotor's. It

began as an "emporium" (market and trading center) for Greek seamen, and extremely valuable jewelry uncovered here indicates that some pretty important people spent time in Budva. And yet, Budva isn't about history; it's about today. As in many Mexican vacation areas, the Old Town is just one more part of the resort experience—it's basically treated as a backdrop for outdoor dining and nightclubs.

A 10-minute stroll tells you all you need to know about Budva. The layout is simple and intuitive—a peninsula (flanked by beaches) with a big Venetian-style bell tower. From the parking lot, a pedestrian-only, tree-and-café-lined boulevard runs away from the Old Town. But to see the historic core of town, go instead through the Old Town walls and wander up the main drag, Njegoševa; just before the small square, on the right, is the **TI** (July-Sept daily 9:00-21:00, shorter hours off-season, at #28, tel. 033/452-750, www.budva.travel).

Out at the tip of town, you'll pop out into a small café-lined square with a **Catholic church** (on the left, with an unusually modern 1970s mosaic behind the altar depicting St. John preaching on the Montenegrin coast) facing the Orthodox **Holy Trinity Church,** with gorgeous and colorful Orthodox decorations inside. Beyond that is a huge **citadel** that's imposing on the outside but dull on the inside; it's not worth paying the €2 to tour its museum of model ships, antiquarium (old library), restaurant, and less-than-thrilling sea views (daily May-Sept 9:00-24:00, April and Oct-Nov 9:00-20:00, Dec-March 9:00-17:00).

MONTENEGRO

Sveti Stefan

Like a mirage hovering just offshore, the famously exclusive luxury hotel that makes up the resort peninsula of Sveti Stefan beckons curious travelers to come, see, snap a photo...and then wish they'd spent more time elsewhere. While scenic, there's not much to actually experience at Sveti Stefan (unless you've got a thousand bucks to rent a room); while it's a great photo op, it disappoints many who make the trip. But for those caught up in Robin Leach-ian memories of this hotel's glory days, it's worth a pilgrimage.

Once an actual, living town (connected to the mainland only by a narrow, natural causeway), Sveti Stefan was virtually abandoned after World War II. The Yugoslav government developed it into a giant resort hotel in the 1950s. As old homes were converted to hotel rooms, the novelty of the place—and its sterling location, surrounded by pebbly beaches and lush scenery—began to attract some seriously wealthy guests.

During this resort's heyday in the 1960s and 1970s, it ranked with Cannes or St-Tropez as *the* place to see or be seen on Europe's beaches. You could rent a room, a house, an entire block of houses, or even the entire peninsula. Anonymity was vigilantly protected, as the nicest "rooms" had their own private pools (away from public scrutiny), lockable gates, and security guards. Lured by Sveti Stefan's promise of  privacy, celebrities, rock stars, royalty, and dignitaries famously engaged in bidding wars to decide who'd be granted access to the best suites: Whoever put the most money in a sealed envelope and slipped it to the manager, won. (According to local legend, Sly Stallone's money talked.) Guests were pampered—indulged no matter how outrageous their requests. Sophia Loren, Kirk Douglas, Doris Day, and Claudia Schiffer are just a few of the big names who basked on Sveti Stefan's beaches.

By the late 2000s, Sveti Stefan had experienced a dramatic decline. Warfare in nearby places (such as Dubrovnik and Kosovo) kept visitors away, its cachet faded, and the resort grew a bit rough around the edges. Then the Indian company Aman Resorts swept in with ambitious plans to restore the island to its former status as one of the world's most exclusive, crème-de-la-crème resorts (cheapest Db-€700, www.amansvetistefan.com). These days, no-neck thugs guard the causeway, letting only guests (no exceptions) cross over into the fantasy world of Sveti Stefan. If you're desperate to check it out, you can reserve a meal at the restaurant (€25 per person minimum, but count on paying far more). If you want to relax on the beaches flanking the causeway, most areas charge €30-50 per person for the day, but there are a few free areas—ask the guard for details.

Even if you can't enter the peninsula, let your imagination run as you gaze upon it. Strolling through the dead town, peeking through gates, visitors hope to spot a withered old celebrity who forgot to go home. "Rooms" come with varying degrees of privacy (each more expensive than the last): no fence, small fence, big fence. At the far end is the biggest and most famous "suite," where guests have an entire corner of the peninsula to themselves. At the top of the peninsula is a big Russian Orthodox church and a smaller Serbian Orthodox church—though both are little more than hotel decorations today.

Across the water from Sveti Stefan, on its own little cove, is one of Tito's former vacation villas (Villa Miločer, also part of the Aman resort).

Getting to Sveti Stefan: Sveti Stefan is just three miles (5 km) beyond Budva. Coming around the bay from Budva (following signs toward *Bar*), you'll pass above the peninsula on the main road, watching for the well-marked pull-out on the right that offers classic views. After snapping your photos, if you want to get closer, continue down and turn off to the right, following signs to *Hotel Sveti Stefan*; you can park in the pay lot (€1/hour) and walk along the beach as far as the causeway.

From Sveti Stefan to Dubrovnik: Figure 1.5 hours to the Croatian border (if you go via Tivat—rather than Kotor—and use the shortcut ferry across the Bay of Kotor, described on page 388), then another 45 minutes to Dubrovnik.

MONTENEGRO

BOSNIA-HERZEGOVINA

Bosna i Hercegovina

BOSNIA-HERZEGOVINA

 The mid-1990s weren't kind to Bosnia-Herzegovina: War. Destruction. Genocide. But apart from the tragic way it separated from Yugoslavia, the country has long been—and remains—a remarkable place, with ruggedly beautiful terrain, a unique mix of cultures and faiths, kind and welcoming people who pride themselves on their hospitality, and some of the most captivating sightseeing in southeastern Europe.

Little Bosnia-Herzegovina is a country with three faiths, three languages, and two alphabets. While the rest of Yugoslavia has splintered into countries dominated by one ethnicity, Bosnia remains an uneasy mix of scattered communities, with large contingents of all three major Yugoslav groups: Muslim Bosniaks, Eastern Orthodox Serbs, and Catholic Croats. These same three factions fought each other in that brutal war just two decades ago, and today they're struggling to reconcile, work together, and put the country back on track.

A visit here offers a fascinating opportunity to sample the cultures of these three major faiths within a relatively small area. In the same day, you can inhale incense in a mystical-feeling Serbian Orthodox church, hear the subtle clicking of rosary beads in a Roman Catholic church, and listen to the Muslim call to prayer echo across a skyline of prickly minarets. Few places in Europe—or the world—cram so much diversity into such a small space.

About half of the people in Bosnia are "Bosniaks"—that is, Muslims. Travel in Bosnia offers an illuminating and unique glimpse of a culture that's both devoutly Muslim and fully European. Here, just a short drive from the touristy Dalmatian Coast, you can step into a mosque and learn about Islam directly from a Muslim. The country also holds one of the most important pilgrimage sites of the Roman Catholic world: Međugorje, where six residents have reported seeing visions of the Virgin Mary.

More than any other country in this book, Bosnia rearranges your mental furniture. While repairs are ongoing, you'll still be confronted by vivid and thought-provoking scars of the 1990s war, especially outside of the tourist zones. Poignant roadside memori-

Bosnia-Herzegovina

Bosnia-Herzegovnia Political Regions
- Republika Srpska
- Muslim-Croat Federation

100 Kilometers
50 Miles

als to fallen soldiers, burned-out husks of buildings, unmistakable starburst patterns in the pavement, and bullet holes in walls

are a constant reminder that the country is still recovering—physically and psychologically. Driving through the countryside, you'll pass between Muslim, Croat, and Serb towns—each one decorated with its own provocative sectarian symbols. In an age when we watch news coverage of conflicts abroad with the same detachment we accord Hollywood blockbusters, Bosnia teaches an essential lesson about how real—and destructive—war and interethnic strife truly are.

Bosnia-Herzegovina Almanac

Official Name: Bosna i Hercegovina (abbreviated "BiH"); the *i* means "and"—Bosnia and Herzegovina (the country's two regions). For simplicity, I generally call it "Bosnia" in this book. "Bosna" (literally "running water") is the name of a major river here, while the tongue-twisting name "Herzegovina" (hert-seh-GOH-vee-nah) comes from the German word for "dukedom" (*Herzog* means "duke").

Snapshot History: Bosnia-Herzegovina's early history is similar to the rest of the region: Illyrians, Romans, and Slavs (oh, my!). In the late 15th century, Turkish rulers from the Ottoman Empire began a 400-year domination of the country. Many of the Ottomans' subjects converted to Islam, and their descendants remain Muslims today. Bosnia-Herzegovina became part of the Austro-Hungarian Empire in 1878, then Yugoslavia after World War I, until it declared independence in the spring of 1992. The bloody war that ensued came to an end in 1995. (For details, see the Understanding Yugoslavia chapter.)

Population: About 4.6 million. (There were about 100,000 identified casualties of the recent war, but many estimates of total casualties are double that number.) Someone who lives in Bosnia-Herzegovina, regardless of ethnicity, is called a "Bosnian." A southern Slav who practices Islam is called a "Bosniak." Today, about half of all Bosnians are Bosniaks (Muslims), a little more than a third are Orthodox Serbs, and about 15 percent are Catholic Croats.

Area: 19,741 square miles (about the size of West Virginia). In both size and population, Bosnia is comparable to Croatia.

Geography: Bosnia and Herzegovina are two distinct regions that share the same mountainous country. Bosnia constitutes the majority of the country (in the north, with a continental climate), while Herzegovina is the southern tip (about a fifth of the total area, with a hotter Mediterranean climate). The nation's capital, Sarajevo, has an estimated 310,000 people; Mostar is

In this book I focus on a few key destinations, including several fascinating, user-friendly places within easy reach of the Dalmatian Coast: the Turkish-flavored city of Mostar (with its restored Old Bridge—one of Europe's most inspiring sights), some nearby attractions offering a more complete view of Herzegovina (Blagaj, Počitelj, and Stolac), and the Catholic shrine at Međugorje. A longer trip from Dalmatia—but well worth the trek—is the Bosnian capital of Sarajevo, with a spectacular mountain-valley setting, a multilayered history, powerful wartime stories, and a resilient populace of proud Sarajevans eager to show you their fine city.

Bosnia is highly recommended as a detour—both geographi-

Herzegovina's biggest city (with approximately 130,000 people) and unofficial capital.

Red Tape: To enter Bosnia-Herzegovina, Americans and Canadians need only a passport (no visa required).

Economy: The country's economy has struggled since the war—the per capita GDP is just $6,600, and the official unemployment rate is around 43 percent.

Currency: The official currency is the Convertible Mark (Konvertibilna Marka, abbreviated KM locally, BAM internationally). The official exchange rate is $1 = about 1.40 KM. But merchants are usually willing to take euros, and (in Mostar) they'll often accept Croatian kunas, roughly converting prices with a simple formula:

2 KM = €1 = 8 kn (= about $1.40)

Telephones: Bosnia-Herzegovina's country code is 387. If calling from another country, first dial the international access code (00 in Europe, 011 in the US), then 387, then the area code (minus the initial zero), then the number.

Flag: The flag of Bosnia-Herzegovina is a blue field with a yellow triangle along the top edge. The three points of the triangle represent Bosnia-Herzegovina's three peoples (Bosniaks, Croats, Serbs), and the triangle itself resembles the physical shape of the country. A row of white stars underscores the longest side of the triangle. These stars—and the yellow-and-blue color scheme—echo the flag of the European Union (a nod to the EU's efforts to bring peace to the region). While this compromise flag sounds like a nice idea, almost no Bosnian embraces it as his or her own; each group has its own unofficial but highly prized symbols and flags (such as the fleur-de-lis for the Bosniaks, the red-and-white checkerboard shield for the Croats, and the cross with the four C's for the Serbs)—many of which offend the other groups.

cal and cultural—from the Croatian and Slovenian mainstream. Inquisitive visitors come away from a visit to Bosnia with a more nuanced understanding of the former Yugoslavia. Practically speaking, Bosnia offers lower prices and a warmer welcome than you'll find on the Croatian coast.

Nervous travelers might be tempted to give Bosnia-Herzegovina a miss. The country can be unsettling, because of its in-your-face war damage and exotic mélange of cultures that seems un-European. But to me, for exactly these reasons, Bosnia ranks alongside Croatia and Slovenia as a rewarding destination. Overcome your jitters and dive in.

Bosnian History

With its mountainous landscape, remote from the more mainline areas of the western Balkans, Bosnia's evolution has followed a unique course. Even now, the people of Bosnia struggle with being outsiders—afloat on an oddball cultural island flanked by the Roman Catholic West (Croatia) and the Orthodox East (Serbia), borrowing elements from both but not fully belonging to either.

After periods of rule by the Illyrians (ancestors of today's Albanians) and the Romans, Bosnia fostered its own thriving Slavic culture during the Middle Ages. This was the time of the Bogomil culture: A homegrown branch of Christianity that was neither Catholic nor Orthodox—and was viewed with suspicion by both faiths. The Bogomil (literally "dear to God") faith was simple, ascetic, and somewhat mystic, combining elements of Slavic, Illyrian, and Celtic traditions. The Bogomils—who comprised a majority of the population of medieval Bosnia—had a thriving civilization. Vivid artifacts of the Bogomil kingdom are still around, such as their engraved burial grave markers, called *stećaks* (some of the best-preserved are in Stolac, near Mostar).

When the Ottomans (from what's now called Turkey) took over this land in the 15th century, they tolerated different faiths... but offered economic and political incentives to those who converted to Islam. In negotiating their religious freedoms with the sultans, Bosnia's Roman Catholics (who identified as Croats) and Eastern Orthodox (who identified as Serbs) both had the support of larger church hierarchies outside of Bosnia. But the Bogomils had no bargaining power, and were more likely to swap one monotheistic faith for another—creating the Muslim South Slav ethnicity that would come to be known as "Bosniak."

Under the Ottomans, Bosnia flourished. The Ottoman sultans invested in infrastructure (primarily bridges—including Mostar's Old Bridge—and fountains) and architecture, including many mosques, hammams (baths), caravanserais (inns), madrassas (theological schools), and so on. Bosnian Muslims rose through the ranks of the empire, becoming military generals, religious leaders, beloved poets, and even grand viziers (top-level advisors to the sultans).

After four centuries of rule, the Ottoman Empire entered a steep decline. Unable to continue to rule over its vast holdings, in 1878 the sultan passed control of Bosnia-Herzegovina to its Habsburg rival, the Austro-Hungarian Empire (which already controlled neighboring Croatia and Slovenia). The Habsburgs quickly moved to modernize Bosnia, erecting buildings and investing in infrastructure. But just 40 years later, that empire, too, would topple—losing a war that began when its heir, the Archduke Franz Ferdinand, was assassinated in Sarajevo (see sidebar on page 485).

Following World War I, Bosnia was swept up in the movement to create a union of the South Slavs. The original incarnation of Yugoslavia, called "the Kingdom of the Serbs, Croats, and Slovenes," ignored the Bosniaks both in name and in political influence—they were merely along for the ride.

During World War II, Bosnia was part of the so-called "Independent State of Croatia" (run by the Nazis' puppet Ustaše government). Some of the most dramatic WWII battles between the Yugoslav Partisans and the Nazis took place here in Bosnia. The postwar communist state of Yugoslavia was born in the Bosnian town of Jajce on November 29, 1943, when Partisan generals met to outline the future of a hoped-for post-Nazi state. But in the new incarnation of Yugoslavia, many Bosniaks still felt like second-class citizens. Local Muslims recall that Yugoslav government-issued textbooks reinforced negative stereotypes. For example, they might say "Sasha [a typically Serb name] is working," but "Mujo [a typically Muslim name] is a bad boy."

Even after the outbreak of violence between breakaway republics Slovenia and Croatia and Serb-dominated Yugoslavia in 1991, things stayed strangely calm in Bosnia. When the Bosnian conflict finally erupted in 1992, it was war of the most brutal kind. The early to mid-1990s saw the worst human, architectural, and cultural devastation in Bosnian history. Sarajevo, Srebrenica, and Mostar became synonymous with sectarian strife, horrific sieges, and shocking genocide. (For more details on the war, see page 684 of the Understanding Yugoslavia chapter.)

The Dayton Peace Accords that ended the conflict here in 1995 gerrymandered the nation into three separate regions: the Federation of Bosnia and Herzegovina (FBiH, shared by Bosniaks and Croats, roughly in the western and central parts of the country), the Republika Srpska (RS, dominated by Serbs, generally to the north and east), and the Brčko District (BD, a tiny corner of the country, with a mix of the ethnicities). For the most part, each of the three native ethnic groups stay in "their" part of this divided country, but tourists can move freely between them.

On your visit, tune into the many ways that the Bosniaks, Croats, and Serbs of Bosnia work hard to coexist. To satisfy the country's various factions, the currency uses both the Roman and the Cyrillic alphabets, and bills have different figureheads and symbols (some bills feature

Fundamentalist Islam in Bosnia?

Islam is a hot topic in today's Europe, where many citizens are blaming Muslim immigrants for their society's woes. And even though Bosnia's Muslims are indigenous, they're not immune to the criticism—especially from their Serb and Croat rivals. While Bosniaks have a long history as a peace-loving people, critics allege that elements of the population are experimenting with some alarming fundamentalist Islamic ideologies.

These allegations do have some basis in fact. During the war and genocide of the 1990s, many Bosniaks felt abandoned by their western allies in Europe and the US, who were too timid to step in and "take sides" to end the violence. In his people's darkest hour, desperate Bosnian President Alija Izetbegović recruited assistance from the only group willing to offer help: Muslim fundamentalists from the Middle East and North Africa. Several hundred mujahideen (Islamic jihadists) came to Bosnia to train Bosniak soldiers, and participated in bloody massacres of Serbs and Croats. They brought with them the dangerous ideas of Wahhabism—an ultraconservative movement bent on "purifying" Islam, often through violent means. According to reports, Izetbegović was even in contact with Osama bin Laden. In some cases, the mujahideen offered donations to widows of *šehid*s (Bosniak martyrs).

While waning, these groups' influence persists. Muslim countries have helped to fund the postwar reconstruction of Bosnia, especially the building and rebuilding of mosques and madrassas. Just as the end of atheistic, communist Yugoslav rule kick-started a passion for Catholicism in Croatia and the Orthodox faith in Serbia, many Muslims in Bosnia are today actively pursuing their faith. You may even see women wearing traditional Muslim headscarves—a rare sight before the war, when most Bosniaks dressed just like their Serb and Croat neighbors.

Meanwhile, some of the fundamentalist Muslims who came to fight in the war are still here (although they were supposed to leave the country under the Dayton Peace Accords). Mujahideen who fought were initially rewarded with Bosnian citizenship (these passports were revoked in 2007). Some of them married local women, however, and are pursuing a Wahhabist agenda in Bosnia. Small pockets of Wahhabists live in remote areas high in the mountains, separate from mainstream Bosnian society—indeed, the typical Bosniak on the street is as wary of them as you might be. The violent element of Bosnian Wahhabists are just one more example of a terrorist "cell" in a country that doesn't want them. The majority of practicing Muslims in Bosnia explicitly denounce the Wahhabists. As in any country, Bosnia has its share of fanatics—but they make up a tiny fringe in this predominantly peaceful nation.

Bosniaks, others Serbs). Until very recently, the alphabet used on road signs changed with the territory: Roman alphabet in Muslim and Croat areas, Cyrillic alphabet in Serb lands. But now all road signs throughout Bosnia-Herzegovina are required to appear in both alphabets—though that doesn't prevent vandals from spray-painting over the alphabet they don't like. License plates also used different alphabets, but this led to vandalism to cars that crossed into the "other side." Today's license plates use only letters that are common to both alphabets.

Towns with mixed populations are either effectively divided in half, or have buildings clearly marked with symbols indicating the ethnicity of the occupant. Small-town schoolhouses often operate "two schools under one roof," with separate entrances and staggered shifts for the Bosniak and Croat kids...who, virtually from birth, are constantly told they are very different from each other. In some towns, a beautifully restored Orthodox church may sit across from the battered footprint of a long-gone mosque (or vice versa).

Bosnia has a central government, but each population group also has its own autonomous government and sub-agencies, resulting in four different, essentially redundant bureaucracies. The country is also divided into 10 state-like cantons, each of which also has some governmental authority. What's more, these various levels of governments refuse to cooperate—imagine the inefficiency. (For example, nobody knows how many people live in Bosnia, because there's no agreement on how to conduct a national census.) On top of all this, Bosnia is still navigating the complex transition from communism to capitalism, and rebuilding from a devastating war. It's a miracle that things here work as well as they do.

Nearly 20 years later, the delicate compromises that were necessary to end a horrifying war have become almost too complicated to maintain. For Bosnia-Herzegovina to fully recover, all three groups must learn to truly set aside their differences and work together. Pessimists (who are abundant in this region) don't like Bosnia's chances, and Bosnian Serbs still talk loudly about secession (their president, Milorad Dodik, is a separatist who has floated several proposals to hold a referendum for independence). But others see signs of hope, such as the young people from the three faiths now beginning to cautiously intermingle, as their ancestors did for centuries. Will Bosniak, Serb, and Croat youth manage to transcend the fear and anger that tainted their parents' and grandparents' country in the 20th century? Stay tuned.

Bosnian Food

Bosnia-Herzegovina dines on grilled meat, stewed vegetables, soft cheeses, and other foods you may think of as "Turkish" or "Greek."

BOSNIA-HERZEGOVINA

Balkan Flavors

All of the countries of the Balkan Peninsula—basically from Slovenia to Greece—have several foods in common: The Ottomans from today's Turkey, who controlled much of this territory for centuries, imported some goodies that remained standard fare here long after they left town. Whether you're in Bosnia-Herzegovina, Slovenia, Croatia, Montenegro, Serbia, Kosovo, or Albania, it's worth seeking out some of these local tastes.

A popular, cheap fast food you'll see everywhere is **burek** (BOO-rehk)—phyllo dough filled with meat, cheese, spinach, or apples. The more familiar **baklava** is phyllo dough layered with honey and nuts.

Grilled meats are a staple of Balkan cuisine. You'll most often see **čevapčići** (cheh-VAHP-chee-chee), or simply **čevap** (cheh-VAHP)—minced meat formed into a sausage-link shape, then grilled. **Ražnjići** (RAZH-nyee-chee) is small pieces of steak on a skewer, like a shish kebab. **Pljeskavica** (plehs-kah-VEET-suh) is similar to čevapčići, except the meat is in the form of a hamburger-like patty.

While Balkan cuisine favors meat, a nice veggie complement is **đuveđ** (JOO-vedge)—a spicy mix of stewed vegetables, flavored with tomatoes and peppers.

And you just can't eat any of this stuff without the ever-present condiment **ajvar** (EYE-var). Made from red bell pepper and eggplant, ajvar is like ketchup with a kick. Many Americans pack a jar of this distinctive sauce to remember the flavors of the Balkans when they get back home. (You may even be able to find it at specialty grocery stores in the US—look for "eggplant/red pepper spread.") Particularly in Bosnia, another side-dish you'll see is the soft, spreadable—and tasty—cheese called **kajmak. Lepinje** is a pita-like grilled bread, which is often wrapped around čevapčići or pljeskavica to make a sandwich.

Ajvar, kajmak, lepinje, and diced raw onions are the perfect complement to a **"mixed grill"** of various meats on a big platter—the quintessence of Balkan cuisine on one plate.

For a rundown of the most common items you'll eat in Bosnia—and throughout the Balkans—see the "Balkan Flavors" sidebar.

Bosnia produces some wine, but it's mostly consumed domestically. Sarajevso Pivo, brewed in the capital, is the favored brand of beer. In Bosnia, "coffee" is *kafa* (not *kava*, as in Croatia and Slovenia).

Bosnian Language

Technically, Bosnia-Herzegovina has three languages—Bosnian, Serbian, and Croatian. But all three are mutually intelligible variants of what was until recently considered a single language: Serbo-Croatian. The Croatian survival phrases on page 729 work fine throughout Bosnia-Herzegovina. Bosniaks and Croats use basically the same Roman alphabet we do, while Serbs use the Cyrillic alphabet. You'll see both alphabets on currency, official documents, and road signs, but the Roman alphabet predominates in virtually every destination covered in this book. Many people also speak English.

MOSTAR and NEARBY

Mostar • Blagaj • Počitelj • Stolac • Međugorje

Mostar (MOH-star) encapsulates the best and the worst of Yugoslavia. During the Tito years, its residents enjoyed an idyllic mingling of cultures—Catholic Croats, Orthodox Serbs, and Muslim Bosniaks living together in harmony, their differences spanned by an Old Bridge that epitomized an optimistic vision of a Yugoslavia where ethnicity didn't matter. But then, as the country unraveled in the early 1990s, Mostar was gripped by a gory three-way war among those same peoples...and that famous bridge crumbled into the Neretva River.

Mostar is still rebuilding, and the bullet holes and destroyed buildings are ugly reminders that the last time you saw this place, it was probably on the nightly news. Western visitors may also be struck by the immediacy of the Muslim culture that permeates Mostar—at this crossroads of civilizations, minarets share the horizon with church steeples. During the Ottomans' 400-year control of this region, many Slavic subjects converted to Islam (see sidebar on page 432). And, although they retreated in the  late 19th century, the Ottomans left behind a rich architectural, cultural, and religious legacy that has forever shaped Mostar. Five times each day, loudspeakers on minarets crackle to life, and the call to prayer warbles through the streets. In many parts of the city, you'd swear you were in Turkey.

If these images intrigue you, read on—Mostar has so much

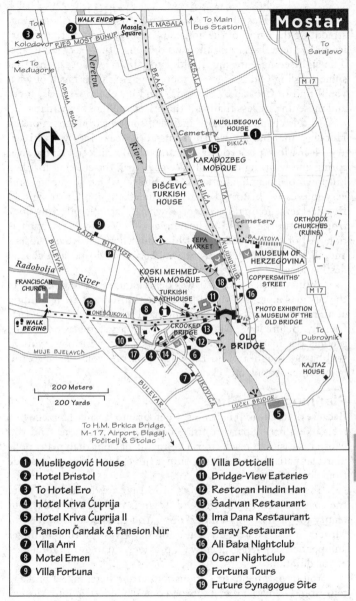

Mostar

❶	Muslibegović House	❿	Villa Botticelli
❷	Hotel Bristol	⓫	Bridge-View Eateries
❸	To Hotel Ero	⓬	Restoran Hindin Han
❹	Hotel Kriva Ćuprija	⓭	Šadrvan Restaurant
❺	Hotel Kriva Ćuprija II	⓮	Ima Dana Restaurant
❻	Pansion Čardak & Pansion Nur	⓯	Saray Restaurant
❼	Villa Anri	⓰	Ali Baba Nightclub
❽	Motel Emen	⓱	Oscar Nightclub
❾	Villa Fortuna	⓲	Fortuna Tours
		⓳	Future Synagogue Site

more to offer. Despite the scars of war, its setting is stunning: straddling the banks of the gorgeous Neretva River, with tributaries and waterfalls carving their way through the rocky landscape. The sightseeing—mosques, old Turkish-style houses, and that spine-tingling Old Bridge—is more engaging than much of what you'll find in Croatia or Slovenia. And it's cheap—hotels, food, and museums are less than half the prices you'll pay in Croatia.

In this chapter, I've also included some nearby attractions in Herzegovina that are worth trying to squeeze into your itinerary. Near Mostar is a trio of other mostly Bosniak sights: the river spring and whirling dervish house at Blagaj, the striking fortified hill town of Počitelj, and workaday Stolac, which sits upon some very impressive history. I've also included the top Croat sight in Bosnia-Herzegovina: Međugorje, where Catholic pilgrims flock from around the world to hear tales of a Virgin Mary apparition. All of these places are within a half-hour's drive of Mostar, and all are more or less on the way between Mostar and coastal destinations.

While a visit to Mostar was depressing just a few years ago, the city gets more uplifting all the time: Mostarians are rebuilding at an impressive pace and working hard to make Mostar tourist-friendly. Before long, Mostar will reclaim its status as one of the premier destinations in the former Yugoslavia. Visit now, while it still has its rough-around-the-edges charm—you'll have seen it before it really took off.

Planning Your Time

Because of its cultural hairiness, a detour into Bosnia-Herzegovina feels like a real departure from a Dalmatian vacation. And yet, Mostar is easier to reach from Dubrovnik or Split than many popular Dalmatian islands (it's within a three-hour drive or bus ride from either city).

The vast majority of tourists in Mostar are day-trippers from the coast, which means the Old Town is packed at midday, but empty in the morning and evening. You can get a good feel for Mostar in just a few hours, but a full day gives you time to linger and ponder. My self-guided walk provides a framework for a visit of any duration.

You have three basic options for getting here: take a package tour from Dalmatia; rent a car for a one-day side-trip into Mostar; or (my favorite) spend the night here en route between Croatian destinations. To work a Mostar overnight into your itinerary, consider a round-trip plan that takes you south along the coast, then back north via Bosnia-Herzegovina (for example, Split-Hvar-Korčula-Dubrovnik-Mostar-back to Split).

Getting Around Herzegovina

The destinations I've covered in this chapter aren't as easy to reach as they could be from the Dalmatian Coast, but connections are workable.

By Car: Coming with your own car gives you maximum flexibility, and a number of interesting routes connect Mostar to the coast (for detailed route information, see "Route Tips for Drivers" on page 448). If you do plan to drive here, let your car-rental company know in advance, to ensure you have the appropriate paperwork for crossing the border. If you're not up for driving yourself, consider splurging on a **driver** to bring you here (for drivers based in Dubrovnik, see page 294; for a Mostar-based driver, see page 425). Drivers may suggest several detours en route. Do your homework to know which ones interest you (for example, Međugorje isn't worth the extra time for most visitors), and don't hesitate to say you want to just max out on time in Mostar itself.

By Bus: Especially if you're spending the night in Mostar, bus connections with destinations on the Dalmatian Coast (especially Split and Dubrovnik) are workable—though getting clear and consistent schedule information can be a headache. For details, see "Mostar Connections," page 446.

By Package Tour: Taking a package excursion from a Dalmatian resort town seems like an efficient way to visit Mostar or Međugorje. Unfortunately, in reality it can be less rewarding than doing it on your own—count on lots and lots of hours on a crowded bus, listening to a lackluster, multilingual tour guide reading from a script, and relatively little time in the destinations themselves. But if you just want a quick one-day look at these places, an excursion could be a necessary evil. These all-day tours are sold from Split, Hvar, Korčula, Dubrovnik, and other Croatian coastal destinations for about €50-60. The best tours focus almost entirely on Mostar (it still won't be enough time); avoid tours that include a pointless boat trip on the Neretva River or time in Međugorje. Those that add a quick visit to the worthwhile town of Počitelj are a better deal. Ask for details at any travel agency in Dalmatia.

Orientation to Mostar

(country code: 387; area code: 036)

Mostar—a mid-sized city with just over 100,000 people—is situated in a basin surrounded by mountains and split down the middle by the emerald-green Neretva River. Bosniaks live mostly on the east side of the river (plus a strip on the west bank) and Croats in the modern sprawl to the west. The populations are beginning to mix again, albeit with tentative baby steps. Virtually all of the sights are in the Bosniak zone, but visitors move freely throughout the city, and most don't even notice the division. The cobbled, Turkish-feeling Old Town (called the "Stari Grad" or—borrowing a Turkish term—the "Stara Čaršija") surrounds the town's centerpiece, the Old Bridge.

The skyline is pierced by the minarets of various mosques, but none is as big as the two major Catholic (Croat) symbols in town, both erected since the recent war: the giant white cross on the hilltop (marking the place from where Croat forces shelled the Bosniak side of the river, including the Old Bridge); and the enormous (almost 100-foot-tall) bell tower of the Franciscan Church of Sts. Peter and Paul. A monumental Orthodox cathedral once stood on the hillside across the river, but it was destroyed in the war when the Serbs were forced out. Funds are now being collected to rebuild it.

A note about safety: Mostar is as safe as any city its size, but it doesn't always *feel* safe. You'll see bombed-out buildings everywhere, even in the core of the city. Some are marked with *Warning! Dangerous Ruin* signs, but for safety's sake, never wander into any building that appears damaged or deserted. In terms of petty theft, the Old Town has as many pickpockets as any tourist zone in Europe: Watch your valuables, especially on the Old Bridge.

Tourist Information

The virtually worthless TI shares a building with a tour office, but it does give out a free town map and a few other brochures on Mostar and Herzegovina (sporadic hours, generally open June-Sept daily 9:00-17:00, maybe later in busy times, likely closed Oct-May, just a block from the Old Bridge on Rade Bitange street, tel. 036/580-275, www.bhtourism.ba).

Arrival in Mostar

By Bus or Train: The **main bus station** (where most buses arrive in town) sits next to the giant but mostly deserted **train station,** north of the Old Town on the east side of the river. At the bus station, you'll find ticket windows and a left-luggage counter (2 KM/bag) in the Autoprevoz lobby facing the bus stalls. You can check schedules and buy tickets in this office for most buses *except* the many connections operated by Globtour, whose office is nearby (exit Autoprevoz, turn left, and walk to the end of the bus-station area). Because these two companies don't cooperate, you have to check with both to get the complete schedule. To find your way to the town center, walk through the bus stalls and parking lot and turn left at the big road, which leads you to the Old Town area in about 15 minutes. A taxi into town costs about 10 KM.

If you're arriving by bus it's possible (though unlikely) that you'll arrive at Mostar's makeshift secondary bus station, called **"Kolodvor,"** on the west/Croat side of town. From here, it's a dreary 15-minute walk into town: Turn right out of the bus station area, turn left down the busy Dubrovačka street, and head straight to the river to reach the main bus station. From the station, head south along the river into the Old Town.

For details on both stations—and how to get reliable schedule information—see "Mostar Connections," later.

By Car: For tips on driving to Mostar from the Dalmatian Coast, see page 448.

Helpful Hints

Local Cash: Need Convertible Marks? The most convenient ATM in town is to the left of Fortuna Tours' door, right at the top of Coppersmiths' Street (but on a short visit, you can generally skip a trip to the ATM, as most vendors here also accept Croatian kunas and euros).

Travel Agency: The handy **Fortuna Tours** travel agency, right in the heart of the Old Town (at the top of Coppersmiths' Street), sells all the tourist stuff, can book you a local guide, and answers basic questions (open long hours daily, Kujundžiluk 2, tel. 036/551-887, main office tel. 036/552-197, fax 036/551-888, www.fortuna.ba, fortuna_mostar1@bih.net.ba).

Local Guides: Hiring a guide is an excellent investment to help you understand Mostar. I've enjoyed working with **Alma Elezović,** a warm-hearted Bosniak who loves sharing her city and her wartime stories with visitors (€20/person, up to €70/group for 2-3-hour tour, includes entrance to a Turkish house and a mosque, tel. 036/550-514, mobile 061-467-699, aelezovic @gmail.com). If Alma is busy, various companies around town can arrange for a local guide at extremely reasonable prices (2-hour tour—€30/2 people, €40/4 people, includes entrance to mosque and/or Turkish house); try **Fortuna Tours,** listed previously.

If someone approaches you offering to be your guide, ask the price in advance (many charge ridiculously high rates). If they seem cagey or overpriced, decline politely. The official guides are better anyway.

Local Driver: Ermin Elezović, husband of local guide Alma (see above), is a gregarious, English-speaking driver who enjoys taking visitors on day trips from Mostar. You can also hire him for a transfer between Mostar and destinations anywhere in Croatia (prices for a van for up to 6 people: €100 for one-way transfer to Sarajevo, Split, or Dubrovnik, or €150 to add some extra time for sightseeing en route; €200 round-trip from Mostar to Sarajevo, Split, or Dubrovnik; tel. 036/550-514, mobile 061-908-597, elezovicermin@gmail.com).

Sights in Mostar

Mostar's major sights line up along a handy L-shaped axis. I've laced them together as an enjoyable orientation walk: From the Franciscan Church, you'll walk straight until you cross the Old Bridge. Then you'll turn left and walk basically straight (with a couple of detours) to the big square at the far end of town.

• *Begin at the...*

▲Franciscan Church of Sts. Peter and Paul

In a town of competing religious architectural exclamation points, this spire is the tallest. The church, which adjoins a working Franciscan monastery, was built in 1997, after the fighting subsided (the same year as the big cross on the hill). The tower, which looks at first glance like a minaret on steroids, is actually modeled after typical Croatian/Venetian campanile bell towers. Step inside to see how the vast and coarse concrete shell awaits completion. In the meantime, the cavernous interior is already hosting services. (Sunday Mass here is an inspiration.)

• *The church fronts the busy boulevard called...*

▲Bulevar

"The Boulevard" was once the modern main drag of Mostar. In the early 1990s, this city of Bosniaks, Croats, and Serbs began to fracture under the pressure of politicians' propaganda. In October 1991, Bosnia-Herzegovina—following Croatia's and Slovenia's example, but without the blessing of its large Serb minority—began a process of splitting from Yugoslavia. Soon after, the Serb-dominated Yugoslav People's Army invaded. Mostar's Bosniaks and Croats joined forces to battle the Serbs and succeeded in claiming the city as their own, forcing out the Serb residents.

But even as they fended off the final, distant bombardments of Serb forces, Mostar's Bosniaks (Muslims) and Croats (Catholics)

began to squabble. Neighbors, friends, and even relatives took up arms against each other. As fighting raged between the Croat and Bosniak forces, this street became the front line—and virtually all of its buildings were destroyed. Then as now, the area to the east of here (toward the river) was held by Bosniaks, while the western part of town was Croat territory.

While many of the buildings along here have been rebuilt, some damage is still evident. Stroll a bit, imagining the hell of a split community at war. Mortar craters in the asphalt leave poignant scars. During those dark war years, the Croats on the hill above laid siege to the Bosniaks on the other side, cutting off electricity, blocking roads, and blaring Croatian rabble-rousing pop music and Tokyo Rose-type propaganda speeches from loudspeakers. Through '93 and '94, when the Bosniaks dared to go out, they sprinted past exposed places, for fear of being picked off by a sniper. Local Bosniaks explain, "Night was time to live" (in black clothes). When people were killed along this street, their corpses were sometimes left here for months, because it wasn't safe to retrieve the bodies. Tens of thousands fled. Scandinavian countries were the first to open their doors, but many Bosnians ended up elsewhere in Europe, the US, and Canada.

The stories are shocking, and it's difficult to see the war impartially. But looking back on this complicated war, I try not to broadly cast one side as the "aggressors" and another as the "victims." Bosniaks were victimized in Mostar, just as Croats were victimized during the siege of Dubrovnik (explained on page 302). And, as the remains of a destroyed Orthodox cathedral on the hillside above Mostar (not quite visible from here) attest, Serbs also took their turn as victims. Every conflict has many sides, and it's the civilians who often pay the highest toll—no matter their affiliation.

Cross the boulevard and head down Onešćukova street. A few steps down on the left, the vacant lot with the menorah-ornamented metal fence will someday be the **Mostar Synagogue.** While the town's Jewish population has dwindled to a handful of families since World War II, many Jews courageously served as aid workers and intermediaries when Croats and Bosniaks were killing each other. In recognition of their loving help, the community of Mostar gave them this land for a new synagogue.

• *Continue past the synagogue site, entering the Old Town and following the canyon of the...*

Radobolja River Valley

Cross the creek called Radobolja, which winds over waterfalls and several mills on its way to join the Neretva, and enter the city's cobbled historic core (keeping the small river on your

MOSTAR AND NEARBY

right). As you step upon the smooth, ankle-twisting river stones, you suddenly become immersed in the Turkish heritage of Mostar. Around you are several fine examples of Mostar's traditional heavy limestone-shingled roofs. From the arrival of the Ottomans all the way through the end of World War II, Mostar had fewer than 15,000 residents—this compact central zone was pretty much all there was to the city. It wasn't until the Tito years that it became industrialized and grew like crazy. As you explore, survey the atmospheric eateries clinging to the walls of the canyon—and choose one for a meal or drink later in the day (I've noted a couple under "Eating in Mostar," later).

Walk straight ahead until you reach a square viewpoint platform on your right. It's across from a charming little mosque and above the stream (you may have to squeeze between souvenir stands to get there). The mosque is one of 10 in town. Before the recent war, there were 36, and before World War II, there were even more (many of those damaged or destroyed in World War II were never repaired or replaced, since Tito's communist Yugoslavia discouraged religion). But the recent war inspired Muslims to finally rebuild. Each of the town's newly reconstructed mosques was financed by a Muslim nation or organization (this one was a gift from an international association for the protection of Islamic heritage). Some critics (read: Croats) allege that these foreign Muslim influences—which generally interpret their faith more strictly than the extremely progressive and laid-back Bosniaks—are threatening to flood the country with a rising tide of Islamic fundamentalism. For more on this debate, see page 416.

• *Spanning the river below the mosque is the...*

▲Crooked Bridge (Kriva Ćuprija)

This miniature Old Bridge was built nearly a decade before its more famous sibling, supposedly to practice for the real deal. Damaged—but not destroyed—during the war, the bridge was swept away several years later by floods. The bridge you see today is a recent reconstruction.

• *Continue deeper on the same street into the city center. After a few steps, a street to the left (worth a short detour) leads to the TI, then a copper-domed hammam (Turkish bathhouse), which was destroyed in World War II and only recently rebuilt. A happening nightlife and restaurant scene tumbles downhill toward the river from here, offering spectacular views of the Old Bridge.*

Back on the main drag, continue along the main shopping zone, past several market stalls, to the focal point of town, the...

▲▲▲Old Bridge (Stari Most)

One of the most evocative sights in the former Yugoslavia, this iconic bridge confidently spanned the Neretva River for more than

four centuries. Mostarians of all faiths love the bridge and speak of "him" as an old friend. Traditionally considered the point where East meets West, the Old Bridge is as symbolic as it is beautiful. Dramatically arched and flanked by two boxy towers, the bridge is stirring—even if you don't know its history.

Before the Old Bridge, the Neretva was spanned only by a rickety suspension bridge, guarded by *mostari* ("watchers of the bridge"), who gave the city its name. Commissioned in 1557 by the Ottoman Sultan Süleyman the Magnificent, and completed just nine years later, the Old Bridge was a technological marvel for its time..."the longest single-span stone arch on the planet." (In other words, it's the granddaddy of the Rialto Bridge in Venice.) Because of its graceful keystone design—and the fact that there are empty spaces inside the structure—it's much lighter than it appears. And yet, nearly 400 years after it was built, the bridge was still sturdy enough to support the weight of the Nazi tanks that rolled in to occupy Mostar. Over the centuries, it became the symbol of the town and region—a metaphor in stone for the way the diverse faiths and cultures here were able to bridge the gaps that divided them.

All of that drastically changed in the early 1990s. Beginning in May of 1993, as the city became engulfed in war, the Old Bridge frequently got caught in the crossfire. Old tires were slung over its sides to absorb some of the impact from nearby artillery and shrapnel. In November of 1993, Croats began shelling the bridge from the top of the mountain (where the cross is now—you can just see its tip peeking over the hill from the top of the bridge). The bridge took several direct hits on November 8; on November 9, another shell caused the venerable Old Bridge to lurch, then tumble in pieces into the river. The mortar inside, which contained pink bauxite, turned the water red as it fell in. Locals said that their old friend was bleeding.

The decision to destroy the bridge was partly strategic—to cut off a Bosniak-controlled strip on the west bank from Bosniak forces on the east. (News footage from the time shows

Bosniak soldiers scurrying back and forth over the bridge.) But there can be no doubt that, like the Yugoslav Army's siege of Dubrovnik, the attack was also partly symbolic: the destruction of a bridge representing the city's Muslim legacy.

After the war, city leaders decided to rebuild the Old Bridge. Chunks of the original bridge were dredged up from the river. But the limestone had been compromised by soaking in the water for so long, so it couldn't be used (you can still see these pieces of the old Old Bridge on the riverbank below). Having pledged to rebuild the bridge authentically, restorers cut new stone from the original quarry, and each block was hand-carved. Then they assembled the stones with the same technology used by the Ottomans 450 years ago: Workers erected wooden scaffolding and fastened the blocks together with iron hooks cast in lead. The project was overseen by UNESCO and cost over $13 million, funded largely by international donors.

It took longer to rebuild the bridge in the 21st century than it did to build it in the 16th century. But on July 23, 2004, the new Old Bridge was inaugurated with much fanfare and was immediately embraced by both the city and the world as a sign of reconciliation.

Since its restoration, another piece of bridge history has fully returned, as young men once again jump from the bridge 75 feet down into the Neretva (which remains icy cold even in summer). Done both for the sake of tradition and to impress girls, this custom was carried on even during the time when the destroyed bridge was temporarily replaced by a wooden one. Now the tower on the west side of the bridge houses the office of the local "Divers Club," a loosely run organization that carries on this long-standing ritual. On hot summer days, you'll see divers making a ruckus and collecting donations at the top of the bridge. They tease and tease, standing up on the railing and pretending they're about to jump... then getting down and asking for more money. (If he's wearing trunks rather than Speedos, he's not a diver—just a teaser.) Once they collect about €30, one of them will take the plunge.

Before moving on, see how many of the town's 10 mosques you can spot from the top of the bridge (I counted seven minarets).

• *If you'd like to see one of the best* **views** *in town—looking up at the Old Bridge from the riverbank below—backtrack the way you came into the shopping zone, take your first left (at the recommended Šadrvan restaurant—a good place to try the powerful "Bosnian coffee"), then find*

MOSTAR AND NEARBY

the steps down to the river on the left.

When you're ready to continue, hike back up to the Old Bridge and cross to the other side. After the bridge on the right are two different exhibits worth a quick visit.

Bookstore near the Old Bridge

This excellent bookstore has a good, free photo exhibition of powerful images of war-torn Mostar, displayed inside a former mosque for soldiers who guarded the bridge. They play a montage of videos and photos of the bridge—before, during, and after the war—that's nearly as good as the similar film shown at the Museum of Herzegovina (described later). The shop also sells an impressively wide range of books about the former Yugoslavia and its troubled breakup.

Cost and Hours: Free, daily 7:00-24:00.

• *Just beyond the bookstore, tucked into the corner on the right, look for the stairs leading up to the...*

Museum of the Old Bridge (Muzej Stari Most)

Located within one of the Old Bridge's towers, this museum features a film and photos about the reconstruction of the bridge, archaeological findings, and a few other paltry exhibits about the history of the town and bridge, all in English. First climb up the stairs just after the bridge and buy your ticket, before hiking the rest of the way up to the top of the tower, where you can enjoy fine views through grubby windows. Then go around below to the archaeological exhibit. The museum offers more detail than most casual visitors need; consider just dropping into the smaller, free photo exhibition described previously, then moving along.

Cost and Hours: 5 KM, Tue-Sun 10:00-18:00, closed Mon, lots of stairs, Bajatova 4, mobile 061-707-307.

• *After the Old Bridge, the street swings left and leads you along...*

▲▲Coppersmiths' Street (Kujundžiluk)

This lively strip, with the flavor of a Turkish bazaar, offers some of the most colorful shopping this side of Istanbul. You'll see Mostar's characteristic bridge depicted in every possible way, along with blue-and-white "evil eyes" (believed in the Turkish culture to keep bad spirits at bay), old Yugoslav Army kitsch, and hammered-copper decorations (continuing the long tradition that gave the street its name). Partway up, the homes

The Muslims of Bosnia

While Muslim immigrants have only recently become a fixture in many European cities, Bosnia-Herzegovina is one place where Muslims have continuously been an integral part of the cultural tapestry for centuries.

During the more than 400 years that Bosnia was part of the Ottoman Empire, the Muslim Turks did not forcibly convert their subjects (unlike some Catholic despots at the time). However, it was advantageous for non-Turks to adopt Islam (for lower taxes and better business opportunities), so many Slavs living here became Muslims. In fact, within 150 years of the start of Ottoman rule, half of the population of Bosnia-Herzegovina was Muslim.

The Ottomans became increasingly intolerant of other faiths as time went on, and uprisings by Catholics and Orthodox Christians eventually led to the end of Ottoman domination in the late 19th century. But even after the Ottomans left, many people in this region continued practicing Islam, as their families had been doing for centuries. These people constitute an ethnic group called "Bosniaks," and many of them are still practicing Muslims today (following the Sunni branch of the Muslim faith). Most Bosniaks are Slavs—of the same ethnic stock as Croats and Serbs—and look pretty much the same as their neighbors; however, some Bosniaks have ancestors who married into Turkish families, and they may have some Turkish features.

The actions of a small but attention-grabbing faction of Muslim extremists have burdened Islam with a bad reputation in the Western world. But judging Islam based on Osama bin Laden and al-Qaeda is a bit like judging Christianity based on the Oslo gunman and the Ku Klux Klan. Visiting Mostar is a unique opportunity to get a taste of a fully Muslim society, made a bit less intimidating because it wears a more-familiar European face.

Here's an admittedly basic and simplistic outline (written by

with the colorfully painted facades double as galleries for local artists. The artists live and work upstairs, then sell their work right on this street. Pop into the *atelier d'art* ("Ðul Emina") on the right to meet Sead Vladović and enjoy his impressive iconographic work (daily 9:00-20:00). This is the most touristy street in all of Bosnia-Herzegovina, so don't expect any bargains. Still, it's fun. As you stroll, check out the fine views of the Old Bridge.

• *Continue uphill. After the street levels out, about halfway along the street on the left-hand side, look for the entrance to the...*

▲Koski Mehmed-Pasha Mosque (Koski Mehmed-Paša Džamija)

Mostar's Bosniak community includes many practicing Muslims. Step into this courtyard for a look at one of Mostar's many

a non-Muslim) designed to help travelers from the Christian West understand a very rich but often misunderstood culture that's worthy of respect:

Muslims, like Christians and Jews, are monotheistic. They call God "Allah." The most important person in the Islamic faith is Muhammad, Allah's most important prophet, who lived in the sixth and seventh centuries A.D.

The "five pillars" of Islam are the same among Muslims in Bosnia-Herzegovina, Turkey, Iraq, Indonesia, the US, and everywhere else. Followers of Islam should:

1. Say and believe, "There is only one God, and Muhammad is his prophet."

2. Pray five times a day, while facing Mecca. Modern Muslims explain that it's important for this ritual to include several elements: washing, exercising, stretching, and thinking of God.

3. Give to the poor (one-fortieth of your wealth, if you are not in debt).

4. Fast during daylight hours through the month of Ramadan. Fasting is a great social equalizer and helps everyone to feel the hunger of the poor.

5. Visit Mecca. This is interpreted by some Muslims as a command to travel. Muhammad said, "Don't tell me how educated you are, tell me how much you've traveled."

Good advice for anyone, no matter what—or if—you call a higher power.

mosques. This mosque, dating from the early 17th century, is notable for its cliff-hanging riverside location, and because it's particularly accessible for tourists. But Mostar's other mosques share many of its characteristics—much of the following information applies to them as well.

Cost and Hours: 4 KM to enter mosque, 4 KM more to climb minaret, daily April-Oct 9:00-18:00, until 19:00 at busy times, Nov-March 9:00-15:00; if it seems crowded with tour groups, you can enter a very similar mosque later on this walk instead.

Touring the Mosque: The **fountain** *(šadrvan)* in the courtyard allows worshippers to wash before entering the mosque, as directed by Islamic law. This practice, called ablution, is both a literal and a spiritual cleansing in preparation for being in the presence of Allah. It's also refreshing in this hot climate, and the sound of running water helps worshippers concentrate.

The **minaret**—the slender needle jutting up next to the dome—is the Islamic equivalent of the Christian bell tower, used to call people to prayer. In the old days, the *muezzin* (prayer leader) would climb the tower five times a day and chant, "There is only one God, and Muhammad is his prophet." In modern times, loudspeakers are used instead. Climbing the minaret's 89 claustrophobic, spiral stairs is a memorable experience, rewarding you at the top with the best views over Mostar—and the Old Bridge—that you can get without wings (entrance to the right of mosque entry).

Because this mosque is accustomed to tourists, you don't need to take off your shoes to enter (but stay on the green carpet), women don't need to wear scarves, and it's fine to take photos inside. Near the front of the mosque, you may see some of the small, overlapping rugs that are below this covering (reserved for shoes-off worshippers).

Once **inside,** notice the traditional elements of the mosque. The niche *(mihrab)* across from the entry is oriented toward Mecca (the holy city in today's Saudi Arabia)—the direction all Muslims face to pray. The small stairway *(mimber)* that seems to go nowhere is symbolic of the growth of Islam—Muhammad had to stand higher and higher to talk to his growing following. This serves as a kind of pulpit, where the cleric gives a speech, similar to a sermon or homily in Christian church services. No priest ever stands on the top stair, which is symbolically reserved for Muhammad.

The balcony just inside the door is traditionally where women worship. For the same reason I find it hard to concentrate on God at yoga classes, Muslim men decided prayer would go better without the enjoyable but problematic distraction of bent-over women between them and Mecca. These days, women can also pray on the main floor with the men, but they must avoid physical contact.

Muslims believe that capturing a living creature in a painting or a sculpture is inappropriate. (In fact, depictions of Allah and the prophet Muhammad are strictly forbidden.) Instead, mosques are filled with ornate patterns and Arabic calligraphy (of the name "Muhammad" and important prayers and sayings from the Quran). You'll also see some floral and plant designs, which you'd never see in a more conservative, Middle Eastern mosque.

Before leaving, ponder how progressive the majority of Mostar's Muslims are. Most of them drink alcohol, wear modern European clothing (you'll see virtually no women wearing head scarves or men with beards), and almost never visit a mosque to pray. In so many ways, these people don't fit our preconceived notions of Islam...and yet, they consider themselves Muslims all the same.

The mosque's **courtyard** is shared by several merchants. When you're done haggling, head to the terrace behind the mosque for the best view in town of the Old Bridge.

• *Just beyond this mosque, the traffic-free cobbles of the Old Town end. Take a right and leave the cutesy tourists' world. Walk up one block to the big...*

▲▲New Muslim Cemetery

In this cemetery, which was a park before the war, every tomb is dated 1993, 1994, or 1995. As the war raged, more exposed

cemeteries were unusable. But this tree-covered piece of land was relatively safe from Croat snipers. As the casualties mounted, locals buried their loved ones here under cover of darkness. Many of these people were soldiers, but some were civilians. Strict Muslim graves don't display images of

people, but here you'll see photos of war dead who were young, less-traditional members of the Muslim community. The fleur-de-lis shape of many of the tombstones is a patriotic symbol for the nation of Bosnia. The Arabic squiggles are the equivalent of an American having Latin on his or her tombstone—old-fashioned and formal.

• *Go up the wide stairs to the right of the cemetery (near the mosque). At #4 on the right, just before and across from the bombed-out tower, you'll find the...*

Museum of Herzegovina (Muzej Hercegovine)

This humble little museum is made worthwhile by a deeply moving **film**, rated ▲▲, that traces the history of the town through its Old Bridge: fun circa-1957 footage of the diving contests; harrowing scenes of the bridge being pummeled, and finally toppled, by artillery; and a stirring sequence showing the bridge's reconstruction and grand reopening on that day in 2004—with high-fives, Beethoven's *Ode to Joy*, fireworks, and more divers.

The museum itself displays fragments of this region's rich history, including historic photos and several items from its Ottoman period. There are sparse English descriptions, but without a tour guide the exhibits are a bit difficult to appreciate. Topics include the Turkish period, Herzegovina under the Austro-Hungarian

Empire, village life, and local archaeology. One small room com-memorates the house's former owner, Dzemal Bijedić, who was Tito's second-in-command during the Yugoslav period until he was killed in a mysterious plane crash in 1977. (If Bijedić had lived, many wonder whether he might have succeeded Tito...and suc-ceeded in keeping Yugoslavia together.)

Cost and Hours: 5-KM museum entry includes 12-minute film, no narration—works in any language, ask about "film?" as you enter; Mon-Fri 9:00-14:00, Sat 10:00-12:00, closed Sun; Bajatova 4—walking up these stairs, it's the second door that's marked for the museum, under the overhanging balcony, www.muzej hercegovine.com.

• *Backtrack to where you left the Old Town. Notice the* **Tepa Market**, *with locals buying produce, in the area just beyond the pedestrian zone. Now walk (with the produce market on your left) along the lively street called* **Braće Fejića**. *(There's no sign, but the street is level and busy with cafés.) You're in the "new town," where locals sit out in front of boisterous cafés sipping coffee while listening to the thumping beat of distinctly Eastern-sounding music.*

Stroll down this street for a few blocks. At the palm trees (about 50 yards before the minaret—look for sign to Ottoman House*), you can side-trip a block to the left to reach...*

▲Bišćević Turkish House (Bišćevića Ćošak)

Mostar has three traditional Turkish-style homes that are open for tourists to visit. The Bišćević House is the oldest, most inter-esting, and most convenient for a quick visit, but two others are described at the end of this listing. Dating from 1635, the Bišćević House is typical of old houses in Mostar, which mix Oriental style with Mediterranean features.

Cost and Hours: 4 KM, daily March-Oct 8:00-19:00 or 20:00, Nov-Feb 9:00-15:00—but can close unexpectedly, Bišćevića 13.

Touring the House: First you'll step through the outer (or animals') garden, then into the inner (or family's) garden. This inner zone is surrounded by a high wall—protection from the sun's rays, from thieves...and from prying eyes, allowing women to take off the veil they were required to wear in public. Enjoy the geometrical patters of the smooth river stones in the floor (for example, the five-sided star), and keep an eye out for the house's pet turtles. It's no coincidence that the traditional fountain *(šadrvan)* resembles those at the entrance to a mosque—a reminder of the importance of running water in Muslim culture. The little white building is a kitchen—cleverly located apart from the house so that the heat and smells of cooking didn't permeate the upstairs living area.

Buy your ticket and take off your shoes before you climb up the wooden staircase. Imagine how a stairway like this one could be pulled up for extra protection in case of danger (notice that this one has a "trap door" to cover it). The cool, shady, and airy living room is open to the east—from where the wind rarely blows. The overhanging roof also prevented the hot sun from reaching this area. The loom in the corner was the women's workplace—the carpets you're standing on would have been woven there. The big chests against the wall were used to bring the dowry when the homeowner took a new wife. Study the fine wood carving and the heavy stonework of the roof.

Continue back into the main gathering room *(divanhan)*. This space—whose name comes from the word "talk"—is designed in a circle so people could face each other, cross-legged, for a good conversation while they enjoyed a dramatic view overlooking the Neretva. The room comes with a box of traditional costumes—great for photo fun. Put on a pair of baggy pants and a fez and really lounge.

Other Turkish Houses: If you're intrigued by this house, consider dropping by Mostar's two other Turkish houses. The **Muslibegović House** (Muslibegovića Kuća) feels newer because it dates from 1871, just a few years before the Ottomans left town. This homey house—which also rents out rooms to visitors (see "Sleeping in Mostar," later)—has many of the same features as the Bišćević House. If they're not too busy, Sanela or Gabriela can give you an English tour (4 KM, mid-April-mid-Oct daily 10:00-18:00, closed to visitors off-season, just two blocks uphill from the Karađozbeg Mosque at Osman Đikića 41, tel. 036/551-379, www.muslibegovichouse.com). To find it, go up the street between the Karađozbeg Mosque and the cemetery, cross the busy street, and continue a long block uphill on the alley. The wall with the slate roof on the left marks the house.

The **Kajtaz House** (Kajtazova Kuća), hiding up a very residential-feeling alley a few blocks from the Old Bridge, feels lived-in because it still is (in the opposite direction from most of the other sights, at Gaše Ilića 21).

• *Go back to the main café street and continue to the...*

▲Karađozbeg Mosque (Karađozbegova Džamija)

The city's main mosque was completed in 1557, the same year work began on the Old Bridge. This mosque, which welcomes visitors, feels less touristy than the one back in the Old Town. Before entering the gate into the complex, look for the picture showing the recent war damage sustained here. You'll see that this mosque has most of the same elements as the Koski Mehmed-Pasha Mosque (described earlier), but some of these decorations are original. Across the street is another cemetery with tombstones from that terrible year, 1993.

Cost and Hours: 4 KM to enter mosque, 4 KM more to climb minaret, daily May-Sept 9:00-19:30, Oct-April 10:00-15:00. Inside the mosque, either stay on the green carpet or remove your shoes.

• *Now continue into modern, urban Mostar along the street in front of the Karađozbeg Mosque. This grimy, mostly traffic-free street is called...*

▲Braće Fejića

Walking along the modern town's main café strip, enjoy the opportunity to observe this workaday Bosniak town. You'll see the humble offices of the ragtag B&H Airlines; a state-run gambling office taxing its less-educated people with a state lottery; and lots of cafés that serve drinks but no food. People generally eat at home before going out to nurse an affordable drink. (Café ABC has good cakes and ice cream; the upstairs is a popular pizza hangout for students and families.)

At the small mosque on the left, obituary announcements are tacked to the outer wall, listing the bios and funeral times for locals who have recently died. A fig tree grows out of the mosque's minaret, just an accident of nature illustrating how that plant can thrive with almost no soil (somehow, the Bosniaks can relate). Walking farther, look up to see a few ruins—still ugly nearly two decades after the war. There's a messy confusion about who owns what in Mostar. Surviving companies have no money. Yugo Bank, which held the mortgages, is defunct. No one will invest until clear ownership is established. Until then, the people of Mostar sip their coffee and rip up their dance clubs in the shadow of these jagged reminders of the warfare that wracked this town not so long ago.

Near the end of the pedestrian zone, through the parking lot on the right, look for the building with communist-era reliefs of 12th-century Bogomil tomb decor—remembering the indigenous culture that existed here even before the arrival of the Ottomans.

When you finally hit the big street (with car traffic), head left one block to the big **Masala Square** (literally, "Place for Prayer").

The Dawn of War in Mostar

Mostar was always one of the most stubbornly independent parts of the former Yugoslavia. It had one of the highest rates of mixed-ethnicity marriages in all of Bosnia-Herzegovina. In the early 1990s, Mostar's demographics were proportioned more-or-less evenly—about 35 percent of its residents were Bosniaks, 34 percent Croats, and 19 percent Serbs. But this delicate balance was shattered in a few brutal months of warfare.

On April 1, 1992, Bosnia-Herzegovina—led by Muslim president Alija Izetbegović—declared independence from Yugoslavia. Very quickly, the Serb-dominated Yugoslav People's Army moved to stake their claim on territory throughout the country, including the important city of Mostar. On April 3, Serb forces occupied the east end of town (including the Ottoman Old Town), forcing many residents—predominantly Croats and Bosniaks—to hole up in the western part of the city. Meanwhile, Serbian and Croatian leaders were secretly meeting to divvy up Bosnian territory, and by early May, they'd agreed that Croatia would claim Mostar. Several weeks later, when the joint Croat-Bosniak forces crossed back over the river, the Serb forces mysteriously withdrew from the city (having been directed to capitulate), and retreated to the mountaintops above town, where they watched...and waited. The Croats and Bosniaks, believing they'd achieved peace, began putting their city back together. During this time, some factions also rounded up, tortured, and killed Serbs still living in Mostar. Many Bosniaks moved back to their homes on the east side of town, but, rather oddly, many of the Croats who had previously resided there instead stayed in the west—in many cases, moving into apartments vacated by Serbs who had fled.

On May 9, 1993—the Yugoslav holiday of "Victory over Fascism Day"—Mostarians were rocked awake by the terrifying sounds of artillery shells. Croat military forces swept through the city, forcibly moving remaining Bosniaks from the west part of town into the east. Throughout that summer, Bosniak men were captured and sent to concentration camps, while the Croats virtually sealed off the east side of town—creating a giant ghetto with no way in or out. The long and ugly siege of Mostar had begun.

Historically this was where pilgrims gathered before setting off for Mecca on their hajj. This is a great scene on balmy evenings, when it's a rendezvous point for the community. The two busts near the fountain provide perfect goal posts for budding soccer stars.

• *For a finale, you can continue one block more out onto the bridge to survey the town you just explored. From here, you can backtrack to linger in the places you found most inviting. Or you can venture into...*

Western (Croat) Mostar

Most tourists stay on the Bosniak side of town. For a complete look at this divided city, consider a stroll to the west. While there are few attractions here, and it's not particularly pretty—it feels like any dreary mid-size Balkan city—it provides an interesting contrast to the Muslim side of town.

Crossing the river and Bulevar, the scarred husks of destroyed buildings begin to fade away, and within a block you're immersed in concrete apartment buildings—making it clear that, when the city became divided, the Muslims holed up in the original Ottoman Old Town, while the Croats claimed the modern Tito-era sprawl. The relative lack of war damage (aside from a few stray bullet holes) emphasizes that it was the Croats laying siege to the Muslims of Mostar. Looking at a map, you'll notice that many streets on this side of town are named for Croatian cities (Dubrovačka, Splitska, Vukovarska) or historical figures (Kralja Tomislava, for the duke who first united the Croats in the 10th century). This side of town also has several remnants of Habsburg rule (including genteel buildings that look like they'd be at home in Vienna, and fine boulevards lined with plane trees). A few of these streets converge at the big roundabout called the Rondo, where *Centar* signs pointedly direct traffic *away* from the (Bosniak) Old Town. Also notice the many road signs pointing toward Široki Brijeg—a Bosnian Croat stronghold. A block toward the Old Town from the Rondo, notice the big cemetery with Muslim tombstones from the early 1990s. These are the graves of those killed during the first round of fighting, when the Croats and Bosniaks teamed up to fight the Serbs. You'll also notice some glitzy new shopping centers and more pizza and pasta restaurants than *ćevapčići* joints (in other words, even the food over here is more Croatian than Bosnian).

Nightlife in Mostar

Be sure to enjoy the local scene after dark in Mostar. Though the town is touristy, it's also a real urban center with a young population riding a wave of raging hormones. The meat market in the courtyard next to the old Turkish bathhouse near the TI is fun to observe. The Old Bridge is a popular meeting place for locals as well as tourists (and pickpockets). A stroll from the Old Bridge down the café-lined Braće

Fejića boulevard, to the modern Masala Square at the far end of town (described earlier), gives a great peek at Mostarians socializing away from the tourists.

Ali Baba is an actual cave featuring a fun, atmospheric, and youthful party scene. Order a cocktail or try a Turkish-style hub-

bly-bubbly (*šiša,* SHEE-shah). Ask to have one of these big water pipes fired up for you and choose your flavored tobacco: apple, cappuccino, banana, or lemon (20 KM per pipe per group, 8-KM cocktails, open late daily; look for low-profile, cave-like entrance along Coppersmiths' Street, just down from the Old Bridge—watch for "Open Sesame" sign tucked down a rocky alley).

Oscar Nightclub is a caravanserai for lounge lizards—an exotic world mixing babbling streams, terraces, lounge chairs, and big sofas where young and old enjoy 5-10-KM cocktails and *šiša* (10 KM will last you about 40 minutes; June-Aug open "non-stop," closed Sept-May, up from the Old Bridge on Onešćukova street, near the Crooked Bridge at the end of the pedestrian zone).

Sleeping in Mostar

The Bristol and Ero are big, full-service hotels, but a bit farther from the charming Old Town. The rest are small, friendly, accessible, affordable guest houses in or very near the Old Town. Many hotels and pensions in town promise "parking," but it's often street parking out front—private lots are rare. Mostar's Old Town can be very noisy on weekends, with nightclubs and outdoor restaurants rollicking into the wee hours. If you're a light sleeper, consider Villa Fortuna and the Muslibegović House, which are quieter than the norm.

$$$ The Muslibegović House, a Bosnian national monument that also invites tourists in to visit during the day, is in an actual

Turkish home dating from 1871. The complex houses 10 homey rooms and two suites, all of which combine classic Turkish style (elegant and comfortable old beds, creaky wooden floors with colorful carpets, lounging sofas; guests remove shoes at the outer door) with modern comforts (air-con, free Wi-Fi, flatscreen TVs). Situated on a quiet residential lane just above the bustle of Mostar's main pedestrian drag and Old Town zone, this

Sleep Code

($1 = about 1.40 KM, €1 = about $1.40, country code: 387, area code: 036)

S = Single, **D** = Double/Twin, **T** = Triple, **Q** = Quad, **b** = bathroom. Unless otherwise noted, prices include breakfast.

Rates: If I list two rates separated by a slash, the first is for peak season (June-Sept), and the second is for off-season (Oct-May).

Price Ranges: To help you sort easily through these listings, I've divided the accommodations into three categories based on the price for a double room with bath during peak season:

$$$ Higher Priced—Most rooms €70 or more.

$$ Moderately Priced—Most rooms between €40-70.

$ Lower Priced—Most rooms €40 or less.

Prices can change without notice; verify the hotel's current rates online or by email. For other updates, see www .ricksteves.com/update.

is a memorable experience (Sb-€55, Db-€90/€75, "pasha suite"-€105, includes a tour of the house, closed Nov-Feb, 2 blocks uphill from the Karađozbeg Mosque at Osman Đikića 41, tel. 036/551-379, www.muslibegovichouse.com, muslibegovichouse@gmail .com; Taž, Sanela, and Gabriela).

$$$ Hotel Bristol is the only business-class place near central Mostar. Its 47 rooms don't quite live up to their four stars, but the location is handy, overlooking the river a 10-minute walk from the heart of the Old Town (Sb-€42, Db-€76, apartment-€90, extra bed-€16, air-con, elevator, free Internet access and Wi-Fi, some street noise, limited parking, Mostarskog Bataljona, tel. 036/500-100, fax 036/500-502, www.bristol.ba, info@bristol.ba).

$$$ Hotel Ero, a 20-minute walk north of the Old Town, is a good big-hotel option, with 91 fine rooms and a professional staff. This was one of the only big buildings in the center not damaged during the war, since it hosted journalists and members of the international community and was therefore off-limits (Sb-€51, Db-€86, suite-€110, air-con, elevator, free Wi-Fi, some traffic noise, ulica Dr. Ante Starčevića, tel. 036/386-777, fax 036/386-700, www.ero.ba, hotel.ero@tel.net.ba).

$$ Hotel Kriva Ćuprija ("Crooked Bridge"), by the bridge of the same name, is tucked between waterfalls in a picturesque valley a few steps from the Old Bridge. It's an appealing oasis with five rooms, four apartments, and a restaurant with atmospheric outdoor seating (Sb-€39, Db-€65, apartment-€75, extra bed-€18, 10 percent discount on rooms and food with this book, can be noisy, air-con, free Wi-Fi, free parking, call to reconfirm if arriving after 19:00, enter at Onešćukova 23 or Kriva Ćuprija 2, tel. 036/550-953, mobile 061-135-286, www.motel-mostar.ba, info@motel-mostar.ba, Sami). Their second location—**Hotel Kriva Ćuprija II**—offers 10 modern rooms with a business-class vibe in a Habsburg-style building overlooking the river from a drab urban street, about 200 yards to the south (same prices, discount, amenities, and contact information as main hotel; some traffic noise, Maršala Tita 186, next to the Lučki Bridge, reception tel. 036/554-125).

$$ Pansion Čardak, run by sweet Suzana and Nedžad Kasumović, has four rooms sharing a kitchen and Internet nook in a stone house set just back from the bustling Crooked Bridge area (Db-€50/€45, Tb-€75/€60, Qb-€90/€75, cash only, no breakfast, air-con, free Wi-Fi, free parking, Jusovina 3, tel. 036/578-249, mobile 061-385-988, www.pansion-cardak.com, info@pansion -cardak.com).

$$ Pansion Nur, run by Feđa, a relative of Suzana and Nedžad (above), also has four rooms and a shared kitchen (twin Db-€40/€35, Db-€50/€40, Tb-€70/€60, suite-€80/€70, cash only, no breakfast, air-con, free Wi-Fi, free parking, Jusovina 8b, tel. 036/580-296, mobile 062-160-872, www.pansion-nur.com, info @pansion-nur.com).

$$ Villa Anri, a bit more hotelesque than other pensions in Mostar, sits a block farther from the bustle near the Bulevar. The stony facade hides seven rooms (five with balconies) combining old Herzegovinian style and bright colors. The big draw is the rooftop terrace, shared by two rooms, which enjoys grand views over the Old Bridge area (Db-€60/€50, Db with grand terrace-€70/€60, Tb-€85/€70, Tb with grand terrace-€100/€80, Qb-€110/€90, cash only, air-con, free Wi-Fi, free parking, Braće Đukića 4, tel. 036/578-477, www.villa-anri-mostar.ba, villa.anri@gmail.com).

$$ Motel Emen has six modern, sleek rooms overlooking a busy café street a few cobbled blocks from the Old Bridge (Sb-€50, Db-€70, bigger Db with balcony-€80, all rooms €10 less Oct-May, air-con, free Internet access and Wi-Fi, free parking, Onešćukova 32, tel. 036/581-120, www.motel-emen.com, info@motel-emen .com).

$ Villa Fortuna is an exceptional value, located in a nondescript urban neighborhood a few minutes' walk farther away from the Old Bridge. Owners Nela and Mili Bijavica rent eight tasteful, modern rooms above the main office of Fortuna Tours. The courtyard in front offers free, secure parking, and in back there's a pleasant garden with a traditional Herzegovinian garden cottage

(Sb-€30, Db-€40, apartment-€80, these prices if you book direct, breakfast-€5, non-smoking, air-con, free Wi-Fi, Rade Bitange 34, tel. & fax 036/580-625, mobile 063-315-017, www.villafortuna .ba, villa_fortuna@bih.net.ba). Fortuna Tours can also put you in touch with locals renting rooms and apartments.

$ **Villa Botticelli,** overlooking a charming waterfall garden just up the valley from the Crooked Bridge, has five colorful rooms (Sb-€30, Db-€40, Tb-€60, breakfast-€3, air-con, free Wi-Fi, Muje Bjelavca 6, enter around back along the alley, mobile 063-809-658, www.villabotticelli.com, botticelli@bih.net.ba, Snježana and Zoran).

Eating in Mostar

Most of Mostar's tourist-friendly restaurants are conveniently concentrated in the Old Town. If you walk anywhere that's cobbled, you'll stumble onto dozens of tempting restaurants charging the same reasonable prices and serving rustic, traditional Bosnian food. In my experience, the menus at most places are virtually identical—though quality and ambience can vary greatly. As eateries tend to come and go quickly here, and little distinguishes these places anyway, don't be too focused on a particular spot. Grilled meats are especially popular—read the "Balkan Flavors" sidebar, on page 418, before you dine. Another specialty is *dolma*—a pepper stuffed with minced meat, vegetables, and rice. On menus, look for the word *domaća*—"homemade." Sarajevska beer is on tap at most places.

On the Embankment, with Old Bridge Views

For the best atmosphere, find your way into the several levels of restaurants that clamber up the riverbank and offer perfect views of the Old Bridge. In terms of the setting, this is the most memorable place to dine in Mostar—but be warned that the quality of the food along here is uniformly low, and prices are relatively high (figure 8-15 KM for a meal). If you want a good perch, it's fun and smart to drop by earlier in the day and personally reserve the table of your choice.

To reach two of the most scenic eateries, go over the Old Bridge to the west side of the river, and bear right on the cobbles until you get to the old Turkish bathhouse (with the copper domes on the roof). To the right of the bathhouse is the entrance to a lively courtyard surrounded with

Enter the Dragon

The city's oddest monument is a testament to how reconciliation can come about in strange and unexpected ways. In the
early 2000s, idealistic young Mostarians formed the Urban
Movement of Mostar, which searched for a way to connect the
still-feuding Catholic and Muslim communities. As a symbol
of their goals, they chose Bruce Lee, the deceased kung-fu
movie star, who is beloved by both Croats and Bosniaks for
his characters' honorable struggle against injustice. A life-size
bronze statue of Lee was unveiled with fanfare in November
2005 in Veliki Park. Unfortunately, soon after, the statue was
damaged. Whether or not the vandalism was ethnically motivated is unclear, but many locals hope the ideals embodied in
the statue will continue to bring the city together.

cafés. Continuing toward the river from the courtyard, stairs lead
down to several riverfront terraces belonging to two different restaurants: **Teatar,** a bit closer to the bridge, has unobstructed views
and lower-quality food, while **Babilon** has slightly better (but still
not great) food and nearly as good views. Poke around to find your
favorite bridge panorama before settling in for a drink or a meal.

Two other places (including a pizzeria) are a bit closer to the
bridge—to reach these, look for the alley on the left just before the
bridge tower.

Near the Old Bridge

While they lack the Old Bridge views, these places are just as central as those listed above, and serve food that's generally a step up.
The first three places are in the atmospheric Old Town, while the
last one is in the modern part of town.

Restoran Hindin Han is pleasantly situated on a woody
terrace over a rushing stream. It's respected locally for its good
cooking and fair prices (big 12-16-KM salads, 7-13-KM grilled
dishes, 12-20-KM fish and other main dishes, Sarajevsko beer on
tap, daily 11:00-24:00, Jusovina 10, tel. 036/581-054). To find it,
walk west from the Old Bridge, bear left at the Šadrvan restaurant,
cross the bridge, and you'll see it on the left.

Šadrvan ("Fountain"), situated smack-dab in the center of the
tourist zone, where cobbled paths converge near the Old Bridge, is
undoubtedly touristy. But it also has fine service, good food, and
pleasant outdoor seating under a tree around its namesake fountain. This is also a good place to nurse a "Bosnian coffee"—like
Turkish coffee, unfiltered, with "mud" in the bottom of the cup
(7-10-KM vegetarian options, 10-15-KM pastas, 7-20-KM main
dishes, daily 7:00-23:00, Jusovina 11, tel. 036/579-057).

Ima Dana ("Someday") is woven into a tangle of terraces over a rushing little stream facing the Crooked Bridge, with good food and a pleasant riverside setting (7-10-KM pizzas and pastas, 7-18-KM meat and fish meals, daily 11:00-24:00, on Jusovina street at the end of the Crooked Bridge, head waiter Miro's mobile is 061-529-408).

Local Alternative in the New Town: **Saray** is an untouristy, nondescript little eatery just uphill from the Karadozbeg Mosque in the modern part of town. They have a basic menu of cheap and very tasty grilled meats—specializing in the classic *čevapčići* (little sausage-shaped meat patties)—and outdoor seating overlooking a playground that offers good people- and kid-watching while you eat (4-10-KM grilled meat dishes, big 6-7-KM salads, daily 9:00-17:00, Karadozbegova 3, mobile 062-062-301).

Mostar Connections

By Bus

Not surprisingly for a divided city, Mostar has two different, autonomous bus terminals, each served by different companies. Mostar's **main bus station** (called "Autobusna Stanica") is on the east/Bosniak side of the river, about a 15-minute walk north of the Old Town (for details, see "Arrival in Mostar," earlier). Most buses you're likely to take use this station; for information on the other station (on the west/Croat side of town), see the end of this section.

Schedules and Tickets: At the main station, two primary companies (one Bosniak, one Croat) operate independent offices, providing schedule information and tickets only for their own buses. Because the companies refuse to cooperate, there's no single information or ticket office for all Mostar buses—so it's essential to visit both companies to know your options before buying tickets. (You may be lucky and encounter a helpful person in one office who'll clue you in on options at the other, but don't count on it—they're just as likely to pretend the other company doesn't exist.) As you face the bus station, near the left end is the Bosniak company **Autoprevoz** (tel. 036/551-900, www.autoprevoz-bus.ba); they also sell tickets for a few other companies (including Eurolines and Bogdan Bus). Near the right end is the Croat-owned **Globtour** (tel. 036/318-333, www.globtour.com), which sells tickets only for its own buses. Local and regional connections (not listed below) are operated by Mostar Bus, whose buses depart from across the street from the main bus station (www.mostarbus.ba).

Tracking down reliable **schedule** information in Mostar is tricky, but you can start by checking the websites listed above, then calling or visiting both companies at the station to confirm your options and buy tickets. While this may sound intimidating, it's workable—just be sure to double-check your plans. Note that buses to seasonal destinations (such as along the Dalmatian Coast) run more frequently in peak season, roughly June through mid-September. The prices I've listed are estimates; it can depend on the company.

From Mostar's Main Bus Station to: Međugorje (6-7/day, 40 minutes, all operated by Globtour, 4-5 KM), **Sarajevo** (at least hourly, 2.5 hours, several different companies—check with both offices to know all your options, 20 KM), **Zagreb** (4/day on Globtour, 1/day on Autoprevoz, 8-9.5 hours, includes a night bus, 45 KM), **Split** (2/day with Globtour, 2-3/day with Autoprevoz, 4-4.5 hours, plus 1 night bus with Eurolines/Autoprevoz, 20-30 KM), **Dubrovnik** (2/day with Globtour, 1/day with Eurolines/Autoprevoz—or 3/day in summer, 4-5 hours, 25-30 KM). The important Dubrovnik connection is tricky: Most days, all Dubrovnik buses depart early in the day, making an afternoon return from Mostar to Dubrovnik impossible. In summer, however, Eurolines adds two more departures each day—including a handy 17:30 departure, which makes day-tripping from Dubrovnik workable (tickets sold at Autoprevoz office). Globtour also runs a handy bus to Montenegro's **Bay of Kotor** (departs Mostar at 7:00, arrives at Kotor at 12:30 and Budva at 13:30, then returns the same day).

From Mostar's West/Croat Bus Station: A few additional buses, mostly to Croatian destinations and to Croat areas of Bosnia-Herzegovina, depart from the west side of town. These use a makeshift "station" (actually a gravel lot behind a gas station) on Vukovarska street, called "Kolodvor." It's about a 15-minute walk due west of the main bus station. Most buses using the Kolodvor station are operated by the Euroherc company. In addition to one daily bus apiece to **Zagreb, Split,** and **Sarajevo,** this station has several departures to **Metković** (at the Croatian border, with additional connections to Croatian destinations; 8/day) and to **Međugorje** (7/day Mon-Fri, 3/day Sat, none Sun, 5 KM). Additionally, some Croat buses leave from a bus stop near the Franciscan Church. But since the connections from this side are sparse, the location is inconvenient, and the "station" is dreary, I'd stick with the main bus station and ignore this option unless you're desperate.

By Train

Mostar is on the train line that runs from Ploče (on the Croatian coast between Split and Dubrovnik) to Zagreb, via Mostar and Sarajevo. This train—which leaves from next to the main bus station—generally runs once daily, leaving **Ploče** soon after 6:00 in the morning, with stops at **Mostar** (1.75 hours), **Sarajevo** (4.25 hours), and **Zagreb** (13.5 hours; bus is faster). Going the opposite direction, the train leaves Zagreb at about 9:00 in the morning. There's also a night train connection running in both directions along the same track (leaving Ploče northbound at 16:25, arriving in Mostar at 18:35, Sarajevo at 20:59, and Zagreb at 6:44; and southbound leaving Zagreb at 21:24, arriving in Sarajevo at 6:39 and Mostar at 9:31). Train info: tel. 036/550-608.

Route Tips for Drivers:
From Dubrovnik to Mostar

You have two ways to drive between Dubrovnik and Mostar: easy and straightforward along the coast, or adventurous and off the beaten path through the Herzegovinian mountains. I've narrated each route as you'd encounter it driving from Dubrovnik to Mostar, but you can do either one in reverse—just hold this book upside-down. (For driving directions from Mostar to Sarajevo, see the end of the Sarajevo chapter.)

The Main Coastal Road

The vast majority of traffic from Dubrovnik to Mostar follows the coastal road north, then cuts east into Bosnia. Because this is one of the most direct routes, it can be crowded (allow about 2.5 hours). It's also a bit inconvenient, as you have to cross the border three times (into and out of Bosnia at Neum, and into Bosnia again at Metković).

Begin by driving north of Dubrovnik, passing some of the places mentioned in the Near Dubrovnik chapter: **Trsteno** (with its arboretum), and **Ston** and **Mali Ston** (with a mighty wall and waterfront restaurants, respectively). After passing the Ston turn-off, you'll see the long, mountainous, vineyard-draped **Pelješac Peninsula** across the bay on your left.

Soon you'll come to a surprise border crossing, at **Neum.** Here you'll cross into Bosnia-Herzegovina—then, six miles later, cross back out again (for details on this odd little stretch of Bosnian coast, see page 357).

You won't be back in Croatia for long. Just north of Neum, the main coastal road jogs away from the coast and around the striking **Neretva River Delta**—the extremely fertile "garden patch of Croatia," which produces a significant portion of Croatia's fruits and vegetables. The Neretva is the same river that flows under Mostar's Old Bridge upstream—but in Metković, it spreads out into 12 branches as it enters the Adriatic, flooding a vast plain and creating a bursting cornucopia in the middle of an otherwise rocky and arid region. Enjoying some of the most plentiful sunshine on the Croatian coast, as well as a steady supply of water for irrigation, the Neretva Delta is as productive as it is beautiful.

At the Neretva Delta, turn off for the town of **Metković;** at the far end of that town, you'll cross the border into **Bosnia-Herzegovina,** then continue straight on the main road (M17) directly into Mostar. As you drive, you'll see destroyed buildings and occasional roadside memorials bearing the likenesses of fresh-faced soldiers who died in the recent war.

Along the way are a few interesting detours: In Čapljina, you can turn off to the left to reach **Međugorje** (see page 455). If you stay on the main road, keep your eyes peeled soon after the Čapljina turnoff for a mountaintop castle tower (on the right side of the road), which marks the medieval town of **Počitelj** (see page 453). With extra time, just before Mostar (in Buna), you can detour a few miles along the Buna River into **Blagaj** (see page 452).

Approaching **Mostar** on M17, you'll pass the airport, then turn left at your first opportunity to cross the river. After crossing the bridge, bear right onto Bulevar street, and continue on that main artery for several blocks (passing several destroyed buildings). At the street called Rade Bitange (just after the giant church bell tower), turn right to find the public parking lot (2 KM/hour, 10 KM/8 hours)—less than a 10-minute walk from the Old Bridge. Be warned that signage is poor; if you get lost, try asking for directions to "Stari Most" (STAH-ree most)—the Old Bridge.

Rugged-but-Scenic Backcountry Journey through Serb Herzegovina

While the coastal route outlined above is the most common way to connect Dubrovnik to Mostar, I enjoy getting out of the tourist rut by twisting up the mountains behind Dubrovnik and cutting across the scenic middle of Herzegovina. (If you're traveling by road between Dubrovnik and Split at another point in your trip, you'll see the coastal road anyway—so this alternative helps you avoid the rerun.) This route feels much more remote, but the roads are good and the occasional gas station and restaurant break up the journey. I find this route particularly interesting because it offers an easily digestible taste of the **Republika Srpska** part of Herzegovina—controlled by the country's Serb minority, rather than its Bosniak and Croat majority. You'll see Orthodox churches and monasteries, the Cyrillic alphabet, and various symbols of the defiantly proud Serb culture (such as the red, white, and blue flag with the four golden C's). You can't get a complete picture of the former Yugoslavia without sampling at least a sliver of Serb culture. (Because this road goes through the Serbian part of Herzegovina, it's not popular among Bosniaks or Croats—in fact, locals might tell you this road "does not exist." It does.) If you want a little taste of Republika Srpska, consider just day-tripping into Trebinje—

especially on Saturday, when the produce market is at its liveliest.

The first step is to climb up into the mountains and the charming market town of Trebinje. From there, two different roads lead to Mostar: via Stolac or via Nevesinje. If you take the Stolac route, the whole journey from Dubrovnik to Mostar takes about as long as the coastal road (and potentially even faster, thanks to the light traffic and lack of an extra border). The Nevesinje route takes a good hour longer than the Stolac route, and immerses you in an even more remote landscape.

Dubrovnik to Trebinje: From Dubrovnik, head south toward Cavtat, the airport, and Montenegro. Shortly after leaving Dubrovnik, watch for—and follow—signs on the left directing you to *Brgat Gornji*. (Signage completely ignores the large Serb town of Trebinje, just past this obscure border village.) As you drive through the border into Bosnia-Herzegovina, notice the faint remains of a long-abandoned old rail line cutting sharp switchbacks up the hill. This once connected Dubrovnik to Mostar and Sarajevo. The charred trees you may see are not from the war, but from more recent forest fires.

Carry on across the plateau, where you may begin to notice Cyrillic lettering on signs: You've crossed into the Republika Srpska. About 20 minutes after the border, you'll come upon **Trebinje** (Требиње)—a pleasant and relatively affluent town with a leafy main square that hosts a fine Saturday market. Trebinje is a good place to stretch your legs, get some Bosnian Convertible Marks (ATMs are scattered around the town center), and maybe nurse a coffee while people-watching on the main square. Overlooking  the town from its hilltop perch is the striking Orthodox Church of Nova Gračanica, built to resemble the historically important Gračanica Monastery in Kosovo. If you have time, drive up to the church's viewpoint terrace for great views over Trebinje and the valley, and step inside the church to immerse yourself in a gorgeously vibrant world of Orthodox icons.

From Trebinje, you have two options for getting to Mostar: The faster route via Stolac, or the very rugged slower route via Nevesinje.

Stolac Route: As you enter Trebinje, after crossing the river, follow signs for *Mostar* and *Ljubinje*. Follow the Trebišnjica River into a high-altitude karstic basin, where waterwheels power a primitive irrigation system. From here, the river flows down to the coast—providing hydroelectric power for Dubrovnik—before detouring south and emptying into the sea near Herceg Novi, Montenegro...one river, three countries, in just a few miles. This area is blanketed with vineyards and dotted with old monasteries. Passing the village of Mesari ("Butchers"), you'll also see flocks of sheep. In this part of the Balkans, Croats were traditionally the city-dwellers, while Serbs were farmers. There used to be sheep like these in the pastures near Dubrovnik, but when the Serbs left during the war, so did the sheep.

The large field you're driving along is called **Popovo Polje** ("Priests' Field"). Because it floods easily, the canal was built to remove floodwater. Pull over at one of the humble, slate-roofed Orthodox chapels by the road. In the cemeteries, many of the gravestones are from 1991—when soldiers from this area joined the war effort against Dubrovnik.

At the fork, carry on straight to Ljubinje. Climbing up into the mountains, you'll see garbage along the side of the road—an improvised dump in this very poor land, where a fractured government struggles to provide even basic services. Twisting up through even higher mountains, you'll wind up in the town of **Ljubinje** (Љубиње). In this humble burg, roadside stands with *med* signs advertise homegrown honey. The partially built houses are not signs of war damage (the war didn't reach here); it's a form of "savings" in the Balkans, where people don't trust banks: Rather than deposit money in an account, they spend many years gradually adding on to a new house.

Continuing toward Mostar, you'll pass through more desolate countryside to the town of **Stolac** (Столац); the town's defiant mosque minaret tells you that you've crossed from Serb territory into Bosnia's Muslim-Croat Federation. Stolac is home to some fascinating history, and worth a stroll if you have the time (see page 453). Leaving Stolac, keep an eye out (on the left) for its interesting **necropolis**—a cluster of centuries-old traditional Bosnian tombstones (worth a quick photo-op stop, and described on page 454).

Past Stolac, you'll soon pop out at an intersection with the main road between Mostar and the coast. From here, turn right to head into **Počitelj** (see page 453), then the turnoff for **Blagaj** (page 452) and on to **Mostar.** (If you want to go to **Međugorje**—see page 455—turn left here, then turn right once you get to Čapljina.) For arrival tips in Mostar, see the end of the driving directions above.

Nevesinje Route: This longer, more remote, middle-of-nowhere adventure takes about an hour longer than the Stolac route. But if you're adventurous, it's a fun ride. From Trebinje,

drive north toward **Bilećko Lake**—a vast, aquamarine lake you'll
see on your right (the Vikiovac Restaurant offers a great viewpoint). Then you'll go through the town of **Bileća** (Билећа), turning west at the gloomy industrial town of **Gacko** (Гацко, with a
giant coal mine), and onward to the humble but proud little town
of **Nevesinje** (Невесиње). From Nevesinje, it's a quick drive up
over the mountains, then down into Mostar—passing spectacular
views of Herzog Stjepan's imposing castle over the town of Buna.
Follow signs on into Mostar.

Near Mostar

While Mostar has its share of attractions, there's also plenty to see
within a short drive. Ideally try to splice one or two of these stops
into your trip between Mostar and the coast (see my "Route Tips
for Drivers," earlier, for tips on linking them up).

Blagaj

Blagaj (BLAH-gai, rhymes with "pie") was the historical capital
of this region until the arrival of the Ottomans. This is the site

of a mountain called Hum, which
is topped by the ruins of a hilltop castle that once belonged to
Herzog ("Duke") Stjepan, who
gave Herzegovina its name. Deep
in Blagaj is an impressive cliff
face with a scenic house marking
the source of the Buna River. The
building, called the Tekija, is actually a former monastery for Turkish
dervishes (an order that emphasizes
poverty and humility, famous for
the way they whirl in a worshipful
trance); inside is a modest museum
with the graves of two important dervishes. Today the area is surrounded by gift shops and a big restaurant with fine views over the
river and cliff.

Blagaj is easiest to see on the way to or from Mostar—just
turn off from the main road and follow the Buna River to the big
parking lot.

Počitelj

Počitelj (POTCH-ee-tell) is an artists' colony filled with a compelling mix of Christian and Muslim architecture. Ideally situated

right along the main Mostar-to-Croatia road, it's one of the most popular rest stops for passing tour buses, so it's hardly undiscovered. But it's still worth a stop for its dramatically vertical townscape and beautifully restored Ottoman architecture.

Park your car and hike across the riverstone cobbles to the open square at the base of town, with a handy restaurant, lots of gift shops, and aggressive vendors. The multidomed building is an old hammam (bathhouse). Then hike

up the steep stairs (dodging costumed vendors, and enjoying fine aerial views on those hammam domes) to reach the **mosque.** It's free to enter (women must cover their heads). The interior is bigger, though not necessarily better decorated, than the mosques in downtown Mostar (for a description of a typical Bosnian mosque interior, see page 432). A photo on the porch shows the building circa 1993, destroyed to its foundation.

Continue up the stairs behind the mosque, which lead steeply all the way up to the **fortress,** which was originally built in the

15th century by Hungarian King Mátyás Corvinus (who pushed the Ottomans back, briefly reclaiming some territory—including this region—for the forces of Christian Europe). There's virtually nothing to see inside (the stairs inside the tower are extremely steep and narrow—

tread carefully), but the views are sensational. The best views are from the flat terrace out front. It's clear just how strategic this location is, with perfect views up and down the Neretva Valley, constricted as it is here between steep cliffs.

Stolac

One of the most historic spots in Herzegovina, Stolac (STOH-lats) was a cradle of early Balkan civilization. Unless you're fascinated by archaeology, Stolac isn't worth a long detour—but since it's on the way between Mostar and Dubrovnik (on the back-roads route), consider stopping off if you have a little time to spare.

About 15,000 to 16,000 years ago—long before the Greeks or Romans arrived in this region—the Illyrians (ancestors of today's Albanians) lived in this area's caves, where they left behind some drawings. On a hill above the modern town are the overgrown remains of the once-fearsome dry-stone Illyrian fortress that watched over this strategic road in the third and fourth centuries B.C. The Romans were

later supplanted by the local Bogomil civilization, an indigenous Christian society. Stolac's most impressive attraction dates from this era: On the outskirts of town (on the road toward Mostar), you'll find a **necropolis** with a bonanza of giant tombstones called *stećak*s (from the 13th-15th centuries), engraved with evocative reliefs. Soon after these were erected, the Ottomans arrived, and conversions to Islam followed.

Archaeological treasures aside, today's Stolac is a workaday village with little tourism—trudging along, largely oblivious to the ancient treasures embedded all around. The town was particularly hard-hit during the recent war, when it was taken over by Croat forces and its majority Muslim residents forced to flee to Mostar. Today the war crimes tribunal in The Hague has an entire division devoted to "Stolac Crimes"—at least 80 civilians were killed here. The mosque and surrounding area were completely leveled; it's now rebuilt, and the town's population is divided evenly between Croats and Bosniaks. Tension still hangs heavy in the air. Local Croats have erected crosses in front of several buildings in town, and the main square features a giant monument engraved with the names of Croats killed in the fighting here. In a recent soccer match between the Croatian and Turkish national teams, local Bosniaks backed the Turks...and things got very tense.

If you're interested in learning more, it's well worth hiring local guide **Sanel Marić** to show you around. Sanel is an industrious young man who works for a local organization that strives to help the people of Stolac transcend the scars of the recent war. He can both show you some of the ancient sights around town, and fill you in on recent events (€30 for a tour around town, mobile 061-071-830, sanell_m@yahoo.com).

Međugorje

Međugorje is an unassuming little village "between the hills" (as its name implies) that ranks with Lourdes, Fátima, and Santiago de Compostela as one of the most important pilgrimage sites in all of Christendom. To the cynical non-Catholic, it's just a strip of crassly commercial hotels, restaurants, and rosary shops leading up to a dull church, all tied together by a silly legend about a hilltop apparition. But if you look into the tear-filled eyes of the pilgrims who've journeyed here, it's clear that to some, this place offers much more than what you see on the surface. Strolling through the grounds, you can hear the hushed sounds of prayer whispering through the bushes.

For true believers, Međugorje represents a once-in-a-lifetime opportunity to tread on sacred soil: a place where, over the last three decades, the Virgin Mary has appeared to six local people. Even though the Vatican has declined to recognize the apparitions, that doesn't stop hundreds of thousands of Catholics from coming here each year. More than 30 million pilgrims have visited Međugorje since the sightings began—summer and winter, war (which didn't touch Međugorje) and peace, rain and shine. People make the trek here from Ireland, Italy, Germany, Spain, the US, and just about anywhere else that has Catholics.

Planning Your Time

Unless you're a pilgrim (or think you might be a pilgrim), skip Međugorje—it's an experience wasted on nonbelievers. (The only "attractions" are an unexceptional modern church, a couple of hilltop hikes, and pilgrim-spotting.)

If you do go, the easiest way is to take a day-trip excursion from the Dalmatian Coast (sold from Split, Dubrovnik, and Korčula). By public bus, you can day-trip into Međugorje from Split, but not from Dubrovnik. Consider spending the night here, or sleep in Mostar two nights and day-trip into Međugorje.

Orientation to Međugorje

(country code: 387; area code: 036)
Međugorje (MEDGE-oo-gor-yeh, sometimes spelled "Medju-gorje" in English) is basically a one-street town—most everything happens in the half-mile between its post office (where the bus

Međugorje Mary

What compels millions to flock to this little village in the middle of nowhere? The official story goes like this: On the evening of June 24, 1981, two young women were gathering their sheep on the hillside above Mostar. They came across a woman carrying a baby who told them to come near. Terrified, they fled, only to realize later that this might have been a vision of the Virgin Mary. They returned the next night with some friends and saw the apparition again.

In the nearly three decades since, six different locals (including the two original seers) claim to have seen the vision, and some of them even say they see it regularly to this day. They also say that Mary has given them 10 secrets—predictions of future events that will portend Judgment Day. Written on a piece of parchment, these are kept safely at the home of one of the seers. They have said they will reveal each of these secrets, 10 days before the event occurs, to the local parish priest, who will then alert the world.

But official representatives of the Vatican are not among the believers. According to Catholic law, such visions must be "certified" by the local bishop—and the one around here didn't buy it. One cause for suspicion is that the six seers, before witnessing the visions, were sometimes known to be troublemakers. (In fact, they later admitted that they went up the hill that fateful night not to chase wayward sheep, but to sneak a smoke.) One investigator even suggested that they invented the story as a prank, only to watch it snowball out of control once they told it to the local priest. After decades of reluctance, in mid-2010 the Vatican formed a commission to determine whether to officially endorse this "miracle." (For now, priests are allowed to accompany pilgrimages to Međugorje, but not to *lead* them.)

Whether or not the story is true is, to a certain extent, beside the point—that people *believe* it's true is why they come here.

stop is) and the main church, St. James (Crkva Sv. Jakova). On the hills behind the church are two trails leading to pilgrimage sites. Many travel agencies line the main strip; at any of these, you can find a room, rent a car, hire a local guide, buy ferry tickets for Croatia, and use the Internet.

By the way, Međugorje is clearly a "Croat" sight. While this may seem odd (after all, you're in Bosnia-Herzegovina, not

Croatia), remember that any Catholic from the former Yugoslavia is called a Croat. Virtually every local person you'll meet in Međugorje is, strictly speaking, a Bosnian Croat.

Sights in Međugorje

The center of pilgrim activity is **St. James' Church** (Crkva Sv. Jakova), which was built before the apparitions. The exterior and interior are both pretty dull, but that doesn't stop pilgrims from worshipping here at all times of day (inside and outside). The inside, like the outside, is modern and monochromatic—with a soothing yellow color, and modern stained-glass windows lining the nave. Out in front of the church are posted maps that are useful for getting oriented, and a white statue of the Virgin Mary that attracts a lot of attention from pilgrims. Outside, along the left side of the church, notice the long row of multilingual confessional booths—each one marked with the language spoken by the priest inside, who stands at the ready.

As you face the church, you'll see two trails leading up to the hills. Behind and to the left of the church is **Apparition Hill** (at Podbrdo), where the sightings occurred (a 1-mile hike, topped by a statue of Mary). Directly behind the church is the **Great Hill** (Križevac, or "Cross Mountain"), where a giant hilltop cross, which predates the visions, has become a secondary site of pilgrimage (1.5-mile hike). Note that the paths up to the hilltops are embedded with rocks. If you wonder why they don't make it easier to climb up, remember that an act of pilgrimage is supposed to be challenging. In fact, pilgrims often do one or both of these hikes barefoot, as a sign of penitence.

Around back of the church is a makeshift amphitheater with benches, used for outdoor services. Beyond that is a path, lined with scenes from the life of Jesus. Farther along, on the right, is a giant statue of the **Resurrected Savior** (Uskrsli Spasitelj), also known as the "Weeping Knee." While the elongated, expressionistic sculpture—exemplifying Christ's suffering—is inherently striking, the eternal dampness of its right knee attracts the most attention from pilgrims. Miraculously (or not), it's always wet—go ahead and touch

the spot that's been highly polished by worshippers and skeptics alike.

Believers and nonbelievers both appreciate the parade of

kitsch that lines the **main street** leading up to the church. While rosaries are clearly the big item, you can get basically anything you want stamped with Catholic imagery (Mary is particularly popular, for obvious reasons).

Sleeping in Međugorje

The main street has dozens of hotels and pensions to accommodate pilgrims.

$ Hotel Martin, well-run by Martin Ilić, is set back slightly from the main road. With 45 comfortable, modern rooms—all with balconies—it's an easy choice (Db-€44, cash only, air-con, elevator, tel. 036/651-541, fax 036/651-505, www.martin.ba, martin .ilic@tel.net.ba). Don't confuse this with the Pansion Martin, much farther out of town.

Eating in Međugorje

The main street is lined with straightforward, crank-'em-out eateries catering to tour groups. For something a little more atmospheric and fun, head for **Gardens Restaurant** (near the post-office end of the main drag). The ground-floor bar, which feels a bit like a transplanted British pub, serves only drinks; you can order tasty international cuisine in the classy dining room upstairs, and the namesake garden terrace out back. Somewhat youthful, but still respectable, it's a nice place to unwind at the end of a long pilgrimage (8-13-KM pastas and pizzas, 14-22-KM main courses, daily 10:00-23:00, Antunovića 66, tel. 036/650-499, www.clubgardens .com).

Sleeping and Eating near Međugorje

Considering how drab the town itself is, if you're determined to sleep or eat near Međugorje, you might as well do it at a pleasant new facility just outside town (leaving town, follow signs for *Split/ Ljubuški,* and look for it on the left between warehouses). **Herceg Etno Selo** (Herceg Ethno Village) is a completely artificial but undeniably appealing faux-village of brand-new but old-looking Bosnian dry-stone buildings wedged between industrial areas and office parks. With slate roofs, inviting ponds, playgrounds, a vineyard, a small farm, and a big amphitheater, this sprawling complex includes 50 buildings, housing a restaurant, a big hotel, gift shops, and more. Designed as a retreat center for church groups on pilgrimage, it's a restful place. If Epcot had a low-rent "Croat Herzegovina" pavilion, it would look a lot like this—completely

artificial but utterly charming. The industrial-sized, smoky restaurant has a menu of very well-executed Bosnian and Croatian food
(6-15-KM starters, 13-25-KM main dishes), while the hotel has 71
rooms (Db-€82, Tromeđa bb, tel. 036/653-400, www.etno-herceg
.com, info@etno-herceg.com).

SARAJEVO

Spectacularly set in a mountain valley blanketed with cute Monopoly houses, Sarajevo (sah-rah-YEH-voh) is a sight to behold. It's a cruel irony that for a few short years, Sarajevo became synonymous with sectarian strife, because for virtually its entire history, this beautiful city was a model of the opposite: Muslims, Catholics, Orthodox Christians, and Jews living together in cooperation and harmony. (One of its many nicknames is "Little Jerusalem.") Squeezed into its narrow valley, Sarajevo never even had the option of splitting itself up into ethnic ghettos, so people lived side-by-side. To this day, there are several places in the city where you can see a mosque, synagogue, Catholic church, and Orthodox church with a turn of the head.

Sarajevo is the delightful product of a rich, if occasionally tumultuous, history. The Ottoman-style Old Town, the Baščaršija, feels as if it could have been transplanted here from Istanbul. Then you'll turn a corner and suddenly feel lost in an almost Viennese cityscape. Though torn by war two decades ago, Sarajevo is now a comfortable and safe place to visit.

Listen to the Muslim call to prayer and Catholic and Orthodox church bells playfully jostle above the characteristic lanes of a bazaar-like marketplace. Ponder the scars of war, hunch over to squeeze through the tunnel that was the besieged Sarajevans' lifeline to the world, and listen to a Sarajevan relate personal stories from the harrowing time of the siege. Then relax in a café with a cup of "Bosnian coffee" or nibble on some of the best *bureks* (savory, flaky pies) this side of the Bosphorus. Go ahead—it's OK to enjoy Sarajevo.

Planning Your Time

Sarajevo demands a minimum of a day. Side-tripping here from Mostar lets you scratch the surface, but you won't regret having one, two, or even three nights here. With whatever time you have, begin in the characteristic Turkish quarter, the Baščaršija. My four-part self-guided walk takes you all the way through town, with opportunities to stop at virtually everything worth seeing (except the Sarajevo War Tunnel Museum, which requires a long but worthwhile detour).

Note that Sarajevo is a 2.5-hour trip beyond Mostar, making it a logistical deadhead that's not really "on the way" to other destinations in this book. To maximize efficient use of your time, consider flying in or out (for example, Croatia Airlines has reasonable flights to Zagreb). But be aware that in winter, heavy morning fog often grounds flights here.

Orientation to Sarajevo

(country code: 387; area code: 033)
With approximately 310,000 people (660,000 in the greater Sarajevo area)—filling a city that held up to 525,000 at its prewar peak—Sarajevo is barely contained by its valley. It's surrounded by steep mountains on all sides, with its houses scampering up the valley walls (more recently joined by wartime cemeteries occupying what once were forested parks). It's a long, skinny city, lining up along its humble Miljacka River and main thoroughfare. You can trace the city's historical and architectural development from east to west, starting with the historic Old Town core, called the Baščaršija. West of that is the Austrian-feeling part of town (along Ferhadija street), and beyond that, the modern, concrete skyscraper zone called Marijin Dvor. From here, the city's busy main drag rumbles west (it's called Zmaja od Bosne close to downtown, and Bulevar Meše Selimovića farther out; in wartime it was known as "Sniper Alley").

Terminology: When it comes to the wars of the 1990s, the terminology for the various parties is particularly sensitive—and can vary depending on who you're talking to. During the siege, the citizens of Sarajevo were majority Muslim/Bosniak, but also included Croats, Serbs, Jews, and others; many think of themselves not as a specific ethnicity, but as "Sarajevans" or "Bosnians." Meanwhile, the army surrounding the city was made up almost entirely of Serbs, but not all Serbs supported them—so to call

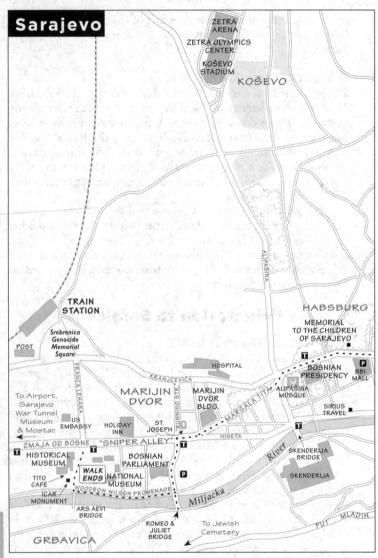

Sarajevo

SARAJEVO

them simply "Serbs" is incomplete. Sarajevans (conscientious not to disrespect the many Serbs who were among those besieged) prefer to call the aggressors "the Bosnian Serb Army," "Army of Republika Srpska" (abbreviated VRS), "Karadžić's forces," or "Četniks." But the term "Četnik" is a loaded one: It was first used to describe the fierce Serb fighting force that ethnically cleansed parts of Yugoslavia during World War II. The troops who surrounded the city evoked this earlier image and called themselves

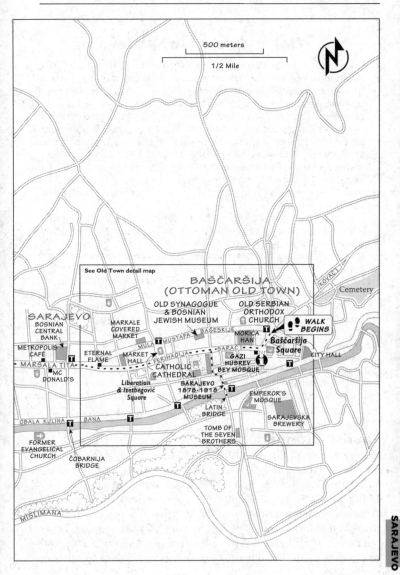

"Četniks," and many Sarajevans have followed suit. However, in other contexts, calling a Serb (who was not involved in the siege) a "Četnik" is a serious insult that could put you on the receiving end of the infamous Balkan temper. It's similar to calling an everyday German a "Nazi": The rare German who actually has Nazi sympathies may consider it a badge of honor, but the vast majority would be justifiably hurt and angry.

War and Peace in Sarajevo

When the Ottomans arrived in this valley in the 15th century, what had been a humble settlement of Bogomil kings and Franciscans from Dubrovnik was swiftly converted into a major trading center—thanks to its strategic location along the mountainous passage from the Croatian coast to the Ottoman-held lands farther east. Sarajevo's location, nestled in the mountains, was near silver and coal mines, and came with an ample supply of fresh spring water and mountain runoff—providing constantly running water, so valued by Muslim culture. The Ottomans harnessed that water to build baths and fountains for Sarajevo's mosques. The town became a thriving population center and, eventually, the capital of the area.

The city's growth was set back temporarily in 1697, when Prince Eugene of Savoy—leading his Habsburg-funded army on an offensive against the Ottomans—burned Sarajevo to the ground. Later, as the Ottoman Empire declined in the late 19th century, it turned the keys to Bosnia and Sarajevo over to the Habsburgs, who gladly sent urban planners and architects to spiff up the humble Ottoman burg to Viennese standards. Under the Austro-Hungarian Empire, Sarajevo was modernized and grew quickly. But within only a few decades, the Habsburgs, too, fell from power—thanks to a war that started with the assassination of the heir to the throne in this very city (see "The Shot Heard 'Round the World," on page 485).

During the Yugoslav era, Sarajevo enjoyed a privileged status as a town that exemplified Tito's idealistic vision of the various Yugoslav ethnicities living and working together. It was

Tourist Information

Sarajevo's helpful TI is on the main pedestrian drag through the old Ottoman quarter (May-Aug Mon-Fri 9:00-22:00, Sat-Sun 10:00-18:00; Sept-April Mon-Fri 10:00-18:00, Sat-Sun 10:00-15:00; Sarači 58, tel. 033/580-999, www.sarajevo-tourism.com). Another branch is at the airport. At either TI, you can pick up maps of town, the *Sarajevo Navigator* monthly planner, and other brochures. The TI can give you a list of hotels, and can call around to check availability, but they aren't legally allowed to sell you anything.

Arrival in Sarajevo

By Bus or Train: Sarajevo's bus and train stations sit next to each other one very long, urban block up from the Marijin Dvor area (former "Sniper Alley," Holiday Inn, and museums). It's a long 30-minute walk into the Old Town (Baščaršija) and most hotels; instead, hop on tram #1 to the Baščaršija, or pay 6-10 KM for a taxi.

chosen to represent Yugoslavia to the world as the host of the 1984 Winter Olympics. Sarajevo seemed poised to emerge as a leading world-class city.

But then its fate took an appalling turn for the worse. As Yugoslavia broke apart, multiethnic Bosnia became ground zero for hashing out old grudges between the union's dominant ethnic groups. Sarajevans woke up one morning in the spring of 1992 to discover that their hometown was under siege, completely surrounded by the heavy artillery of Radovan Karadžić's Bosnian Serb army and paramilitary groups. Overnight, their city—once a proud showpiece—became a shooting gallery, and the Sarajevan people were the targets. They were bombarded without warning and picked off by distant snipers as they crossed the street. For three years and eight months, Sarajevo endured the longest siege of modern European history. The Sarajevans—Bosniaks, Croats, and Serbs alike—were forced to improvise to create shelter, heat, food, and entertainment. They dug a half-mile-long tunnel to get basic supplies and did whatever they could to keep going. For more on this dark time, see "The Siege of Sarajevo" on page 476.

Since 1996, peace has returned to Sarajevo, and the rebuilding of the city is well underway. While you'll see some completely restored historical buildings and brand-new glass skyscrapers, you'll also see the skeletons of bombed-out buildings, and lots of bullet holes and shrapnel scars. Sarajevo is a city in transition—and much remains to be done.

By Car: If you're driving into Sarajevo from Mostar, see "Route Tips for Drivers" at the end of this chapter.

By Plane: Sarajevo's small, sleepy airport sits on the southwestern edge of town (airport code: SJJ, tel. 033/289-100, www.sarajevo-airport.ba). It has ATMs and a TI kiosk. Unfortunately, there's no handy public-transportation connection into town, so the easiest option is a taxi; the fair metered rate to downtown is around 20 KM, but most taxi drivers demand 30 KM. If you'd like to take public transit, walk straight out the front door of the airport and continue on foot about 10 minutes directly ahead to the Dobrinja neighborhood, where you can catch trolley bus #103 to the Latin Bridge in the Old Town, or bus #31E to near the old City Hall, also in the Old Town (both run about 3-4/hour, buy ticket from kiosk or driver, see tram description next page). If you'll be at the airport, it's convenient to visit the nearby War Tunnel Museum (pay no more than 10 KM for the taxi ride from the airport).

Getting Around Sarajevo

Almost everything that's worth seeing in town (with the notable exception of the War Tunnel Museum) is within long walking distance of each other. But you may need to make use of the city's public transportation network, which includes trams, buses, and trolley buses. A single ticket costs 1.60 KM if you buy it at a kiosk, or 1.80 KM if you buy it on board (good for one ride only—if you transfer, you must buy a new ticket). A day ticket costs 4.60 KM (good for one calendar day). The handy tram #3 does a big loop from one end of town to the other, starting in the Old Town (several stops, including at the Latin Bridge/Latinska Ćuprija, at the City Hall/Vijećnica, at the Baščaršija stop near the main square on Kovači street, and behind the cathedral), then along the main drag (former "Sniper Alley") to the west end of town (Ilidža stop, a short taxi ride to the Sarajevo War Tunnel Museum), and back again (7.5 miles and 40 minutes one-way).

Helpful Hints

Travel Agency: Sirius Travel, run by can-do Bakir and Sakiba Zagorica (who used to live in Florida), can arrange accommodations and transfers (€10 to the airport), tours around town (€50/2-hour walking tour, €80/4-hour walking tour plus drive to panoramic viewpoints), or anything else you might need in Sarajevo (along the river at Obala Kulina Bana 5, tel. 033/550-940, www.sirius-travel.ba, siriustravel@bih.net.ba).

Internet Access: You'll find Internet cafés all over the Old Town. Wi-Fi is widely available at hotels and cafés.

Tours in Sarajevo

▲▲▲**Local Guides**—With such a powerful and challenging-to-grasp recent history, and with the ready availability of extremely good and affordable local guides, it's virtually obligatory to hire a guide for your Sarajevo time. For the price of joining an organized walking tour in many European cities, you can hire your very own Sarajevan for the day, who will likely be willing to speak frankly about their experiences during the siege. If at all possible, arrange to hire **Amir Telibečirović,** a journalist, war veteran, and historian who explains Sarajevo's sights and history—from ancient to recent—with brilliant clarity. Amir can add immeasurably to your Sarajevo experience (€15/person for a tour of any length, mobile 061-304-966, walteraga@yahoo.com). If Amir is busy, **Jadranka Šuster** is worth considering for her professional, by-the-book approach (€40/2 hours, €15/extra hour, €120/all day, more for 4 or more people; also offers special activities such as cooking classes, coppersmithing, and wood-burning crafts; mobile 061-828-400, www.sarajevo-tour.com, sarajevotour@gmail.com). Other guides are also available for similar rates; to arrange, contact Sirius Travel (see "Helpful Hints," earlier).

Insider Tours—This company runs various itineraries around the city, departing from their office near the Latin Bridge (at Zelenih Beretki 30). Options include their introductory free tour (tips expected, 2 hours, daily at 16:30); Insider Walks (€7, 1.5 hours, daily at 10:00); Times of Misfortune, detailing the siege (€25, 3 hours, daily at 11:00); and a tour of the War Tunnel Museum (€12, 2 hours, daily at 14:00). They also offer excursions to other parts of Bosnia (including the Srebrenica massacre site, a river-rafting trip, Mostar, and the so-called Bosnian pyramid). Call ahead to reserve and confirm the details (mobile 061-190-591, tel. 033/534-353, www.sarajevoinsider.com).

Adventure Excursions—Sarajevo's spectacular setting lends itself to adventure travel—hiking, mountain biking, river rafting, skiing, and so on. **Green Visions** offers eco-friendly excursions into the Bosnian countryside (tel. 033/717-291, www.green visions.ba).

Self-Guided Walk

▲▲▲Welcome to Sarajevo

This walk begins where most tourist visits do, in the Ottoman-influenced Old Town—the Baščaršija—then strolls through history as it traverses the Habsburg quarter and finally reaches the notorious "Sniper Alley" of the 1992-1996 siege (and the nearby National Museum and Historical Museum). Architecturally, it moves more or less forward through history (though the sights jump around a bit). This walk provides a useful spine for visiting virtually all of the sights mentioned under "Sights in Sarajevo," later (except the War Tunnel Museum, which is farther out). If you're in a hurry and want to focus on the Old Town, you can just do Parts 1 and 2; Parts 3 and 4 take you deeper into the urban part of town, including several sights relating to the siege, and are also worthwhile if you can spare the time. Doing the entire walk without entering any of the sights could take as little as two hours—but with sightseeing stops, it can fill an entire day.

• *Begin at the main square of the Old Town (Baščaršija), with the iconic fountain at the top.*

Part 1: Ottoman Old Town (Baščaršija)

"Pigeon Square": Though it's nicknamed for its many winged residents, this square is officially called Baščaršija. Literally translated as "Main Marketplace," this unmistakably Ottoman-flavored square has given its name to the entire Old Town. The fountain,

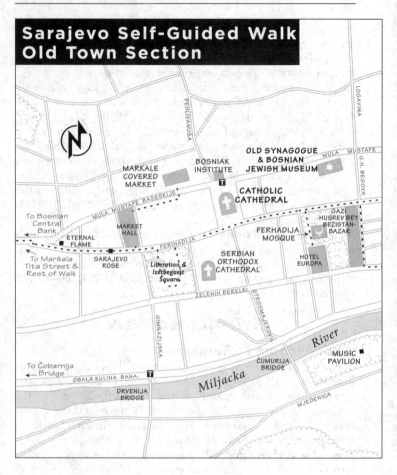

Sarajevo Self-Guided Walk
Old Town Section

SARAJEVO

called **Sebilj,** is an icon of Sarajevo. According to local legend, visitors who drink water from this fountain will return to Sarajevo someday. The original was built in 1753, but this restored version dates from the 19th century. There's a replica of this fountain in Belgrade—a gift from the people of Sarajevo. Although it's the centerpiece of the "Turkish" Old Town, the fountain is more Persian in style. The Ottoman Empire (of which Sarajevo was a part) enjoyed influences from throughout both the Islamic and the European worlds: art, literature, and poetry from Persia (today's Iran); religious influence (i.e., Sunni Islam) from the Arabic

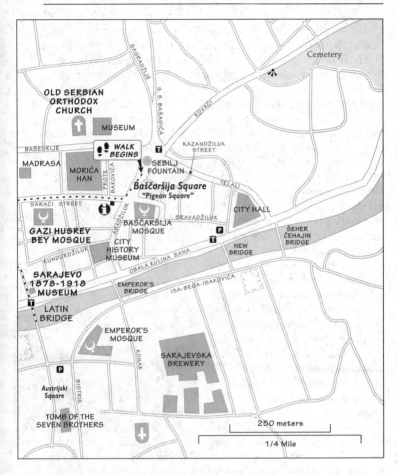

world; diplomacy from the Germanic world; and herbal pharmacology and music from the Jewish world.

Branching off to the right as you face the fountain, find the narrow and delightfully atmospheric **Coppersmiths' Street**

(Kazandžiluk). Craftsmen along this cozy drag still carry out their work, hammering beautiful works of art out of copper—you can hear their little hammers tapping from their workshops. This might be the most touristy street in Sarajevo, so the prices aren't a bargain, but it's a fun stroll.

At the bottom of the square is the **Baščaršija Mosque,** the first of many we'll see throughout town (though this one is closed to the public). The walk also features a pair of covered market halls *(bezistan);* the one across from the mosque (Brusa Bezistan), dating from 1551, holds the **City History Museum,** with a great model of late 19th-century Sarajevo and other good exhibits (described later). Extending away from the market hall (past the mosque), **Bravadžiluk** means "Locksmiths' Street"—but locals call it "Čevap Street" for its many *čevabdžinica* (shops selling the tasty minced-meat, grilled sausages called *čevapčići*). This also leads (in one long block) to the **City Hall** (Vijećnica)—the best example of Austrian Historicist-style architecture from the 40 years of Habsburg rule. It's also the place where, on June 28, 1914, that empire's heir, Archduke Franz Ferdinand, began a fateful drive through town. (We'll see where that trip ended later on this walk.) Later converted into the City Library, this landmark building—and its books—were destroyed by shells in 1992; today it's being restored.

• *Across from the mosque, walk down the main street through town.*

Sarači Street: Lined with shops, *čevap* joints, and the TI, this busy pedestrian street is a handy artery for sightseeing. Like so many streets in the Baščaršija, this is named for a type of craftsman who worked here—in this case, "Leathermakers." After a short block, on the left, is the **TI.** Across the street is the lane called **Prote Bakovića,** crammed with characteristic (if touristy) eateries. Bakovića also leads to the **Old**

Serbian Orthodox Church, well worth a visit (described later). None of the four Serbian Orthodox Churches in Sarajevo was vandalized during the siege, though they were all damaged by shrapnel launched at nearby targets by the Bosnian Serb Army.

Just beyond the TI, on the right, dip into the courtyard of the **Morića Han,** an old Ottoman caravanserai—like an inn, where passing merchants could find food and accommodations. It serves a similar purpose today, with several atmospheric café tables offering the chance to taste the high-octane, unfiltered "Bosnian coffee" (described on page 498—stop now if you need to get caffeinated for all the sightseeing coming up).

A block farther along, on the left, you'll see the courtyard of Sarajevo's top mosque, the **Gazi Husrev Bey Mosque**—definitely worth a visit, and described later. Across the street from the mosque courtyard is the **Kuršumilja Madrasa,** originally built as an Islamic theological school. Step into the courtyard, which is sometimes filled with special exhibits. The modern school next door still teaches the Islamic faith.

Continuing past the mosque, after the next corner you reach another covered market on the left—this one still functioning as a market: **Gazi Husrev Bey Bezistan-Bazar.** Cut through the market hall, pop out the far end, and turn right to find a field (squeezed between the market and Hotel Europa) littered with ruins from a 16th-century Ottoman caravanserai.

• *Now walk back past the end of the covered market, take the first right, and walk a short block down to the...*

Miljacka River: The last building on your left before the riverfront houses the **Sarajevo 1878-1918 Museum** (described later). The museum outlines the brief but prolific four decades of Austrian Habsburg rule here—and, more importantly, the story of how Gavrilo Princip's assassination of the Habsburg heir, Archduke Franz Ferdinand, took place right on this corner. The shooting set off a chain reaction of allegiances and grudges that swiftly pulled all of Europe—and, eventually, much of the world—into a Great War that would end the age of empires and inaugurate a new era of modern nations. (For the full story, see "The Shot Heard 'Round the World" on page 485.)

Go across the street to the Turkish-style **Latin Bridge** (Latinska Ćuprija)—so named because during Ottoman times,

this was an area populated by many Catholics (who said Mass in Latin). After World War I, the bridge was renamed "Principov Most" for the assassin who had asserted Bosnian Serb nationalism against the Habsburgs. But after the 1992-1996 siege, Sarajevans couldn't stand calling the bridge after a Bosnian Serb, and went back to the old name.

Looking down, you'll see that the Miljacka is hardly a rushing river (like the Neretva in Mostar)—up here in the Bosnian highlands, this is still just a trickle. While not navigable for trade, the river's current could be harnessed to spur the development of the old Ottoman town. From here, you're near three sights that may be worth a detour later. Looking across the bridge to the left, you'll see the copper-domed **Emperor's Mosque** (Careva Džamija)—the city's most elegant and oldest, built in 1457 to honor the Ottoman Sultan Mehmet the Conqueror (though it's been rebuilt and expanded many times since then). Just behind the mosque, a short walk from here, is the **Sarajevsko Pivo** brewery, a huge facility that churns out every Bosniak's favorite brew. Because it's fed by a natural spring, this was one of the few factories that was able to keep working through the siege. It's also a fine place for a meal in their atmospheric old beer hall (see "Eating in Sarajevo," later). Those intrigued by Sarajevo's spiritual history might consider a five-minute detour from here to the **Tomb of the Seven Brothers** (described later; go straight across the river and up the hill, past the park with the charming little music pavilion/tea house, to the top of the parking lot).

• *Backtrack all the way past the covered market to the main drag where we started, turn left, and continue along this strip. This street has now changed its name to Ferhadija. Without the slightest transition, you step from the extremely Ottoman-feeling "little Istanbul" of the Baščaršija into the Viennese-feeling Habsburg Quarter.*

Part 2: Habsburg Sarajevo (Ferhadija Street)

With the precipitous decline of the Ottoman Empire in the late 1800s, the Habsburgs—who ruled the vast Austro-Hungarian

Empire from Vienna—saw an opportunity to fill the vacuum left in this part of Europe. With the swirl of a pen in 1878, Bosnia went from Ottoman to Austrian rule. As they had throughout their realm, the Habsburgs stepped in and immediately began to modernize Sarajevo, rolling out new infrastructure and buildings like crazy. While they ruled Sarajevo for only 40 years, the Habsburgs left it a far more modern city than they'd found it.

After a few steps on Ferhadija, an alley on the right leads up to the **Old Synagogue and Bosnian Jewish Museum** (described later)—offering a fascinating look at another of this city's many faiths.

Just a bit farther, set back from the street on the left, is the small but pretty **Ferhadija Mosque.** (Just to the right of the mosque, notice the Club Bill Gates. I wonder if they pay him royalties?) If you go beyond the mosque and duck into the **Hotel Europa,** you'll find a genteel, chandeliered, Viennese-style coffee house interior. The architect who gave Sarajevo its Austrian look—including this hotel—was actually a Czech, Karel Pařík. He lived here for nearly 60 years and designed some 70 buildings in town, including the City Hall, the big Evangelical Church across the river, and the National Museum where this walk ends.

Continuing two more blocks along Ferhadija street, on the right, you can't miss the **Catholic Cathedral** (described later). Notice that this is the fourth different house of worship we've seen (Muslim, Orthodox Christian, Jewish, Catholic) in just the short distance since we began our walk. Behind the cathedral is an old Ottoman bathhouse *(hamam)*, with telltale copper domes. Today it's part of a private cultural center called the **Bosniak Institute**.

A block farther along Ferhadija, on the left, is a parklike square once called Liberation Square—recently renamed **Liberation and Izetbegović Square** to honor the wartime Bosnian president. The square is ringed with busts of important Bosnian writers, and the *Multicultural Man Builds the World* statue in the middle—

of a naked man doing jumping jacks, with a highly polished member—was donated by an Italian artist to beautify the war-torn city. You'll see many such examples of donated public art through Sarajevo—quite a few of them are "white elephants" not entirely embraced by the cynical, siege-hardened Sarajevans. At the far end of the square, local old-timers gather to play giant-size chess—carefully strategizing while a rogues' gallery of onlookers cheers and jeers for each move. It's an enjoyably local scene that testifies to the resilience of the Bosnian spirit—and the ability of unemployed locals to find ways to entertain themselves in a miserable economy.

At the end of the square is yet another house of worship: The bold facade and towers of the **Serbian Orthodox Cathedral.** This was built from 1863-1869, during Ottoman rule. In this ecumenical

city, the funds came from all quarters: donations from the Romanovs, Russia's ruling family; from the Ottoman sultan; and from a Serbian prince. Like many houses of worship in this town, the church's architecture demonstrates the mingling of faiths: It looks like an Orthodox church with a Catholic bell tower. (Bell towers are atypical enough for Orthodox churches, but this one even uses Catholic-style Roman numerals.) The interior is cavernous and sparsely decorated, and (as of this writing) many of the icons are missing for restoration, but it's still worth a quick look (free, daily 8:00-17:30).

Just after the park, on your right, is a **market hall.** Go through (or alongside) this hall and emerge on the other side, then walk to the right one block along the busy street. On the left side of this street, look for Sarajevo's **Markale covered market.** This busy, completely untouristy market gained infamy during the Siege of

Sarajevo as the site of two cruel bombings that targeted civilians and claimed more than a hundred innocent lives—Sarajevans who were simply shopping for paltry foodstuffs to keep their families fed and alive through impossibly tough conditions. Two plaques along the back walls of the market commemorate the 67 Sarajevans who died during an attack on February 5, 1994 (plus another 144 wounded), and the 43 who died (and 90 wounded) on August 28, 1995. These ruthless bombardments were a turning point in the siege—when the international community began to sit up and pay attention, and realize that this was not simply a standard-issue war between equal parties, but a barbaric siege that was destroying the lives of countless peace-loving civilians who wanted no part of the violence. It was the 1995 attack, in part, that prompted NATO air strikes against Karadžić's forces two days later. "Operation Deliberate Force" ultimately led to the Dayton Peace Accords, which finally ended the violence—although Sarajevans wish NATO hadn't been quite so "deliberate" as to wait three and a half years before taking action.

Head back to the main walking street and continue on your way. As you walk, in the pavement in front of the Tally Weijl shop (at #12, on the left), look for the distinctive starburst indentation that's colored in red. This is one of the increasingly rare **Sarajevo**

roses. Immediately following the war, about 1,000 of the impact craters in the streets of Sarajevo were filled with a red resin, instantly creating a poignant memorial. For example, the plaque on the Tally Weijl shop explains that on May 27, 1992, 26 *Građana Sarajeva* ("citizens of Sarajevo") were killed by an artillery shell while waiting in line to buy bread at a bakery here. As the city has resurrected itself from the rubble, most of these Sarajevo roses have been replaced with new asphalt. Only a few remain, and those are tended to by a local preservation group. (It's possible that the one I'm describing will also have disappeared by the time you read this.)

The street angles and takes you up to an intersection with the busy Maršala Tita street, named for the WWII Partisan military hero and president-for-life of communist Yugoslavia—Marshal Tito. (Recent plans to rename this drag for wartime

Bosnian President Alija Izetbegović—a Muslim—were scuttled when Bosnian Serbs protested.) On the right at the corner is an **eternal flame** honoring Partisan fighters. If you're here in cold weather, you may notice that the practical Sarajevans—who learned during the lean years of the siege never to waste resources—use it to warm up as they pass by.

Part 3: Maršala Tita Street

Crowded with cars, trucks, trams, and buses, this artery feels more urban and less atmospheric than the Ottoman and Austrian zones we just left. During the siege, this was one of the safest major boulevards in town, since it's relatively narrow and well-protected from snipers by tall buildings. The exposed side-streets were blocked off to create what was called a "Road of Life," where people could walk without fear of being picked off by distant gunmen. We'll follow this street several blocks to ground zero of the former war zone.

After a block, on the right, his-and-hers Atlases flank the doors of the **Bosnian Central Bank** building—where the fledg-

ling Convertible Mark currency is administered. The all-purpose lights spanning the street here are lit up to celebrate local festivals and (in this multifaith city) a wide range of religious holidays: Ramadan, Catholic Christmas, Orthodox Christmas, and New Year's.

Farther along, on the left, is the local **McDonald's,** which caused an uproar when it finally opened here in July of 2011. The opening was delayed for four years, as local *ćevap* vendors—scandalized by the notion of a multinational conglomerate challenging the loyalty of local palates—did whatever they could to block it. For weeks after it opened, there were long lines down the street of Sarajevans curious to try the American burgers. But within a few weeks, the furor died down, the crowds dispersed, and the *ćevap* sellers were satisfied that Bosnians wouldn't abandon the grilled meats they've enjoyed for centuries.

Two blocks later, the street opens up. On the right is a fine park with one of the most emotionally devastating memorials in this tragedy-laden city: the **Memorial to the Children of Sarajevo.**

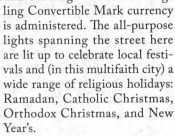

The Siege of Sarajevo

Most travelers know that Bosnia-Herzegovina was torn apart by a war when Yugoslavia broke up in the early to mid-1990s (see the Understanding Yugoslavia chapter). But few realize that in that country's capital, Sarajevo, the "war" was not conventional fighting between armies, but a medieval-style siege designed to cut off the city from food, water, electricity, telephone, medicine, and other critical supplies. The Siege of Sarajevo lasted for more than 1,300 days, making it the longest siege in modern European history (longer than the infamous WWII-era Siege of Leningrad, a.k.a. St. Petersburg). How could a modern city of some 300,000 people be cut off in this way?

In early 1992, the people of Bosnia-Herzegovina voted in favor of independence from Yugoslavia; although many Serbs boycotted the ballot box, 64 percent of Bosnians turned out, and 98 percent of them voted yes. Over the next month, Bosnian Serb leader Radovan Karadžić and Bosnian President Alija Izetbegović traded heated rhetoric about what the new nation of Bosnia-Herzegovina would look like. Meanwhile, each one built a makeshift army: Izetbegović's Bosnian Army asserted control over Sarajevo's city center, while Karadžić's well-supplied Bosnian Serb troops from the Yugoslav People's Army fortified their positions on the hills ringing the capital.

On April 1, a Serb militia group invaded the town of Bijeljina in eastern Bosnia, massacring many innocent civilians. On April 5, some 100,000 Sarajevans—of all ethnic stripes—came to the busy intersection in front of the Bosnian Parliament to stage a peace rally. They occupied the parliament chamber and demanded the security that the government had failed to provide. Karadžić watched nervously from his office in the Holiday Inn across the street. When the protesters turned their attention to his building, he commanded his snipers to open fire on the unarmed crowd, killing six. Karadžić fled to the hills above town, while Izetbegović's police moved in and arrested the snipers. After Izetbegović refused Karadžić's ultimatum to release the snipers, Karadžić began shelling the city.

For the next month, the situation degraded in other parts of the country, as Bosnian Serb paramilitary groups carried out ethnic cleansing. On May 2, 1992, the Bosnian Serb Army began their advance on the capital in earnest, bombarding Sarajevo's city center, blowing up its central post office to disable telephone communication, and erecting barricades, completely cutting off the Sarajevans from the outside world. The city was defended by a motley collection of policemen, professional soldiers who had defected from the Yugoslav army, and even criminal street gangs who came together to defend their hometown. About 12 percent of the army was made up of Serbs. It wasn't necessarily a "pro-Bosnia" army—just Sarajevans desperate to preserve their way of life. This wasn't patriotism: It was survival.

Both sides dug in for a long struggle. Yugoslavia's leader,

Slobodan Milošević, sent a ruthless general, Ratko Mladić, to take command of the Bosnian Serb forces. His orders: "Target the Muslim neighborhoods...Shell them until they're at the edge of madness." Snipers monitored exposed streets, immediately firing upon any Sarajevan who dared to walk past.

Horrifying as the tales of besieged Sarajevo are, it's equally uplifting to hear about the irrepressible human spirit shown during these times. The people of Sarajevo survived thanks to the tireless efforts of those who dug and used a tunnel to break the siege (see the "Sarajevo War Tunnel Museum" on page 491); and to international relief organizations, including the Red Cross as well as Islamic, Orthodox, Catholic, and Jewish humanitarian groups.

Food was a major concern. The UN took responsibility for humanitarian aid through the siege, and about 90 percent of food was provided by UN airlifts. Sarajevans remember European Community-donated mystery meat in an *ICAR* can, which they ate happily while trying not to think of where it came from (now immortalized by a monument behind the Historical Museum).

Amazingly, people did not simply give up. Even if they lacked basic resources, they continued dressing well and keeping up appearances—if only to preserve their own sanity. Barbers, for example, had a very valuable skill that they could barter for other goods and services.

Throughout even the darkest days of the siege, Sarajevans had art galleries, cafés for socializing, and even a film festival (the famous Sarajevo Film Festival, still going strong, began in 1993). One well-known figure—Vedran Smailović, the so-called "Cellist of Sarajevo"—played his instrument in the bombed-out ruins around town. In 1993, a "Miss Sarajevo" beauty pageant was held in a basement; at the end, all of the contestants held up a banner pleading, "Don't let them kill us." (The pageant was immortalized in U2's "Miss Sarajevo" music video.)

Sarajevans managed to keep their sense of humor even through the difficult times. One night, a pro-Serb vandal spraypainted on a Sarajevo post office, "This is Serbia!" The next day, it was rebutted with a new message: "No, this is a post office, you idiot!" On another occasion, someone graffitied on a building: "Tito, come back!" The next day's response: "No thanks, I'm not crazy!"

In mid-1995, thanks to NATO bombing raids and joint action by the Croatian and Bosnian armies, the siege started to weaken. On Feb. 29, 1996—the four-year anniversary of the independence referendum that had sparked the war—the government officially declared that the siege was over. It's impossible to know exact figures, but most estimates suggest that about 300,000 to 350,000 lived through the siege, including around 50,000 to 70,000 Serbs who decided to stay in their home city. During the siege, about 10,000 Sarajevans died—including nearly 1,600 children—and 56,000 to 70,000 were wounded.

Look closely at the symbolism-packed fountain. The glass sculpture in the middle represents a sandcastle, but one that is not—and never will be—finished...the innocent play of a child cut short by an untimely death. The footprints embedded in the concrete basin belong to the young siblings

of children who were killed in the war. The silver pillars to the left can be spun to see names of young victims of the fighting. Nearly 1,600 children were among those killed during the siege.

Scattered in the hillsides of the **park** beyond the fountain, notice a few Ottoman-style gravestones, shaped like turbans—the earliest dating from the early 17th century. In the pavement at the far end of this park, look for a Sarajevo rose.

A block later, on the left, is the **Bosnian Presidency** (the local "White House"). During the early days of the war, this building was the focus of street-by-street fighting; if the Bosnian Serb forces had claimed it, they could have declared victory. At one point, they were within 50 yards of this building, but the defense held. As part of the compromise to end the war, today Bosnia's "Presidency" is made up of a committee of three members: one Bosniak, one Croat, and one Serb, with a rotating chairmanship. Difficult as it is to get things done with one president, imagine how impossible the situation is when you need agreement among three people who are predisposed to mistrust each other. While critical for ending the war, this compromise has made it even more difficult to move forward with postwar recovery.

In the park next to the Presidency is the 16th-century Alipašina Mosque. A long walk directly up the hill from here (about a mile up Alipašina street) would take you to the **Zetra Olympics Center** (not worth a detour now, but worth considering if you're curious and have time later). This complex includes Koševo Stadium, which held the opening ceremony for the 1984 Olympics (and, in 1997, hosted visits by both Pope John Paul II and the band U2—both of whom had spoken out in support of the besieged

Sarajevans), and Zetra Arena, which was used for Olympic skating events (this is where Torvill and Dean thrilled the world with their ice dancing) and for the closing ceremony. Today the complex houses a museum about those games. Poignantly, the stadium that

once commanded the world's attention is now surrounded by a vast field of headstones—mostly of Sarajevans killed during the war. The ice arena's basement was used as a makeshift morgue, and its wooden seats were used to build coffins for the deceased.

Continuing a few short blocks along Maršala Tita street—passing another park (with a conspicuously modern sculpture that was another artist's "white elephant" gift to Sarajevo)—you reach a building called **Marijin Dvor** (on the right). While pretty dreary-looking today, this was built in the Habsburg period (1895) as the palace of an aristocrat's wife, giving its name to what would later become Sarajevo's city center—where we're headed next.

• *Where Maršala Tita street merges with another big street, you're in the center of modern Sarajevo and the start of the city's main thorough-fare (Zmaja od Bosne).*

Part 4: Modern Sarajevo and "Sniper Alley"

This neighborhood is officially called Marijin Dvor (roughly "Maria's Castle," after the palace we just passed)—a strangely romantic name for a concrete skyscraper jungle turned war zone. These days it's better known as "Sniper Alley," the nickname given it by foreign journalists who covered the besieged city.

• *Begin your visit to this part of Sarajevo with a...*

"Sniper Alley" Spin-Tour: Stand near the tram stop at the big intersection across the street from the church, so you can see between the buildings across the river to the hillside. High on that hill, the patch of land with the grave markers is the city's main **Jewish cemetery;** during the siege, Karadžić's snipers found this an ideal position from which to rain bullets down on the innocent civilians below. People would cross this street only at night, by cover of darkness, or occasionally by running behind a moving UN armored vehicle that provided cover. Just two decades ago, if you stood here long enough to read this paragraph, you'd be dead.

Spin to the right to see the towering, glassy skyscraper—the **Bosnian Parliament** building. While freshly rebuilt today, this was utterly destroyed during the war.

Looking farther to the right, up the big boulevard, you'll see the prominent, bright-yellow facade of the **Holiday Inn.** When it was built for the 1984 Olympics, this was the premier hotel in Sarajevo, fit for visiting dignitaries. But less than a decade later, the first shots of the Bosnian War were fired right here. As tensions were rising throughout Bosnia-Herzegovina, tens of thousands of peace protesters filled this street on April 5, 1992. Karadžić instructed snipers positioned in the hotel to open fire on the unarmed crowd, killing six and wounding many others. Later, the hotel housed foreign journalists and dignitaries, and was therefore virtually the only safe space in the entire city center—though even this enclave suffered its share of incidental damage. Since the war, the hotel has been fully renovated.

Turning to the right, you see the Catholic **Church of St. Joseph** (built by the Czech architect Karel Pařík). The street to the left of the church, with a clear view from the sniper's nest in the Jewish cemetery, is called Tršćanska ("Trieste Street")—but locals began calling it Trćanska, "Running Street," where it was deadly to walk at a normal pace. Behind the church stands a **hospital.** While the side of the hospital facing away from the hillside sniper's nest was a safe place for injured and ill Sarajevans to recover, the side facing the hill was exposed to sniper fire...a lesson learned in the worst possible way when snipers shot through the windows of the hospital to kill patients lying in their beds.

• *From here, if you want to go straight to the National Museum, continue up the main street past the Bosnian Parliament, then carry on another long block to reach the museum (on your left). But for a more interesting approach—dotted with significant siege locations—take the scenic back way along the river. Walk down the street alongside the Bosnian Parliament to the river and the...*

"Romeo and Juliet Bridge": This bridge was originally named "Vrbanja Bridge," but now it's officially called "Suada Dilberović and Olga Sučić Bridge" for the two young women who were the first documented victims of the Siege of Sarajevo. Dilberović was a Dubrovnik-born Bosniak pursing her medical degree at the University of Sarajevo, and Sučić was a Croat resident of Sarajevo; both were killed by sniper bullets while standing on this bridge during the Holiday Inn peace rally massacre. But this bridge is internationally better known as "Romeo and Juliet Bridge," for two other victims of the war. Two young Sarajevans—Admira Ismić (a Bosniak) and Boško Brkić (a Serb)—were lovers who wanted to escape to a better life together. Brkić used his connections to Serb officials to obtain promise of safe passage out of the city. On May 19, 1993, the couple made it as far as this bridge before snipers opened fire; both were hit and fell to the ground. Boško died instantly; Admira crawled to her beloved, and died clutching his body in her arms. The bodies could not be retrieved and buried for fear of further sniper attacks,

so they lay on the bridge for another week, locked in a heart-wrenching embrace. After four days, American war correspondent Kurt Schork issued a dispatch describing the corpses, grabbing the attention of people around the world with this example of the horrifying conditions in the Bosnian capital. The ill-fated "Romeo and Juliet of Sarajevo" have been immortalized in film, song, and news accounts. Sarajevans embrace the couple for the way they embody a united Sarajevo—with people of various ethnicities living together under siege. As Ismić's father said in Schork's dispatch, "Love took them to their deaths. That's proof this is not a war between Serbs and Muslims. It's a war between crazy people, between monsters."

Directly across this bridge is the **Grbavica** neighborhood, the closest Bosnian Serb forces got to the city center during the siege—which is why the area we just passed through was so deadly. The snipers were just a couple of blocks away.

• *Turn right and stroll along the river for a couple of blocks, along the...*

Woodrow Wilson Promenade (Vilsonovo Šetalište): Though this was a deadly no-man's-land just two decades ago, today it's a pleasant, tree-lined riverside park. But here in Sarajevo, even a pretty park has a sinister edge: The trees here survived only because they were too close to enemy lines to safely cut down for fuel.

Soon you reach the **Ars Aevi Bridge,** designed by Paris' Pompidou Centre architect Renzo Piano, who has also drawn up plans for the nearby future home of Sarajevo's contemporary art museum. At this bridge, turn right and head away from the river. You're facing two museums: On the right, the genteel mansion housing the **National Museum;** and on the left, the gloomy concrete home of the **Historical Museum** (both described later). On your way to these museums, pause to appreciate a few artsy and ironic landmarks.

The field on the left is the future site for the Ars Aevi contemporary art museum (www.arsaevi.ba). Nearby, look for the  **monument** shaped like a giant tin can with an *ICAR* label. This is a (somewhat ironic) thank-you for international relief supplies sent to Sarajevo during the siege, including the canned meat that sometimes appeared in care packages from the European Community. Understandably, Sarajevans have a love-hate nostalgia for this "siege Spam." Just beyond that, tucked into the back wall of the Historical Museum, are the outdoor tables of the **Tito Café.** This kitschy hangout celebrates the dictator of

communist Yugoslavia with preachy red flags, lots of old photos, camouflage stools, and a bust of the beloved leader, as well as an old jeep and other Yugoslav military vehicles scattered out front. The clientele seems split between those who really do miss Tito, and those who are here ironically...but either way, they're having fun. (While nursing a drink here, read the "Tito" sidebar on page 680.) Continuing up the sidewalk between the two museums, you'll pass another ironic monument, a big **stone slab,** on the left (next to the stairs to the Historical Museum). This reads, "Under this stone there is a monument to the victims of the war and cold war."

• *Our long walk through Sarajevo—and its history—is finished. From here, you can visit the two nearby museums; walk or ride a tram (#2, #3, or #5) back to your starting point in the Old Town; or take a taxi or tram #3 (plus a short taxi ride) out to the War Tunnel Museum.*

Sights in Sarajevo

I've organized Sarajevo's main sights as you'll reach them while you follow my self-guided walk, above.

In the Ottoman Old Town (Baščaršija)

▲**City History Museum (in Brusa Bezistan Covered Market)**—Filling a big indoor bazaar right on old Sarajevo's main square, this good museum features a giant model of the city in 1878, at the apex of the Ottoman period and just before the new Austrian rulers renovated and expanded Sarajevo. The rest of the collection offers a fine historical overview of the city in English, with actual artifacts, traditional costumes, and a good video tracing Sarajevo's story (with English subtitles).

Cost and Hours: 5 KM, 3-KM audioguide, Mon-Fri 10:00-16:00—until 18:00 mid-April-mid-Oct, Sat 10:00-15:00, closed Sun, Abadžiluk 10, tel. 033/239-590, www.muzejsarajeva.ba.

▲**Old Serbian Orthodox Church**—While fully Orthodox inside and out, this 16th-century church has features that resemble a synagogue or a mosque—hinting at the mingling of faiths that has characterized Sarajevo for most of its history. Stepping inside, notice that the church (which was built on the site of an even earlier one) is set about three feet below street level. Because the Ottomans wouldn't allow churches to be taller than mosques, the builders went down instead of up. Also notice how—with its

split-level design and upstairs gallery—
it feels like a synagogue with an iconostasis. You may see worshippers making a
fuss over a small coffin, which contains
the body of a child; this is believed to
have healing power, especially for infer-
tile women. Across the small courtyard
is a museum with old icons, incense
burners, vestments, and manuscripts
in Cyrillic. Look for the document in
squiggly Arabic script—a written confirmation from the Ottoman sultan
permitting worshippers to practice the
Orthodox Christian faith here.

Cost and Hours: 2 KM, includes church and museum, Mon-
Sat 8:00-18:00, Sun 8:00-16:00, Mula Mustafe Bašeskije 59.

▲▲**Gazi Husrev Bey Mosque (Gazi Husrev Begov
Džamija)**—Called "Begova Mosque" for short, this is Sarajevo's
most important and most historic mosque. For more on Bosnia's
Muslim faith, see page 432.

Cost and Hours: Outer courtyard-free; mosque-2 KM—buy
ticket at little house to the left as you enter courtyard; specific opening times vary depending on prayer schedule and are
posted at ticket office—generally May-Sept daily 9:00-12:00 &
14:30-16:00 & 17:30-19:00, Oct-April open sporadically, closed
to visitors during Ramadan, Sarači, tel. 033/532-144, www.vakuf
-gazi.ba.

Courtyard: Start in the outer courtyard. The **fountain** in the
middle (with water piped in from the mountains three miles away)
is for washing before prayer. Around the left side, look for the
two freestanding **mausoleums** (you can't enter them, but you can
peek through the windows around the side). The larger one holds
the remains of the mosque's founder and namesake, Gazi Husrev
Bey (1480-1541; *bey* is an Ottoman aristocratic title, like "Lord"
or "Sir"). He was a governor of Bosnia who donated vast sums to
improving Sarajevo (throughout the Old Town, look for plaques
that say *Gazi Husrev Begov-Vakuf*—marking his gifts to the city).
The smaller mausoleum holds his assistant and secretary, a highly
educated Croat named Tardić who had been captured in a battle.
He accepted Gazi Husrev Bey's offer of a job, a precondition of
which was that he convert to Islam, and went on to become the
governor's most trusted advisor. The **cemetery** behind the mausoleums has graves both old and new; one of the most recent holds
the remains of the imam from the destroyed mosque in Banja
Luka, a Serb stronghold in northern Bosnia.

Interior: Buy a ticket at the office and step into the mosque's

interior (women must cover their heads). You'll see many of the same elements as other Bosnian mosques (see description on page 433). Appreciate the remarkably spacious-feeling architecture. Many of the carpets are gifts from Muslim nations and date from the Tito era. As an anchor

of the non-aligned world, which included many Muslim countries (in North Africa and the Middle East), Tito had particularly good relations with Islamic leaders. The electric lighting—the world's first in a mosque—was installed by the Habsburg rulers in 1898 (the same year they lit up Vienna's Schönbrunn Palace), suggesting how deeply the Habsburgs respected the local Islamic faith. The besieging Bosnian Serb forces in the 1990s didn't share this respect, and used the mosque's minaret for target practice. Looking through the windows, you can see the walls are six feet thick—which helped save it from utter destruction. The mosque was badly damaged, and renovated in 1996 using funds largely from Saudi Arabia; the interior is still less ornately decorated than it once was.

Nearby: The **clock tower** across the narrow street is also part of the mosque complex; notice that its "noon" lines up with sunset—critical in establishing the five times each day that Muslims pray. Under the clock tower you'll find a free public WC and a little hole-in-the-wall bakery that's open late.

▲▲**Sarajevo 1878-1918 Museum and Archduke Franz Ferdinand Assassination Site**—Worth ▲▲▲ and ample goose

bumps to historians with vivid imaginations, and interesting to anyone, this is the nondescript street corner where the heir to the vast but declining Austro-Hungarian Empire met a bloody fate at the hands of a Bosnian Serb separatist, plunging Europe into the War to End All Wars (until the next war). The shots were fired as Franz Ferdinand and his wife Sophie sat, JFK-and-Jackie style, in an open-top car during a visit to the Bosnian capital (for the full story, see the sidebar). The street corner where it happened, across from the Latin Bridge (Latinska Ćuprija), is now home to a plaque and a humble one-room museum, which shows a good video montage in its window that helps illustrate the story. The **Sarajevo 1878-1918 Museum** traces the four decades when this

SARAJEVO

The Shot Heard 'Round the World

On June 28, 1914, Archduke Franz Ferdinand and his wife, Archduchess Sophie, visited Sarajevo on the anniversary of the Battle of Kosovo Polje (the same 14th-century battle that, several decades later, Slobodan Milošević would exploit to whip up Serbian nationalism and ignite the wars of the 1990s). While they were in town, a local pan-Slavic movement to liberate Bosnia from the Austro-Hungarian Empire (affiliated with a movement called the Black Hand) plotted an assassination. Early in the day, one attempt failed when the bomb intended for the archduke's car instead wounded other members of his party. Believing the plot to be foiled, the archduke continued on his way, visiting the City Hall a few blocks up the river.

A 19-year-old Bosnian Serb named Gavrilo Princip, who was in on the plot, was waiting for Ferdinand's car along the river by the Latin Bridge (across the street from today's museum, by the bus stop). But when that area became too crowded, he crossed to the corner now marked by a plaque, and stepped into a nearby delicatessen. Meanwhile, after leaving the City Hall, Franz Ferdinand decided at the last moment to change his schedule and visit the people who had been wounded by the bomb. Confused by the last-minute change, the driver took a wrong turn up this street and paused in a moment of indecision, causing the car to stall...directly in front of Princip. The assassin raised his gun and fired at Franz Ferdinand and General Oskar Potoriek; he shot the archduke and missed the general, but hit Archduchess Sophie—killing the imperial couple.

Princip and the other plotters were arrested. The Habsburgs wanted to send investigators into Serbia to root out the co-conspirators; Serbia's refusal to grant them access kicked off a chain reaction that brought all of Europe to war. While historians stress that Ferdinand's assassination was merely the event that ignited the tinderbox of World War I—not the "cause" of the war—its significance is undeniable.

The epilogue: Because Princip was too young to be executed, he was given a 20-year sentence at Theresienstadt prison outside of Prague (which the Nazis later converted into Terezín Concentration Camp). The terrible conditions at the camp led to Princip's early death at age 24. Much of the world considered him a monster, but by the end of World War I, the nascent nation of Yugoslavia—which emerged from the ashes of that war exactly as Princip and his accomplices had dreamed—celebrated him as a hero, even giving his name to the bridge near the place where he happened to be standing when he stumbled into his opportunity to change history.

city was part of the Vienna-ruled Austro-Hungarian Empire, with a special emphasis on the assassination. Just inside the entrance, look for the symbolic footprints of the assassin, Gavrilo Princip. Beyond that, the museum holds one well-presented room featuring the trappings of the age, a map showing the sites relating to the assassination, life-size mannequins of Franz Ferdinand and Sophie, and clips from a 1970s-vintage Yugoslav film about the assassination, all with English labels.

Cost and Hours: 2 KM, Mon-Fri 10:00-16:00, Sat 10:00-15:00, closed Sun, Zelenih Beretki 1, tel. 033/533-288, www.muzej sarajeva.ba.

Near the Old Town (Baščaršija)

Tomb of the Seven Brothers—The nondescript mosque at the top of the parking lot across the Latin Bridge from the Old Town

is a favorite spot for Sarajevo superstition. Along the right, outer wall of the mosque are a door and seven windows marking tombs of (according to legend) innocent people who were unjustly sentenced to death; a strange light was reported to be emanating from their graves at night. It's believed that if you put a coin of the same value in each of these eight slots, you can make a wish or a request. Then you are supposed to walk around the top of the mosque, turn left, and walk down the little lane. Listen carefully—the first words you hear as you walk along this street will help you divine the answer you seek. Interestingly—but not surprisingly for this fundamentally ecumenical town—even non-Muslim Sarajevans come here when they are searching for enlightenment.

Cemeteries and Viewpoint just Above the Baščaršija—If

you walk about 10 minutes up Kovači street from the Sebilj fountain, you'll come to a fine viewpoint over the Old Town, as well as some large, thought-provoking cemeteries from the siege years. Looking even higher in the hills, you'll see more sprawling cemeteries blanketing the hillsides. People were buried in these places either at night or in heavy fog, when gravediggers could be safe from snipers. In the cemetery at the top of Kovači street is the ceremonial domed grave of wartime president Alija

Izetbegović (a museum dedicated to him is nearby). Just above this area is a neighborhood called Vratnik (roughly "Gateway"), the oldest part of town.

In the Habsburg Quarter

Immediately west of the Ottoman quarter is the more modern part of town, built at the end of the 19th century after Bosnia became part of the Austro-Hungarian Empire. While several of the sights scattered through this area are much older, most of the buildings here are evocative of those in the capital at the time, Vienna.

▲▲**Old Synagogue (Stari Hram) and Bosnian Jewish Museum (Muzej Jevreja BiH)**—Combining a classic old 16th-century synagogue with an excellent and insightful museum chronicling the Jewish faith in this country, this building was modeled after a synagogue in Toledo, Spain. Soon after the Jews were expelled from that kingdom in the late 15th century, Sephardic Jews made their way to Bosnia, which they found to be an unusually tolerant place (typical of its entire history). Unlike many Central and Eastern European cities, Sarajevo did not relegate its Jews to a ghetto; they lived amidst their non-Jewish neighbors. Local Sephardi used "Ladino," a unique language mixing Spanish and Hebrew (even today, rabbis greet each other not with *Shalom*, but with *Buenos días*).

Cost and Hours: 3 KM, 5-KM guidebook, Mon-Fri 10:00-16:00—until 18:00 May-mid-Oct, Sun 10:00-13:00, closed Sat, Josipa Štadlera 32, tel. 033/475-740.

Touring the Synagogue and Museum: Buy your ticket and step into the central hall, with the *bima* (altar-like raised area) in

the center and the wooden doors that hold the Torah. Women, who in accordance with Jewish tradition worship separately from men, stand up in the arcades ringing the hall. Climb up the stairs to see the exhibits filling those arcades. On the first floor up, you'll see a replica of the important Sarajevo Haggadah book (see sidebar, next page); a tombstone from a Jewish cemetery on the hill across the river, which is the second biggest in Europe (after Prague's) and was tragically used as a sniper's nest during the siege; and a model of the original appearance of this synagogue. The next floor shows more Jewish religious items and illustrates how local Jews adopted local culture (for example, you'll see Jews wearing Muslim-style fezzes). The replica of an Ottoman-era "pharmacy" with herbal cures is a reminder that such businesses were typically run by Jewish Sarajevans.

SARAJEVO

The Sarajevo Haggadah

An ancient Jewish text telling the story of the Exodus—used as a sort of "order of service" for the Passover Seder—the Haggadah is considered the third most important book of the Jewish faith (after the Torah and Talmud). The Sarajevo Haggadah is filled with colorful illustrations as well as wine stains—indicating that it has been used at many Passover dinner tables. While the book's exact origins are unclear, it likely dates from around 1350 and was brought here from Spain by Sephardic transplants in the 16th century. Appropriately for a book about the Exodus, it has had quite an unlikely journey through a landscape of hardship since then. Bosnians—who, regardless of their ethnicity, consider the Sarajevo Haggadah a part of their national cultural heritage—proudly explain that the book has been protected time after time by people of a wide variety of faiths (not just Jews). During the WWII occupation, when an SS officer came here to claim the Haggadah, the Muslim curator of the museum lied about its whereabouts, and carried it on horseback into the mountains to hide it away under the doorstop of a village mosque. Soon after the siege began in 1992, the room in the National Museum that held the Haggadah was almost entirely destroyed by mortar shells—except the book itself, which was secured in a steel box. The building was exposed to sniper fire, so under cover of darkness, Bosnian Army troops snuck to the museum, rescued the book, and stored it in the vault of the Bosnian Central Bank. Recently the National Museum renovated an appropriately secure place to store the Sarajevo Haggadah (visitors can peek through a door to see it), while the Haggadah replica in the Old Synagogue's museum lets you get a closer look.

The top floor focuses on the dark 20th century, including the Holocaust. The exhibit profiles Bosnians who were designated as "Righteous Among the Nations"—an honorific for non-Jews who risk their own lives to save their Jewish neighbors. Among these is Derviš Korkut, the Muslim museum curator who saved the Sarajevo Haggadah from Nazi investigators. Some Jewish women were smuggled out of Nazi-occupied areas by disguising themselves in Muslim veils. You'll also see Nazi-mandated armbands identifying Jews, photos of resistance fighters, and an exhibit on the reprehensible Jasenovac Concentration Camp on today's Bosnian-Croatian border—where Jews, Serbs, Roma (Gypsies), antifascist Muslims and Croats, communists, and other enemies of the Ustaše-controlled state were savagely executed. Jasenovac lacked the "high-tech" gas chambers of other Nazi camps, so they resorted to more medieval methods, murdering their victims by knife, sword, or even a hammer to the skull. And yet, even through that dark history, Sarajevo has remained a place where cultures coexist side-by-side: Position yourself so that you can look through the Star of David window to see a minaret.

Catholic Cathedral—Dating from 1884-1889, this Historicist structure mingles different architectural styles (typical of Viennese buildings of that age): a Neo-Gothic exterior and a Neo-Byzantine/Neo-Baroque interior. Inside and on the left, look for the grave of the church's founder and a plaque commemorating Pope John Paul II's visit here on April 12, 1997.

Cost and Hours: Free, daily 9:00-16:00, Trg Fra Grge Martića 2.

Near "Sniper Alley"

For the most interesting approach to this area from the Old Town (Baščaršija), see my self-guided walk, earlier.

▲**National Museum (Zemaljski Muzej)**—This humble museum, always desperate for founding, will very likely be closed during your visit—be sure it's open before making the trip. If open, it gives you the chance to peek (through a glass door) at one of the world's most priceless books, the Sarajevo Haggadah (see sidebar).

Cost and Hours: 5 KM; mid-April-mid-Oct Tue-Fri 10:00-17:00, Sat 9:00-13:00, Sun 10:00-14:00, closed Mon; mid-Oct-mid-April Tue-Fri 10:00-15:00, Sun 10:00-14:00, closed Mon and Sat; Zmaja od Bosne 7, tel. 033/262-710, www.zemaljskimuzej.ba.

Touring the Museum: Unfortunately, the **Sarajevo Haggadah** is kept in a glass case inside a room you can't enter—you can only look through its door, keeping you several feet away. Beyond the Haggadah, the large museum—filling four buildings surrounding a central garden—can be seen quickly. Because the collection is often in flux and the different wings can close and reopen without warning, it's best just to wander around and see what's on display.

The **Archaeology** section (to the right in the building where you enter) includes third-century mosaics from Stolac on the ground floor, and, upstairs, artifacts from the Dark Ages and Middle Ages (including the Sarajevo Haggadah).

Head out into the central garden and turn left to find the good **Ethnology** section, which is like an open-air Bosnian folk museum moved inside—with six authentic, mostly wooden interiors from buildings around the country. The rooms are arranged to emphasize how the various cultures that lived here influenced

SARAJEVO

each other. You'll learn about traditional Bosnian lifestyles—how people would sit on the floor around a table to eat, sharing one very long napkin, and how backyards were often connected so that Muslim women could pass between houses without covering up. On the steps out front are *stećak*s, large engraved tombstones from the Bogomil times of the 12th to the 14th centuries (the best collection of these is on the outskirts of Stolac, described on page 454).

The **Natural History** section (in the building directly across the garden from the main building) displays huge collections of butterflies and bugs, plant life, birds, and rocks.

▲**Historical Museum of Bosnia-Herzegovina (Historijski Muzej BiH)**—Filling a still-bombed-out-feeling, Tito-era building next to the National Museum, this features a very small and ramshackle, but—if you take the time to examine and appreciate the items and photos—fascinating exhibit explaining the Siege of Sarajevo. While there are some English labels, they're sparse, and it helps to have a Sarajevan explain the items firsthand; this is a good place to come with a local guide.

Cost and Hours: 4 KM, dry 10-KM book, Mon-Fri 9:00-19:00, Sat-Sun 9:00-14:00, Zmaja od Bosne 5, tel. 033/226-098, www.muzej.ba.

Touring the Museum: Formerly the "Museum of the Revolution," the building's stairwell still features Socialist Realist mosaics from the communist period, and a statue of Tito stands in the inner courtyard. Head upstairs to the two-part exhibit. First (to the right at the top of the stairs) is a brief overview of Bosnian history from prehistoric times through the late 20th century, with mostly photographs and a scant few actual artifacts. But the highlight is on the other side, the **"Sarajevo Surrounded"** exhibit. Follow the chronological exhibit, which uses photographs, news clippings, and other items to tell the story of the siege. Most illuminating are the many actual items that show how Sarajevans improvised ways to carry on during the three and a half years under siege. For example, look for photos of the "Sarafix" technique—invented here, out of necessity—which allowed doctors to set a broken bone with a metal frame with pins instead of a traditional cast. The display of cigarettes explains how smokes were used as a sort of currency; even through the siege, the local cigarette factory kept working, though the product sometimes had to be packaged in makeshift wrappers.

The mockup of a typical siege-time **apartment** shows how people were forced to make do. The windows and roof are covered with a plastic tarp donated by the international community. The TV, telephone, refrigerator, and other appliances were useless without electricity. (The power might come on sporadically, but never for very long.) Look around at the so-called "Sarajevo

inventions," created by desperate and clever people to keep going. Notice the makeshift stove (a collection of several other, smaller stoves is nearby). During the frigid Sarajevo winters, trees were cut down to fuel fires. When the trees were gone, firewood was in short supply (a bundle might cost the equivalent of $50), so besieged residents burned their furniture, shoes, old toys—anything flammable. And they bundled up in as many clothes as possible. After 1994, natural gas was available in some areas; notice the recycled IV tube (still bloody inside) used to power the gas lamp.

The **market stall** displays the paltry essentials that Sarajevans considered themselves lucky to find during wartime. Imagine picking over these meager offerings—rusty canned goods, military rations, plastic bags stuffed with grains—and trying to figure out how to use them to feed your family. Notice the Monopoly-like money that was the city's ersatz legal tender during the siege. Sarajevans learned how to stretch a "one-day ration" for up to two weeks. (Many nations sent old military rations—Sarajevans might find themselves eating leftover US rations from the Vietnam War.) Lawns were converted into makeshift produce gardens. Everyone came up with "siege recipes," replacing unavailable ingredients with whatever they could. For example, during a time when rice was relatively plentiful, they'd mix it with flour to make bread, or use it as filling for *bureks* (savory pastries). Instead of spinach filling for a *burek*, they might use greens from buttercup flowers.

A few more things to look for: The actual shells and weapons were used in the fighting. The elaborate satellite telephone was, for a time, the only way that Bosnian President Alija Izetbegović could communicate with the outside world. One case shows ways that people created light, including a candle made of pork fat with a wick made from carpet fibers. Viewing these items, the desperate ingenuity of the besieged Sarajevans is positively inspiring.

Outer Sarajevo

▲▲**Sarajevo War Tunnel Museum (Sarajevski Ratni Tunel)**—In the countryside on the southwestern outskirts of

SARAJEVO

Sarajevo, near the airport, is a small but fascinating museum celebrating the ingenuity and determination of the besieged Sarajevans to continue supplying their city. Here you can walk through a small stretch of the actual half-mile supply tunnel they dug to stay alive during the siege. The still battle-scarred house that marks its entrance holds a small museum, displaying actual items used in the tunnel.

Cost and Hours: 5 KM, 5-KM English booklet, daily 9:00-15:30, Tuneli 1, mobile 061-213-760.

Getting There: The tunnel is on the outskirts of Sarajevo beyond the airport, a long detour from anyplace else in town. Therefore, the most convenient option is to take a guided tour that includes transportation from downtown and a clear explanation of what happened here. Various companies offer these tours, including Insider Tours (see "Tours in Sarajevo," earlier). By taxi, the fair metered rate from downtown is 15-20 KM one-way—just tell them "*tunel.*" Alternatively, you can take tram #3 or bus #32 from the Old Town to the end of the line (Ilidža stop, about 40 minutes one-way), then walk 2.5 miles or pay 5-6 KM one-way for a taxi from there. If you're flying into or out of the city, this combines well with your trip to the airport.

Background: With the city almost entirely surrounded by the Bosnian Serb Army, the Sarajevans' lone connection to the outside world was a mountain pass. But between them and that pass was the city's airport—which couldn't be crossed by either side because it was controlled by the impartial UN. Sarajevans could only gaze across the runway at the mountains that could be their lifeline. So, rather than go through the airport, they went beneath it—digging a half-mile-long tunnel under the runway. Coal-mine engineers spent four months and four days in 1993 digging a passageway that was about five feet tall and three feet wide. Once completed, Sarajevans could enter the basement of an apartment building, hunch over and hike through thickly humid air for 20 minutes, and emerge at a house on the other end. (After a heavy rain, the tunnel would fill with water, making the hike even more unpleasant.) From the house, they could hike over the mountains to get supplies. While money was scarce, cigarettes produced at Sarajevo's factory could be traded for what was needed, which was carried back over the mountains and through the tunnel. Eventually the tunnel was wired to also supply electricity and natural gas into the city, and was equipped with rails to more efficiently transport goods on wheeled carts. The tunnel was open to any Sarajevan—and people used it to shuttle back and forth, day and night—but it was carefully monitored for smugglers who might use it to profit from the tragedy inside the city. While the besieging enemy knew about the tunnel, its nonlinear course underground made it impossible for them to know exactly where it was—and even if they had known, to destroy it they'd have had to go through the UN-controlled airport. The best they could do was to relentlessly bombard the tunnel's entrances.

Touring the Museum and Tunnel: Get oriented by watching the good 20-minute film that illustrates the construction and use of the tunnel. One room contains gifts brought here by ambassadors from many nations. In the hallway, look for the chair on wheels used to push President Izetbegović through the tunnel—hardly presidential transport, but the only way he could safely get in and out of the city for meetings with the international community.

Then you can actually climb down the tight stairs and squeeze through an 80-foot-long stretch of the tunnel itself. Imagine yourself walking, crouched over, 30 times this far from one end to the other.

Out back are several places to sit and look at a map of the besieged city—superimposed, not without irony, over a map from the 1984 Olympic Games. The actual airport sits on the horizon. (Locals say that when they saw a UN plane taking off—likely carrying international officials to safety—they knew trouble was brewing.) In 1993, for the first time, Bosnia-Herzegovina selected a band to represent the newly independent country at the Eurovision Song Contest (a Europe-wide TV extravaganza somewhat like the finale to *American Idol*). The band, Fazla, was trapped in Sarajevo by the siege. Determined to make it to the show in Ireland, they ran across the UN-controlled airport runway with their instruments, which they then carried over the mountains to freedom. By the time the band returned, the siege tunnel under the airport was finished, and they were able to easily sneak back into the city. Even many people who managed to leave the city chose to return and remain under siege with their families and neighbors, rather than abandon their unique city and way of life.

▲▲**City View**—This vertical city's gorgeous setting is best seen from high up. Unfortunately, most viewpoints are not easily reachable by public transportation. One option is to walk from the Old Town up Kovači street for a decent (if not sky-high) view over town (see page 486). Or you can take a taxi up to the

SARAJEVO

popular viewpoint called White Bastion (Bijela Tabija), at an old fortress (a taxi from the Old Town should cost you about 10 KM round-trip). Bus tours around the city include at least one panoramic viewpoint offering grand vistas over one of Europe's most spectacularly set cities.

Sleeping in Sarajevo

The city enjoys a wide variety of good accommodations, ranging from budget hostels to cozy and warmly run little pensions to plush hotels. All of my listings are in or very near the Old Town (Baščaršija) and the start of my self-guided walk. Places that are actually in the Baščaršija come with some nighttime noise.

$$$ Hotel Central is a well-located, very plush splurge right in the heart of the Old Town. The public areas and rooms are done in a very trendy, modern style. Given the central location, request a quiet room (Sb-€100, Db-€120, junior suite-€150; look online for cheaper deals—likely Sb-€95, Db-€100-110, junior suite-€110-120; air-con, free Wi-Fi, pool/sauna, Ćumurija 8, tel. 033/561-800, www.hotelcentral.ba, info@hotelcentral.ba).

$$ Hotel Michele is a friendly, slightly quirky guest house facing a school in a quiet neighborhood; it's a 10-minute, fairly steep walk uphill from Maršala Tita street. The 10 huge rooms and eight gargantuan apartments are gaudy, decorated with antique furniture. This place has hosted several celebrities in town for the

---

Sleep Code

($1 = about 1.40 KM, €1 = about $1.40, country code: 387, area code: 033)

S = Single, **D** = Double/Twin, **T** = Triple, **Q** = Quad, **b** = bathroom. Unless otherwise noted, the staff speaks English, credit cards are accepted, and prices include breakfast. Sarajevo's hotels quote prices in euros.

To help you sort easily through these listings, I've divided the accommodations into three categories based on the price for a standard double room with bath in peak season:

  $$$ Higher Priced—Most rooms €100 or more.
    $$ Moderately Priced—Most rooms between €70-100.
      $ Lower Priced—Most rooms €70 or less.

Prices can change without notice; verify the hotel's current rates online or by email. For other updates, see www.ricksteves.com/update.

Sarajevo Film Festival...it doesn't take much prompting to get the receptionist to do some name-dropping (Sb-€75, Db-€85, much bigger "luxury" room for €20 more, apartments-€120-150, air-con, free Wi-Fi, free parking garage, Ivana Cankara 27, tel. 033/560-310, mobile 061-338-177, www.hotelmichele.ba, contact@hotel michele.ba).

$$ Ada Hotel is a soothing oasis with a charming facade and breakfast room. Its wooden staircase leads to eight nicely appointed, modern rooms. Popular with visitors to the US Embassy, it's a five-minute uphill walk above the Old Town, near a large wartime cemetery (Sb-€51, Db-€77, air-con, free W-Fi, Abdesthana 8, tel. 033/475-870, www.adahotel.ba, adahotel@adahotel.ba).

$$ Hotel Safir, while slightly overpriced, is nicely located near (but not *too* near) to the Old Town action. The eight rooms are modern, with blue tile accents and small kitchenettes, but a bit sterile (Sb-€60, Db-€82, air-con, free Wi-Fi, Jagodića 3, tel. 033/475-040, www.hotelsafir.ba, info@hotelsafir.ba).

$$ Hotel Old Town, while a bit impersonal, has 15 new-feeling rooms right in the heart of the Old Town (Sb-€55, Db-€82, Tb-€117; prices soft in slow times—more like Db-€76; air-con, free Wi-Fi, Mali Čurčiluk 11A, tel. 033/574-200, www.hotelold town.ba, info@hoteloldtown.ba).

$ Halvat Guest House is very tight but homey, offering five stylish-for-the-price rooms and one apartment squeezed into a modern shell. It's on a nondescript urban street that's a quick walk from the heart of the Old Town. The staff, led by Valida and Mumo, are friendly and welcoming (Sb-€46, Db-€68, Tb-€86; apartment-€46/person for up to three; skip breakfast to save €4/person, cash only, air-con, free Wi-Fi, Kasima Efendije Dobrače 5, tel. 033/237-714, www.halvat.com.ba, halvat@bih.net.ba).

$ Kandilj Pension ("Candle") has 10 simple, comfortable rooms in a traditional Ottoman-style house with a snug break-fast cellar. It's up a gentle hill and next to the Tomb of the Seven Brothers across the river from the Old Town (Sb-€40, Db-€62, Tb-€73, air-con, free Internet access and Wi-Fi, Bistrik/potok 12A, tel. 033/572-510, mobile 063-714-222, www.kandilj.com, info@kandilj.com).

$ B&B Divan offers nine very centrally located rooms right in the heart of the Old Town. Some rooms face the busy road, while others face a popular restaurant and café zone, so you may have some noise (€15 dorm beds, breakfast-€5 extra; Sb-€50, Db-€60—these rooms include breakfast; air-con, free Wi-Fi, laundry service-€10, Mula Mustafe Bašeskije 54, tel. 033/238-677, mobile 061-150-035, www.pansiondivan.ba, info@pansion divan.ba).

Sarajevo Hotels & Restaurants

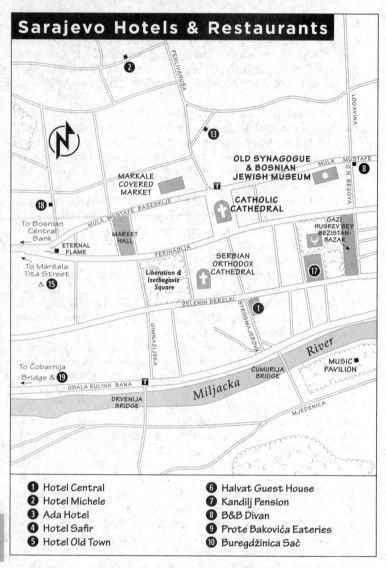

1 Hotel Central
2 Hotel Michele
3 Ada Hotel
4 Hotel Safir
5 Hotel Old Town
6 Halvat Guest House
7 Kandilj Pension
8 B&B Divan
9 Prote Bakovića Eateries
10 Buregdžinica Sač

Eating in Sarajevo

Cosmopolitan Sarajevo boasts a wide array of good eateries, serving not only traditional Bosnian food but a wide range of international flavors. I've focused my recommendations on the area in and near the Old Town (Baščaršija).

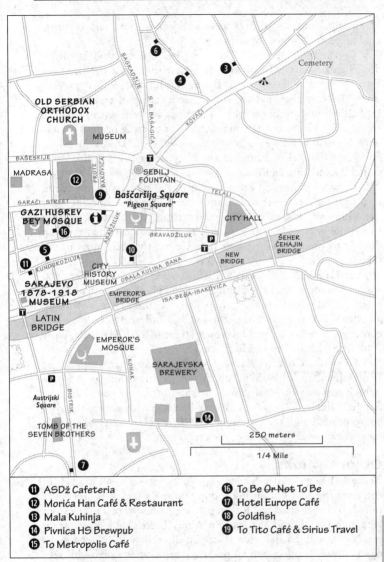

Restaurants

⓫ ASDž Cafeteria
⓬ Morića Han Café & Restaurant
⓭ Mala Kuhinja
⓮ Pivnica HS Brewpub
⓯ To Metropolis Café

⓰ To Be Or Not To Be
⓱ Hotel Europe Café
⓲ Goldfish
⓳ To Tito Café & Sirius Travel

Traditional Bosnian Food

The Baščaršija is crowded with tourist-oriented eateries sling-ing good, if somewhat overpriced, traditional Bosnian fare (for a primer, see the "Balkan Flavors" sidebar on page 418).

Several obvious choices line the street called **Prote Bakovića**, which juts up from the main drag just a block over from "Pigeon Square" (across from the TI). Along here are a variety of crowd-pleasing cafés and restaurants, including Dveri, Pod Lipom, and

Dženita. Comparison-shop menus and take your pick. But first read up on the cheaper options below.

Burek: These delicious "Bosnian pies," made with flaky phyllo dough and savory fillings, are available throughout the Balkans. But the best I've tasted are at **Buregdžinica Sač,** a tiny hole-in-the-wall where they're made with fresh ingredients and baked the traditional way, under a metal lid that's covered with hot coals *(ispod saća).* Order at the counter, then take away or grab a table outside—this is Sarajevo's best quick meal (5 KM/portion, Mon-Sat 8:30-20:00, closed Sun, in the alley off of Bravadžiluk street called Bravadžiluk Mali).

Ćevapčići: Around every corner in the Baščaršija, you'll run into a *ćevabdžinica*—the word for a cheap eatery selling the tasty little sausage-shaped minced-meat patties. Bosnians agree that this is the best place in the country to get this local answer to hot dogs or hamburgers. The places here are mostly interchangeable—take your pick.

Aščinica: An *aščinica* is a Turkish-style cafeteria, where you survey your options at the display case and point to what you want. It's an efficient, affordable, and relatively untouristy way to get a taste of Bosnian cooking. The *aščinica* called **ASDž** is a good choice on a nondescript Old Town street (6-12 KM meals, daily 7:00-19:00, Mali Čurčiluk 3, tel. 033/238-500).

Bosnian Coffee *(Bosanska kafa):* Known elsewhere as "Turkish coffee," this thick, unfiltered, highly caffeinated sludge (which leaves a layer of "mud" at the bottom of your cup) is a Sarajevo staple. Choose any Baščaršija table with a view that you enjoy, or poke into the atmospheric **Morića Han** courtyard, a former caravanserai (which also has a restaurant).

Other Options

Mala Kuhinja ("Little Kitchen") is just that—a small kitchen in the corner of its tight dining room, where six tables of diners get to watch chefs Senad and Rasim prepare Asian fusion cuisine from whatever they found at today's market. There's no menu and no servers—you'll discuss what you want directly with the chefs. It's open only for lunch or early dinner, and reservations are highly rec-ommended (18-20-KM lunches, 25-KM early dinners, bring your own alcohol, daily 9:00-18:00, Josipa Štadlera 6, mobile 061-144-741, tel. 033/200-727).

Sarajevska Brewery's **Piv-nica HS** brewpub is a big, rollicking beer hall that also manages to feel cozy. Tucked in the back of the sprawling, spring-fed Sarajevska complex, this place has two levels of diners, a double-decker bar, a wide variety of Sarajevsko beers on tap, and a long menu of pub grub (8-10-KM pastas and starters, 13-22-KM main dishes, daily 10:00-1:00 in the morning, Franjevačka 15, tel. 033/239-740).

Metropolis is a mod, trendy-feeling, split-level café serving coffee, cakes, and good, eclectic, international food in the modern part of town, along Maršala Tita (5-10-KM sandwiches, wraps, pastas, and pizzas, 13-KM wok dishes, open long hours daily, Maršala Tita 21, tel. 033/203-315).

To Be Or Not To Be, in the Old Town, is a popular, intimate little place (with six tables on two floors, plus some outdoor seating) where Amer serves up international meals. On the sign notice that "or not" is crossed out—during the siege, everyone here decided they definitely wanted to be (6-15-KM omelets and pastas, 14-20-KM meat and fish dishes, daily 11:00-23:00, Čizmedžiluk 5, tel. 033/233-265, mobile 061-508-008).

Cafés

Being at the intersection of two cultures famous for enjoying a cup of coffee (Viennese and Ottoman), Sarajevo has more than its share of cozy cafés. Explore the streets—both in the Old Town and in the modern areas—to find just the right spot. For Ottoman atmosphere, explore the Baščaršija, or just cut to the chase and head for the **Morića Han** courtyard (described earlier). For Viennese-style splendor, you'll stumble on many fine options, but likely none as impressive as the chandeliered café inside the **Hotel Europe.** For a claustrophobic, cluttered old room that feels like Antiques Roadshow, head for the quirky **Goldfish** (Kaptol 5). And if you're nostalgic for the Red old days, it's obligatory to visit **Tito Café** behind the Historical Museum (see page 490).

Sarajevo Connections

From Sarajevo by Bus to: Mostar (hourly, 2.5 hours, 20 KM), **Split** (5/day in summer, 3/day in winter, 5.5-6 hours, 50 KM), **Dubrovnik** (3/day in summer, 1/day in winter, 5-6.5 hours, 60 KM), **Zagreb** (3/day including one night bus, 8 hours, 54 KM). Many (but not all) buses are operated by Eurolines (www.centro trans.com); the general number for bus information at the main station is tel. 033/213-100. A few additional buses depart from the predominantly Serb area of East Sarajevo (info tel. 057/317-377).

By Train: Sarajevo sits on the middle of a train line that goes south to **Mostar** and **Ploče** (on the Croatian coast between Split and Dubrovnik), and north to **Zagreb** (2/day in each direction; 1.75 hours to Mostar, 4.25 hours to Ploče, 9 hours to Zagreb).

Route Tips for Drivers:
From Mostar to Sarajevo

Whether you're driving or taking the bus from Mostar to Sarajevo, you're in for a scenic mountain journey that takes you past some interesting sights of historic interest. Even if you're not stopping along the way, keep track of these landmarks as you roll.

You'll begin by heading up the dramatically scenic Neretva River Canyon, which surrounds a thrusting river that powers many hydroelectric dams. The first major town you pass is **Jablanica,** famous among Bosnians as the best place to enjoy spit-grilled lamb (look for restaurants along the road)—and as the site of a WWII battle that demonstrated Tito's brilliance as a military tactician. (To mislead the Nazis, his troops first destroyed five bridges across this river, then quickly repaired one of them, allowing for a movement of Partisan forces that caught the Nazis off-guard. In 1969, the victory was immortalized in the Oscar-nominated *Battle of Neretva,* which featured Yul Brenner, Orson Welles, and other big names lured by the Yugoslav government's extremely generous funding.)

The next major town is **Konjic,** known for its traditional woodworking. The mountains above Konjic are a popular place for whitewater rafting. The town's old bridge (which you'll see on the right as you drive over the modern bridge) dates from the same era as Mostar's Old Bridge. Both Jablanica and Konjic were held by Muslim forces during the 1990s war, which made them relatively safe havens, especially compared to Mostar or Sarajevo.

From Konjic, the road climbs up to **Ivan Planina** mountain, the geographical boundary between Herzegovina and Bosnia. Along this rugged road, you'll pass the deserted village of **Bradina** (unmarked, just before the tunnel), which was the birthplace of Ante Pavelić—the Bosnian Croat who led the ruthless Nazi-puppet Ustaše forces during World War II.

Passing through the **Ivan Tunnel** (nearly a half-mile long), you enter Kanton Sarajevo (*kanton*, based on the Swiss canton model, means roughly "county"). In addition to separating Herzegovina from Bosnia, this tunnel marks a dramatic weather divide—from the balmy, Mediterranean climate around Mostar to the chilly, continental climate of Sarajevo.

Winding down into the plain around **Sarajevo,** you'll enter the city limits. Just before the Hotel Radon Plaza is a destroyed retirement home—marking what was the front line of the besieged area of wartime Sarajevo. Everything you'll pass from here on out was under constant sniper fire for three and a half years (you're driving straight up what was called "Sniper Alley"). As you continue to drive into town along the main drag, watch for these landmarks: on the right, the UN offices (in the former university student center); on the left, the national TV headquarters; on the right, a huge new mosque built with donations from Indonesia (one of 10 in town financed by wealthy investors from the Muslim world); on the left, the distinctive blue Avaz Twist Tower, hosting the offices of Bosnia's main newspaper (*Dnevni Avaz,* "Daily Voice"); also on the left, the US Embassy, followed by the famous Holiday Inn (built for the 1984 Olympics, and later a safe haven for wartime journalists); and, across the street from the Holiday Inn, the newly restored Bosnian Parliament building. From here, keep following the river into the city center—going through the Austro-Hungarian part of town, passing the place where Archduke Franz Ferdinand was assassinated, and winding up at Sarajevo's Old Town, the Baščaršija.

It's important to find secure parking in Sarajevo. Small lots are scattered around the Old Town area; for a bigger, more secure garage, head for the BBI shopping center (on Maršala Tita street—see map on page 496).

SLOVENIA
Slovenija

SLOVENIA

Tiny, overlooked Slovenia is one of Europe's most unexpectedly charming destinations. At the intersection of the Slavic, German, and Italian worlds, Slovenia is an exciting mix of the best of each culture. Though it's just a quick trip away from the tourist throngs in Venice, Munich, Salzburg, and Vienna, Slovenia has stayed off the tourist track—making it a handy detour for in-the-know Back Door travelers. Be warned: I've never met anyone who visited Slovenia and didn't wish they'd allotted more time for this delightful, underrated land.

Today, it seems strange to think that Slovenia was ever part of Yugoslavia. Both in the personality of its people and in its landscape, Slovenia feels more like Austria. Slovenes are more industrious, organized, and punctual than their fellow former Yugoslavs...yet still friendly, relaxed, and Mediterranean. Locals like the balance. Visitors expecting minefields and rusting Yugo factories are pleas-

antly surprised to find Slovenia's rolling countryside dotted instead with quaint alpine villages and the spires of miniature Baroque churches, with breathtaking, snowcapped peaks in the distance.

Only half as big as Switzerland, Slovenia is remarkably diverse for its size. Travelers can hike on alpine trails in the morning and explore some of the world's best caves in the afternoon, before relaxing with a seafood dinner on the Adriatic.

Slovenia enjoys a powerhouse economy—the healthiest of all of Europe's former communist countries. The Austro-Hungarian Empire left it with a strong industrial infrastructure, which the Yugoslav government expanded. By 1980, 60 percent of all Yugoslav industry was in little Slovenia (which had only 8 percent of Yugoslavia's population and 8 percent of its territory). With independence, Slovenia continued this trend, pushing their

mighty little economy into the future. Of the 12 new nations that have joined the European Union since 2004, Slovenia was the only one rich enough to be a net donor (with a higher per-capita income than the average), and the first one to join the euro currency zone (it adopted the euro in January 2007). Thanks to its long-standing ties to the West and can-do spirit, Slovenia already feels more "Western" than any other destination in this book.

The country has a funny way of making people fall in love with it. Slovenes are laid-back, easygoing, stylish, and fun. They won't win any world wars (they're too well-adjusted to even try)... but they're exactly the type of people you'd love to chat with over a cup of coffee.

The Slovenian language is as mellow as the people. While Slovenes use Serb, German, and English curses in abundance, the worst they can say in their native tongue is, "May you be kicked by a horse." For "Darn it!" they say, "Three hundred hairy bears!"

Coming from such a small country, locals are proud of the few things that are distinctly Slovenian, such as the roofed hayrack. Foreigners think that Slovenes' fascination with these hayracks is strange...until they visit and see them absolutely everywhere (especially in the northwest). Because of the frequent rainfall, the hayracks

SLOVENIA

Slovenia Almanac

Official Name: Republika Slovenija, or simply Slovenija.

Snapshot History: After being dominated by Germans for centuries, Slovenian culture proudly emerged in the 19th century. In the aftermath of World War I, Slovenia merged with its neighbors to become Yugoslavia, then broke away and achieved independence for the first time in 1991.

Population: Slovenia's two million people (a count similar to Nevada's) are 83 percent ethnic Slovenes who speak Slovene, plus a smattering of Serbs, Croats, and Muslim Bosniaks. Almost 60 percent of the country is Catholic.

Latitude and Longitude: 46° N and 14° E (latitude similar to Lyon, France; Montreal, Canada; or Bismarck, North Dakota).

Area: At 7,800 square miles, it's about the size of New Jersey, but with one-fourth the population.

Geography: Tiny Slovenia has four extremely different terrains and climates: the warm Mediterranean coastline (just 29 miles long—about one inch per inhabitant); the snow-capped, forested alpine mountains in the northwest (including 9,400-foot Mount Triglav); the moderate-climate, central limestone plateau that includes Ljubljana and the cave-filled Karst region; and to the east, a corner of the Great Hungarian Plain (the Prekmurje region, near Maribor and Ptuj). If you look at a map of Slovenia and squint your eyes a bit, it looks like a chicken running toward the east.

Biggest Cities: Nearly one in five Slovenes lives in the two biggest cities: Ljubljana (the capital, pop. 270,000) and Maribor (in the east, pop. 158,000). Half of the population lives in rural villages.

Economy: With a Gross Domestic Product of $56 billion and a GDP per capita of $28,000, Slovenia's economy is extremely healthy (especially compared to most other post-communist states). Slovenia's wealth comes largely from manufactured metal products (trucks and machinery), which are traded with a diverse group of partners.

Currency: Slovenia uses the euro: €1 = about $1.40.

Government: The country is led by the prime minister (currently Janez Janša), who heads the leading vote-getting party in legislative elections. He governs along with the figurehead president (currently Danilo Türk). Slovenia's relatively peaceful secession is credited largely to former Prime Minister Milan Kučan, who remains a popular figure. The National Assembly consists of about 90 elected legislators; there's also a second house of parliament, which has much less power. Despite the country's small size, it is divided into some 200 municipalities.

Flag: Three horizontal bands of white (top), blue, and red. A shield in the upper left shows Mount Triglav, with a wavy-line sea below and three stars above.

The Average Slovene: The average Slovene skis, in this largely alpine country, and is an avid fan of team handball (yes, handball). He or she lives in a 250-square-foot apartment, earns $1,400 a month, watches 16 hours of TV a week (much of it in English with Slovene subtitles), and enjoys a drink-and-a-half of alcohol every day.

Notable Slovenes: A pair of prominent Ohio politicians—perennial presidential candidate Dennis Kucinich and former Senator George Voinovich, both from the Cleveland area—are each half-Slovene. (In 1910, Cleveland had the biggest Slovenian population of any city in the world—just ahead of Trieste and Ljubljana.) Classical musicians might know composers Giuseppe Tartini and Hugo Wolf. Even if you haven't heard of architect Jože Plečnik yet, you'll hear his name a hundred times while you're in Slovenia—especially in Ljubljana (see page 546). Perhaps most famous of all is the illustrious Melania Knauss—a GQ cover girl who's also the current Mrs. Donald Trump.

Sporty Slovenes: If you follow alpine sports or team handball, you'll surely know some world-class athletes from Slovenia. NBA fans might recognize basketball players Primož Brezec and Bostjan Nachbar, as well as some other lesser players. Slovenian hockey player Anže Kopitar plays in the NHL. The athletic Slovenes—perhaps trying to compensate for the miniscule size of their country—have accomplished astonishing feats: Davo Karničar has skied down from the summits of some of the world's tallest mountains (including Everest, Kilimanjaro, and McKinley). Benka Pulko became the first person ever to drive a motorcycle around the world (that is, all seven continents, including Antarctica; total trip: 118,000 miles in 2,000 days—also the longest solo motorcycle journey by a woman; www.benka pulko.com). Dušan Mravlje ran across all the continents (www .dusanmravlje.si). And ultra-marathon swimmer Martin Strel has swum the entire length of several major rivers, including the Danube (1,775 miles), the Mississippi (2,415 miles), the Yangtze (3,915 miles), and the Amazon (3,393 miles; for more, see www .martinstrel.com).

are covered by a roof that allows the hay to dry thoroughly. The most traditional kind is the *toplar*, consisting of two hayracks connected by one big roof. It looks like a skinny barn with open, fenced sides. Hay hangs on the sides to dry; firewood, carts, tractors, and other farm implements sit on the ground inside; and dried hay is stored in the loft above. But these wooden *toplarji* are firetraps, and a stray bolt of lighting can burn one down in a flash. So in recent years, more farmers are moving to single hayracks *(enojni);* these are still roofed, but have posts made of concrete, rather than wood. You'll find postcards and miniature wooden models of both kinds of hayracks (a fun souvenir).

Another good (and uniquely Slovenian) memento is a cre-atively decorated front panel from a beehive *(panjske končnice)*. Slovenia has a strong beekeeping tradition, and beekeepers once believed that painting the fronts of the hives made it easier for bees to find their way home. Replicas of these panels are available at gift shops all over the country. (For more on the panels and Slovenia's beekeeping heritage, see page 591.)

Slovenia is also the land of polka. Slovenes claim that polka music was invented here, and singer/accordionist Slavko Avsenik—from the village of Begunje near Bled—cranks out popular oompah songs that make him bigger than the Beatles (and therefore, presumably, Jesus) in Germany. You'll see the Avsenik ensemble and other oompah bands on Slovenian TV, where hokey Lawrence Welk-style shows are a local institution.

To really stretch your euros, try one of Slovenia's more than 400 farmhouse B&Bs, called "tourist farms" *(turistične kmetije)*. These are actual, working farms (often organic) that sell meals and/or rent rooms to tourists to help make ends meet. You can use a tourist farm as a home base to explore the entire country—remember, the farthest reaches of Slovenia are only a day trip away. A comfortable, hotelesque double with a private bathroom—plus a traditional Slovenian dinner and a hearty breakfast—costs as little as €50. Request a listing from the Slovenian Tourist Board (see page 693), or find information at www.slovenia.info.

Most visitors to Slovenia are, in my experience, completely charmed by the place. With all it has going for it, it's hard to believe that Slovenia is not already overrun with tourists. Somehow, this little country continues to glide beneath the radar. Exploring its mountain trails and meeting its friendly locals, you'll feel like you're in on a secret.

Helpful Hints

Sunday Closures: Slovenia can be extremely sleepy on Sundays, even in the larger towns and cities, where virtually all shops are closed. Plan ahead. Fortunately, many restaurants remain open, plus a select few grocery stores.

Smoking Ban: Smoking is prohibited in public places, unless it's a specially designated (and well-ventilated) smoking room. Larger hotels still have some "smoking" rooms, but smoking isn't allowed in public areas.

Telephones: Slovenian phone numbers beginning with 080 are toll-free; 090 and 089 denote expensive toll lines. Most mobile phone numbers begin with 030, 031, 040, 041, 051, 059, 070, or 071. For more details on how to dial to, from, and within Slovenia, see page 696.

Toll Sticker: To drive on Slovenia's expressways *(avtocesta)*, you'll need to display a toll sticker *(vinjeta,* veen-YEH-tah; €15/week, €30/month). If renting your car in Slovenia, it probably comes with a toll sticker (but ask just to be sure); if you're driving in from elsewhere, such as Croatia, you can buy one at a gas station, post office, or some newsstands. **Be warned:** This rule is taken very seriously. If you're found driving on expressways without the sticker, you'll immediately be fined €150.

Cruise Port: The Slovenian coastal town of **Koper** (see page 672) is becoming a popular port of call for Mediterranean cruises. As the country is so small, it's possible to see just about any of the Slovenia destinations covered in this book in a single day in port (provided you use your time efficiently and have a private driver—I recommend Tina Hiti and Sašo Golub, listed on page 571).

Slovenian History

Slovenia has a long and unexciting history as part of various larger empires. Charlemagne's Franks conquered the tiny land in the eighth century, and, ever since, Slovenia has been a backwater of the Germanic world—first as a holding of the Holy Roman Empire and later, the Habsburg Empire. Slovenia seems as much German as Slavic. But even as the capital, Ljubljana, was populated by Austrians (and called Laibach by its German-speaking residents), the Slovenian language and cultural traditions survived in the countryside.

Ljubljana rose to international prominence for half a decade (1809-1813) when Napoleon named it the capital of his "Illyrian Provinces," stretching from Austria's Tirol to Croatia's Dalmatian Coast. During this time, the long-suppressed Slovene language was used for the first time in schools and the government. This

Slo-what?-ia

The only thing I know about Slovakia is what I learned first-hand from your foreign minister, who came to Texas.

—George W. Bush, to a Slovak journalist (Bush had actually met with Dr. Janez Drnovšek, who was then Slovenia's prime minister)

Maybe it's understandable that many Americans confuse Slovenia with Slovakia. Both are small, mountainous countries that not too long ago were parts of bigger, better known, now defunct nations. But anyone who has visited Slovenia and Slovakia will set you straight—they feel worlds apart.

Slovenia, wedged between the Alps and the Adriatic, is a tidy, prosperous country with a strong economy. Until 1991, Slovenia was one of the six republics that made up Yugoslavia. Historically, Slovenia has had very strong ties with Germanic culture—so it feels like its neighbor to the north, Austria.

Slovakia—two countries away, to the northeast—is slightly bigger. Much of its territory is covered by the Carpathian Mountains, most notably the dramatic, jagged peaks of the High Tatras. In 1993, the Czechs and Slovaks peacefully chose to go their separate ways, so the nation of Czechoslovakia dissolved into the Czech Republic and the Slovak Republic (a.k.a. Slovakia).

To make things even more confusing, there's also **Slavonia.** This is the thick, inland "panhandle" that makes up the northeast half of Croatia, along Slovenia's southeast border. Much of the warfare in Croatia's 1991-1995 war took place in Slavonia (including Vukovar; see the Understanding Yugoslavia chapter).

I won't tell on you if you mix them up. But if you want to feel smarter than a former president, do a little homework and get it right.

kicked off a national revival movement (as in so many other Central and Eastern European countries at the time)—asserting the worthiness of the Slovenian language and culture compared to the dominant Germanic worldview of the time. Inspired by the patriotic poetry of France Prešeren, national pride surged.

The last century saw the most interesting chapter of Slovenian history. Some of World War I's fiercest fighting occurred at the Soča (Isonzo) Front in northwest Slovenia—witnessed by young Ernest Hemingway, who drove an ambulance (see sidebars on pages 607 and 616). After the war, from 1918 to 1991, Slovenia was Yugoslavia's smallest, northernmost, and most affluent republic. Concerned about Serbian strongman Slobodan Milošević's nationalistic politics, Slovenia seceded in 1991. Because more than 90 percent of the people here were ethnic Slovenes, the break with Yugoslavia was simple and virtually uncontested. Its war for independence lasted just 10 days and claimed only a few dozen lives. (For more details, see the Understanding Yugoslavia chapter, page 682.)

After centuries of looking to the West, in May of 2004 Slovenia became the first of the former Yugoslav republics to join the European Union. The Slovenes have been practical about this move, realizing it's essential for their survival as a tiny nation in a modern world. But there are trade-offs, and "Euroskeptics" are down on EU bureaucracy. As borders disappear, Slovenes are experiencing more crime. Traditional farms are grappling with strict EU standards. Slovenian businesses are having difficulty competing with big German and other Western European firms. Before EU membership, only Slovenes could own Slovenian land. But now wealthy foreigners are buying property, driving up the cost of real estate.

Yet EU membership seems to be agreeing with the Slovenes. For one thing, it allowed this generally low-key, conflict-averse little country a rare chance to flex its political muscles when, in 2009, Slovenia temporarily vetoed Croatia's bid for EU membership over a longstanding border rivalry along the Istrian coastline (for details, see page 48). Slovenia also became the first post-communist country to adopt the euro currency in January of 2007. Despite the worldwide economic crisis, business here is booming. As throughout their history, the Slovenes are adjusting to the 21st century with their characteristic sense of humor and easygoing attitude.

Slovenian Food

Slovenian cuisine offers more variety and better quality than Croatian fare. Slovenes brag that their cuisine melds the best of

Italian and German cooking—but they also embrace other international influences, especially French. Like Croatian food, Slovenian cuisine also features some pan-Balkan elements: The savory phyllo-dough pastry *burek* is the favorite fast food here, and when Slovenes host a backyard barbecue, they grill up *čevapčiči* and *ražnjiči*, topped off with the eggplant-and-red-bell-pepper condiment *ajvar* (see the "Balkan Flavors" sidebar on page 418). Slovenia enjoys Italian-style fare, with a pizza or pasta restaurant on seemingly every corner. Hungarian food simmers in the northeast corner of the country

Pršut

In Slovenia, Croatia, and Montenegro, *pršut* (purr-SHOOT) is one of the essential food groups. This air-cured ham (like Italian prosciutto) is soaked in salt and sometimes also smoked. Then it hangs in open-ended barns for up to a year and a half, to be dried and seasoned by the howling Bora wind. Each region produces a slightly different *pršut*. In Dalmatia, a layer of fat keeps the ham moist; in Istria, the fat is trimmed, and the *pršut* is dryer.

Since Slovenia joined the European Union, strict new standards have swept the land. Separate rooms must be used for the slaughter, preparation, and curing of the ham. While this seems fair enough for large producers, small family farms that want to produce just enough *pršut* for their own use—and maybe sell one or two ham hocks to neighbors—find they have to invest thousands of euros to be compliant.

(where many Magyars reside). And in most of the country, traditional Slovenian food has a distinctly Germanic vibe—including the "four S's": sausages, schnitzels, strudels, and sauerkraut.

Traditional Slovenian dishes are prepared with groats—a grainy mush made with buckwheat, barley, or corn. Buckwheat, which thrives in this climate, often appears on Slovenian menus. You'll also see plenty of *štruklji* (dumplings), which can be stuffed with cheese, meat, or vegetables. *Repa* is turnip prepared like sauerkraut. Among the hearty soups in Slovenia is *jota*—a staple for Karst peasants, made from *repa*, beans, and vegetables.

The cuisine of Slovenia's Karst region (the arid limestone plain south of Ljubljana) is notable. The small farms and wineries of this region have been inspired by Italy's Slow Food movement—their owners believe that cuisine is meant to be gradually appreciated, not rushed—making the Karst a destination for gourmet tours. Karstic cuisine is similar to France's nouvelle cuisine—several courses in small portions, with a focus on unusual combinations and preparations—but with a Tuscan flair. The Karst's tasty air-dried ham *(pršut)*, available throughout the country, is worth seeking out (see sidebar). Istria (the peninsula just to the south of the Karst, in southern Slovenia and Croatia) produces truffles that, locals boast, are as good as those from Italy's Piedmont (see page 156).

Voda is water, and *kava* is coffee. Radenska, in the bottle with the three little hearts, is Slovenia's best-known brand of mineral water—good enough that the word *Radenska* is synonymous with bottled water all over Slovenia and throughout the former Yugoslavia. It's not common to ask for (or receive) tap water, but you can try requesting *voda iz pipe*.

Adventurous teetotalers should forego the Coke and sample Cockta, a Slovenian cola with an unusual flavor (which supposedly comes from berry, lemon, orange, and 11 herbs). Originally called "Cockta-Cockta," the drink was introduced during the communist period, as an alternative to the difficult-to-get Coca-Cola. This local variation developed a loyal following...until the Iron Curtain fell, and the real Coke became readily available. Cockta sales plummeted. But in recent years— prodded by the slogan "The Taste of Your Youth"—nostalgic Slovenes are drinking Cockta once more.

To toast, say, *"Na ZDROW-yeh!"*—if you can't remember it, think of "Nice driving!" The premier Slovenian brand of *pivo* (beer) is Union (OO-nee-ohn), but you'll also see a lot of Laško (LASH-koh), whose mascot is the Zlatorog (or "Golden Horn," a mythical chamois-like animal).

Slovenia produces some fine *vino* (wine). The Celts first made wine in Slovenia; the Romans improved the process and spread it throughout the country. Slovenia has three primary wine regions. Podravje, in the northeast, is dominated by *laški* and *renski riesling*. Posavje, in the southeast, produces both white and red wines, but is known mostly for the light, russet-colored *cviček* wine. Primorska, in the southwest, has a Mediterranean climate and produces mostly reds. One of the most popular is *teran*, made from *refošk* grapes, which grow in iron-rich red soil *(terra rossa)*—infusing them with a high lactic acid content that supposedly gives the wine healing properties.

Slovenia's national dessert is *potica*, a rolled pastry with walnuts and sometimes also raisins. For more tasty treats, see the "Bled Desserts" sidebar on page 585. Locals claim that Ljubljana has the finest gelato outside of Italy—which, after all, is just an hour down the road.

Slovenian Language

Slovene is surprisingly different from languages spoken in the other former Yugoslav republics. While Serbian and Croatian are mutually intelligible, Slovene is gibberish to Serbs and Croats. Most Slovenes, on the other hand, know Serbo-Croatian because, a generation ago, everybody in Yugoslavia had to learn it.

Linguists have identified some 46 official dialects of Slovene, and there are probably another 100 or so unofficial ones. Locals can tell which city—or sometimes even which remote mountain valley—someone comes from by their accent.

The tiny country of Slovenia borders Italy and Austria, with important historical and linguistic ties to both. For self-preservation, Slovenes have always been forced to function in many different languages. All of these factors make them excellent linguists. Most young Slovenes speak effortless, flawless English—then admit that they've never set foot in the United States or Britain, but love watching American movies and TV shows (which are always subtitled, never dubbed).

Slovene pronunciation is very similar to Croatian (see page 695). Remember, *c* is pronounced "ts" (as in "cats"). The letter *j* is pronounced as "y"—making "Ljubljana" easier to say than it looks (lyoob-lyee-AH-nah). Slovene only has one diacritical mark: the *strešica*, or "little roof." This makes *č* sound like "ch," *š* sound like "sh," and *ž* sound like "zh" (as in "measure"). The letter *v* is pronounced like "u"—so the Slovenian word *avto* sounds like "auto," and the mountain Triglav is pronounced "TREE-glau" (rhymes with "cow").

The only trick: As in English, which syllable gets the emphasis is unpredictable. Slovenes use many of the same words as Croatians, but put the stress on an entirely different place.

Learn some key Slovenian phrases (see the Slovenian survival phrases on page 731). You'll make more friends and your trip will go more smoothly.

LJUBLJANA

Slovenia's capital, Ljubljana (lyoob-lyee-AH-nah), with a lazy Old Town clustered around a castle-topped mountain, is often likened to Salzburg. It's an apt comparison—but only if you inject a healthy dose of breezy Adriatic culture, add a Slavic accent, and replace favorite son Mozart with local architect Jože Plečnik.

Ljubljana feels smaller than its population of 270,000. While big-league museums are in short supply, the town itself is an idyllic place that sometimes feels too good to be true. Festivals fill the summer, and people enjoy a Sunday stroll any day of the week. Fashion boutiques and al fresco cafés jockey for control of the Old Town, while the leafy riverside promenade crawls with stylishly dressed students sipping *kava* and polishing their near-perfect English. Laid-back Ljubljana is the kind of place where graffiti and crumbling buildings seem elegantly atmospheric instead of shoddy. But more and more of those buildings have been getting a facelift recently, as a spunky mayor has been spiffing up the place and creating gleaming traffic-free zones left and right—making what was already an exceptionally livable city into a true pedestrians' paradise.

Batted around by history, Ljubljana has seen cultural influences from all sides—most notably Prague, Vienna, and Venice. This has left the city a happy hodgepodge of cultures. Being the midpoint between the Slavic, Germanic, and Italian worlds gives Ljubljana a special spice. People often ask me: What's the "next Prague"? And I have to answer Kraków. But Ljubljana is the *next* "next Prague."

The Story of Ljubljana

In ancient times, Ljubljana was on the trade route connecting the Mediterranean (just 60 miles away) to the Black Sea (toss a bottle off the bridge here, and it can float to the Danube and, eventually, all the way to Russia). Legend has it that Jason and his Argonauts founded Ljubljana when they stopped here for the winter on their way home with the Golden Fleece. The town was Romanized (and called Emona) before being overrun by Huns, only to be resettled later by Slavs.

In 1335, Ljubljana fell under the jurisdiction of the Habsburg emperors (who called it Laibach). After six centuries of Habsburg rule, Ljubljana still feels Austrian—especially thanks to its abundant Austrian Baroque and Viennese Art Nouveau architecture—but it has a Mediterranean flair.

Napoleon put Ljubljana on the map when he made it the capital of his Illyrian Provinces, a realm that stretched from the Danube to Dubrovnik, and from Austria to Albania (for just four short years, 1809-1813). For the first time, the Slovene language was taught in schools, awakening a newfound pride in Slovenian cultural heritage. People still look back fondly on this very brief era, which was the first (and probably only) time when Ljubljana rose to prominence on the world stage. After more than 600 years of being part of the Habsburg Empire, Ljubljana has no "Habsburg Square"...but they do have a "French Revolution Square."

In the mid-19th century, the railway connecting Vienna to the Adriatic (Trieste) was built through town—and Ljubljana boomed. An earthquake hit the city in 1895, damaging many buildings.

Planning Your Time

Ljubljana deserves a full day. While there are few must-see sights, the city's biggest attraction is its ambience. You'll spend much of your time strolling the pleasant town center, exploring the many interesting squares and architectural gems, shopping at the boutiques, and sipping coffee at sidewalk cafés along the river.

Here's the best plan for a low-impact sightseeing day: Begin on Prešeren Square, the heart of the city. Cross the Triple Bridge and wander through the riverside produce market before joining the town walking tour at 10:00 (at 11:00 in Oct-March). After the tour, wander south along the Ljubljanica River and through the Krakovo gardens to my favorite Ljubljana museum, the Jože Plečnik House (as this sight may close for renovation, confirm it's open before making the trip). In the afternoon, commit some quality time to people-watching at a riverside café, window-shop at some colorful boutiques, or consider more sightseeing (good

Locals cleverly exaggerated the impact (propping up buildings that were structurally sound, and even tearing down unwanted old houses that had been unharmed) in preparation for the visit of Emperor Franz Josef—who took pity on the city and invested generously in its reconstruction. Ljubljana was made over in the Art Nouveau style so popular in Vienna, its capital at the time. A generation later, architect Jože Plečnik bathed the city in his distinctive, artsy-but-sensible, classical-meets-modern style.

In World War II, Slovenia was occupied first by the Italians, then by the Nazis. Ljubljana had a thriving resistance movement that the Nazis couldn't suppress—so they simply fenced off the entire city and made it a giant prison for three years, allowing only shipments of basic food supplies to get in. But the Slovenes—who knew their land far better than their oppressors did—continued to slip in and out of town undetected, allowing them to agitate through the end of the war.

In 1991, Ljubljana became the capital of one of Europe's youngest nations. Today the city is filled with university students, making it a very youthful-feeling town. Ljubljana has always felt free to be creative, and recent years—with unprecedented freedoms—have been no exception. This city is on the cutting edge when it comes to architecture, public art, fashion, and trendy pubs—a tendency embodied by its recent mayor-turned-parliamentarian, Zoran Janković (see page 532). And yet, Ljubljana's scintillating avant-garde culture has soft edges—hip, but also nonthreatening and user-friendly.

options include the Serbian Orthodox Church and Tivoli Park, with the Contemporary History Museum, west of downtown; or the Slovenian Ethnographic Museum and other sights in Metelkova, north of downtown).

Plenty of good day trips are a short distance from Ljubljana. With a second day, visit Lake Bled (see next chapter), or head for one of the two impressive caves (Škocjan or Postojna) and nearby sights in the Karst region south of the city (see The Karst chapter).

Ljubljana is dead and disappointing on Sundays (virtually all shops are closed and the produce market is quiet, but museums—except for the Jože Plečnik House—are generally open, a modest flea market stretches along the riverfront, and the TI's walking tour still runs). The city is also relatively quiet in August, when the students are on break and many locals head to beach resorts. They say that in August, even homeless people go to the coast.

LJUBLJANA

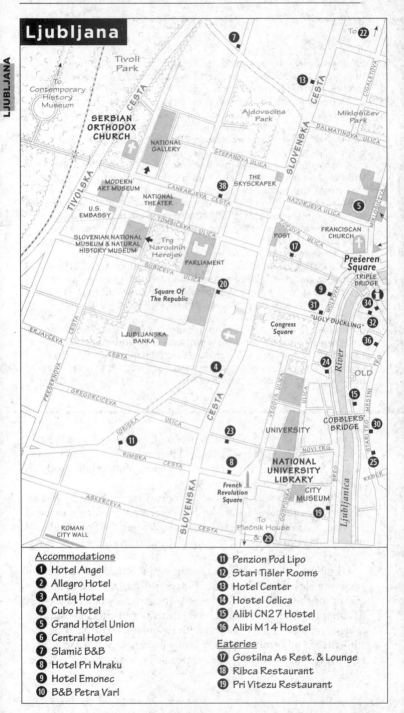

Ljubljana

Accommodations

1. Hotel Angel
2. Allegro Hotel
3. Antiq Hotel
4. Cubo Hotel
5. Grand Hotel Union
6. Central Hotel
7. Slamič B&B
8. Hotel Pri Mraku
9. Hotel Emonec
10. B&B Petra Varl
11. Penzion Pod Lipo
12. Stari Tišler Rooms
13. Hotel Center
14. Hostel Celica
15. Alibi CN27 Hostel
16. Alibi M14 Hostel

Eateries

17. Gostilna As Rest. & Lounge
18. Ribca Restaurant
19. Pri Vitezu Restaurant

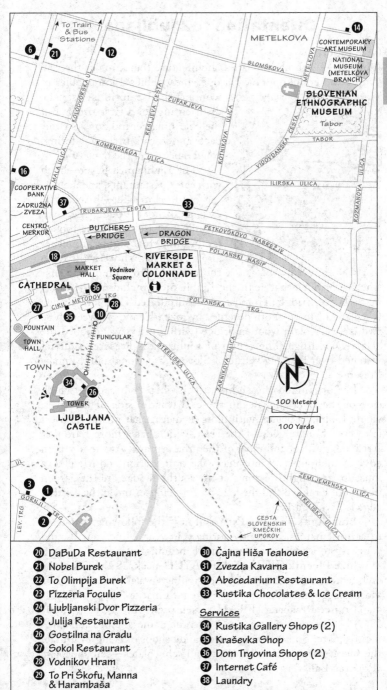

LJUBLJANA

20 DaBuDa Restaurant	**30** Čajna Hiša Teahouse
21 Nobel Burek	**31** Zvezda Kavarna
22 To Olimpija Burek	**32** Abecedarium Restaurant
23 Pizzeria Foculus	**33** Rustika Chocolates & Ice Cream
24 Ljubljanski Dvor Pizzeria	
25 Julija Restaurant	**Services**
26 Gostilna na Gradu	**34** Rustika Gallery Shops (2)
27 Sokol Restaurant	**35** Kraševka Shop
28 Vodnikov Hram	**36** Dom Trgovina Shops (2)
29 To Pri Škofu, Manna & Harambaša	**37** Internet Café
	38 Laundry

Orientation to Ljubljana

(area code: 01)

Ljubljana—with narrow lanes, architecture that mingles the Old World and contemporary Europe, and cobbles upon cobbles of

wonderful distractions—can be disorienting for a first-timer. But the charming central zone is compact, and with a little wandering, you'll quickly get the hang of it.

The Ljubljanica River—lined with cafés, restaurants, and a buzzing outdoor market—bisects the city, making a 90-degree turn around the base of a castle-topped mountain. Most sights are either along or just a short walk from the river. Visitors enjoy the distinctive bridges that span the Ljubljanica, including the landmark Triple Bridge (Tromostovje) and pillared Cobblers' Bridge (Čevljarski Most)—both designed by Jože Plečnik. Between these two is a very plain wooden bridge (with great views) dubbed the "Ugly Duckling." The center of Ljubljana is Prešeren Square, watched over by a big statue of Slovenia's national poet, France Prešeren.

I've organized the sights in this chapter based on which side of the river they're on: the east (castle) side of the river, where Ljubljana began, with more medieval charm; and the west (Prešeren Square) side of the river, which has a more Baroque/ Art Nouveau feel and most of the urban sprawl. At the northern edge of the tourist's Ljubljana is the train station and Metelkova museum and nightlife zone; at the southern edge are the garden district of Krakovo and the Jože Plečnik House; and at the western edge is Tivoli Park.

Ljubljana's Two Big Ps: You'll hear the following two easy-to-confuse names constantly during your visit. Mind your Ps, and your visit to Ljubljana becomes more meaningful:

Jože Plečnik (YOH-zheh PLAYCH-neek, 1872-1957) is the architect who shaped Ljubljana, designing virtually all of the city's most important landmarks. For more information, see page 546.

France Prešeren (FRAHN-tseh preh-SHAY-rehn, 1800-1849) is Slovenia's greatest poet and the namesake of Ljubljana's main square. Some civic-minded candy shops—trying to imitate the success of Austria's "Mozart Ball" chocolates—sell chocolate "Prešeren Balls."

Tourist Information

Ljubljana's helpful, businesslike TI has a useful website (www .visitljubljana.si) and three branches: at the **Triple Bridge,** across from Prešeren Square (daily June-Sept 8:00-21:00, Oct-May 8:00-19:00, Stritarjeva 1, tel. 01/306-1215); at the upper corner of the **market** (with pay Internet access, bike rental, and information about the rest of Slovenia; June-Sept daily 8:00-21:00; Oct-May Mon-Fri 8:00-19:00, Sat-Sun 9:00-17:00; Krekov trg 10, tel. 01/306-4575); and at the **train station** (June-Sept daily 8:00-22:00; Oct-May Mon-Fri 10:00-19:00, Sat 8:00-15:00, closed Sun; Trg O.F. 6, tel. 01/433-9475).

At any TI, pick up a pile of free resources: the big city map, the *Tourist Guide,* the monthly *Where to?* events guide, and a wide range of informative brochures. The TI also offers a free room-finding service. The **Ljubljana Tourist Card,** which includes access to public transportation and covers entry to many city museums as well as the TI's walking tours and boat trips, could save busy sight-seers some money (€23/24 hours, €30/48 hours, €35/72 hours).

Arrival in Ljubljana

By Train: Ljubljana's modern, user-friendly train station (Železniška Postaja) is at the northern edge of the city center. Emerging from the passage up to track 1a, turn right and walk under the long canopy along the train tracks to find the yellow arrivals hall. Everything is well-signed in English, including a **TI,** the handy train-information office next door (with useful handouts outlining trips to several domestic and international destinations, daily 5:30-21:30), and—near the front of the station—a big **ticket office** with clearly marked ticket windows and an **ATM** (office open daily 5:00-22:00). Arrivals are *prihodi,* departures are *odhodi,* and track is *tir.*

The main square is an easy 10-minute **walk** from the station; you can walk to any of my recommended hotels within about 20 minutes (often less). To reach Prešeren Square at the city's center, leave the arrivals hall to the right and walk a long block along the busy Trg Osvobodilne Fronte (or "Trg O.F." for short, with the bus station in the middle). After passing all of the bus stalls, turn left across Trg O.F. and go down Miklošičeva, at the building with the round red-brick columns. This takes you past some of Ljubljana's most appealing architecture to Prešeren Square.

Unscrupulous **taxis** crouch in front of the station, waiting to spring on unsuspecting tourists. The fair metered rate to any of my recommended hotels is around €3 (maybe up to €4-5 in heavy traffic or after hours). But, because the city refuses to regulate taxi tariffs, train-station taxis uniformly charge exorbitant rates—generally around €3-5 per kilometer (plus an extra fee of around €2-3 for bags), which is exponentially more than the €1 per kilometer charged by legitimate outfits. Simply put, it's impossible to hail a taxi on the street in front of the station and get anything resembling a fair fare. But all hope is not lost—to avoid giving these crooks the satisfaction, you can simply call for a taxi that charges fair rates (dial 041-731-831 or 080-1190); if you're uncomfortable calling yourself, just ask the train station TI to call for you (since they're familiar with the situation, they're usually happy to do this if they're not too busy). Taking the time to call, then waiting just a few more minutes for your cab, could easily save you €10 or more. For more on taxis—and how to avoid rip-offs—see "Getting Around Ljubljana—By Taxi," later.

By Bus: Ljubljana's bus station (Autobusna Postaja) is a low-profile building (with ticket windows, Internet access, a bakery, and newsstands) in the middle of Trg O.F., right in front of the train station. To get into the city center, see "By Train," above.

By Car: As you approach Ljubljana on the expressway, the toll road ends. Once you're on the ring road, simply follow signs for *Center*. Once you get into the city center, you'll begin to see directional signs to individual hotels. Ask your hotel about parking—most have some available, usually for a price. If you need to gas up your rental car before returning it, you'll find a huge gas station on Tivolska Cesta (just west of the train station, near the big Union brewery). Otherwise, your options in the center are limited—it's better to look for a gas station on the expressway before you reach the city.

By Plane: See "Ljubljana Connections," at the end of this chapter.

Helpful Hints

Pedestrian Safety: Many Ljubljana residents commute by bike. As a pedestrian, I've had many close calls with bikes whizzing by. Keep your eyes open and stay out of the designated bike lanes on the sidewalks (often marked in red).

Closed Days: Most Ljubljana museums (except the castle and a few less-important museums) are closed on Mondays. The recommended Jože Plečnik House is closed Sundays, Mondays, and Fridays, and might be closed entirely for restoration during your visit.

Markets: In addition to the regular **market** that sprawls along the riverfront (described under "Sights in Ljubljana"), a colorful **flea market** hops along the Ljubljanica River's Breg embankment (across the river from the castle) every Sun 8:00-14:00. On summer Saturdays, there's also a lively and colorful **arts and handicrafts market** in the same place (Sat 8:00-14:00).

Ljubljana Essentials

English	Slovene	Pronounced
Ljubljana Castle	Ljubljanski Grad	lyoob-lyee-AHN-skee grahd
Prešeren Square	Prešernov trg	preh-SHEHR-nohv turg
Congress Square	Kongresni trg	kohn-GREHS-nee turg
French Revolution Square	Trg Francoske Revolucije	turg frant-SOH-skeh reh-voh-LOOT-see-yeh
Square of the Republic	Trg Republike	turg-reh-POOB lee-keh
Triple Bridge	Tromostovje	troh-moh-STOHV-yeh
Cobblers' Bridge	Čevljarski Most	chehv-LAR-skee mohst
Dragon Bridge	Zmajski Most	ZMAY-skee mohst
Jože Plečnik, the architect	Jože Plečnik	YOH-zheh PLAYCH-neek
France Prešeren, the poet	France Prešeren	FRAHN-tseh preh-SHAY-rehn

Money: Most banks are open Mon-Fri 8:00-12:00 & 15:00-17:00, a few also open Sat 9:00-12:00, closed Sun.

Internet Access: Most hotels offer free Internet access and/ or Wi-Fi for their guests. The **TI** at the upper end of the market has several terminals (€1/30 minutes, see "Tourist Information," earlier). **Cyber Café Xplorer** is twice as expensive but has longer hours (Mon-Fri 10:00-22:00, Sat-Sun 12:00-22:00, Cankarjeva 9).

Post Office: The main post office *(pošta)* is in a beautiful yellow Art Nouveau building a block up Čopova from Prešeren Square, at the intersection with the busy Slovenska cesta (Mon-Fri 8:00-19:00, Sat 8:00-13:00, closed Sun).

Architecture Guidebooks: Ljubljana is a turn-on for architecture buffs. If you want to learn more about this city's quirky buildings, consider the excellent €27 *Let's See the City: Ljubljana* architecture guidebook, or the €17 book about Jože Plečnik's work (sold at the Jože Plečnik House, some TIs, and many bookstores).

Laundry: Most hotels can do your laundry, but it's pricey. **Hostel Celica** serves as the town's self-serve launderette—but it has only one machine, and hostel guests have priority (€7/ load, not very central at Metelkova 8). For full service, try

Tekstilexpress, between the city center and Tivoli Park (€2.25/kilo, figure about €12-15 for a full load, takes 24 hours, Mon-Fri 7:00-19:00, Sat 9:00-13:00, closed Sun, Cankarjeva 10B, tel. 01/252-7354).

Car Rental: Figure about €60 per day (includes tax and insurance, no extra charge for drop-off elsewhere in Slovenia). Handy options include **Hertz** (Trdinova 9, tel. 01/434-0147, www.hertz.si), **Europcar** (in City Hotel at Dalmatinova 15, mobile 031-382-052, www.europcar.si), **Avis** (Čufarjeva 2, tel. 01/430-8010, www.avis.si), **Budget** (in Grand Hotel Union at Miklošičeva 3, tel. 01/421-7340, www.budget.si), and **Sixt** (at the train station, tel. 01/234-4650).

Best Views: The Skyscraper's observation deck offers the best views in town (see page 542). Views from the castle are nearly as good. At street level, my favorite views are from the wooden bridge called the "Ugly Duckling" (between the Triple and Cobblers' bridges), especially at night. On sunny, blue-sky days, the colorful architecture on and near Prešeren Square pops, and you'll take photos like crazy along the river promenade.

Getting Around Ljubljana

By Bus: Virtually all of Ljubljana's sights are easily accessible by foot, so public transportation probably isn't necessary. And it's a bit of a headache: To ride a bus, you first have to buy a plastic "Urbana" card for €2 (nonrefundable), which you then load with credit to pay for rides. A ride costs €0.80, and you can't pay the driver—you have to use the card (shareable by up to three people). You can buy the Urbana card at any TI, the bus station, and some newsstands. Transit info: www.lpp.si.

By Taxi: Always call for a cab, or you'll get ripped off. Because cabbies can legally charge whatever they want, even if they use the meter you'll still pay way too much. Legitimate taxis usually start at about €1.50, and then charge €1 per kilometer. But because city leaders refuse to regulate taxi tariffs, many unscrupulous cabbies (including all of those that wait at the train station) legally charge far more, and tack on bogus additional "surcharges." Crooked cabbies are a big problem in Ljubljana, but you can avoid this headache entirely by always calling a reputable taxi company instead of hailing one on the street. If you do this, Ljubljana is a fantastic taxi town with very affordable rates—a ride within the city center (such as from the station to a hotel) should run only a few euros, generally less than €5. Good companies include **Yellow Taxi** (mobile 041-731-831) and **Metro Taxi** (tel. 080-1190). Don't be intimidated—dispatchers speak English, and your hotel, restaurant, or maybe the TI (if they're not too busy) can call a cab for you.

By Bike: Ljubljana is a cyclist's delight, with lots of well-marked bike lanes. A few hotels have rental or loaner bikes, or you can rent bikes at the market square TI (€1/2 hours, €5/day; see "Tourist Information," earlier). Like many European cities, Ljubljana has a subsidized bike-rental program (called BicikeLJ) with 30 locations around the city center. While this program is cheap, it requires advance registration with a credit card, and you have to get the local public-transit Urbana card—probably not worth it for a short visit (for details, see http://en.bicikelj.si).

Tours in Ljubljana

Most of Ljubljana's museums are disappointing; the town's ambience, architecture, and public art are its best attractions. To help you appreciate it all, taking a walking tour—either through the TI or by hiring your own local guide—is worth ▲▲.

Walking Tour—The TI organizes excellent two-hour guided town walks of Ljubljana in English, led by knowledgeable guides. In summer, the walk also includes either a trip up to the castle (by funicular or tourist train) or a 30-minute boat ride on the river. From April through September, there are three tours daily: at 10:00, 14:00, and 17:00. From October through March, the walking tour goes daily at 11:00 (€10, or €9 if you pay at TI, meet at Town Hall around corner from Triple Bridge TI).

Local Guides—Having an expert show you around his or her hometown for two hours for €50 has to be the best value in town. Ljubljana's hardworking guides lead tours on a wide variety of topics and can tailor their tour to your interests (figure €60/2 hours, 50 percent more for same-day booking, contact TI for details, arrange at least 24 hours before). **Marijan Krišković,** who leads tours for me throughout Europe, is an outstanding guide (mobile 040-222-739, kriskovic@yahoo.com). **Barbara Jakopič,** soft-spoken and extremely knowledgeable, is also good (mobile 040-530-870, b_lucky2@yahoo.com). **Minka Kahrič,** who's traveled to the North Pole, also leads tours closer to home—including walks around Ljubljana and excursions into the countryside (€60/2-hour walking tour; driving: €100/up to 4 hours, €140/up to 8 hours; mobile 041-805-962, polarnimedo@yahoo.com).

Boat Cruise—Consider seeing the town from the Ljubljanica River. You have two options for your one-hour cruise: with English commentary from a live guide (€10, 2/day in summer), or unguided (€8, hourly in summer 10:00-20:00). For details, check with the TI (weather permitting, departs from near the Triple Bridge—about one block along the embankment away from the market). Because Ljubljana is a small town that's easily seen by foot, this trip is more romantic than informative.

Bike Tour—The TI offers a bike tour of the city by request (€15, 2 hours, 4-person minimum, arrange at least 24 hours ahead, get details at TI).

Excursions from Ljubljana—Slovenia is a tiny country with many worthwhile sights that are near Ljubljana but tricky to reach by public transportation. To hit several efficiently in one day, consider joining an excursion. Tour companies tend to come and go here—drop by any TI to ask about the latest options and which companies have the best reputations. You'll find fliers everywhere. Two relatively well-established outfits are **Roundabout** (their one-day "Karst and Coast Mystery" tour takes you to Predjama Castle, Škocjan Caves, Lipica, and Piran for €45 plus admission to the caves; www.roundabout.si) and **Slovenia Explorer** (their ambitious "Slovenia in 1 Day" trip visits Lake Bled, Lake Bohinj, and Postojna Caves for €115; www.slovenia-explorer.com).

Self-Guided Spin-Tour

▲▲Prešeren Square

The heart of Ljubljana is lively Prešeren Square (Prešernov trg). It's always been bustling, but now it's more people-friendly than ever, since the mayor recently outlawed buses and taxis here.

The city's meeting point is the large **statue of France Prešeren,** Slovenia's greatest poet, whose works include the lyr-

ics to the Slovenian national anthem (and whose silhouette adorns Slovenia's €2 coin). The statue shows Prešeren, an important catalyst of 19th-century Slovenian nationalism, being inspired from above by a Muse. This statue provoked a scandal and outraged the bishop when it went up a century ago—a naked woman sharing the square with a church! To ensure that nobody could be confused about the woman's intentions, she's conspicuously depicted with typi-

cal Muse accessories: a laurel branch and a cloak. Even so, for the first few years they covered the scandalous statue with a tarp each night. And the model who posed for the Muse was so disgraced that no one in Slovenia would hire her—so she emigrated to South America and never returned.

Stand at the base of the statue to get oriented. The bridge crossing the Ljubljanica River is one of Ljubljana's most important landmarks, Jože Plečnik's **Triple Bridge** (Tromostovje). The middle (widest) part of this bridge already existed, but Plečnik

added the two side spans
to more efficiently funnel
the six streets of traffic on
this side of the bridge to
the one street on the other
side. The bridge's Venetian
vibe is intentional: Plečnik
recognized that Ljubljana,

located midway between Venice and then-capital Vienna, is itself
a bridge between the Italian and Germanic worlds. Across the
bridge are the TI, WCs, ATMs, market and cathedral (to the left),
and the Town Hall (straight ahead).

Now turn 90 degrees to the right, and look down the first
street after the riverbank. Find the pale woman in the picture
frame on the second floor of the first yellow house. This is **Julija,**
the unrequited love of Prešeren's life. Tour guides spin romantic
tales about how the couple met. But the truth is far less exciting:
He was a teacher in her father's house when he was in his 30s and
she was four. Later in life, she inspired him from afar—as she does
now, from across the square—but they never got together. She may
have been his muse, but when it came to marriage, she opted for
wealth and status.

When Ljubljana was hit by an earthquake in 1895, locals
took the opportunity (and an ample rebuilding fund from the

Austro-Hungarian Empire)
to remake their city in style.
Today Ljubljana—especially
the streets around this square—
is an architecture-lover's paradise. The **Hauptmann House,**
to the right of Julija, was the
only building on the square to
survive the quake. A few years

later, the owner redecorated it in the then-trendy Viennese Art
Nouveau style you see today, using bright colors (since his family
sold dyes). All that remains of the original structure is the little
Baroque balcony above the entrance.

Just to the right of the Hauptmann House is a car-sized
model of the city center—helpful for orientation. The street
next to it (with the McDonald's) is **Čopova,** once the route of
Ljubljana's Sunday promenade. A century ago, locals would put
on their Sunday best and stroll from here to Tivoli Park, listening to musicians and dropping into cafés along the way. Plečnik
called it the "lifeline of the city," connecting the green lungs of the
park to this urban center. Today, Slovenska avenue and railroad
tracks cross the route, making the promenade less inviting. But in

Ljubljana at a Glance

▲▲▲People-Watching Ljubljana's single best activity is sitting at an outdoor café along the river and watching the vivacious, stylish, fun-loving Slovenes strut their stuff. **Hours:** 24/7.

▲▲Riverside Market Lively market area in the Old Town with produce, clothing, and souvenirs. **Hours:** Best in the morning, especially Sat; market hall open Mon-Fri 7:00-16:00, Sat 7:00-14:00, closed Sun.

▲▲Serbian Orthodox Church of Sts. Cyril and Methodius Beautifully decorated house of worship giving insight into the Orthodox faith. **Hours:** Sun 9:00-12:00 & 17:00-18:00, Mon 8:00-9:00 & 17:00-18:00, Tue-Sat 8:00-12:00 & 14:00-18:00.

▲▲National and University Library Jože Plečnik's pièce de résistance, with an intriguing facade, piles of books, and a bright reading room. **Hours:** Main staircase open Mon-Fri 9:00-20:00, Sat 9:00-14:00, closed Sun; student reading room open to the public only mid-July-mid-Aug Mon-Fri 14:00-20:00.

▲▲Jože Plečnik House Final digs of the famed hometown architect who shaped so much of Ljubljana, explained by an enthusiastic guide. **Hours:** English tours begin at the top of each hour Tue-Thu 10:00-18:00, Sat 9:00-15:00, last tour departs one hour before closing, closed Sun-Mon and Fri, and possibly closed at other times while undergoing renovation—call ahead.

the last decade, Ljubljana has been trying to recapture its golden age, and some downtown streets are pedestrian-only on weekends once again. The new evening *paseo* thrives along the river from the Triple Bridge all the way up the river.

Continue looking to the right, past the big, pink landmark Franciscan Church of St. Mary. The characteristic glass awning marks **Centromerkur**—the first big post-quake department store, today government-protected. At the top of the building is Mercury, god of commerce, watching over the square that has been Ljubljana's commercial heart since the city began. (If you look carefully, you can see the mustachioed face of the building's owner hiding in the folds of cloth by Mercury's left foot.) Since this area was across the river from medieval Ljubljana (beyond the town's limits...and the long arm

▲▲**Slovenian Ethnographic Museum** Engaging, well-presented collection celebrating Slovenian culture. **Hours:** Tue-Sun 10:00-18:00, closed Mon.

▲**Cathedral** Italian Baroque interior and highly symbolic, intricately carved doors. **Hours:** Open long hours daily but closed 12:00-15:00.

▲**Dragon Bridge** Distinctive Art Nouveau bridge adorned with the city's mascot. **Hours:** Always roaring.

▲**Ljubljana Castle** Tower with good views and so-so 3-D film. **Hours:** Grounds open daily April-Sept 9:00-23:00, Oct-March 10:00-21:00; castle open daily April-Sept 9:00-21:00, Oct-March 10:00-18:00, film plays all day on the half-hour.

▲**Contemporary History Museum** Baroque mansion in Tivoli Park, with exhibit highlighting Slovenia's last 100 years. **Hours:** Tue-Sun 10:00-18:00, closed Mon.

▲**City Museum of Ljubljana** Modern, high-tech exhibit on the city's history. **Hours:** Tue-Sun 10:00-18:00, Thu until 21:00, closed Mon.

▲**Cobblers' Bridge** Columned bridge that epitomizes Jože Plečnik's distinctive architectural style. **Hours:** Always open.

of its tax collector), it was the best place to buy and sell goods. Today this recently restored, fine old building houses the top-end Galerija Emporium fashion mall, making it the heart of Ljubljana's boutique culture. Step inside for a glimpse at the sumptuous interior, with a grand staircase that gives way to a modern zone.

The street between Centromerkur and the pink church is **Miklošičeva cesta,** which connects Prešeren Square to the train station. When Ljubljana was rebuilding after the 1895 earthquake, town architects and designers envisioned this street as a showcase of its new, Vienna-inspired Art Nouveau image.

Up Miklošičeva street and on the left is the prominent **Grand Hotel Union,** with a stately domed spire on the corner. When these buildings were designed, Prague was the cultural capital of the Slavic world. The new look of Ljubljana paid homage to "the golden city of a hundred spires" (and copied Prague's romantic image). The city actually had a law for several years that new corner buildings had to have these spires. Even the trees you'll see around town were part of the vision. When the architect Plečnik designed the Ljubljanica River embankments a generation later, he planted tall, pointy poplar trees and squat, rounded willows—imitating the spires and domes of Prague.

Detour a block up Miklošičeva cesta to see two more architectural gems of that era (across from the Grand Hotel Union): First is a Secessionist building—marked **Zadružna Zveza**—with classic red, blue, and white colors (for the Slovenian flag). Next is the noisy, pink, zigzagged **Cooperative Bank.** The bank was designed by Ivan Vurnik, an ambitious Slovenian architect who wanted to invent a distinctive national style after World War I,

when the Habsburg Empire broke up and Eastern Europe's nations were proudly emerging for the first time.

Prešeren Square is the perfect springboard to explore the rest of Ljubljana. Now that you're oriented, visit some of the areas listed next.

Sights in Ljubljana

Ljubljana is bursting with new, well-presented, we-try-harder museums celebrating Slovenian history and culture. These include the Slovenian History Exhibition at the castle, the City Museum of Ljubljana, and the Contemporary History Museum in Tivoli Park. Those of us who've fallen in love with this city and country find each of these museums fascinating in its own right, but—since they're similar and largely overlapping—some visitors might find them redundant and dull. If you get museumed out easily, just visit the one that's handiest to your sightseeing plan.

East of the River, Under the Castle: The Market and Old Town

The castle side of the river is the city's most colorful and historic quarter, packed with Old World ambience.

▲▲**Riverside Market (Tržnice)**—In Ljubljana's thriving Old Town market, big-city Slovenes enjoy buying directly from the producer. Prices go down as the day gets late and as the week goes on. The market, worth an amble anytime, is best on Saturday mornings, when the townspeople take their time wandering the stalls. In this tiny capital of a tiny country, you may even see the president searching for the perfect melon.

Begin your walk through the market at the Triple Bridge (and TI). The riverside **colonnade,** which echoes the long-gone medieval

city wall, was designed by (who else?) Jože Plečnik. This first stretch—nearest the Triple Bridge—is good for souvenirs: woodcarvings, miniature painted frontboards from beehives, honey products (including honey brandy), and lots of colorful candles (bubbly Marta will gladly paint a special message on your candle for no extra charge).

Farther in, the market is almost all local, and the colonnade is populated by butchers, bakers, fishermen, and lazy cafés. Peek down at the actual river and see how the architect wanted the town and river to connect. The lower arcade (which you can access directly from the Triple Bridge, or by going down the spiral staircase by the beehive panels) is a people zone, with public WCs, inviting cafés, and a stinky fish market *(ribarnica)* offering a wide variety. The recommended restaurant just below, **Ribca,** serves fun fishy plates, beer, and coffee with great riverside seating.

Across from the stairs that lead down into the fish market, about where the souvenir stands end, you reach the first small market square. On your right, notice the 10-foot-tall concrete **cone.** Plečnik wanted to make Ljubljana the "Athens of the North" and imagined a huge hilltop cone crowning the center of a national acropolis—a complex for government, museums, and culture. This ambitious plan didn't make it off the drawing board, but part of Plečnik's Greek idea came true: this marketplace, based on an ancient Greek *agora.* Plečnik's cone still captures the Slovenes' imaginations...and adorns Slovenia's €0.10 coin.

At the top of this square, you'll find the 18th-century **cathedral** standing on the site of a 13th-century Romanesque church (check out its finely decorated doors and consider going inside; for a complete description, see later).

The building at the end of the first market square is the seminary palace. In the basement is a **market hall,** with vendors selling cheeses, meats, baked goods, dried fruits, nuts, and other goodies (Mon-Fri 7:00-16:00, Sat 7:00-14:00, closed Sun). This place is worth a graze. Most merchants are happy to give you a free sample (point to what you want, and say *probat, prosim*—"a taste, please").

Leaving the market hall, notice where the colonnade ends at a modern bridge. Jože Plečnik designed a huge, roofed **Butchers' Bridge** to be built here, but—like so many of his designs—the plans were scuttled. Decades later, aware of Plečnik's newfound touristic currency, some town politicians dusted off the old plans and proposed building the bridge. The project stalled for years

Zoran Janković

The latest chapter in Ljubljana's story has been written by a recent mayor, Zoran Janković. As chairman of the huge Mercator supermarket chain, Janković was famous for prowling around the front lines of his stores, micromanaging all the day-to-day business. After corporate political shuffling forced him out, Janković turned his attention to the municipal realm—and, in 2006, was elected mayor of Ljubljana in a landslide.

The people of this city, who had grown accustomed to well-intentioned but ineffectual leaders who proposed, then cancelled, ambitious projects, were stunned to see Janković's corporate-minded, no-nonsense follow-through. Project after project materialized, on time and under budget: the funicular to the castle, several new bridges (including the Butchers' Bridge at the market), the creation of quaintly cobbled traffic-free zones throughout almost the entire town center, and the pedestrianization of miles of riverfront embankment. The sweeping changes have had their critics—among them elderly people who can no longer easily drive to their homes in the now-traffic-free center—but ultimately most Ljubljanans are thrilled with the transformation. It's a good example of how a progressive electorate can trust a capable leader to wisely invest public funds in urban-beautification projects that benefit the common good.

After winning re-election to the mayor's office in another landslide in 2010, Janković turned his sights to the national arena. In the parliamentary elections of December, 2011, the party he formed—Positive Slovenia—eked out a nationwide victory. Fittingly, it was the Ljubljana vote that put him over the top. However, some last-minute political wrangling among members of his coalition cost him the prime ministership—he merely has a seat in the parliament. While some Slovenes were optimistic about what this bold innovator might do on a national scale, others were troubled by his virtually complete lack of foreign policy experience. Will Janković's mastery at managing the capital city ultimately translate to nationwide success in challenging economic times? Stay tuned.

until the arrival of Mayor Zoran Janković, who swiftly constructed this modern version of the bridge. While it looks nothing like Plečnik's original plans, the bridge kept the old name and has been embraced by the community (there's a handy public WC down below on the lower level). The sculptures on the bridge, by local artist Jakov Brdar, were originally intended to be temporary—but people loved them, so they stayed. Notice the mournful pose of the Adam and Eve statues (being evicted from the Garden of Eden) at the market end of the bridge. And don't miss the bizarre smaller sculptures along the railing—such as the ones that look like mischievous lizards breaking out of their eggs. Almost as soon as it was built, the bridge's railings were covered with padlocks—part of the recent Europe-wide craze for young couples to commemorate their love by locking a padlock to a bridge railing. But all those locks are just too much for the railing to support—they are regularly cut off, soon to be replaced by new ones.

Sprawling up from the bridge is the **main market square,** packed with produce and clothing stands. (The colorful flower

market hides behind the market hall.) The vendors in the row nearest the colonnade sell fruit from all over, but the ones located deeper in the market sell only locally grown produce. These producers go out of their way to be old-fashioned—a few of them still follow the tradition of pushing their veggies on wooden carts (called *cizas*) to the market from their garden patches in the suburbs. Once at the market, they simply display their goods on top of their cart, turning it into a sales kiosk. Tell the vendor what you want—it's considered rude for customers to touch the fruits and vegetables before they're bought. Over time, shoppers develop friendships with their favorite producers. On busy days, you'll see a long line at one stand, while the other merchants stand bored. Your choice is simple: Get in line, or eat subpar produce.

Near the market hall, look for the little **scales** in the wooden kiosks marked *Kontrolna Tehtnica*—allowing buyers to immediately check whether the producer cheated them (not a common problem, but just in case). The Habsburg days left locals with the old German saying, "Trust is good; control is better." Nearby, look for the innovative "Nonstop Mlekomat" stand, a vending machine that lets you buy a plastic bottle, then fill it with a liter of raw, unskimmed, farm-fresh milk for €1.

Two more sights are immersed in the market action (both described next); the cathedral sits at the top of the market area, near the Triple Bridge, while the Dragon Bridge spans the river just beyond the end of the market colonnade.

▲**Cathedral (Stolnica)**—Ljubljana's cathedral is dedicated to St. Nicholas, protector against floods and patron saint of the fishermen and boatmen who have long come to sell their catch at the market. While the interior is worth a peek (free, open long hours daily but closed 12:00-15:00), the intricately decorated doors—created for Pope John Paul II's visit here in 1996—are even more interesting.

Go under the high arch, then take a close look at the remarkable side **door** on the left. Buried deeply in the fecund soil of their ancient and pagan history, the nation's linden tree of life sprouts with the story of the Slovenes. The ceramic pots represent the original Roman settlement here. Just to the left, above the tree, are the Byzantine missionaries Cyril and Methodius, who came here to convert the Slavs to Christianity in the ninth century. Just above, Crusaders and Ottomans do battle. Near the top, see the Slovenes going into the cave—entering the dark 20th century (World War I, World War II, and communism). At the top is Pope John Paul II (the first Slavic pontiff, who also oversaw the fall of communism). Below him are two men who are on track to becoming Slovenia's first saints; the one on the right is Frederic Baraga, a 19th-century bishop who became a missionary in Michigan and codified Chippewa grammar (notice the Native American relief on the book he's holding). In the upper right-hand corner is a sun, which has been shining since Slovenia gained its independence in 1991. Around back of the cathedral is a similar door, carved with images of the six 20th-century bishops of Ljubljana.

The cathedral's **interior** is stunning Italian Baroque. The transept is surrounded by sculptures of four bishops of Roman Ljubljana (when it was called Emona, or Aemon). Left of the main altar, notice the distinctive chair. This was designed by the very religious Jože Plečnik, whose brother was a priest here. Look up over the nave to enjoy the recently restored, gorgeous ceiling fresco.

▲Dragon Bridge (Zmajski Most)—The dragon has been the symbol of Ljubljana for centuries, ever since Jason (of Argonauts and Golden Fleece fame) supposedly slew one in a nearby swamp. This is one of the few notable bits of Ljubljana architecture not by Plečnik (but by Jurij Zaninović, a fellow student of Vienna architect Otto Wagner). While the dragon is the star of this very photo-

genic Art Nouveau bridge, the bridge itself was officially dedicated to the 40th anniversary of Habsburg Emperor Franz Josef's reign (see the dates on the side: 1848-1888). Tapping into the emp's vanity got new projects funded—vital as the city rebuilt after the 1895 earthquake. But the Franz Josef name never stuck; those dragons are just too darn memorable.

From the Dragon Bridge, it's an easy funicular ride or steep hike up to Ljubljana Castle (described later). Or you can head back through the market to reach the Town Square and Old Town (see next).

▲Town Square (Mestni Trg) and the Old Town—Ljubljana's Town Square, just across the Triple Bridge and up the street from Prešeren Square, is home to the **Town Hall** (Rotovž), highlighted by its clock tower and pillared loggia. Step inside the Renaissance courtyard to see paintings, artifacts, and a map of late 17th-century Ljubljana. Studying this map, notice how the river, hill, and wall worked together to fortify the town. Courtyards like this (but humbler) are hidden throughout the city. As rent in these old places is cheap, many such courtyards host funky and characteristic little businesses. Be sure to get off the main drag and poke into Ljubljana's nooks and crannies.

In the square is a recent replica of the **Fountain of Three Carniolian Rivers,** inspired in style and theme by Rome's many

fountains. (The original is in a museum.) The figures with vases represent this region's three main rivers: Ljubljanica, Sava, and Krka. This is one of many works in town by Francesco Robba, an Italian who came to Ljubljana for a job, fell in love with a Slovene, and stayed here the rest of his life—decorating the city's churches with beautiful Baroque altars. At the nearby corner, check out the wild interior of the Nova KBM Bank, which looks more like a cutting-edge nightclub.

In the early 19th century, Ljubljana consisted mainly of this single street, running along the base of Castle Hill (plus a small "New Town" across the river). Stretching south from here are two other "squares"—Stari trg (Old Square) and Gornji trg (Upper Square)—which have long since grown together into one big, atmospheric promenade lined with quaint boutiques, great restaurants, and cafés (perfect for a stroll). Virtually every house along this drag has a story to tell of a famous resident or infamous incident. As you walk, keep your eyes open for Ljubljana's mascot dragon—it's everywhere. Near the Town Hall, look for a pair of interesting spots on the left: At #4, Čupterija Bar has one of the most creative interiors in this very creative town. Next door at #5, Café Galerija is the city art gallery, with changing exhibits and a cool café in back. Continuing along this drag, stow your guidebook and enjoy some boutique window-shopping and people-watching; you'll also pass some recommended eateries (see "Eating in Ljubljana," later). At the end of the pedestrian zone (at Gornji trg), look uphill and notice the village charms of some of the oldest buildings in town (four medieval houses with rooflines slanted at the ends, different from the others on this street).

▲Ljubljana Castle (Ljubljanski Grad)—The castle above town offers enjoyable views of Ljubljana and the surrounding country-side. There has probably been a settle-ment on this site since prehistoric times, though the first fortress here was Roman. The 12th-century version was gradually added on to over the cen-turies, until it fell into disrepair in the 17th century. Today's castle was rebuilt in the 1940s, renovated in the 1970s, and is still technically unfinished (sub-ject to ongoing additions). The castle houses a climbable tower, a good

exhibit about Slovenian history, a fine restaurant, the good Rustika gift shop, temporary exhibition halls, and a Gothic chapel with Baroque paintings of the coat of arms of St. George (Ljubljana's patron saint, the dragon-slayer). Above the restaurant are two wedding halls—Ljubljana's most popular places to get married (free for locals). The castle is also home to the Ljubljana Summer Festival, with concerts throughout the summer (tel. 01/306-4293, www.ljubljanafestival.si). While the castle and its attractions are ho-hum, the views are worth the trip.

Cost and Hours: You can hike up to the castle and wander the grounds for free (daily April-Sept 9:00-23:00, Oct-March 10:00-21:00). But if you want to enter the three sights at the cas-tle (history exhibition, film, and castle tower), you'll pay €4 (€6 combo-ticket also includes funicular; €8 combo-ticket includes sights, funicular, and guided tour; sights open daily April-Sept 9:00-21:00, Oct-March 10:00-18:00, tel. 01/232-9994, www .ljubljanskigrad.si).

Tours: Guided tours of the castle in Slovene and English leave from the castle information center daily June through mid-September at 10:00, 11:00, 14:00, and 16:00 (€6, or included in €8 combo-ticket with castle sights and funicular; tour lasts 1-1.5 hours; winter tours possible to arrange upon request for at least 3 people—call a day ahead).

Getting to the Castle: A slick **funicular** whisks visitors to the top in a jiff (€1.50 one-way, €3 round-trip, also included in combo-tickets described above, runs every 10 minutes, 1-minute ride, daily April-Sept 9:00-23:00, Oct-March 10:00-21:00, catch it at Krekov trg—across the street from the market square TI). From the top, you'll find free WCs and a few easy flights of stairs up into the heart of the castle complex (or take the elevator). Another sweat-free route to the top is via the **tourist train** that leaves at the top of each hour (or more frequently with demand) from in front of the Town Hall (€3 round-trip, daily in summer 9:00-21:00, shorter hours off-season, doesn't run in snow or other bad weather). There are also two handy **trails** to the castle. The steeper-but-faster route begins near the Dragon Bridge: Find Študentovska lane, just past the statue of Vodnik in the market. This lane dead-ends at a gravel path, which you'll follow up to a fork. Turn left to zigzag up the steepest and fastest route, which deposits you just below the castle wall; from here, turn left again and curl around the wall to reach the main drawbridge. Slower but a bit less steep is Reber, just off Stari trg, a few blocks south of the Town Hall: Walk up to the top of Reber, and, at the dead end, turn right and start climbing up the stairs. From here on out, keep bearing left, then go right when you're just under the castle (follow *Grad* signs).

Sights at the Castle: Three sights cluster around the tallest tower: You can see a **film** about the history of Ljubljana (plays all day on the half-hour); climb the 92 steps up to the **castle tower,** with one of the best views in town; or tour the good exhibition about Slovenian history. From a sightseeing perspective, the castle's highlight is its **Slovenian History Exhibition,** which offers a concise but engaging overview of this little country's story. As you enter, ask to borrow the free audioguide, then head downstairs and work your way up. Dark display cases light up when you approach, revealing actual artifacts, video clips, and touchscreens with more information. A unique feature of the museum is that you're invited to touch replicas of important historic items (generally displayed next to the original items). Don't miss the top floor of the exhibit (go up the glassed-in staircase), which is the most interesting—covering the tumultuous 20th century. You'll learn about topics ranging from the battlefields of World War I, to the creation of the first Yugoslavia, to the fascist occupation and harrowing Italian-run concentration camps of World War II, to the cult of personality around Partisan war hero-turned-Yugoslav president Tito, to Slovenia's bid for independence.

Eating: Combine your visit to the castle with a meal at the recommended **Gostilna na Gradu,** with the best traditional Slovenian food in town (in the castle courtyard; described later, under "Eating in Ljubljana").

West of the River, Beyond Prešeren Square: The Museum Zone and Tivoli Park

The Prešeren Square (west) side of the river is the heart of modern Ljubljana, and home to several prominent squares and fine museums. These sights are listed roughly in order from Prešeren Square and can be linked to make an interesting walk.

• *Leave Prešeren Square in the direction the poet is looking, bear to your left (up Wolfova, by the picture of Julija), and walk a block to...*

Congress Square (Kongresni Trg)—This grassy, tree-lined square is ringed by some of Ljubljana's most important buildings: the University headquarters, the Baroque Ursuline Church of the Holy Trinity, a classical mansion called the Kazina, and the Philharmonic Hall. Once clogged with traffic, the area around the square was recently pedestrianized, including the broad strip along the far side. At the top end of the square, by the entry to a pedestrian underpass, a Roman sarcophagus sits under a gilded statue of a **Roman citizen**—a replica of an artifact from 1,700 years ago, when this town was called Emona. The busy street above you has been the main trading route through town since ancient Roman times. This square hosts the big town events.

• *Take the underpass beneath Slovenska avenue (the town's main traffic thoroughfare—which may be open only to buses in the coming years). As you go down into the underpass, you can turn left to find a surviving chunk of the old Roman wall. Continuing through the underpass and emerging at the far end, walk straight through the gap in the shopping mall into the...*

▲Square of the Republic (Trg Republike)—This unusual square is essentially a parking lot ringed by an odd collection of buildings. While hardly quaint, the Square of the Republic gives you a good taste of a modern corner of Ljubljana. And it's historic—this is where Slovenia declared its independence in 1991.

The **twin office towers** (with the world's biggest digital watch, flashing the date, time, and temperature) were designed by Plečnik's protégé, Edvard Ravnikar. As harrowing as these structures seem, imagine if the builders had followed the original plans—the towers would be twice as tall as they are now, and connected by a bridge, representing the gateway to Ljubljana. These buildings were originally designed as the Slovenian parliament, but they were scaled back when Tito didn't approve (since it would have made Slovenia's parliament bigger than the Yugoslav parliament in Belgrade). Instead, the **Slovenian Parliament** is across the square, in the strangely low-profile office building with the sculpted entryway. The carvings are in the Socialist Realist style, celebrating the noble Slovenian people conforming to communist ideals for the good of the entire society. Completing the square

are a huge conference center (Cankarjev Dom, the white building behind the skyscrapers), a shopping mall, and some public art.

• *Just a block north, through the grassy park (Trg Narodni Herojev), you'll find the...*

Slovenian National Museum (Narodni Muzej Slovenije) and Slovenian Museum of Natural History (Prirodoslovni Muzej Slovenije)—These two museums share a single historic

building facing a park behind the Parliament. While neither collection is particularly good, they're both worth considering if you have a special interest or if it's a rainy day.

The **National Museum** occupies the ground floor, featuring a lapidarium with carved-stone Roman monuments and exhibits on Egyptian mummies. (Temporary exhibits are also on this level.) Upstairs and to the right are more exhibits of the National Museum, with archaeological findings ranging from old armor and pottery to the museum's two prized possessions: a fragment of a 45,000-year-old Neanderthal flute fashioned from a cave bear's femur, supposedly the world's oldest musical instrument; and the "figural situla," a beautifully decorated bronze bucket from 500 B.C.

Upstairs and to the left is the **Natural History** exhibit, featuring the flora and fauna of Slovenia. You'll see partial skeletons of a mammoth and a cave bear, plenty of stuffed reptiles, fish, and birds, and an exhibit on "human fish" (*Proteus anguinus*—long, skinny, pale-pink, sightless salamanders unique to caves in this part of Europe).

Cost and Hours: €3 for each museum, or €5 for both, some English descriptions, free audioguide for Natural History Museum, both open daily 10:00-18:00, Thu until 20:00, Prešernova 20, tel. 01/241-4400, www.nms.si and www.pms-lj.si.

• *At the far end of the building is a glassed-in annex displaying Roman stone monuments (free). Turning left around the museum building and walking one block, you'll see the...*

US Embassy—This pretty yellow chalet (with brown trim and

a red roof, at Prešernova cesta 31) wins my vote for quaintest embassy building in the world. Resist the urge to snap a photo... those guards are all business.

• *Just up Prešernova street from the embassy are two decent but skippable art museums.*

National Gallery (Narodna Galerija)—This museum has three

parts: European artists (in the new building), Slovenian artists (in the old building), and temporary exhibits. Find the work of Ivana Kobilca, a late 19th-century Slovenian Impressionist. Art-lovers enjoy her self-portrait in *Summer*. If you're going to Bled, you can get a sneak preview with Marko Pernhart's huge panorama of the Julian Alps.

Cost and Hours: €7, more for special exhibits, permanent collection free first Sun of the month, open Tue-Sun 10:00-18:00, closed Mon, enter through old-fashioned facade at Cankarjeva 20, another entrance is at the big glass box between two older buildings at Prešernova 24, tel. 01/241-5418, www.ng-slo.si.

Museum of Modern Art (Moderna Galerija Ljubljana)— Newly renovated, this museum has a permanent collection of modern and contemporary Slovenian artists, as well as temporary exhibits by both Slovenes and international artists. To explore the "Continuities and Ruptures" permanent collection (aptly named for a place with such a fractured, up-and-down recent history), borrow the English floor plan and take a chronological spin through the 20th century. Unusual for a "modern" art museum is the room with Partisan art, with stiff, improvised, communist-style posters from the days when Tito and his crew were just a ragtag militia movement.

Cost and Hours: €5, Tue-Sun 10:00-18:00, closed Mon, Tomšičeva 14, tel. 01/241-6800, www.mg-lj.si.

• *By the busy road near the art museums, look for the distinctive Neo-Byzantine design (tall domes with narrow slits) of the...*

▲▲Serbian Orthodox Church of Sts. Cyril and Methodius— Ljubljana's most striking church interior isn't Catholic, but Orthodox. This church was built in 1936, soon after the Slovenes joined a political union with the Serbs. Wealthy Slovenia attracted its poorer neighbors from the south—so it built this church for that community. Since 1991, the Serb population continues to grow, as people from the struggling corners of the former Yugoslavia flock to prosperous Slovenia.

Step inside for the best glimpse of the Orthodox faith this side of Dubrovnik. The church is colorfully decorated without a hint of the 21st century, mirroring a very conservative religion. You'll see Cyrillic script in this building, which feels closer to Moscow than to Rome. Notice that there are no pews, because worshippers stand throughout the service. On the left, find the little room with tubs of water, where the faithful light tall, skinny beeswax candles (purchased at the little window in the back corner). The painted screen, or iconostasis, is believed to separate our material world from the spiritual realm behind it. Ponder the fact that several centuries ago, before the Catholic Church began to adapt to a changing world, all Christians worshipped this way. For more on the Orthodox faith, see the sidebar on page 318.

Cost and Hours: Free, Sun 9:00-12:00 & 17:00-18:00, Mon

8:00-9:00 & 17:00-18:00, Tue-Sat 8:00-12:00 & 14:00-18:00

• *On the other side of the busy street is...*

Tivoli Park (Park Tivoli)—This huge park, just west of the center, is where Slovenes relax on summer weekends. The easiest access

is through the graffiti-covered underpass from Cankarjeva cesta (between the Serbian Orthodox Church and the Museum of Modern Art). As you emerge, the Neoclassical pillars leading down the promenade clue you in that this part of the park was designed by Jože Plečnik. Along this "main boulevard" of the park, various changing photographic exhibitions are displayed.

• *Aside from taking a leisurely stroll, the best thing to do in the park is visit the...*

▲Contemporary History Museum (Muzej Novejše Zgodovine)—In a Baroque mansion (Cekinov Grad) in Tivoli Park, a well-done exhibit called "Slovenians in the 20th Century" traces the last hundred years of Slovenia—essentially from the end of World War I to independence in 1991. Out front is a T-55 Yugoslav tank that was commandeered by the Slovenes during their war for independence. Inside, the ground floor displays temporary exhibits, and upstairs you'll find several rooms using models, dioramas, light-and-sound effects, and English explanations to creatively tell the story of one of Europe's youngest nations. While it's a little difficult to fully appreciate, the creativity and the spunky spirit of the place are truly enjoyable.

Cost and Hours: €3.50, permanent exhibit free first Sun of the month, guidebook-€15, open Tue-Sun 10:00-18:00, closed Mon, in Tivoli Park at Celovška cesta 23, tel. 01/300-9610, www .muzej-nz.si.

Getting There: The museum is a 20-minute walk from the center, best combined with a wander through Tivoli Park. The fastest approach: As you emerge from the Cankarjeva cesta underpass into the park, climb up the stairs, then turn right and go straight ahead for five minutes. You'll continue straight up the ramp, then turn left after the tennis courts and look for the big pink-and-white mansion on the hill.

Touring the Museum: The exhibit begins at the dawn of the 20th century, during Slovenia's waning days as part of the Austro-Hungarian Empire. You'll walk through a simulated trench from the Soča Front, then learn about the creation of the post-World War I Kingdom of Serbs, Croats, and Slovenes (or, as this exhibit pointedly puts it, "Kingdom of Slovenes, Croats, and Serbs").

Your footfalls echo loudly as you enter the room describing Slovenia's WWII experience (ask them to start the 12-minute "multivision" wrap-around slideshow, with music and sound effects). You'll learn how during that war, Slovenia was divided between neighboring fascist powers Germany, Italy, and Hungary. Each one tried (but failed) to exert linguistic and cultural control over the people, hoping to eradicate the Slovenian national identity. Video screens show subtitled interviews with people who lived through those war years.

Passing through the ballroom, you reach the "Slovenia 1945-1960" exhibit, outlining both the good (modernization) and the bad (prison camps and secret police) of the early Tito years. Despite his ruthless early rule, Tito remains popular here; under his stern bust, page through the photo album of Tito's visits to Slovenia. Find the display of the country's former currencies. Examining the Yugoslav dinar, notice that the figureheads on that communist currency were generic, idealized workers, farmers, and other members of the proletariat...except for a few notable individuals (including Tito). Meanwhile, Slovenia's short-lived post-Yugoslav currency, the *tolar* (1991-2006), featured artists and scientists rather than heads of state and generals.

The most evocative room has artifacts from the Slovenes' brave declaration of independence from a hostile Yugoslavia in 1991. The well-organized Slovenes had only to weather a 10-day skirmish to gain their freedom. It's chilling to think that at one point bombers were en route to level this gorgeous city. The planes were called back at the last minute, by a Yugoslav People's Army officer with allegiances to Slovenia.

• *Hungry? Straight ahead and down the stairs from the museum, look for the "Hot Horse" food kiosk, selling €4 horseburgers (no joke). A local institution, this is a popular place to get together with friends and neighbors. The giant, modern, blocky, light-blue building across the busy road is the* **Pivovarna Union**—*the brewery for Ljubljana's favorite brew.*

On your way back to the center, consider stopping by...

▲**The Skyscraper (Nebotičnik)**—This 1933 Art Deco building was the first skyscraper in Slovenia, for a time the tallest building in Central Europe, and one of the earliest European buildings that was clearly influenced by American architecture. The Skyscraper's top floor, which hosts a pricey restaurant, café, and observation deck, offers the best view of Ljubljana's skyline. Zip up in the elevator just to take a peek, or stay for a drink or meal. There are three levels: The best is the open-air, top-level terrace (floor #12—ride up to #11 and walk up the spiral stairs), where you can enjoy unobstructed views over the city and castle. While up on the terrace, you can enjoy a light meal (€4-9), cocktail (€5-8), or beer, wine, or coffee (€3). One floor below (#11) is the indoor club/lounge, with a similar menu. And on the next floor down is the restaurant (floor #10), with pricey food (€8-10 starters, €12-14 pastas, €20-24 main dishes) and less-impressive views. I'd skip the restaurant and the club, and just grab a drink or snack up on the terrace.

Cost and Hours: Free to ride the elevator up for a peek, but you should buy at least a drink if you want to stick around; terrace and club open Sun-Wed 9:00-1:00 in the morning, Thu-Sat 9:00-3:00 in the morning; restaurant open Mon-Sat 12:00-21:00, closed Sun; 2 blocks from Prešeren Square at Štefanova 1, tel. 040-601-787, www.neboticnik.si.

• *A few blocks south, near several Jože Plečnik sights (see next section) at the river end of French Revolution Square, you'll find the...*

▲**City Museum of Ljubljana (Mestni Muzej Ljubljana)**—This thoughtfully presented museum, located in the recently restored Auersperg Palace, offers a high-tech, in-depth look at the story of this city. You'll learn how Ljubljana has belonged to 10 different states over the last 200 years, ranging from the genteel Habsburg Empire to the oppressive Nazi regime to membership in the benevolent EU. You'll begin your visit in the cellar, with Roman ruins (including remains of the original Roman road and sewer system, found right here) and layers of medieval artifacts. You may see one of the museum's prize pieces, the world's oldest wooden wheel on an axle, dating from around 3200 B.C. and discovered in the Ljubljana marshlands (often not on display because it's incredibly fragile). Rounding out the collection is an evolving permanent collection and a range of temporary exhibits (generally on the second floor). Though everything is well-described in English (and touchscreens provide more information), a student on the museum's staff might be able to show you around if it's not too busy—ask.

Cost and Hours: €4, Tue-Sun 10:00-18:00, Thu until 21:00, closed Mon, kid-friendly, Gosposka 15, tel. 01/241-2500, www.mestnimuzej.si.

Nearby: Included in your ticket is an audio/videoguide that leads you on a walking tour to two nearby archaeological sites.

• *If visiting the museum, don't miss the nearby National and University Library and French Revolution Square—both described in the next section.*

South of Prešeren Square: Jože Plečnik's Architecture

Jože Plečnik is to Ljubljana what Antoni Gaudí is to Barcelona: a homegrown and amazingly prolific genius who shaped his town with a uniquely beautiful vision. And, as in Barcelona, Ljubljana has a way of turning people who couldn't care less about architecture into Plečnik fans. There's plenty to see. In addition to the

Triple Bridge, the riverside market, and the sights listed here, Plečnik designed the embankments along the Ljubljanica and Gradaščica Rivers in the Trnovo neighborhood; the rebuilt Roman wall along Mirje street, south of the center; the Church of St. Francis, with its classicist bell tower; St. Michael's Church on the Marsh; Orel Stadium; Žale Cemetery; and many more buildings throughout Slovenia.

Some of the best Plečnik sights are near the river, just south of Congress and Prešeren squares. I've linked them up in the order of a short self-guided walk.

• *From Prešeren Square, stroll south along the river. After the plain wooden bridge called the "Ugly Duckling," you'll come to the...*

▲**Cobblers' Bridge (Čevljarski Most)**—Named for the actual cobblers (shoemakers) who set up shop along the river in olden times, the bridge encapsulates

Plečnik's style perhaps better than any other structure: simple, clean lines adorned with classical columns. Ideal for people-watching (with the castle hovering scenically overhead), this is one of Ljubljana's most appealing spots.

• *Continue past the Cobblers' Bridge on the right side of the river, past the fountain. After about a block, turn right up the parked-up street called Novi trg. At the top of this street, on the left, is a red-brick building embedded with gray granite blocks in an irregular checkerboard pattern. This is the...*

▲▲**National and University Library (Narodna in Univerzitetna Knjižnica, or NUK)**—Widely regarded as Plečnik's masterpiece, this building is a bit underwhelming...until an under-

standing of its symbolism brings it to life. On the surface, the red-and-gray color scheme evokes the red soil and chunks of granite of the Karst region, south of Ljubljana. But on a deeper level, the library's design conveys the message of overcoming obstacles to attain knowledge. The odd-sized and -shaped blocks in the facade represent a complex numerological pattern that suggests barriers on the path to enlightenment. The sculpture on the river side is Moses—known for leading his people through 40 years of hardship to the Promised Land. On the right side of the building, find the horse-head doorknobs—representing the winged horse Pegasus (grab hold, and he'll whisk you away to new levels of enlightenment). Step inside. The main staircase is dark and gloomy—modeled after an Egyptian tomb. But at the top, through the door marked *Velika Čitalnica*, is the bright, airy main reading room: the ultimate goal, a place of learning. The top-floor windows are shaped roughly like open books.

Aside from being a great work of architecture, the building also houses the most important library in Slovenia, with more than two million books (about one per Slovene). The library is supposed to receive a copy of each new book printed in the country. In a freaky bit of bad luck, this was the only building in town damaged in World War II, when a plane crashed into it. But the people didn't want to see their books go up in flames—so hundreds of locals formed a human chain, risking life and limb to save the books from the burning building.

Cost and Hours: Free, staircase open Mon-Fri 9:00-20:00, Sat 9:00-14:00, closed Sun. The quiet main reading room is officially open for visitors only during very limited hours (mid-July-mid-Aug Mon-Fri 14:00-20:00). If you're not here during that one-month span, and you're really determined to see it, you can go up the stairs and try sticking close to a student going inside the reading room—but note that the guards frown on uninvited visitors. To get out, follow another student or push gently on the door (it'll likely open easily).

• *Directly behind the library is a mellow square with an obelisk in the middle. This is...*

French Revolution Square (Trg Francoske Revolucije)—Plečnik designed the **obelisk** in the middle of the square to commemorate Napoleon's short-lived decision to make Ljubljana the capital of his Illyrian Provinces. It's rare to find anything honoring Napoleon outside of Paris, but he was good to Ljubljana. Under his rule, Slovenian culture flourished, schools were established, and roads and infrastructure were improved. The monument contains ashes of the unknown French soldiers who died in 1813, when the region went from French to Austrian control.

The Teutonic Knights of the Cross established the nearby **monastery** (Križanke, ivy-capped wall and gate, free entry) in 1230. The adaptation of these monastery buildings into the Ljubljana Summer Theatre was Plečnik's last major work (1950-1956).

• *From here, it's a scenic 10-minute walk to the next sight. From the*

Jože Plečnik
(1872-1957)

There is probably no other single architect who has shaped one city as Jože Plečnik (YOH-zheh PLAYCH-neek) shaped Ljubljana. From libraries, office buildings, cemeteries, and stadiums to landscaping, riverside embankments, and market halls, Plečnik left his mark everywhere. While he may not yet register very high on the international Richter scale of important architects, the Slovenes' pride in this man's work is understandable.

Plečnik was born in Ljubljana and trained as a furniture designer before his interest turned to architecture. He studied

in Vienna under the Secessionist architect Otto Wagner. His first commissions, done around the turn of the 20th century in Vienna, were pretty standard Art Nouveau stuff. Then Tomáš Masaryk, president of the new nation of Czechoslovakia, decided that the dull Habsburg design of Prague Castle could use a new look to go with its new independence. But he didn't want an Austrian architect; it had to be a Slav. In 1921, Masaryk chose Jože Plečnik, who sprinkled the castle grounds with his distinctive

touches. By now, Plečnik had perfected his simple, eye-pleasing style, which mixes modern and classical influences, with lots of columns and pyramids—simultaneously austere and playful.

By the time Plečnik finished in Prague, he had made a name

obelisk, walk down Emonska toward the twin-spired church. You'll pass (on the left) the delightful Krakovo district—a patch of green countryside in downtown Ljubljana. Many of the veggies you see in the riverside market come from these carefully tended gardens. When you reach the Gradaščica stream, head over the bridge (also designed by Plečnik) and go around the left side of the church to find the house.

▲▲**Jože Plečnik House (Plečnikova Zbirka)**—Ljubljana's favorite son lived here from 1921 until his death in 1957. He added on to an existing house, building a circular bedroom for himself and filling the place with bric-a-brac he designed, as well as artifacts, photos, and gifts from around the world that inspired him as he shaped Ljubljana. Living a sim-

LJUBLJANA

for himself. His prime years were spent creating for the Kingdom of Yugoslavia (before the ideology-driven era of Tito). Plečnik returned home to Ljubljana and set to work redesigning the city, both as an architect and as an urban planner. He lived in a humble house behind the Trnovo Church (now a tourable and recommended museum), and on his walk to work every day, he pondered ways to make the city even more livable. Wandering through town, notice how thoughtfully he incorporated people, nature, the Slovenian heritage, town vistas, and symbolism into his works—it's feng shui on a grand urban scale.

For all of Plečnik's ideas that became reality, even more did not. After World War II, the very religious Plečnik fell out of favor with the new communist government and found it more difficult to get his projects completed. (It's fun to imagine how this city might look if Plečnik had always gotten his way.) After his death in 1957, Plečnik was virtually forgotten by Slovenes and scholars alike. His many works in Ljubljana were taken for granted.

But in 1986, an exposition about Plečnik at Paris' Pompidou Center jump-started interest in the architect. Within a few years, Plečnik was back in vogue. Today, scholars laud him as a genius who was ahead of his time...while locals and tourists enjoy the elegant simplicity of his works.

ple, almost monastic lifestyle, Plečnik knew what he liked, and these tastes are mirrored in his house.

Today the house is decorated exactly as it was the day Plečnik died, containing much of his equipment, models, and plans. The house can be toured only with a guide, whose enthusiasm brings the place to life. There are very few barriers, so you are in direct contact with the world of the architect. Still furnished with unique, Plečnik-designed furniture, one-of-a-kind inventions, and favorite souvenirs from his travels, the house paints an unusually intimate portrait of an artist.

While the house initially underwhelms some visitors, it's a ▲▲▲ pilgrimage for those who get caught up in Ljubljana's idiosyncratic sense of style. As you tour the place, be patient. Listen to its stories. Appreciate the subtle details. Notice how reverently your guide (and other Slovenes) speak of this man. Contrast the humbleness of Plečnik's home with the dynamic impact he had on the cityscape of Ljubljana and the cultural heritage of Slovenia. Wandering Plečnik's hallways, it's hard not to be tickled by this man's sheer creativity and by the unique world he forged for himself to live in. As a visitor to his home, you're in good company. He invited only his closest friends here—except during World War II, when Ljubljana was occupied by Nazis and the university was closed, Plečnik allowed his students to work with him here.

Possible Closure: As the house is slated to be closed for restoration sometime soon, it's important to ask the TI, check the website, or call the museum to be sure it's open before making the trek out here.

Cost and Hours: €4, Tue-Thu 10:00-18:00, Sat 9:00-15:00, 45-minute English tours begin at the top of each hour, last tour departs one hour before closing, closed Sun-Mon and Fri, Karunova 4, tel. 01/280-1600, www.mgml.si, info@mgml.si. It's well-run by Ana and Natalija, who sometimes lead the tours.

Getting There: It's directly behind the twin steeples of the Trnovo Church. The 15-minute stroll from the center—the same one Plečnik took to work each day—is nearly as enjoyable as the house itself. You can either walk south along the river, then turn right onto Gradaška and stroll along the stream to the church; or, from French Revolution Square, head south on Emonska. Either way, you'll pass through the garden-patch district of Krakovo, where pea patches and characteristic Old World buildings gracefully cohabitate. On the way to or from the museum, consider getting a meal in Krakovo (three restaurants—Pri Škofu, Manna, and Harambaša—are described later, under "Eating in Ljubljana").

Museums in Metelkova, Northeast of Prešeren Square

These three museums, about a 10-minute walk northeast of Prešeren Square in the dull but up-and-coming district of Metelkova, face each other on a slick modern plaza next to the park called Tabor.

▲▲**Slovenian Ethnographic Museum (Slovenski Etnografski Muzej)**—Housed in a brand-new facility, this delightful museum is Ljubljana's most underrated attraction. With both permanent and temporary exhibits, the museum strives to explain what it is to be Slovene, with well-presented and well-described cultural artifacts from around the country. If you've caught the Slovenian folk culture itch, this is the place to scratch it.

Cost and Hours: €4.50, free last Sun of month, Tue-Sun 10:00-18:00, closed Mon, great café, Metelkova 2, tel. 01/300-8745, www.etno-muzej.si.

Touring the Museum: The ground and first floors have good temporary exhibits, while upstairs you'll find two permanent exhibits.

The best exhibit, filling the third floor, is called **"Between Nature and Culture."** As you exit the elevator, turn left and consider the surprisingly frank exhibit that acknowledges the shortsighted tendency for museum curators—including at this museum—to emphasize things that are foreign or different. Continue through collections of "Distant Worlds" (non-European cultures) to reach the core of the collection, which focuses on Slovenia. A good but slow-moving film visits the country's four major regions. Another exhibit ponders how people half a world away—in Slovenia and in North America—simultaneously invented a similar solution (snowshoes) for a common problem. One display deconstructs Slovenian clichés (including this country's odd fascination with its traditional hayracks). The arrangement of the collection emphasizes the evolution of an increasingly complicated civilization, from basic farming tools to ceramics to modern technology. The children's "Ethnoalphabet" area features an A-to-Ž array of engaging, hands-on activities.

The other permanent exhibit, on the second floor (from the elevator, turn left to find the entrance), is called **"I, We, and Others."** A bit too conceptual for its own good, this heady exhibit ponders the notion of belonging. Designed for Slovenes more than foreigners (with very limited posted English information—borrow the free English audioguide from the ticket desk before heading up), it considers various aspects of how people define who they are, from individual and family to community and nation. Videos and sounds enhance the exhibits, and the curators neatly juxtapose well-known icons from different cultures (such as various national parliament buildings) in thought-provoking ways. While it's easy to get lost amid the navel-gazing, there is something particularly poignant about this topic here in the identity-obsessed Balkans.

Slovenian National Museum-Metelkova (Narodni Muzej Slovenije)—Next door to the Ethnographic Museum is this facility, where items from the Slovenian National Museum that were formerly tucked away in storage are now displayed on two floors. The very pretty historical bric-a-brac is neatly presented without much context—it's just an excuse to get a bunch of interesting stuff out into public view. Each room has a different collection: furniture, pottery and ceramics, church vestments, weapons and armor, and more. The painting gallery is nicely organized by century and style. Everything's labeled in English, and on weekday afternoons (after 15:00) and all day on weekends, a guide can show you around, if they're not too busy.

Cost and Hours: €3, Tue-Sun 10:00-18:00, closed Mon, Maistrova 1, tel. 01/230-7032.

Contemporary Art Museum—This brand-new collection, featuring changing exhibitions of present-day, mostly Slovenian artists, is scheduled to open next to the National Museum in 2012.

Shopping in Ljubljana

Ljubljana, with its easygoing ambience and countless boutiques, is made to order for whiling away an afternoon shopping. It's also a fun place to stock up on souvenirs and gifts for the folks back home. Popular items include wood carvings and models (especially of the characteristic hayracks that dot the countryside), different flavors of schnapps (the kind with a whole pear inside—cultivated to actually grow right into the bottle—is considered a particularly classy gift), honey mead brandy (*medica*—sweet and smooth), and those adorable painted panels from beehives (described on page 592). Rounding out the list of traditional Slovenian items are wrought-iron products from Kropa, crystal from Rogaska, lace from Idrija, salt from Piran, and Peko shoes (similar to high-fashion Italian models, but cheaper; the name is an abbreviation of its founder's name: Peter Kozina).

Souvenirs: The most atmospheric trinket-shopping is in the first stretch of the **market colonnade,** along the riverfront next to the Triple Bridge (described earlier, under "Sights in Ljubljana"). If you're looking for serious handicrafts rather than trinkets, drop by the **Rustika** gallery, just over the Triple Bridge (on the castle side). In addition to beehive panels, they also have lace, painted chests and boxes, and other tasteful local-style mementos (daily 9:00-20:00, Stritarjeva 9, mobile 031-459-509). There's another Rustika location up at the castle courtyard. **Kraševka** sells high-quality artisanal products (mostly foods) from the Karst region, and also acts as a sort of information office for that area (Mon-Fri 9:00-19:00, Sat 9:00-15:00, closed Sun, Ciril-Metodov trg 10, tel. 01/232-1445). A somewhat more downscale souvenir shop with a wide variety is **Dom Trgovina,** with two locations: One is a block across the Triple Bridge from Prešeren Square and facing the Town Hall (Mon-Fri 9:00-19:00, Sat 9:00-15:00, closed Sun, Mestni trg 24, tel. 01/241-8390), and the other is across from the TI on the main market square (Mon-Fri 8:00-19:00, Sat 8:00-15:00, closed Sun, Ciril-Metodov trg 5).

Boutiques and Galleries: Of the many fun and funky boutique streets in town, my two favorites are along the main drag through the **Old Town** (Mestni trg/Stari trg/Gornji trg), and along **Trubarjeva street,** a block up from the river (easy to find from Prešeren Square).

Sleeping in Ljubljana

Ljubljana has a good range of accommodations in all price ranges. I've focused my listings in or within easy walking distance of the city center. To get the best value, book ahead. The most expensive hotels raise their prices even more during conventions (Sept-Oct, and sometimes also June). The TI can give you a list of cheap private rooms *(sobe)*. To locate the following accommodations, see the map on page 518.

   $$$ *Boutique Hotels in the Old Town:* Three similar (but unrelated), expensive boutique hotels cluster idyllically on a cobbled square in Ljubljana's Old Town. While a bit overpriced (catering to deep-pocketed business travelers), they offer Old World charm with upscale touches (the rates listed are for May-mid-June and Sept-Oct, followed by mid-June-Aug, then Nov-April). **Hotel Angel,** part of the Lesar group, has 12 rooms with crisp white decor and hardwoods (Db-€165/€120/€110, pricier suites, air-con, free Wi-Fi, Gornji trg 7, tel. 01/425-5089, www.angelhotel.si, info@angelhotel.si). **Allegro Hotel** has a musical theme and 16 rooms around a checkerboard-tiled garden courtyard (classic Db-€140/€130/€100, superior Db-€170/€150/€120, air-con, free Internet access and Wi-Fi, Gornji trg 6, tel. 059/119-620, www.allegrohotel.si, info@allegrohotel.si). The family-run **Antiq Hotel** has 16 idiosyncratically decorated rooms sprawling through two buildings with lots of stairs and a mazelike floor plan (small S-€80, Sb-€125-145, small D-€120, Db-€157-180, price depends

---

Sleep Code

(€1 = about $1.40, country code: 386, area code: 01)
S = Single, **D** = Double/Twin, **T** = Triple, **Q** = Quad, **b** = bathroom. Unless otherwise noted, credit cards are accepted and breakfast is included, but the modest tourist tax (about €1 per person, per night) is not. Everyone listed here speaks English.

   To help you easily sort through these listings, I've divided the accommodations into three categories based on the price for a double room with bath during high season:

   $$$ Higher Priced—Most rooms €110 or more.
   $$ Moderately Priced—Most rooms between €70-110.
   $ Lower Priced—Most rooms €70 or less.

   Prices can change without notice; verify the hotel's current rates online or by email. For other updates, see www.ricksteves.com/update.

on size, air-con, free Internet access and Wi-Fi, some rooms have low beams and doors, Gornji trg 3, tel. 01/421-3560, fax 01/421-3565, www.antiqhotel.eu, info@antiqhotel.eu).

$$$ Cubo Hotel is a jolt of trendy minimalism on Ljubljana's hotel scene. Its 26 rooms are the best place in town for sleek, mod elegance. Choose between streetside rooms, which enjoy castle views but get some traffic noise, or quieter courtyard rooms (very flexible rates but generally Sb-€135, Db-€140-180, palatial suite-€200-250, cheaper off-season, non-smoking, air-con, elevator, free Wi-Fi, Slovenska cesta 15, tel. 01/425-6000, fax 01/425-6020, www.hotelcubo.com, reception@hotelcubo.com).

$$$ Grand Hotel Union is Ljubljana's top address, as much an Art Nouveau landmark as a hotel. You'll pay dearly for its Old World elegance, hundred years of history, professional staff, big pool, and perfect location (right on Prešeren Square). While their rack rates are outrageously high, you can often snare a great deal in the summer (July-Aug), winter, and on many weekends. The 194 plush "Executive" rooms are in the main building (official rates: Sb-€194, Db-€224; in slow times maybe as low as Sb-€110, Db-€120; non-smoking floors, air-con, elevator, free Wi-Fi, Miklošičeva cesta 1, tel. 01/308-1877, fax 01/308-1015, www.gh-union.si, hotel.union@gh-union.si). Its 133 "Business" rooms next door are not as luxurious, almost as expensive, and a lesser value (official rates: Sb-€178, Db-€208; same potential deals as "Executive" rooms, non-smoking floors, air-con, elevator, free cable Internet, Miklošičeva cesta 3, tel. 01/308-1170, fax 01/308-1914, www.gh-union.si, hotel.business@gh-union.si). Both branches have access to parking (€17/day), as well as a pool and sauna on the top floor of the Business branch, and a free Internet terminal in the Executive branch. Because of a noisy nearby disco, request a quieter room at either building if you're here on a weekend.

$$$ Central Hotel, technically part of the Grand Hotel Union up the street, has 74 rooms similar to (but slightly smaller than) the "Business" rooms at the main hotel, but cheaper and in a friendlier, less-pretentious package. The hotel is conveniently situated between Prešeren Square and the train station (official rates: Sb-€139, Db-€167; much lower prices likely July-Aug, in winter, and on weekends—maybe as low as Sb-€75, Db-€90; extra bed-€27, non-smoking rooms, air-con, elevator, free Internet access and cable Internet, parking garage-€19/day, Miklošičeva cesta 9, tel. 01/308-4300, fax 01/230-1181, www.centralhotel.si, central.hotel@gh-union.si).

$$ Slamič B&B has 11 modern rooms with hardwood floors, tasteful decor, and absentee management. Over an upscale café in a nondescript neighborhood, this is a fine spot for affordable elegance (Sb-€65-75, Db-€95-99, price depends on size; suite:

Sb-€135, Db-€165; air-con, lots of stairs with no elevator, free Wi-Fi, Kersnikova 1, tel. 01/433-8233, fax 01/433-8022, www .slamic.si, info@slamic.si). As the café hours are limited (Mon-Thu 7:30-22:00, Fri 7:30-21:00, Sat 9:00-16:00, closed Sun), clearly communicate your arrival time.

$$ Hotel Pri Mraku has 35 comfortable, slightly overpriced rooms in a pleasant neighborhood near French Revolution Square. While it's a bit rough around the edges and not without its quirks, this trusty old place is my sentimental favorite in Ljubljana (Sb-€73, Db-€106, ground-floor and top-floor rooms have air-con and cost €4-5 extra, 8 percent discount for Rick Steves readers if you reserve ahead, extra bed-€23, cheaper mid-Oct-April, non-smoking floor, elevator, free Internet access and Wi-Fi, lunch restaurant with terrace under an old vine, Rimska 4, tel. 01/421-9650, fax 01/421-9655, www.daj-dam.si, hotelmrak@daj-dam.si).

$$ Hotel Emonec (eh-MOH-nets), with some of the most centrally located cheap beds in Ljubljana, hides just off Wolfova lane between Prešeren and Congress squares. Its 41 sleek rooms—in two buildings across a courtyard from each other—feel institutional and characterless, with tight bathrooms and a shoestring staff, but the price and location are hard to beat. As it's near a noisy disco, light sleepers should try requesting a quiet room (Sb-€64, small Db-€67, bigger "standard" Db-€77, Tb-€90-96, Qb-€105-111, price depends on demand, cheaper Nov-April, pay Internet access, free Wi-Fi in some areas, free cable Internet in rooms, free loaner bikes for guests, Wolfova 12, tel. 01/200-1520, fax 01/200-1521, www.hotel-emonec.com, hotelemonec@siol.net).

$ B&B Petra Varl offers comfortable, affordable, nicely appointed rooms on a courtyard across from the bustling riverside market. Petra, who's an artist and speaks good English, will help you feel at home. As this place is Ljubljana's top budget option, book early (Db-€60, extra bed-€10, includes kitchenette with basic do-it-yourself breakfast, cash only, air-con, free Wi-Fi, go into courtyard at Vodnikov trg 5 and look for *B&B* sign at 5A, mobile 041-389-470, petra@varl.si).

$ Penzion Pod Lipo has 10 rooms above a restaurant in a mostly residential area about a 12-minute walk from Prešeren Square. While the rooms are old and simple, it's thoughtfully run by Marjan (Db-€65, Tb-€75, Qb-€100, breakfast in restaurant-€3.50 extra, cash only, reception open 8:00-22:00, non-smoking, free Internet access, free cable Internet, guest kitchen, putting green on terrace, tel. 01/251-1683, mobile 031-809-893, www.penzion-podlipo.com, info@penzion-podlipo.com).

$ Stari Tišler ("Old Carpenter") is a good budget option in a characteristically old, time-warp house immersed in a commercial zone a 10-minute walk from Prešeren Square. Its four modern rooms—which are nicely appointed (with mod, colorful splashes) for this price range—share two toilets and one shower, keeping prices low. It's above a restaurant that's popular at lunchtime with local businesspeople (D-€50, T-€75, breakfast-€5, air-con, up 2 flights of stairs, free Wi-Fi, Kolodvorska 8, tel. 01/430-3370, www.stari-tisler.com, info@stari-tisler.com, Sandra).

$ Hotel Center (not to be confused with "Central Hotel," listed earlier) is a good value. Marko's eight small, modern rooms deliver on his promise of "three-star furnishings at two-star prices." While the location, just across Slovenska avenue from the main part of town, is convenient, this place suffers from noise—from the busy road on one side, and from the bar downstairs on the other...bring earplugs (Db-€60-66 depending on season, breakfast-€4.20, free Wi-Fi, down the passage at Slovenska cesta 51 and around back, mobile 041-263-347, www.hotelcenter.si, info@hotelcenter.si).

Hostels

Ljubljana has several good hostels. The ones listed here are particularly well-established.

$ Hostel Celica, a proud, innovative, and lively place, is funded by the city and run by a nonprofit student organization.

This former military prison's 20 cells *(celica)* have been converted into hostel rooms—each one unique, decorated by a different designer (tours of the hostel daily at 14:00). The top floor features more typical hostel rooms (each with its own bathroom, for 3-12 people). The building also houses an art gallery, tourist information,  Internet access and Wi-Fi, self-service laundry (€8/load), good restaurant, and shoes-off "Oriental café" (all prices listed are per person—cell rooms: S-€53-61, D-€28-32, T-€25-30; bed in top-floor rooms with bathrooms: 3- to 5-bed room-€25-30, 7-bed dorm-€23-27, 12-bed dorm-€21-25; price depends on demand—most expensive on June-Sept weekends, cheaper Nov-March; includes breakfast, sheets, towels, and tax; no curfew, non-smoking, bike and car rental, active excursions around Slovenia, Metelkova 8, a dull 15-minute walk to Prešeren Square, 8 minutes to the train station, tel. 01/230-9700, fax 01/230-9714, www.hostelcelica.com, recepcija@hostelcelica.com). Light sleepers take note: The hostel hosts live music events about two nights per week until around 24:00, but otherwise maintains "quiet time" after 23:00. However, the surrounding neighborhood—a bit run-down and remote, but safe—is a happening nightlife zone, which can make for noisy weekends.

$ Alibi Hostel, an official IYHF hostel creatively run by Gorazd, has two very different branches. For a grungy, funky backpacker-slumbermill scene, head for **Alibi CN27,** with 100 beds (including 20 private rooms). The rooms are colorful and scruffy, and it's ideally located right on Ljubljana's main riverfront-café drag. The imaginative graffiti murals—featuring a stripper with memorable piercings and a certain cowboy president—are guaranteed to offend just about anyone over 30 (dorm bed–€17, or €19 Fri-Sat; D–€50, or €60 Fri-Sat; includes sheets and tax, cheaper Oct-May, no breakfast, free Internet access and Wi-Fi, self-service laundry, lockers, Cankarjevo nabrežje 27, tel. 01/251-1244, www.alibi.si). When backpackers grow a bit older and more sedate, they're more interested in comfort than socializing—and it's time to head for **Alibi M14,** across the street from Grand Hotel Union, a few steps off Prešeren Square. With four small but well-appointed private rooms with private bathrooms, seven private rooms with shared baths, a 10-bed dorm (sharing one bathroom), and a pleasant kitchen—but not a lot of rowdy hangout areas—it's a good compromise (dorm bed–€15-19, €1 extra Fri-Sat; D–€40-50, €6 extra Fri-Sat; Db–€50-60, €6 extra Fri-Sat; cheaper Oct-May, includes sheets and towels, free Internet access and Wi-Fi, self-service laundry, lockers, Miklošičeva cesta 14, tel. 01/232-2770, www.alibi.si, m14@alibi.si).

Eating in Ljubljana

At this crossroads of cultures (and cuisines), Italian and French flavors are just as "local" as meat-and-starch Slovenian food. This cosmopolitan city also dabbles in other cuisines; you'll find Thai, Indian, Chinese, Mexican, and more. To locate these restaurants, see the map on page 518.

In the City Center

Gostilna As ("Ace"), tucked into a courtyard just off Prešeren Square, offers fish-lovers the best blowout in town. It's dressy, pricey, and pretentious (waiters ignore the menu and recommend what's fresh). Everything is specially prepared each day and beautifully presented. It's loosely based on the Slow Food model: Servings are small, and you're expected to take your time and order two or three courses (mostly fish and Italian, €6-15 starters, €18-30 main courses, daily 12:00-24:00, reservations smart, Čopova 5A, or enter courtyard with *As* sign near image of Julija on Wolfova, tel. 01/425-8822). For cheaper food from the same kitchen, eat at their attached **As Lounge.** This much livelier, more casual spot features drinks, €8-11 salads and sandwiches, €7-10 pastas, and €11-19 main courses. You'll sit in the leafy courtyard or the glassed-in winter garden (food served daily 12:00-23:00, longer hours for drinks). The courtyard also has a couple of other fun eateries—and, in the summer only, live music and a much-loved gelato stand.

Ribca ("Fish") hides under the first stretch of market colonnade near the Triple Bridge. This is your best bet for a relatively quick and cheap riverside lunch. Choose between the two straightforward menus: grilled fillets or fried small fish. With the fragrant fish market right next door, you know it's fresh. If you just want to enjoy sitting along the river below the bustling market, this is also a fine spot for a coffee or beer (€6-7 salads, €4 seafood salads, €4-8 main courses, €7.50 lunches, Mon-Fri 8:00-16:00, Sat 8:00-14:00, closed Sun).

Pri Vitezu is well-respected for its seasonal menu of classic Mediterranean dishes. It sits along the newly spiffed-up Breg embankment, just beyond the Cobblers' Bridge; sit out on the pedestrian mall, or in the Old World-elegant interior. This place is especially worth considering for its excellent-value €9 lunch special, which includes soup, salad bar, a main dish, and a dessert (available Mon-Fri, on Sat they have a €14 traditional Slovenian lunch; otherwise €10-18 starters, €14-28 main dishes, €40 five-course meal, Mon-Fri 11:00-23:00, Sat 12:00-22:00, closed Sun, Breg 18-20, tel. 01/426-6058).

Asian Fusion: **DaBuDa** is the best spot in Ljubljana for Asian cuisine, featuring good Thai dishes (salads, curries, wok meals, and noodles) in a very mod, dark-wood, split-level setting frequented by hip young professionals (good-value €6-7 lunch specials, €8-14 main courses at dinner, Mon-Fri 11:00-23:00, Sat-Sun 12:00-23:00, also a few outdoor tables, between Congress Square and Square of the Republic at Šubičeva 1A, tel. 01/425-3060).

Fast and Cheap: *Burek,* the typical Balkan phyllo-dough snack (see the "Balkan Flavors" sidebar on page 418), can be picked up at street stands around town. Most are open 24 hours and charge about €2 for a hearty portion. An easy choice is **Nobel Burek,** next to Miklošičeva cesta 30; but many locals prefer **Olimpija Burek,** around the corner at Pražakova 14 (across from the post office).

Pizzerias: Ljubljana has lots of great sit-down pizza places. Expect to pay €5-10 for an average-sized pie (wide variety of toppings). **Pizzeria Foculus,** tucked in a boring alleyway a few blocks up from the river, has a loyal local following, a happening atmosphere, an innovative leafy interior, a few outdoor tables, and Ljubljana's best pizza (over 50 types for €6-10, €6-8 salads, daily 11:00-24:00, just off French Revolution Square across the street from Plečnik's National and University Library at Gregorčičeva 3, tel. 01/251-5643). **Ljubljanski Dvor** enjoys the most convenient and scenic location of any pizzeria in town. On a sunny summer day, the outdoor riverside terrace is unbeatable. The interior has a simple pizza parlor downstairs (€5-11 pizzas and pastas), with a more refined dining room upstairs (selling the same pizzas and pastas, plus €12-20 Italian main courses; pizza parlor open daily 10:00-24:00, upstairs restaurant opens at 12:00, just 50 yards from Cobblers' Bridge at Dvorni trg 1, tel. 01/251-6555). Ljubljanski Dvor also has a handy, cheap pizza **take-out window** (go around back to the walk-up window on Congress Square, €2 slices to go, picnic in the park or down on the river—plenty of welcoming benches, Mon-Fri 7:00-24:00, Sat 9:00-24:00, Sun 12:00-24:00).

In the Old Town

The main drag through the Old Town (which starts at the Town Hall and changes names as it goes: Mestni trg, then Stari trg, then Gornji trg) is lined with inviting eateries. Tables spill into the cobbled pedestrian street, filled with happy diners. If you're at a loss for where to eat in town, stroll here to survey your options, then pick your favorite menu and ambience. As many restaurants along here are uniformly good, no one place really has the edge. One popular choice is **Julija,** with homey country-Slovenian decor inside, great outdoor seating, Mediterranean-Slovenian cuisine, and good €10 lunch deals (otherwise figure €8-12 starters, €12-19 main dishes, daily 12:00-22:00, Stari trg 9, tel. 01/425-6463). **Romeo,** across the street, is a lowbrow bar serving unexceptional Mexican food... but the name sure is clever (get it? "Romeo and Julija"). I've also enjoyed a great salad lunch at the **Čajna Hiša** teahouse (described later, under "Coffee, Tea, and Treats.")

Traditional Slovenian Food

Because Slovenes head into the countryside when they want traditional fare, Ljubljana isn't the best place to find authentic Slovenian grub. And, frankly, most visitors prefer the Mediterranean/international restaurants that are more common in the capital anyway. But you do have some good options in the city center.

Gostilna na Gradu, in the castle courtyard high above town, is your single best option for true Slovenian food in Ljubljana—if you don't mind going up to the castle to get it (the handy funicular costs €3 round-trip). Run by a well-respected chef, it serves up a seasonal menu of traditional flavors with modern flair. The portions are small, but the prices are surprisingly affordable. Choose between the dull vaulted interior, the glassed-in arcade, or the out-door tables. Reservations are recommended before you make the trip up here (€8-12 pastas, €6-15 main dishes, €30 five-course meal lets you sample several flavors, Sun-Fri 10:00-24:00, Sat 10:00-16:00, Grajska Planota 1, mobile 031-301-777).

Touristy but Acceptable Options: Two places near the market are easy and popular options for Slovenian dishes. Both of these places cater mostly to tourists—so don't expect top quality or a great value. **Sokol,** with brisk, traditionally clad waiters, fills a fun, sprawling Slovenian-village interior with jaunty polkas on the soundtrack and a very central location. It's in all the guidebooks and deluged by tourists, so don't expect an authentic experience (€9-21 main courses, a few veggie options, Mon-Sat 7:00-23:00, Sun 10:00-23:00, on castle side of Triple Bridge at Ciril-Metodov trg 18, tel. 01/439-6855). A few blocks away, across from the main market square, **Vodnikov Hram** has an Old World interior and outdoor tables overlooking a parking lot. While a variation on the same theme as Sokol, it's marginally less touristy, and has slightly lower prices (€7-8 pastas, €7-24 main courses, Mon-Sat 9:00-24:00, Sun 10:00-24:00, Vodnikov trg 2, tel. 01/234-5260).

In Krakovo

The Krakovo district—just south of the city center, where garden patches nearly outnumber simple homes—is a pleasant area to wander. It's also home to a trio of tasty restaurants. Consider combining a meal here with your trip to the Jože Plečnik House (which is just beyond Krakovo).

Pri Škofu ("By the Bishop") is a laid-back, informal place with mostly outdoor seating and a focus on freshness, serving international cuisine with a Slovenian flair. There's no menu—the waiter tells you what's good today...and it is. They'll ask what kind of pasta or meat you want, then help you narrow down your options (sauces, sides, etc.) to get to your ideal meal. This hidden gem is deliciously memorable and worth seeking out. Reservations are essential (creative €3 soups, €7-8 lunches, €7-23 main courses at dinner, homemade €3 desserts, Mon-Fri 10:00-24:00, Sat-Sun 12:00-24:00, Rečna 8, tel. 01/426-4508).

Manna, with artfully presented Slovenian-Mediterranean fusion cuisine, sits along the pleasant Gradaščica canal. The interior is pure Secession—the Gustav Klimt-era, early 20th-century, gold-accented Viennese style that was so influential in Ljubljana. I prefer the more artistic, café-like downstairs to the stuffy upstairs dining room, but the seating out front is hard to beat on a nice day (€12 lunch special Mon-Fri, otherwise €7-12 starters, €9-25 main dishes, Mon-Sat 12:00-24:00, closed Sun, Eipprova 1A, tel. 01/283-5294).

Harambaša is the closest thing to a ticket to Sarajevo. Serving Balkan grilled meats, this popular-with-students eatery has Bosnian-flavored decor, old pictures, and cuisine reminiscent of the Bosnian capital. For a refresher on the meat dishes, see "Balkan Flavors" on page 418. The menu is limited, which makes ordering easy. Their handy €7 *pola-pola* combo-plate—with lotsa meat combined with chopped onions, *kajmak* (a soft cheese spread), and *lepinja* (pita bread)—makes for a simple but filling lunch. Also consider the Bosnian coffee (a high-octane brew with "mud" at the bottom) and baklava. Vegetarians need not apply (€5-7 main courses, Mon-Fri 10:00-22:00, Sat 12:00-22:00, Sun 12:00-18:00, Vrtna 8, mobile 041-843-106).

Coffee, Tea, and Treats

Riverfront Cafés: Enjoying a coffee, beer, or ice-cream cone along the Ljubljanica River embankment (between the Triple and

Cobblers' bridges) is Ljubljana's single best experience—worth ▲▲▲. Tables spill into the street, and some of the best-dressed, best-looking students on the planet happily fill them day and night. (A common question from first-time visitors to Ljubljana: "Doesn't anybody here have a job?") This is some of the top people-watching in Europe. Rather than recommend a particular place (they're all about the same), I'll leave you to explore and find the spot with the breezy ambience you like best. When ordering, the easiest choice is a *bela kava*— "white coffee," basically a caffè latte.

Teahouse: If coffee's not your cup of tea, go a block inland to the teahouse **Čajna Hiša.** They have a shop (called "Cha") with over 100 varieties of tea, plus porcelain teapots and cups from all over (Mon-Fri 9:00-20:00, Sat 9:00-15:00, closed Sun). The café serves about 50 different types of tea, light food (including great salads), and desserts (€2-4 cakes and sandwiches, €7-9 salads, Mon-Fri 9:00-22:30, Sat 9:00-15:00 & 18:00-22:00, closed Sun, on the atmospheric main drag in the Old Town a few steps from Cobblers' Bridge at Stari trg 3, tel. 01/252-7010).

Cakes: **Zvezda Kavarna,** a trendy, central place at the bottom of Congress Square, is a local favorite for cakes, pastries, and ice cream (decadent €3-5 cakes, Mon-Sat 7:00-23:00, Sun 10:00-20:00, a block up from Prešeren Square at Wolfova 14, tel. 01/421-9090). **Abecedarium** (ah-beh-tseh-dah-ree-oom, like the alphabet) serves up delicious €4 Nutella-banana cake (and other food) with indoor or outdoor seating near the Triple Bridge. It's located in the oldest house in town, named for a work by one of Slovenia's greatest thinkers, who once lived in the house (daily 8:00-24:00, Ribji trg 2, tel. 01/426-9514).

Chocolates and Ice Cream: **Rustika** is a local chain that sells tasty homemade chocolates (€3.80/100 grams), cookies (including one kind with four different types of chocolate), and a wide variety of unusual and delicious artisan ice cream flavors. The menu changes from day to day, but highlights can include balsamic vinegar with vanilla or strawberry, very dark chocolate, Kanada (with maple syrup and walnuts), and Greek yogurt with honey and nuts. The handiest location is about an eight-minute walk from Prešeren Square, and comes with a delightful stroll along colorful Trubarjeva street (€1.20/scoop, ice cream available summer only, Mon-Fri 8:00-19:00, Sat 9:00-13:00, closed Sun, Trubarjeva 44, mobile 059-935-730). Don't confuse this sweet shop with the Rustika gift shop.

More Ice Cream: Ljubljana is known for its Italian gelato-style ice cream. You'll see fine options all along the Ljubljanica River embankment. Favorites include **Rustika,** the courtyard garden at **Gostilna As** (summer only), and **Zvezda Kavarna** (all described earlier).

Ljubljana Connections

As Slovenia's transportation hub, Ljubljana is well-connected to both domestic and international destinations. When checking schedules, be aware of name variations: In Slovene, Vienna is "Dunaj" and Budapest is "Budimpešta."

Getting to Croatia

To reach **Istria** by public transportation, you have two relatively straightforward options: In summer (June-late Sept), a direct bus departs Ljubljana for Rovinj once each day (around 13:45, 5.5 hours, €21, also stops en route in Piran and Poreč; off-season runs 2/week—generally Mon and Fri, departing 16:30). From mid-July through August, there's also a train connection to Pula (Thu-Sun only, 4.75 hours, transfer in Hrpelje-Kozina); once in Pula, you can connect by bus to other Istrian destinations. On off-season weekends, you might have to get creative (try connecting through Rijeka).

If connecting directly to Croatia's **Dalmatian Coast,** you have three options: Train to Zagreb (2.5 hours), where you can catch a cheap Croatia Air flight or a bus (see "Zagreb Connections" on page 82); take the long, once-daily train connection from Ljubljana to Split (9 hours, requires a change in Zagreb); or, much slower, take the train to Rijeka, then cruise on a boat down the coast from there.

By Train

From Ljubljana by Train to: **Lesce-Bled** (roughly hourly, 40-60 minutes—but bus is better because it goes right to Bled town center), **Postojna** (nearly hourly, 1 hour), **Divača** (close to Škocjan Caves and Lipica, nearly hourly, 1.75 hours), **Sežana** (close to Lipica, nearly hourly, 2 hours), **Piran** (direct bus is better—see below; otherwise allow 4 hours, train to Koper, 4/day, 2.5 hours; then bus to Piran, 7/day, 30 minutes), **Maribor** (hourly, 2-3 hours, more with a transfer in Zidani Most), **Ptuj** (3/day, 2.5 hours, more with transfer in Pragersko), **Zagreb** (7/day, 2.5 hours), **Rijeka** (2/day direct, 2.75 hours), **Pula** (1/day mid-July-Aug Thu-Sun only, 4.75 hours, transfer in Hrpelje-Kozina), **Split** (1/day, 9 hours, transfer in Zagreb), **Vienna** (that's *Dunaj* in Slovene, 1/day direct, 6 hours; otherwise 4/day with transfer in Maribor, 6-7 hours), **Budapest** (that's *Budimpešta* in Slovene; 2/day direct, 8-9 hours, other connections possible with 1-2 changes but complicated, night train departs Ljubljana around 1:50 in the morning), **Venice** (1/day with a change to a bus in Villach, 6.75 hours; bus may be faster—see www.drd.si), **Salzburg** (2/day direct, 4-5 hours, more with transfer in Villach), **Munich** (3/day direct, 6 hours, including 1 night train; otherwise transfer in Salzburg). Train info: tel. 01/291-3332, www.slo-zeleznice.si.

By Bus

The bus station is a low-profile building in front of the train station. Buses depart from the numbered stalls in the middle of the street. For any bus, you have to buy tickets at the bus station ticket windows or at the automated e-kart kiosk (pay with credit card or cash), not from the driver. For bus information, pick up one of the blue phones inside the station to be connected to a helpful English-speaking operator. Bus info: www.ap-ljubljana.si, toll tel. 1991 (about €0.75/minute).

By Bus to: **Bled** (Mon-Sat hourly—usually at the top of each hour, fewer on Sun, 1.25 hours, €6.30), **Postojna** (at least hourly, 1 hour, €6), **Divača** (close to Škocjan Caves and Lipica, about every 2-3 hours, 1.5 hours, €7.90), **Piran** (5/day Mon-Fri, 2/day Sat, 4/day Sun, 2.5 hours, €12), over the **Vršič Pass** to **Bovec** (1/day June-Sept, departs Ljubljana 6:30, arrives Bovec 10:45, €14, none Oct-May), **Rovinj** (1/day June-late Sept, departs Ljubljana around 13:45, 5.5 hours, €21; off-season: 2/week, generally Mon and Fri, departs 16:30), **Rijeka** (2/day in summer, sporadic off-season, 2.5 hours, €23), **Zagreb** (1/day Mon-Fri only, €12).

By Plane

Slovenia's only **airport** (airport code: LJU) is 14 miles north of Ljubljana, about halfway to Bled. Confusingly, the airport goes by three names: Ljubljana Airport (the international version); Brnik (for the town that it's near); and Jože Pučnik Airport (a politician for whom it was controversially renamed in 2007). Most flights are operated by Slovenia's national airline, Adria Airways (www .adria-airways.com), but additional flights are run by easyJet (www.easyjet.com), Wizz Air (www.wizzair.com), Czech Airlines (www.csa.cz), and others. If you need to kill time here, follow signs (around to the left as you exit the terminal) to *Razgledna Terasa* and *Terasa Avionček* and ride the elevator up to the rooftop terrace with a café (daily 9:00-19:00). Here you can sip a coffee while you watch planes land and take off. Airport info: tel. 04/206-1000, www.lju-airport.si.

Getting Between Downtown Ljubljana and the Airport: Two kinds of buses connect the airport with Ljubljana's bus station: **public bus** #28 (to the right as you exit the airport; Mon-Fri hourly until 20:00, only 7/day Sat-Sun, 45 minutes, €4.10), and a **minibus** (to the left as you exit the airport, scheduled to depart after various arriving flights—look for schedule posted near bus stop). Two different companies run the minibus transfers, which take about 30 minutes: Markun (€5 to train station, €9 to your hotel, mobile 041-792-865) and Marko Nowotny (€9 regardless of your destination, mobile 040-771-771, www.mnj.si). I'd take whichever one is departing first. For a transfer *to* the airport, your hotel or any TI can make arrangements with one of these companies a day or so in advance (same price). Unfortunately, certain evening arrivals don't coordinate well with either the bus or the minibus, so you might have to wait a while or take a pricey **taxi** (figure €20-25 to the airport if you call a reputable company, but more like €42 *from* the airport—since you have to use the pricey taxi stand out front).

The Austrian Alternative: Since Ljubljana's airport is the only one in the country (and thus charges extremely high taxes and airport fees), many Slovenes prefer to fly out of Austria. The airport in **Klagenfurt** (airport code: KLU, also known as "Alpe-Adria Airport"), just over the Austrian border to the north, is subsidized by the local government to keep prices low and compete with Ljubljana's airport. Especially if you're connecting to Bled, it's somewhat handy to reach (from Ljubljana or Bled, take the train to Villach, then to Klagenfurt's Annabichl station, which is a 5-minute walk from the airport; total trip 3 hours from Ljubljana, or 2 hours from Bled; www.klagenfurt-airport.com). A taxi transfer to Bled runs a hefty €120 and takes about an hour (see "By Taxi" on page 570). Austrian Airlines (www.austrian.com) flies from Klagenfurt, as do low-cost carriers such as Ryanair (www .ryanair.com), TUIfly (www.tuifly.com), Germanwings (www .germanwings.com), and Air Berlin (www.airberlin.com).

LAKE BLED

Lake Bled—Slovenia's leading mountain resort—comes complete with a sweeping alpine panorama, a fairy-tale island, a cliff-hanging medieval castle, a lazy lakeside promenade, and the country's most sought-after desserts. There are few more enjoyable places to simply be on vacation.

Since the Habsburg days, Lake Bled (locals pronounce it "blayd") has been *the* place where Slovenes wow visiting diplomats. Tito had one of his vacation homes here (today's Hotel Vila Bled), and more recent visitors have included Prince Charles, Madeleine Albright, and Laura Bush. But above all, Lake Bled feels like a place that Slovenes enjoy alongside their visitors.

Lake Bled has plenty of ways to idle away an afternoon. While the lake's main town, also called Bled, is more functional than quaint, it offers postcard views of the lake and handy access to the region. Hike up to Bled Castle for intoxicating vistas. Make a wish and ring the bell at the island church. Wander the dreamy path around the lake. Sit on a dock, dip your feet in the water, and feed some of the lake's resident swans. Then dive into some of Bled's famous cakes while you take in the view of Triglav, Slovenia's favorite mountain (see "Mount Triglav" sidebar on page 605). Bled quiets down at night—there's no nightlife beyond a handful of pubs—giving hikers and other holiday-makers a chance to recharge. Bled is also a great jumping-off point for a car trip through the Julian Alps (see next chapter).

Planning Your Time

Bled and its neighboring mountains deserve two days. With one day, spend it in and around Bled (or, to rush things, spend the morning in Bled and the afternoon day-tripping). With a second day and a car, drive through the Julian Alps using the self-guided tour in the next chapter. The circular route takes you up and over the stunning Vršič Pass, then down the scenic and historic Soča River Valley. Without a car, skip the second day, or spend it doing nearby day trips: Bus or bike to Radovljica to see the bee museum, hike to Vintgar Gorge, or visit the more rustic Lake Bohinj (all described under "Near Lake Bled," later in this chapter).

Orientation to Lake Bled

(area code: 04)

The town of Bled is on the east end of 1.5-mile-long Lake Bled. The lakefront is lined with cafés and resort hotels. A 3.5-mile path meanders around the lake. As no motorized boats are allowed, Lake Bled is particularly peaceful.

The tourists' center of Bled is a cluster of big resort hotels, dominated by the giant, red Hotel Park (dubbed the "red can"). The busy street called **Ljubljanska cesta** leads out of Bled town toward Ljubljana and most other destinations. Just up from the lakefront, across Ljubljanska cesta from Hotel Park, is the modern **commercial center** (Trgovski Center Bled), with a travel agency, grocery store, ATM, shops, and a smattering of lively cafés. Nicknamed "Gaddafi" by the people of Bled, the commercial center was designed for a Libyan city, but the deal fell through—so the frugal Slovenes built it here instead. Just up the road from the commercial center, you'll find the post office and library (with Internet access).

Bled's less-touristy Old Town is under the castle, surrounding the pointy spire of St. Martin's Church. There you'll find the bus station, some good restaurants, a few hostels, and more locals than tourists.

The mountains poking above the ridge at the far end of the lake are the Julian Alps, crowned by the three peaks of Mount Triglav. The big mountain behind the town of Bled is Stol ("Chair"), part of the Karavanke range that defines the Austrian border.

Tourist Information

Bled's helpful TI is in the long, lakefront casino building across the street from the big, red Hotel Park (as you face the lake, the TI is hiding around the front at the far left end, overlooking the lake). Pick up the good map (with the lake on one side and the whole

Lake Bled

To Podhom & Vintgar Gorge
To Zasip

Ⓟ **Pletna Boat Dock**
Ⓡ **Rowboat Rental**

Recika River

CESTA V VINTGAR

634

RECIŠKA CESTA

KOLODVORSKA CESTA

See Bled Town Detail Map

PREŠERNOVA CESTA

BLED TOWN

CASTLE   CHURCH

To Lesce (Train Station), Radovljica & Ljubljana

BLED JEZERO STATION

ROWING CENTER

SWIMMING POOL

LJUBLJANSKA CESTA

COMMERCIAL CENTER

Lake   *Bled*

Bled Island

CHURCH OF THE ASSUMPTION

99 STEPS

Ⓟ

CAMP-GROUND

Ⓡ

SUMMER LUGE

ALP PENZION & ESSENSE SPA

▲ Mt. Straža

VILA BLED

CESTA SVOBODE

MLINO

ADVENTURE PARK

1 Kilometer

1/2 Mile

To Lake Bohinj   209

DEVA PURI GALLERY

LAKE BLED

region on the other) and the free Bled information booklet. Get advice on hikes and day trips, confirm transit schedules, and if you're doing any serious hiking, spring for a good regional map (July-Aug Mon-Sat 8:00-21:00, Sun 9:00-18:00; May-June and Sept-Oct Mon-Sat 8:00-19:00, Sun 11:00-17:00; Nov-April Mon-Sat 8:00-18:00, Sun 8:00-13:00; Cesta Svobode 10, tel. 04/574-1122, www.bled.si). The TI can give you a list of accommodations, and if they're not too busy, they may be able to call around to check availability for you (Kompas Bled travel agency has a room-booking service—see "Helpful Hints," later).

For more details on hiking in Triglav National Park, visit the **Triglav National Park Information Center** on the main road out of town (free information, maps and guidebooks for sale; May-Sept daily 10:00-18:00; Oct-April Mon-Fri 12:00-16:00, Sat-Sun 10:00-18:00; Ljubljanska cesta 27, tel. 04/578-0205, www.tnp.si).

Arrival in Bled

By Train: Two train stations have the name "Bled." The **Bled Jezero** ("Bled Lake") station is across the lake from Bled town and is used only by infrequent, slow, tourist-oriented trains into the mountains. You're much more likely to use the **Lesce-Bled** station

LAKE BLED

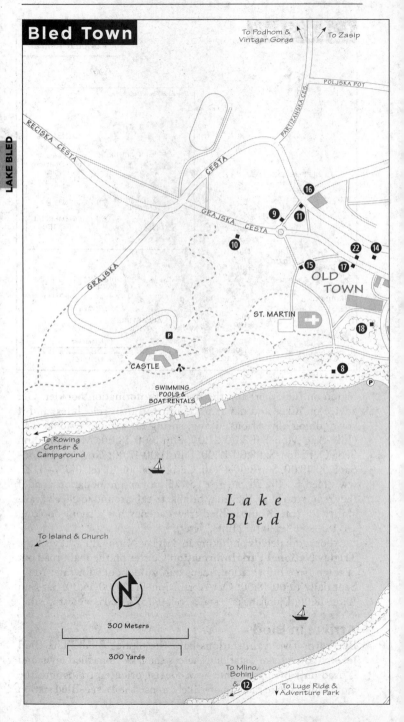

Bled Town

To Podhom &
Vintgar Gorge

To Zasip

POLJSKA POT

REČIŠKA CESTA

PARTIZANSKA CES.

CESTA

GRAJSKA CESTA

16

9   11

10

22   14

15   17

OLD
TOWN

GRAJSKA

ST. MARTIN

18

P

CASTLE

8

P

SWIMMING
POOLS &
BOAT RENTALS

To Rowing
Center &
Campground

To Island & Church

N

300 Meters

300 Yards

L a k e
B l e d

To Mlino,
Bohinj
&   12

To Luge Ride &
Adventure Park

LAKE BLED

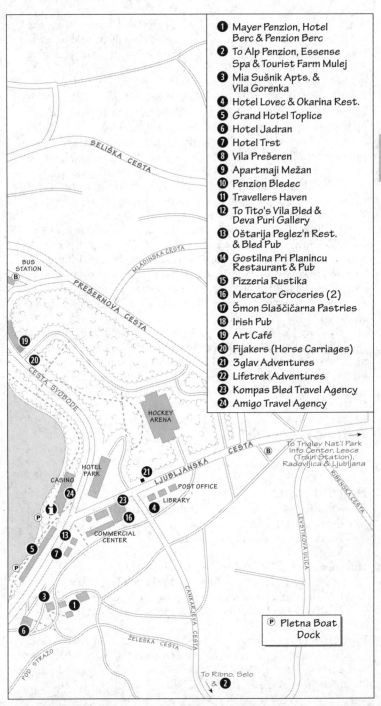

1. Mayer Penzion, Hotel Berc & Penzion Berc
2. To Alp Penzion, Essense Spa & Tourist Farm Mulej
3. Mia Sušnik Apts. & Vila Gorenka
4. Hotel Lovec & Okarina Rest.
5. Grand Hotel Toplice
6. Hotel Jadran
7. Hotel Trst
8. Vila Prešeren
9. Apartmaji Mežan
10. Penzion Bledec
11. Travellers Haven
12. To Tito's Vila Bled & Deva Puri Gallery
13. Oštarija Peglez'n Rest. & Bled Pub
14. Gostilna Pri Planincu Restaurant & Pub
15. Pizzeria Rustika
16. Mercator Groceries (2)
17. Šmon Slaščičarna Pastries
18. Irish Pub
19. Art Café
20. Fijakers (Horse Carriages)
21. 3glav Adventures
22. Lifetrek Adventures
23. Kompas Bled Travel Agency
24. Amigo Travel Agency

Ⓟ Pletna Boat Dock

in the nearby village of Lesce. The Lesce-Bled station is on the main line and has far better connections to Ljubljana and international destinations. So if you're buying a train ticket or checking schedules, request "Lesce-Bled" rather than just "Bled." (This is so important, I'll remind you again later.)

The small **Lesce-Bled station** is in the village of Lesce, about 2.5 miles from Bled. The nearest ATM is upstairs in the shopping center across the street (at the Gorenjska Banka on the third floor, across the parking lot from Mercator supermarket). From the Lesce station, you can take the bus into Bled town (2/hour, 10 minutes, €1.30, catch it across the street from the train station); or pay about €10 for a taxi into town. If taking the train out of Lesce-Bled, you can buy tickets at this station or on the train—nobody in Bled town sells tickets.

By Bus: Bled's main bus station is just up from the lake in the Old Town. To reach the lake, walk straight downhill on Cesta Svobode. Note that many buses also stop on the way into town, along Ljubljanska cesta; this stop is handier for walking to many of my recommended accommodations—though some bus drivers may not want to stop here (for details, see "Sleeping in Bled," later).

By Car: Coming from Ljubljana, you'll wind your way into Bled on Ljubljanska cesta, which rumbles through the middle of town before swinging left at the lake. There's a short-term parking lot just above the commercial center, but it's often full; for a longer stay, turn right at the traffic light by Gostilna Union to reach a larger lot that's not far from the lake (near the sports hall). If you're sleeping in town, ask your hotel about parking. Also see "Route Tips for Drivers" on page 587.

By Plane: For details on getting from Ljubljana's airport to Bled, see "Lake Bled Connections," later.

Helpful Hints

Money: Bled town's handiest ATMs are at **SKB Banka** (upstairs in round building at commercial center) and **Gorenjska Banka** (at far end of Hotel Park; this ATM does not accept Visa cards).

Internet Access: Most hotels offer free Internet access and/or Wi-Fi for their guests. In a pinch, the public library has terminals with fast access (free up to one hour per day, Mon-Fri 10:00-19:00, Sat 8:00-12:00, closed Sun, next to the post office on Ljubljanska cesta).

Post Office: If you're coming up from the lake on Ljubljanska cesta, it's just past the commercial center and library (Mon-Fri 8:00-19:00, Sat 8:00-12:00, closed Sun, slightly longer hours July-Aug, tel. 04/575-0200).

Bled and the Julian Alps Essentials

English	Slovene	Pronounced
Slovenia's Biggest Mountain	Triglav	TREE-glau
Lake Bled	Blejsko Jezero	BLAY-skoh YAY-zay-roh
The Island	Otok	OH-tohk
Bled Castle	Blejski Grad	BLAY-skee grahd
Town near Bled with Train Station	Lesce	lest-SEH
Town with Bee Museum	Radovljica	rah-DOH-vleet-suh
Gorge near Bled	Vintgar	VEENT-gar
Rustic Lake near Bled	Bohinj	BOH-heen
Scenic High-Mountain Pass	Vršič	vur-SHEECH
Historic River Valley	Soča	SOH-chah

Laundry: Most hotels can do laundry for you, but it's expensive (priced by the piece). You'll get a better deal from a can-do local, **Anže Štalc.** Call Anže to arrange drop-off (possibly at the Amigo travel agency, Cesta Svobode 15, next to the Casino), and pick it up cleaned and folded 24 hours later (€15/load, €5 more for same-day express service, mobile 041-575-522).

Car Rental: The Julian Alps are ideal by car. Several big chains rent cars in Bled—figure €60 per day, including tax, insurance, and unlimited mileage (generally no extra charge for drop-off elsewhere in Slovenia). Various major companies have branches in Bled, including **Europcar** (mobile 031-382-055), **Budget** (mobile 041-644-626), **Sixt** (mobile 030-645-350), **Hertz** (tel. 04/574-5588), and the local **Avantcar** (mobile 041-400-980); as the offices tend to move around, inquire in Bled about the current locations.

Travel Agency: Kompas Bled, in the commercial center, rents bikes, sells books and maps, offers a room-booking service (including many cheap rooms in private homes—though most are away from the lake), and sells various tours around the region (May-Sept Mon-Sat 8:00-19:00, Sun 8:00-12:00 & 16:00-19:00; Oct-April Mon-Sat 8:00-19:00, closed Sun; Ljubljanska cesta 4, tel. 04/572-7500, www.kompas-bled.si, kompas.bled@siol.net).

Massage: If you're here to relax, consider a massage at the **Essense** wellness center at the recommended Alp Penzion. This modern, classy facility—hiding in the countryside about a 15-minute walk or 5-minute taxi ride above the lake—offers a wide range of spa treatments, including pedicures and Thai massage. A standard 50-minute massage will run you about €36 (call first to arrange, Cankarjeva cesta 20A, tel. 04/576-7450, www.alp-penzion.com).

Getting Around Lake Bled (Literally)

By Bike: You can rent a mountain bike at the TI or at Kompas Bled travel agency (both listed earlier) for the same rates (€3.50/hour, €6/3 hours, €8/half-day, €11/day). The TI also has electric bikes, which give you a much-appreciated boost once you get them moving—well worth the small extra cost if you don't bike much (€5/1 hour, €10/4 hours, €15/8 hours). While walking around the lake is slo-mo bliss, biking it lets you fast-forward between the views of your choice. Biking is also a great way to reach Vintgar Gorge—perfect for combining a countryside pedal with a walk immersed in nature. For a longer pedal, ask for the TI's excellent biking map, with various great bike trips clearly marked and described. The bike path to the nearby town of Radovljica (and its bee museum) is about four miles one-way (get details at the TI).

By Horse and Buggy: Buggies called *fijakers* are the romantic, expensive, and easy way to get around the lake. Hire one along the lakefront between Hotel Park and the castle (around the lake-€40, one-way up to castle-€40, round-trip to castle with 30-minute wait time-€50, mobile 041-710-970).

By Tourist Train: A little train makes a circuit around the lake every 40 minutes in summer (€3, daily 9:00-21:00 in peak season, shorter hours off-season, weather-dependent, mobile 051-337-478).

By Tourist Bus: A handy but pricey shuttle bus passes through Bled once daily in summer. It leaves the bus station at 10:00, stops at a few hotels (including Grand Hotel Toplice), then goes up to the castle and on to the Vintgar Gorge entrance (€3.50 one-way to any stop, June-Sept only, confirm schedule at TI or bus station).

By Taxi: Your hotel can call a taxi for you. Or contact **Bled Tours,** run by friendly, English-speaking driver Sandi Demšar and his girlfriend Cvetka (€10 to the castle or to Lesce-Bled train station, €14 to Radovljica, €50 to Ljubljana airport, €120 to Klagenfurt airport in Austria, office at Ljubljanska cesta 19, mobile 031-205-611, www.bledtours.si, info@bledtours.si).

By Boat: For information on renting your own boat, see "Boating," page 577. For details on riding the characteristic *pletna* boats, see "Getting to the Island," page 574.

By Private Plane: If you have perfect weather and deep pockets, there's no more thrilling way to experience Slovenia's high-mountain scenery than from a small propeller plane soaring over the peaks. Flights depart from a grass airstrip near the village of Lesce, a 10-minute drive or taxi ride from Bled. Expensive...but unforgettable (€75 for 15-minute hop over Lake Bled only, €135 for 30-minute flight that also buzzes Lake Bohinj, €195 for deluxe 45-minute version around the summit of Triglav, arrange at least a day in advance, tel. 04/532-0100, www.alc-lesce.si, info@alc-lesce.si).

Tours at Lake Bled

Local Guides—**Tina Hiti** and **Sašo Golub,** an energetic young couple, are both excellent guides who enjoy sharing the town and region they love with American visitors. Hiring one of them can add immeasurably to your enjoyment and understanding of Bled and the surrounding area (€45/2-hour tour of Bled, arrange several days in advance, info@pg-slovenia.com, Tina's mobile 040-166-554, Sašo's mobile 040-524-774, www.pg-slovenia.com). Tina and Sašo are especially handy for side-tripping into the countryside if you don't want to drive yourself. I've spent great days with both of them and was thankful they were behind the wheel. Their most popular trip is a day in the Julian Alps (€150 round-trip from Bled, €180 to pick up or drop off in Ljubljana—these prices are for two people; it's more expensive for three or more people, since they have to rent a van), but they also offer many other options, including all-day shore excursions from the cruise port in Koper (€230 for a day visiting Ljubljana and Bled) and trips in the Slovenian countryside to research your roots (price depends on distance). As Tina and Sašo both lead tours for me in Europe—and have two young kids—they may send you off with a well-trained substitute, such as Tina's father, Gorazd, a former Yugoslav Olympian (in ice hockey) who brings the older generation's perspective to the trip.

Excursions—To hit several far-flung day-trip destinations in one go, you could take a package tour from Bled. Destinations range from Ljubljana and the Karst region to the Austrian Lakes to Venice. For example, an all-day Julian Alps trip to the Vršič Pass and Soča Valley runs about €36 per person (sold by various agencies, including Kompas Bled). This tour is handy, but two people can rent a car for the day for about the same price and do it at their own pace using the self-guided driving tour in the next chapter.

Adventure Trips—Various Bled-based companies specialize in taking tourists on active, outdoorsy excursions into the surrounding countryside and mountains. One popular, all-day trip is white-water rafting on the Soča River (around €90/person). Other options include canyoning, river tubing, mountain biking, paragliding, rock climbing, and more. Various outfits cluster near the commercial center; these include **3glav Adventures** (just above commercial center at Ljubljanska cesta 1, mobile 041-683-184, www.3glav-adventures.com), **Lifetrek Adventures** (near the bus station at Grajska 4, mobile 040-508-853, www.lifetrek-slovenia .com), and **Amigo** (next to the Casino at Cesta Svobode 15, tel. 05/597-3250, www.amigo.si). Note that these companies tend to attract a young, sometimes rowdy crowd that enjoys lubricating their adventures with alcohol.

Sights at Lake Bled

Bled doesn't have many "sights," but there are plenty of rewarding and pleasant activities.

▲▲▲**Walk Around the Lake**—Strolling the 3.5 miles around the lake is enjoyable, peaceful, and scenic. At a leisurely pace, it takes about an hour and a half...not counting stops to snap photos of the ever-changing view. On the way, you'll pass some great villas, mostly from the beginning of the 19th century. The most significant one was a former residence of Marshal Tito— today the Hotel Vila Bled, a fine place to stop for a coffee and pretend Tito invited you over for a visit (described next). For the more adventurous, hiking paths lead up into the hills surrounding the lake (ask TI for details and maps; or hike to Vintgar Gorge, described on page 588).

▲**Tito's Vila Bled**—Before World War II, this villa on Lake Bled was the summer residence for the Yugoslav royal family. When Tito ran Yugoslavia, the part-Slovene communist leader took over the place and had it renovated using plans from the architect Jože Plečnik. During his heyday, Tito entertained international guests here (big shots from the communist and non-aligned world, from Indira Gandhi to Nikita Khrushchev to Kim Il Sung to Raúl Castro). Since 1984, it's been a classy hotel and restaurant, offering guests grand Lake Bled views and James Bond ambience. The garden surrounding the villa is filled with exotic trees, brought here by Tito's guests from distant lands.

The terrace has a restaurant that welcomes visitors to drop in for a meal, a piece of cake, or just a cup of coffee. Tito fans might want to splurge for an overnight (standard Db-€230, tel. 04/575-3710, www.vila-bled.si). But even if you're not a guest here, the hotel's staff is generally tolerant of curious tourists poking around the public areas inside. From the marbled lobby, head upstairs. This is where Tito sympathizers have a nostalgic opportunity to

send an email from his desk, sip tea in his lounge, and gawk at his **Socialist Realist wall murals.** Those murals, decorating the upper walls of a vast ballroom on the second floor, are a fascinating peek at the propaganda of the time. Follow the rousing story of the origins of postwar Yugoslavia, starting on the upper left as you enter: First you see the Nazi destruction of Belgrade in 1941, a dark moment that inspired the South Slavs to band together to fight these foreign occupiers. See Tito raising his ragtag army, then leading them into pivotal battles in Bosnia-Herzegovina (notice the minaret and the destroyed bridge over the Neretva River), followed by a winter spent enduring hardship. At the end of this long wall, Tito's victorious Partisans crush the final vestiges of the Nazis; in the upper-right corner, the spring blossoms represent a promising future for the people of Yugoslavia. The large panel at the end of the room trumpets the idealized postwar world that Tito envisioned: proud workers from all walks of life coming together for the betterment of Yugoslavia. In the shadow of a mighty factory—a symbol of heavy industry, which communists embraced as the way of the future—notice that the ironworker and the farmer are holding hands in unity. The room's focal point is the mother hoisting a young child with one arm, and the flag of the nascent Socialist Federal Republic of Yugoslavia with the other.

Getting There: The villa is a 20-minute lakeside walk from the town of Bled at Cesta Svobode 26 (it's the big, white villa with the long staircase at the southern end of the lake, just beyond the village of Mlino). You can also ask your *pletna* gondolier to drop you off here after visiting the island. Those hiking around the lake will pass the gate leading up through Tito's garden to the restaurant and lobby.

▲▲**The Island (Otok)**—Bled's little island—capped by a super-

cute church—nudges the lake's quaintness level over the top. Locals call it simply "The Island" *(Otok).* While it's pretty to look at from afar, it's also fun to visit.

The island has long been a sacred site with

a romantic twist. On summer Saturdays, a steady procession of brides and grooms, cheered on by their entourages, heads for the island. Ninety-nine steps lead from the island's dock up to the Church of the Assumption on top. It's tradition for the groom to carry—or try to carry—his bride up these steps. About four out of five are successful (proving themselves "fit for marriage"). During the communist era, the church was closed, and weddings were outlawed here. But the tradition re-emerged—illegally—even before the regime ended, with a clandestine ceremony in 1989.

An eighth-century Slavic pagan temple dedicated to the goddess of love and fertility once stood here; the current Baroque ver-

sion (with Venetian flair—the bell tower is separate from the main church) is the fifth to occupy this spot. Go inside (€3, daily May-Sept 9:00-19:00, April and Oct until 18:00, Nov-March until 16:00) and find the rope for the church bell, hanging in the middle of the aisle just before the altar. A local superstition claims that if you can get this bell to ring three times with one big pull of the rope, your dreams will come true. Worth a try.

If you're waiting for a herd of tourists to ring out their wishes, pass the time looking around the front of the church. When the church was being renovated in the 1970s, workers dug up several medieval graves (you can see one through the glass under the bell rope). They also discovered Gothic frescoes on either side of the altar, including, above the door on the right, an unusual ecclesiastical theme: the *bris* (Jewish circumcision ritual) of Christ.

A café (with a WC) and souvenir shop (with an exhibit of nativity scenes) are near the church at the top of the steps.

To descend by a different route, walk down the trail behind the church, then follow the path around the island's perimeter back to where your *pletna* boat awaits.

Getting to the Island: The most romantic route to the island is to cruise on one of the distinctive *pletna* boats (€12 per person round-trip, includes 30-minute stay on the island; catch one at several spots around the lake—most convenient from in front of Grand Hotel Toplice or just below Hotel Park, might have to wait for more passengers to fill the boat; generally run from dawn, last boat leaves one hour before church closes—see hours above; replaced by enclosed electric boats in winter—unless the lake freezes, in which case there are no boats; mobile 031-316-575). Other places to catch a *pletna* include the village of Mlino, partway around the lake; the

Pletna Boats

The *pletna* is an important symbol of Lake Bled. In addition to providing a pleasant way to reach the island, these boats

also carry on a tradition dating back for generations. In the 17th century, Habsburg Empress Maria Theresa granted the villagers from Mlino—the little town along the lakefront just beyond Bled—special permission to ferry visitors to the island. (Since Mlino had very limited access to farmland, the people needed another source of income.) Mlino residents built their *pletnas* by hand, using a special design passed down from father to son for centuries—like the equally iconic gondolas of Venice. Eventually, this imperial decree and family tradition evolved into a modern union of *pletna* oarsmen, which continues to this day.

Today *pletna* boats are still hand-built according to that same centuries-old design. There's no keel, so the skilled

oarsmen work hard to steer the flat-bottomed boat with each stroke—boats piloted by an inexperienced oarsman can slide around on very windy days. There are 21 official *pletnas* on Lake Bled, all belonging to the same union. The gondoliers dump all of their earnings into one fund, give a cut to the tourist board, and divide the rest evenly among themselves. Occasionally a new family tries to break into the cartel, underselling his competitors with a "black market" boat that looks the same as the official ones. While some see this as a violation of a centuries-old tradition, others view it as good old capitalism. Either way, competition is fierce.

bottom of the grand staircase leading up to Vila Bled (it's a shorter trip from here—though the same cost—as it's much closer to the island); and at the campground. For more on these characteristic little vessels, see the "*Pletna* Boats" sidebar. You can also **rent your own boat** to row to the island (see "Boating," later). It's even possible to **swim** to the island, especially from the end of the lake nearest the island (see "Swimming," later), but you're not allowed into the church in your swimsuit. Guess you'll just have to go in naked.

▲**Bled Castle (Blejski Grad)**—Bled's cliff-hanging castle, dating in one form or another from 1,000 years ago, was the seat of the Austrian Bishops of Brixen, who controlled Bled in the Middle Ages. Today it's merely a fine tourist attraction with a little history and lots of big views. The various sights at the castle are more cute than interesting, but the real reason to come up here is to bask in the sweeping panoramas over Lake Bled and the surrounding mountainscapes.

Cost and Hours: €8, daily May-Oct 8:00-20:00, Nov-April 9:00-18:00, tel. 04/572-9782, www.blejski-grad.si.

Getting to the Castle: To really earn those views, you can **hike** up the steep hill (20-30 minutes). The handiest trails are behind big St. Martin's Church: Walk past the front door of the church with the lake at your back, and look left after the first set of houses for the *Grad* signs marking the steepest route (follow the wooden stakes all the way up the steep switchback steps); or, for a longer but less steep route, continue past the church on the same street about five minutes, bearing uphill (left) at the fork, and find the *Grad 1* sign just after the Pension Bledec hostel on the left. Once you're on this second trail, don't take the sharp-left uphill turn at the fork (instead, continue straight up, around the back of the hill). If you'd rather skip the hike, you can take the 10:00 **tourist bus** (see "Getting Around Lake Bled," earlier), your **rental car,** a **taxi** (around €10), or—if you're wealthy and romantic—a **horse and buggy** (€40, €10 extra for driver to wait 30 minutes and bring you back down). However, these options take you only to the parking lot, from which it's still a steep and slippery-when-wet five-minute hike up to the castle itself.

Touring the Castle: Your castle admission includes a newly spruced-up castle museum (described next); a small theater continuously showing a fun 20-minute movie about Bled (under the restaurant); a tiny chapel with 3-D frescoes that make it seem much bigger than it is (next to the museum entrance); and a rampart walk with an "herbal gallery" (gift shop of traditional-meets-modern herbal brandies, cosmetics, and perfumes—find the stairs up to the right as you enter the castle complex).

The **museum** strains to make the story of Bled, the castle, and the surrounding region of Carniola interesting. The ground floor has exhibits about old furniture, geology, and the seasonal life cycle of the region, while upstairs are a cool 3-D model of the surrounding mountains, smaller models illustrating the growth of the building, and exhibits on the development of tourism at Lake

Bled (including its many fine vacation villas). While video screens and some English information are helpful, there's really not much to say.

In addition, the castle is home to a pair of interesting, old-fashioned shops: You can visit Mojster Janez's working replica of a **printing press** *(grajska tiskarna/manufaktura)* from Gutenberg's time and print your own custom-made souvenir certificate for €8-14 (next to the castle's oldest tower—from the 11th century). There's also an exhibition in English about early printing methods and the importance of moveable type for advancing the Protestant Reformation, whose goal was to get the word of God more easily into the hands of everyday people. Near the "herbal gallery" (to the right as you enter the castle) is a **wine cellar** *(grajska klet de Adami)* where you can bottle and cork your own bottle of wine (€12-15). Slovenian wines are well-explained by one of two guys (both, coincidentally, named Andrej) who dress as monks, since winemaking was a monastic responsibility in the Middle Ages. Both the printing press and the wine cellar may close earlier than the castle grounds (possibly around 18:00).

Eating at the Castle: The **restaurant** at the castle is fairly expensive, but your restaurant reservation gets you into the castle grounds for free (international cuisine and some local specialties, €12-14 pastas, €18-25 main courses, daily in summer 10:00-22:00, less off-season, tel. 04/579-4424). Better yet, bring your own picnic to munch along the wall with million-dollar views over Lake Bled (buy sandwiches at the Mercator grocery store in the commercial center before you ascend—described later, under "Eating in Bled").

Boating—Bled is the rowing center of Slovenia. Town officials even lengthened the lake a bit so it would perfectly fit the standard two-kilometer laps, with 100 meters more for the turn (on maps, you can see the little divot taken out of the far end). Bled hosted its fourth world championship in August of 2011. The town has produced many Olympic medalists, winning gold in Sydney and silver in Athens. You'll notice that local crew team members are characters—with a tradition of wild and colorful haircuts. You'll likely see them running or rowing. This dedication to rowing adds to Bled's tranquility, since no motorized boats are allowed on the lake.

If you want to get into the action, you'll find **rental rowboats** at the swimming pool under the castle (small 3-person boat: first hour-€15, additional hours-€8 each; bigger 5-person boat: first hour-€17, additional hours-€9 each; daily in summer 10:00-18:00, last rental at 17:00). Two other places farther from Bled town also rent rowboats (4-person boat-€10/hour, closed in bad weather and off-season): Pension Pletna in Mlino (a 15-minute walk around the lake past Grand Hotel Toplice) and the campground on the far end of the lake.

Swimming—Lake Bled has several suitable spots for a swim. The swimming pools under the castle are filled with lake water and routinely earn the "blue flag," meaning the water is top-quality (swim all day—€7, less for afternoon only, June-Sept daily 8:00-19:00, closed Oct-May and in bad weather, tel. 04/578-0528). Lake Bled's main beach is at the campground at the far end of the lake, though you can also swim near the village of

Mlino. If you swim to the island, remember that you can't get into the church in your swimsuit.

Luge Ride (Polento Sankanje)—Bled's "summer toboggan" luge ride, atop Mount Straža overlooking the lake, allows you to scream down a steep, curvy metal rail track on a little plastic sled. A chairlift takes you to the top of the track, where you'll sit on your sled, take a deep breath, and remind yourself: Pull back on the stick to slow down, push forward on the stick to go faster. You'll drop 480 feet in altitude on the 570-yard-long track, speeding up to about 25 miles per hour as you race toward the lake. You'll see the track on the hillside just south of town, beyond the Grand Hotel Toplice.

Cost and Hours: €8/ride, cheaper for multiple rides, chairlift only—€4, weather-dependent—if it rains, you can't go; mid-June-Aug daily 10:00-20:00; May-mid-June and Sept Sat-Sun only 11:00-18:00, closed Mon-Fri; Oct Sat-Sun only 11:00-16:30; most of April Sat-Sun only 11:00-17:00; closed Nov-early April.

Nearby: The affiliated **Adventure Park** (Pustolovski Park), next to the luge, has a series of five high-ropes courses designed for everyone from five-year-olds to adults (same hours as luge, €18 for adults, €13 for kids 7-14, €10 for kids under 7; various combotickets—for example, €23 covers the lift, adventure park, and one luge ride; mobile 031-761-661, www.pustolovski-park-bled.si).

Deva Puri Gallery—Just away from the lake (on the road to Lake Bohinj, behind Vila Bled), this gallery hosts good, rotating exhibits of mostly modern art. You'll see the latest exhibits advertised around town; recent installations have included Picasso's ceramics and Slovenian Impressionism. While the gallery is a bit out of town (a long walk or a quick bike, car, or taxi ride), it's worth the trek for art-lovers.

Cost and Hours: Price depends on exhibit but generally around €7, daily 10:00-19:00, open roughly mid-summer through Nov, Pristava, mobile 051-336-834, www.deva.si.

Day Trips—For details on some easy and enjoyable nearby side-trips—including a scenic gorge hike, a quirky bee museum, an old blacksmithing town, and a more remote lake experience—see "Near Lake Bled" later in this chapter.

Nightlife in Bled

Bled Pub Crawl

Bled is quiet after hours. However, the town does have a few fun bars that are lively with a young crowd (all open nightly until late). Since many young people in Bled are students at the local tourism school, they're likely to speak English...and eager to practice with a native speaker. Try a "Smile," a Corona-type Slovenian lager. *Šnops* (schnapps) is a local specialty—popular flavors are plum *(slivovka)*, honey *(medica)*, blueberry *(borovničevec)*, and pear *(hruškovec)*.

Kick things off with the fun-loving local gang at **Gostilna Pri Planincu** near the bus station (described later, under "Eating in Bled"). Then head down Cesta Svobode toward the lake; just below Hotel Jelovica, you'll find the rollicking **Irish Pub** (a.k.a. "The Pub"), with Guinness and indoor or outdoor seating. For a more genteel atmosphere, duck across the street and wander a few more steps down toward the lake to find the **Art Café,** with a mellow ambience reminiscent of a Van Gogh painting. Around the lake near the commercial center, **Bled Pub** (a.k.a. "The Cocktail Bar" or "Troha"—for the family that owns it) is a trendy late-night spot where bartenders sling a dizzying array of mixed drinks to an appreciative crowd (between the commercial center and the lake, above the recommended Oštarija Peglez'n restaurant). If you're still standing, several other, more low-key bars and cafés percolate in the commercial center.

Sleeping in Bled

Bled is dominated by a few giant, gradually decaying, communist-era convention hotels. Some have been nicely renovated, but most are stale, outmoded, and overpriced. (It's a strange, incestuous little circle—the majority of the town's big hotels and restaurants are owned by the same company.) Instead, I prefer staying in smaller, pension-type accommodations in the countryside—many of them are just a short walk above the lake. These quaint little family-run pensions book up early with Germans and Brits; reserve as far ahead as possible. I've listed the high-season prices (May-Oct) unless noted. Off-season, prices are typically 10-20 percent lower. For even cheaper beds, consider one of the many *sobe* (rooms in private homes) scattered around the lake (about €21 per person in peak season, €16 per person if you stay three nights or longer,

Sleep Code

(€1 = about $1.40, country code: 386, area code: 04)
S = Single, **D** = Double/Twin, **T** = Triple, **Q** = Quad, **b** = bathroom. Unless otherwise noted, credit cards are accepted and breakfast is included, but the modest tourist tax (about €1 per person, per night) typically is not. Everyone listed here speaks English.

To help you easily sort through these listings, I've divided the accommodations into three categories based on the price for a double room with bath during high season:

$$$ Higher Priced—Most rooms €100 or more.
$$ Moderately Priced—Most rooms between €60-100.
$ Lower Priced—Most rooms €60 or less.

Prices can change without notice; verify the hotel's current rates online or by email. For other updates, see www.ricksteves.com/update.

breakfast-€6 extra). Kompas Bled travel agency can book you a *soba* (see page 569), but be sure the location is convenient before you accept.

Above the Lake

These friendly, cozy, characteristic accommodations are Bled's best values. The only catch is that they're perched on a hilltop a steep five- to ten-minute climb up from the lake (easier than it sounds). There are two ways to find them from the town center: Walk around the lake to Grand Hotel Toplice, then go up the stairs around the right side of the Hotel Jadran (on the hill across the street from Grand Hotel Toplice). Or, from the main road into town (Ljubljanska cesta), take the small service road just above the commercial center (in front of Hotel Lovec), and loop up around the big Kompas and Golf hotels. Some buses (including those to/from Ljubljana) stop at a bus stop higher up on Ljubljanska cesta, just above the traffic light; this stop is handier to these hotels than the main bus station (though bus drivers don't always want to stop since it's a hassle to open the luggage compartment here—try asking nicely). From the bus stop, you can walk down Ljubljanska cesta and take the road just above the post office, which leads up to this area. If you're sleeping up here, Mayer Penzion's restaurant is the easiest choice for dinner (described later, under "Eating in Bled").

$$ Mayer Penzion, thoughtfully run by the Trseglav family, comes with 13 great-value rooms, a helpful staff, a tasty restaurant,

an atmospheric wine-tasting cellar, and beautifully handcrafted
Slovenian woodwork inside
and out. They book up fast in
summer with return clients, so
reserve early (Sb-€57, Db-€82,
€5 less for 3 nights or more, extra
bed-€20, family deals, elevator,
free Internet access and Wi-Fi,
Želeška cesta 7, tel. 04/576-5740, fax 04/576-5741, www.mayer-sp.si,
penzion@mayer-sp.si). They also rent a cute, newly restored two-
story Slovenian farm cottage next door (Db-€120, Tb/Qb-€150).

$$ Hotel Berc and **Penzion Berc** (pronounced "berts"), run
by the Berc brothers, are next door to Mayer Penzion. Both have
cozy public spaces, free Internet access and Wi-Fi, and free loaner
bikes, and are worth reserving ahead (both cash only, www.berc
-sp.si). The new hotel building has 15 rooms with pleasantly woody
decor (Sb-€40-50, Db-€70-80; price depends on size, season, and
length of stay; all rooms have balconies, Pod Stražo 13, tel. 04/576-
5658, fax 04/576-5659, hotel@berc-sp.si, run by Luka). The older,
adjacent *penzion* offers 11 cheaper, older, but nearly-as-nice rooms
(Sb-€40, Db-€65, €5 more for 1-night stays, 10 percent cheaper
off-season, most rooms have balconies, closed Nov-Christmas
and sporadically off-season, Želeška cesta 15, tel. 04/574-1838, fax
04/576-7320, penzion@berc-sp.si, run by Miha).

$$ Alp Penzion is in a tranquil countryside setting amid
hayfields. It's a long hike beyond the others listed here, but still
within a 15-minute walk of the lake (better for drivers or for those
who don't mind the walk). With 12 rooms (some with balconies),
this place is enthusiastically run by the Sršen family, who offer
lots of fun extras, including a tennis court and summer barbecue grill/outdoor pub (June-Sept: Sb-€60, Db-€75-80—higher
price for rooms with balcony; Oct-May: Sb-€45, Db-€68; extra
bed-€15, 3 percent cheaper if you pay cash, prices can be flexible—
based on demand, family rooms, dinner possible—ask when you
book, air-con, free Internet access and Wi-Fi, free loaner bikes,
Cankarjeva cesta 20A, tel. 04/574-1614, fax 04/574-4590, www
.alp-penzion.com, bled@alp-penzion.com). Just next door is the
relaxing Essense spa (described earlier, under "Helpful Hints").

$ Friendly Mia Sušnik rents out two comfortable apart-
ments. Modern, tidy, and equipped with kitchens, these are a good
budget choice for families (Db-€57, Tb-€68, Qb-€79, 20 percent
extra for fewer than 3 nights, includes tax, no breakfast, cash
only, free Wi-Fi, laundry service-€10, free parking, Želeška cesta
3, tel. 04/574-1731, www.bled-holiday.com, susnik@bled-holiday
.com). It's just toward the lake from the bigger pensions, with a

big crucifix out front. Her sister Ivanka also rents apartments, but they're farther from the lake.

$ Tourist Farm Mulej, farther out of town than my other listings and better for drivers, is a new but traditional farmhouse in a tranquil valley about a half-mile from the lake (1.5 miles from Bled town). Damjana and Jože, who run a working farm, rent out eight modern rooms and four apartments—all with balconies—and serve breakfasts and dinners made with food they produce (Db-€60, or €80 with dinner; €30 per extra person in apartments, or €40 with dinner; 20 percent extra for 1- or 2-night stays in June-Aug, cash only, family rooms, free cable Internet, free loaner bikes, horseback riding, Selo pri Bledu 42a, tel. & fax 04/574-4617, www.mulej-bled.com, info@mulej-bled.com). It's in the farm village of Selo—drive along the lakeside road south from Bled, then turn off in Mlino toward Selo, and look for the signs (to the right) once in the village.

$ Vila Gorenka is your non-hostel, low-budget option. The Žerovec family's old-fashioned house has 10 basic, faded, musty rooms sharing two bathrooms (S-€20, D-€36, cash only, no extra charge for 1-night stays, no breakfast, free Internet access and Wi-Fi, just below the bigger pensions at Želeška cesta 9, mobile 040-958-624, http://freeweb.siol.net/mz2, vila.gorenka@siol.net, Janez).

Near the Lake

You'll pay a premium to be closer to the lake—but it's hard to argue with the convenience.

$$$ Hotel Lovec (LOW-vets), a Best Western Premier, sits in a convenient (but non-lakefront) location just above the commercial center. Gorgeously renovated inside and out, and run by a helpful and friendly staff, it's a welcoming, cheery, well-run alternative to Bled's many old, dreary communist hotels. Its 60 plush rooms come with all the comforts (Sb-€128, Db-€151, €20 more for a lake-view balcony, very soft rates fluctuate with demand—email to ask for best price, cheaper Nov-Feb, family and "executive" suites available, delicious breakfast, elevator, free Internet access and Wi-Fi, indoor pool, free parking garage for guests, Ljubljanska cesta 6, tel. 04/620-4100, fax 04/576-8625, www.lovechotel.com, booking@kompas-lovec.eu).

$$$ Grand Hotel Toplice (TOHP-leet-seh) is the grande dame of Bled, with 87 high-ceilinged rooms, parquet floors, a genteel lakeview café/lounge, posh decor, all the amenities, and a long list of high-profile guests—from Madeleine Albright to Jordan's King Hussein to Slovene-by-marriage Donald Trump (ask to see their "wall of fame"). Once elegant, this place is a bit faded these days, but it's still a classic. Rooms in the back are cheaper, but have no lake views and overlook a noisy street—try to get one as high up as possible (I've listed the official rates followed by what you'll likely pay in slower times—non-view: Sb-€150/€110, Db-€170/€140; lake view: Sb-€180/€160, Db-€230/€200; suites with lake views-€280; 15-20 percent less Nov-April, very flexible rates—check online, air-con, elevator, free Internet access and cable Internet, free one-hour boat rental for guests, free parking, Cesta Svobode 12, tel. 04/579-1000, fax 04/574-1841, www.hotel-toplice.com, ghtoplice @hotelibled.com). The hotel's name—*toplice*—means "spa"; guests are free to use the hotel's swanky, natural-spring-fed indoor swimming pool (a chilly 72 degrees Fahrenheit). This hotel also runs two smaller, far less luxurious hotels nearby with very dated and faded rooms and lower rates (Hotel Trst and Hotel Jadran, details at Toplice's website).

$$$ Vila Prešeren has eight stylish, pricey rooms above a popular restaurant right on the lake. As the rooms are an afterthought to the busy restaurant, don't expect much personal attention from the staff (Sb-€112, Db-€150, apartment-€200-214 depending on size, cheaper mid-Oct-early May, no reception—check in at the restaurant, air-con, free Wi-Fi, Veslaška promenada 14, tel. 04/575-2510, www.vilapreseren.si, vilapreseren@sprtinaresorts.si).

$ Apartmaji Mežan, run by young couple Janez and Saša, has three apartments in a modern home buried in the middle of town, just uphill from the church. As it's next to an old barn, it's technically a tourist farm (Db-€50, cash only, no breakfast, free Internet access and Wi-Fi, Riklijeva 6, mobile 041-210-290 or 041-516-688, www.apartmaji-mezan.si, sasa.mezan@gmail.com).

$ Penzion Bledec (BLED-ets), a family-run, official IYHF hostel, is just below the castle at the top of the Old Town. Each of the 12 rooms has its own bathroom. They have dorms (bed in 4- to 7-bed dorm-€22-24 depending on number of bunks) as well as rooms that can be rented as doubles (though "doubles" are actually underutilized triples and quads, with separate beds pushed together—so they might not be reservable July-Aug or at other busy times, Db-€54, Tb-€72; cheaper Nov-April, members pay 10 percent less, includes sheets and breakfast, great family rooms, free Internet access and Wi-Fi, full-service laundry for guests-€9/load, restaurant, Grajska 17, tel. 04/574-5250, fax 04/574-5251, www .youth-hostel-bledec.si, bledec@mlino.si).

$ Travellers Haven is a low-key hostel run by Mirjam and Karmen. The 27 beds fill six rooms in a nicely renovated hundred-year-old villa in the Old Town. The lodgings are well-maintained and the hangout areas are inviting, though the tight bathrooms offer little privacy (€19 for a bunk in a 4- to 6-bed room, D-€48, no breakfast but guest kitchen, reception open 8:00-13:00 & 16:00-23:00; free Internet access, Wi-Fi, laundry machines, and loaner

bikes; Riklijeva cesta 1, mobile 031-704-455 or 041-396-545, www
.travellers-haven.si, travellers-haven@t-2.net).

Eating in Bled

Bled has several good restaurants, but most everything is quite
similar. For variety, wait for Ljubljana.

Okarina, run by charming, well-traveled Leo Ličof, serves a
diverse array of cuisines, all of them well-executed: international
fare, traditional Slovenian specialties, and Indian (Himalayan)
dishes. Leo has a respect for salads and vegetables and a passion
for fish. Creative cooking, fine presentation, friendly service, and
an atmosphere as tastefully eclectic as the food make this place a
great splurge (€9-14 pastas, €10-23 main courses, plus a few pricier
splurges, daily 12:00-15:00 & 18:00-24:00, next to Hotel Lovec
at Ljubljanska cesta 8, tel. 04/574-1458). In the back of the menu,
look for the copy of the guest book page with Paul McCartney's
visit from May 2005. Around the left side of the building, Leo
runs a smaller pavilion restaurant out back, with different ambience and food (as the details are expected to change, ask when you
arrive).

Oštarija Peglez'n ("The Old Iron"), conveniently located on
the main road between the commercial center and the lake, cooks
up tasty Slovenian and Mediterranean meals, with an emphasis
on fish and fun, family-style shareable plates. Choose between the
delightful Slovenian cottage interior or the shady streetside terrace. Reservations are smart in summer (€7-9 salads and pastas,
€11-19 main courses, daily 12:00-23:00, Cesta Svobode 19A, tel.
04/574-4218).

Vila Prešeren is the best choice for lakeside dining, with
a giant terrace reaching all the way down to the lakefront path.
Featuring tasteful, mod decor, international cuisine, and slow service, this is a great spot to linger over a meal, a drink, or a classic
Lake Bled dessert (€10-12 salads, €8-14 pastas, €11-21 main courses,
daily 7:00-23:00, Veslaška promenada 14, tel. 04/575-2510).

Mayer Penzion, just up the hill from the lakefront, has a
dressy restaurant with good traditional cooking that's worth the
short hike. This is where a Babel of international tourists come to
swap hiking tips and day-trip tales. As this is the only real restaurant in the pension neighborhood, it can be very busy—reserve
ahead (€8-21 main courses, Tue-Sun 18:00-24:00, closed Mon,
indoor or outdoor seating, above Hotel Jadran at Želeška cesta 7,
tel. 04/576-5740).

Gostilna Pri Planincu ("By the Mountaineers") is a homey,
informal bar coated with license plates and packed with fun-loving
and sometimes rowdy natives. A larger dining area sprawls behind

Bled Desserts

While you're in Bled, be sure to enjoy the town's specialty, a cream cake called **kremna rezina** (KRAYM-nah ray-ZEE-nah; often referred to by its German-derived name, **kremšnita,** KRAYM-shnee-tah). It's a layer of cream and a thick layer of vanilla custard art-fully sandwiched between sheets of delicate, crispy crust. Heavenly. Slovenes travel from all over the country to sample this famous dessert.

Slightly less renowned—but just as tasty—is **grmada** (gur-MAH-dah, "bonfire"). This dessert was developed by Hotel Jelovica as a way to get rid of their day-old left-overs. They take yesterday's cake, add rum, milk, custard, and raisins, and top it off with whipped cream and chocolate syrup.

Finally, there's *prekmurska gibanica*—or just **gibanica** (gee-bah-NEET-seh) for short. Originating in the Hungarian corner of the country, *gibanica* is an earthy pastry filled with poppy seeds, walnuts, apples, and cheese, and drizzled with rum.

These desserts are typically enjoyed with a lake-and-mountains view—the best spots are the terrace at Vila Prešeren, the Panorama restaurant by Grand Hotel Toplice, and the terrace across from the Hotel Park (figure around €5 for cake and coffee at any of these places). For a more local (but non-lake view) setting, consider Šmon Slaščičarna (only slightly cheaper; see next page).

the small, local-feeling pub, and there's outdoor seating out front and on the side patio. The menu features huge portions of stick-to-your-ribs Slovenian pub grub, plus Balkan grilled-meat specialties (€9-19 main courses). Look for their €6-8 daily specials—huge, home-style traditional dishes. Upstairs is a timbered pizzeria sell-ing €5-9 wood-fired pies (daily 9:00-23:00, pizzeria open from 11:00, Grajska cesta 8, tel. 04/574-1613). The playful cartoon mural along the outside of the restaurant shows different types of moun-taineers (from left to right): thief, normal, mooch ("gopher"), climber, and naked (...well, almost).

Pizzeria Rustika, in the Old Town, offers wood-fired piz-zas and salads. Its upstairs terrace is relaxing on a balmy evening (€6-9 pizzas, daily 12:00-23:00, service can be slow when it's busy, Riklijeva cesta 13, tel. 04/576-8900).

The **Mercator** grocery store, in the commercial center, has the makings for a bang-up picnic. They sell pre-made sandwiches for about €3, or will make you one to order (point to what you want). This is a great option for hikers and budget travelers (Mon-Fri 7:00-19:00, Sat 7:00-15:00, Sun 8:00-12:00). There's another location closer to the Old Town and castle (Mon-Sat 7:00-20:00, Sun 8:00-16:00).

Dessert: While tourists generally gulp down their cream cakes on a hotel restaurant's lakefront terrace, local residents favor the desserts at **Šmon Slaščičarna** (a.k.a. the "Brown Bear," for the bear on the sign). It's nicely untouristy, but lacks the atmosphere of the lakeside spots (€2-3 cakes, daily 7:30-21:00, near bus station at Grajska cesta 3, tel. 04/574-1616).

Lake Bled Connections

The most convenient train connections to Bled leave from the Lesce-Bled station, about 2.5 miles away (see details under "Arrival in Bled," earlier). Remember, when buying a train ticket to Lake Bled, make it clear that you want to go to the Lesce-Bled station (not the Bled Jezero station, which is poorly connected to the main line). No one in the town of Bled sells train tickets; buy them at the station just before your train departs (open Mon-Fri 5:30-21:00, Sat 7:00-15:00, Sun 14:30-19:30). If the ticket window there is closed, buy your ticket on board from the conductor (who will likely waive the €2.50 additional fee).

Note that if you're going to **Ljubljana,** the bus (which leaves from Bled town itself) is better than the train (which leaves from the Lesce-Bled train station).

From Lesce-Bled by Train to: Ljubljana (roughly hourly, 40-60 minutes), **Salzburg** (5/day, 4 hours, some change in Villach, Austria), **Munich** (5/day, 6 hours, some change in Salzburg), **Vienna** (that's *Dunaj* in Slovene, 5/day, 6 hours, transfer in Villach or Salzburg), **Venice** (3/day with transfer in Villach—likely part-way by bus, 6 hours), **Zagreb** (6/day direct, 3/day with a change in Ljubljana, 3.5 hours).

By Bus to: Ljubljana (Mon-Sat hourly—usually at :30 past the hour, fewer on Sun, 1.25 hours, €6.30), **Radovljica** (Mon-Fri at least 2/hour, Sat hourly, Sun almost hourly, 15 minutes, €1.80), **Lesce-Bled train station** (2/hour, 10 minutes, €1.30), **Lake Bohinj** (hourly, 40 minutes and €3.60 to Bohinj Jezero stop, 50 minutes and €4.10 to Bohinj Vogel or Bohinj Zlatorog stop, 3/day in summer continue all the way to Savica Waterfall trailhead), **Podhom** (15-minute hike away from Vintgar Gorge, Mon-Fri 5/day in the morning, 1/day Sat, none Sun, 15 minutes, €1.30), **Spodnje Gorje**

(also 15-minute hike from Vintgar Gorge, take bus in direction of Krnica, hourly, 15 minute, €1.30). Confirm times at the TI or using the schedules posted at the unstaffed Bled bus station. Buy tickets on the bus.

By Plane: Ljubljana Airport is between Lake Bled and Ljubljana, about a 45-minute drive from Bled. Connecting by taxi costs around €40-50 (set price up front—since it's outside of town, they don't use the meter; be sure to use a Bled-based taxi, rather than a Ljubljana-based taxi, which will likely be more expensive). The Zup Prevozi shuttle bus is a more affordable option at €13, but it runs only three times each day (generally coordinated to meet easyJet flights). However, at other times you can arrange for a shuttle from Zup Prevozi for a bit less than a taxi (€34/1 person, €35/2 people, €37/3 people, €39/4 people, mobile 031-304-141, www.zup-prevozi.eu). The bus connection from Bled to the airport is cheap (total cost: about €5.40) but complicated and time-consuming: First, go to Kranj (Mon-Fri 12/day, Sat-Sun 8/day, 35 minutes), then transfer to a Brnik-bound bus (at least hourly, 20 minutes). Many Bled residents prefer to fly from Klagenfurt, Austria. For details on both the Ljubljana and Klagenfurt airports, see page 561.

Route Tips for Drivers: Bled is less than an hour north of Ljubljana on the slick A2 expressway. The exit is marked for *Lesce*, but you'll also see signs for *Bled*, which will lead you directly to the lake (where the road becomes Ljubljanska cesta).

To reach Radovljica (bee museum) or Lesce (train station), drive out of Bled on Ljubljanska cesta toward the expressway. Watch for the turnoff to those two towns on the right. They're on the same road: Lesce first (to reach train station, divert right when entering town), then Radovljica. Also along this road, between Lesce and Radovljica, is the well-marked turnoff to the road to Kropa (with its Iron Forging Museum).

Near Lake Bled

The countryside around Bled offers several day trips that can be done easily without a car (bus connection information is described in each section). The four trips listed here are the best (two small-town/museum experiences, two hiking/back-to-nature options). They're more convenient than can't-miss, but each is worthwhile on a longer visit, and all give a good taste of the Julian Alps. For a self-guided driving tour through farther-flung (and even more striking) parts of the Julian Alps, see the next chapter.

Vintgar Gorge

Just north of Bled, the river Radovna has carved this mile-long, picturesque gorge into the mountainside. For hikers, Vintgar (VEENT-gar) Gorge is worth ▲▲.

Boardwalks and bridges put you right in the middle of the action of this "poor man's Plitvice." You'll cross over several waterfalls and marvel at the clarity of the water. The easy hike is on a boardwalk trail with handrails (sometimes narrow and a bit slippery). At the end of the gorge, you'll find a snack stand, WCs, and a bridge with a fine view. Go back the way you came, or take a prettier return to Bled (see "Scenic Hike Back to Bled," later). The gorge is easily reachable from Bled by bus or foot and is the best option for those who are itching for a hike but don't have a car.

Cost and Hours: €4 to enter gorge, open daily May-late Oct 8:00-19:00 or until dusk, June-Aug maybe until 20:00, closed late Oct-April, tel. 04/572-5266.

Getting to Vintgar Gorge: The gorge is 2.5 miles north of Bled. To reach the gorge entrance, you can walk (takes at least one hour one-way), pedal a rental bike (about 30 minutes, easiest with an electric bike rented at the TI), take a bus (15-minute ride plus 15-minute walk, or 30-minute ride on summer tourist bus), or drive (less than 10 minutes).

Walkers and **cyclists** leave Bled on the road between the castle and St. Martin's Church and take the uphill (left) road at the fork. Just after the little yellow chapel, turn right on the road with the big tree, then immediately left at the Mercator grocery store. When the road swings left, continue straight onto Partizanska (marked for *Podhom* and a walking sign for *Vintgar;* ignore the bus sign for *Vintgar* pointing left). At the fork just after the little bridge, go left for Podhom, then simply follow signs for *Vintgar*.

In summer, the easy **tourist bus** takes you right to the gorge entrance in 30 minutes (see "Getting Around Lake Bled," page 570). Otherwise, you can take a **local bus** to one of two stops: Podhom (Mon-Fri 5/day in the morning, 1/day Sat, none Sun, 15 minutes, €1.30) or Spodnje Gorje (take bus in direction of Krnica, hourly, 15 minutes, €1.30). From either the Podhom or the Spodnje Gorje bus stop, it's a 15-minute walk to the gorge (follow signs for *Vintgar*).

Drivers follow signs to *Podhom,* then *Vintgar* (see walking/cycling instructions).

Near Lake Bled

To Italy

109

Kranjska Gora

206

202

Mojstrana

Vršič Pass

SLOVENIA

Mount Triglav

JULIAN ALPS

(TUNNEL)

To Villach and Klagenfurt Airport

85

AUSTRIA

KARAVANKE MTNS

Jesenice

A2

Stol Mtn.

VINTGAR GORGE

Podhom

Spodnje Gorje

Krnica

LESCE-BLED STATION

Begunje

Bled Town

Mlino

BLED JEZERO STATION

Radovljica

To Airport & Ljubljana

Lake Bled

Sava River

Savica Waterfall

HOTEL ZLATOROG & STARE PENSION

Lake Bohinj

Bohinjska Bistrica

Ribčev Laz

209

Sava Bohinjska R.

Kropa

To Ljubljana

WWI CEMETERY

(Lift)

Polje

Vogel Mtn.

Car Train to Most na Soči & Nova Gorica

Podbrdo

N

5 Kilometers

5 Miles

.... Lake Boats

LAKE BLED

Scenic Hike Back to Bled: If you still have energy once you reach the end of the gorge, consider this longer hike back with panoramic views. Behind the snack stand deep in the gorge, find the trail marked *Katarina Bled.* You'll go uphill for 25 strenuous minutes (following the red-and-white circles and arrows) before cresting the hill and enjoying beautiful views over Bled town and the region. Continue straight down the road 15 minutes to the typical, narrow, old village of Zasip, then walk (about 30 minutes) or take the bus back to Bled.

Radovljica

The town of Radovljica (rah-DOH-vleet-suh, "Radol'ca" for

short), perched on a plateau above the Sava River, has the charming Old Town that Bled lacks. The traffic-free core of the town, once hemmed in by a stout wall (still faintly visible in some areas), is jammed with historic buildings that surround the long, skinny main square called Linhartov trg. While Radovljica's Old Town is a pleasant place to stroll or nurse a coffee, you can see it all in a few minutes. The main reason to visit here is to tour its offbeat but strangely fascinating beekeeping museum—despite only having a few rooms, it still ranks as one of Europe's biggest on the apiarian arts. Skip the town on Mondays, when the museum is closed (and be aware that the museum closes for a three-hour lunch break off-season).

Getting to Radovljica

Buses to Radovljica generally leave Bled every half-hour (fewer on weekends, €1.80, buy ticket from driver, trip takes about 15 minutes). To reach the town center and the bee museum from the bus station, leave the station going straight ahead, cross the bus parking lot and the next street, then turn left down the far street (following brown sign for *Staro Mesto*). In five minutes, you'll reach the start of the pedestrianized Linhartov trg (with the TI—on the right—and the start of my "Old Town Stroll").

Drivers leave Bled on Ljubljanska cesta, then turn right at the sign for *Radovljica* and go through the village of Lesce; the road dead-ends at Radovljica's pedestrian zone, where you'll find a parking lot (by the rustic garage), the TI, and the start of my "Old Town Stroll."

A handy **bike** path scenically and peacefully connects Bled with Radovljica (about 4 miles, get details at TI).

Orientation to Radovljica

Tourist Information

The enthusiastic TI loves to help visitors appreciate the town of "Radol'ca" (daily May-Sept 9:00-19:00, Oct-April 9:00-18:00, Linhartov trg 1, tel. 04/531-5112, www.radolca.si)

Sights in Radovljica

Old Town Stroll

Whether arriving by bus or by car, you'll enter the Old Town next to the TI. If you curl around below the main road, you'll find the scant remains of the city's original **moat**—the only surviving one in Slovenia.

Continuing into the Old Town, after a half-block you'll pass a fun little **secondhand shop** on the right—crammed with everything from beat-up modern appliances to genuine Slovenian antiques.

Beyond that, the street opens up into **Linhartov trg,** a charming square fronted by historic buildings. On the left is the **Magušarjeva Hiša,** a fine old Gothic house where potter Urban

Magušar lives, has a studio and exhibition space, and teaches pottery classes—if you're curious, step into the courtyard and ask him if you can see the house (Trubarjeva 1, mobile 041-734-808, www.magusarjevahisa.si for the house, www.vajadelamojstra.si for the gallery). Nearby are a Renaissance building now housing a youth hostel and fine café, and the traditional, recommended **Lectar** restaurant, with a "living museum" in the basement where you can watch bakers making traditional gingerbread ornaments (€1 entry).

Across the street is a monument to local benefactor **Josepina Hučevar,** who funded the town's water system (see the old well nearby) and financed schools (a student holds the big medallion with her image). Next to that is the **Šivičeva Hiša,** an atmospheric late-Gothic house that's open to the public. If you go a block down any street to the right, you'll come to a fine valley **viewpoint** emphasizing Radovljica's dramatic position on a long promontory.

Dominating the main part of the square is the big, yellow **town "castle"** (actually a mansion); upstairs you'll find the Apicultural Museum (described next), the Linhart Museum, and the Baroque Hall—once divided into 10 small offices, but recently restored to its previous grandeur.

Beyond the mansion (and connected to it by a gallery) is **St. Peter's Church;** to its right is its rectory, where you can dip into the pretty courtyard. Poke around past the church to reach the edge of the ravine. If you circle around the small building

behind the church, burrowed into the hillside you'll find a **World War II-era bunker** left behind by the Nazis. Peeking into the window of the bunker, you'll see it's been turned into a chapel dedicated to Edith Stein, a 20th-century Polish Jew who became a Carmelite nun but was arrested by the Nazis and executed at Auschwitz. She was later made a saint by Pope John Paul II (notice the menorah and Star of David inside the chapel). While she actually has no official ties to Radovljica, locals are inspired by Edith's example.

▲Apicultural Museum (Čebelarski Muzej)

This museum celebrates Slovenia's long and very proud beekeeping heritage. Since the days before Europeans had sugar, Slovenia has been a big honey producer. Slovenian farmer Anton Janša is considered the father of modern beekeeping and was Europe's first official teacher of this art (in Habsburg Vienna). And even today, beekeeping is considered a crucial part of Slovenian culture. The surrounding area (Carniola) has about 6,000 inhabitants, including 65 beekeepers who manage 5,000 hives—the most bees per capita of any place in Europe. Slovenes reserve an importance and affection for bees that's rare in our modern times. For example, the Slovene language has two different words for "to give birth" and "to die": One they use exclusively for humans and bees, and a different one for all other animals. If a beekeeper dies, it's believed (with some pretty incontrovertible evidence) that the new beekeeper must be formally "introduced" to the hive by going there and explaining to the bees what has happened; otherwise, they become confused and agitated, and often die themselves.

Cost and Hours: €3, good English descriptions, €1.60 English guidebook is a nice souvenir; May-Oct Tue-Sun 10:00-18:00, closed Mon; March-April and Nov-Dec Wed and Sat-Sun 10:00-12:00 & 15:00-17:00, Tue and Thu-Fri 8:00-15:00, closed Mon; Jan-Feb Tue-Fri 8:00-15:00, closed Sat-Mon; upstairs at Linhartov trg 1, tel. 04/532-0520, www.muzeji-radovljica.si.

◎ Self-Guided Tour: Everything is well-described in English, but this commentary will help you locate the highlights.

The first room of the museum traces the history of beekeeping, from the time when bees were kept in hollowed-out trees to the present day. The bust celebrates beekeeper extraordinaire Anton Janša.

In the second room are old-fashioned tools. When a new queen bee is born, the old queen takes half the hive's bees to a new location. Experienced beekeepers used the long, skinny instrument (a beehive stethoscope) to figure out when the swarm was ready to fly the coop. Then, once the bees had moved to a nearby tree, the beekeeper used the big spoons to retrieve the queen—surrounded by an angry ball of her subjects—from her new home before she could get settled in. The beekeeper transferred the furious gang into a manmade hive designed for easier, more sanitary collection of the honey. You can also see the tools beekeepers used to create smoke, which makes bees less aggressive. Even today, some of Slovenia's old-fashioned beekeepers simply light up a cigarette and blow smoke on any bees that get ornery.

The third room features the museum's highlight: whimsically painted beehive frontboards (called *panjske končnice*). Beekeepers, believing these paintings would help the bees find their way home, developed a tradition of decorating their hives with religious, historical, and satirical folk themes.

The oldest panel dates from 1758, but the practice really took off in the 19th century. Take your time perusing these delightful illustrations. The depiction of a hunter's funeral shows all the animals happy...except his dog. One popular panel shows two farmers fighting over a cow, while a lawyer milks the cow. There's everything from portraits of Habsburg emperors, to a "true crime" sequence of a man murdering his family as they sleep, to proto-"Lockhorns" cartoons of marital strife, to 18th-century erotica (one with a woman showing some leg and another with a flip-up, peek-a-boo panel). A few panels blur the line between humorous and misogynistic: Look for the devil sharpening a woman's tongue on a wheel, or the man carrying a cross—and his wife—on his back. The life-size wooden statues were used to "guard" the beehives—and designed to look like fearsome Ottoman and Napoleonic soldiers.

The fourth room examines the biology of bees. In the summer only, look for the actual, functioning beehive. Try to find the queen—she's usually marked with a dot on her back. The surround-sound hive nearby lets you step inside to hear the noise of a buzzing queen.

Finally, you'll have the opportunity to watch a good but dry, detailed 14-minute film about the Carniolan bee, and check out special exhibits. Back at the entrance, the ticket desk sells a few choice souvenirs, including hand-painted replicas of frontboards, honey brandy, candles, ornaments, and other bee products.

Nearby: Sharing a ticket desk with the bee museum, the **Linhart Museum** celebrates one of Slovenia's leading Enlightenment thinkers. Radovljica-born Anton Linhart was an 18th-century playwright, politician, pedagogue, and historian who wrote some of the first plays in the Slovenian language and set the stage for France Prešeren. While he's important to Slovenes, it's hard to drum up much excitement for this earnest two-room museum devoted to a man who is not that interesting to outsiders (€5 combo-ticket with Apicultural Museum, same hours).

Eating in Radovljica

Several Radovljica restaurants near the bee museum have view terraces overlooking the surrounding mountains and valleys.

Lectar offers pricey, hearty Slovenian fare in a rural-feeling setting with a user-friendly, super-traditional menu. Its several heavily decorated rooms are often filled with tour groups, but in good weather, don't miss the terrace out back. Come here if you want to linger over rustic Slovenian specialties—not if you're in a hurry. The restaurant is known for its heart-shaped gingerbread cookies (called *lect*), inscribed with messages of love. In the cellar is a €1 "living museum" where you can watch costumed bakers make and decorate these hearts according to the traditional recipe (€6-10 starters, €9-14 main courses, Wed-Mon 12:00-22:00, closed Tue, family-friendly, Linhartov trg 2, tel. 04/537-4800).

Gostilna Avguštin, across the street, is the simpler local alternative for unpretentious, stick-to-your-ribs Slovenian fare. Their terrace in back enjoys an even better view than Lectar's (€6-8 starters, €10-19 main dishes, daily 10:00-24:00, Linhartov trg 15, tel. 04/531-4163).

Grajska Gostilnica, outside of the Old Town and closer to the bus station, dishes up good, basic pub grub (salads, pizza, pastas, open long hours daily, across from the bus station and to the left, inside Hotel Grajski Dvor at Kranjska 2, tel. 04/531-5585).

Kropa

Tucked in a narrow gully below the Jelovica Plateau, the modest metalworking village of Kropa has a big history as one of the earliest and most prolific industrial centers of Europe. Like other early-industry sights in Europe (such as England's Ironbridge Gorge), Kropa thrills engineers—for whom it merits ▲▲—but may leave others cold.

Beginning in the 15th century, the people of Kropa took advantage of their substantial natural resources: iron ore from nearby mines; plenty of wood to keep the furnaces burning; and water from their rushing river diverted into channels to power waterwheels. By the 16th century, Kropa was already known as one of the most important blacksmithing towns in Europe, and was granted a prized semi-autonomous status by the Habsburg Empire. Blacksmiths here specialized in spikes and nails, producing 127 different types—from small tacks for shoes, to bigger nails for horseshoes, to huge spikes used for major construction projects all over Europe. For example, the romantic wooden pilings in the Venice lagoon are held together with Kropa spikes.

By the 18th century—still well before the dawn of the Industrial Age—Kropa was one of the most industrially developed places in Europe, churning out high volumes of products. Its 70 houses were packed with 1,400 people, and men, women, and children all worked in the foundries. But by the late 18th century, local iron ore deposits were depleted, the industry collapsed, and some 800 local residents died of disease and other poverty-related causes. The 19th century saw another boost, as Kropa spikes were in demand to build the Vienna-

Trieste railway. By modern times, the nail and spike industry had been replaced by decorative blacksmithing (especially at the big Uko factory across from the museum), which included items such as fancy gates and mailboxes. Today, Kropa's 90 houses now hold a more reasonable population of 200.

Getting There: Kropa is poorly connected by bus (sporadic weekday connections to Radovljica); skip it unless you have a car. Drivers can find the well-marked road to Kropa off the road that runs between Lesce and Radovljica.

▲Iron Forging Museum (Kovaški Muzej)

Worth ▲▲ to engineers, this modest but engaging exhibit traces the history of this metalworking burg. Filling two floors of a typical old Kropa house, the displays have little English explanation but capture the blacksmithing spirit of Kropa.

Cost and Hours: €3; May-Oct Tue-Sun 10:00-18:00, closed Mon; March-April and Nov-Dec Tue and Thu-Fri 8:00-15:00, Wed and Sat-Sun 10:00-12:00 & 15:00-17:00, closed Mon; Jan-Feb Tue-Fri 8:00-15:00, closed Sat-Mon; Kropa 10, tel. 04/533-7200, www.muzeji-radovljica.si.

Touring the Museum: When you buy your ticket, ask Metka if she's willing to show you around the museum; unless they're busy with groups, she can take you through the collection and really bring the (otherwise poorly explained) exhibits to life. If she's busy, the following describes some things to look for on your own.

Go up to the first floor and enter the room with the big town model of Kropa as it was in the 19th century—which makes it clear

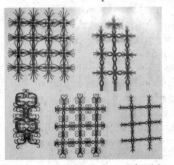

just how ingeniously the town channeled its water supply to use its raw power for its foundries. The next room shows big chunks of iron ore, and the buckets used to gather and carry it. (Many workers here farmed during the summer and were miners in the winter.) Although the big model of a blast furnace seems like fairly sophisticated and "modern" industrial engineering, Kropa used facilities like this all the way back in the mid-15th century. Water was used to turn a wheel to pump bellows onto a wood fire, superheating it to melt down the raw iron ore to create impure "pig iron." The second, smaller chimney was a second furnace used for refining the pig iron into useable iron. Look at the blacksmiths' tools and pass through the room with several huge bellows, then enter the room with decorative iron gratings and other decorations, dating from Kropa's later era of blacksmithing, between the two World Wars. Near the base of the stairs is a big music box with a piano, drums, and cymbals (Metka can start it for you).

Climb the stairs to the top floor, where you'll see a model of a typical family home, as well as mannequins of the family in period dress. The next room displays the vast range of nails and spikes that were produced here. A worker was expected to produce 2,000 of these spikes in one day.

Nearby: The museum's fascinating **spike forge** (up at the top of town), where you can watch an actual blacksmith making spikes the traditional way, costs €1 extra. Unfortunately, it's open almost exclusively for groups with a prior reservation, and because they need to stoke a real fire, they can't keep it open at other times for walk-in visitors. When you visit, you can try asking Metka if they happen to have the fires going that day; if so, a blacksmith may be willing to do a demonstration for you—but no guarantees.

Kropa Town

Take a stroll from the museum up through this hardworking yet charming village. Notice the **canals** that have been split off from the main river to channel water to turn waterwheels (you'll see a replica waterwheel by the Uko factory).

The main **bridge** through town offers a good view up and down the thundering river, so packed with energy for harnessing—

making it clear why this was an attractive place for early industry. The blocky, boldly communist-era **monument** next to the bridge honors the Partisans who died during World War II while evicting the Nazis from Yugoslavia. Although its aesthetic is off-putting Socialist Realism, its content—with locally made iron decorations—is unique to Kropa. Notice the depiction of a Kropa resident handing over his hammer in exchange for a rifle. While this is a heroic image, most people from Kropa have long enjoyed military exemption—since their metalworking prowess was so valuable to the war effort. The communist Yugoslav government—always eager to celebrate industry for its role in advancing the cause of the proletariat—made Kropa Slovenia's first town to be protected as a cultural monument, in 1953.

Crossing the bridge and continuing up the road, near the top of town on the left you'll pass a traditional **forge** with firewood stacked out front. This working facility—which still merges the power of wood, water, and a blacksmith's arm to create spikes—is part of the Iron Forging Museum, but unfortunately, it's rarely open to individual visitors (explained earlier). For most of its history, Kropa had 15 such forges.

Lake Bohinj

The pristine alpine Lake Bohinj (BOH-heen), 16 miles southwest of Bled, enjoys a quieter scene and (in clear weather) even better vistas of Triglav and the surrounding mountains. This is a real back-to-nature experience, with just a smattering of hotels and campgrounds, rather than the well-oiled resort machine of Bled. Some people adore Bohinj; others are bored by it. While spectacular in clear, sunny weather, it's disappointing in the clouds (and, because of its position deep in the mountains, it can be socked in here even when it's clear in Bled). But if the weather is great and you're finding Bled too touristy to allow you to really enjoy nature, go to Bohinj.

Getting to Lake Bohinj: From Bled, hourly **buses** head for Bohinj, stopping at three different destinations: Bohinj Jezero (the village of Ribčev Laz, 40 minutes, €3.60), then Bohinj Vogel (a 10-minute walk from the base of the Vogel Mountain cable car, 50 minutes, €4.10), and finally a few hundred yards more to Bohinj Zlatorog (Hotel Zlatorog and the one-hour hike to the Savica waterfall trailhead, 50 minutes, €4.10). In summer, a few buses continue all the way to the Savica Waterfall trailhead (see details under "Savica Waterfall," later). Off-season, there are fewer buses—confirm times before you depart.

Drivers leave Bled going south along the lakefront road, Cesta Svobode; in the village of Mlino, you'll peel off from the lake and follow signs to *Boh Bistrica* (a midsize town near Lake Bohinj). Once in the town of Bohinjska Bistrica, turn right, following *Boh Jezero* signs. The road takes you to the village of Ribčev Laz and along the lakefront road with all the attractions—the drive from Bled to the lake takes about 30 minutes. You can follow this road all the way to the Vogel cable-car parking lot; at the Vogel turnoff, you can continue straight ahead to reach the Savica Waterfall trailhead, or turn right and cross the bridge to curl around the far end of the lake and see the pristine river that feeds the lake (which flows out of the pool at the base of the Savica Waterfall).

Sights at Lake Bohinj

A visit to Bohinj has three parts: a village (offering boat trips on the lake), a cable car (and nearby cemetery), and a waterfall hike. I've listed them as you'll reach them along the main road from Bled, which runs along the south side of the lake. If you plan to do everything (boat trip, cable car, waterfall hike), ask at the TI in Ribčev Laz about a combo-ticket to save some money.

Ribčev Laz Village—Coming from Bled, your first views of Bohinj will be from the little village called Ribčev Laz (loosely translated as "Good Fishin' Hole")

at the southeast corner of the lake. Here you'll find a TI, a handful of hotels and ice-cream stands, and the Bohinj Jezero bus stop. The town's main landmark is its picturesque lakefront church, **St. John the Baptist** (to your right as you face the lake, past the stone bridge; not open to visitors).

A five-minute stroll down the main lakefront road is a dock where you can catch an electric **tourist boat** to make a silent circuit around the lake (€10 round-trip, €7 one-way, daily 10:00-18:00, runs hourly, less off-season). The boat stops at the far end of the lake, at Camp Zlatorog—a 10-minute walk from the Vogel cable car (see below). Across from the Ribčev Laz dock is a fun concrete 3-D model of Triglav. Finally, a few more steps down the road, just beyond a boat rental dock, you'll see a statue of Zlatorog, the "Golden Horn"—a mythical chamois-like creature native to the Julian Alps.

▲Vogel Mountain Cable Car—For a mountain perch without the sweat, take the cable car up to the top of Vogel Mountain, offering impressive panoramic views of Mount Triglav and the Julian

Alps. On a clear day, this is the best mountain panorama you can get without wings (the light is best in the morning). The summit is a ski-in-winter, hike-in-summer area with a pasture filled with grazing cows (summer only) and smaller chairlifts to various recreation areas. The first, short chairlift you'll see is designed for skiers and doesn't run in summer, but if you hike down into the little valley, you can take the second chairlift up the adjacent summit (Orlove Glave) for views into another valley on the other side. Then, from Orlove Glave, you can hike or ride the chairlift back to where you started. With plenty of time and very strong knees, you could even hike from Orlove Glave all the way back down to Lake Bohinj. If you need a break near the cable-car station, the alpine hut Merjasec ("Wild Boar") offers tasty strudel and a wide variety of local brandies (including the notorious "Boar's Blood"—a concoction of several different flavors guaranteed to get you snorting).

Cost and Hours: €13 round-trip, Dec-Oct daily 8:00-18:00, runs every 30 minutes in summer and continuously in winter, closed Nov, www.vogel.si.

Getting There: To reach the cable-car station, drivers follow signs to *Vogel* (to the left off the main lakefront road); by bus, get off at the Bohinj Vogel stop (request this stop from driver) and hike about 10 minutes up the steep road on the left (away from the lake).

World War I Cemetery—Back down below the cable car, on the main road just beyond the cable-car station and Bohinj Vogel bus stop, look for the metal gate on the left marking a World War I cemetery—the final resting place for some Soča Front soldiers (see sidebar on page 616). While no fighting occurred here (it was mostly on the other side of these mountains), injured soldiers were brought to a nearby hospital, and those who didn't recover ended up here. Notice that many of the names are not Slovenian, but Hungarian, Polish, Czech, and so on—a reminder that the entire multiethnic Austro-Hungarian Empire was involved in the fighting. If you're walking down from the cable-car station, the cemetery makes for a poignant detour on your way to the main road (look for it through the trees).

Savica Waterfall (Slap Savica)—Up the valley beyond the end of the lake is Bohinj's final treat, a waterfall called Slap Savica (sah-VEET-seh). Hardy hikers enjoy following the moderate-to-strenuous uphill trail (including 553 stairs) to see the cascade, which dumps into a remarkably pure pool of aquamarine snowmelt.

Cost and Hours: €2.50, daily in summer from 8:00 until dusk, allow up to 1.5 hours for the round-trip hike.

Getting There: Drivers follow the lakefront road to where it ends, right at the trailhead. Without a car, getting to the trailhead is a hassle. Boats on the lake, as well as most public buses from Bled, take you only as far as the Bohinj Zlatorog stop—

the end of the line, and still a one-hour hike from the trailhead (from the bus stop, follow signs to *Slap Savica*). However, during the summer (Mon-Sat late June-Sept only, none Sun or off-season), three buses a day run from Bled all the way to the Savica trailhead (likely departing Bled at 10:00, 14:20, and 16:20, about an hour to the trailhead, returning at 15:20 and 18:20—but confirm times locally before making the trip). But frankly, if the connections don't fit your itinerary, it's not worth worrying about.

Sleeping at Lake Bohinj

If you'd like to get away from it all and settle in at Bohinj, consider **$$ Stare Pension** (STAH-reh). Well-run by mild-mannered Jože, it has 10 older, rustic, but well-maintained rooms (five of them with balconies) in a pristine setting at the far end of the lake (Db-€80 July-Aug, €70 May-June and Sept, €60 Oct-April, €5 less without balcony, half-board-€10 per person, free Internet access and Wi-Fi, Ukanc 128, mobile 040-558-669, www.impel-bohinj .si, info@impel-bohinj.si).

THE JULIAN ALPS

Vršič Pass • Soča River Valley • Bovec • Kobarid

The countryside around Lake Bled is plenty spectacular. But to top off your Slovenian mountain experience, head for the hills. The northwestern corner of Slovenia—within yodeling distance of Austria and Italy—is crowned by the Julian Alps (named for Julius Caesar). Here, mountain culture has a Slavic flavor.

The Slovenian mountainsides are laced with hiking paths, blanketed in deep forests, and speckled with ski resorts and vacation chalets. Beyond every ridge is a peaceful alpine village nestled around a quaint Baroque steeple. And in the center of it all is Mount Triglav—ol' "Three Heads"—Slovenia's national symbol and tallest mountain.

The single best day in the Julian Alps is spent driving up and over the 50 hairpin turns of breathtaking Vršič Pass (vur-SHEECH, open May-Oct) and back down via the Soča (SOH-chah) River Valley, lined with offbeat nooks and Hemingway-haunted crannies. As you curl on twisty roads between the cut-glass peaks, you'll enjoy stunning high-mountain scenery, whitewater rivers with superb fishing, rustic rest stops, thought-provoking World War I sights, and charming hamlets.

A pair of Soča Valley towns holds watch over the region. Bovec is all about good times (it's the whitewater adventure-sports hub), while Kobarid attends to more serious matters (WWI history). Though neither is a destination in itself, both Bovec and Kobarid are pleasant, functional, and convenient home bases for exploring this gloriously beautiful region.

Getting Around the Julian Alps

The Julian Alps are best by **car.** Even if you're doing the rest of your trip by train, consider renting a car here for maximum mountain day-trip flexibility. I've included a self-guided driving tour that incorporates the best of the Julian Alps (Vršič Pass and Soča Valley).

If you're without your own wheels, hiring a **local guide with a car** can be a great value, maximizing not only what you see, but what you learn. Cheaper but less personalized, you could join a day-trip **excursion** from Bled. (Both options are explained under "Tours at Lake Bled," page 571.) A public **bus** follows more or less the driving-tour route described below, leaving Ljubljana each morning at 6:30, arriving in Bovec at 10:45 (daily July-Aug, Sat-Sun only June and Sept, none Oct-May). Or stay closer to Bled, and get a taste of the Julian Alps by taking advantage of easy and frequent bus connections to more convenient day-trip destinations (the Vintgar Gorge and Lake Bohinj—both described under "Near Lake Bled" in the previous chapter).

Self-Guided Driving Tour

This all-day, self-guided driving tour—rated ▲▲▲—takes you over the highest mountain pass in Slovenia, with stunning scenery and a few quirky sights along the way. From waterfalls to hiking trails, World War I history to queasy suspension bridges, this trip has it all.

Orientation to the Julian Alps

Most of the Julian Alps are encompassed by Triglav National Park (Triglavski Narodni Park). This drive is divided into two parts: the Vršič Pass and the Soča River Valley. While not for stick-shift novices, all but the most timid drivers will agree that the scenery is worth the many hairpin turns. Frequent pull-outs offer plenty of opportunities to relax, stretch your legs, and enjoy the vistas.

Planning Your Time: This drive can be done in a day, but consider spending the night along the way for a more leisurely pace. You can start and end in Bled or Ljubljana. You can return to your starting point, or do this trip one-way as a very scenic detour between these two destinations.

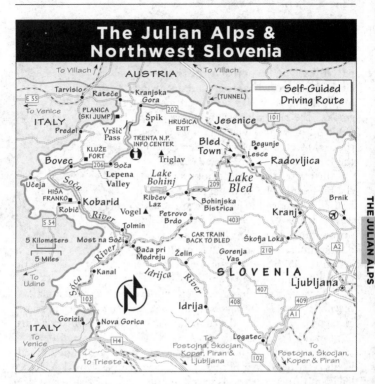

The Julian Alps & Northwest Slovenia

Self-Guided Driving Route

Length of This Tour: These rough estimates do not include stops: Bled to the top of Vršič Pass—1 hour; Vršič Pass to Trenta (start of Soča Valley)—30 minutes; Trenta to Bovec—30 minutes; Bovec to Kobarid—30 minutes; Kobarid to Ljubljana or Bled—2 hours (remember, it's an hour between Ljubljana and Bled). In other words, if you started and ended in Bled and drove the entire route without stopping, you'd make it home in less than five hours...but you'd miss so much. It takes at least a full day to really do the region justice.

Tourist Information: The best sources of information are the Bled TI (see page 564), the Triglav National Park Information Centers in Trenta (page 608) and Bled (page 565), and the TIs in Bovec and Kobarid (both listed in this chapter).

Maps: Pick up a good map before you begin (available at local TIs, travel agencies, and gas stations). The all-Slovenia *Autokarta Slovenija* or the TI's *Next Exit: Goldenhorn Route* map both include all the essential roads, but several more detailed options are also available. The 1:50,000 Kod & Kam *Posoče* map covers the entire Vršič Pass and Soča Valley (but doesn't include the parts of the drive near Bled and Ljubljana).

OK...let's ride.

Part 1: Vršič Pass

From Bled or Ljubljana, take the A2 expressway north, enjoying views of Mount Triglav on the left as you drive. About 10 minutes past Bled, you'll approach the industrial city of **Jesenice,** whose iron- and steelworks once filled this valley with multicolored smoke. The city, which was known as the "Detroit of Yugoslavia," plans to convert these old factories (most of which closed in the 1980s) into a sort of theme park.

Just after the giant smokestack with the billboards, the little gaggle of colorful houses on the right (just next to the freeway) is **Kurja Vas** ("Chicken Village"). This unassuming place is locally famous for producing hockey players: 18 of the 20 players on the 1971 Yugoslav hockey team—which went to the World Championships—were from this tiny hamlet.

As you zip past Jesenice, keep your eye out for the exit marked *Jesenice-zahod, Trbiž/Tarvisio, Kr. Gora,* and *Hrušica* (it's after the gas station, just before the tunnel to Austria). When you exit, turn left toward *Trbiž/Tarvisio* and *Kranjska Gora* (yellow sign).

Just after the exit, the big, blue building surrounded by tall lights was the former border station (the overpass you'll go under leads into Austria). Locals have fond memories of visiting Austria during the Yugoslav days, when they smuggled home forbidden Western goods. Some items weren't available back home (VCRs, Coca-Cola, designer clothes), while other goods were simply better in Austria (chocolate, coffee, dishwasher soap).

Slovenes brag that their country—"with 56 percent of the land covered in forest"—is Europe's second-greenest. As you drive toward Kranjska Gora, take in all this greenery...and the characteristic Slovenian hayracks (recognized as part of the national heritage and now preserved; see page 505). The Vrata Valley (on the left) is a popular starting point for climbing Mount Triglav. Paralleling the road on the left is a "rails-to-trails" bike path—converted from an old railway bed—that loops from here through Italy and Austria, allowing bikers to connect three countries in one day. On the right, watch for the statue of Jakob Aljaž, who actually bought Triglav, back when such a thing was possible (he's pointing at his purchase). Ten minutes later, in Gozd Martuljek, you'll cross a bridge and enjoy a great head-on view of Špik Mountain.

Kranjska Gora was once Yugoslavia's leading winter resort, and remains popular with Croatian skiers. As every Slovene and Croatian wants a ski bungalow here, it has some of the highest property values in the country. Entering Kranjska Gora, you'll see

Mount Triglav

Mount Triglav ("Three Heads") stands watch over the Julian Alps, and all of Slovenia. Slovenes say that its three peaks are the guardians of the water, air, and earth. This mountain defines Slovenes, even adorning the nation's flag: You'll often see the national seal, with three peaks (the two squiggly lines under it represent the Adriatic). Or take a look at one of Slovenia's €0.50 coins.

From the town of Bled, you'll see Triglav peeking up over the ridge on a clear day. (You'll get an even better view from nearby Lake Bohinj.)

It's said that you're not a true Slovene until you've climbed Triglav. One native took these words very seriously and climbed the mountain 853 times...in one year. Climbing to the summit—at 9,396 feet—is an attainable goal for any hiker in decent shape. If you're here for a while and want to become an honorary Slovene, befriend a local and ask if he or she will take you to the top.

If mountain climbing isn't your style, relax at an outdoor café with a piece of cream cake and a view of Triglav. It won't make you a Slovene...but it's close enough on a quick visit.

THE JULIAN ALPS

a turnoff to the left marked for *Bovec* and *Vršič*. This leads up to the pass, but winter sports fanatics may first want to take a 15-minute detour to see the biggest ski jump in the world, a few miles ahead (stay straight through Kranjska Gora, then turn left at signs for **Planica**, the last stop before the Italian border). Every few years, tens of thousands of sports fans flock here to watch the ski-flying world championships. This is where a local boy was the first human to fly more than 100 meters (328 feet) on skis. Today's competitors routinely set new world records (currently 784 feet—that's 17 seconds in the air). From the ski jump, you're a few minutes' walk from Italy or Austria. This region—spanning three nations—lobbied unsuccessfully under the name Senza Confini (Italian for "without borders") to host the 2006 Winter Olympics. This philosophy is in tune with the European Union's vision for a Europe of regions, rather than nations.

Back in Kranjska Gora, follow the signs for *Vršič*. Before long, you'll officially enter **Triglav National Park** and come to the first of this road's 50 hairpin turns (24 up, then 26 down)—each one numbered and labeled with the altitude in meters. Notice that the turns are cobbled to provide better traction. If the drive seems daunting, remember that 50-seat tour buses routinely conquer this pass...if they can do it, so can you. Better yet, imagine the bicyclists who regularly pedal to the top. The best can do it in less than 30 minutes—faster than driving.

After switchback #8, with the cute waterfall, park your car on the right and hike up the stairs on the left to the little **Russian**

chapel. This road was built during World War I by at least 10,000 Russian POWs of the Austro-Hungarian Empire to supply the front lines of the Soča Front. The POWs lived and worked in terrible conditions, and several hundred died of illness and exposure. On March 8, 1916, an avalanche thundered down the mountains, killing hundreds more workers. This chapel was built where the final casualty was found. Take a minute to pay your respects to the men who built the road you're enjoying today. Because it's a Russian Orthodox chapel, notice that the crosses topping the steeples have three crossbars. (For more on the Orthodox faith, see page 318.)

Back on the road, after #17, look as high as you can on the cliff face to see sunlight streaming through a **"window"** in the rock. This natural formation, a popular destination for intrepid hikers, is big enough for the Statue of Liberty to crawl through.

After #22, at the pullout for Erjavčeva Koča restaurant, you may see tour-bus groups making a fuss about the mountain vista. They're looking for a ghostly face in the cliff wall, supposedly belonging to the mythical figure **Ajda.** This village girl was cursed by the townspeople after correctly predicting the death of the Zlatorog (Golden Horn), a magical, beloved, chamois-like animal. Her tiny image (with a Picasso nose) is just above the tree line, a little to the right—try to get someone to point her out to you (you can see her best if you stand at the signpost near the road).

After #24, you reach the **summit** (5,285 feet). Consider getting out of the car to enjoy the views (in peak season, you'll pay an attendant to park here). Hike up to the hut for a snack or drink on the grand view terrace. On the right, a long gravel chute gives hikers a thrilling glissade. (From the pullout just beyond #26, it's easy to view hikers "skiing" down.)

Hemingway in the Julian Alps

It was against the scenic backdrop of the Slovenian Alps that a young man from Oak Park, Illinois, first came to Europe—the continent with which he would forever be identified. After graduating from high school in 1917 and working briefly as a newspaper reporter, young Ernest Hemingway wanted to join the war effort in Europe. Bad vision kept him out of the army, but he craved combat experience—so he joined the Red Cross Ambulance Corps instead.

After a short detour through Paris, Hemingway was sent to the Italian Front. On his first day, he was given the job of retrieving human remains—gruesomely disfigured body parts—after the explosion of a munitions factory. Later he came to the Lower Piave Valley, not far from the Soča Front. In July 1918, his ambulance was hit by a mortar shell. Despite his injuries, he saved an Italian soldier who was also wounded. According to legend, he packed his own wound with cigarette butts to stop the flow of blood.

Sent to Milan to recuperate, Hemingway fell in love with a nurse, but she later left him for an Italian military officer. A decade later, Hemingway wrote about Kobarid (using its Italian name, Caporetto), the war, and his case of youthful heartbreak in the novel *A Farewell to Arms*.

THE JULIAN ALPS

As you begin the descent, keep an eye out for old WWI debris. A lonely guard tunnel stands after #28, followed by a tunnel marked *1916* (on the left) that was part of the road's original path. Then you'll see abandoned checkpoints from when this was the border between Italy and the Austro-Hungarian Empire. At #48 is a statue of **Julius Kugy,** an Italian botanist who wrote books about alpine flora.

At #49, the road to the right (marked *Izvir Soče*) leads to the **source of the Soča River.** If you feel like stretching your legs after all that shifting, drive about five minutes down this road to a restaurant parking lot. From here, you can take a challenging 20-minute uphill hike to the Soča source. This is also the starting point for the well-explained, 12-mile Soča Trail (Soška Pot), which leads all the way to the town of Bovec, mostly following the road we're driving on today.

Nearing the end of the switchbacks, follow signs for *Bovec*. Crossing the Soča River, you begin the second half of this trip.

Part 2: Soča River Valley

During World War I, the terrain between here and the Adriatic made up the Soča (Isonzo) Front. As you follow the Soča River south, down what's nicknamed the "Valley of the Cemeteries," the scenic mountainsides around you tell the tale of this terrible war-fare. Imagine a young Ernest Hemingway driving his ambulance through these same hills (see sidebar).

But it's not all so gloomy. There are plenty of other diversions—interesting villages and churches, waterfalls and suspension bridges, and lots more. Perhaps most impressive is the remarkable clarity and milky-blue color of the Soča itself, which Slovenes proudly call their "emerald river."

After switchback #49, you'll cross a bridge, then pass a church and a botanical garden of alpine plants (Alpinum Juliana). Across the street from the garden (on the right) is the parking lot for the Mlinarica Gorge. While the gorge is interesting, the bridge leading to it was damaged in a severe storm and hasn't yet been rebuilt—so it's best left to hardy hikers.

The last Vršič switchback (#50) sends you into the village of **Trenta.** As you get to the cluster of buildings in Trenta's "downtown," look on the left for the **Triglav National Park Information Center,** which also serves as a regional TI (daily July-Aug 8:00-20:00, May-June and Sept-Oct 10:00-18:00, Dec-April 10:00-14:00, closed Nov, tel. 05/388-9330, www.tnp.si). The €5 museum here provides a look (with English explanations) at the park's flora, fauna, traditional culture, and mountaineering history. An AV

show celebrates the region's forests, and a poetic 15-minute slideshow explains the wonders and fragility of the park (included in museum entry, ask for English version as you enter).

After Trenta, you'll pass through a tunnel; then, on the left, look for a classic **suspension bridge.** Pull over to walk out for a bounce, enjoying the river's crystal-clear water and the spectacular mountain panorama.

About five miles beyond Trenta, in the town of Soča, is the **Church of St. Joseph** (with red onion dome, hiding behind the big tree on the right). The church was damaged in the earthquakes of 1998 and 2004, so the interior is likely covered with scaffolding. But if it's not covered, you'll see some fascinating art. During World War II, an artist hiding out in the mountains filled this church with patriotic symbolism. The interior is bathed in Yugoslav red, white, and blue—a brave statement made when such nationalistic sentiments were dangerous. On the ceiling is St. Michael (clad in Yugoslav colors) with Yugoslavia's three WWII enemies at his feet: the eagle (Germany), the wolf (Italy), and the serpent

(Japan). The tops of the walls along the nave are lined with saints, but these are Slavic, not Catholic. Finally, look carefully at the Stations of the Cross and find the faces of hated Yugoslav enemies:

Hitler (fourth from altar on left) and Mussolini (first from altar on right). Behind the church, the stylized cross on the hill marks a **WWI cemetery**—the final resting place of some 600 Austro-Hungarian soldiers who were killed in action.

For another good example of how the Soča River cuts like God's band saw into the land, stop about two minutes past the church at the small gravel lot (on the left) marked ***Velika Korita Soče*** ("Grand Canyon of Soča"). Venture out onto the suspension bridge over the gorge...and bounce if you dare. Just beyond this bridge is the turnoff (on the left) to the Lepena Valley, home of the recommended Pristava Lepena ranch, with accommodations and Lipizzaner horses (described later, under "Sleeping in Bovec").

Roughly five miles after the town of Soča, you exit the national park, pass a WWI graveyard (on the left), and come to a fork in the road. The main route leads to the left, through Bovec. But first,

take a two-mile detour to the right (marked *Trbiž/ Tarvisio* and *Predel/Kluže*), where the WWI **Kluže Fort** keeps a close watch over the narrowest part of a valley leading to Italy (€3; July-Aug daily 9:00-20:00; June and Sept Sun-Fri 9:00-17:00, Sat 9:00-18:00; May and Oct Sat-Sun 10:00-17:00, closed Mon-Fri; closed Nov-April; www.kluze.net). In the 15th century, the Italians had a fort here to defend against the Ottomans. Half a millennium later, during World War I, it was used by Austrians to keep Italians out of their territory. Notice the ladder rungs fixed to the cliff face across the road from the fort—allowing soldiers to quickly get up to the mountaintop.

Back on the main road, continue to **Bovec**. This town, which saw some of the most vicious fighting of the Soča Front, was hit hard by earthquakes in 1994 and 1998 (and by another tremor in 2004). Today, it's been rebuilt and remains the adventure-sports capital of the Soča River Valley—also known as the "Adrenaline Valley," famous for its whitewater activities. (Since the water comes from high-mountain runoff, the temperature of the Soča never goes above 68 degrees Fahrenheit.) For a good lunch stop in Bovec, take the turnoff as you first reach the town, and you'll pass an inviting restaurant terrace on the right (Martinov Hram; for details, see "Eating in Bovec," later). But if you're not eating or spending the night in Bovec, you could skip the town entirely and not miss much (continue along the main road to bypass the town center).

Heading south along the river—with water somehow both perfectly clear and spectacularly turquoise—watch for happy kayakers. When you pass the intersection at Žaga, you're just four miles from Italy. Along the way, you'll also pass a pair of **waterfalls:** the well-known Boka ("Slovenia's second-longest waterfall," on the right just before Žaga) and the hidden gem Veliki Kozjak (on the left just before Kobarid). It's possible—but challenging—to hike to either fall (Boka's trailhead is just after the bridge on the right, but it's an extremely strenuous hike; Veliki Kozjak is a bit more manageable, but still not level or easy—for details, see page 620).

Signs lead to the town of **Kobarid,** home to a sleepy main square and some fascinating WWI sights. Even if you don't think you're interested in the Soča Front, consider dropping in to the Kobarid Museum. Driving up to the Italian mausoleum hovering over the town is a must. (These sights are described later, under "Sights in Kobarid.")

Leaving Kobarid, continue south along the Soča to **Tolmin.** Before you reach Tolmin, decide on your preferred route back to civilization...

Finishing the Drive

While you could go back over the pass the way you came, there are various ways to make your trip a loop by circling through some more varied scenery. Which way you go depends on your final destination: Ljubljana or Bled.

To Ljubljana (or Southern Slovenia/Croatia)

From Tolmin, you have two possible driving routes to the capital. Either option brings you back to the A1 expressway south of Ljubljana, and will get you to the city in about two hours (though the second route has fewer miles).

Nova Gorica Route: The option you'll encounter first (turnoff to the right before Tolmin) is the smoother, longer route southwest to Nova Gorica. Along this road, you'll pass a hydroelectric dam and go under a 1906 rail viaduct that once connected this area to the port of Trieste (now in Italy). In the charming town of Kanal, you'll cross over the Soča on a picturesque bridge that's faintly reminiscent of Mostar's (as in that city, young people stage a competition for jumping off this bridge into the raging river below). Father along, the striking Solkan Bridge (another link in the Trieste rail line) is the longest single-span stone arch bridge in the world. Soon after, you arrive in Nova Gorica. This fairly dull city is divided in half by the Italian border (the Italian side is called "Gorizia"). Because Italians aren't allowed to gamble in their home towns, Nova Gorica is packed with casinos catering to Italian gamblers. In fact, it's home to Europe's biggest casino. Rocks spell out the name "TITO" on a hillside above town—a strange relic of an earlier age. From Nova Gorica, you can hop on the H4 expressway, which links easily to the main A1 expressway. Also notice that the road from Nova Gorica to Ljubljana takes you through the heart of the Karst region—if you have time and daylight to spare, you could tour a cave, castle, or Lipizzaner stud farm on your way back up to Ljubljana (see the Karst chapter).

Idrija Route: For a more off-the-beaten-path, ruggedly scenic approach, take this rural option: Continue through Tolmin, then head southeast through the hills back toward Ljubljana. Along the way, you could stop for a bite and some sightseeing at the town of Idrija (EE-dree-yah), known to all Slovenes for three things: its tourable mercury mine, fine delicate lace, and tasty *žlikrofi* (like ravioli). Back at the expressway (at Logatec), head north to Ljubljana.

To Bled

To reach Bled, you could follow either of the Ljubljana-bound routes outlined above, then carry on northward for another hour to Bled (allow about 3 hours total). But the following options are more direct.

Car Train: The fastest option is to load your car onto a "Car Train" (Autovlak) that cuts directly through the mountains. The train departs at 18:30 from Most na Soči (just south of Tolmin, along the Idrija route described above) and arrives at Bohinjska Bistrica, near Lake Bohinj, at 19:14 (€12 for the car; confirm schedule at the Bled TI before making the trip). From Bohinjska Bistrica, it's just a half-hour drive back to Bled. No reservations are necessary, but arrive at the train station about 30 minutes before the scheduled departure to allow time to load the car.

Through Italy via Predel Pass: Although this route requires some backtracking, it also includes a detour through Italy. From Kobarid, drive back the way you came (through Bovec), then turn off for the Kluže Fort (described on page 609), marked for *Predel* and Italy. In a few miles, after passing the fort, the road curves up through two small villages (first Log pod Mangartom, then

Strmec na Predelu directly above it). Continue past the ruined fortress and cross the Italian border (there's no need to stop). Then curl down a few hairpin turns past the end of Lake Predel, and continue straight through the ghost city of Cave del Predil (a former lead-mining town) and along the valley road, following signs for Slovenia. Approaching Tarvisio, turn right (continuing to follow signs for Slovenia); from here, it's about a half-hour (10 miles) back across the Slovenian border to Kranjska Gora. This is where you first began your ascent of the Vršič Pass—just retrace your steps back to Bled.

Other Driving Routes: The fastest route (about 2 hours) is partially on a twisty, rough, very poor-quality road (go through Tolmin, turn off at Bača pri Modreju to Podbrdo, then from Petrovo Brdo take a very curvy road through the mountains into Bohinjska Bistrica and on to Bled). For timid drivers, it's more sane and not too much longer to start out on the Idrija route toward Ljubljana (described above), but turn off in Želin (before Idrija) toward Škofja Loka and Kranj, then continue on to Bled.

Bovec

The biggest town in the area, Bovec (BOH-vets) has a happening main square and all the tourist amenities. It's best known as a hub for whitewater adventure sports. While not exactly quaint, Bovec is charming enough to qualify as a good lunch stop or overnight home base. If nothing else, it's a nice jolt of civilization wedged between the alpine cliffs.

Orientation to Bovec

Tourist Information
The helpful TI on the main square offers fliers on mountain biking and water sports (flexible hours, generally June-Sept daily 9:00-19:00; off-season Mon-Fri 9:00-17:00, Sat-Sun 9:00-14:00 & 14:30-17:00; Trg Golobarskih Žrtev 8, tel. 05/384-1444, www.bovec.si).

Arrival in Bovec
The main road skirts Bovec, but you can turn off (watch for signs on the right) to take the road that goes through the heart of town, then rejoins the main road farther along. As you approach the city center, you can't miss the main square, Trg Golobarskih Žrtev, with the TI and a good restaurant (described later, under "Eating in Bovec").

Sleeping in Bovec

$$$ Hotel Mangart is a big, modern, chalet-style hotel with 36 rooms on the edge of Bovec (toward the Vršič Pass). All of the rooms have balconies, except the cheaper bunkbed hostel rooms (Db-€110 in July-Aug, €100 in May-June and Sept, €90 in Oct, cheaper Nov-April, bigger superior rooms have bathtubs and nicer decor—not worth the extra €20; hostel rooms are a great value-€25/person in a small 2-, 4-, or 6-bed room with a tight bathroom; elevator, free Wi-Fi, Mala vas 107, tel. 05/388-4250, www.hotel-mangart.com, booking@hotel-mangart.com).

$$ Martinov Hram has 11 nice, modern rooms over a popular restaurant a few steps from Bovec's main square. While the rooms are an afterthought to the busy restaurant (reception at the bar), they're comfortable (very flexible rates, in peak season figure Sb-€40, Db-€70, a few euros less off-season, no extra charge for 1-night stays, rooms on sunny side have air-con, free Wi-Fi in restaurant and cable Internet in rooms, Trg Golobarskih Žrtev 27, tel. 05/388-6214, www.martinov-hram.si, sara.berginc@gmail.com).

Near Bovec

$$$ Pristava Lepena is a relaxing oasis hiding out in the Lepena Valley just north of Bovec. Well-run by Milan and Silvia Dolenc, this place is its own little village: a series of rustic-looking cabins, a restaurant, a sauna/whirlpool, and an outdoor swimming pool. Hiding behind the humble split-wood shingle exteriors is surprising comfort: 13 cozy apartments (with wood-burning stoves, TV,

THE JULIAN ALPS

Sleep Code

(€1 = about $1.40, country code: 386, area code: 05)
S = Single, **D** = Double/Twin, **T** = Triple, **Q** = Quad, **b** = bathroom. Unless otherwise noted, credit cards are accepted and breakfast is included, but the modest tourist tax (about €1 per person, per night) is not. Everyone listed here speaks English.

To help you easily sort through these listings, I've divided the accommodations into three categories based on the price for a double room with bath during high season:

$$$ Higher Priced—Most rooms €100 or more.
$$ Moderately Priced—Most rooms between €50-100.
$ Lower Priced—Most rooms €50 or less.

Prices can change without notice; verify the hotel's current rates online or by email. For other updates, see www.ricksteves.com/update.

telephone, Wi-Fi, and all the amenities) that make you feel like relaxing. This place whispers "second honeymoon" (Db-€138 in July-Aug, €122 in May-June and Sept, €106 in early Oct and late April, closed in winter except mid-Dec-early Jan, multinight stays preferred, 1-night stays may be possible for 20 percent extra, dinner-€19, lunch and dinner-€31, nonrefundable 30 percent advance payment when you reserve; just before Bovec, turn left off the main road toward Lepena, and follow the white horses to Lepena 2; tel. 05/388-9900, fax 05/388-9901, www.pristava-lepena.com, pristava .lepena@siol.net). The Dolences also have three Welsh ponies and five purebred Lipizzaner horses (two mares, three geldings) that guests can ride (in riding ring-€16/hour, on trail-€20/hour, riding lesson-€24; non-guests may be able to ride for a few euros more—call ahead and ask).

$$ **Boka Pension** fills a big modern-but-tasteful building squeezed between the road and the Soča, near the big Boka waterfall. The 20 rooms are simple but have nice woody touches (Db-€66 in mid-July-Aug, €62 in May-mid-July and Sept, cheaper off-season, €10 more for a bigger suite, elevator, free cable Internet, some road noise, Žaga 156a, tel. 05/384-5512, www.boka-bovec.si, penzion@boka-bovec.si).

$ **Tourist Farm Pri Plajerju** is on a picturesque plateau at the edge of Trenta (the first town at the bottom of the Vršič Pass road). Run by the Pretner family (gregarious Marko is a park ranger, shy Stanka is "the boss"), this organic farm raises sheep and rents five apartments in three buildings separate from the main house. As the Soča Valley doesn't have many tourist farms, this is one of your best options if you want to stay at one. However, its location deeper in the mountains makes it a bit less convenient for side-tripping—it's 30 minutes to Bovec, and 45 minutes to Kobarid (July-Aug: Db-€45-55, Tb-€55-65, Qb-€68-78; Sept-June: Db-€40-50, Tb-€50-60, Qb-€63-70; price depends on size, breakfast-€7, dinner-€11—available some but not all nights, watch for signs to the left after coming over the pass and going through the village of Trenta, Trenta 16a, tel. & fax 05/388-9209, mobile 041-600-590, www.eko-plajer.com, info@eko-plajer.com).

Eating in Bovec

Martinov Hram, run by the Berginc family, has an inviting outdoor terrace under a grape trellis. Inside, the nicely traditional decor goes well with Slovenian specialties with a focus on sheep (good homemade bread, €7-12 pastas, €8-20 main courses, Tue-Sun 10:00-23:00, closed Mon, on the main road through Bovec, just before the main square on the right at Trg Golobarskih Žrtev 27, tel. 05/388-6214).

Kobarid

Kobarid (KOH-bah-reed) feels older, and therefore a bit more appealing, than its big brother Bovec. This humble settlement was immortalized by a literary giant, Ernest Hemingway, who drove an ambulance in these mountains during World War I. He described Kobarid as "a little white town with a campanile in a valley. It was a clean little town and there was a fine fountain in the square." Sounds about right. Even though Kobarid loves to tout its Hemingway connection, historians believe that Papa did not actually visit Kobarid until he came back after the war to research his book.

Aside from its brush with literary greatness, Kobarid is known as a hub of information about the Soča Front (with an excellent WWI museum, a hilltop Italian mausoleum, and walks that connect the nearby sights). You won't find the fountain Hemingway wrote about—it's since been covered up by houses (though the town government hopes to excavate it as a tourist attraction). You will find a modern statue of Simon Gregorčič (overlooking the main intersection), the beloved Slovenian priest-slash-poet who came from and wrote about the Soča Valley.

Orientation to Kobarid

(area code: 05)
The main road cuts right through the heart of little Kobarid, bisecting its main square (Trg Svobode). The Kobarid Museum is along this road, on the left before the square. To reach the museum from the main square, simply walk five minutes back toward Bovec.

Tourist Information
The TI has good information on the area, and Internet access (May-June Mon-Fri 9:00-13:00 & 14:00-18:00, Sat-Sun 10:00-14:00; July-Sept daily 9:00-19:00; Oct-April Mon-Fri 9:00-13:00 & 14:00-16:00, Sat-Sun 10:00-14:00; on the main square at Trg Svobode 16—follow the white footprints behind the statue of Gregorčič, tel. 05/380-0490, www.dolina-soce.com and www.kobarid.si).

The Soča (Isonzo) Front

The valley in Slovenia's northwest corner—called Soča in Slovene and Isonzo in Italian—saw some of World War I's fiercest fighting. While the Western Front gets more press, this eastern border between the Central Powers and the Allies was just as significant. In a series of 12 battles involving 22 different nationalities along a 60-mile-long front, 300,000 soldiers died, 700,000 were wounded, and 100,000 were declared MIA. In addition, tens of thousands of civilians died. A young Ernest Hemingway, who drove an ambulance for the Italian army in nearby fighting, would later write the novel *A Farewell to Arms* about the battles here (see "Hemingway in the Julian Alps" sidebar on page 607).

On April 26, 1915, Italy joined the Allies. A month later, it declared war on the Austro-Hungarian Empire (which included Slovenia). Italy unexpectedly invaded the Soča Valley, quickly taking the tiny town of Kobarid, which it planned to use as a home base for attacks deeper into Austro-Hungarian territory. For the next 29 months, Italy launched 10 more offensives against the Austro-Hungarian army, which was encamped on higher ground on the mountaintops. All of these Italian offensives were unsuccessful, even though the Italians outnumbered their opponents three to one. This was unimaginably difficult warfare—Italy had to attack uphill, waging war high in the mountains, in the harshest of conditions. Trenches had to be carved into rock instead of mud, and many unprepared conscripts—brought here from faraway lands and unaccustomed to the harsh winter conditions atop the Alps—froze to death. During one brutal winter alone, some 60,000 soldiers were killed by avalanches.

Visitors take a look at this tight valley, hemmed in by seemingly impassible mountains, and wonder: Why would people fight so fiercely over such inhospitable terrain? At the time, Slovenia was the natural route from Italy to the Austro-Hungarian capital

Sights in Kobarid

▲▲▲Kobarid Museum (Kobariški Muzej)—This modest but world-class museum, offering a haunting look at the tragedy of the Soča Front, was voted Europe's best museum in 1993. The tasteful exhibits, with fine English descriptions and a pacifist tone, take an even-handed approach to the fighting—without getting hung up on identifying the "good guys" and the "bad guys." The museum's

at Vienna. The Italians believed that if they could hold this valley and push over the mountains, Vienna—and victory—would be theirs. Once committed, they couldn't turn back, and the war devolved into one of attrition—who would fall first?

In the fall of 1917, Austro-Hungarian Emperor Karl appealed to his ally Germany, and the Germans agreed to assemble an army for a new attack to retake Kobarid and the Soča Valley. In an incredible logistical accomplishment, they spent just six weeks building and supplying this new army by transporting troops and equipment high across the mountaintops under cover of darkness...above the heads of their oblivious Italian foes dozing in the valley below.

On October 24, Austria-Hungary and Germany launched an attack that sent 600,000 soldiers down into the town of Kobarid. This crucial 12th battle of the Soča Front, better known as the Battle of Kobarid, was the turning point—and saw the introduction of battlefield innovations that are commonplace in the military today. German field commanders were empowered to act independently on the battlefield, reacting immediately to developments rather than waiting for approval. Also, for the first time ever, the Austrian-German army used elements of a new surprise-attack technique called *Blitzkrieg*. (One German officer, Erwin Rommel, made great strides in the fighting here, and later climbed the ranks to become famous as Hitler's "Desert Fox" in North Africa.)

The attack caught the Italian forces off-guard, quickly breaking through three lines of defense. Within three days, the Italians were forced to retreat. (Because the Italian military worked from the top down, the soldiers were sitting ducks once they were cut off from their commanders.) The Austrians called their victory the "Miracle at Kobarid." But Italy felt differently. The Italians see the battle of Caporetto (the Italian name for Kobarid) as their Alamo. To this day, when an Italian finds himself in a mess, he might say, "At least it's not a *Caporetto*."

A year later, Italy came back—this time with the aid of British, French, and US forces—and easily retook this area. On November 4, 1918, Austria-Hungary conceded defeat. After more than a million casualties, the fighting at Soča was finally over.

focus is not on the guns and heroes, but on the big picture of the front and on the stories of the common people who fought and died here.

Cost and Hours: €5, good selection of books; April-Sept Mon-Fri 9:00-18:00, Sat-Sun 9:00-19:00; Oct-March Mon-Fri 10:00-17:00, Sat-Sun 9:00-18:00; Gregorčičeva 10, tel. 05/389-0000, www.kobariski-muzej.si.

Tours: History buffs can call ahead to arrange a private guide to lead them through the collection (€20/hour), or tour the sights outside (€25/hour). You can also arrange a guide through the Walk of Peace Visitors Center, listed later.

◐ Self-Guided Tour: The entry is lined with hastily made cement and barbed-wire gravestones, flags representing all the nationalities involved in the fighting, and pictures of soldiers and nurses from diverse backgrounds who were brought together here (for example, the men wearing fezzes were from Bosnia-Herzegovina, which was annexed by the Austro-Hungarian Empire shortly before the war).

Buy your ticket and ask to watch the English version of the 19-minute film on the history of the Soča Front (informative but dry, plays on top floor).

The first floor up is divided into several rooms. The White Room, filled with rusty crampons, wire-cutters, pickaxes, and shovels, explains wintertime conditions at the front. What looks like a bear trap was actually used to trap enemy soldiers. The Room of the Rear shows the day-to-day activities away from the front line, from supplying troops to more mundane activities (milking cows, washing clothes, getting a shave, lifting weights, playing with a dog). The Black Room is the museum's most somber, commemorating the more than one million casualties of the Soča Front. These heartbreaking exhibits honor the common people whose bodies fertilized the battlefields of Europe. Horrific images of war injuries are juxtaposed with a display of medals earned—prompting the question, was it worth it? The little altar was purchased by schoolchildren, who sent it to the front to offer the troops some solace.

Through the door marked *Room of the Krn Range* (also on the first floor up), find your way to the Kobarid Rooms, which trace the history of this region from antiquity to today. High on the wall, look for the timelines explaining the area's turbulent history. The one in the second room shows wave after wave of invaders (including Ottomans, Habsburgs, and Napoleon). In the next room, above a display case with military uniforms, another timeline shows the many flags that flew over Kobarid's main square during the 20th century.

On the top floor, across from the room where the film plays (described above), you'll see a giant model of the surrounding mountains, painstakingly tracing the successful Austrian-German *Blitzkrieg* attack during the Battle of Kobarid.

▲▲Italian Mausoleum (Kostnica)—The 55 miles between here and the Adriatic are dotted with more than 75 cemeteries, reminders of the countless casualties of the Soča Front. One of the most dramatic is this mausoleum, overlooking Kobarid. The access road,

across Kobarid's main square from the side of the church, is marked by stone gate towers (with the word *Kostnica*—one tower is topped with a cross and the other with a star for the Italian army).

Take the road up Gradič Hill—passing Stations of the Cross—to the mausoleum. Built in 1938 (when this was still part of Italy) around the existing Church of St. Anthony, this octagonal pyramid holds the remains of 7,014 Italian soldiers. The stark, cold, Neoclassical architecture is pure Mussolini. Names are listed alphabetically, along with mass graves for more than 1,700 unknown soldiers *(militi ignoti)*.

Walk behind the church and enjoy the **view.** Find the WWI battlements high on the mountain's rock face (with your back to church, they're at 10 o'clock). Incredibly, the fighting was done on these treacherous ridges; civilians in the valleys only heard the distant battles. Looking up and down the valley, notice the "signal churches" evenly spaced on hilltops, each barely within view of the next—an ancient method for quickly spreading messages or warnings across long distances.

If the **church** is open, go inside and look above the door to see a brave soldier standing over the body of a fallen comrade, fending off enemies with nothing but rocks.

When Mussolini came to dedicate the mausoleum, local revolutionaries plotted an assassination attempt that they believed couldn't fail. A young man planned to suicide-bomb Mussolini as the leader came back into town from this hilltop. But as Mussolini's car drove past, the would-be assassin looked at his fellow townspeople around him, realized the innocent blood he would also spill, and had a last-minute change of heart. Mussolini's trip was uneventful, and fascism continued to thrive in Italy.

▲**Walk of Peace (Pot Miru)**—This relatively new walking route—which, as of a 2012 expansion, extends more than 140 miles from these mountains all the way to the Adriatic—is designed to link museums, cemeteries, churches, and other sites related to the warfare of the Soča Front. In addition to the excellent museum here in Kobarid, several other "outdoor museums" in the area let you get close to the places where the fighting actually occurred. Some are reachable by car, while others require a challenging mountain hike. To learn more about all of these options, visit the **Walk of Peace Foundation Information Center,** across the street from the Kobarid Museum. They hand out good, free maps and

THE JULIAN ALPS

booklets about these places, and sell a fine €10 guidebook to WWI sights in the area. They also plan a new exhibition featuring a touchscreen map of the route, a film offering a bird's-eye view over the territory of the front, and photographs of the area (free; July-Aug Mon-Fri 9:00-13:00 & 14:00-19:00, Sat-Sun 10:00-13:00 & 14:00-19:00; April-June and Sept-Oct slightly shorter hours; Nov-March Sat-Sun only 10:00-15:00, closed Mon-Fri; Gregorčičeva 8, tel. 05/389-0167, www.potmiru.si). They also arrange guides that can join you for part of the walk (€25/hour for up to 4 hours, €20/hour for longer tours), and in the summer, they offer excursions to related sights nearby (for example, to the open-air museum in Kolovrat, 2/week, €15).

Kobarid Historical Walk—This shorter walk to WWI sights around Kobarid is well-explained by the free brochure available at the TI, museum, and information center (3 miles, mostly uphill, allow 3-5 hours; or you can just do a shorter, easier stretch along the river, 1-2 hours).

Alpine Cheese Museum—This humble exhibit, at the big Planika ("Edelweiss") dairy at the edge of town, examines the history of cheesemaking in this area since ancient times.

Cost and Hours: €2, May-mid-Sept Mon-Sat 10:00-18:00; March-April and mid-Sept-Oct Mon-Sat 10:00-16:00, closed Sun and off-season; Gregorčičeva 32, www.mlekarna-planika.si /muzej.

Great Kozjak Waterfall (Veliki Kozjak) Hike—If you have time to kill in Kobarid and want to go for a sturdy hike, consider trekking to the Great Kozjak Waterfall—a dramatic cascade that flows through an extremely narrow gorge and plunges 50 feet into a beautiful pool. While local signs clock the hike at 30 minutes from the town center, plan on closer to 45 minutes each way. The trailhead is at the Bovec end of Kobarid: As you approach town from Bovec, turn right into the town, then take an immediate and sharp left to go back under the main road, following signs for *Kamp Koren*. Wind down to cross the bridge over the Soča, then turn left and head up the hill (you'll pass Kamp Koren). You can park in the big gravel lot across the street from the camp, or, to get closer to the trailhead, turn left just after Kamp Koren at the *Slap Kozjak* sign and follow the gravel road (park your car at the pullout after the multicolored beehives). Continue walking along the gravel path down into the ravine, passing views of a smaller waterfall. Go right at the fork, continue into the gorge, and take the high, narrow bridge over the stream (which has no railing—a little nerve-wracking for those afraid of heights). Finally, follow the boardwalk as it curls around a cliff for great views of the falls.

Sleeping in Kobarid

(€1 = about $1.40, country code: 386, area code: 05)
My first listing is right on the main square. The other two hide on side streets about a block off the main road through town, between the museum and the main square (about a 3-minute walk to either).

$$$ Hotel Hvala is the only real hotel in town. Run by the Hvala family, its 32 contemporary rooms are comfortable, and the location can't be beat. The mural on the wall in the elevator shaft tells the story of the Soča Valley as you go up toward the top floor (mid-July-Aug: Sb-€76, Db-€112, cheaper third-floor "mansard" Sb-€62, Db-€98; Sept-mid-July: Sb-€72, Db-€104, cheaper third-floor "mansard" Sb-€58, Db-€90; pricier superior Db with air-con and sleek new decor-€160-200; cheaper off-season, hotel closed parts of Feb and Nov, elevator, free Internet access and Wi-Fi, Trg Svobode 1, tel. 05/389-9300, fax 05/388-5322, www.hotelhvala.si, topli.val@siol.net).

$ Apartmaji Lia, run by sweet Alenka Likar, has six tidy apartments in two buildings in the town center (Db-€40, extra adult-€20, kids under 15-€10, cash only, no breakfast, some rooms have air-con, free Wi-Fi, main house at Volaričeva 9, mobile 051-415-058, www.apartmaji-lia.si, apartmajilia@gmail.com).

$ Picerija Fedrig is a pizzeria that rents five simple but fine rooms upstairs (Db-€40, less for more than 1 night, 10 percent more in Aug, between the main square and the Kobarid Museum at Volaričeva 11, tel. 05/389-0115, fedrig@t-2.net).

Eating in Kobarid

Topli Val ("Heat Wave"), Hotel Hvala's restaurant, is pricey but good, with a menu that emphasizes fish (€8-16 pastas, €9-23 main courses, lengthy list of Slovenian wines, daily 12:00-15:00 & 18:00-23:00, Trg Svobode 1, tel. 05/389-9300).

Kotlar Restaurant, across the square from Hotel Hvala, is similarly priced and well-regarded (Thu-Mon 12:00-15:00 & 18:00-22:00, closed Tue-Wed, Trg Svobode 11, tel. 05/389-1110). Kotlar also rents rooms if you're in a pinch.

Picerija Fedrig (also listed under "Sleeping in Kobarid," above) serves up good €5-7 pizzas (Tue-Thu 17:00-22:00, Fri-Sun 12:00-22:00 closed Mon, also closed Tue in Nov-April, Volaričeva 11, tel. 05/389-0115).

Sleeping and Eating near Kobarid

$$$ Hiša Franko is a gourmet restaurant that also rents 10 rooms less than a five-minute drive outside of Kobarid. The modern-style rooms in the main building are upscale and comfortable, while the rooms in the adjacent yellow house are much simpler, dated, and affordable (main-building Db-€110-135 depending on size and amenities, yellow-house Db-€80, includes breakfast, free Wi-Fi, bike rental-€7, Staro Selo 1, tel. 05/389-4120, www.hisafranko.com, info@hisafranko.com).

What brings most people here is the upscale **restaurant,** which combines Slovenian cuisine and ingredients with modern international influences to create a memorable, if pricey, meal. The dining room is spiffy but casual and unpretentious, and the service is attentive and welcoming (€12-15 starters, €22-24 main dishes, €50-75 fixed-price meals, Wed-Sun 12:00-15:00 & 17:00-23:00, closed Mon-Tue).

Getting There: To reach Hiša Franko, leave Kobarid heading toward Robič on the pleasant tree-lined road, and look for the sign on the right.

THE JULIAN ALPS

LOGARSKA DOLINA
and THE NORTHERN VALLEYS

 The Julian Alps around Lake Bled are Slovenia's most accessible and most famous pincushion of peaks. But the high-mountain thrills don't end there. Stretching to the east, along the border with Austria, is the Kamniško-Savinjske range—home to several very remote valleys. One particularly inviting nook between the cut-glass peaks is the time-passed valley called Logarska Dolina. To get way, way, way off the beaten track—with gravel roads, unpasteurized milk, and the few Slovenes who still don't speak English—head to Logarska Dolina, its surrounding valleys, and the breathtaking Panoramic Road above them all. Slovenes like to keep this getaway a secret; it's one of their favorite escapes from the daily grind (and, along with Lake Bled, one of the country's most popular places to get married). Travelers who find Lake Bled too touristy prefer Lake Bohinj (see page 597). But travelers who think Bohinj is too touristy...love Logarska Dolina.

Logarska Dolina—very loosely translated as "Woodsman's Valley"—is best left to adventurous drivers, true back-to-nature nuts, and those intrigued by old-fashioned farming lifestyles...or, better yet, travelers who are all of the above. Most of all, Logarska Dolina is the ideal excuse for a long drive on high-mountain roads to one of Slovenia's most traditional corners.

Planning Your Time

A trip to Logarska Dolina can be done as a long full-day circular drive from either Bled or Ljubljana. With more time, you could spend the night. If you're heading between Ljubljana/Bled and Ptuj/Maribor on the A1 expressway, Logarska Dolina is roughly on the way (though it's still an hour off the expressway).

Logarska Dolina

Kamniško

Road ——
Path - - - -

Not to scale:
Solčava to Entry Kiosk
is a 7-Minute Drive.

Ojstrica
7,710'

Robanov Kot

Raduha
6,765'

Luče

To Ljubljana

4

SAVINAJA

LOGARSKA DOLINA

1 Hotel Plesnik
2 Vila Palenk
3 Na Razpotju Guesthouse
4 Tourist Farm Govc-Vršnik
5 Tourist Farm Žibovt
6 Tourist Farm Perk
7 Tourist Farm Klemenšek
8 Orlovo Gnezdo Mountain Hut

Solčava

RIVER

PANORAMIC
ROAD

Getting to Logarska Dolina

I'd skip this region without a car. Public transportation to the northern valleys is extremely time-consuming. In summer only, one **bus** a day goes from the city of Celje to Solčava, then on to Logarska Dolina. But once you're there, many of the region's best attractions (such as the Panoramic Road) are unreachable by public bus.

On the other hand, Logarska Dolina is made to order by **car.** The valley is nearly due north from Ljubljana. But because of the mountains that lie between them, you'll need to boomerang substantially to the east to get there. From Ljubljana, take the A1 expressway east (toward Celje) to the Šentrupert exit. From here, most of the route is well-marked with *Log Dolina* signs (usually brown). Head north on road 225 along the Savinja River, past Mozirje and Nazarje, then continue northwest on road 428 through Ljubno, Luče, and Solčava. (For details on getting around the valleys once you're in Solčava, see "Route Tips for Drivers," later.) Figure about an hour from Ljubljana to the Šentrupert exit, then another hour to Solčava.

A good, detailed map is essential. The *Avtokarta Slovenija* map will do, but consider getting one with even more detail for

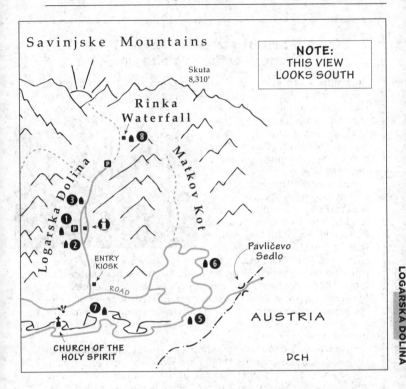

this region (such as the 1:50,000 *Zgornja Savinjska Dolina* map, available locally).

The route I've described above is the best. Detailed maps will show some seeming "shortcuts" that appear to take you more directly between Ljubljana and Logarska Dolina—but these will actually cost you time. I've tried both of the most likely options: the easier version, through Kamnik, then over the mountains via Gornji Grad to pick up the main road into Solčava (near Ljubno); and the off-road version of this route, cutting the corner from Krivčevo north (on unpaved roads—impassable outside of summer) through Podvolovljek to Luče. These alternatives come with some beautiful scenery and save you miles, but they are very time-consuming. Another seeming shortcut via Kranj—dipping into Austria on the impossibly twisty Jezersko-Pavličevo Sedlo road, through Vellach—is also possible, and also time-consuming.

Orientation to Logarska Dolina

(area code: 03)

The region is tucked in the northern corner of Slovenia, just a few miles from Austria. This chapter's sights branch off from an

Farming in (and Above) the Northern Valleys

For many visitors, the most striking thing about a visit to this region is the ingenious way the intrepid locals have learned to eke out a living in such an inhospitable land. Just as throughout the Alps, the valleys and plateaus here are carefully manicured, creating cow-filled pastures wherever there's a flat patch of earth. But what's special in Logarska Dolina is the way farmers also cultivate the land at the very tops of hills. Especially from the Panoramic Road, you can see that the  highest points of various ridges and foothills are shaved bare—rounded hilltops sticking up here and there like bald heads in a crowd. Cows graze even on this sharply angled land. Locals joke that these farms are so steep that cows' front legs are shorter than their rear legs to make it easier for them to climb uphill—and dogs have to hang on to the grass with their teeth and bark through their rear ends.

You'll see more traditional houses here than just about anywhere else in the country. Many have wooden roofs and siding. These shingles are generally made of hard, durable larch wood, and the boards are not cut, but split. Each house has a tiled stove

east-west axis formed by the valley of the Savinja River. The main attraction here is the valley called **Logarska Dolina,** which cuts through the mountainscape south from the Savinja River Valley. Roughly parallel to Logarska Dolina are two smaller valleys: gentle **Robanov Kot** to the east and rugged **Matkov Kot** to the west. (*Dolina* means "valley;" *kot*—literally, "corner"—is a short valley.) Running along the top of the Podolševa ridge above the Savinja River is the rough, gravelly **Panoramic Road** (Panoramska Cesta)—with spectacular views over the entire region.

Tourist Information

Logarska Dolina has a modest TI kiosk, across the parking lot from Hotel Plesnik (described later, under "Sleeping in Logarska Dolina"). The TI can help you find a room or plan a hike, and can arrange activities such as guided hikes, bike rental, horseback riding, rock climbing, archery, and paragliding (very flexible hours but generally May-Oct daily 9:00-15:00, closed Nov-April and in bad weather, take left fork to hotel after you enter Logarska Dolina

for heat, and a patch of grass to feed livestock.

It's a rough lifestyle. A farming family's primary source of income is their animals—mostly cows used for milk and meat, but also pigs and goats. Some of the farms in the Savinja River Valley raise yaks imported from Scotland, which are bred for their meat. A second source of income is forestry: The trees on a farm's property can be harvested and sold. Finally, farmers make a living from you and me, in the form of overnights or meals eaten at their farms.

All the tourist farms *(turistična kmetija)* in this region are a recent phenomenon. During the Yugoslav era, people who lived here stopped farming and moved or commuted into nearby towns in the valley to work in factories. But Slovenia's industry was designed to work as a cog in the Yugoslav machine—other regions provided raw materials, and a large, ready-made market to buy the finished product. After the Slovenes declared independence from Yugoslavia, many of the factories closed, and the farmers-turned-workers returned to their ancestral farming ways. To supplement their income, many families have converted their working farms into tourist farms, inviting guests to visit, stay, and dine with them, and appreciate their unique lifestyles. (I've listed several of these farms under "Sleeping in Logarska Dolina" and "Eating in Logarska Dolina," later.) Even though many of the farms in Logarska Dolina seem as though they could be generations old, some date from only the mid-1990s.

to Logarska Dolina 9, tel. 03/838-9004, www.logarska-dolina.si). If it's closed—as is the case off-season—the nearby Hotel Plesnik also provides basic tourist information. There are also TIs along the main road in Luče (tel. 03/839-3555) and in Solčava (tel. 03/839-0710). Both have similar hours to the Logarska Dolina TI.

Sights in Logarska Dolina

The road along the Savinja River, and the Panoramic Road up above, are connected at both ends—forming a handy loop that allows drivers to see everything efficiently. I suggest driving the Panoramic Road first, to get a good overview of the region, then winding down along the Savinja River to see the valleys. (If you have bad morning weather that looks like it may clear up in the afternoon, do the opposite.)

Route Tips for Drivers: The town of Solčava is the gateway to the region. In Solčava, you can twist up to the Panoramic Road (follow signs to *Podolševa*). At the far (west) end of this sky-high road, you'll come to a fork: Going left drops you directly down into Logarska Dolina, while going right takes you toward the Austrian border at Pavličevo Sedlo, and a very rugged, gravelly loop around the top, then bottom, of Matkov Kot (easy to miss—follow signs for tourist farms).

After visiting Logarska Dolina, take the Savinja River road back to Solčava. If you have time, you can detour into the valley of Robanov Kot when you head south from Solčava.

▲▲▲**Panoramic Road (Panoramska Cesta)**—The Logarska Dolina valley itself (described later) is beautiful. But the region's

spectacular highlight is the Panoramic Road twisting along the top of the cliff above it. At an altitude of around 4,000 feet (compared to about 2,500 feet in Logarska Dolina), this road offers one thrilling drive.

As you rattle along the rough road, all around you are vast swaths of mountain forests, broken only by hilltops covered with patches of green grass. Each of these hills is its own farm, which raises grass to feed livestock (see sidebar). Several stretches of the Panoramic Road are what Slovenes poetically call "white roads"—that is, gravel (no pavement). Realize that you're just an avalanche's tumble from the Austrian border.

About halfway along the Panoramic Road, the late 19th-century **Church of the Holy Spirit** (Sveti Duh) hovers on a hilltop above the hamlet of Podolševa.

Climb up to the church for sweeping views over Logarska Dolina. If the church is open, duck inside and find a very unusual relief of three men representing the Holy Trinity. God is in the center, Jesus is on the left, and on the right, it's...the Holy

Spirit, depicted not as a dove but as a balding man.

The Panoramic Road is lined with inviting tourist farms offering beds and meals to travelers—just follow the views to the farm of your choice (Tourist Farm Klemenšek, listed under "Eating in Logarska Dolina," is one good option). Some farms, such as Tourist Farm Žibovt (near the end of the Panoramic Road, listed under "Sleeping in Logarska Dolina"), serve *kislo mleko*, or "soured milk"...which is exactly what it sounds like (about €3 per bowl). Fresh, unpasteurized milk is set out in the open air, usually in a darkened room. The fat rises to the top and forms a skin on top. The bottom of the milk is like yogurt, white and relatively flavorless. Meanwhile, the yellowish top layer comes with a kick: a pungent barnyard aftertaste. I tried it—once—and enjoyed it...the experience, if not the flavor.

▲▲**Logarska Dolina**—This valley, 4.5 miles long and about a quarter-mile wide, is the region's main draw. A flat, broad meadow

 surrounded on all sides by sheer alpine cliffs, it's an idyllic place for a drive, hike, or bike ride. Various sights—caves, waterfalls, old log cabins, and so on—surround the valley, but it's most appealing simply as a place to commune with gorgeous Slovenian nature.

Though you can enter the valley year-round, you'll have to pay a €5 entry fee per car April through October (at other times, or if there's bad weather and the entry kiosk is closed, it's free). After the valley entrance, the road forks. Take the left fork to reach the TI (see "Tourist Information," earlier) and hotels; or take the right fork to bypass them (the two forks eventually rejoin).

At the far end of the valley, you'll find a parking lot with some snack stands. From here, you can follow the *Slap Rinka—10 min* signs up the moderately strenuous path to the **Rinka Waterfall.** Relax at the little mountain hut called Orlovo Gnezdo ("Eagle's Nest") and enjoy a drink with a view of the falls, which plunge 300 feet down from the adjacent cliffs.

With more time, Logarska Dolina offers an inviting, mostly level place to go for a longer **hike,** surrounded by cow-filled meadows and towering peaks. The "Nature-Ethnographic Trail" is a two-hour, four-mile (one-way) hike that starts near the entrance of the valley and leads to the end of the valley. As you enter Logarska Dolina, pick up the brochure that describes the route. It's available at the TI, along with information about more adventurous hikes up into the mountains around Logarska Dolina.

Robanov Kot and Matkov Kot—These smaller, sleepier valleys, dotted with traditional farm buildings, flank Logarska Dolina. They offer the same surrounded-by-mountains feeling, but are less cultivated and less crowded than Logarska during the peak season. With extra time, poke into one or both of these mini-valleys simply to enjoy the peaceful views. **Robanov Kot,** near Solčava, is more accessible, with better and more level roads (well-marked with a brown sign just south of Solčava; home to recommended Tourist Farm Govc-Vršnik). The **Matkov Kot** road is more rugged, with cliff-hanging gravel roads (it's easy to miss this poorly marked valley—look for signs to the tourist farms; the recommended Tourist Farm Perk is on this road).

Sleeping in Logarska Dolina

The accommodations listed here are situated in four very different settings. The hotel/villa and guesthouse are in the heart of the Logarska Dolina valley; the first tourist farm is in the side-valley called Robanov Kot; the second tourist farm is on the Panoramic Road, capping the ridge above the valleys; and the last farm is in the side-valley called Matkov Kot.

$$ Hotel Plesnik and **Vila Palenk,** both part of the only big hotel outfit in the area, sit proudly in the middle of Logarska Dolina. The hotel, with lively public spaces and 30 modern rooms with traditional farmhouse furnishings, is a big, classy, overpriced splurge (Sb-€96, Db-€154, €5 cheaper without balcony, elevator). The nearby, smaller Vila Palenk has 11 rustic rooms with more character (Sb-€79, Db-€126, no elevator, breakfast at the main hotel). The staff at both places speak English. Reservations for both are handled through the same office (no extra charge for 1-night stays, €12 per person for lunch or dinner at hotel restaurant, check online for weekend deals, indoor swimming pool, Logarska Dolina 10, tel. 03/839-2300, fax 03/839-2312, www.plesnik.si, info@plesnik .si). After entering Logarska Dolina, you'll come to a fork; bear left to reach the hotel.

$$ Na Razpotju Guesthouse, affiliated with the hotel, has 10 straightforward rooms. It's family-friendly and a better value than the hotel, but communication can be challenging (Sb-€45, Db-€70, a quarter-mile from Hotel Plesnik toward the far end of the valley, Logarska Dolina 14, tel. 03/839-1650, razpotje@siol .net).

Near Logarska Dolina

$ Tourist Farm Govc-Vršnik, the most modern and accessible of my tourist farm listings, is in the smaller, relaxing valley of Robanov Kot, a 15-minute drive from Logarska Dolina. This working farm, run by the English-speaking Vršnik family, has a traditional beehive and 10 cozy rooms with bright, woody decor (Db-€58, or €72 with dinner, 20 percent more for 1- or 2-night stays, €6 less mid-Oct-late April, cash only, free Wi-Fi, Robanov Kot 34, tel. 03/839-5016, fax 03/839-5017, www.govc-vrsnik.com, govc.vrsnik@siol.net). As you enter the valley of Robanov Kot (just south of Solčava), just watch for signs (it's the second tourist farm on the left).

$ Tourist Farm Žibovt is dramatically situated at the far end of the Panoramic Road, a few minutes' walk from the Austrian bor-

LOGARSKA DOLINA

Sleep Code

(€1 = about $1.40, country code: 386, area code: 03)
S = Single, **D** = Double/Twin, **T** = Triple, **Q** = Quad, **b** = bathroom. These accommodations include breakfast. The hotel accepts credit cards, but the tourist farms are cash only and charge 20-30 percent extra for stays of fewer than three nights. These prices don't include the modest tourist tax (about €1 per person, per night). Unless otherwise noted, everyone listed here speaks English (or has a neighbor or relative who can help translate).

To help you easily sort through these listings, I've divided the accommodations into two categories based on the price for a double room with bath during high season:

   $$ Higher Priced—Most rooms €60 or more.
   $ Lower Priced—Most rooms less than €60.

Prices can change without notice; verify the hotel's current rates online or by email. For other updates, see www.ricksteves.com/update.

der. It perches on a ledge with fine views of a tranquil meadow that ends at a sheer cliff plunging to the bottom of Logarska Dolina. In addition to renting six cheery rooms, the Poličnik family serves meals and turns out a wide range of dairy products—including the unforgettable *kislo mleko* ("soured milk"). Near this farm is a modest marble quarry (Db-€52, or €70 with dinner, cash only, minimal English spoken, Logarska Dolina 24, tel. 03/584-7118, www.nad1000m.si/zibovt, kmetija.zibovt@gmail.com, Žarko and Martina Poličnik). The farm is well-marked at the far end of the Panoramic Road (near the Austrian border crossing at Pavličevo Sedlo).

$ Tourist Farm Perk is the most rustic of my listings, with seven rooms (some of which have a private bathroom on the hall). It's scenically perched on the particularly remote-feeling gravel road high above Matkov Kot (D/Db-€48, or €60 with dinner, cash only, Logarska Dolina 23, tel. 03/584-7120, mobile 041-282-485, www.perk.si, krivec.neza@siol.net, Krivec family).

Eating in Logarska Dolina

Many of the region's tourist farms serve full meals to passersby in summer and light meals and snacks at other times. **Tourist Farm Klemenšek,** set on a grassy ridge with spectacular views, has the classic Logarska Dolina setting, home cooking, and indoor or outdoor tables (July-Aug daily 11:00-21:00; May-June and

Sept-mid-Oct Sat-Sun only 11:00-21:00, closed Mon-Fri; closed mid-Oct-April; halfway between Sveti Duh and the end of the Panoramic Road, tel. 03/838-9024, www.na-klemencem.si). **Hotel Plesnik** and **Na Razpotju Guesthouse,** listed earlier, also serve food to non-guests. But the best option is to bring a **picnic** with you and eat whenever you find the scenic perch you like best. You'll find small grocery stores along the main road in both Luče and Solčava, but few opportunities to buy groceries once in the valley.

Near Logarska Dolina: Velenje Castle

This scenic, 700-year-old, hill-capping castle seems out of place over the modern industrial town of Velenje (which was once named "Titovo Velenje" for the Yugoslav dictator, Tito). Even more unusual is the eclectic, extensive, and endearing museum it houses. While it's not worth going far out of your way to see, a trip to the castle makes a good rainy-day activity or a fine diversion if you've got extra time at the end of your Logarska Dolina day.

You'll find a surprising diversity of exhibits surrounding the tranquil castle courtyard: replicas of a circa-1930s general store and pub; a Czech professor's three-room collection of African art and everyday items; a survey of regional history through the Middle Ages, including a replica of a countryside home; a city history overview (the town was founded only after World War II, so much of the story dates from Tito's Yugoslav era); various Slovenian paintings and sculptures; and temporary exhibits. Separate buildings house a collection of Baroque church art and an exhibit on mastodons (the remains of two of these extinct tusked mammals were found near here in 1964).

Only some of the exhibits are described in English, but you can borrow the good one-page English descriptions when you enter. If the guides aren't busy, one of them can show you around (included in ticket price). Better yet, call ahead to see if an English tour is scheduled, or to request a tour for yourself.

Cost and Hours: €2.50, Tue-Sun 10:00-18:00, closed Mon, Ljubljanska cesta 54, tel. 03/898-2630, www.muzej-velenje.si.

Getting There: Velenje Castle is easy to visit en route to or from Logarska Dolina, especially if you're headed east on the expressway. From the road connecting Logarska Dolina to the expressway, you can detour east just south of Mozirje (via Gorenje) into Velenje, where you'll look for easy-to-miss brown signs to turn off for the castle. From Velenje, you can head south straight to the expressway.

PTUJ and MARIBOR

The vast majority of Slovenia's attractions are concentrated in the western third of the country: the mountains, the sea, the capital city, and the Karst. East of Ljubljana, the mountains gradually merge into plains, the towns and cities become less colorful, and "oh, wow!" turns into "so what?" But there's hope, in the form of Slovenia's oldest town (and winner of the "funniest name" award): Ptuj (puh-TOOey—the "P" is almost silent; and yes, it really does sound like someone spitting). For a big-city complement to Ptuj, drop into Maribor—the country's second city, and the de facto capital of eastern Slovenia. Expect some contrasts from the more popular parts of Slovenia. Even in this tiny country, rivalry rages between cities—and people here in the "02 Zone" (the area-code-derived nickname that Slovenes use for this region) have their own personality, dialect, and political priorities.

Planning Your Time

With a week or more in Slovenia and a desire to delve into the less-touristed areas of the country, Ptuj deserves a short visit. A few hours are enough to feel you've mastered the town; if you're a restless sightseer, it's tough to fill an entire day here. Begin by touring the castle, then enjoy a wander through the Old Town and consider Ptuj's other museums. Let your pulse slow and take a mini-vacation from your vacation. If you can't sit still that long, consider spending a few more hours on a side-trip into Maribor.

Ptuj and Maribor are conveniently located on the train network, and are easy to reach from Ljubljana, as well as from international destinations like Zagreb, Vienna, and Budapest.

Ptuj

With a storied past, a much-vaunted castle, and easygoing locals who act like they've never met a tourist, Ptuj is charming. Populated since the Early Stone Age, Ptuj has a long and colorful history that reads like a Who's Who of Central Europe: Celts and Romans, Dominican friars and Habsburg counts, Nazis and Yugoslavs...not to mention a fuzzy monster named Kurent. The people of Ptuj are particularly proud of their Roman era, when "Poetovio" was a bustling metropolis of 40,000 people (nearly quadruple today's size). But even as it clings to its noble past, today's Ptuj is refreshingly real, with a sleepy small-town ambience and an interesting castle-museum.

While it hosts plenty of visitors (mostly Germans and Austrians, who call it "Pettau"), Ptuj is hardly a tourist town. Real people, not nightclubs or souvenir shops, populate the Old Town. If this makes Ptuj feel a bit less polished than the big-name sights in western Slovenia, so much the better—think of it as a diamond in the rough.

Orientation to Ptuj

(area code: 02)

Ptuj is squeezed between its historic castle and the wide Drava River. With just 11,000 people (23,000 in greater Ptuj), it still ranks as Slovenia's eighth-largest town. The Old Town is shaped roughly like a triangle, with the castle and the two monasteries as its three points. You can walk from one end of the Old Town to the other in about 10 minutes, but since the town slopes uphill from the river to the castle, there's a bit of up and down.

Tourist Information

Ptuj's TI shares the square called Slovenski trg with its landmark City Tower. Pick up the information magazine, which contains a city map marked with sights, hotels, and restaurants. The TI also publishes an events guide and has free Internet access (daily May–Sept 9:00–20:00, Oct–April 9:00–18:00, Slovenski trg 5, tel. 02/779-6011, www.ptuj.info).

Arrival in Ptuj

The humble **train** station is about a 10-minute walk from the center. Exit the station to the left, then cross the busy road to the **bus** station. From the bus station, the Old Town is just on the other side of the big commercial center. **Drivers** will find a handy park-

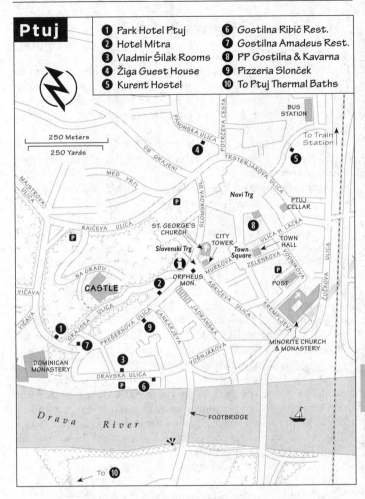

Ptuj

1. Park Hotel Ptuj
2. Hotel Mitra
3. Vladmir Šilak Rooms
4. Žiga Guest House
5. Kurent Hostel
6. Gostilna Ribič Rest.
7. Gostilna Amadeus Rest.
8. PP Gostilna & Kavarna
9. Pizzeria Slonček
10. To Ptuj Thermal Baths

ing lot on the riverfront, next to the recommended Gostilna Ribič restaurant.

Helpful Hints

Internet Access: The town has a few Internet cafés, but the easiest access is at the free terminal inside the TI (see earlier).

Local Guide: To arrange your own private guide, contact the **Ptujske Vedute agency** (€40 for up to a one-hour tour of the Old Town, also possible for half-day or full-day tours, tel. 02/778-8780, ptuj@vedute.si). The TI can also help you find a guide.

Sights in Ptuj

▲▲Ptuj Castle (Ptujski Grad)

The modest castle is Ptuj's top sight, and proudly claims to be Slovenia's most-visited museum. Overlooking the town from its perch over the Drava River, it's less than thrilling from afar. But the horseshoe-shaped castle complex hosts a series of surprisingly rich and engaging exhibits.

Cost and Hours: €5, daily 9:00-17:00, May-mid-Oct until 18:00, July-Aug Sat-Sun until 20:00, tel. 02/748-0360, www .muzej-ptuj-ormoz.si.

Information and Tours: Good English descriptions are posted in most rooms. English tours are rare, but you can call to ask if one is scheduled that you can join (included in €5 entry fee). Or you can call ahead to arrange your own private tour for €15 extra (depends on guide availability, email at least one day ahead to ptuj@vedute.si). But my self-guided tour, below, covers the highlights. For more in-depth information, pick up the thorough €7 guidebook.

Getting There: You can't miss the castle, sitting over the city. It's about a 10-minute cobbled hike above the Old Town. Several different trails lead up from the Old Town, all well-marked with *Grad* signs (easiest to find is the lane called Grajska ulica, near the TI).

◑ Self-Guided Tour: The core of the Ptuj Castle collection shows off the lifestyles of the castle's historic residents, while other exhibits display weapons, musical instruments, and traditional costumes used for the annual Kurentovanje festival. You'll follow a one-way route. The entrances to each exhibit are not all well-marked, but attendants are always around to direct you to what you want to see. Touring the whole shebang takes about two hours.

After buying your ticket, go up the stairs near the ticket office and turn right. Look over the **courtyard** for this quick history lesson: In the 11th century, the archbishops of Salzburg built a fortress here. In the 12th century, the Lords of Ptuj, who watched over the Salzburgers' land, moved in. The LoP's died out in the mid-15th century, and from then on, the castle changed hands frequently. Over the next several centuries, Ptuj Castle gradually acquired its current appearance: a Romanesque core (part of a 14th-century fortress, barely visible now) with a Renaissance arcaded

courtyard (designed by Italian experts who came to fortify the castle against the Ottomans), accentuated by an austere Baroque addition (the outermost wing, with the decorated stone window frames). Most of what you'll see in today's exhibit dates from the time of the Counts of Herberstein (1873-1945).

Now look over the door at the end of the arcade to see the **castle seal,** a hodgepodge of symbols representing previous owners. What's an English phrase doing on a seal for a castle in Slovenia? It's because of a Hungarian princess. In the Middle Ages, when a princess of Hungary moved to Scotland to be with her new husband, she took with her a particularly protective chamberlain. When the chamberlain buckled the princess to her horse for a treacherous river crossing, he'd fasten her on with three belts instead of just one, and shout "Grip fast!" when they came to any rough patches. That chamberlain's descendants took the name Leslie and eventually bought this castle in 1656. The family crest became those three buckles the chamberlain had used to protect his princess (in the left shield). You'll spot this insignia throughout the castle.

• *Going through the door, you enter the...*

Feudal Dwelling Culture Collection: This exhibit displays artifacts belonging to the castle's previous owners. The route takes you more or less clockwise in a roughly chronological order, from the 16th to the 19th centuries. In the first few rooms—where receptions were held and guests were (hopefully) impressed—you'll see several 17th-century tapestries from Brussels depicting the travels of Ulysses. Notice that nearly every big room has its own ceramic stove (fed from behind the wall by servants). Looking up, you'll see that while some of the rooms have exposed wooden-beam ceilings, others are adorned with cake-frosting stucco work—it's original, was created by highly skilled masters, and is still intact after nearly 300 years. At the end of the first hall is a gallery of portraits of the Herbersteins, who furnished this part of the castle and were eager to establish their legitimacy as a ruling family.

• *Looping back to where you began, head down the hallway into the residential part of the castle (in the hall, notice the 700-year-old Herberstein family tree on your right). The first big room is the...*

Countess' Salon: Also called the "Chinese Salon," this room reveals the fascination many 17th- and 18th-century Europeans had for foreign cultures. But the European artists who created these works never actually visited China, instead basing their visions on stories they heard from travelers who may or may not have had firsthand experience there. The results—European depictions of imagined Chinese culture—are highly inaccurate at best, and flights of pure fantasy at worst (look around for animals and instruments that never existed). This European interest in Chinese

Kurentovanje

Ptuj is famous for its distinctive Mardi Gras celebration, called Kurentovanje (koo-rent-oh-VAWN-yeh). Locals dress up in elaborate costumes and parade through the streets, celebrating the end of winter and heralding the arrival of spring. Nearby villages have similar, smaller, and more traditional processions.

It seems quaint today, but in the Middle Ages, Kurentovanje was deadly serious. The winter is particularly harsh here, so when spring began to approach, the peasants wanted to offer encouragement. They'd put on frightening masks and costumes and parade around making as much noise as possible to scare off the winter.

Kurentovanje's most notable character is Kurent, a fun-loving Slavic pagan god of hedonism—sort of the Slovenian Bacchus. A Kurent is covered with fur and has a long, red tongue, horns, a snout, whiskers, two red-ringed eyes, a wooden club with a spiny hedgehog skin wrapped around one end, and red or green socks. It wears a chain of five bells around its waist, and jumps around and swings its hips to get them clanging as loudly as possible. Kurents travel together in packs, so the combined noise can be deafening.

culture is known as *chinoiserie*. We'll see a similar fixation on Turkish culture soon.

• *Head through the next few rooms (countess' bedroom, countess' dressing room, old chapel, chambermaid's room). Before entering the 14th-century core—and oldest part—of the castle, keep your head up to see a very unusual chandelier: an anatomically correct (or surgically enhanced, by the look of it) female dragon. Continue into the...*

Bedrooms: The first shows off what prim and proper 17th-century Europeans considered to be "erotic" art (with a mythical creature trying to woo a woman), while the second is decorated in Napoleonic-era Empire-style furniture. In this room, pay special attention to the stove: Water (which could be scented) was poured into the top, and emerged at the bottom in the form of steam. Fancy. The third bedroom brings the survey of furniture up to date: 19th-century Biedermeier...simple, practical, comfortable, but still beautiful.

• *Going into the arcade, turn left to find the...*

Festival Hall: Then as now, this hall was a preferred place for banquets and concerts. Decorating the walls is Europe's biggest

Traditionally the role of Kurent was played by young men of the village—they were able to pull it off physically (the costume could weigh 90 pounds) and used it as an opportunity to catch the eye of a potential wife. (As the Kurents parade through the streets, young women still toss them handkerchiefs in approval.) Leading up to the procession, the young man would make his own costume in secret. That way, the monster would be all the more frightening and impressive when it was finally revealed. Ideally, they'd use the stinkiest animal hides they could find, to make the beast smell as hideous as it looked and sounded.

These processions have evolved into modern extravaganzas. These days, men and women of any age buy their Kurent costumes in a store, and Kurentovanje's daytime parades are followed by evenings of music, celebration, and general debauchery. In recent years, in a sort of "creature exchange" program, characters from Mardi Gras celebrations in other countries have come to take part in Kurentovanje.

Imagine about 350 of these hairy beasts, each one with five huge bells clanging at top volume, stomping down Prešernova street. Or come the Sunday before Ash Wednesday, and see for yourself. For details on all the festivities, check out www.kurento vanje.net.

Kurentovanje ends at midnight on Shrove Tuesday (before Ash Wednesday), when people move into the more pensive season of Lent... confident that spring will return with ease.

collection of *turqueries*. Like the faux-Chinese stuff we saw earlier, this is a (usually highly inaccurate) European vision of Turkish culture. After the Habsburg armies defeated the Ottomans and forced them out of Central Europe, the two powers began a diplomatic relationship. In the late 17th century, many Austrian officers went to Turkey and came back with souvenirs and tall tales, which were patched together to form the idiosyncratic vision of the Ottoman Empire you see here.

The left wall shows Ottoman politicians of the day—many with European features (presumably painted by artists who'd never laid eyes on an actual Turkish person). Along the back wall, we see portraits of four sultans' wives. Imagine how astonishing the notion of a harem must have been in the buttoned-down Habsburg days. But even though these paintings are unmistakably titillating, they're still appropriately repressed. The first woman (on left) wears two different layers of semi-transparent clothing (what's the point?). And the fourth woman (on right) reaches for some fruit (symbolic of...well, you know) and teasingly pulls open her dress so we can see what's underneath, which is...more clothes.

Finally, look on the right wall, with 17th-century Eurofied visions of people from other cultures: Africans, Native Americans, and Asians, all with exaggerated features.

This quirky collection is typical of Slovenian museums: Since they can't afford great works by famous artists, they collect items that may seem obscure, but actually have an interesting story to tell.

• *Backtrack to where you entered, and go straight ahead along the arcade to the end of the hall, where you'll take the tight, medieval spiral staircase up one level. At the top, turn left.*

Medieval Knights, Founders, and Patrons of the Arts: This exhibit tells the story of the Lords of Ptuj.

• *Continue into the two big rooms.*

Castle Gallery: The first room displays works of art from the Baroque period, including an army of sandstone dwarfs. The second (darkened) room highlights the Middle Ages. The first three sculptures on the left (#10-12) are especially precious, done by the greatest local masters of the day.

• *Exit to the right, and walk to the end of the arcade. And now for something completely different.*

Carnival Masks Collection: Ptuj's Mardi Gras celebration, called Kurentovanje, is well-known for its processions of fanciful masked characters (see sidebar). This exhibit—as colorful as an episode of *Sesame Street*—offers an entertaining look at the complete Kurentovanje experience. The costume of the old woman carrying the old man on her back seems whimsical, but it represents a powerful theme: We carry the memory of the deceased with us always. The bear costume is a reminder of times when Roma (Gypsy) entertainers actually did bring trained bears to town. The plow is used to symbolically "wake up the soil" and set the stage for a season of bountiful crops. The horse (called Rusa) is taken by a farmer from house to house, trying to "sell" it to neighbors. But the horse is unruly and obnoxious—supposedly good luck for the health and fertility of livestock. The Kurent costumes (in the last room) are especially striking—from old homemade costumes (turn an old coat inside-out to reveal the fur lining) to today's store-bought version (they run about €500).

After the Carnival Masks Collection, you might pass through an ethnographic collection (farm implements, traditional tools, etc.), which the museum hopes to move soon to a more suitable location.

• *Head back down to the courtyard. Ask one of the attendants to direct you (across the courtyard from the ticket office) to the...*

Collection of Musical Instruments: This fun and well-presented exhibit groups instruments by type of music, which you'll hear as you enter each room. The first section celebrates Ptuj's civic marching band, a prized local tradition. The next section displays ancient Roman instruments. The tibia (in the display case), dating from the second century A.D., is the only one ever found; it had two pipes made of bone leading to a single mouthpiece (illustrated on the wall). The next section features woodwinds and strings, including a rare, preserved lute. And the last section shows off a Bösendorfer piano and other keyboard instruments.

• *As you exit, you can ask to be directed to the anticlimactic finale (to the right), the...*

Collection of Arms: Squeezed into one corner of a huge, vaulted room is an armory collection spanning several centuries, from the 1400s through World War I. They're displayed on racks, as they would have been in a real armory.

• *Your castle visit is over. Enjoy the views, then head back down into town.*

Old Town

The sights in Ptuj's Old Town are simple and not very time-consuming. Wander around, take them in at your own pace, then reward yourself with a relaxing drink on a square.

▲**Slovenski Trg**—Once Ptuj's main square, and now its most atmospheric, Slovenski trg is fronted by the TI, Hotel Mitra, and the City Tower. Around this square are several reminders of Ptuj's Roman past.

The white marble slab in the middle of the square, known as the **Orpheus Monument,** was commissioned by a Roman mayor in the second century A.D. to honor an esteemed figure: himself. Notice the musician playing the lyre (near the top, center of slab, below the naked woman). Since the lyre is commonly associated with Orpheus, the monument's nickname stuck. When Rome fell, so did many of its structures, including this one. It became buried in history, only to reappear in the 16th century as the town pillory, where criminals were punished (secured by chains that were embedded in the holes you still see in the slab). In the Middle Ages, the town judge would come out onto the balcony over the door of his white house at the top of the square (at #6) to witness justice being served.

The **City Tower** was built in the late 16th century to defend against Ottoman invaders (who were likely to pass by here on their way to lay siege to Vienna). The tower used to be another story taller, but the top burned in a devastating fire (one of four that swept the city in the late 17th and early 18th centuries). The newly shorter tower was capped with this jaunty Baroque steeple.

Embedded in the staircase at the back of the tower are more fragments from Ptuj's Roman era. This so-called **"open-air museum"** is just a taste of the vast Roman material unearthed in Ptuj. In the middle of the staircase, make out the letters: POETOVIONA—a longer version of Ptuj's Roman name, Poetovio. (For an even more extensive Roman collection, head for the Dominican Monastery.)

Just behind the City Tower is **St. George's Parish Church** (Cerkev Svetega Jurija), which dates back before any other building in Slovenia. The current Gothic version is packed with diverse ecclesiastical art. If it's open, go inside (daily 7:00-11:00 & 18:00-18:30). As you enter, notice (on your left) the gorgeous circa-1380 statue of St. George, Ptuj's patron saint, slaying the dragon. Then go to the first big pillar on the right, where you'll see a glass-covered relief depicting throngs of admirers adoring the Baby Jes... wait—where's Jesus? (Not to mention Mary's hands?) Several years ago, Jesus was stolen from this pillar. To help prevent further vandalism, the priests reduced the opening times (notice the seven-hour midday break).

Prešernova Street (Prešernova Ulica)—Stretching away from the City Tower is Ptuj's main drag and oldest street. It's wider than most streets in town because it led to what was once the medieval market square (now Slovenski trg), and merchants would set up market stalls all along the street. Many of the houses here have long since been renovated in Renaissance or Baroque style, making it Ptuj's most picturesque thoroughfare.

Town Square (Mestni Trg)—Today Ptuj's main square, this lively people zone (just down Murkova street from Slovenski trg) is a hub of activity. Major events and festivals—including the Kurentovanje Mardi Gras festival—take place here.

The square is watched over by the distinctive **Town Hall,** built by a visionary mayor a century ago. The three flags represent (left to right) the European Union, Slovenia, and the Municipality of Ptuj. Over the left door (on the corner) are two statues commemorating Ptuj's Roman history: on the right, Emperor Trajan, who granted Ptuj city status in the early second century A.D.; and on the left, St. Viktorin, a Ptuj bishop who wrote scholarly works on ecclesiastical themes during the late third century A.D., until he was martyred by Emperor Diocletian.

In the middle of the square is a statue of **St. Florian,** who traditionally protects towns against fire. Ptuj was devastated by four different fires in the late 17th and early 18th centuries. This statue is a 1993 replica of one that was built here after the fourth fire, in 1744. Miraculously, the town never burned again...or maybe not so miraculously, since they rebuilt it with stone instead of wood. Largely as a result of Ptuj's frequent fires, its rival Maribor (to the north) gradually supplanted it as the region's main center of commerce and winemaking. Ptuj's fate was sealed a century later, when the rail line between Vienna and Trieste was routed through Maribor. Today Maribor has 10 times as many people as Ptuj—and 10 times the industry, congestion, and urban gloominess. Hmm... maybe Ptuj got the better end of the deal, after all.

Ptuj Cellar (Ptujska Klet)—Ptuj is highly regarded for its wines, and this is the main facility for the major Pullus brand. Simple wine was produced in this region as far back as the Celts. The Romans advanced the art, only to have it disappear in the Dark Ages, then be revived in the 13th century by Minorite monks. Today this enormous cellar, branching out under the Old Town, continues this proud tradition—and holds a staggering 1.3 million gallons of wine (about 85 percent of it white). The cellar is also home to a "wine archive" with bottles dating back to 1917. This precious archive survived World War II because it was sealed off from the Nazis behind a giant barrel.

The winemakers are proudest of their award-winning Sauvignon Blanc (€4/bottle), but their best seller—at a million bottles a year—is a local wine called Haložan (a semi-dry blend of four whites, €2/bottle).

Tours and Tastings: Cellar tours and wine-tastings are possible if you call ahead (Mon-Sat 9:00-17:00, call Tanja at mobile 041-394-896). While these are often available in English, you may wind up joining a German- or Slovene-language tour. Either way, you'll pay €9 for the experience. The cellar tour comes with some hokey lighting effects and is followed by an even hokier audio-visual presentation during the tasting.

Shop: If you just want to pick up a bottle, stop by their wine shop, next door to the cellar (Mon-Fri 9:00-17:00, closed Sat-Sun, Vinarski trg 1, tel. 02/787-9810, www.pullus.si).

Minorite Church and Monastery (Minoritski Samostan)—This church, dedicated to Saints Peter and Paul, was one of the only buildings in town destroyed in World War II. (The Allies believed that the occupying Nazis were storing munitions here.) Only the foundation at the back end of the church (the part that's yellow instead of white) survived, and it was left in ruins for decades. In 1989, friars celebrated their 750th anniversary in Ptuj by rebuilding the back part of the church. About a decade later, the front (white) half was also reconstructed. They followed the original plans carefully, but something's missing: Those empty niches above the door, once occupied by statues, are a sobering reminder of wartime devastation. But step into the contemporary interior. There, at the altar, are the original statues that once adorned the church facade. At the chapel at the back of the church (on the right), you'll see very contemporary Stations of the Cross. Then go through the door on the right into the peaceful cloister. A handful of friars can still be seen roaming these tranquil halls, and you're welcome to stroll here, too.

Cost and Hours: Free, daily 7:30-18:30, Minoritski trg.

Dominican Monastery (Dominikanski Samostan)—This monastery, at the opposite end of the Old Town, is no longer operative, but instead hosts a wide range of Roman artifacts—many of which are displayed on the lawn. Inside you'll find more Roman fragments scattered around a cloister with sparse explanations (though the collections may be closed for renovation).

Cost and Hours: €5, mid-April-Dec daily 9:00-17:00, closed in winter, Muzejski trg 1, tel. 02/787-9230.

Ptuj Thermal Baths (Terme Ptuj)—This gigantic bath complex, a 15-minute walk across the river from Ptuj's Old Town, is a fun place to splash around on a longer visit. The "Thermal Park" has multiple swimming pools, whirlpools, and slides, including the "longest slide in Slovenia." The complex also offers various spa treatments.

Cost and Hours: €12, cheaper after 15:00, outdoor pools daily 9:00-20:00, indoor pools daily 8:00-22:00, Pot v Toplice 9, tel. 02/749-4100, www.terme-ptuj.si.

Sleeping in Ptuj

Central Ptuj has only a few hotels, a hostel, and a handful of *sobe/* guest houses. While the options seem limited, the rooms are generally a good value compared to the western part of the country. Several of the cheaper places don't serve breakfast, but you can get a €5 buffet breakfast at Hotel Mitra even if you're not staying there (included for guests).

$$$ Park Hotel Ptuj is doing its best to be big-time stylish in a small-time town. Its 15 rooms come with slick modern decor, but it doesn't quite live up to the high prices. This place

Sleep Code

(€1 = about $1.40, country code: 386, area code: 02)
S = Single, **D** = Double/Twin, **T** = Triple, **Q** = Quad, **b** = bathroom.
No hotel in Ptuj has an elevator, but everyone listed here
speaks English. Unless otherwise noted, credit cards are
accepted and breakfast is included, but the modest tourist
tax (about €1 per person, per night) is not.

To help you easily sort through these listings, I've divided
the accommodations into three categories based on the price
for a double room with bath:

$$$ Higher Priced—Most rooms €80 or more.
  $$ Moderately Priced—Most rooms between €30-80.
   $ Lower Priced—Most rooms €30 or less.

Prices can change without notice; verify the hotel's
current rates online or by email. For other updates, see www
.ricksteves.com/update.

recently closed, but hopes to reopen soon (Sb-€57, Db-€97-107
depending on size, air-con, free Wi-Fi, Prešernova 38, tel. 02/749-
3300, fax 02/749-3319, www.parkhotel-ptuj.si, info@parkhotel
-ptuj.si).

$$$ Hotel Mitra enjoys Ptuj's best location: right on its most
appealing street, a few steps from the landmark City Tower. It's
the closest thing in town to a business-class hotel. Each of the
29 rooms has its own historical theme (Sb-€64, bigger Sb-€70,
Db-€109, Db suite-€149, €5 less per person mid-Oct-April, lots of
stairs, free Wi-Fi, Prešernova 6, tel. 02/787-7455, fax 02/787-7459,
www.hotel-mitra.si, info@hotel-mitra.si).

$$ Vladmir Šilak rents 16 comfortable rooms around a
charming courtyard in his gorgeously renovated, circa-1513 Old
Town home. If you want to sleep in a 500-year-old house with
huge medieval vaults and three-foot-thick walls, this is the
place (Sb-€31-33, Db-€44, Tb-€57, Qb-€68, five-person apart-
ment-€64-83 depending on size of room, no breakfast, about €10
more if you want your own kitchen, no extra charge for 1-night
stays, free Wi-Fi, bike rental, Dravska 13, tel. 02/787-7447, mobile
031-597-361, www.rooms-silak.com, info@rooms-silak.com).

$$ Žiga Guest House is simpler, slightly cheaper, and less
memorable. Located on a nondescript street between the bus sta-
tion and the Old Town, this reliable budget option has 10 out-
moded rooms (Sb-€22, Db-€35, no breakfast, cash only, some
noise from nearby bar on weekends, free Wi-Fi, Panonska 1,

PTUJ

tel. 02/748-1683, fax 02/748-1684, www.prenocisca-ziga.com, prenocisce.ziga@gmail.com, run with care by the Šoštarić family).

$ Kurent Youth Hostel, an IYHF hostel, is institutional, comfortable, and clean. It has 53 bunks in two- to six-bed rooms, each with its own bathroom (€16 per bed, €1.50 less with hostel membership, breakfast €0.50 extra, Internet access, self-service laundry-€4.50/load, reception open daily 8:00-12:00 & 16:00-20:00, Osojnikova 9, tel. 02/771-0814, fax 02/771-0815, www.youth-hostel .si, ptuj@youth-hostel.si). It's hiding in the big, pinkish commercial center (with the Spar supermarket) near the bus station.

Eating in Ptuj

Little Ptuj isn't known for its high cuisine. You'll spot several breezy cafés and packed pizzerias, but high-quality eateries are in short supply.

Gostilna Ribič is every local's first recommendation for a splurge dinner. One of the most popular (and expensive) places in town, it has a short menu that's focused on fish. Sit in the classy interior or outside on the relaxing riverside terrace (€7 pastas, €10-20 main courses, Tue-Sun 10:00-23:00, closed Mon, Dravska ulica 9, tel. 02/749-0635). If you're ready for a break from Slovenian cuisine, the Chinese restaurant (Kitajski Vrt) across the street is surprisingly good.

Gostilna Amadeus serves up traditional Slovenian cuisine to tour groups, individual tourists, and a few locals. They're especially proud of their €4 *štruklji* (ravioli-like filled dumplings). The bar, with outdoor seating, is downstairs; to eat a meal, head upstairs to their nicely appointed dining room (€6 pastas, €7-15 main courses, Mon-Sat 12:00-23:00, Sun 12:00-16:00, Prešernova 36, tel. 02/771-7051).

PP is frequented by locals who enjoy its inexpensive, unpretentious, stick-to-your-ribs fare—lots of meat and potatoes, plus fried...everything. With a gaudy pub ambience, this Slovenian answer to T.G.I. Friday's is on the town's main shopping square (Novi trg), surrounded by supermarkets and malls. The Kavarna (café) has light food and outdoor seating; to eat a full meal, look for the indoor Gostilna (filling €4-9 main courses, Mon 9:00-22:00, Tue-Sat 9:00-20:00, closed Sun, Kavarna open until 22:00, Novi trg 2, tel. 02/749-0622). The name stands for Perutnina Ptuj, a chicken conglomerate that owns half the town (including this place, Gostilna Ribič, and the big wine cellar)—you'll see their logo everywhere.

Pizzeria Slonček has a great location right on Prešernova, with outdoor tables and good pizzas for less than €5 (daily 9:00-22:00, Prešernova 19, tel. 02/776-1311).

Ptuj Connections

From Ptuj by Train to: Maribor (8/day, 45-60 minutes, some connections are faster with a transfer in Pragersko rather than direct), **Ljubljana** (3/day direct including 2 early, 2.5 hours; many more with transfer in Pragersko, 2-3 hours), **Zagreb** (3/day, 3.5-4.25 hours, usually requires 2 transfers), **Budapest** (4/day, 6.75-8 hours, 2-3 changes, one handy direct train leaves daily at 11:27 and arrives Budapest 17:45), **Vienna** (that's *Dunaj* in Slovene, 6/day, 5-6.25 hours, most require 1-2 changes). For destinations in western Slovenia, first go to Ljubljana.

Maribor

The second-biggest city in Slovenia (with 158,000 people), Maribor lives forever in the shadow of its much glitzier big sister, Ljubljana. Maribor is too small to offer an exciting big-city experience and too big to be charming. But this home of industry, business, and one of Slovenia's three universities is worth a quick look if you want to round out your Slovenian experience.

The lazy provincial town of Maribor woke up fast in 1846, when the Habsburgs built the train line from Vienna to the coast through here. It quickly modernized, losing some of its quaintness but gaining an urban, industrial flavor. However, Maribor was devastated in World War II (unlike other Slovenian cities), when it served as a headquarters for occupying Nazi forces. Since the city's factories also produced plane engines and other supplies, it became a "secondary target," where Allied warplanes—mostly Americans—would drop their bombs if unable to hit their primary targets in Germany or Austria.

Today, rebuilt Maribor feels mellow for its size. Nestled up against a gentle vineyard-covered hill, it's almost cozy. From a tourist's perspective, the town is pleasant enough, but pretty dull—there's little to do other than wander its pedestrians-only streets. But being named a European Capital of Culture for 2012 has helped boost Maribor's appeal. The city doesn't merit a detour, but it's worth  a couple of hours for a stroll if you're passing through or have run out of diversions in Ptuj.

MARIBOR

The countryside surrounding Maribor—called Mariborsko Pohorje—is an inviting recreational area, with vine-strewn hills lively with hikers and bicyclists in summer and with skiers in winter. Maribor is also the center of a thriving wine-growing region—especially popular among Austrians, who flow over the border to sample wines here, then stumble home. If you have time to spare, ask the TI for details about either of these outlying activities.

Orientation to Maribor

Maribor lines up along the bank of the Drava River. At the center of its concrete sprawl is the mostly traffic-free Old Town, with a variety of fine squares.

Tourist Information

The main TI is at the northeast corner of the Old Town, on the far side of the Franciscan Church from Trg Svobode (Mon-Fri 9:00-19:00, Sat-Sun 9:00-18:00, Partizanska 6a, tel. 02/234-6611, www.maribor-pohorje.si). Pick up the handy city map and any other brochures that interest you. The TI can also give you a list of hotels or help you arrange for a local guide.

Arrival in Maribor

The train station (which has big lockers) is a 10-minute walk east of the Old Town. Exit the station to the left and head up busy Partizanska cesta. Follow Partizanska as it swings right at the bus station, then continue three more blocks toward the Franciscan Church, with its twin red-brick spires. The main TI is in front of the church, and the Old Town is immediately behind the church.

Self-Guided Walk

Welcome to Maribor

Maribor's Austrian-feeling Old Town lacks big-league sights, but its squares and lanes are worth a wander. This very lightly narrated walk will give you the lay of the land. You could do it in less than a half-hour, not including stops.

Entering the Old Town from the train station (on Partizanska, near the Franciscan Church with its two red-brick spires—see "Arrival in Maribor," earlier), you find yourself on **Trg Svobode.** The oddly bulbous monument honors local Partisans (Yugoslav freedom-fighters) who were executed by Nazis during World War II. Wine cellars honeycomb the earth under this square (most can be toured only with a group—ask at the TI).

At the end of the square, with the tall tower, is the town's

castle (Mestni Grad), which houses a good regional museum.

Adjoining Trg Svobode is a second square, **Grajski trg**—Maribor's liveliest, bustling with cafés and restaurants (including the recommended Štajerc brewpub). At the top of the square is the venerable **Café Astoria,** a local landmark (open long hours daily).

Recent-history buffs may want to take a detour from here to Maribor's most interesting museum: the **Maribor National Liberation Museum** (Muzej Narodone Osvoboditve Maribor), about a five-minute walk up the street at the top of Grajski trg (between Café Astoria and the castle). This collection features a hodgepodge of items from the city's history, mostly focusing on Slovenia's turbulent 20th century. A permanent exhibit covers the early Tito years (1945-1955) and is supplemented by temporary exhibits. Enjoy the idealized Socialist Realist propaganda posters of happy Yugoslavs, eagerly pitching in to build a new nation (€2, Mon-Fri 8:00-17:00, Sat 9:00-12:00, closed Sun, Ulica Heroja Tomšiča 5, tel. 02/235-2600, www.muzejno-mb.si).

Back on Grajski trg, follow lively **Slovenska ulica,** lined with characteristic cafés, sweet shops, and happy al fresco diners. Take a left at Gosposka, then turn right on 10 Oktobra to find the big parking-lot square called Slomškov trg, with the city **cathedral** (skip the tower climb—the view is nothing special).

From the cathedral, walk straight down toward the river, cutting through Rotovški trg. You'll wind up on the long, narrow **Glavni trg,** surrounded by historic buildings (including the City Hall) and presided over by an impressive 18th-century plague column.

If you continue down to the riverbank, you'll find yourself in the district called **Lent,** where vintners traditionally offer tastings of their wines. While it's usually pretty quiet, this area hops each summer when Maribor hosts its Lent Festival (late June-early July, http://lent.slovenija.net). Along this embankment, look for the locally revered "old vine" stretching along a railing—it's supposedly 400 years old and still produces wine-worthy grapes.

Eating in Maribor

Štajerc is a popular local watering hole that brews its own beer and serves up heavy, starchy, traditional food. They're particularly known for their distinctive emerald-green beer, Štajerc Zeleno. Sit inside, or enjoy the outdoor seating on Maribor's most happening square, Grajski trg (€5-12 meals, closed Sun, Vetrinjska 30, tel. 02/234-4234).

MARIBOR

Maribor Connections

From Maribor by Train to: Ptuj (8/day, 45-60 minutes), **Ljubljana** (hourly, 2-3 hours, some direct, others transfer in Zidani Most), **Vienna** (that's *Dunaj* in Slovene, 2/day direct, 3.75 hours).

THE KARST

Caves, Castles, and Horses

In Slovenia's Karst region, about an hour south of Ljubljana on the A1 expressway, you'll find some of the most impressive cave systems on the planet, a chance to see the famous Lipizzaner stallions for a fraction of what you'd pay in Vienna, and one of Europe's most dramatically situated castles—built into the face of a mountain.

The word "karst" is used worldwide to refer to an arid limestone plateau, but Slovenia's is the original. In fact, that term comes from the Slovenian word "Kras"—a specific region near the Italian border. Since this limestone terrain is easily dissolved by water, karstic regions are punctuated by remarkable networks of caves and underground rivers.

Your top Karst priority is a cave visit. Choose between Slovenia's two best caves, Škocjan or Postojna—each with a handy side-trip nearby (to help you pick, see the sidebar on page 657). In the neighborhood of Škocjan is Lipica, where the Lipizzaner stallions strut their stuff. Just up the road from Postojna is Predjama Castle, picturesquely nestled into the side of a cliff.

I've listed public-transit possibilities for several of these destinations, but most of them are very challenging to reach without a car. To efficiently hit several in one day, consider taking a guided excursion from Ljubljana (see page 526).

Sleeping: To sleep in the heart of the Karst—a short drive from all these sights—consider **Tourist Farm Hudičevec** (hoo-DEE-cheh-vets), midway between Škocjan and Postojna. This kid-friendly complex, with seven rooms and two apartments, is run by the farming Simčič family. A roomy, hotelesque, spick-and-span double with a private bathroom—including a Slovenian dinner and

farm-fresh eggs for breakfast—
costs only €64 for two people
(Db without dinner-€46, big
apartment-€80 plus €9 per person for optional dinner, cash
only, free Wi-Fi, tel. 05/703-
0300, fax 05/703-0320, www
.hudicevec.si, info@hudicevec
.si). Idyllic and remote as this

place sounds, it's actually right next to the expressway (which
makes it easy to reach, but also means it comes with some road
noise, and large tour groups may show up for dinner). Take the
Razdrto exit from the expressway, turn right toward Postojna,
then start looking right away for the low-profile sign directing you
back under the road.

Škocjan Caves and Lipica Stud Farm

Drivers can easily combine these two attractions, which are just
a short drive from each other. By public transportation, it's more
challenging. The main transit hubs for this area are the towns of
Divača and Sežana, both served by train and bus from Ljubljana.
A shuttle bus goes between the Divača train station and Škocjan
Caves (10 minutes, 2/day in high season only, coordinated to meet
some trains—check schedules at Ljubljana TI). To reach Lipica,
you'll have to take a taxi from one of the train stations.

▲▲▲Škocjan Caves (Škocjanske Jame)

Škocjan (SHKOHTS-yahn) offers good formations and a spectacularly vast canyon with a raging underground river. You'll end up
walking about two miles, going up and down more than 400 steps.
While anyone in good shape can enjoy Škocjan, those who have
trouble walking or tire easily are better off touring the Postojna
Caves instead (described later).

Cost and Hours: €15, guided tour is mandatory, usually in
English, and takes about two hours; June-Sept tours daily at the
top of each hour 10:00-17:00, Oct-May tours daily at 10:00 and
13:00 and sometimes also at 15:00 or 15:30, call or pick up current brochure—which you'll find everywhere in Slovenia—to confirm schedule before making the trip; tel. 05/708-2110, www.park
-skocjanske-jame.si.

Getting to Škocjan: By car, take the A1 expressway south
from Ljubljana about an hour and get off at the Divača exit (also
marked with brown signs for *Lipica* and *Škocjanske jame*) and follow signs for *Škocjanske jame*. (Before or after Škocjan, drivers can
easily visit the Lipica Stud Farm, described next.) The caves have

THE KARST

free and easy parking.

By public transportation, it's trickier. Take the train or bus to Divača (see "Ljubljana Connections," page 560), which is about three miles from the caves. To get from the Divača train station to the caves, you can either take the local shuttle bus (2/day, only in summer); rent a bike (often possible in summer); hike about 45 minutes; or take a taxi (around €8-10, taxi stand in front of Divača train station).

Touring the Caves: Upon arrival, get a ticket for the next tour (they rarely fill up). You'll pass waiting time at a covered terrace with a gift kiosk, a bar serving light meals and drinks, and an interactive educational center with exhibits about the caves. At tour time, your guide (toting an industrial-strength flashlight) calls everyone together, and you march silently for 10 minutes to the cave entrance. There you split into language groups and enter the cave.

The first half of the experience is the "dry caves," with a wide array of wondrous formations and what seem like large caverns. The

experience builds and builds as you go into ever-more-impressive grottoes, and you think you've seen the best. But then you get to the truly colossal "finale" cavern, with a mighty river crashing through the bottom. You feel like a bit player in a sci-fi thriller. It's a world where a thousand evil *Wizard of Oz* monkeys could comfortably fly in formation. You hike high above the river for about a mile, crossing a breathtaking (but stable-feeling) footbridge 150 feet above the torrent. Far below, the scant remains of century-old trails from the early days of tourism are evocative. The cave finally widens, sunlight pours in, and you emerge—like lost creatures seeking daylight—into a lush canyon. A steep, somewhat strenuous hike leads to a small funicular, which lifts you back to the ticket booth/café/shop.

Museum: A small museum about the local geology and the history of Škocjan spelunking is in the Jurjev Barn, about a 10-minute walk from the entrance (admission covered by cave ticket in summer, open June-Sept daily 11:30-19:30; €4 Oct-May, open by request only).

▲Lipica Stud Farm (Kobilarna Lipica)

The Lipica (LEE-peet-suh) Stud Farm, a 10-minute drive from the Škocjan Caves, was founded in 1580 to provide horses for the Habsburg court in Vienna. Horse-loving Habsburg Archduke

The Karst Region

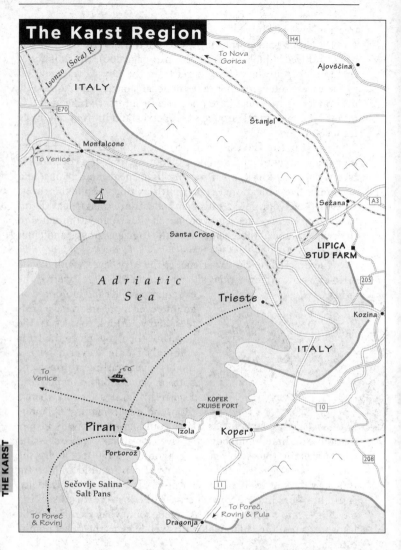

Charles wanted to create the perfect animal: He imported Andalusian horses from his homeland of Spain, then bred them with a local line to come up with an extremely intelligent and easily trainable breed. Charles' creation, the Lipizzaner stallions—known for their noble gait and Baroque shape—were made famous by Vienna's Spanish Riding School. Italian and

Arabian bloodlines were later added to tweak various characteristics. These regal horses have changed shape with the tenor of the times: They were bred strong and stout during wars, frilly and slender in more cultured eras. But they're always born black, fade to gray, and turn a distinctive white in adulthood. Until World War I, Lipica bred horses for Austria's needs. Now Austria breeds its own line, and these horses prance for Slovenia—a treasured part of its cultural heritage (and featured on Slovenia's €0.20 coin).

Today you can tour the Lipizzaner stables to visit these magnificent animals, whose stalls are labeled with their purebred bloodlines. Unlike in Vienna, it's cheap and easy to get tickets to see the horses perform. While the show is less polished than in Vienna, the Lipizzaners' clever routine—stutter-stepping sideways to the classical beat—still thrills visitors. This up-close horse encounter is worth a visit only if you're a horse enthusiast, or if you have a car and it fits your schedule.

By the way, the hills less than a mile away are in Italy. Aside from the horses, Lipica's big draw is its casino. Italians across the border are legally forbidden from gambling in their own town's casinos—for fear of addiction—so they flock here to Slovenia to try their luck.

Visiting the Stud Farm: There are three activities at Lipica—you can tour the farm for a look at the horses, watch a training session, and, on some days, see a more elaborate performance of the prancing stallions. If you're coming all the way to Lipica, you might as well time it so that you can do both the one-hour tour and a training session (10:00-12:00) or—better yet—a full performance. Call ahead or check online to confirm performance and tour times before you make the trip (tel. 05/739-1580, www.lipica .org). Note that in summer, Monday is the only day you can't see the horses training or performing (but the tour still runs).

Cost: Stud farm tour only-€11, tour plus training session-€13, tour plus performance-€18.

Tours: July-Aug daily on the hour 9:00-18:00 except 12:00; April-June and Sept-Oct daily on the hour 9:00-17:00 except 12:00 (also at 18:00 Sat-Sun); March daily on the hour 9:00-15:00 except 12:00 (also at 16:00 Sat-Sun); Nov-Feb daily at 11:00, 13:00, 14:00, and 15:00. Note that on days when there's a performance (see next), the 15:00 tour is canceled.

Performances: April-Oct Tue, Fri, and Sun at 15:00, none Nov-March.

Training Sessions: April-Oct Tue-Sun 10:00-12:00, none Mon or Nov-March.

Getting to Lipica: The Lipica Stud Farm is in Slovenia's southwest corner (a stone's throw from Trieste, Italy). By car, exit the A1 expressway at Divača and follow brown *Lipica* signs. (As you drive into the farm, you'll go through pastures where the stallions often roam.) It's a hassle by public transportation. You can take the train or bus from Ljubljana to Divača (about six miles from Lipica) or to Sežana (about four miles from Lipica). From those places, you can hire a taxi (€15 from Divača, €10 from Sežana) or rent a bike (often possible in summer).

Postojna vs. Škocjan: Which Caves to Visit?

The recipe for creating a cave is simple: Begin with limestone. Then, just add water and wait for 2 million years. (Serves half a million tourists each year.)

The Karst has two big cave systems: Postojna and Škocjan. Each one is massive. Stalagmites and stalactites—in

a slow-motion love story—silently work their way toward each other, a third of an inch per century, until that last drip never drops. Minerals picked up by the water as it seeps through various rocks create the different colors (iron makes red, limestone makes white, and so on). Both caves were excavated and explored in the mid-19th century.

However, what you'll see inside each cave system—and how you'll see it—is quite different. Slovenes debate long and hard about which cave system is better. The formations at Postojna are slightly more abundant, varied, and colorful, with stalagmites and stalactites as tall as 100 feet. Postojna is easier to reach by public transportation and far less strenuous to visit than Škocjan—of the three-mile route, you'll walk only about a mile (the rest of the time, you're on a speedy underground train). But Postojna is also more expensive and much more touristy (they get about 500,000 visitors each year, five times as many as Škocjan)—you'll wade through tour buses and tacky souvenir stands on your way to the entrance. Most importantly, Postojna lacks Škocjan's spectacular, massive-cavern finale. Škocjan also comes with a fairly strenuous hike, leaving you feeling like you really did something adventurous. Finally, the choice of likely side-trip might help you decide: Near Postojna is the cliff-hanging Predjama Castle, while Škocjan is closer to the Lipica Stud Farm.

No matter which cave you visit, you'll find it chilly, but not really cold (a light sweater is fine). Both caves technically forbid photography (a laughable rule that nobody takes seriously).

These caves are also home to a unique little cave-dwelling creature—the so-called "human fish" (a.k.a. olm or *Proteus anguinus*), which is a long, skinny, pale-pink salamander-like creature with fingers and toes. The world's biggest cave-dwelling animal, these amphibians can grow up to a foot long, live for about a century, and survive up to a decade without eating (the live specimens on display in Postojna are never fed during the four months they're on view). As they're endemic to Slovenia, the "human fish" are celebrated as a sort of national mascot.

Postojna Caves and Predjama Castle

These two sights are easy to connect for drivers, since they're along the same road. If you're using public transportation, it's not too difficult to reach the caves, but expensive and/or time-consuming to see the castle.

▲▲Postojna Caves (Postojnska Jama)

Postojna (poh-STOY-nah) is the most accessible—and most tour-isty—cave experience in the region. It's the biggest cave system in Slovenia, with more than 12 miles of explored caves (three of which you'll see on the tour). It's also the easiest to visit, since much of the tour is on a fast-moving train, and the rest is well-paved, well-lit, and not too steep. All of this makes it Slovenia's single most popular tourist attraction.

Cost and Hours: €23, tours leave daily at the top of each hour July-Aug 9:00-18:00; May-June and Sept 9:00-17:00; April and Oct at 10:00, 12:00, 14:00, and 16:00; Nov-March at 10:00, 12:00, and 15:00; tours last 1.5 hours, call to confirm schedule or pick up brochure at any TI, Jamska cesta 30, tel. 05/700-0100, www.postojna-cave.com. If you're visiting several sights here—including the Vivarium and Predjama Castle interior—do the math to see if the advertised combo-tickets save you money.

Crowd Control: From mid-May through August, try to show up 30 minutes early for the morning tours (popular with tour buses); otherwise, aim for 15 minutes ahead.

Getting to Postojna: The caves are just outside the town of Postojna, about 45 minutes south of Ljubljana on the A1 express-way. By **car,** take the expressway south from Ljubljana and get off at the Postojna exit. Leaving the expressway, turn right and follow the *jama/grotte/cave* signs through town until you see the tour buses. Drivers pay to park 200 yards from the cave entry. By **train,** you'll arrive at the train station in the town of Postojna; from here, you can walk to the caves in about 20 minutes, or pay for a taxi. If coming on the bus from Ljubljana, you'll be dropped just a five-minute walk from the caves.

Touring the Caves: A visit here is basically an easy, lightly guided stroll through an amazing underground cavern. Whether you arrive by car, tour bus, or on foot, you'll walk past a paved out-door mall of shops, eateries, and handicraft vendors to the gaping hole in the mountain. Buy your ticket at the kiosk, then climb up the stairs and wait with the mob to board the little open-air train, which slings you deep into the mountain, whizzing past wonder-ful formations. (The ride alone is exhilarating.) Then you get out, assemble into language groups, and follow a guide on a well-lit, circular, paved path through more formations.

First you'll hike uphill into the "Big Mountain"—the highest point inside the caves, and (surprisingly) actually higher than where you entered. You're surrounded by a sea of fairy-chimney stalagmites and stalactites, some of them a hundred feet tall. Then you'll hike downhill and cross a bridge over a canyon into "Spaghetti Hall," named for the long, skinny stalactites that seem to be dripping from the ceiling. Also in this area are some amazing, translucent "curtains" of rock. Circling down beneath the bridge you just crossed, you'll come to some huge, white, melting-ice-cream formations (including one called "The Organ," for

obvious reasons). You'll wind up in the impressively vast cavern called the "Concert Hall," peering into an aquarium with the strange "human fish." Then you'll load back onto the train and return to the bright daylight. Exiting the train, notice that the ceiling of this part of the cavern is charred black. The only coloring in the cave caused by humans, this is residue from a huge WWII explosion; the Partisan Army blew up a fuel and ammo depot the Nazis kept here.

"Vivarium": This disappointing exhibit, which fills a smaller cave next to the ticket booth, gives you the chance to learn more about karstic caves and speleobiology (the study of cave-dwelling animal life). You'll be given a flashlight and sent to look for 17 different species of animals—but since the cave-dwellers (naturally) hide from view, you just wind up squinting into empty aquariums most of the time. One interesting feature is a wall with graffiti signatures from past visitors—some dating all the way back to the 13th century. Upstairs is a "butterfly collection"—two dozen frames filled with samples of butterflies around a big conference room (not worth the outrageous €4 extra fee). While troglodytes, science nuts, and those who just can't get enough of those human fish may get a charge out of this exhibit, it's basically just an attempt to wring a little more cash out of gullible tourists (€4, €8 including butterfly exhibit, opens 30 minutes before first cave tour, closes 30 minutes after the last tour).

▲Predjama Castle (Predjamski Grad)

Burrowed into the side of a mountain close to Postojna is dramatic Predjama Castle (prehd-YAH-mah), one of Europe's most scenic castles (despite its dull interior). Predjama is a hit with tourists for its striking setting, exciting exterior, and romantic legend.

Notice as you approach that you don't even see Predjama—

660 Rick Steves' Croatia & Slovenia

crouching magnificently in its cave—until the last moment. The first castle here was actually a tiny ninth-century fortress embedded deep in the cave behind the present castle. Over the centuries, different castles were built here, and they gradually moved out to the mouth of the cave. While the original was called "the castle in the cave," the current one is *pred jama*—"in front of the cave."

While enjoying the view, ponder this legend: In the 15th century, a nobleman named Erasmus killed the emperor's cousin in a duel. He was imprisoned under Ljubljana Castle and spent years nursing a grudge. When he was finally released, he used his castle—buried deep inside the cave above this current version—as a home base for a series of Robin Hood-style raids on the local nobility and merchants. (Actually, Erasmus stole from the rich and kept for himself—but that was good enough to make him a hero to the peasants, who hated the nobles.)

Soldiers from Trieste were brought in to put an end to Erasmus' raids, laying siege to the castle for over a year. Back then, the only way into the castle was through the cave in the valley below—then up, through an extensive labyrinth of caves, to the top. While the soldiers down below froze and starved, Erasmus' men sneaked out through the caves to bring in supplies. (They liked to drop their leftovers on the soldiers below to taunt them, letting them know that the siege wasn't working.)

Eventually, the soldiers came up with a plan. They waited for Erasmus to visit the latrine—which, by design, had to be on the thin-walled outer edge of the castle—and then, on seeing a signal by a secret agent, blew Erasmus off his throne with a cannonball. Erasmus is supposedly buried under the huge linden tree in the parking lot.

As the legend of Erasmus faded, the function of the castle changed. By the 16th century, Predjama had become a castle for hunting more than for defense—explaining its current picturesque-but-impractical design.

After driving all the way here, it seems a shame not to visit the interior—but it's truly skippable. The management (which also runs the nearby Postojna Caves) is very strict about keeping the interior 16th-century in style, so there's virtually nothing inside except 20th-century fakes of 16th-century furniture, plus a few forgettable paintings and cheesy folk displays. English descriptions are sparse, and the free English history flier is not much help. But for most, the views of the place alone are worth the drive.

THE KARST

Cost and Hours: €10 to go inside, daily July-Aug 9:00-19:00, May-June and Sept 9:00-18:00, April and Oct 10:00-17:00, Nov-March 10:00-16:00. Information: tel. 05/751-6015.

Cave Tours: If you're already visiting the caves at Postojna or Škocjan, a visit to the caves under this castle is unnecessary (€9, 45 minutes; May-Sept daily at 11:00, 13:00, 15:00, and 17:00; no tours Oct-April).

Getting to Predjama: Predjama Castle is on a twisty rural road 5.5 miles beyond Postojna Caves. By car, just continue on the winding road past Postojna, following signs for *Predjama* and *Predjamski Grad* (coming back, follow signs to *Postojna*). If using public transportation, you can take the train to the town of Postojna, but from there you'll have to pay for a taxi. If you're in a pinch, consider hitching a ride between Predjama and Postojna with a friendly tour bus or tourist's car, as most visitors do both sights.

PIRAN

Croatia's 3,600-mile-long coast gets all the press, but don't overlook Slovenia's own 29 miles of Adriatic coastline. The Slovenian coast has only a handful of towns: big, industrial Koper; lived-in and crumbling Izola; and the swanky but soulless resort of Portorož. But the Back Door gem of the Slovenian Adriatic is Piran. Most Adriatic towns are all tourists and concrete, but Piran has kept itself charming and in remarkably good repair while holding the tourist sprawl at bay. In peak season, it's overrun with Italian vacationers. But as you get to know it, Piran becomes one of the most pleasant and user-friendly seaside towns this side of Dubrovnik.

Planning Your Time

You can see everything in Piran (including a pop into the Maritime Museum and a hike up the bell tower) in a quick, hour-long walk. Then feel free to just bask in the town's ambience. Enjoy a gelato or a *kava* (coffee) on the sleek, marbled Tartini Square, surrounded by Neoclassical buildings and watched over by the bell tower. Wander Piran's piers and catch its glow at sunset.

Piran also works as a base for visiting the caves, horses, and castles of the nearby Karst region (see previous chapter). Notice, too, that it's conveniently on the way between Ljubljana/the Karst and Croatia's Istria (see "Route Tips for Drivers" at the end of this chapter).

Orientation to Piran

(area code: 05)
Piran (pee-RAHN) is small; everything is within a few minutes' walk. Crowded onto the tip of its peninsula, the town can't grow. Its population—7,500 a century ago—has dropped to about 4,200 today, as many young people find more opportunity in bigger cities.

Piran clusters around its boat-speckled harbor and main showpiece square, Tartini Square (Tartinijev trg). Up the hill behind Tartini Square is the landmark bell tower of the Cathedral of St. George. A few blocks toward the end of the peninsula from Tartini Square is the heart of the Old Town, May 1 Square (Trg 1 Maja).

From Tartini Square and the nearby marina, a concrete promenade—lined with rocks to break the storm waves and with expensive tourist restaurants to break your budget—stretches along the town's waterfront, inviting you to stroll.

Tourist Information

The TI is on Tartini Square facing the marina (daily June-Aug 9:00-20:00, Sept-May 9:00-17:00, at #2, tel. 05/673-4440, www.portoroz.si). For **Internet access**, get online at the Val Youth Hostel (described later, under "Sleeping in Piran"). You can **rent a bike** at the Maona travel agency (€6/2 hours, €20/24 hours, Cankarjevo nabrežje 7, tel. 05/673-4520).

Arrival in Piran

By Car: In peak season (June-early Sept), you have to park at the big harborside garage called Arze, just outside the gate into town (€1.20/hour, €12/day, frequent shuttle buses take you right to Tartini Square, or you can walk 10 minutes). If you're staying in town, you can drive in to drop things off at your hotel, but you'll likely need to take your car right back to the harborside lot. Off-season, you may be able to find some marked tourist spaces inside the Old Town area, but they're expensive (€5 for the first hour, €3/hour after that, get a ticket as you enter the gate and pay as you exit)—be careful to park only in spaces designated for tourists.

By Bus: Piran has two bus stops. Shuttle buses from the harborside parking lot and nearby towns (such as Portorož) stop right at Tartini Square; buses to long-distance destinations (such as Ljubljana) use the low-profile main bus station along the water, near the entrance to town.

Sights in Piran

In Piran

▲**Tartini Square (Tartinijev trg)**—Tartini Square, with its polished marble, was once part of a protected harbor. In 1894, the harbor smelled so bad that they decided to fill it in. Today, rather than fishing boats, it's filled with skateboarding kids.

The statue honors **Giuseppe Tartini** (1692-1770), a composer and violinist once known throughout Europe. While the Church of St. Peter has overlooked this spot since 1272, its current facade is Neoclassical, from the early 1800s. The Neo-Renaissance Town Hall dates from the 1870s.

The fine little red palace in the corner (at #4) evokes Venice.

This **"Venetian House"** (c. 1450) is the oldest preserved house on the square. Classic Venetian Gothic, it was built by a wealthy Venetian merchant and comes with a legend: The merchant fell in love with a simple local girl when visiting on business, became her sugar daddy, and eventually built her this flat. When the townsfolk began to gossip about the relationship, he answered them with the relief you see today (with the Venetian lion, between the two top windows): *Lassa pur dir* ("Let them talk").

May 1 Square (Trg 1 Maja)—This square marks the center of medieval Piran, where its main streets converged. Once the administrative center of town, today it's the domain of local kids and ringed by a few humble eateries. The stone rainwater cistern dominating the center of the square was built in 1775 after a severe drought. Rainwater was captured here with the help of drains from roofs and channeled by hardworking statues into the system. The water was filtered through sand and stored in the well, clean and ready for townspeople to draw—or, later, pump—for drinking.

Cathedral and Bell Tower of St. George (Stolna Cerkev Sv. Jurija)—Piran is proud of its many churches, which number more than 20. While none are of any real historic or artistic importance, the Cathedral of St. George is worth a look. This cathedral dates from the 14th century and was decorated in the Baroque style by Venetian artists in the 17th century. It dominates the Old Town

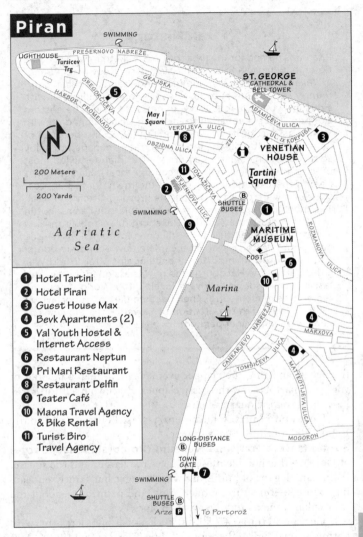

Piran

SWIMMING

PREŠERNOVO NABREŽE

LIGHTHOUSE

Tursicev Trg

GRAJSKA

ST. GEORGE
CATHEDRAL &
BELL TOWER

GREGORČIČEVA

HARBOR PROMENADE

ADAMIČEVA ULICA

May 1 Square

VERDIJEVA ULICA

OBZIDNA ULICA

ZEL.

UL. IX KORPUSA

VENETIAN HOUSE

200 Meters

200 Yards

TOMAŽIČEVA

Adriatic Sea

SMERNOVA ULICA

Tartini Square

B SHUTTLE BUSES

SWIMMING

Marina

MARITIME MUSEUM

POST

ROZMANOVA ULICA

❶ Hotel Tartini
❷ Hotel Piran
❸ Guest House Max
❹ Bevk Apartments (2)
❺ Val Youth Hostel &
    Internet Access
❻ Restaurant Neptun
❼ Pri Mari Restaurant
❽ Restaurant Delfin
❾ Teater Café
❿ Maona Travel Agency
    & Bike Rental
⓫ Turist Biro
    Travel Agency

CANKARJEVO NABREŽE

MARXOVA

TOMBLCEVA ULICA

MATTEOTIJEVA ULICA

MOGORON

LONG-DISTANCE
B BUSES

TOWN GATE ❼

SWIMMING

SHUTTLE **B** BUSES
P
Arze

↓ To Portorož

with its bell tower *(campanile)*, a miniature version of the more famous one on St. Mark's Square in Venice. The tower (with bells dating from the 15th century) welcomes tourists willing to climb 146 rickety steps for the best view in town and a chance for some bell fun. Stand inside the biggest bell. Chant, find the resonant

Piran History

Piran was named for the fires (*pyr* in Greek) that were lit at the tip of its peninsula to assist passing ships. Known as "Pirano" in *Italiano*, the town is home to a long-standing Italian community (about 1,500 today)—so it's legally bilingual, with signs in two languages. As with most towns on the eastern Adriatic, it has a Venetian flavor. Piran wisely signed on with Venice as part of its trading empire in 933, and because of its valuable salt industry and strong trade, managed to enjoy some autonomy in later centuries. After plagues killed most of Piran's population in the 15th century, local Italians let Slavs fleeing the Ottomans repopulate the town. Piran's impressive walls were built to counter the growing Ottoman threat. Too much rain ruined the town's valuable salt basins, but in the 19th century, the Austrian Habsburg rulers rebuilt the salt industry (these salt fields are still open for tourist visits—see next page). With that change came a new economic boom, and Piran grew in importance once again. After World War I, this part of the Habsburg Empire was assigned to Italy, but fascism never sat well with the locals. After World War II, the region was made neutral, then became part of Yugoslavia in 1956. In 1991, with the creation of Slovenia, the Slovenes of Piran were finally independent.

frequency, and ring the clapper ever so softly. Snap a portrait of you, your partner, and the rusty clapper. Brace yourself for *fortissimo* clangs on the quarter-hour.

Cost and Hours: Church entry-free, bell tower–€1, daily 10:00-17:00, until 19:00 in summer.

Sergej Mašera Maritime Museum (Pomorski Muzej Sergej Mašera)—This humble museum faces the harbor and the square, filling an elegant old building with meager but faintly endearing exhibits—furniture, model ships, and paintings—about the "Slovenian seamen" and the town's history.

Cost and Hours: €3.50, €0.50 English booklet, otherwise borrow scant English descriptions; July-Aug Tue-Sun 9:00-12:00 & 17:00-21:00, closed Mon; Sept-June Tue-Sun 9:00-17:00, closed Mon; Cankarjevo nabrežje 3, tel. 05/671-0040, www.pommuz-pi.si.

Harborfront Stroll—Wandering along the harborfront is a delight: almost no pesky mopeds or cars, and virtually no American or Japanese tourists—just Slovenes and Italians. Children sell shells on cardboard boxes. Husky sunbathers lie like large limpets on the rocks. Walk around the lighthouse at the tip of the town and around the corner, checking out the cafés and fish restaurants along the way.

Swimming—While there is no sandy beach, the water is warm and clean, and swimming is a major activity in Piran. There are two pebbly beaches: one just outside of town before the big parking lot, and the other at the end of the harbor promenade past the lighthouse. Two designated swimming areas are accessible from the promenade—both with ladders, showers, and some very slippery concrete embankments (one in front of Hotel Piran, the other around the corner from the lighthouse).

Near Piran
▲**Sečovlje Salina Nature Park (Krajinski Park Sečoveljske Soline)**—A few miles south of Piran, a literal stone's throw from the Croatian border, are enormous salt fields that have been used since the Middle Ages for harvesting this precious mineral—back when it was more valuable than gold. As you drive by on the way to Croatia, you'll wonder what this massive complex is—so why not stop for a visit? This "nature park" has two parts: Lera, to the north, harvests salt using 700-year-old techniques; while Fontanigge, to the south (closer to Croatia), is no longer in operation, but has a good museum to explain traditional salt-harvesting methods to tourists. I never thought salt could be so interesting.

The **Lera** section has a visitors center, restaurant, and guided tours (€30, 1.5-hour guided walk through the salt fields, reserve ahead at www.kpss.si/en/visiting/guided-tours). This is also where you're most likely to see salt being harvested just as it was from medieval times up until the Austrians arrived in 1904. Museum docents do it the way their ancestors did: First, they fill up large shallow pans with seawater, then they seal them off and allow the water to naturally evaporate, leaving behind those precious deposits.

At **Fontanigge** (within a few feet of the Croatian border, which is just over the little river), you can tour the Salt-Making Museum. Well-explained by posted English information and a knowledgeable docent, the exhibit demonstrates tools and methods, illustrating the lifestyles of the people who eked out a hard living on these salty marshes (for example, since they all shared a communal oven, each family had their own stamp for marking their loaves of bread). The catch: The museum is about a mile and a half off the main road, reachable only by a 30-minute walk down a very bumpy gravel road (or an easy boat trip from Piran—see "Getting There," below).

Cost and Hours: €5 covers entry to both Fontanigge and Lera salt fields and the museum; salt fields open daily 8:00-21:00 in summer, 8:00-17:00 off-season; museum open daily April-Oct 9:00-18:00, closed Nov-March; tel. 05/671-0040, www.kpss.si.

Getting There: Both salt fields are between Piran and the

PIRAN

Croatian border. For **drivers** heading south toward Croatia (see "Route Tips for Drivers," later), you'll pass the entrance to the Lera salt field and visitors center on the right, just after entering the town of Seča. To visit Lera, go down a steep cobbled stretch, then cross a bridge over a channel to reach the visitors center. For Fontanigge—farther along the main road—it's more complicated: You'll actually have to cross the Slovenian border, then a few feet later, just before you reach the Croatian border post, you'll see a gravel road on the right, leading to the salt field. It's a five-minute drive to the gate, where you'll park and walk about 30 minutes to the museum. (Though there is a very rough gravel road to the museum, they prefer that visitors avoid driving on it, in order to protect this fragile landscape.)

If you don't have a car, the only possibility is to take the very sporadic *Solinarka* **boat** from Piran (goes right to the museum, frequency depends on demand and sometimes not at all—ask at the Piran TI).

Sleeping in Piran

Piran's accommodations options are limited: two comparable hotels, a colorful guest house, some youth hostels, and *sobe* (rooms in private homes).

$$$ Hotel Tartini faces the main square 50 yards from the waterfront. Its 46 rooms are jaunty, colorful, and a bit faded. Don't miss the upstairs terrace cocktail bar, with great views over Tartini Square (Sb-€88/€82/€76, Db-€124/€110/€102; €10 more for seaside room with balcony; air-con, elevator, free Wi-Fi, Tartinijev trg 15, tel. 05/671-1000, fax 05/671-1665, www.hotel-tartini-piran.com, info@hotel-tartini-piran.com).

$$$ Hotel Piran is right on the water, with a concrete "beach" directly in front of it. Its 89 rooms are more business than resort, with a complex pricing scheme (seaview superior Sb-€88/€80/€77, non-view superior Db-€108/€102/€98, seaview standard Db-€116/€108/€104, seaview superior Db-€132/€122/€118; "superior" rooms have air-con, a bigger bathroom, and more soundproof windows; elevator, pay Internet access and Wi-Fi, Stijenkova 1, tel. 05/690-7000, fax 05/690-7008, www.hoteli-piran.si, booking@bernardin group.si).

$$ Guest House Max is a clean-yet-funky place just under the town's bell tower. Mellow and friendly Max welcomes travelers with six simple, mod, and comfy rooms up a tight staircase over a cozy breakfast room. Since Max is a one-man show (and usually takes a mid-afternoon siesta), it's essential to carefully settle on an arrival time with him (Db-€70/€60, higher price is for July-late Aug, €10 less for Sb, cash only, no extra charge for 1-night stays,

Sleep Code

(€1 = about $1.40, country code: 386, area code: 05)
S = Single, **D** = Double/Twin, **T** = Triple, **Q** = Quad, **b** = bathroom. Unless otherwise noted, credit cards are accepted and breakfast is included, but the modest tourist tax (about €1 per person, per night) is not. Everyone listed here speaks English.

Rates: If I've listed three sets of rates, separated by slashes, the first price is for peak season (mid-July-late Aug), the second is for shoulder season (June-mid-July and late Aug-Sept), and the third is for the rest of the year (though some rates go even lower in winter). The dates for seasonal rates vary by hotel, and prices can change without notice; verify the hotel's current rates online or by email. For other updates, see www.ricksteves.com/update.

Price Ranges: To help you sort easily through these listings, I've divided the accommodations into three categories based on the price for a double room with bath during high season:

$$$ Higher Priced—Most rooms €85 or more.
  $$ Moderately Priced—Most rooms between €50-85.
    $ Lower Priced—Most rooms €50 or less.

fans, portable air-con unit may be available on very hot days, free Wi-Fi, ulica 9 Korpusa #26, tel. 05/673-3436, mobile 041-692-928, www.maxpiran.com, info@maxpiran.com).

$$ Bogdan and Jana Bevk rent six good apartments in two different buildings with roof terraces; both are buried in a quiet part of the Old Town (Db-€60/€50/€40, €10 more for newer apartments with sauna, 50 percent more for 1-2-night stays, no breakfast, air-con, free Wi-Fi, lots of stairs, Marxova 13 and Preži-hova 4, mobile 051-623-682, tel. 05/902-2111, www.bevk.si, info @bevk.si).

$ Val Youth Hostel rents the cheapest beds in town. It's a friendly place, a half-block off the waterfront (55 beds in 22 two-, three-, or four-bed rooms; €27/€23 per person, lower price is for mid-Sept-mid-May, €5 more for 1-night stays in peak season, includes breakfast and sheets, prices are the same regardless of room size, free self-service laundry, kitchen; free Internet access for guests, or €1/hour for non-guests; 20 yards in from waterfront near tip of peninsula at Gregorčičeva 38A, tel. 05/673-2555, fax 05/673-2556, www.hostel-val.com, yhostel.val@siol.net).

$ Sobe: To track down a private room, try two local travel agencies: **Maona** (Cankarjevo nabrežje 7, tel. 05/673-4520, www .maona.si, maona@siol.net) or **Turist Biro** (Tomažičeva 3, tel. 05/673-2509, www.turistbiro-ag.si, info@turistbiro-ag.si). As with those who rent rooms in coastal Croatia, Piran's *sobe* hosts charge 30-50 percent extra for one- or two-night stays.

Eating in Piran

Pricey tourist bars and restaurants face the sea (figure about €20 per main course), while the laid-back, funky, and colorful local joints seem to seek an escape from both the tourists and the sun in the back lanes. Get off the beaten track to find one of my recommended restaurants, and you'll enjoy a seafood-and-pasta feast for half what you'd pay in Venice (just across the sea).

Restaurant Neptun, with fresh seafood and pastas in a fish-net-strewn dining room, is far classier than the tacky tourist fish joints. The Grilj family and their three cooks work hard to please six tables of diners. Everything's made to order with fish straight out of the Adriatic—nothing's frozen. I can't resist their gnocchi with scampi (€6-10 pastas, €8-18 meat and fish dishes, daily 12:00-16:00 & 18:00-24:00, open all day in summer, Župančičeva 7, tel. 05/673-4111). Don't confuse this with Neptun Café, at the waterfront bus station.

Pri Mari Restaurant is about a 10-minute walk from Tartini Square, near the entrance to town. Gregarious Mara and Tomaž will welcome you into their cheery dining room like an old friend, then treat you to tasty Venetian-style cooking (€7-12 pastas, €8-16 meat and fish dishes, Tue-Sat 12:00-22:00, Sun 12:00-18:00—or until 22:00 in July-Aug, closed Mon, Dantejeva 17, tel. 05/673-4735).

Restaurant Delfin is a crank-'em-out fish restaurant with a good reputation. Run by the Pašalič family, it has a pleasant dining room as well as tables out on the Old Town's May 1 Square (€6-7 pastas, €8-12 meat dishes, €11-18 fish dishes, daily 11:00-24:00, Kosovelova 4, tel. 05/673-2448).

Drinks: **Teater Café** is *the* place for drinks with Adriatic views and a characteristic old interior. Catching the sunset here is a fine way to kick off your Piran evening (open long hours daily, Stjenkova 1).

Piran Connections

The best way to connect Piran with **Ljubljana** is by **bus** (5/day Mon-Fri, 2/day Sat, 4/day Sun, 2.5 hours, €12, toll tel. 1991—about €0.75/minute, www.ap-ljubljana.si). By **train,** the trip takes four hours (bus between Piran and Koper, then train between Koper and Ljubljana).

To Croatia's Istria

By Bus: In summer (June-late Sept), a handy bus goes each afternoon from Piran to Rovinj (also stops in Poreč en route; about 2.5 hours from Piran to Rovinj; may run twice a week off-season). Year-round, there are also buses going from Piran to Poreč and Pula (2/day Mon-Fri, 1/day Sat-Sun); from those towns, you can transfer to reach Rovinj. There are additional bus connections between Piran and Umag (at the northern end of Istria; 3/day Mon-Fri, 2/day Sat-Sun). From Umag, buses run to other destinations in Istria (including Rovinj and Pula). Additional connections into Istria depart from Portorož, the large resort town next to Piran.

By Boat: Trieste Lines runs boats from Trieste (Italy) to Piran, Poreč, and Rovinj—potentially handy for connecting Piran to those Istrian destinations (2/week, €18 one-way between Piran and Rovinj; as schedule is in flux, check details at www.trieste lines.it).

By Boat to Venice

A boat called the *Prince of Venice*—designed for day-trippers, but also convenient for one-way transport—sails from the nearby town of Izola to Venice two or three times each week in peak season (roughly May-Sept, with a few departures in April and Oct, 3-hour trip each way; €50-60 round-trip depending on season, 30 percent less for one-way; departs from Izola at 8:00 and arrives in Venice at 11:00, shuttle bus picks up at Piran's Tartini Square one hour before departure; boat returns from Venice on the same day at 17:00, arriving Izola at 20:00; book through Kompas Travel Agency, www.kompas-online.net, prince@kompas.si).

Commodore Cruises also runs a ship called *Dora* from Piran to Venice, but the schedule is more sporadic (check your latest option at www.commodore-cruises.hr).

Route Tips for Drivers

Piran is a natural stopover between Ljubljana and Croatia's Istria. You can do the Karst sights on the way down (lined up conveniently along the A1 expressway), sleep in Piran, then continue to Istria; or simply make a beeline to Piran and see the town before moving on to sleep in Istria.

From Ljubljana to Piran: Piran is about 1.5 hours from Ljubljana. From Ljubljana, take the A1 expressway south to Koper; once in Koper, follow *Portorož/Portorose* signs, then *Piran/Pirano*. For arrival and parking instructions, see "Arrival in Piran," earlier.

From Piran to Croatia's Istria: Leaving Piran, go through Portorož, then Lucija, then follow signs to *Pula*. Just after you enter Seča, signs on the right point to the salt fields. The border is just a few minutes straight ahead. (If you want to see the salt museum, remember that it's between the Slovenian and Croatian border posts—just after leaving Slovenia, keep an eye on the right for the very easy-to-miss gravel road.) Once in Croatia, follow *Pula* signs to get on the *ipsilon* highway that zips you down through the middle of Istria.

Koper Cruise Port

The big city a half-hour to the north of Piran, Koper, is a gloomy industrial burg (pop. 25,000) that is also emerging as a popular cruise port. In 2011, 120,000 passengers (including some arriving on Norwegian, Royal Caribbean, Princess, Thomson, Seabourn, and Crystal cruises) called here. Ships put in right in front of the Old Town, which is enjoyable to explore briefly—check in at the small TI kiosk, which they set up when ships are in town (TI tel. 05/664-6403, www.koper.si). Koper's adjacent train and bus stations are beyond the far end of the Old Town, about a 20-minute walk from the port—but when cruise ships put in, some buses stop right along the harborfront.

The town of Koper itself isn't worth a day, but there's plenty to see nearby. The easiest option is to ride a bus to **Piran** (1-3/hour, 45 minutes, €3.10 one-way). To reach this bus, exit the ship, turn left toward the port, walk about five minutes, and watch for the bus stop. From the main bus station, you can ride the bus into the nearby Italian port city of **Trieste** (6/day, none on Sun, 45-60 minutes)—the historic port of the Austro-Hungarian Empire, with a fine Old Town and a romantic harbor.

To go farther afield, you can head north to **Ljubljana.** Reaching the capital takes about 2.5 hours by bus or by train, but connections are sparse (about 4/day on either, though the only times convenient for cruisers are the 10:03 train or the 10:50 bus—both Mon-Fri only).

As the drive to Ljubljana takes an hour less (about 1.5 hours each way), Koper is a good place to consider hiring your own **guide/driver** to efficiently link together several worthwhile Slovenian stopovers. A popular round-trip from Koper is to visit both Ljubljana and Lake Bled before returning to your ship; if you skip Bled, you'll have time to tour one of the great caves (Škocjan or Postojna) or other sights (such as the Lipica Stud Farm) between the coast and Ljubljana. Bled-based guides Tina Hiti and Sašo Golub can take you on an all-day excursion to see the best of Slovenia for €230 (for details, see page 571).

UNDERSTANDING YUGOSLAVIA

Americans struggle to understand the complicated breakup of Yugoslavia—especially when visiting countries that have risen from its ashes, such as Croatia, Slovenia, and Bosnia-Herzegovina. Talking to the locals can make it even more confusing: Everyone in the former Yugoslavia seems to have a slightly different version of events. A very wise Bosniak once told me, "Listen to all three sides—Muslim, Serb, and Croat. Then decide for yourself what you think." That's the best advice I can offer. But since you likely won't have time for that on your brief visit, here's an admittedly oversimplified, as-impartial-as-possible history to get you started.

Balkan Peninsula 101

For starters, it helps to have a handle on the different groups who've lived in the Balkans—the southeastern European peninsula between the Adriatic and the Black Sea, stretching from Hungary to Greece. The Balkan Peninsula has always been a crossroads of cultures. The Illyrians, Greeks, and Romans had settlements here before the Slavs moved into the region from the north around the seventh century. During the next millennium and a half, the western part of the peninsula—which would become Yugoslavia—was divided by a series of cultural, ethnic, and religious fault lines.

The most important religious influences were **Western Christianity** (i.e., Roman Catholicism, first brought to the western part of the region by Charlemagne and later reinforced by the Austrian Habsburgs), **Eastern Orthodox Christianity** (brought to the east from the Byzantine Empire), and **Islam** (brought to the south by the Ottomans).

Two major historical factors made the Balkans what they are today: The first was the **split of the Roman Empire** in the fourth century A.D., dividing the Balkans down the middle into Roman

Catholic (west) and Byzantine Orthodox (east)—roughly along today's Bosnian-Serbian border. The second was the **invasion of the Islamic Ottomans** in the 14th century. The Ottoman victory at the Battle of Kosovo Polje (1389) began five centuries of Islamic influence in Bosnia-Herzegovina and Serbia, further dividing the Balkans into Christian (north) and Muslim (south).

Because of these and other events, several distinct ethnic identities emerged. The major ethnicities of Yugoslavia—Croat, Slovene, Serb, and Bosniak—are all considered South Slavs. The huge Slav ethnic and linguistic family—some 400 million strong—is divided into three groups: South (the peoples of Yugoslavia, explained next, plus Bulgarians), West (Poles, Czechs, and Slovaks), and East (Russians, Ukrainians, and Belarusians).

The South Slavs, who are all descended from the same ancestors and speak closely related languages, are distinguished by their religious practices. Roman Catholic **Croats** or **Slovenes** are found mostly west of the Dinaric Mountains (Croats along the Adriatic coast and Slovenes farther north, in the Alps); Orthodox Christian

Who's Who in Yugoslavia

Yugoslavia was made up of six republics, which were inhabited by eight different ethnicities (not counting small minorities such as Jews, Germans, and Roma). This chart shows each ethnicity and the republic(s) in which they were most concentrated. Not coincidentally, the more ethnically diverse a region was, the more conflict it experienced.

	Serbia*	Croatia	Bosnia-Herz.	Slovenia	Montenegro	Macedonia
Serbs (Orthodox)	X	X	X		X	
Croats (Catholic)		X	X			
Bosniaks (Muslims)			X			
Slovenes (Catholic)				X		
Macedonians (like Bulgarians)						X
Montenegrins (like Serbs)					X	
Albanians	X		X			X
Hungarians	X	X		X		

*Within Serbia were two "autonomous provinces," each of which was dominated by a non-Slavic ethnic group: Hungarians in Vojvodina and Albanians in Kosovo.

Serbs live mostly east of the Dinaric range; and Muslim **Bosniaks** (whose ancestors converted to Islam under the Ottomans) live mostly in the Dinaric Mountains. Two other, smaller Orthodox ethnicities have been influenced by other large groups: the **Montenegrins** (shaped by centuries of Croatian and Venetian Catholicism) and the **Macedonians** (with ties to Bulgarians and Greeks). To complicate matters, the region is also home to several non-Slavic minority groups, including **Hungarians** (in the northern province of Vojvodina) and **Albanians,** concentrated in Kosovo (descended from the Illyrians, who lived here long before the Greeks and Romans).

Of course, these geographic divisions are extremely general. The groups overlapped a lot—which is exactly why the breakup of Yugoslavia was so contentious. One of the biggest causes of

YUGOSLAVIA

this ethnic mixing came in the 16th century. The Ottomans were threatening to overrun Europe, and the Austrian Habsburgs wanted a buffer zone—a "human shield." The Habsburgs encouraged Serbs who were fleeing from Ottoman invasions to settle along today's Croatian-Bosnian border (known as *Vojna Krajina*, or "Military Frontier"). The Serbs stayed after the Ottomans left, establishing homes in predominantly Croat communities.

After the Ottoman threat subsided in the late 17th century, some of the Balkan states (basically today's Slovenia and Croatia) became part of the Austrian Habsburg Empire. The Ottomans stayed longer in the south and east (today's Bosnia-Herzegovina and Serbia)—making the cultures in these regions even more different. By the mid-19th century, the Ottoman Empire had become the dysfunctional "Sick Man of Europe," which made it easy for Serbia to gain its independence; meanwhile, Bosnia-Herzegovina was taken into the Habsburg fold. But before long, World War I erupted, after a disgruntled Bosnian Serb nationalist killed the Austrian archduke and heir to the Habsburg throne during a visit to Sarajevo (see page 485).

South Slavs Unite

When the Austro-Hungarian Empire fell at the end of World War I, the map of Europe was redrawn for the 20th century. After centuries of being governed by foreign powers, the South Slavs began to see their shared history as more important than their differences. A tiny country of a few million Croats or Slovenes couldn't have survived on its own. Rather than be absorbed by a non-Slavic power, the South Slavs decided that there was safety in numbers, and banded together as a single state—first called the Kingdom of the Serbs, Croats, and Slovenes (1918), later known as the Kingdom of Yugoslavia (Land of the South Slavs—*yugo* means "south"). "Yugoslav unity" was in the air, but this new union was fragile and ultimately bound to fail (not unlike the partnership between the Czechs and Slovaks, formed at the same time and for similar reasons).

From the very beginning, the various ethnicities struggled for power within the new Yugoslavia. The largest group was the Serbs (about 45 percent), followed by the Croats (about 25 percent). Croats often felt they were treated as lesser partners under the Serbs. For example, many Croats objected to naming the country's official language "Serbo-Croatian"—why not "Croato-Serbian"? Serbia already had a very strong king, Alexander Karađorđević, who immediately attempted to give his nation a leading role in the federation. A nationalistic Croat politician named Stjepan Radić, pushing for a more equitable division of powers, was shot by a Serb during a parliamentary session in 1928. Karađorđević abolished the parliament and became dictator. Six years later, infuriated Croat separatists killed him. By the time World War II came to Yugoslavia, the kingdom was already on the verge of collapse. The conflicts between the various Yugoslav groups set the stage for a particularly complex and gruesome wartime experience.

World War II

Observers struggle to comprehend how it was possible for inter-ethnic conflict to escalate so quickly here in the early 1990s. Most of the answers can be found in the war that shook Europe 50 years earlier. In the minds of the participants, the wars of the 1990s were a continuation of unresolved conflicts from World War II.

The Nazis invaded Yugoslavia in April 1941; within 11 days, the country had surrendered. The core of the nation (much of today's Croatia and Bosnia-Herzegovina) became the misnamed Independent State of Croatia, which was actually run by a Nazi puppet government called the Ustaše. (Meanwhile, much of today's Serbia was occupied by Nazi Germany, and Montenegro by Mussolini's Italy.) Many Croat nationalists supported the Ustaše in the hopes that it would be their ticket to long-term indepen-dence from Serbia.

Emboldened by their genocide-minded Nazi overlords, Ustaše leaders used death camps to exterminate their enemies—specifi-cally, the Serbs who, they felt, had wronged them in the days of the Kingdom of Yugoslavia. Not only were Jews, Roma, and other Nazi-decreed "undesirables" murdered in Ustaše concentration camps, but also hundreds of thousands of Serbs living in Croatia and Bosnia. Other Serbs were forced to flee the country or convert to Catholicism. Most historians consider the Ustaše camps to be the first instance of ethnic cleansing in the Balkans. (Half a cen-tury later, the Serbs justified their ruthless treatment of Croats and Bosniaks as retribution for these WWII atrocities.)

Meanwhile, in the eastern mountains of Yugoslavia rose the Četniks—a fearsome paramilitary band of mostly Serbian men fighting to re-establish a Serb-dominated monarchy. Wearing long beards and traditional mountain garb, and embracing a skull-and-crossbones logo adorned with the motto "Freedom or Death" in Cyrillic, the Četniks were every bit as brutal as their Ustaše enemies. In pursuit of their goal to create a purely Serb state, the Četniks expelled or massacred Croats and Muslims living in the territory they held. (To this day, if a Croat wants to really insult a Serb, he'll call him a "Četnik," and a Serb might use "Ustaše" to really hit a Croat where it hurts.)

Fighting against both the Četniks and the Ustaše was the ragtag Partisan Army, led by Josip Broz—better known by his code name, Tito. The clever and determined Partisans had dual aims: to liberate Yugoslavia as a free nation on its own terms, and to make that new state a communist one. Even while the war was still underway, the Partisan leadership laid the foundations for what would become a postwar, communist Yugoslavia.

After years of largely guerrilla fighting among these three groups, the Partisans emerged victorious. And so, as the rest of Eastern Europe was being "liberated" by the Soviets, the Yugoslavs regained their independence on their own. After the short but rocky Yugoslav union between the World Wars, it seemed that no one could hold the southern Slavs together in a single nation. But one man could, and did: Tito.

Tito's Yugoslavia

Communist Party president and war hero Tito emerged as a political leader after World War II. With a Slovene for a mother, a Croat for a father, a Serb for a wife, and a home in Belgrade, Tito was a true Yugoslav. Tito had a compelling vision that this fractured union of the South Slavs could function.

Tito's new incarnation of Yugoslavia aimed for a more equitable division of powers. It was made up of six republics, each with its own parliament and president: **Croatia** (mostly Catholic), **Slovenia** (mostly Catholic), **Serbia** (mostly Orthodox), **Bosnia-Herzegovina** (the most diverse—mostly Muslim Bosniaks, but with very large Croat and Serb populations), **Montenegro** (mostly Orthodox—sort of a Serb/Croat hybrid), and **Macedonia** (with about 25 percent Muslim Albanians and 75 percent Orthodox Macedonians). Within Serbia, Tito set up two autonomous provinces, each dominated by an ethnicity that was a minority in greater Yugoslavia: Albanians in **Kosovo** (to the south) and Hungarians in **Vojvodina** (to the north). By allowing these two provinces some degree of independence—including voting rights—Tito hoped they would balance the political clout of Serbia, preventing a single republic from dominating the union.

Each republic managed its own affairs, but always under the watchful eye of president-for-life Tito, who said that the borders between the republics should be "like white lines in a marble column." Nationalism was strongly discouraged, and Tito's tight—often oppressive—control kept the country from unraveling. For more on Tito, see the sidebar on page 680.

Tito's Yugoslavia was communist, but it wasn't Soviet communism; you'll find no statues of Lenin or Stalin here. Despite strong pressure from Moscow, Tito refused to ally himself with the Soviets—and therefore received good will (and $2 billion) from the United States. He ingeniously played the East and the West against each other. He'd say to both Washington and Moscow, "If you don't pay me off, I'll let the other guy build a base here."

Everyone paid up.

Economically, Tito's vision was for a "third way," in which Yugoslavia could work with both East and West without being dominated by either. Yugoslavia was the most free of the communist states. While large industry was nationalized, Tito's system allowed for small businesses. This experience with a market economy benefited Yugoslavs when Eastern Europe's communist regimes eventually fell. And even during the communist era, Yugoslavia remained a popular tourist destination for visitors from both East and West, keeping its standards more in line with Western Europe than the Soviet states. Meanwhile, Yugoslavs, uniquely among communist citizens, were allowed to travel to the West. In fact, because Yugoslavs could travel relatively hassle-free in both East and West, their "red passports" were worth even more on the black market than American ones.

Things Fall Apart

With Tito's death in 1980, Yugoslavia's six constituent republics gained more autonomy, with a rotating presidency. But before long, the fragile union Tito had held together started to unravel.

The breakup began in the late 1980s, with squabbles in the autonomous province of Kosovo between the Serb minority and the ethnic-Albanian majority. But, even though 9 of every 10 Kosovans were Albanian, the region remained important to the Serbs, who consider Kosovo the cradle of their civilization—the medieval homeland of their most important monasteries and historic sites. Most significantly, it was the location of the Battle of Kosovo Polje ("Field of Blackbirds"), an epic 14th-century battle that formed the foundation of Serbian cultural identity...even though the Serbs lost to the Ottoman invaders (sort of the Serbian Alamo). One Serb told me, "Kosovo is the Mecca and Medina of the Serb people."

Serbian politician Slobodan Milošević saw how the conflict could be used to Serbia's (and his own) advantage. In April of 1987, Milošević delivered a rabble-rousing speech in Kosovo, pledging that Serbia would come to the aid of its Kosovar-Serb brothers (famously asserting, "No one has the right to beat you"). He returned two years later for the 600th anniversary of the Battle of Kosovo Polje and delivered another inflammatory speech ("Six centuries later, now, we are being again engaged in battles....They are not armed battles, although such things cannot be excluded yet"). With these visits, Milošević upset the delicate balance that Tito had so carefully sought, while setting the stage for his own rise to the Serbian presidency.

When Milošević-led Serbia annexed Kosovo soon after, other republics (especially Slovenia and Croatia) feared that he would

YUGOSLAVIA

Tito
(1892-1980)

The Republic of Yugoslavia was the vision of a single man, who made it reality. Josip Broz—better known as Marshal Tito—presided over the most peaceful and prosperous era in this region's long and troubled history. Three decades after his death, Tito is beloved by many of his former subjects...and yet, he was a communist dictator known for torturing and executing his political enemies. This love-him-and-hate-him autocrat is one of the most complex figures in the history of this very complicated land.

Josip Broz was born in 1892 to a Slovenian mother and a Croatian father in the northern part of today's Croatia, which then belonged to the Austro-Hungarian Empire. After growing up in the rural countryside, he was trained as a metalworker. He was drafted into the Austro-Hungarian army, went to fight on the Eastern Front during World War I, and was captured and sent to Russia as a prisoner of war. Freed by Bolsheviks, Broz fell in with the Communist Revolution...and never looked back.

At war's end, Broz returned home to the newly independent Yugoslavia, where he worked alongside the Soviets to build a national Communist Party. As a clandestine communist operative, he adopted the code name he kept for the rest of his life: Tito. (Some people half-joke that the name came from Tito's authoritarian style: *"Ti, to!"* means "You, do this!")

When the Nazis occupied Yugoslavia, Tito raised and commanded a homegrown, communist Partisan Army. Through guerilla tactics, Tito's clever maneuvering, and sheer determination, the Partisans liberated their country. And because they did so mostly without support from the USSR, Yugoslavia was able to set its own postwar course.

The war hero Tito quickly became the "president for life" of postwar Yugoslavia. But even as he introduced communism to his country, he retained some elements of a free-market economy—firmly declining to become a satellite of Moscow. He also led the creation of the worldwide Non-Aligned Movement, joining with nations in Africa, the Middle East, Asia, and Latin America in refusing to ally with the US or USSR (see page 144). Stubborn but suitably cautious, Tito expertly walked a tightrope between East and West.

There was a dark side to Tito. In the early years of his regime, Tito resorted to brutal, Stalin-esque tactics to assert his control. Immediately following World War II, the Partisan Army massacred tens of thousands of soldiers who had supported the Nazis. Then Tito systematically routed out other Nazi supporters, arresting, trying, torturing, or executing those who did not accept his new regime (including the Croatian archbishop Alojzije Stepinac, whom Tito imprisoned for five years—see page 46). Those whose lives were ruined during this reign of terror will never forgive Tito for what he did.

But once he gained full control, Tito moved away from strong-arm tactics and into a warm-and-fuzzy era of Yugoslav brotherhood. Tito believed that the disparate peoples of Yugoslavia could live in harmony. For example, every Yugoslav male had to serve in the People's Army, and Tito made sure that each unit was a microcosm of the complete Yugoslavia—with equal representation from each ethnic group. This meant that Yugoslavs from diverse backgrounds were forced to work together and socialize, and as a result, they became friends.

Tito's reign is a case study in the power of the cult of personality. Rocks on hillsides throughout Yugoslavia were rearranged to spell "TITO," and his portrait hung over every family's dinner table. Each of the six republics renamed one of its cities for their dictator. The main street and square in virtually every town were renamed for Tito (many have kept the name). Tito also had vacation villas in all of Yugoslavia's most beautiful areas, including Lake Bled, the Brijuni Islands, and the Montenegrin coast. People sang patriotic anthems to their Druža (Comrade) Tito: "Comrade Tito, we bow to you."

Tito died in 1980 in a Slovenian hospital. His body was loaded onto his Blue Train and went on a grand tour of the Yugoslav capitals: Ljubljana, Zagreb, Sarajevo, and Belgrade, where he was buried before hundreds of thousands of mourners, including more heads of state than at any other funeral in history.

The genuine outpouring of support at Tito's death might seem unusual for a man who was, on paper, an authoritarian communist dictator. But even today, many former Yugoslavs—especially Slovenes and Bosniaks—believe that his iron-fisted government was a necessary evil that kept the country strong and united. The eventual balance Tito struck between communism and capitalism, and between the competing interests of his ethnically diverse nation, led to this region's most stable and prosperous era. Pictures of Tito still hang in many Croatians' homes. In a recent poll in Slovenia, Tito had a higher approval rating than any present-day politician, and 80 percent of Slovenes said they had a positive impression of him.

And yet, the Yugoslavs' respect for their former leader was not enough to keep them together. Tito's death began a long, slow chain reaction that led to the end of Yugoslavia. As the decades pass, the old joke seems more and more appropriate: Yugoslavia had eight distinct peoples in six republics, with five languages, three religions (Orthodox Christian, Catholic, and Muslim), and two alphabets (Roman and Cyrillic), but only one Yugoslav—Tito.

gut their nation to create a "Greater Serbia," thereby destabilizing the friendly coalition of diverse Yugoslav republics. Some of the leaders—most notably Milan Kučan of Slovenia—tried to avoid warfare by suggesting a plan for a loosely united Yugoslavia, based on the Swiss model of independent yet confederated cantons. But other parties, who wanted complete autonomy, refused. Over the next decade, Yugoslavia broke apart, with much bloodshed.

The Slovene Secession

Slovenia was the first Yugoslav republic to hold free elections, in the spring of 1990. Voters wanted the communists out, and they wanted their own independent nation. The most ethnically homogeneous of the Yugoslav nations, Slovenia was also the most Western-oriented, prosperous, and geographically isolated—so secession just made sense. But that didn't mean it would be achieved without violence.

After months of stockpiling weapons, Slovenia closed its borders and declared independence from Yugoslavia on June 25, 1991. Belgrade sent in the Yugoslav People's Army to take control of Slovenia's borders with Italy and Austria, figuring that whoever controlled the borders had a legitimate claim on sovereignty. Fighting broke out around these borders. Because the Yugoslav People's Army was made up of soldiers from all republics, many Slovenian troops found themselves fighting their own countrymen. (The army had cut off communication between these conscripts and the home front, so they didn't know what was going on—and often didn't realize they were fighting their friends and neighbors until they were close enough to see them.)

Slovenian civilians bravely entered the fray, blockading the Yugoslav barracks with their own cars and trucks. Most of the Yugoslav soldiers—now trapped—were young and inexperienced, and were terrified of the improvised (but relentless) Slovenian militia, even though their own resources were far superior.

After 10 days of fighting and fewer than a hundred deaths, Belgrade relented. The Slovenes stepped aside and allowed the Yugoslav People's Army to leave with their weapons and to destroy all remaining military installations as they went. When the Yugoslav People's Army cleared out, they left the Slovenes with their freedom.

The Croatian Conflict

In April of 1990, a retired general and historian named Franjo Tuđman—and his highly nationalistic, right-wing party, the HDZ (Croatian Democratic Union)—won Croatia's first free elections (for more on Tuđman, see page 48). Like the Slovenian reformers, Tuđman and the HDZ wanted more autonomy from Yugoslavia.

But Tuđman's methods were more extreme than those of the gently progressive Slovenes. Tuđman invoked the spirit of the Ustaše, who had ruthlessly run Croatia's puppet government under the Nazis. He reintroduced symbols that had been embraced by the Ustaše, including the red-and-white checkerboard flag and the kuna currency. (While many of these symbols predated the Ustaše by centuries, they had become irrevocably tainted by their association with the Ustaše.) The 600,000 Serbs living in Croatia, mindful that their grandparents had been massacred by the Ustaše, saw the writing on the wall and began to rise up.

The first conflicts were in the Serb-dominated Croatian city of Knin. Tuđman had decreed that Croatia's policemen must wear a new uniform, which was strikingly similar to Nazi-era Ustaše garb. Infuriated by this slap in the face, and prodded by Slobodan Milošević's rhetoric, Serb police officers in Knin refused. Over the next few months, tense negotiations ensued. Serbs from Knin and elsewhere began the so-called "tree trunk revolution"—blocking important Croatian tourist roads to the coast with logs and other barriers. Meanwhile, the Croatian government—after being denied support from the United States—illegally purchased truckloads of guns from Hungary. (A UN weapons embargo, which was designed to prevent the outbreak of violence, had little effect on the Serb-dominated Yugoslav People's Army, which already had its own arsenal. But it was devastating to separatist Croatian and—later—Bosnian forces, which were just beginning to build their armies.) Croatian policemen and Serb irregulars from Knin fired the first shots of the conflict on Easter Sunday 1991 at Plitvice Lakes National Park.

By the time Croatia declared its independence (on June 25, 1991—the same day as Slovenia), it was already embroiled in the beginnings of a bloody war. Croatia's more than half-million Serb residents immediately declared their own independence from Croatia. The Serb-dominated Yugoslav People's Army swept in, supposedly to keep the peace between Serbs and Croats—but it soon became obvious that they were there to support the Serbs. The ill-prepared Croatian resistance, made up mostly of policemen and a few soldiers who defected from the People's Army, were quickly overwhelmed. The Serbs gained control over the parts of inland Croatia where they were in the majority: a large swath around the Bosnian border (including Plitvice) and part of Croatia's inland panhandle (the region of Slavonia). They called this territory—about a quarter of Croatia—the **Republic of Serbian Krajina** (*krajina* means "border"). This new "country" (hardly recognized by any other nations) minted its own money and raised its own army, much to the consternation of Croatia—which was now worried about the safety of Croats living in Krajina.

As the Serbs advanced, hundreds of thousands of Croats fled to the coast and lived as refugees in resort hotels. The Serbs began a campaign of ethnic cleansing, systematically removing Croats from contested territory—often by murdering them. The bloodiest siege was at the town of **Vukovar,** which the Yugoslav People's Army surrounded and shelled relentlessly for three months. By the end of the siege, thousands of Croat soldiers and civilians had disappeared. Many were later discovered in mass graves; hundreds remain missing, and bodies are still being found. In a surprise move, Yugoslav forces also attacked the tourist resort of **Dubrovnik**—which resisted and eventually repelled the invaders (see page 302). By early 1992, both Croatia and the Republic of Serbian Krajina had established their borders, and a tense ceasefire fell over the region.

The standoff lasted until 1995, when the now well-equipped Croatian army retook the Serb-occupied areas in a series of two offensives—**"Lightning"** *(Blijesak),* in the northern part of the country, and **"Storm"** *(Oluja),* farther south. Some Croats retaliated for earlier ethnic cleansing by doing much of the same to Serbs—torturing and murdering them, and dynamiting their homes. Croatia quickly established the borders that exist today, and the Erdut Agreement brought peace to the region. But most of the 600,000 Serbs who had once lived in Croatia/Krajina were forced into Serbia or were killed. While Serbs have long since been legally invited back to their ancestral Croatian homes, relatively few have returned—afraid of the "welcome" they might receive from the Croat neighbors who killed their relatives or blew up their houses just two decades ago.

The War in Bosnia-Herzegovina

As violence erupted in Croatia and Slovenia, Bosnia-Herzegovina was suspiciously quiet. Even optimists knew it couldn't last. At the crossroads of Balkan culture, Bosnia-Herzegovina was even more diverse than Croatia; it was populated predominantly by Muslim Bosniaks (43 percent of the population), but also by large numbers of Serbs (31 percent) and Croats (17 percent). Bosniaks tended to live in the cities, while Serbs and Croats were more often farmers.

In the fall of 1991, Bosnia-Herzegovina's president, Alija Izetbegović, began to pursue independence. While most Bosnian Croats and virtually all Bosniaks supported this move, Bosnia's substantial Serb minority resisted it. Bosnian Serbs preferred to remain part of an increasingly dominant ethnic group in a big country (Yugoslavia) rather than become second fiddle in a new, small country (Bosnia-Herzegovina). And so the Serbs within Bosnia-Herzegovina created their own "state," called the Republic of the Serb People of Bosnia-Herzegovina. Its president, Radovan Karadžić, enjoyed the semisecret military support of Slobodan Milošević and the Yugoslav People's Army. The stage was set for a bloody secession.

In the spring of 1992, as a referendum on Bosnian independence loomed, the Serbs made their move. To legitimize their claim to "their" land, the Serbs began a campaign of ethnic cleansing against Bosniaks and Croats residing in Bosnia. Initially Karadžić's forces moved to take control of a strip of Muslim-majority towns (including Foča, Srebrenica, Goražde, Višegrad, and Zvornik) along the Drina River, between Serbia proper and Serb-controlled areas closer to Sarajevo. They reasoned that their claim on this territory was legitimate, because the Ustaše had decimated the Serb population there during World War II. The well-orchestrated Karadžić forces secretly notified Serb residents to evacuate before they invaded each mixed-ethnicity town, then encircled the remaining Bosniaks and Croats with heavy artillery and sniper fire in an almost medieval-style siege. Many people were executed on the spot, while others were arrested and taken to concentration camps. Survivors were forced to leave the towns their families had lived in for centuries.

It was during this initial wave of Bosnian Serb ethnic cleansing—orchestrated by Radovan Karadžić and his generals—that the world began to hear tales as horrifying as anything you can imagine. Militia units would enter a town and indiscriminately kill anyone they saw—civilian men, women, and children. Pregnant women mortally wounded by gunfire were left to die in the street. Fleeing residents crawled on their stomachs for hours to reach cover, even as their family and friends were shot and blown up right next to them. Soldiers rounded up families, then forced parents to watch as they slit the throats of their children—and then the parents were killed, too. Dozens of people would be lined up along a bridge to have their throats slit, one at a time, so that their lifeless bodies would plunge into the river below. (Villagers downstream would see corpses float past, and know their time was coming soon.) While in past conflicts houses of worship had been considered off-limits, now Serbs actively targeted mosques and Catholic churches. Perhaps most despicable was the establishment of so-called "rape camps"—concentration camps where mostly Bosniak women were imprisoned and systematically raped by Serb soldiers. Many were intentionally impregnated and held captive until they had come to term (too late for an abortion), when they were released to bear and raise a child forced upon them by their hated enemy. These are the stories that turned "Balkans" into a dirty word.

The Bosnian Serb aggressors were intentionally gruesome and violent. Leaders roused their foot soldiers with hate-filled propaganda (claiming, for example, that the Bosniaks were intent on creating a fundamentalist Islamic state that would do even worse to its Serb residents), then instructed them to carry out unthinkable atrocities. For the people who carried out these attacks, the war represented a cathartic opportunity to exact vengeance for decades-old perceived injustices. But their superiors had even more dastardly motives. They sought not only to remove people from "their" land, but to ensure that the various groups could never again tolerate living together.

Bosnia-Herzegovina was torn apart. Even the many mixed families were forced to choose sides. If you had a Serb mother and a Croat father, you were expected to pick one ethnicity or the other—and your brother might choose the opposite. The majority of people, who did not want this war and couldn't comprehend why it was happening, now faced the excruciating realization that their neighbors and friends were responsible for looting and burning their houses, and shooting at their loved ones. As families and former neighbors trained their guns on each other, proud and beautiful cities such as Mostar were turned to rubble, and people throughout Bosnia-Herzegovina lived in a state of constant terror.

Even as the Serbs and Croats fought brutally in the streets, their leaders—Slobodan Milošević and Franjo Tuđman, respectively—were secretly meeting to carve up Bosnia into Serb and Croat sectors, at the Bosniaks' expense (the so-called Karađorđevo Agreement). Bosniak President Alija Izetbegović was completely left out of the discussion. For his part, Izetbegović desperately pleaded with the international community to support the peaceful secession of a free Bosnian state. Motivated more by fear than by nationalism, Izetbegović insisted that the creation of an independent Bosnia-Herzegovina was the only way to protect the lives of the Bosniak people. He said, "I would sacrifice peace for a sovereign Bosnia-Herzegovina, but for that peace in Bosnia-Herzegovina I would not sacrifice sovereignty."

At first, the Bosniaks and Croats teamed up to fend off the Serbs. But even before the first wave of fighting had subsided, Croats and Bosniaks turned their guns on each other. The Croats split off their own mini-state, the Croatian Republic of Herzeg-Bosnia. A bloody war raged for years among the three groups: the Serbs (with support from Serbia proper), the Croats (with support from Croatia proper), and—squeezed between them—the internationally recognized Bosniak government, with little support from anybody.

The United Nations Protection Force (UNPROFOR)—dubbed "Smurfs" both for their light-blue helmets and for their ineffectiveness—exercised their very limited authority to provide humanitarian aid. Their charge allowed them only to feed civilians caught in the crossfire—an absurd notion in places like Sarajevo, where civilians were forced to live like soldiers. (A political cartoon from the time shows a Bosnian Serb preparing to murder a Bosniak with a knife. A UN solider appears and says, "Not so fast!" He proceeds to feed the Bosniak...then walks away, mission accomplished, while the Serb murders his victim.) Later, the UN tried to designate "safe areas" where civilians were protected, but because the UNPROFOR troops were not allowed to use force, even in self-defense, they became impotent witnesses to atrocities. This ugly situation was brilliantly parodied in the film *No Man's Land* (which won the Oscar for Best Foreign Film in 2002), a very dark comedy about the absurdity of the Bosnian war.

For three and a half years, the capital of Sarajevo—still inhabited by a united community of Sarajevans (who largely eschewed their individual ethnicities as Bosniaks, Croats, and Serbs)—was surrounded by Karadžić's Bosnian Serb army (for more on the Siege of Sarajevo, see page 476). Other Bosniak cities were also besieged, most notoriously Srebrenica in July 1995. After surviving as a UN-designated safe area, this mid-sized, predominantly Bosniak town near the Serbian border was left unprotected early that summer when UNPROFOR troops vacated. Bosnian Serb forces, led by General Ratko Mladić, swept in and rounded up all the men and boys in Srebrenica—about 8,000 civilians—and took them into the woods under cover of darkness. They were never again seen alive, and mass graves are still being found in the Srebrenica woods. Additionally, 35,000 to 40,000 Bosniak women and children were forcibly removed from the city; many of them (including babies) died en route.

After four long years, the mounting mass of atrocities—including the siege of Srebrenica and the bombing of innocent civilians at a market in Sarajevo—finally persuaded the international community to act. In the late summer of 1995, NATO began bombing Bosnian Serb positions, forcing them to relax their siege and come to the negotiating table. The Dayton Peace Accords—brokered by US diplomats at Wright-Patterson Air Force Base near Dayton, Ohio—finally brought an end to the wars of Yugoslav succession.

The Dayton Peace Accords carefully divided Bosnia-Herzegovina into three different units: the Federation of Bosnia and Herzegovina (Bosniaks and Croats), the Serb-dominated Republika Srpska, and the mixed-ethnicity Brčko District. While this compromise helped bring the war to an end, it also created a nation with four independent and redundant governments—further crippling this war-torn and impoverished region.

The Fall of Milošević

After years of bloody conflicts, public opinion among Serbians had decisively swung against their president. The transition began gradually in early 2000, spearheaded by Otpor, a nonviolent, grassroots, student-based opposition movement, and aided by similar groups. Using clever PR strategies, these organizations convinced Serbians that real change was possible. As anti-Milošević sentiments gained momentum, opposing political parties banded together behind one candidate, Vojislav Koštunica. Public support for Koštunica mounted, and when the arrogant Milošević called an early election in September 2000, he was soundly defeated. Though Milošević tried to claim that the election results were invalid, determined Serbs streamed into their capital, marched on their parliament, and—like the Czechs and Slovaks a decade before—peacefully took back their nation.

In 2001, Milošević was arrested and sent to The Hague, in the Netherlands, to stand trial before the International Criminal Tribunal for the Former Yugoslavia (ICTY). Milošević served as his own attorney as his trial wore on for five years, frequently delayed due to his health problems. Then, on March 11, 2006—as his trial was coming to a close—Milošević was found dead in his cell. Ruled a heart attack, Milošević's death, like his life, was controversial. His supporters alleged that Milošević had been denied suitable medical care, some speculated that he'd been poisoned, and others suspected that he'd intentionally worsened his heart condition to avoid the completion of his trial. Whatever the cause, in the end Milošević escaped justice—he was never found guilty of a single war crime.

More War Leaders on Trial

On July 18, 2008, Serbian police announced that they had captured Radovan Karadžić, the former leader of the Bosnian Serb state who is considered one of the worst culprits in the brutal ethnic cleansing during the war.

Karadžić, who went into hiding shortly after the war (in 1996), had been living for part of that time in a residential neighborhood of Belgrade, posing as an alternative-medicine healer named Dr. Dragan David Dabić. (Karadžić had previously received training as a psychiatrist.) This expert on what he called "Human Quantum Energy" had his own website and even presented at conferences.

How did one of the world's most wanted men effectively disappear in plain sight for 12 years? He had grown a very full beard

and wore thick glasses as a disguise, and frequented a neighborhood bar where a photo of him, in his earlier life, hung proudly on
the wall...and yet, he was undetected even by those who saw him
every day. It's alleged that at least some Serb authorities knew of
his whereabouts, but, considering him a hero, refused to identify
or arrest him.

After his arrest, Karadžić was indicted at The Hague for war
crimes, including genocide. In May of 2011, the last "most wanted"
criminal of the conflict—Karadžić's military leader, General Ratko
Mladić—was found and arrested. As of this writing, Karadžić and
Mladić are each standing trial in The Hague.

Montenegro and Kosovo: Europe's Newest Nations

After the departures of Croatia, Slovenia, Bosnia-Herzegovina,
and Macedonia (which peacefully seceded in 1991), by the late
1990s only two of the original six republics of Yugoslavia remained
united: Serbia (which still included the provinces of Kosovo and
Vojvodina) and Montenegro. But in 2003, Montenegro began a
gradual secession process that ended when it peacefully tiptoed its
way to independence in 2006. (For all the details, see "Montenegro:
Birth of a Nation" on page 384.)

The Yugoslav crisis concluded in the place where it began: the
Serbian province of Kosovo. Kosovo's majority Albanians rebelled
against Serbian rule in 1998, only to become victims of Milošević's
ethnic cleansing (until US General Wesley Clark's NATO warplanes forced the Serbian army out). For nearly a decade, Kosovo
remained a UN protectorate within Serbia—still nominally part of
Serbia, but for all practical purposes separate and self-governing
(under the watchful eye of the UN).

But on Sunday, February 17, 2008, Kosovo's provisional government unilaterally declared its independence as the "Republic
of Kosovo." The US, UK, France, Germany, and several other
countries quickly recognized the new republic, but the UN didn't
officially endorse it. Serbia opposed the move, and was backed
by several countries involved in their own internal disputes with
would-be breakaway regions: Russia (areas of Georgia), China
(Taiwan), and Spain (Catalunya, the Basque Country, and others).

The new Kosovo government carefully stated that it would
protect the rights of its minorities, including Serbs. But the Serbs
deeply believed that losing Kosovo would also mean losing their
grip on their own history and culture. They also feared for the
safety of the Serb minority there (and potential retribution from
Albanians who had for so long been oppressed themselves). For
a few tense months, international observers watched nervously,
worrying that war might erupt in the region once more. There
have been a few scuffles, especially in some of the larger Serb

settlements. But as of this writing, Kosovo's independence appears to be holding—representing, perhaps, the final chapter of a long and ugly Yugoslav succession. Kosovo is the seventh country to emerge from the breakup of Yugoslavia.

Finding Their Way: The Former Yugoslav Republics

Today, Slovenia and Croatia are as stable as Western Europe, Bosnia-Herzegovina has made great strides in putting itself back together, Macedonia feels closer to Bulgaria than to Belgrade, and the sixth and seventh countries to emerge from "Yugoslavia"—Montenegro and Kosovo—are fledgling democracies.

And yet, nagging questions remain. Making the wars even more difficult to grasp is the uncomfortable reality that there were no clear-cut "good guys" and "bad guys"—just a lot of ugliness on all sides. When considering specifically the war between the Croats and the Serbs, it's tempting for Americans to take Croatia's "side" because we saw them in the role of victims first; because they're Catholic, so they seem more "like us" than the Orthodox Serbs; and because we admire their striving for independence. But in the streets and the trenches, it was never that straightforward. The Serbs believe that *they* were the victims first—back in World War II, when their grandparents were executed in Croat-run Ustaše concentration camps. And when Croats retook the Serb-occupied areas in 1995, they were every bit as brutal as the Serbs had been a few years before. Both sides resorted to genocide, both sides had victims, and both sides had victimizers.

Even so, many can't help but look for victims and villains. During the conflict in Bosnia-Herzegovina, several prominent and respected reporters began to show things from one "side" more than the others—specifically, depicting the Bosniaks (Muslims) as victims. This reawakened an old debate in the journalism community: Should reporters above all remain impartial, even if "showing all sides" might make them feel complicit in ongoing atrocities?

As for villains, it's easy to point a finger at Slobodan Milošević, Radovan Karadžić, Ratko Mladić, and other military leaders who have been arrested and tried at The Hague. Others condemn the late Croatian President Franjo Tuđman, who, it's now known, secretly conspired with Milošević to redraw the maps of their respective territories. And of course, the foot soldiers of those monstrous men—who followed their immoral orders—cannot be excused.

And yet, you can't paint an entire group with one brush. While some Bosnian Serbs did horrifying things, only a small fraction of all Bosnian Serbs participated in the atrocities. Travelers to this region quickly realize that the vast majority of people they meet here never wanted these wars. And so finally comes the inevitable question: Why did any of it happen in the first place?

Explanations tend to gravitate to two extremes. Some observers consider this part of the world to be inherently warlike—a place where deep-seated hatreds and age-old ethnic passions unavoidably flare up. This point of view sees an air of inevitability about the recent wars and the potential for future conflict. And it's hard to deny that the residents of the region tend to obsess about exacting vengeance for wrongdoings (real or imagined) that happened many decades or even centuries in the past.

For others, however, this theory is an insulting oversimplification. Sure, animosity has long simmered in the Balkans, but for centuries before World War II, the various groups had lived more or less in harmony. The critical component of these wars—what made them escalate so quickly and so appallingly—was the single-minded, self-serving actions of a few selfish leaders who exploited existing resentments to advance their own interests. It wasn't until Milošević, Karadžić, Tuđman, and others expertly manipulated the people's grudges that the region fell into war. By vigorously fanning the embers of ethnic discord, polluting the airwaves with hate-filled propaganda, and carefully controlling media coverage of the escalating violence, these leaders turned what could have been a healthy political debate into a holocaust.

Tension still exists throughout the former Yugoslavia—especially in the areas that were most war-torn. Croatians and Slovenes continue to split hairs over silly border disputes, Bosnia-Herzegovina groans under the crippling inefficiency of four autonomous governments, and Serbs ominously warn that they'll take up arms to reclaim Kosovo. Observers can't escape the painful truth that, just as grudges held over from World War II were quickly ignited in the 1990s, holdover tensions from the recent wars could someday ignite a new wave of conflict. When the people of this region encounter other Yugoslavs in their travels, they instantly evaluate each other's accent to determine: Are they one of us, or one of them?

For the visitor, it's tricky to get an impartial take on the current situation, or even on historical "facts." People you meet will tell you their stories, and sometimes it's just as important to listen to the tone and subtext of their tale as it is to try to judge its veracity. Are they preaching a message of reconciliation or one of provocation?

With time, hard feelings are fading. The appealing prospect of European Union membership is a powerful motivator for groups to set aside their differences and cooperate. The younger generations don't look back—teenaged Slovenes no longer learn Serbo-Croatian, have only known life in an independent little country, and get bored (and a little irritated) when their old-fashioned parents wax nostalgic about the days of a united Yugoslavia. A middle-aged Slovene friend of mine thinks fondly of his months of compulsory service in the Yugoslav People's Army, when his unit was made up of Slovenes, Croats, Serbs, Bosniaks, Albanians, Macedonians, and Montenegrins—all of them countrymen, and all good friends. To the young Yugoslavs, ethnic differences didn't matter. My friend still often visits with an army buddy from Dubrovnik—600 miles away, not long ago part of the same nation—and wishes there had been a way to keep the country all together. But he says, optimistically, "I look forward to the day when the other former Yugoslav republics also join the European Union. Then, in a way, we will all be united once again."

APPENDIX

Contents

Tourist Information

Before Your Trip

National tourist offices are a wealth of information. Before your trip, get the free general information packet and request any specifics you may want (such as regional and city maps and festival schedules).

Croatian Tourist Office: Ask for their free brochures and maps. In the US, call 212-279-8672 or visit http://us.croatia.hr (cntony@earthlink.net).

Slovenian Tourist Office: They have a *Slovenia Invigorates* brochure, map, and information on various regions, with details on hiking, biking, winter travel, and tourist farms. From the US, call Slovenian tel. 01/306-4575 or visit www.slovenia.info (info @slovenia.info).

Bosnia-Herzegovina Tourist Office: From the US, call Bosnian tel. 33/233-886 or visit www.bhtourism.ba (tourinfo@bih .net.ba).

In Croatia, Slovenia, and Bosnia-Herzegovina

Your best first stop in every town is generally the tourist information office—abbreviated **TI** in this book (though locally, you may see them marked *TZ*, for *turistička zajednica*). Throughout Croatia and Slovenia, you'll find TIs are usually well-organized and always have an English-speaking staff; Bosnian TIs can be more hit-or-miss.

TIs are good places to get a city map and information on public transit (including bus and train schedules), walking tours, special events, and nightlife. Many TIs have information on the entire country or at least the region, so try to pick up maps for destinations you'll be visiting later in your trip. If you're arriving in town after the TI closes, call ahead or pick up a map in a neighboring town.

The TIs in these countries are run by the government, which means their information isn't colored by a drive for profit. I find TIs in Croatia and Slovenia to be better informed and more helpful than in most other parts of Europe. Local TIs are not allowed to make money by running a room-booking service—though they can almost always give you a list of local hotels and private rooms. If they're not too busy, they can call around for you to check on availability. While every major town has at least one travel agency with a room-booking service, even if there's no "fee," you'll save yourself and your host money by going direct with the listings in this book.

Communicating

Hurdling the Language Barrier

The language barrier in Croatia and Slovenia is actually smaller than in France, Italy, or Spain. You'll find that most people in the tourist industry—and virtually all young people—speak excellent English. Bosnia and Montenegro also have many English-speakers.

Of course, not *everyone* speaks English. Be reasonable in your expectations, especially when trying to communicate with clerks or service workers. It always helps to know a few words of the local language. Croatian and Slovene are closely related, but not identical. Still, they're similar enough that the same basic words work in both. For example, "hello" is *dobar dan* in Croatian, but *dober dan* in Slovene. I've listed the essential phrases near the end of this book (beginning on page 729).

Europe's Best Linguists

Why do Croatians and Slovenes speak English so well?

Residents of big, powerful Western European countries, such as Germany or Italy, might think that foreigners should learn *their* language. But Croatians and Slovenes are as practical as Germans and Italians are stubborn. They realize that it's unreasonable to expect an American to learn Croatian (5 million speakers worldwide) or Slovene (2 million). When only a few million people on the planet speak your language, it's essential to find a common language with the rest of the world—so they learn English early and well.

In Croatia, all schoolchildren start learning English in the third grade. (I've had surprisingly eloquent conversations with Croatian grade-schoolers.) And, since American television programs here are subtitled rather than dubbed, people get plenty of practice hearing American English (with a nonstop simultaneous translation). This means Croatians and Slovenes speak not textbook English, but *real* English—and can be more proficient in slang than some Americans.

Whenever I've heard a Croatian and a foreigner (say, a Norwegian) conversing in English, it's a reminder to me that as Americans, we're lucky to speak the world's new lingua franca.

Croatians and Slovenes pronounce a few letters differently than in English, and they add a few diacritics—little markings that signal a particular pronunciation. Here are a few rules of thumb for sounding out unfamiliar words:

J / j sounds like "y" as in "yellow"

C / c sounds like "ts" as in "bats"

Č / č and **Ć / ć** sound like "ch" as in "chicken"

Š / š sounds like "sh" as in "shrimp"

Ž / ž sounds like "zh" as in "leisure"

Đ / đ (only in Croatian) is like the "dj" sound in "jeans"

Croatian and Slovene are notorious for their seemingly unpronounceable consonant combinations. Most difficult are hv (as in *hvala*, "thank you") and nj (as in Bohinj, a lake in Slovenia). Foreigners are notorious for over-pronouncing these combinations. In the combination hv, the h is nearly silent; if you struggle with it, simply leave off the h (for *hvala*, just say "VAH-lah"). When you see nj, the j is mostly silent, with a slight "y" sound that can be omitted: for Bohinj, just say BOH-heen. Listen to locals and imitate.

A few key words are helpful for navigation: *trg* (pronounced "turg," square), *ulica* (OO-leet-sah, road), *cesta* (TSEH-stah, avenue), *autocesta* (OW-toh-tseh-stah, expressway), *most* (mohst, bridge), *otok* (OH-tohk, island), *trajekt* (TRAH-yehkt, ferry), and *Jadran* (YAH-drahs, Adriatic). If you forget the word for "thank you" *(hvala)*, just think of "koala."

Note that Bosnia and Montenegro each have their own languages, but both are very closely related to Croatian—using virtually all of the same letters and words listed above.

Throughout Croatia and Slovenia, German can be a useful second language (especially in Croatia, which is popular among German-speaking tourists). And a few words of Italian can also come in handy, especially in bicultural Istria.

Learn the key phrases and travel with a phrase book. Consider Lonely Planet's good *Eastern Europe Phrasebook,* which includes both Croatian and Slovene, or their in-depth, stand-alone *Croatian Phrasebook.*

Don't be afraid to interact with locals—a friendly greeting in their language is an easy icebreaker. Give it your best shot, and the natives will appreciate your efforts.

Telephones

Smart travelers use the telephone to reserve or reconfirm rooms, get tourist information, reserve restaurants, confirm tour times, or phone home. This section covers dialing instructions, phone cards, and types of phones (for more in-depth information, see www .ricksteves.com/phoning.)

How to Dial

Calling from the US to Europe, or vice versa, is simple—once you break the code. The European calling chart in this chapter will walk you through it.

Dialing Domestically Within Croatia or Slovenia

Croatia and Slovenia, like much of the US, use an area-code dialing system. This means you dial the local number when calling within a city, and add the area code (which starts with a 0) if calling long distance within the same country. For example, Dubrovnik's area code is 020, and the number of one of my recommended Dubrovnik B&Bs is 453-834. To call the B&B within Dubrovnik, just dial 453-834. To call it from Split, dial 020/453-834. (Bosnia and Montenegro work the same way.)

In Croatia, mobile phone numbers begin with 091, 098, or 099, and numbers beginning with 060 are pricey toll lines. Slovenian phone numbers beginning with 080 are toll-free; 090 and 089 denote expensive toll lines. Mobile phone numbers in Slovenia usually begin with 031, 041, 051, 040, or 070.

Dialing Internationally to or from Croatia and Slovenia

If you want to make an international call, follow these steps:

• Dial the international access code (00 if you're calling from Europe, 011 from the US or Canada).

• Dial the country code of the country you're calling (385 for Croatia, 386 for Slovenia, 387 for Bosnia-Herzegovina, 382 for Montenegro, or 1 for the US or Canada).

• Dial the area code (if applicable) and the local number—keeping in mind that you must drop the initial zero of the area code when calling from another country to Croatia, Slovenia, Bosnia, or Montenegro (the European calling chart lists specifics per country).

Calling from the US to Croatia: To call a recommended Dubrovnik B&B from the US, dial 011 (the US international access code), 385 (Croatia's country code), 20 (Dubrovnik's area code minus the initial zero), then 453-834 (local number). The same formula works for Slovenia, Bosnia, and Montenegro.

Calling from any European country to the US: To call my office in Edmonds, Washington, from anywhere in Europe, I dial 00 (Europe's international access code), 1 (the US country code), 425 (Edmonds' area code), and 771-8303.

Note: You might see a + in front of a European number. When dialing the number, replace the + with the international access code of the country you're calling from (00 from Europe, 011 from the US or Canada).

Prepaid Phone Cards

To make calls from public phones, you'll need a prepaid phone card. There are two kinds of phone cards: insertable (usable only in pay phones) and international (usable from any phone).

Insertable Phone Cards: This type of card is a convenient way to pay for calls from public pay phones and can be purchased at newsstands and post offices. Simply take the phone off the hook, insert the prepaid card, wait for a dial tone, and dial away. The price of the call (local or international) is automatically deducted while you talk. These cards only work in the country where you buy them (so your Slovenian phone card is worthless in Croatia). Insertable phone cards are a good deal for calling within Europe, but calling the US can be pricey (at least 50 cents/minute). Be aware that with the prevalence of mobile phones, public phones are getting harder to find.

International Phone Cards: Although common throughout much of Europe, prepaid phone cards are relatively rare in Croatia and Slovenia, and the savings aren't that enticing (calls to the US generally cost around 25-50 cents per minute). They work from any type of phone, including your hotel-room phone (but ask at the

European Calling Chart

Just smile and dial, using this key:
AC = Area Code, LN = Local Number.

European Country	Calling long distance within ...	Calling from the US or Canada to ...	Calling from a European country to ...
Austria	AC + LN	011 + 43 + AC (without the initial zero) + LN	00 + 43 + AC (without the initial zero) + LN
Belgium	LN	011 + 32 + LN (without initial zero)	00 + 32 + LN (without initial zero)
Bosnia-Herzegovina	AC + LN	011 + 387 + AC (without initial zero) + LN	00 + 387 + AC (without initial zero) + LN
Britain	AC + LN	011 + 44 + AC (without initial zero) + LN	00 + 44 + AC (without initial zero) + LN
Croatia	AC + LN	011 + 385 + AC (without initial zero) + LN	00 + 385 + AC (without initial zero) + LN
Czech Republic	LN	011 + 420 + LN	00 + 420 + LN
Denmark	LN	011 + 45 + LN	00 + 45 + LN
Estonia	LN	011 + 372 + LN	00 + 372 + LN
Finland	AC + LN	011 + 358 + AC (without initial zero) + LN	999 (or other 900 number) + 358 + AC (without initial zero) + LN
France	LN	011 + 33 + LN (without initial zero)	00 + 33 + LN (without initial zero)
Germany	AC + LN	011 + 49 + AC (without initial zero) + LN	00 + 49 + AC (without initial zero) + LN
Gibraltar	LN	011 + 350 + LN	00 + 350 + LN
Greece	LN	011 + 30 + LN	00 + 30 + LN
Hungary	06 + AC + LN	011 + 36 + AC + LN	00 + 36 + AC + LN
Ireland	AC + LN	011 + 353 + AC (without initial zero) + LN	00 + 353 + AC (without initial zero) + LN

European Country	Calling long distance within...	Calling from the US or Canada to...	Calling from a European country to...
Italy	LN	011 + 39 + LN	00 + 39 + LN
Montenegro	AC + LN	011 + 382 + AC (without initial zero) + LN	00 + 382 + AC (without initial zero) + LN
Morocco	LN	011 + 212 + LN (without initial zero)	00 + 212 + LN (without initial zero)
Netherlands	AC + LN	011 + 31 + AC (without initial zero) + LN	00 + 31 + AC (without initial zero) + LN
Norway	LN	011 + 47 + LN	00 + 47 + LN
Poland	LN	011 + 48 + LN	00 + 48 + LN
Portugal	LN	011 + 351 + LN	00 + 351 + LN
Slovakia	AC + LN	011 + 421 + AC (without initial zero) + LN	00 + 421 + AC (without initial zero) + LN
Slovenia	AC + LN	011 + 386 + AC (without initial zero) + LN	00 + 386 + AC (without initial zero) + LN
Spain	LN	011 + 34 + LN	00 + 34 + LN
Sweden	AC + LN	011 + 46 + AC (without initial zero) + LN	00 + 46 + AC (without initial zero) + LN
Switzerland	LN	011 + 41 + LN (without initial zero)	00 + 41 + LN (without initial zero)
Turkey	AC (if there's no initial zero, add one) + LN	011 + 90 + AC (without initial zero) + LN	00 + 90 + AC (without initial zero) + LN

- The instructions above apply whether you're calling a land line or mobile phone.

- The international access code (the first numbers you dial when making an international call) is 011 if you're calling from the US or Canada. It's 00 if you're calling from virtually anywhere in Europe (except Finland, where it's 999 or another 900 number, depending on the phone service you're using).

- To call the US or Canada from Europe, dial 00, then 1 (the country code for the US and Canada), then the area code and number. In short, 00 + 1 + AC + LN = Hi, Mom!

front desk if there are any fees for toll-free calls). To use the card, you'll dial a toll-free access number, then enter your scratch-to-reveal PIN code. But a few of the cards I've tried have an access number that's not toll-free—which means that you pay both for the call, and for the time being deducted from your card. If you want to experiment with international phone cards, try looking for fliers advertising long-distance rates, or ask about the cards at Internet cafés, newsstands, souvenir shops, and youth hostels. Buy a low denomination in case the card is a dud. These cards generally work only in the country where you buy them.

US Calling Cards: These cards, such as the ones offered by AT&T, Verizon, or Sprint, are the worst option. You'll nearly always save money by using a pay phone and a locally purchased, insertable phone card instead.

Types of Phones
Public Pay Phones
Coin-op phones are virtually extinct. You will need an insertable phone card (see above) to make a call.

Hotel-Room Phones
Calling from your hotel room can be cheap for local calls (ask for the rates at the front desk first), but is often a rip-off for long-distance calls (unless you use an international phone card, explained above). Some hotels charge a fee for dialing supposedly "toll-free" numbers, such as the one for your international phone card—ask before you dial. Incoming calls are free, making this a cheap way for friends and family to stay in touch (provided they have a good long-distance plan for calls to Europe—and a list of your hotels' phone numbers).

If you're sleeping in my recommended *sobe* (B&Bs), be aware that you're unlikely to have a telephone in your room.

Metered Phones
These are available in phone offices and sometimes in bigger post offices. You can talk all you want, then pay the bill when you leave—but be sure you know the rates before you have a lengthy conversation.

Mobile Phones
Many travelers enjoy the convenience of traveling with a mobile phone.

Using Your Mobile Phone: Your US mobile phone works in Europe if it's GSM-enabled, tri-band or quad-band, and on a calling plan that includes international calls. Phones from AT&T and T-Mobile, which use the same GSM technology that Europe does, are more likely to work overseas than Verizon or Sprint phones (if you're not sure, ask your service provider). Most US providers charge $1.29-1.99 per minute while roaming internationally to make or receive calls, and 20-50 cents to send or receive text messages.

You'll pay cheaper rates if your phone is electronically "unlocked" (ask your provider about this); then, in Europe, you can simply buy a tiny **SIM card,** which gives you a European phone number. SIM cards are sold at mobile-phone stores and some newsstand kiosks for $5-15, and generally include several minutes' worth of prepaid domestic calling time. When you buy a SIM card, you may need to show ID, such as your passport. Insert the SIM card in your phone (usually in a slot on the side or behind the battery), and it'll work like a European mobile phone. Before purchasing a SIM card, always ask about fees for domestic and international calls, roaming charges, and how to check your credit balance and buy more time. In the SIM card's home country, domestic calls are reasonable, and incoming calls are free. You'll pay more if you're roaming in another country.

Buying a European Mobile Phone: Mobile-phone shops all over Europe sell basic phones. The mobile-phone desk in a big department store is another good place to check. Phones that are "locked" to work with a single provider start around $40; "unlocked" phones (which allow you to switch out SIM cards to use your choice of provider) start around $60. You'll also need to buy a SIM card and prepaid credit for making calls.

Renting a European Mobile Phone: Car-rental companies and mobile-phone companies offer the option to rent a mobile phone with a European number. While this seems convenient, hidden fees (such as high per-minute charges or expensive shipping costs) can really add up—which usually makes it a bad value. One exception is Verizon's Global Travel Program, available only to Verizon customers.

Data Downloading on a Smartphone: Many smartphones, such as the iPhone, Android, and BlackBerry, work in Europe (note that some older Verizon iPhones don't work abroad). For voice calls and text messaging, smartphones work the same as other US mobile phones (explained earlier). But beware of sky-high fees for data downloading (checking email, browsing the Internet, streaming videos, and so on). The best solution: Disable data roaming entirely, and only use your device when you find free Wi-Fi. You can ask your mobile-phone provider to cut off your account's data-roaming capability, or you can manually turn it off on your phone (look under the "Network" menu).

If you want Internet access without being limited to Wi-Fi, you'll need to keep data roaming on—but you can take steps to reduce your charges. Consider paying extra for a limited international data-roaming plan through your carrier, then use data roaming selectively (if a particular task gobbles bandwidth, wait until you're on Wi-Fi). In general, ask your provider in advance how to avoid unwittingly roaming your way to a huge bill. If your smartphone is on Wi-Fi, you can use certain apps to make cheap or free voice calls over the Internet (see next).

Calling over the Internet

Some things that seem too good to be true...actually are true. If you're traveling with a wireless device (such as a laptop or smartphone), you can use VoIP (Voice over Internet Protocol) to make free calls over the Internet to another wireless device (or you can pay a few cents to call from your computer to a telephone). If both devices have cameras, you can even see each other while you chat. The major providers are Skype (www.skype.com, also available as a smartphone app), Google Talk (www.google.com/talk), and FaceTime (this app comes standard on newer Apple devices). With a smartphone, you can get online at a hotspot and use these apps to make calls without ringing up expensive roaming charges (though call quality can be spotty on slow connections).

Useful Phone Numbers
Emergency Needs

For medical or other emergencies, dial 112 in Croatia, Slovenia, Montenegro, and Bosnia-Herzegovina. For police, dial 92 in Croatia, 113 in Slovenia, or 122 in Bosnia-Herzegovina and Montenegro.

US Embassies

In Croatia: Ulica Thomasa Jeffersona 2, Zagreb, passport services available Mon-Thu 13:00-15:00 plus Wed 9:00-11:00, tel. 01/661-2200, after business-hours tel. 01/661-2400, consular services tel. 01/661-2300, http://croatia.usembassy.gov

In Slovenia: Prešernova 31, Ljubljana, passport services available Mon-Fri 9:00-11:30 & 13:00-15:00, tel. 01/200-5595, after business hours tel. 01/200-5500, http://slovenia.usembassy.gov

In Montenegro: Džona Džeksona 2, Podgorica, must call for appointment, tel. 020/410-500, http://podgoricamontenegro.us embassy.gov

In Bosnia-Herzegovina: Ulica Robert C. Frasure 1, Sarajevo, passport services available Mon-Fri 14:00-15:30 plus Fri 8:00-10:30, tel. 033/704-000, http://sarajevo.usembassy.gov. There's also a branch office in Mostar (Husnije Repca 3, tel. 036/580-580).

Canadian Embassies and Consulates

In Croatia: Prilaz Đure Deželića 4, Zagreb, Mon-Thu 10:00-12:00 & 13:00-15:00, Fri 10:00-13:00, tel. 01/488-1200, after-hours emergencies call collect Canadian tel. 613/996-8885, www.canadainternational.gc.ca/croatia-croatie

In Slovenia: Consulate at Trg Republike 3, 12th floor, Ljubljana, Mon-Fri 9:00-13:00, tel. 01/252-4444, after-hours emergencies call collect Canadian tel. 613/996-8885, some services provided through Canadian Embassy in Budapest, Hungary (listed below), www.canadainternational.gc.ca/hungary-hongrie

In Montenegro: Contact the Canadian Embassy in Belgrade, Serbia; from Montenegro dial 00-381-11-306-300000-389-2-322-5630, after-hours emergencies call collect Canadian tel. 613/996-8885, www.canadainternational.gc.ca/serbia-serbie

In Bosnia-Herzegovina: Contact the Canadian Embassy in Budapest, Hungary; from Bosnia-Herzegovina dial 00-36-1-392-3360, for after-hours emergencies call collect Canadian tel. 613/996-8885, www.canadainternational.gc.ca/hungary-hongrie

Travel Advisories

US Department of State: tel. 202/647-5225, www.travel.state.gov
Canadian Department of Foreign Affairs: Canadian tel. 800-267-8376, www.international.gc.ca
US Centers for Disease Control and Prevention: tel. 800-CDC-INFO (800-232-4636), www.cdc.gov/travel

Directory Assistance

Dial 988 in Croatia or Slovenia.

Internet Access

It's useful to get online periodically as you travel—to confirm trip plans, check train or bus schedules, get weather forecasts, catch up on email, blog or post photos from your trip, or call folks back home (explained earlier, under "Calling over the Internet").

   Internet Terminals: Some hotels offer a computer in the lobby with Internet access for guests. If you ask politely, smaller places may sometimes let you sit at their desk for a few minutes just to check your email. If your hotel or *soba* doesn't have access, ask your hotelier to direct you to the nearest place to get online.

   Traveling with a Laptop or Other Wireless Device: Wireless Internet access (Wi-Fi) is becoming commonplace at virtually all accommodations in Slovenia and Croatia. Most accommodations that offer this do so for free, but a few (especially fancier chain hotels) charge by the minute. Other accommodations have a port in your room for plugging in an Ethernet cable. (If you don't have a cable, you can usually borrow one.) You can generally find a café with Wi-Fi or an Internet hotspot in most towns. A cellular modem—which lets your laptop access the Internet over a mobile phone network—provides more extensive coverage, but is much more expensive than Wi-Fi.

Warning: Anytime you access the Internet—especially over a public connection (such as a Wi-Fi signal or at an Internet café)—you're running the risk that someone could be looking over your shoulder, literally or virtually. Be careful about storing personal information (such as passport and credit-card numbers) online. If you're not convinced it's secure, avoid accessing any sites (such as online banking) that could be sensitive to fraud.

Mail
While you can arrange for mail delivery to your hotel (allow 10 days for a letter to arrive), phoning and emailing are so easy that I've dispensed with mail stops altogether.

You can mail one package per day to yourself worth up to $200 duty-free from Europe to the US (mark it "personal purchases"). If you're sending a gift to someone, mark it "unsolicited gift." For details, visit www.cbp.gov and search for "Know Before You Go."

Transportation

By Car or Public Transportation?
Cars are best for three or more traveling together (especially families with small kids), those packing heavy, and those scouring the countryside. Trains, buses, and boats are best for solo travelers, blitz tourists, and city-to-city travelers. While a car gives you more freedom—enabling you to search for hotels more easily and carry your bags along—trains, buses, and boats zip you effortlessly and scenically from town to town, usually dropping you in the center, often near a TI.

Cars are great in the countryside, but a worthless headache in places like Ljubljana and Dubrovnik. But in some parts of Croatia and Slovenia, a car is helpful, if not essential: Istria (especially the hill towns), Rab, the Julian Alps, Logarska Dolina, the Karst, and Montenegro's Bay of Kotor. A trip into Mostar (and on to Sarajevo) is best by car—allowing you to stop off at interesting places en route—but doable by public transportation. In other areas, a car is unnecessary: Ljubljana, Zagreb, and most of the Dalmatian Coast (Dubrovnik, Split, Hvar, and Korčula). For most trips, the best plan is a combination: Use public transportation in some areas, then strategically rent a car for a day or two in a region that merits it. (I've noted which areas are best by car, and offered route tips and arrival instructions throughout this book.)

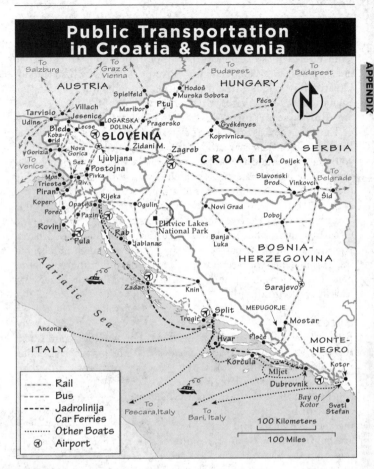

Public Transportation in Croatia & Slovenia

Legend:
- ·-·-· Rail
- - - - Bus
- ▬ ▬ ▬ Jadrolinija Car Ferries
- ········ Other Boats
- ✈ Airport

100 Kilometers

100 Miles

Public Transportation

Throughout this book, I've suggested whether trains, buses, or boats are better for a particular destination (in the "Connections" section at the end of each chapter). When checking timetables *(vozni red)*, arrivals are *prihodi* and departures are *odhodi; svaki dan* means "daily," but some transit doesn't run on Sundays *(nedjeljom)* or holidays *(praznikom)*. You'll notice that many posted schedules list departure times, but not the duration of the trip; try asking for this information at the ticket window.

Trains

Trains are ideal for certain routes in Croatia and Slovenia (such as between Ljubljana and Zagreb) and for connecting to other countries. But their usefulness is limited, and you'll find buses, boats, and flights better for most journeys.

Schedules and Tickets: Pick up train schedules from stations as you go. To study ahead on the Web, check www.bahn.com (Germany's excellent all-Europe timetable). You can also check www.slo-zeleznice.si for Slovenia, and www.hznet.hr for Croatia. Buy tickets at the train station (or on board, if the station is unattended)—you rarely need a reservation.

Railpasses: While railpasses can be a good deal in some parts of Europe, they usually aren't as useful in Croatia or Slovenia. Point-to-point tickets are affordable and often the better option. If your travels are taking you beyond Croatia and Slovenia, consider the flexible Eurail Selectpass, which covers unlimited travel for up to 15 travel days (within a two-month period) in three, four, or five adjacent countries (Croatia and Slovenia are considered a single "country"). A separate combo-pass covers Hungary, Slovenia, and Croatia, and another pass covers Austria, Slovenia, and Croatia. Again, none of these passes is likely to save you much money, but if a pass matches your itinerary, give it a look and crunch the numbers. For options and prices on pertinent Eurail passes, see www.ricksteves.com/rail.

Buses

Buses often take you where trains don't. For example, train tracks run only as far south as Split; for destinations on the Dalmatian Coast farther south, you'll rely on buses (or boats). Even on some routes that are served by trains, buses can be a better option. For instance, Ljubljana and Lake Bled are connected by both train and bus—but the bus station is right in the town center of Bled, while the

train station is a few miles away. Buses can even be convenient for connecting to islands (via ferry, of course). For example, if heading from the island of Korčula to Dubrovnik, the bus connection runs more frequently than the comparable boat connection, and takes about the same amount of time.

Confusingly, a single bus route can be operated by a variety of different companies, making it difficult to find comprehensive schedules. Some big cities have handy websites listing all connections (such as www.ap-ljubljana.si for Ljubljana, www.akz.hr for Zagreb, and www.ak-split.hr for Split), but for smaller towns, the TI is your best source of information. Get creative with checking schedules: If you're going from a small town to Split, and that town doesn't have its own online timetable, try checking the "arrivals" schedules on the Split website instead. If your trip involves a connection at an intermediate station, don't be surprised if it's difficult to get the schedule details for your onward journey. Be patient, and try calling that town's TI (or the TI or bus station at your final destination) for details.

Prices vary among companies, even for identical journeys. For popular routes during peak season, drop by the station to buy your ticket a few hours in advance—or even the day before—to ensure getting a seat (ask the bus station ticket office or the local TI how far ahead you should arrive). Buses have some overhead bag storage on board, but you'll likely check your big bag under the bus (for the extra cost of about $2 per bag).

If you're headed south along the coast, sitting on the right side comes with substantially better scenery (sit on the left for northbound buses). When choosing a seat, also take the direction of the sun into consideration.

Boats

All along the Croatian coast, slow car ferries and speedy catamarans inexpensively shuttle tourists between major coastal cities and quiet island towns. Boats run often in summer (June-early Sept), but frequency drops sharply off-season.

Croatians use the word **"ferry"** *(trajekt)* to describe a boat that takes cars (though walk-on passengers are also welcome). These move slowly but can run in almost any weather. While the number of cars is limited, there's virtually unlimited deck space for walk-on passengers. Watching the ferry crew scurrying around to load and unload cars and trucks onto their boat—especially if it's a small one—is a ▲▲▲ Croatian experience.

Increasingly, popular tourist destinations in Croatia are connected by much faster, passenger-only **catamarans.** These are efficient, but they have to slow down (or sometimes can't run at all) in bad weather. Catamarans are smaller, with limited seats, so they tend to sell out quickly. Because of the high speeds, you'll generally have to stay inside the boat while en route, rather than being outside on the deck.

Most of Croatia's boats are operated by the state-run company called Jadrolinija (yah-droh-LEE-nee-yah), which runs a variety of vessels. Most notable are the four big Jadrolinija car ferries: *Marko Polo* and *Liburnija* go all the way down the coast from Rijeka to Dubrovnik, and cross to Bari, Italy; *Dubrovnik* and *Ivan Zajc* cross between Ancona, Italy and Split. Jadrolinija also runs smaller car ferries along the coast, as well as some faster catamarans (including *Adriana*, which goes between Split, Hvar, and Vela Luka on Korčula Island).

Buy your ticket before boarding the boat. Each town has a Jadrolinija ticket office, which I've listed throughout this book; if the office isn't at the dock itself, there's always a small ticket kiosk that opens at the dock before each departure. The main Jadrolinija office is in Rijeka (tel. 051/666-111, fax 051/213-116, www.jadrolinija .hr). For non-Jadrolinija boats, you may have to buy the tickets at a travel agency, or you might buy  them at the Jadrolinija office. I've tried to list the correct place and time to buy tickets for each boat, but as this changes from year to year, you may have to ask around.

Boat rides are cheap for deck passengers. A short hop, such as from Split to the island of Hvar or Korčula, costs around $5-10 on most boats (strangely, the faster catamarans are usually cheaper than the slow car ferries). For a longer trip, such as from Split to Dubrovnik, figure $20. It's about $65 for a car and driver to ride the ferry from Split to Dubrovnik (less for shorter trips).

Advance reservations are not necessary for walk-on passengers on car ferries; you can almost always find a seat on the deck or in the onboard café. Warning: The catamarans—which have limited space—can fill up, and it's typically not possible to buy tickets a day or more in advance (the exception is Korčula, where tickets for the early-morning *Krilo* boat go on sale the prior evening). If you're here at a busy time, it's worth going out of your way to buy your catamaran tickets early in the day. Then, to get a good seat on board, show up 30-60 minutes before departure time.

Drivers cannot reserve a car space in advance on most routes. This means you'll want to arrive at the dock up to a few hours early,  especially in peak season. Because volumes flex with the season, the local TI is your best resource for advice on how early to get in line. Notice that on some islands, the car ferry port is a long drive from the main tourist town (for example, Vela Luka on Korčula Island is a 1-hour drive from Korčula town; Stari Grad on Hvar Island is a 20-minute drive from Hvar town).

You can buy food and drinks on board most boats. It's not too expensive, but it's not top-quality, either. Bring your own snacks or a picnic instead.

Because Jadrolinija has a virtual monopoly on coastal ferries, their routes don't always cater to customer demand. But a few new, private companies are beginning to compete with Jadrolinija—most notably, the *Krilo* catamaran that connects Split, Hvar, and Korčula (www.krilo.hr), and the *Nona Ana* catamaran between Dubrovnik, Mljet Island, and Korčula (www.gv-line.hr).

The boat schedule information in this book changes every year, without fail. It's essential to confirm before you make your plans. Jadrolinija's website (www.jadrolinija.hr) is useful, but they don't post future schedules very far in advance. Once again, local TIs are the single best source of information for how their town is connected to the rest of the coast.

Renting a Car

If you're renting a car, bring your driver's license. In Slovenia and Bosnia, you're also technically required to have an International Driving Permit (IDP)—a translation of your driver's license (sold at your local AAA office for $15 plus the cost of two passport-type photos; www.aaa.com). While I've frequently rented cars in these countries with just my US license, a few of my readers have been stopped and asked to show their IDP—so you should probably have one.

Rental companies require you to be at least 18 years old and to have held your license for at least one year. Drivers under the age of 25 may incur a young-driver surcharge, and some rental companies do not rent to anyone 75 and over.

Research car rentals before you go. It's cheaper to arrange most car rentals from the US. Call several companies and look online to compare rates, or arrange a rental through your hometown travel agent. Most of the major US rental agencies (such as Alamo/National, Avis, Budget, Dollar, Hertz, and Thrifty) have offices throughout Europe. It can be cheaper to use a consolidator, such as Auto Europe (www.autoeurope.com) or Europe by Car (www.ebctravel.com), which compares rates at several companies to get you the best deal. However, my readers have reported problems with consolidators, ranging from misinformation to unexpected fees; because you're going through a middleman, it can be more challenging to resolve disputes that arise with the rental agency.

Regardless of the car-rental company you choose, always read the contract carefully. The fine print can conceal a host of common add-on charges—such as one-way drop-off fees, airport surcharges, or mandatory insurance policies—that aren't included in the "total price," but can be tacked on when you pick up your

The Rental-Car Conundrum

Virtually everyone planning a trip by car to this region runs into the same problem: International drop-off fees for rental cars are astronomical (usually several hundred dollars). Generally there's no extra charge for picking up and dropping off a car in different towns within the same country (for example, the long 8.5-hour drive between Zagreb and Dubrovnik), but you'll pay through the nose to drop off across the border (including the quick 2-hour drive from Zagreb to Ljubljana). This is especially frustrating when connecting some car-friendly parts of southern Slovenia (such as the Karst) with similar areas in nearby northern Croatia (such as Istria or Plitvice Lakes National Park).

First, compare rates at various rental companies to see if one happens to offer a lower drop-off charge (it happens, but it's rare). If there's no way around the high fee, think creatively to avoid this huge and unnecessary expense.

Let's say you want to pick up a car in Ljubljana, drive through Slovenia's Karst to Istria, then continue to Split and drop your car. But you find out the drop-off fee is $400. Here are two possible alternatives: First, you could do a circuit around the sights of southern Slovenia, then head back up to Ljubljana (fast and easy, thanks to the short distances and speedy expressways), drop your Slovenian car there, and take public transit to northern Croatia (such as the bus to Rovinj, or the train to Zagreb, Rijeka, or Pula). After sightseeing there, you could pick up a second car for your Croatian driving (for example, take the bus from Rovinj—which doesn't generally have handy car-rental offices—to a nearby city that does, such as Pula or Poreč). Or you could begin your trip in Croatia, pick up your rental car there, then loop back up into Slovenia with the Croatian car before continuing to Croatia. There's no doubt that these solutions add some hassle to your itinerary, but they could save you hundreds of dollars.

car. You may need to query rental agents pointedly to find out your actual cost.

For the best rental deal, rent by the week, with unlimited mileage. To save money on fuel, ask for a diesel car. When choosing my car, I normally rent a small, inexpensive model like a Ford Fiesta or Škoda Fabia. Expect to pay about $350 to rent a small economy car for a week with unlimited mileage and basic insurance, plus another $100 or so to cover fuel, tolls, and parking. Note that short rentals cost significantly more per day, while longer rentals can be cheaper per day.

Be warned that dropping a car off in a different country—say, picking up in Ljubljana and dropping in Dubrovnik—can be prohibitively expensive (see the "Rental-Car Conundrum" sidebar for ways around this). Again, I prefer to connect long distances by train or bus, then rent cars for a day or two where they're most useful. But be aware that some companies have a minimum rental period (generally three days); you can keep the car for fewer days, but you'll pay for the minimum period anyway. If you want the car for just a day or two, try to find a company that allows short rentals.

An automatic transmission adds about 50 percent to the car-rental cost over a manual transmission. Almost all rentals are manual by default, so if you need an automatic, you must request one in advance; be aware that these cars are usually larger models (not as maneuverable on narrow, winding roads).

As a rule, always tell your car-rental company up front exactly which countries you'll be entering. Some companies levy extra insurance fees for trips taken with certain types of cars (such as BMWs, Mercedes, and convertibles) in certain countries. Or the company may prohibit driving the car in off-the-beaten-track destinations, such as Bosnia-Herzegovina. As you cross borders, you may need to show the proper paperwork, such as proof of insurance (called a "green card"). Double-check with your rental agent that you have all the documentation you need before you drive off.

You can sometimes get a GPS unit with your rental car for an additional fee (around $15/day; be sure it's set to English and has all the maps you need before you drive off). Or, if you have a portable GPS device at home, consider taking it with you to Europe (buy and upload European maps before your trip). GPS apps are also available for smartphones, but downloading maps on one of these apps in Europe could lead to an exorbitant data-roaming bill.

Big companies have offices in most cities; ask whether they can pick you up at your hotel. Small local rental companies can be cheaper but aren't as flexible. Compare pickup costs (downtown can be cheaper than the airport) and explore drop-off options. Returning a car at a big-city train station can be tricky; get precise details on the car drop-off location and hours. Note that rental offices usually close from midday Saturday until Monday.

When you pick up the rental car, check it thoroughly and make sure any damage is noted on your rental agreement. Find out how your car's lights, turn signals, wipers, and gas cap function, and be sure you know what kind of fuel the car takes. When you return the car, make sure the agent verifies its condition with you.

Car Insurance Options

When you rent a car, you are liable for a very high deductible, sometimes equal to the entire value of the car. Limit your financial risk by choosing one of these three options: Buy Collision Damage Waiver (CDW) coverage from the car-rental company, get coverage through your credit card (free, if your card automatically

Driving: Distance & Time

To Salzburg — 145m • 2.5h

To Vienna — 250m • 4h

AUSTRIA

To Vienna — 260m → 4.5h

300m • 6h

Ptuj

35m 1h — Velenje
20m .5h
55m • 1h

Logarska Dolina — 45m • 1.25h

Bled

Šentrupert exit

60m 2.5h — Kobarid

3.0m • 1h

65m 1.5h

40m • 75h

90m • 2h

220m • 5h

70m • 2h

Ljubljana

SLOVENIA

100m • 2h

Zagreb

ITALY

70m • 1.75h

50m • 1h

Škocjan Caves

75m 2h

140m • 4h

85m • 2h

165m • 3h (via expressway)

155m • 3h

To Venice — 125m • 3h

35m • 5h

Piran

25m 1h — 45m • 1.25h
Rijeka/Opatija

90m • 2.5h

45m 1.5h

Motovun
40m 1.25h

65m • 1.5h

Plitvice Lakes National Park

30m 1h

55m • 1.5h

Rovinj

30m .75h

Pula

Rab

Jablanac (ferry to Rab)

65m • 2.5h

85m • 1.75h

60m • 3h

Zadar

100m • 2h (via expressway)

Adriatic Sea

CROATIA

ITALY

m = miles
h = hours
..... = car ferry

Note: Your times may vary based on traffic, construction, and road conditions.

To Budapest

To Budapest

HUNGARY

100 Kilometers

100 Miles

SERBIA

CROATIA

BOSNIA-HERZEGOVINA

• Sarajevo

Split

90m • 2h

2h

Mostar
20m
.75h

80m • 2.5h

Medugorje

110m • 2.5h
(via Stolac)

MONTE-NEGRO

Hvar

3.75 h

30m
1h

Metković

.5 h

30m
.5h

Korčula

35m • 1h

Ston   35m • 1h

4.5 h

Dubrovnik

20m
1h

Cetinje

55m
2h

Kotor

Bay of
Kotor

15m
.5h

20m
1h

Budva

includes zero-deductible coverage), or buy coverage through Travel Guard.

CDW includes a very high deductible (typically $1,000-1,500). Though each rental company has its own variation, basic CDW costs $15-25 a day (figure roughly 25 percent extra) and reduces your liability, but does not eliminate it. When you pick up the car, you'll be offered the chance to "buy down" the basic deductible to zero (for an additional $15-30/day; this is sometimes called "super CDW").

If you opt for **credit-card coverage,** there's a catch. You'll technically have to decline all coverage offered by the car-rental company, which means they can place a hold on your card (which can be up to the full value of the car). In case of damage, it can be time-consuming to resolve the charges with your credit-card company. Before you decide on this option, quiz your credit-card company about how it works.

Finally, you can buy collision insurance from **Travel Guard** ($9/day plus a one-time $3 service fee covers you up to $35,000, $250 deductible, tel. 800-826-4919, www.travelguard.com). It's valid everywhere in Europe but the Republic of Ireland, and some Italian car-rental companies refuse to honor it. Note that various states differ on which products and policies are available to their residents.

For more on car-rental insurance, see www.ricksteves.com /cdw.

Leasing

For trips of two and a half weeks or more, consider leasing (which automatically includes zero-deductible collision and theft insurance). By technically buying and then selling back the car, you save lots of money on tax and insurance. But leases aren't available in Croatia or Slovenia—you'll have to pick up and drop off the car elsewhere in Europe (such as Germany or Italy). Leasing provides you a brand-new car with unlimited mileage and a 24-hour emergency assistance program. You can lease for as little as 17 days to as long as six months. Car leases must be arranged from the US. One of many companies offering affordable lease packages is Europe by Car (US tel. 800-223-1516, www.ebctravel.com).

Driving

Drivers should be prepared for twisty seaside and mountain roads, wonderful views, and plenty of tempting stopovers.

Road Rules: Seat belts are required, and two beers under those belts are enough to land you in jail. Be aware of typical European road rules; for example, many countries—including all those in this book—require headlights to be turned on at all

times (even in broad daylight) and forbid drivers from talking on mobile phones without a hands-free headset. For more on road rules, ask your car-rental company or check the US State Department website (www.travel.state.gov, click on "International Travel," then specify your country of choice and click "Traffic Safety and Road Conditions").

Fuel: Gas is expensive—often about $6 per gallon. Diesel cars are more common in Europe than back home, so be sure you know what type of fuel your car takes before you fill up. Fuel pumps are color-coded for unleaded gasoline or diesel.

Tolls: Croatia and Slovenia are crisscrossed by an impressive network of expressways (*autocesta* in Croatian, *avtocesta* in Slovene). I don't call them "freeways" because they're not—you'll pay to use them.

In Croatia, you'll pay about 0.38 kunas per kilometer—so a 100-kilometer trip (60 miles), which lasts about an hour, costs 38 kunas ($7.60). You'll take a toll-ticket when you enter the expressway, then submit it when you get off (but don't lose your ticket, or you'll pay the maximum).

Slovenia has done away with its tollbooth system. Instead, drivers who use Slovenia's expressways are required to buy a toll sticker, called a vignette (Slovene: *vinjeta*, veen-YEH-tah; €15/1 week, €30/1 month). Vignettes are sold at gas stations, post offices, and some newsstands. Your rental car might already come with one—ask. If you're caught driving on expressways without one, you will be fined €150 (a hefty penalty that's aggressively enforced).

While Bosnia-Herzegovina and Montenegro don't levy tolls (and, in fact, don't even have expressways), you will pay a €10 eco-tax to enter Montenegro by car.

Road Conditions: Construction on superhighways is ongoing, so it's not unusual to discover that a not-yet-finished expressway unexpectedly ends, requiring a transfer to an older, slower road. For example, the wonderfully speedy A1 expressway goes only about 80 miles south of Split; from there southward to Dubrovnik, you'll follow the winding coastal road. (Likewise, you'll sometimes discover that a much faster road has been built between major destinations since your two-year-old map was published.) For the latest on new expressways in Croatia, see www.hac.hr and www.hak.hr; for Slovenia, see www.dars.si. Secondary roads are usually in good repair, but they can be very twisty—especially along the coast or through the mountains. If you get way off the beaten track, you might find gravel. Locals poetically describe these as "white roads." (Get it? No asphalt.) Keep a close eye out for bikers. You'll see scads of them on mountain roads, struggling to earn a thrilling downhill run.

Maps and Signage: A good map is essential (see page 718). While most roads are numbered, the numbers rarely appear on signs. Instead, do as the Croatians and Slovenes do, and navigate by town name—at every major intersection, directional signs point to nearby towns and cities. The color of the sign tells you what type of road you're approaching: yellow is a normal road, while blue (in Croatia) or green (in Slovenia) indicates that the route is via expressway. Brown indicates a cultural or natural attraction (such as a castle or a cave). Learn the universal road signs. As you approach any town, follow the *Centar* signs (usually also signed with a bull's-eye symbol).

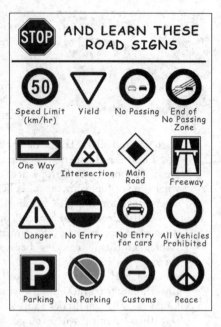

AND LEARN THESE ROAD SIGNS

Speed Limit (km/hr) — Yield — No Passing — End of No Passing Zone — One Way — Intersection — Main Road — Freeway — Danger — No Entry — No Entry for cars — All Vehicles Prohibited — Parking — No Parking — Customs — Peace

Bosnian Detour: If you'll be driving along the Dalmatian Coast, notice that between Split and Dubrovnik, you'll actually pass through Bosnia-Herzegovina for a few miles (through the town of Neum). Don't stress about this international detour—it lasts about 20 minutes, and the borders are a breezy formality (you may need to show your passport, but generally you'll just be waved through; for details, see page 357).

Parking: Get parking advice from your hotel, or look for the blue-and-white *P* signs. Parking is a costly headache in big cities. You'll pay about $15-25 a day to park safely. Rental-car theft can be a problem in cities, so ask at your hotel for advice.

Cheap Flights

Each country has its own national air carrier: Croatia's is **Croatia Airlines** (www.croatiaairlines.com), while Slovenia has **Adria Airways** (www.adria-airways.com). Both airlines offer flights connecting their big cities to destinations within Croatia and Slovenia, and to most major European capitals. And both carriers sell a handful of seats on certain flights at deeply discounted promotional rates. For example, a Croatia Airlines "FlyPromo"

ticket from Zagreb to Split or Dubrovnik can be as inexpensive as $50—cheaper and much faster than taking the bus. These cheap seats sell out fast, so try to book several weeks ahead.

To connect to other parts of Europe, check with the low-cost airlines. Well-known cheapo carriers that fly to cities in Croatia or Slovenia include **easyJet** (www.easyjet.com), **Ryanair** (www.ryanair.com), **Wizz Air** (www.wizzair.com), and **Norwegian Air** (www.norwegian.no). If you're not sure who flies to your destination, check its airport's website for a list of carriers.

Good comparison search engines for international flights include www.kayak.com and www.hipmunk.com. For comparing inexpensive flights within Europe, try www.skyscanner.com.

Be aware of the potential drawbacks of flying on the cheap: nonrefundable and nonchangeable tickets, minimal or nonexistent customer assistance, treks to airports far outside town, and stingy baggage allowances with steep overage fees. If you're traveling with lots of luggage, a cheap flight can quickly become a bad deal. To avoid unpleasant surprises, read the small print before you book.

Europe by Air offers a Flight Pass, charging $99 per leg (plus taxes and airport fees) for flights within Europe. They partner with various well-established airlines, providing good coverage for low prices (most useful for Croatia Airlines flights to and from the Dalmatian Coast; tickets can be purchased only in US, www.europebyair.com, US tel. 888-321-4737).

Resources

Resources from Rick Steves

Rick Steves' Croatia & Slovenia is one of many books in my series on European travel, which includes country guidebooks, city guidebooks (Rome, Florence, Paris, London, etc.), Snapshot guides (excerpted chapters from my country guides), Pocket Guides (full-color little books on big cities), and my budget-travel skills handbook, *Rick Steves' Europe Through the Back Door*. Most of my titles are available as ebooks. My phrase books—for German, French, Italian, Spanish, and Portuguese—are practical and budget-oriented. My other books include *Europe 101* (a crash course on art and history),

Mediterranean Cruise Ports (how to make the most of your time in port), and *Travel as a Political Act* (a travelogue sprinkled with tips for bringing home a global perspective). A more complete list of my titles appears near the end of this book.

Video: My public television series, *Rick Steves' Europe*, covers European destinations in 100 shows, including episodes on Croatia and Slovenia. To watch episodes, visit www.hulu.com/rick-steves -europe; for scripts and other details, see www.ricksteves.com/tv.

Audio: My weekly public **radio show,** *Travel with Rick Steves,* features interviews with travel experts from around the world. This audio content is available for free at Rick Steves Audio Europe, an extensive online library organized by destination. Choose whatever interests you, and download it for free to your computer or mobile device via www.ricksteves.com /audioeurope, iTunes, or the Rick Steves Audio Europe smart-phone app.

Maps

The black-and-white maps in this book are concise and simple, designed to help you locate recommended places and get to local TIs, where you can pick up more in-depth maps of towns or regions (usually free). Better maps are sold at newsstands and bookstores. Before you buy a map, look at it to be sure it has the level of detail you want.

Drivers will want to pick up a good, detailed map in Europe. My favorite maps of the region are by the Slovenian cartographer Kod & Kam (sold all over). Their 1:500,000-scale Croatia map (*Hrvaška* in Slovene, *Hrvatska* in Croatian) covers everything in this book (including Slovenia, Bosnia-Herzegovina, and most of Montenegro) with all the detail you'll need. For just Slovenia, pick up the good 1:300,000 *Autokarta Slovenija* map, sold at tourist shops everywhere (around €8, generally cheaper at TIs than at bookstores or travel agencies). Even better, the Slovenian Tourist Board publishes free excerpts of this same map, divided into three regional zones called "Next Exit"—to save some money, look for these at TIs and skip buying the big map. If you'll be hiking, especially in the Slovenian Alps, you'll find no shortage of excellent, very detailed maps locally.

Since new expressways are constantly being built in these countries, an up-to-date map is essential—it can mean the difference between choosing an old, slow road or saving an hour by finding the new highway.

Begin Your Trip at www.ricksteves.com

At ricksteves.com, you'll discover a wealth of free information on European destinations, including fresh monthly news and helpful tips from thousands of fellow travelers. You'll find my latest guidebook updates (www.ricksteves.com/update), a monthly travel e-newsletter (easy and free to sign up), my personal travel blog, and my free Rick Steves Audio Europe smartphone app (if you don't have a smartphone, you can access the same content via podcasts). You can even follow me on Facebook and Twitter.

Our **online Travel Store** offers travel bags and accessories that I've specifically designed to help you travel smarter and lighter. These include my popular carry-on bags (roll-aboard and backpack versions), money belts, totes, toiletries kits, adapters, other accessories, and a wide selection of guidebooks, planning maps, and DVDs.

Choosing the right **railpass** for your trip—amid hundreds of options—can drive you nutty. (If your trip involves train travel beyond Croatia and Slovenia, a railpass is worth considering.) We'll help you choose the best pass for your needs and ship it to you for free, plus give you a bunch of free extras.

Rick Steves' Europe Through the Back Door travel company offers **tours** with more than three dozen itineraries and more than 450 departures reaching the best destinations in this book...and beyond. We offer a 14-day Adriatic tour that visits Slovenia, Croatia, and a bit of Bosnia-Herzegovina, as well as a 16-day Eastern Europe tour. You'll enjoy great guides, a fun bunch of travel partners (with small groups of generally around 24-28), and plenty of room to spread out in a big, comfy bus. You'll find European adventures to fit every vacation length. For all the details, and to get our Tour Catalog and a free Rick Steves Tour Experience DVD (filmed on location during an actual tour), visit www.ricksteves.com or call the Tour Department at 425/608-4217.

Other Guidebooks

If you're like most travelers, this book is all you need. But if you're heading beyond my recommended destinations, $40 for extra maps and books is money well spent.

The following books are worthwhile, though not updated annually; check the publication date before you buy. The Rough Guides, which individually cover Croatia and Slovenia, are packed with historical and cultural insight. The Lonely Planet guides (with separate Croatia and Slovenia books, and a handy *Western Balkans* book that includes Croatia, Montenegro, Bosnia-Herzegovina, and more) are similar, but are designed more for travelers than for intellectuals. If choosing between these two titles, I'd buy the one that was published most recently.

Dorling Kindersley publishes snazzy Eyewitness Guides, one covering Croatia and another just on Dubrovnik and the Dalmatian Coast. While pretty to look at, these books weigh a ton and are skimpy on actual content.

The British entertainment publication *Time Out* sells a well-researched annual magazine with up-to-date coverage on Croatia, including the latest on hotels, restaurants, and nightlife (look for it at newsstands in Croatia for about $10, www.timeout.com).

If your travels take you to nearby countries, consider *Rick Steves' Eastern Europe,* which covers parts of Croatia and Slovenia, plus Hungary, Poland, the Czech Republic, and Slovakia.

Recommended Books and Movies

To learn about Croatia and Slovenia past and present, check out a few of these books and films.

Books: Lonnie Johnson's *Central Europe: Enemies, Neighbors, Friends* is the best historical overview of Croatia, Slovenia, and their neighboring countries. Rebecca West's classic, bricklike *Black Lamb and Grey Falcon* is the definitive travelogue of the Yugoslav lands (written during a journey between the two World Wars). For a more recent take, Croatian journalist Slavenka Drakulić has written a quartet of insightful essay collections from a woman's perspective: *Café Europa: Life After Communism; The Balkan Express; How We Survived Communism and Even Laughed;* and *A Guided Tour Through the Museum of Communism.* Drakulić's *They Would Never Hurt a Fly* profiles Yugoslav war criminals. For a thorough explanation of how and why Yugoslavia broke apart, read *Yugoslavia: Death of a Nation* (by Laura Silber and Allan Little). Joe Sacco's powerful graphic novel, *Safe Area Goražde,* describes the author's real-life experience living in a mostly Muslim town in Bosnia-Herzegovina while it was surrounded by Serb forces during the wars of the 1990s.

Films: To grasp the wars that shook this region in the early 1990s, there's no better film than the Slovene-produced *No Man's Land,* which won the 2002 Oscar for Best Foreign Film. The BBC produced a remarkable six-hour documentary series called *The Death of Yugoslavia,* featuring actual interviews with all of the key players (it's difficult to find on DVD, but try searching for "Death of Yugoslavia" on YouTube; the book *Yugoslavia: Death of a Nation,* noted above, was a companion piece to this film). Croatian films worth watching include *Border Post* (2006), about various Yugoslav soldiers working together just before the war broke out, and *When Father Was Away on Business* (1985), about a prisoner on the Tito-era gulag island of Goli Otok, near Rab. Other local movies worth watching include *Armin* (2007); *How the War Started on My Island* (1996); *Underground* (1995); and *Tito and Me* (1992).

Holidays and Festivals

This list includes many—but not all—big festivals in this region, plus national holidays. Many sights and banks close down on national holidays—keep this in mind when planning your itinerary. As both Croatia and Slovenia are Catholic, religious holidays— Easter, Ascension Day, Whitsunday, and Whitmonday—are a big deal, and frequent. Muslims (most predominant in Bosnia) observe the month of Ramadan. Before planning a trip around a festival, make sure to verify the dates by checking the festival's website or contacting the national tourist office in Croatia (http://us.croatia .hr) or Slovenia (www.slovenia.info). Unless stated otherwise, all holidays listed here apply to both Croatia and Slovenia.

For sports events, see www.sportsevents365.com for schedules and ticket information.

Jan 1	New Year's Day
Jan 6	Epiphany
Feb	Kurentovanje Carnival, Ptuj, Slovenia (Feb 11-21 in 2012, Feb 2-12 in 2013, www.kurentovanje.net)
Feb 8	National Day of Culture, Slovenia (celebrates Slovenian culture and national poet France Prešeren)
Late March	Ski Flying World Championships, Planica, Slovenia (3 days, www .planica.si)
Easter	April 8 in 2012, March 31 in 2013
April 27	National Resistance Day, Slovenia
May 1	Labor Day, Croatia and Slovenia
Ascension	May 17 in 2012, May 9 in 2013

Whitsunday (Pentecost) and Whitmonday	May 27-28 in 2012, May 19-20 in 2013
Early June	Dance Week Festival, Zagreb, Croatia (www.danceweekfestival.com)
Corpus Christi	June 7 in 2012, May 30 in 2013
June 22	Antifascist Struggle Day, Croatia
June 25	National Day, Slovenia; Statehood Day, Croatia
July 10-Aug 25	Dubrovnik Summer Festival, Croatia (www.dubrovnik-festival.hr)
Early July-late Aug	Ljubljana Summer Festival, Slovenia (www.ljubljanafestival.si)
Ramadan	Muslim holy month (July 20-Aug 18 in 2012, July 9-Aug 7 in 2013)
Late July	International Folklore Festival, Zagreb, Croatia (5 days, costumes, songs, dances from all over Croatia; www.msf.hr)
Aug 5	National Thanksgiving Day, Croatia
Aug 15	Assumption of Mary
Late Aug	Diocletian Days, Split, Croatia (1 week, toga-clad celebrations)
Oct	Tuberfest, Livade, Croatia (Istrian truffle festival, first 3 Sundays)
Oct 8	Independence Day, Croatia
Oct 31	Reformation Day, Slovenia
Nov 1	All Saints' Day/Remembrance Day (religious festival, some closures)
Nov 11	St. Martin's Day (official first day of wine season)
Dec 24-25	Christmas Eve and Christmas Day
Dec 26	Boxing Day/St. Stephen's Day; Independence and Unity Day, Slovenia

Conversions and Climate

Numbers and Stumblers

- Europeans write a few of their numbers differently than we do. 1 = 1, 4 = 4, 7 = 7.
- In Europe, dates appear as day/month/year, so Christmas is 25/12/2012.
- Commas are decimal points and decimals, commas. A dollar and a half is 1,50, one thousand is 1.000, and there are 5.280 feet in a mile.
- When counting with fingers, start with your thumb. If you hold up your first finger to request one item, you'll probably get two.
- What Americans call the second floor of a building is the first floor in Europe.
- On escalators and moving sidewalks, Europeans keep the left "lane" open for passing. Keep to the right.

Metric Conversions (approximate)

A kilogram is 2.2 pounds, and 1 liter is about a quart, or almost four to a gallon. A kilometer is six-tenths of a mile. I figure kilometers to miles by cutting them in half and adding back 10 percent of the original (120 km: 60 + 12 = 72 miles, 300 km: 150 + 30 = 180 miles).

1 foot = 0.3 meter	1 square yard = 0.8 square meter
1 yard = 0.9 meter	1 square mile = 2.6 square kilometers
1 mile = 1.6 kilometers	1 ounce = 28 grams
1 centimeter = 0.4 inch	1 quart = 0.95 liter
1 meter = 39.4 inches	1 kilogram = 2.2 pounds
1 kilometer = 0.62 mile	32°F = 0°C

Clothing Sizes

When shopping for clothing, use these US-to-European comparisons as general guidelines (but note that no conversion is perfect).

- Women's dresses and blouses: Add 30
  (US size 10 = European size 40)
- Men's suits and jackets: Add 10
  (US size 40 regular = European size 50)
- Men's shirts: Multiply by 2 and add about 8
  (US size 15 collar = European size 38)
- Women's shoes: Add about 30
  (US size 8 = European size 38-39)
- Men's shoes: Add 32-34
  (US size 9 = European size 41; US size 11 = European size 45)

Climate

First line is the average daily high; second line, average daily low; third line, average number of rainy days. For more detailed weather statistics for destinations in this book (as well as the rest of the world), check www.worldclimate.com.

	J	F	M	A	M	J	J	A	S	O	N	D
CROATIA • Dubrovnik												
	53°	55°	58°	63°	70°	78°	83°	82°	77°	69°	62°	56°
	42°	43°	57°	52°	58°	65°	69°	69°	64°	57°	51°	46°
	13	13	11	10	10	6	4	3	7	11	16	15
SLOVENIA • Ljubljana												
	36°	41°	50°	60°	68°	75°	80°	78°	71°	59°	47°	39°
	25°	25°	32°	40°	48°	54°	57°	57°	51°	43°	36°	30°
	13	11	11	13	16	16	12	12	10	14	15	15
BOSNIA-HERZEGOVINA • Sarajevo												
	36°	42°	52°	59°	68°	75°	79°	80°	73°	62°	48°	39°
	23°	25°	32°	38°	45°	51°	53°	53°	48°	41°	33°	27°
	16	14	13	13	16	14	12	8	9	12	15	15

Temperature Conversion: Fahrenheit and Celsius

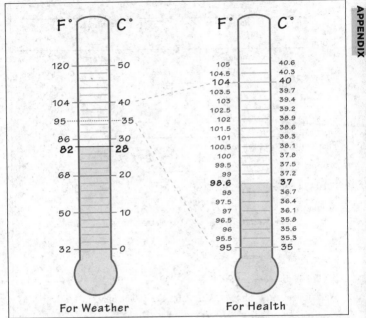

For Weather   For Health

Europe takes its temperature using the Celsius scale, while we opt for Fahrenheit. For a rough conversion from Celsius to Fahrenheit, double the number and add 30. For weather, remember that 28°C is 82°F—perfect. For health, 37°C is just right.

Hotel Reservation

To: _____   _____
           hotel   *email or fax*

From: _____   _____
           name   *email or fax*

Today's date: _____ /_____ /_____
                 day   *month*   *year*

Dear Hotel _____ ,
Please make this reservation for me:

Name: _____

Total # of people: _____   # of rooms: _____   # of nights: _____

Arriving: _____ /_____ /_____   My time of arrival (24-hr clock): _____
              day *month* *year*   (I will telephone if I will be late)

Departing: _____ /_____ /_____
               day *month* *year*

Room(s): Single____   Double ____   Twin____   Triple ____   Quad____

With: Toilet _____   Shower _____   Bath _____   Sink only ____

Special needs: View____   Quiet____   Cheapest ____   Ground Floor____

Please email or fax confirmation of my reservation, along with the type of room reserved and the price. Please also inform me of your cancellation policy. After I hear from you, I will quickly send my credit-card information as a deposit to hold the room. Thank you.

_____
Name

_____
Address

_____
City   *State*   *Zip Code*   *Country*

Before hoteliers can make your reservation, they want to know the information listed above. You can use this form as the basis for your email, or you can photocopy this page, fill in the information, and send it as a fax (also available online at www.ricksteves.com/reservation).

Packing Checklist

Whether you're traveling for five days or five weeks, here's what you'll need to bring. Pack light to enjoy the sweet freedom of true mobility. Happy travels!

- ❏ 5 shirts: long- and short-sleeve
- ❏ 1 sweater or lightweight fleece
- ❏ 2 pairs pants
- ❏ 1 pair shorts
- ❏ 1 swimsuit
- ❏ 5 pairs underwear and socks
- ❏ 1 pair shoes
- ❏ 1 rainproof jacket with hood
- ❏ Tie or scarf
- ❏ Money belt
- ❏ Money—your mix of:
  - ❏ Debit card (for ATM withdrawals)
  - ❏ Credit card
  - ❏ Hard cash (in easy-to-exchange $20 bills)
- ❏ Documents plus photocopies:
  - ❏ Passport
  - ❏ Printout of airline eticket
  - ❏ Driver's license
  - ❏ Student ID and hostel card
  - ❏ Railpass/car rental voucher
  - ❏ Insurance details
- ❏ Daypack
- ❏ Electronics—your choice of:
  - ❏ Camera (and related gear)
  - ❏ Computer/mobile devices (phone, MP3 player, ereader, etc.)
  - ❏ Chargers for each of the above
  - ❏ Plug adapter
- ❏ Empty water bottle

- ❏ Wristwatch and alarm clock
- ❏ Earplugs
- ❏ Toiletries kit
  - ❏ Toiletries
  - ❏ Medicines and vitamins
  - ❏ First-aid kit
  - ❏ Glasses/contacts/sunglasses (with prescriptions)
- ❏ Sealable plastic baggies
- ❏ Laundry soap
- ❏ Clothesline
- ❏ Small towel
- ❏ Sewing kit
- ❏ Travel information (guidebooks and maps)
- ❏ Address list (for sending postcards)
- ❏ Postcards and photos from home
- ❏ Notepad and pen
- ❏ Journal

If you plan to carry on your luggage, note that all liquids must be in 3.4-ounce or smaller containers and fit within a single quart-size sealable baggie. For details, see www.tsa.gov/travelers.

Croatian Survival Phrases

When using the phonetics, pronounce ī / Ī as the long I sound in "light."

Hello. (formal)	Dobar dan.	DOH-bahr dahn
Hi. / Bye. (informal)	Bog.	bohg
Do you speak English?	Govorite li engleski?	GOH-voh-ree-teh lee EHN-glehs-kee
Yes. / No.	Da. / Ne.	dah / neh
I (don't) understand.	(Ne) razumijem.	(neh) rah-ZOO-mee-yehm
Please. / You're welcome.	Molim.	MOH-leem
Thank you (very much).	Hvala (ljepa).	HVAH-lah (LYEH-pah)
Excuse me. / I'm sorry.	Oprostite.	oh-PROH-stee-teh
problem	problem	proh-BLEHM
No problem.	Nema problema.	NEH-mah proh-BLEH-mah
Good.	Dobro.	DOH-broh
Goodbye.	Do viđenija.	doh veed-JAY-neeah
one / two	jedan / dva	YEH-dahn / dvah
three / four	tri / četiri	tree / CHEH-teh-ree
five / six	pet / šest	peht / shehst
seven / eight	sedam / osam	SEH-dahm / OH-sahm
nine / ten	devet / deset	DEH-veht / DEH-seht
hundred / thousand	sto / tisuća	stoh / TEE-soo-chah
How much?	Koliko?	KOH-lee-koh
local currency	kuna	KOO-nah
Write it?	Napišite?	nah-PEESH-ee-teh
Is it free?	Da li je besplatno?	dah lee yeh BEH-splaht-noh
Is it included?	Da li je uključeno?	dah lee yeh OOK-lyoo-cheh-noh
Where can I find / buy...?	Gdje mogu pronaći / kupiti...?	guh-DYEH MOH-goo PROH-nah-chee / KOO-pee-tee
I'd like / We'd like...	Želio bih / Željeli bismo...	ZHEH-lee-oh beeh / ZHEH-lyeh-lee BEES-moh
...a room.	...sobu.	SOH-boo
...a ticket to ___.	...kartu do ___.	KAR-too doh
Is it possible?	Da li je moguće?	dah lee yeh MOH-goo-cheh
Where is...?	Gdje je...?	guh-DYEH yeh
...the train station	...željeznička stanica	ZHEH-lyehz-neech-kah STAH-neet-sah
...the bus station	...autobusna stanica	OW-toh-boos-nah STAH-neet-sah
...the tourist information office	...turističko informativni centar	TOO-ree-steech-koh EEN-for-mah-teev-nee TSEHN-tahr
...the toilet	...vece (WC)	VEHT-SEH
men	muški	MOOSH-kee
women	ženski	ZHEHN-skee
left / right	lijevo / desno	LEE-yeh-voh / DEHS-noh
straight	ravno	RAHV-noh
At what time...	U koliko sati...	oo KOH-lee-koh SAH-tee
...does this open / close?	...otvara / zatvara?	OHT-vah-rah / ZAHT-vah-rah
(Just) a moment.	(Samo) trenutak.	(SAH-moh) treh-NOO-tahk
now / soon / later	sada / uskoro / kasnije	SAH-dah / OOS-koh-roh / KAHS-nee-yeh
today / tomorrow	danas / sutra	DAH-nahs / SOO-trah

In a Croatian Restaurant

English	Croatian	Pronunciation
I'd like to reserve...	Rezervirao bih...	reh-zehr-VEER-ow beeh
We'd like to reserve...	Rezervirali bismo...	reh-zehr-VEE-rah-lee BEES-moh
...a table for one / two.	...stol za jednog / dva.	stohl zah YEHD-nog / dvah
Non-smoking.	Za nepušače.	zah NEH-poo-shah-cheh
Is this table free?	Da li je ovaj stol slobodan?	dah lee yeh OH-vī stohl SLOH-boh-dahn
Can I help you?	Izvolite?	EEZ-voh-lee-teh
The menu (in English), please.	Jelovnik (na engleskom), molim.	yeh-LOHV-neek (nah EHN-glehs-kohm) MOH-leem
service (not) included	posluga (nije) uključena	POH-sloo-gah (NEE-yeh) OOK-lyoo-cheh-nah
cover charge	couvert	KOO-vehr
"to go"	za ponjeti	zah POHN-yeh-tee
with / without	sa / bez	sah / behz
and / or	i / ili	ee / EE-lee
fixed-price meal (of the day)	(dnevni) meni	(duh-NEHV-nee) MEH-nee
specialty of the house	specijalitet kuće	speht-see-yah-LEE-teht KOO-cheh
half portion	pola porcije	POH-lah PORT-see-yeh
daily special	jelo dana	YEH-loh DAH-nah
fixed-price meal for tourists	turistički meni	TOO-ree-steech-kee MEH-nee
appetizers	predjela	PREHD-yeh-lah
bread	kruh	krooh
cheese	sir	seer
sandwich	sendvič	SEND-veech
soup	juha	YOO-hah
salad	salata	sah-LAH-tah
meat	meso	MAY-soh
poultry	perad	PEH-rahd
fish	riba	REE-bah
seafood	morska hrana	MOHR-skah HRAH-nah
fruit	voće	VOH-cheh
vegetables	povrće	POH-vur-cheh
dessert	desert	deh-SAYRT
(tap) water	voda (od slavine)	VOH-dah (ohd SLAH-vee-neh)
mineral water	mineralna voda	MEE-neh-rahl-nah VOH-dah
milk	mlijeko	mlee-YEH-koh
(orange) juice	sok (od naranče)	sohk (ohd NAH-rahn-cheh)
coffee	kava	KAH-vah
tea	čaj	chī
wine	vino	VEE-noh
red / white	crno / bijelo	TSEHR-noh / bee-YEH-loh
sweet / dry / semi-dry	slatko / suho / polusuho	SLAHT-koh / SOO-hoh / POH-loo-soo-hoh
glass / bottle	čaša / boca	CHAH-shah / BOHT-sah
beer	pivo	PEE-voh
Cheers!	Živjeli!	ZHEE-vyeh-lee
More. / Another.	Još. / Još jedno.	yohsh / yohsh YEHD-noh
The same.	Isto.	EES-toh
Bill, please.	Račun, molim.	RAH-choon MOH-leem
tip	napojnica	NAH-poy-neet-sah
Delicious!	Izvrsno!	EEZ-vur-snoh

Slovenian Survival Phrases

When using the phonetics, pronounce ī / Ī as the long I sound in "light."
The vowel "eh" sometimes sounds closer to "ay" (depending on the speaker).

English	Slovenian	Phonetics
Hello. (formal)	Dober dan.	DOH-behr dahn
Hi. / Bye. (informal)	Živjo.	ZHEEV-yoh
Do you speak English?	Ali govorite angleško?	AH-lee goh-voh-REE-teh ahn-GLEHSH-koh
Yes. / No.	Ja. / Ne.	yah / neh
I (don't) understand.	(Ne) razumem.	(neh) rah-ZOO-mehm
Please. / You're welcome.	Prosim.	PROH-seem
Thank you (very much).	Hvala (lepa).	HVAH-lah (LEH-pah)
Excuse me. / I'm sorry.	Oprostite.	oh-proh-STEE-teh
problem	problem	proh-BLEHM
No problem.	Ni problema.	nee proh-BLEH-mah
Good.	Dobro.	DOH-broh
Goodbye.	Na svidenje.	nah SVEE-dehn-yeh
one / two	ena / dve	EH-nah / dveh
three / four	tri / štiri	tree / SHTEE-ree
five / six	pet / šest	peht / shehst
seven / eight	sedem / osem	SEH-dehm / OH-sehm
nine / ten	devet / deset	deh-VEHT / deh-SEHT
hundred / thousand	sto / tisoč	stoh / TEE-sohch
How much?	Koliko?	KOH-lee-koh
local currency	euro	EE-oo-roh
Write it?	Napišite?	nah-PEESH-ee-teh
Is it free?	Ali je brezplačno?	AH-lee yeh brehz-PLAHCH-noh
Is it included?	Ali je vključeno?	AH-lee yeh vuk-LYOO-cheh-noh
Where can I find / buy...?	Kje lahko najdem / kupim...?	kyeh LAH-koh NĪ-dehm / KOO-peem
I'd / We'd like...	Želel / Želeli bi...	zheh-LEEoo / zheh-LEH-lee bee
...a room.	...sobo.	SOH-boh
...a ticket to ___.	...vozovnico do ___.	voh-ZOHV-neet-soh doh
Is it possible?	Ali je možno?	AH-lee yeh MOHZH-noh
Where is...?	Kje je...?	kyeh yeh
...the train station	...železniška postaja	zheh-LEHZ-neesh-kah pohs-TĪ-yah
...the bus station	...avtobusna postaja	OW-toh-boos-nah pohs-TĪ-yah
...the tourist information office	...turistično informacijski center	too-REES-teech-noh een-for-maht-SEE-skee TSEHN-tehr
...the toilet	...vece (WC)	VEHT-SEH
men	moški	MOHSH-kee
women	ženski	ZHEHN-skee
left / right	levo / desno	LEH-voh / DEHS-noh
straight	naravnost	nah-RAHV-nohst
At what time...	Ob kateri uri...	ohb kah-TEH-ree OO-ree
...does this open / close?	...se odpre / zapre?	seh ohd-PREH / zah-PREH
(Just) a moment.	(Samo) trenutek.	(sah-MOH) treh-NOO-tehk
now / soon / later	zdaj / kmalu / pozneje	zuh-DĪ / kuh-MAH-loo / pohz-NEH-yeh
today / tomorrow	danes / jutri	DAH-nehs / YOO-tree

In a Slovenian Restaurant

English	Slovenian	Pronunciation
I'd like to reserve...	Rezerviral bi...	reh-zehr-VEE-rahl bee
We'd like to reserve...	Rezervirali bi...	reh-zehr-VEE-rah-lee bee
...a table for one / two.	...mizo za enega / dva.	MEE-zoh zah EH-neh-gah / dvah
Non-smoking.	Za nekadilce.	zah NEH-kah-deelt-seh
Is this table free?	Ali je ta miza prosta?	AH-lee yeh tah MEE-zah PROH-stah
Can I help you?	Izvolite?	eez-VOH-lee-teh
The menu (in English), please.	Jedilni list (v angleščini), prosim.	yeh-DEEL-nee leest (vuh ahn-GLEHSH-chee-nee) PROH-seem
service (not) included	postrežba (ni) vključena	post-REHZH-bah (nee) vuk-LYOO-cheh-nah
cover charge	pogrinjek	poh-GREEN-yehk
"to go"	za s sabo	zah SAH-boh
with / without	z / brez	zuh / brehz
and / or	in / ali	een / AH-lee
fixed-price meal (of the day)	(dnevni) meni	(duh-NEW-nee) meh-NEE
specialty of the house	specialiteta hiše	speht-see-ah-lee-TEH-tah HEE-sheh
half portion	polovična porcija	poh-loh-VEECH-nah PORT-see-yah
daily special	dnevna ponudba	duh-NEW-nah poh-NOOD-bah
fixed-price meal for tourists	turistični meni	too-REES-teech-nee meh-NEE
appetizers	predjedi	prehd-yeh-DEE
bread	kruh	krooh
cheese	sir	seer
sandwich	sendvič	SEND-veech
soup	juha	YOO-hah
salad	solata	soh-LAH-tah
meat	meso	meh-SOH
poultry	perutnina	peh-root-NEE-nah
fish	riba	REE-bah
seafood	morska hrana	MOHR-skah HRAH-nah
fruit	sadje	SAHD-yeh
vegetables	zelenjava	zeh-lehn-YAH-vah
dessert	sladica	slah-DEET-sah
(tap) water	voda (iz pipe)	VOH-dah (eez PEE-peh)
mineral water	mineralna voda	mee-neh-RAHL-nah VOH-dah
milk	mleko	MLEH-koh
(orange) juice	(pomarančni) sok	(poh-mah-RAHNCH-nee) sohk
coffee	kava	KAH-vah
tea	čaj	chī
wine	vino	VEE-noh
red / white	rdeče / belo	ahr-DEH-cheh / BEH-loh
sweet / dry / semi-dry	sladko / suho / polsuho	SLAHD-koh / SOO-hoh / POHL-soo-hoh
glass / bottle	kozarec / steklenica	koh-ZAH-rehts / stehk-leh-NEET-sah
beer	pivo	PEE-voh
Cheers!	Na zdravje!	nah ZDROW-yeh
More. / Another.	Še. / Še eno.	sheh / sheh EH-noh
The same.	Isto.	EES-toh
Bill, please.	Račun, prosim.	rah-CHOON PROH-seem
tip	napitnina	nah-peet-NEE-nah
Delicious!	Odlično!	ohd-LEECH-noh

Pronouncing Place Names

Remember that *j* is pronounced as "y," and *c* is pronounced "ts." For the special characters, *č* is "ch," *š* is "sh," *ž* is "zh," and *đ* is similar to "j."

Name	Pronounced
Bohinj	BOH-heen
Bovec	BOH-vets
Brijuni (Islands)	bree-YOO-nee
Brtonigla	bur-toh-NEEG-lah
Cavtat	TSAV-taht
Cetinje	TSEH-teen-yeh
Dubrovnik	doo-BROHV-nik
Grožnjan	grohzh-NYAHN
Herzegovina	hert-seh-GOH-vee-nah
Hum	hoom
Hvar	hvahr
Istria	EE-stree-ah
Jadrolinija (Ferry Company)	yah-droh-LEE-nee-yah
Kobarid	KOH-bah-reed
Korčula	KOHR-choo-lah
Lipica (Lipizzaner Stud Farm)	LEE-peet-suh
Ljubljana	lyoob-lyee-AH-nah
Međugorje	medge-oo-gor-yeh
Mljet (National Park)	muhl-YET
Motovun	moh-toh-VOON
Mostar	MOH-star
Njeguši	NYEH-goo-shee
Opatija	oh-PAH-tee-yah
Otočac	OH-toh-chawts
Pelješac	PEHL-yeh-shahts
Piran	pee-RAHN
Plitvice (National Park)	PLEET-veet-seh
Polače	POH-lah-cheh
Pomena	POH-meh-nah
Poreč	poh-RETCH
Postojna (Caves)	poh-STOY-nah
Predjama (Castle)	prehd-YAH-mah
Ptuj	puh-TOOey
Pula	POO-lah
Rab	rob
Radovljica	rah-DOH-vleet-suh
Rijeka	ree-YAY-kah
Rovinj	roh-VEEN
Sarajevo	sah-rah-YEH-voh
Senj	sehn
Škocjan (Caves)	SHKOHTS-yahn
Soča (River Valley)	SOH-chah
Vršič (Pass)	vur-SHEECH
Zagreb	ZAH-grehb

INDEX

INDEX

MAP INDEX

Audio Europe

Rick's Free Travel App

Get your FREE **Rick Steves Audio Europe**™ app to enjoy...

- Dozens of self-guided tours of Europe's top museums, sights and historic walks
- Hundreds of tracks filled with cultural insights and sightseeing tips from Rick's radio interviews
- All organized into handy geographic playlists
- For iPhone, iPad, iPod Touch, Android

With Rick whispering in your ear, Europe gets even better.

Find out more at ricksteves.com

Join a Rick Steves tour

Enjoy Europe's warmest welcome... with the flexibility and friendship of a small group getting to know Rick's favorite places and people. It all starts with our free tour catalog and DVD.

Great guides, small groups, no grumps.

Free information and great gear to

▸ Plan Your Trip

Browse thousands of articles and a wealth of money-saving tips for planning your dream trip. You'll find up-to-date information on Europe's best destinations, packing smart, getting around, finding rooms, staying healthy, avoiding scams and more.

▸ Eurail Passes

Find out, step-by-step, if a railpass makes sense for your trip—and how to avoid buying more than you need. Get free shipping on online orders

▸ Graffiti Wall & Travelers Helpline

Learn, ask, share—our online community of savvy travelers is a great resource for first-time travelers to Europe, as well as seasoned pros.

Rick Steves' Europe Through the Back Door, Inc.

Rick Steves

EUROPE GUIDES

Best of Europe
Eastern Europe
Europe Through the Back Door
Mediterranean Cruise Ports

COUNTRY GUIDES

Croatia & Slovenia
England
France
Germany
Great Britain
Ireland
Italy
Portugal
Scandinavia
Spain
Switzerland

CITY & REGIONAL GUIDES

Amsterdam, Bruges & Brussels
Athens & the Peloponnese
Barcelona
Budapest
Florence & Tuscany
Istanbul
London
Paris
Prague & the Czech Republic
Provence & the French Riviera
Rome
Venice
Vienna, Salzburg & Tirol

SNAPSHOT GUIDES

Barcelona
Berlin
Bruges & Brussels
Copenhagen & the Best of
   Denmark
Dublin
Dubrovnik
Hill Towns of Central Italy
Italy's Cinque Terre
Krakow, Warsaw & Gdansk
Lisbon
Madrid & Toledo
Munich, Bavaria & Salzburg
Naples & the Amalfi Coast
Northern Ireland
Norway
Scotland
Sevilla, Granada & Southern Spain
Stockholm

POCKET GUIDES

Athens
London
Paris
Rome

TRAVEL CULTURE

Europe 101
European Christmas
Postcards from Europe
Travel as a Political Act

Rick Steves guidebooks are published by Avalon Travel,
a member of the Perseus Books Group.

NOW AVAILABLE:
eBOOKS, DVD & BLU-RAY

eBOOKS

Nearly all Rick Steves guides are available as eBooks. Check with your favorite bookseller.

RICK STEVES' EUROPE DVDs

10 New Shows 2011–2012
Austria & the Alps
Eastern Europe
England & Wales
European Christmas
European Travel Skills & Specials
France
Germany, BeNeLux & More
Greece & Turkey
Iran
Ireland & Scotland
Italy's Cities
Italy's Countryside
Scandinavia
Spain
Travel Extras

BLU-RAY

Celtic Charms
Eastern Europe Favorites
European Christmas
Italy Through the Back Door
Mediterranean Mosaic
Surprising Cities of Europe

PHRASE BOOKS & DICTIONARIES

French
French, Italian & German
German
Italian
Portuguese
Spanish

JOURNALS

Rick Steves' Pocket Travel Journal
Rick Steves' Travel Journal

PLANNING MAPS

Britain, Ireland & London
Europe
France & Paris
Germany, Austria & Switzerland
Ireland
Italy
Spain & Portugal

Credits

Contributor
Gene Openshaw

Gene is the co-author of ten Rick Steves books. For this book, he wrote material on Europe's art, history, and contemporary culture. When not traveling, Gene enjoys composing music, recovering from his 1973 trip to Europe with Rick, and living everyday life with his daughter.

Special Thanks

The authors would like to thank our Slovenian and Croatian friends for their invaluable insights. *Hvala lepa* to Marijan Krišković, Tina Hiti, Sašo Golub, Bojan Kočar, and Gorazd Hiti.

Chapter Images

The following list identifies the chapter-opening images and credits their photographers.

Location	Photographer
Title Page: Bled Island, Slovenia	Cameron Hewitt
Introduction: Countryside near Lake Bled, Slovenia	Cameron Hewitt
Croatia (full-page image): Rovinj	Cameron Hewitt
Zagreb: Zagreb Skyline	Cameron Hewitt
Plitvice Lakes National Park: Plitvice	Rick Steves
Istria: Motovun	Cameron Hewitt
Kvarner Gulf: Jablanac	Cameron Hewitt
Split: Riva Promenade and Old Town	Cameron Hewitt
Hvar: Hvar Harbor	Cameron Hewitt
Korčula: View of Old Town	Cameron Hewitt
Dubrovnik: View of Old Town	Cameron Hewitt
Near Dubrovnik: Pelješac	Cameron Hewitt
Montenegro (full-page image): Perast	Cameron Hewitt
Montenegro: Perast and the Bay of Kotor	Cameron Hewitt
Bosnia-Herzegovina (full-page image): Coppersmiths' Street, Mostar	Cameron Hewitt
Mostar: Old Bridge, Mostar	Cameron Hewitt
Sarajevo: Sarajevo Skyline	Cameron Hewitt
Slovenia (full-page image): Julian Alps	Cameron Hewitt
Ljubljana: Ljubljana Castle overlooking Prešeren Square	Cameron Hewitt
Lake Bled: Pletna Boat on Lake Bled	Cameron Hewitt
The Julian Alps: Mountain Hut	Cameron Hewitt
Logarska Dolina and the Northern Valleys: Logarska Dolina	Cameron Hewitt
Ptuj and Maribor: View of Old Town	Cameron Hewitt
The Karst: Predjama Castle	Cameron Hewitt
Piran: Breakwater	Cameron Hewitt

Rick Steves' Guidebook Series

City, Regional, and Country Guides

Rick Steves' Amsterdam, Bruges & Brussels
Rick Steves' Best of Europe
Rick Steves' Budapest
Rick Steves' Croatia & Slovenia
Rick Steves' Eastern Europe
Rick Steves' England
Rick Steves' Florence & Tuscany
Rick Steves' France
Rick Steves' Germany
Rick Steves' Great Britain
Rick Steves' Greece: Athens & the Peloponnese
Rick Steves' Ireland
Rick Steves' Istanbul
Rick Steves' Italy
Rick Steves' London
Rick Steves' Paris
Rick Steves' Portugal
Rick Steves' Prague & the Czech Republic
Rick Steves' Provence & the French Riviera
Rick Steves' Rome
Rick Steves' Scandinavia
Rick Steves' Spain
Rick Steves' Switzerland
Rick Steves' Venice
Rick Steves' Vienna, Salzburg & Tirol

Snapshot Guides

Excerpted from country guidebooks, the Snapshots Guides cover many of my favorite destinations, such as *Rick Steves' Snapshot Barcelona, Rick Steves' Snapshot Scotland,* and *Rick Steves' Snapshot Hill Towns of Central Italy.*

Pocket Guides

My new Pocket Guides are condensed, colorful guides to Europe's top cities, including Paris, London, Rome, and Athens, with more to come. These combine the top self-guided walks and tours from my city guides with vibrant full-color photos, and are sized to slip easily into your pocket.

Rick Steves' Phrase Books

French
French/Italian/German
German
Italian
Portuguese
Spanish

More Books

Rick Steves' Europe 101: History and Art for the Traveler
Rick Steves' Europe Through the Back Door
Rick Steves' European Christmas
Rick Steves' Mediterranean Cruise Ports
Rick Steves' Postcards from Europe
Rick Steves' Travel as a Political Act